SEA OF TROUBLES

ALSO BY IAN RUTLEDGE

ENEMY ON THE EUPHRATES
The Battle for Iraq, 1914–1921

ADDICTED TO OIL
America's Relentless Drive for Energy Security

SEA OF TROUBLES

The European Conquest of the Islamic Mediterranean
and the Origins of the First World War

c. 1750–1918

IAN RUTLEDGE

For Diana, as always

And for my grandchildren
Liam, Amy, Kayley, Jasmine, Alexander, Inara and Rafee

And my step-grandchild, Holly

SAQI BOOKS
Gable House, 18-24 Turnham Green Terrace
London W4 1QP
www.saqibooks.com

Published 2023 by Saqi Books
Copyright © Ian Rutledge 2023

Ian Rutledge has asserted his right under the Copyright, Designs
and Patents Act, 1988, to be identified as the author of this work.

Maps by ML Design

A full CIP record for this book is available from the British Library.

ISBN 978 0 86356 950 0
EISBN 978 0 86356 955 5

Printed and bound by Thomson Press (India)

Europe and the Islamic World have a long, shared past. The very concepts 'Europe' and 'Islamic World' assumed meaning only in their opposition to each other ... Europe had other borders ... but because of its proximity to the vital cultural, religious, and political centres of the two worlds the Mediterranean border has always been the most important.

HENRY LAURENS
(2013)

Contents

Illustrations

Maps

A Note on Terminology and Transliteration

Throughout the book my use of the term 'Mediterranean' is to be understood as 'Mediterranean Region'. In the purely maritime context, it includes the central Mediterranean Sea and its various subsidiary seas – the Aegean, the Adriatic, the Tyrrhenian etc., and the narrows and straights and deltas feeding into and out of it – the Straits of Gibraltar, the Dardanelles, the Sea of Marmara, the Bosphorus and the Nile.

The terrestrial hinterland of the Mediterranean broadly follows its bio-climatic limits but has been drawn considerably deeper inland to reflect the geopolitical context. As such, it is inevitably approximate. This geopolitical Mediterranean incorporates parts of all those current states and their historical predecessors which have a Mediterranean littoral or have colonies or similar dependencies which have a Mediterranean littoral. During the era covered by the book, Britain, although not itself a Mediterranean state, had a Mediterranean presence by virtue of its possession of Gibraltar, Malta, Cyprus, Egypt, Minorca (for a time) and the Ionian Islands (for a time).

To make a comparison with other authors who have taken the 'Mediterranean' as the main theme of their work, it might be said that my definition of 'Mediterranean Region' is narrower than Fernand Braudel's 'Greater Mediterranean',[1] much wider than David Abulafia's 'Great Sea',[2] and more or less the same as John Julius Norwich's 'Middle Sea'.[3]

The Alaouite Empire of Morocco was founded by *Mulay* (Prince) Ali Sharif in southern Morocco in 1631 and unified by his successor in 1659. The name 'Alaouite' derives from the dynasty's claim of descent from the Prophet Muhammad via his son-in law 'Ali ibn Abi Talib and Muhammad's daughter Fatima. It lasted until the French occupation and protectorate in 1911–12. It was reinstated at independence in 1956 under King Muhammad V. The Alaouites' claim to an 'empire' rested on the fact that in its earliest years Moroccan conquests had stretched deep into sub-Saharan Africa. But by the eighteenth century this was no longer the case.

Whenever using the term 'Mediterranean Islam' I am referring to both the Sultanate of Morocco and, of far greater importance, the Ottoman Empire and its Turkish and Arab provinces around the Mediterranean basin. Although many of the Empire's Arab territories had become semi-autonomous by the eighteenth century and are typically allocated only a few pages in most of the historical literature on the Ottoman Empire, by using the historical and spatial construct 'Mediterranean Islam' (or 'the Islamic Mediterranean') my own narrative gives them greater attention.

Finally, throughout the book I unapologetically use the terms 'colonialism' and 'imperialism' interchangeably. In most of the historical literature relating to the European conquest or domination of non-European territories and peoples the reader will find my own usage is common, if not universal. Only Lenin, to the best of my knowledge, ever made a clear distinction between the two; and that was in relation to his own periodisation of the development of capitalism, having nothing to with the presence of colonists, or otherwise.

Transliteration

Transliteration is required when words used in the text do not appear in the English lexicon – or any other European language – and are written in a non-European script. Transliteration aims to turn these 'foreign' words into English etc. in a manner that reflects actual pronunciation. In this book there are two such 'foreign' languages: Ottoman Turkish (a dead language since 1928) and Arabic.

TRANSLITERATION METHODS
These are based on the IJMES Transliteration System for Arabic, Persian, and Turkish (available online), with a few simplifications of my own to avoid excessive use of diacritical marks.

OTTOMAN TURKISH
Ottoman Turkish was written in a slightly modified Arabic script. For transliteration I have Romanised it using one of the two alternatives recommended by IJMES: Modern Turkish orthography.

Unfortunately the glossaries and texts of some historians which I have used do not always transliterate in this conventional manner. Therefore, where appropriate, I have checked these and my own usage against the original Arabic script used in Ottoman Turkish dictionaries: Sir James W. Redhouse, *A Turkish and English Lexicon*, H. Matteosian, Constantinople, 1921; and Ch. Samy bey Fraschery, *Dictionnaire Turc-Francais*, Mihran, Constantinople, 1911.

ARABIC

The symbol ' is used for the letter *'ayn* and the symbol ' for the glottal stop *hamza*; however I have used the *hamza* only when it is in the middle of a word, since at the beginning and end it is not pronounced in normal speech. Arabic also has the complication of having two versions of certain consonants, pronounced differently – the 'soft' and' the 'hard' versions of – 's', 'd', 't' and 'dh' (or z). To keep things simple I have ignored this distinction. So, e.g. a 'hard' t and a 'soft' t are simply written 't' in both cases.

Arabic is also distinguished by having 'long' and 'short' versions of the vowels 'a', 'i' and 'u', where the 'short' versions are actually omitted in modern Arabic orthography. In my own transliteration they are all included, 'long' or 'short', and written as above.

Arabic also has 'broken' plurals which, to Europeans, appear very different to their singulars. With a very few exceptions (See Glossary), in my text I have simply Romanised these plurals by adding an 's' to the singulars.

Place Names

The text covers a huge geographical area. To help the reader manage such a great number of place names, in general, I have used the modern English versions: for example, 'Alexandria', rather than the Arabic 'Iskanderia'. However, where the older (Ottoman or Arabic) name is commonly used in the historical literature, I have sometimes used the Turkish/Arabic name and then added the English name in parentheses, e.g. Izmir (Smyrna).

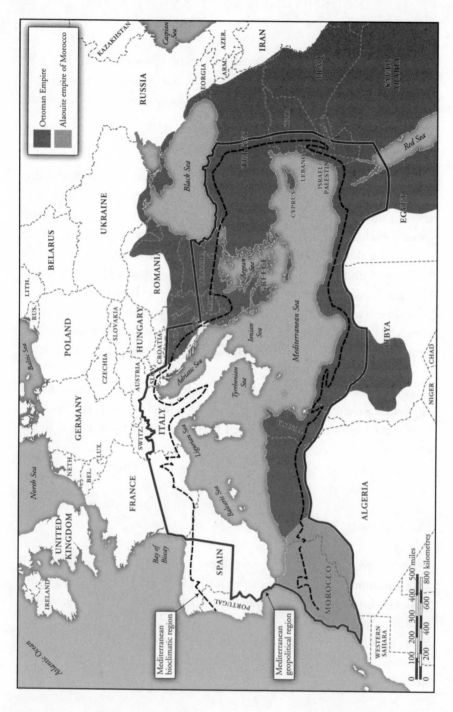

THE ISLAMIC MEDITERRANEAN – THE OTTOMAN EMPIRE AND THE
ALAOUITE 'EMPIRE' OF MOROCCO – C. 1750, AND ITS BIOCLIMATIC
AND GEOPOLITICAL BOUNDARIES

INTRODUCTION

This is the story of how a great and mighty civilisation – Mediterranean Islam – was slowly penetrated and subjugated by the fractious states occupying the lands lying north of the Great Sea. And through that story this book offers a challenging view of European imperialism: it was the Mediterranean and its hinterlands – not sub-Saharan Africa, Asia or the Pacific – which witnessed the most historically and politically significant sphere of imperialism and inter-imperialist rivalry from the early nineteenth to the early twentieth centuries.

There is also one especially important reason why the European conquest of the Islamic Mediterranean was very different from all those better-known episodes of European conquest and colonialism (in the Americas, in Africa and the Pacific). Because the conquest occurred over a much longer period the opponents – the conquerors and the conquered – had known each other for a very long time.

From the Arab conquests of the eighth century to the point at which our narrative begins, the Mediterranean was dominated by Islamic powers. European crusaders reconquered some territory in the twelfth century, but in the mid-fourteenth century the forces of Islam recovered and began an assault on Europe's eastern flank. An Islamised Turkic tribe from Anatolia, the Ottomans, crossed over to Europe at the Dardanelles and subsequently defeated the Christian rulers of the Balkans. In 1453 they captured Constantinople, the capital of the Byzantine Empire and last bastion of Eastern Christianity. The sixteenth century witnessed the spread of Ottoman power south, through Syria and Palestine, and west, along the whole southern shore of the Mediterranean, as they crushed the Mamluk rulers of Egypt and Arab and Berber emirates of the Maghreb. By the mid-eighteenth century around four-fifths of the Mediterranean's shores and hinterlands were in the hands of two Muslim polities, the Ottomans and the Alaouite Sultanate of Morocco, the latter being the only remaining independent Muslim state, shielded by the towering Atlas Mountains.

Of these two, the Ottomans were overwhelmingly the greatest. Contrary to the traditional orientalist historiography, at the moment when the histories of Christian Europeans and Ottoman Muslims became fatally intertwined – the mid-eighteenth century – they were on an equal footing in many relevant respects: culturally, materially, in their level of economic development, and in their living standards. Indeed, Islamic civilisation was still regarded by Christian Europe with awe, fear and, sometimes, admiration.

Our story begins at this time because this was when European powers began to show an interest in exploiting the political difficulties emerging within the Mediterranean's dominant power.[1] In the nineteenth century that interest gradually became one of economic, political and military penetration and engendered an intense rivalry between Britain, France and Russia as they sought domination of the Great Sea and its Islamic hinterlands. At the end of that century this rivalry took a fateful turn as there occurred a major realignment of these imperialist powers; and three more imperialists, Italy, Austria-Hungary and Germany, began to seek their share of the spoils. These developments, in the race to acquire what remained of the Islamic Mediterranean would eventually set off a chain reaction of violence which, in its totality, became the primary cause of the First World War.

*

The Ottomans had been one of the three great patrimonial 'gunpowder empires' of the late Middle Ages – the Mughal (India), the Safavid (Persia) and the Ottoman (Turkey).[2] All three were Islamic polities and all three reached their zenith in the sixteenth century. However, by 1736 Safavid rule had collapsed, and Persia had been conquered by an Afghan warlord. The Mughal emperors of northern India fared little better. By the 1770s they had become mere vassals of the British East India Company. By the eighteenth century these once-powerful Muslim states, together with some smaller Islamic polities like the Mataram Sultanate of Java, had been hollowed out by a common internal breakdown: the Islamic world 'was passing through a crisis in the relationship between commerce, landed wealth and patrimonial authority comparable with that which had convulsed Europe in the first half of the seventeenth century'.[3] This crisis took the form of repeated breakaway movements by newly rich and powerful provincial notables whose strength lay in the growth of large private estates and commercial agriculture on the fringes of empire.

Part One of the book (c. 1750–c. 1815) begins our narrative and paints a picture of the Mediterranean Islamic world at the time when the Ottoman Empire was still mighty. But this was also when Europe began to take an interest in this very different, dangerous but intriguing society that lay on the southern and eastern shores of the Great Sea. Despite the prejudicial descriptions of the Ottoman Empire by (mainly French) observers imbued with the ideas of the eighteenth-century Enlightenment, the Europeans recognised many important similarities between their own world and that of the Muslims.

Nonetheless, a small number of European powers were beginning to probe this empire's weak points, focusing on obtaining commercial privileges and, in doing so, exploiting the centrifugal forces within the Ottoman Empire. In the eighteenth and early nineteenth centuries there were four attempts by European powers to seize Islamic territory in the Mediterranean. These powers were Russia, Spain, France and Britain, and all four failed. Thus, Part One ends at a critical historical juncture. In an era of world history which has been described as the 'first age of global imperialism',[4] the Islamic Mediterranean – while weakened by European commercial penetration and related breakaway attempts – retained its economic and military resilience against European conquest.

Part Two begins in the middle of the Napoleonic wars, but its main narrative is set against the wars' end, when the victors – Britain, Russia, Austria and Prussia, together with a number of lesser monarchical states – met in a series of conferences referred to collectively as the Congress of Vienna, later evolving into a set of diplomatic principles described as the Concert of Europe.* The wars between 1792 and 1815 had been an unmitigated tragedy for the peoples of Europe. Hundreds of thousands had died, not just soldiers but even greater numbers of civilians, as whole cities had been destroyed, thousands of peasant villages burnt to the ground, starvation and disease proliferated. And in some parts of Europe,

---

* 'Concert': A now archaic noun meaning 'agreement', 'conference' or 'convention' with the implication that it is of a permanent or continuing nature.

in particular Portugal, Spain and Russia, war had degenerated into torture, atrocity and massacre. At Paris in 1814 (after Napoleon's initial abdication) and at the subsequent Congress of Vienna in 1815 (after the Battle of Waterloo), the victorious participants met and were determined that such a calamity should never happen again.

However, it was the determination of the Concert of Europe to put an end to the Muslim dominance of the western Mediterranean Sea by the three autonomous regencies of the Ottoman Empire, Algiers, Tunis and Tripoli. Part Two describes how this was eventually achieved by the British and other European navies, strongly assisted by the warships of the US. It was the defeat of the corsair* regencies of the Maghreb that, in 1830, led to the first major act of European imperialism on the Mediterranean's southern shore since Napoleon's invasion of Egypt in 1798: the invasion and occupation of Algiers and its huge hinterland. The invasion was followed by a seventeen-year resistance-struggle by its inhabitants, but one fatally weakened by the fissures between those who wished to retain the link with the Ottoman Empire and those who fought for an embryo Arab nationalism.

The years between 1830 and 1870 also saw the emergence in the Mediterranean of inter-imperialist rivalry between Britain, France and Russia. Meanwhile, Muslim attempts to catch up with the advances of industrial capitalism in Christian Europe largely failed, with the Islamic Mediterranean gradually converted into an economically subordinate role as an agro-exporting region.

Part Three of the book takes us to the age of 'classical imperialism' between 1870 and 1895,[5] at the beginning of which the rulers of Tunisia, Egypt and the remaining Ottoman Empire fell victim to indebtedness and into the hands of European bond-holders. The narrative also describes how the pace of imperialism in the Mediterranean accelerated, with Cyprus, Tunisia and Egypt falling into European hands, while in 1878 only a British fleet anchoring off Istanbul prevented the Russians occupying the Ottoman Capital and the Turkish Straits. Part Three ends with the once-great

---

* A corsair was a state-sanctioned pirate. In the European world they were known as 'privateers'. In the Mediterranean both Muslims and Christians used corsairs to prey upon each other's merchant shipping. The majority of the Christian corsairs were from the Knights of Malta, who also made great use of captured Muslim slaves.

Alaouite Sultanate of Morocco being gradually undermined by debt, crooked European salesmen, exploitative foreign governments, and – in the Sahara region – penetration by French colonialist forces.

The final part of the book describes how, towards the turn of the century, three new imperialist powers, Italy, Austria-Hungary and Germany, appeared on the scene, with ambitions to acquire their share of the old Islamic Mediterranean. It also recounts how the century-long British policy of defending the territorial integrity of Morocco and the Ottoman Empire came to an end with calamitous consequences. Concurrently, between 1894 and 1907 a major realignment of the imperialist powers occurred, with some colonial disputes settled while new ones emerged. And one of these, the Austrian annexation of Bosnia-Herzegovina in 1908, would set in motion a chain reaction of violence leading to the First World War.

*

Initially only three of the five great powers that met in Vienna in 1815 sought to expand their political and economic interests in the Mediterranean region: Russia, France and Britain. Russia's trade was restricted because its only ports with access to world markets – in the Baltic and the White Sea – were ice-bound for the winter months. Until the late 1770s, Russia had no access to the Black Sea. Even after that was achieved in 1774, it had no permanent access into the Mediterranean and its markets. Passage through the Bosphorus and the Dardanelles (the 'Turkish Straits') was often prevented by the Ottomans, with whom Russia had been at war three times in living memory.[6] Consequently, successive Tsars, statesmen and intellectuals believed that a breakthrough into the Mediterranean was essential.

After 1815, the defining features of French imperialism began to emerge. First, there was a determination to recover and maintain what was left of France's pre-revolutionary colonial possessions outside Europe. This objective was partly achieved by agreements made during the Congress of Vienna. Second, as French historian Henry Laurens points out, 'since there could be no question of a military venture within Europe, *the Mediterranean became the outlet*'.[7] France's Mediterranean strategy was to re-establish a land-based empire. This ambition now extended to the whole of the Maghreb, Egypt and Lebanon where French Catholic missionaries were already providing support and assistance to its Christian (Maronite) minority.

Britain's 'Bluewater Empire' in the Mediterranean had been created during the Republican and Napoleonic wars. Extending eastwards from Gibraltar (captured from Spain in 1704) and for a time including the island of Menorca, it stretched to strategically positioned Malta (captured from the French in 1800), and from there to Corfu and the other Greek-populated Ionian Islands (also taken from the French in 1814). Along this maritime highway and as far as Beirut, Britain established consular bases and trading posts which were already providing outlets for its burgeoning exports trades, principally textiles, and income from its rapidly expanding merchant marine.

But it was India, where that old 'gunpowder empire' of the Mughals had largely crumbled away, that Britain valued as its principal imperial possession. When the Mughal emperor was prevailed upon to lease the vastly rich province of Bengal to the East India Company in 1765 the rents extracted from its peasants became an enormous British cash-cow.[8] According to Henry Laurens, 'Bengal defined the Indian routes as the new geopolitical axes which would dominate the next two centuries of history in the Old World.'[9] And those 'Indian routes' passed through the Mediterranean.

From the late eighteenth century onwards, Britain's politicians, state officials and military men believed that maintaining – and when possible, increasing – the flow of revenues from India was of crucial importance to Britain's economic welfare, and behaved as such. In turn, this meant defending the so-called 'overland' route to India which stretched from Alexandria to Cairo, across the Isthmus of Suez, through the Red Sea and into the 'Persian' Gulf, providing a faster means of communication between Britain and India than the older sea route down the coast of Africa, round the Cape and across the Indian Ocean.*

In spite of the emerging three-cornered rivalry between Russia, France and Britain, there was one overriding common interest shared among all the participants of the Vienna Congress, one which, more than any other factor, led them to 'turn south' against the Islamic Mediterranean. Since the sixteenth century the Muslims had dominated the Great Sea itself.

---

*   Before the opening of the Suez Canal there were actually two main 'overland' routes to and from British India: the one described above and the other, less frequently used, through Baghdad and Persia.

They demanded both money and arms from the Europeans as the price for trading in 'their sea', in return for which they agreed 'treaties' and issued 'passports'. Woe betide any merchant ships whose nation refused to play by these rules. Emerging swiftly from their Mediterranean strongholds, the 'Barbary corsairs' would pillage them and enslave their crews.

*

The Safavids, Moghuls and Mataram sultans disappeared from history at the end of the eighteenth century. Yet Mouradgea d'Ohsson, the most reliable contemporary *Christian* authority on the Ottoman state, religion and society, still described it, admiringly, to the King of Sweden as 'a Great Empire'.[10] These words were echoed in 2004 when the British historian Christopher Bayly described the eighteenth-century Ottoman Empire as 'a powerful world class entity'.[11]

However, in Britain, from the 1950s to the early 1970s, a very different and darker portrait of the eighteenth-century Ottoman Empire was being drawn by both academic historians and those writing in a more popular historical genre. It would have a lengthy impact upon how the West viewed Islamic society.

In 1951, the great pre-war Middle-East scholar H. A. R. Gibb and his colleague Harold Bowen depicted the eighteenth-century Ottoman Empire with a relentlessly negative perspective, setting the tone for a succession of 'decline' and 'degeneration' histories. According to Gibb, 'Instead of inspiring its members to earn merit by the exercise of talent and virtue', the Ottoman state, 'taught them they must look to corruption for advancement and might safely neglect their duties.' It had become only 'an engine of feeble tyranny'.[12] Such views became the received wisdom. As one Turkish historian has put it, this body of literature 'framed late Ottoman history in a narrative of imperial collapse to the relentless drumbeat of the march of progress – usually associated with Westernisation, nationalism and secularisation'.[13]

Since the 1980s there has been a florescence of writing on the Ottoman Empire and the Near East generally. With a few exceptions this new literature has studiously avoided the whole question of 'the impact of the West' which so dominated the Eurocentric, Christian-centric and deterministic approaches associated with the 'Eastern Question'* school of historical writing. As another historian has concluded, 'there was nothing inevitable about the way the Eastern Question developed and no historical ordinance which decreed the Ottoman Empire should disappear'.[14]

While the desire of modern scholars to avoid the prejudices of the past is admirable, it has inevitably left a gap: because both the Ottoman Empire and the Sultanate of Morocco *did* suffer certain critical disadvantages compared to 'the West' (disadvantages rarely mentioned in the literature), and they *were* eventually conquered by 'the West'. The disadvantages will become clear as my own narrative progresses; for now, they can be briefly summarised as follows: manpower, money and materials.

We can also include the fact that the Ottoman Empire was itself *an empire* which brought with it fissures and weaknesses. The ruling Turks had an uneven and sometimes hostile relationship with their fellow Muslims – Arabs, Berbers and Kuloğlus – which could impede resistance to European encroachment and attacks. However, this was by no means a universal tendency, as we shall see.

The most serious lacuna in the new literature on the Ottoman Empire is the absence of any reference to imperialism. With one notable exception, in the numerous historical works on the Islamic Mediterranean published over the past thirty years or so, the word 'imperialism' simply does not appear. This is not deliberate or ideological. But it is all the more surprising since, as long ago as 1975, the German historian Winfried Baumgart wrote, 'The carving-out of peripherally located regions (Tunisia, Egypt, Tripoli, Bosnia, regions in the Caucasus) from the Ottoman Empire definitely is imperialism.'[15] If, as the French historian Henry Laurens has argued, it was the Mediterranean which became the fault line between Europe and Islam, it was *also* the Mediterranean – not Africa, as has been often assumed[16] – which was the most politically important region of European imperialist activity from the eighteenth to the early twentieth century, and, in particular, the fulcrum of the greatest inter-imperialist rivalry.

---

*   The term 'Eastern Question' emerged in European political and historical discourse in the mid-nineteenth century and continued in use until the 1960s. Its usage conveyed the idea of the Ottoman Empire as a dying entity whose decay and carve-up had to be somehow 'managed' by the European powers.

Unfortunately, the waters have been muddied by the repeated application of the term 'African' to the most important targets of British and French imperialism in the later nineteenth and early twentieth centuries: Tunisia, Egypt, Libya and Morocco. But while we commonly refer to these as 'North Africa' and their historical development cannot be disentangled from the ties of trade, migration and religion which have crossed that great boundary, the Sahara, historians like Braudel and Abulafia have shown us that in their economy, climate, ecology and culture they are also part of a world which has its centre in a different boundary – the great Mediterranean Sea.

*

Over the past two decades there has been a plethora of historical writing on the origins of the Great War. Much of this literature has acknowledged the need – to use the words of Canadian historian Margaret MacMillan – 'to balance the currents of the past with the human beings who bobbed along on them'.[17] Understanding the latter is the easier part: we have their memoirs, diaries, speeches, etc. Determining the 'currents of the past' is far more difficult. How do we select the more powerful currents from the weaker ones, or those which seemed stronger but whose waves broke and their waters ebbed harmlessly away? And how far back in time do we need to look to see those currents forming? These, of course, are the perennial tasks of the historian.

On this subject let us refer, briefly, to V. I. Lenin's famous text, *Imperialism, the Latest Stage of Capitalism*,[18] a work which has been described as providing 'a theoretical analysis ...of the genesis of war in Europe *after 1900*'[19] (my emphasis). Using data he took from John Hobson's 1902 *Imperialism* and other sources, he concluded that, by 1900, 'the whole world had been divided up'[20] between the great powers during the preceding era of colonialism between 1870 and 1890. Lenin's 'Imperialism' was therefore the 're-partitioning' of a world that had already been 'partitioned'.

However, Lenin wasn't consistent here, because he also concedes that by 1900 the world hadn't been *entirely* partitioned between the great imperialist powers and there was also a continuing struggle to divide up what was left. Lenin identifies a class of 'semi-colonial' countries 'like Persia, China and Turkey [i.e. the Ottoman Empire]',[21] of which the Ottoman Empire was already 'on the way' to becoming a colony, and he concluded: 'It is natural that the struggle for these semi-independent countries should have become particularly bitter ... when the rest of the world had already been divided up.'[22]

Lenin is never clear about the *causal* connections between what he calls 'monopoly and finance capital', post-1900 'imperialism', and the outbreak of the Great War. However, he was correct to see the very end of the nineteenth century as the beginning of the most intense period of inter-imperialist rivalry (as did the great non-Marxist historian of imperialism, William Langer),[23] and recognise that the rivalry over 'what was left to divide up' was extremely fierce.

Part Four of the book demonstrates that it was in what remained of the Ottoman Empire and the 'empire' of Morocco that this struggle became most intense. It shows that between 1908 and 1913 this old Islamic world was destroyed in a chain reaction of inter-imperialist rivalry and violence which finally exploded in the First World War.

The Mediterranean, imperialism, inter-imperialist rivalry, and its ultimate, disastrous consequences: these are the historical parameters which frame the narrative of the book. But there is another, not so explicit, but equally important.

If one examines the narrative literature on British imperialism published over the past thirty years or so (and most of the literature on imperialism *is* about British Imperialism – and written by British historians), what is evident is the absence of any consideration of the actual historical process of conquest. As a consequence the reactions, experiences and beliefs of those who were subjugated by imperialism, those who were 'on the other side', are largely ignored. As one American historian put it, 'Often the voices of the invaded are silent. We look in vain for their reactions to the trauma of invasion and occupation.'[24]

This is reflected in the titles of the many books about British imperialism: almost invariably the actual word 'imperialism' is absent (as is the word 'capitalism').[25] Instead what we get is 'Empire': *Empire, the British Imperial Experience*,[26] *Unfinished Empire*,[27] *The Empire Project*,[28] and so on. In one example of this conventional historical genre the word 'imperial' is considered acceptable, but 'imperialism' is not. Writing in 2002 in the preface to the third edition of his 1976 work *Britain's Imperial Century 1815–1914*, the Cambridge Professor Ronald Hyam remarked approvingly: 'One of the features of the book is that it steers clear of contentious "isms". It is written without resort to those vague and emotive words "imperialism", "colonialism" and "capitalism"', adding rather extraordinarily, 'Even "racism" is avoided.'[29]

Of course, 'imperialism' and 'empire' have very different connotations. 'Empire' implies a settled state of affairs, a *fait accompli*, an end product to be explained, analysed, evaluated. 'Imperialism' suggests something very different: conquest, expropriation, resistance, violence, cruelty, exploitation and racism. So in my narrative I shall try to give voice to those who were on the 'other side', who actually experienced conquest and resisted imperialism, colonialism, capitalism and racism.

This isn't easy because the vast majority of these 'voices' were illiterate. However, at least we can tell the stories – and occasionally hear the actual voices – of those who led them. Men like Cezayirli Gazi Hasan Paşa, the courageous Admiral of the Ottoman fleet whose determination robbed a Russian fleet of total victory in the Mediterranean; 'Abd al-Rahman al-Jabarti, the Egyptian historian who witnessed and recorded Napoleon's occupation; Hamdan ben Othman Khoja, the Kuloğlu notable and publicist who fought the French occupation of Algeria with the pen; Jamal al-Din al-Afghani, the 'modernist' Muslim scholar who opposed British domination in Egypt; 'Umar al-Mukhtar, the Bedouin chieftain who fought against the Italian invasion of Cyrenaica (eastern Libya); and many others.

Sea of Troubles shows that, in the Mediterranean, post-1900 'imperialism' was not only the consequence of the 'colonialism' of 1870–1900, but was the final act in a more than century-long era of European expansion: an era when the Christian powers to the north of the Great Sea began to probe the internal weaknesses of the ageing civilisation on its southern and eastern shores. This historical trajectory began – albeit with failure – in the last part of the eighteenth century. But it resumed after 1815 as the development of capitalism enabled the European powers to utilise their superiority in manpower, money and materials to slowly dominate that old world on their doorstep, politically, financially and territorially. As the Europeans wrestled with their conflicting imperialist objectives and their numbers and rivalry increased, they had no idea that their actions would eventually result in the conflagration which those same powers, meeting in Vienna in 1815, had vowed would never happen again. Those 'currents of the past' may indeed form a long time before their waves finally break.

PART ONE
C. 1750-C. 1815

One only calls a man a 'Turk' if he is brutal and coarse ... All the people of the Empire are designated only by the collective name 'Ottomans' ... And they cannot understand why, in Europe, they are called Turks.

IGNATIUS MOURADGEA D'OHSSON
(1788)

CHAPTER 1

The Islamic and Christian Worlds
of the Eighteenth-Century Mediterranean

> In this enlightened century the only things known about
> the Ottoman Empire are its size, its geographical position,
> never what is behind this colossus. Political analysis has not
> penetrated, nor even perceived the motor forces which drive
> this great machine, only the results, not the causes. For most
> writers the illusion and error which result from long distance,
> superficial and brief observations have only presented
> phantoms.[1]

The man who wrote these words, Ignatius Mouradgea d'Ohsson,* was an
Armenian Catholic, born in Istanbul in 1740, an Ottoman citizen and senior
translator at the Swedish embassy.[2] As such, he was a protégé (protected
person), one of a privileged group of Ottoman citizens who, by virtue of
their attachment to a European embassy, enjoyed exemption from taxation
and the majority of Ottoman judicial procedures.† Perhaps surprisingly for
a Christian, Mouradgea was an admirer of the Ottoman Empire, and his
unfavourable comments about certain 'writers' were presumably aimed at
the eighteenth-century 'Enlightenment' discourse about the 'Orient'. The
keynote of the Enlightenment, especially in its French version, was its
attack on religious obscurantism and the extremes of absolute monarchy;

---

*   Mouradgea added the aristocratic-sounding d'Ohsson only in 1787, to impress his associates
    when visiting Paris.
†   The protégé system – which was later much abused – was part of the so-called 'capitulations'
    agreed between the European Christian states and the Ottoman Empire. A similar system
    developed in the Sultanate of Morocco. See Chapter 3 and especially Chapter 23.

but when French travellers and soldiers spent time in the Ottoman Empire – men like the Comte de Volney (1757–1820) and the Hungarian-born French military officer François Baron de Tott (1733–1793) – they viewed it through the prism of this critique of their own country and its institutions. As we shall see, most of the orientalist tropes found in the 'degeneration and decline' literature ('oriental despotism', 'fanaticism', 'corruption', etc.), which were noted in the Introduction, can be traced back to this Enlightenment image of the Islamic world.[3]

Mouradgea was not a visitor but an Ottoman born and bred, and living in an age when relations between the upper classes of the different religious and ethnic groups within the Empire were relatively harmonious. At the same time he considered himself to be a man of the Enlightenment. But, even as a Christian, he was nevertheless determined to reject those prejudiced accounts of what he considered his own nation. In his great unfinished work, *Tableau Général de l'Histoire Othoman*, whose first volumes were published in French in 1788, he presented what is the most reliable description of the religious, legal and institutional structures of the later eighteenth-century Ottoman Empire. And although he was not averse to offering criticisms, he not only took an optimistic view as to the Empire's future progress but he argued that, whatever its faults, these were derived neither from the religion of Islam, nor from its laws, but merely from popular prejudices.[4]

Mouradgea would have been a teenager, learning his trade at the side of his translator father Ohannes, when, on 30 October 1757, they brought Prince Mustafa from the Cage. As cages go, Istanbul's *kafes*, in which Mustafa had been incarcerated for the past twenty-seven years, was less a forbidding prison than a modest place of compulsory confinement – a small, two-storey suite of rooms within the fourth court of the imperial Topkapı Palace. A marble terrace looked out across a small garden to the confluence of the Bosphorus with the waterway of the Golden Horn. The Cage had originally been surrounded by a high wall with no windows; but Mustafa's predecessor and eldest cousin, Sultan Osman III (r. 1754–57), had somewhat improved conditions in the *kafes*, to make it more open and less oppressive. Indeed, on occasion, Mustafa and his fellow royal prisoners were allowed excursions to other imperial palaces, albeit they were shut up in a similar fashion once they got there. In the rather understated words of

M. Jean-Claude Flachat, a French merchant resident in Istanbul, it was an experience which would 'make a welcome change for them'.⁵ Moreover, the old practice of denying the inmates of the *kafes* the company of women – in case they fathered any children – had now been abolished, although the small number of concubines they were permitted were sterilised to achieve the same objective.

The *kafes* was an innovation of the early seventeenth century. It replaced an earlier custom whereby each new sultan had all his remaining brothers and half-brothers strangled with a silken cord.⁶ The practice had originally been introduced by Sultan Mehmed II, the conqueror of Constantinople in 1453,* and its rationale, in Mehmed's own words, was 'for the order of the World'; in other words to prevent deadly sibling rivalry leading to destructive civil wars. This radical solution reached its apogee at the accession of Mehmed III on 28 January 1595, when a record nineteen male siblings met this fate.⁷ However, by the early seventeenth century it was realised that, in the event of the reigning sultan having no surviving male offspring, mass fratricide carried the attendant risk of wiping out the whole Ottoman dynasty.

Accordingly, it was decided that a less drastic manner of avoiding conflict over the succession should be introduced. And so in 1622 the *kafes* was built, into which all the reigning sultan's younger siblings would be consigned. Accession to the sultanate was henceforth determined by the so-called 'rule of elderness', whereby all the males within an older generation were exhausted before the succession of the male of the next generation.⁸ Consequently, in each of the following twenty-one successions, there were relatively few instances of a son inheriting the throne. One or other of the reigning sultan's surviving brothers could now theoretically get his turn in the succession, but they might be queuing in the *kafes* for decades, languishing in a waiting room of potential Ottoman emperors, most of whom would never live long enough to achieve that lofty eminence.

However, for the forty-year-old Mustafa emerging from his place of

---

* Constantinople was the original Christian name for the Ottoman capital Istanbul, named after the Emperor Constantine established it as the capital of the Roman Empire in 330 CE. After its conquest by the Turks in 1453, Europeans continued to use the name Constantinople until well into the twentieth century.

confinement, his time had finally come. On his release from the *kafes*, he
would have first been met by the green-turbaned *şeyhülislam* (the most
senior Muslim cleric) and the current grand vezir, Mehmed Ragıb Paşa,
in his rich, sable-trimmed, full-length white robe and towering, pointed
white turban. Present also would have been the *silihdar*, resplendent in his
scarlet coat, conical, pointed, scarlet hat and magnificent mustachios, who
was charged with carrying the sultan's sword over his left shoulder, and the
sixty or so members of the imperial divan (State Council).

Portrait of Sultan Mustafa III
(r. 1757–74)

Senior Officers of the Sultan's Court c. 1797

The grand vezir   *The şeyhülislam*   *The silihdar*

After the customary distribution of gifts to the divan and the minting of new coins, Mustafa was conveyed in the imperial galley up the Golden Horn to the mosque complex of Eyüp (Job), reputed to be the burial place of the Prophet Muhammad's friend and standard bearer, killed sometime around 677 CE during the first Arab siege of Constantinople. There, in a ceremony equivalent to coronation, Mustafa was girded by the *şeyhülislam* with the sword of Osman Gazi, the founder of the Ottoman dynasty. Henceforth, according to historic practice, he became the Sultan Mustafa III, Padishah of Islam,[9] Servitor of the Two Holy Places (Mecca and Medina), the Shadow of God on Earth, and recipient of many other honorific titles.

Incarceration in the *kafes* for a lengthy period, accompanied only by selected palace eunuchs, mutes and sterile concubines, was hardly conducive to acquiring the knowledge and experience required for the successful governance of a great empire. Indeed, Mustafa's predecessor had proved a particularly inept ruler in an age when the Empire dearly needed a firm and decisive sultan. Osman III's ministers must have therefore considered it a blessing when he died from apoplexy on 30 October 1757 on receiving news of a particularly grievous catastrophe to afflict the Empire: a few weeks earlier the annual pilgrimage caravan to Mecca and Medina carrying the sultan's *mahmal* (banner) had been attacked by Bedouin tribes on its return journey to Damascus and had virtually been annihilated. The thousands of dead, left helpless to die in the desert, included one of Osman's sisters.[10]

According to Baron de Tott, later artillery advisor to the Ottoman government, Mustafa III was welcomed to the throne because 'the great believed him weak and that they could easily govern him';[11] but at least Mustafa was well educated. He had survived his years of incarceration reasonably well: in captivity he had studied mathematics, medicine and literature and had developed some proficiency in writing poetry. And although he lost no time in enjoying the sybaritic life of the court and its entertainments, he took a greater interest in the running of the Empire than many previous sultans, a task in which he received considerable support from his capable grand vezir, Mehmed Ragıb Paşa, kinsman and close friend. Indeed, de Tott, who accompanied the French minister plenipotentiary M. Charles de Vergennes to Istanbul in May 1755, while generally prejudiced against all things Ottoman, gives a surprisingly even-handed portrait of the man he refers to in his memoirs as the 'famous' Ragıb Paşa.

Ragıb combined an attractive personality with great strength of character. Never did a grand vezir better possess the talents necessary for the role. He could corrupt with skill and intimidate the boldest. Treacherous and immoral, he was also very able and a master of self-control.

And because of his great experience in matters of state

He found everyone ready to carry out his wishes and one soon noticed that his long experience of authority allowed him to exercise it with a strangely light touch.[12]

The matters of state with which Grand Vezir Ragıb Paşa was entrusted encompassed a Mediterranean world whose political geography was very different from the pattern of nation states that would emerge between the mid-nineteenth and early twentieth centuries. Since the crossing of the Dardanelles from Asia in 1352 by Sultan Orhan (r. 1324–60) the Ottomans had become a major European state encompassing the Balkans and Hungary. They had been forced to abandon much previously conquered European territory after their defeat at the Siege of Vienna in 1683. Nevertheless, during the first three decades of the eighteenth century, the Ottomans made a modest recovery. They defeated the Russians under their Tsar Peter the Great on the River Pruth in 1711, drove Venice out of the Greek Peloponnese and Crete in 1715. And at the Treaty of Belgrade in 1739 they recovered Belgrade itself, previously lost to the Austrians. In addition to their Balkan territories, the Islamic Empire of the Ottoman Turks, together with its tribute-paying vassals, controlled around four-fifths of the Mediterranean Sea's coastline and hinterlands. Consequently by the mid-eighteenth century the Ottomans were still one of the world's greatest powers.[13] As French historian Fernand Braudel described it, 'unquestionably ... a world-economy',[14] or as Ignatius Mouradgea simply put it in the dedication to the King of Sweden of his great *Tableau*, 'a Great Empire'.[15]

The Empire's administrative structure, in which Ragıb Paşa was now the most senior government minister, was based on large provinces known as *eyalets* to which the sultan appointed governor-generals (*valis* or *beylerbeyis*) usually with the honorific title paşa (pasha). Each eyalet was divided into a number of *sancaks* (provinces) headed by a district governor, usually addressed as *bey* or *emir* depending on the geographical location.

The provincial *valis*, together with a range of lower-ranking administrators, the army and the various categories of the *ulema* (Muslim clergy and judiciary) traditionally belonged to the Ottoman 'nobility', the tax-exempt *askeris* (literally 'soldiers'). Those they ruled – the peasants, artisans, merchants, servants and urban workers, whether Muslim or non-Muslim – belonged to the tax-paying class, the *reaya* (Ar. *ra'aya*) composed of non-*askeri* Muslim Turks, Muslim Arabs, Christian Arabs (of various denominations), Tatars, Berbers, Kurds and Jews.

Like the other two 'Gunpowder Empires' (the Mughal and the Safavid), the Ottoman state was patrimonial. The sultan was an absolute ruler and most of the land was his personal possession. The *reaya* peasants, who were settled on sultan's land, paid a tithe, typically 10 per cent of the value of their annual harvest. In addition male non-Muslims paid the *cizye* or poll tax, a payment in lieu of the fact that non-Muslims were not required to serve in the armed forces. The tithe and *cizye* were collected by a cavalry officer (*sipahi*) of askeri status. Under this system known as *timar*, the *timarlı* used the tithe to support himself and his entourage and, apart from the *cizye* which had to be handed over to the state, paid his own 'tax' to the sultan

Lesser Officers of the Sultan's Court c. 1797

A member of the sultan's divan   *A servant of the grand vezir*   *The head* terjuman *(translator)*

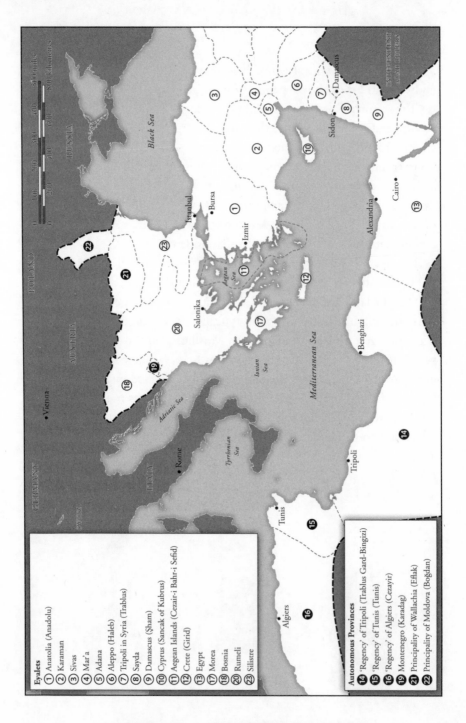

Eyalets
1. Anatolia (Anadolu)
2. Karaman
3. Sivas
4. Mar'a
5. Adana
6. Aleppo (Haleb)
7. Tripoli in Syria (Trablus)
8. Sayda
9. Damascus (Şham)
10. Cyprus (Sancak of Kubrus)
11. Aegean Islands (Cezair-i Bahr-i Sefid)
12. Crete (Girid)
13. Egypt
17. Morea
18. Bosnia
20. Rumeli
23. Silistre

Autonomous Provinces
14. 'Regency' of Tripoli (Trablus Gard-Bingizi)
15. 'Regency' of Tunis (Tunis)
16. 'Regency' of Algiers (Cezayir)
19. Montenegro (Karadag)
21. Principality of Wallachia (Eflak)
22. Principality of Moldova (Boğdan)

EYALETS AND AUTONOMOUS PROVINCES
OF THE OTTOMAN EMPIRE C. 1795

in the form of military service, when required. Although the system had feudal-like features, it was not a heritable landholding and could be revoked at the sultan's will if the military service required was not deemed sufficient.

The patrimonial Ottoman state was ruled by a roughly 1,000-strong bureaucracy. Its members were originally drawn from Christian converts who, together with the standing army and the senior *ulema*, were known as *kapıkulus* (lit. slaves of the state). However, by the eighteenth century the link to Christian converts had largely disappeared and the roughly 55,000 *kapıkulus* based in Istanbul were almost entirely Muslims of the *askeri* strata, of which around 15,000 were 'palace dependents' including the bureaucracy and their households and around 40,000 Janissaries.[16]

One such was the Grand Vezir Ragıb Paşa, whom we have already met. As 'chief executive' of the Empire he was in charge of the two main branches of government, the first and most important of which was the chancery with a staff of around 155, headed by the grand vezir himself. It was situated at the *Bab-ı Ali* ('The High Door', or 'Sublime Porte') leading to the outermost court of the Topkapı Palace.* The second main branch of the bureaucracy was the department of financial affairs, with a staff of about 870, headed by a *baş deftedar* (chief financial officer).[17]

Ragıb Paşa's biography is quite well known to historians, partly because his term of office was memorable as a period when the Empire was completely at peace, and partly because he also distinguished himself as a poet whose works were collected posthumously and published.[18] He was born Mehmed Ragıb in Istanbul in 1698 into a family of middle-ranking *askeri*s. His father, Sevki Mustafa Effendi, was a clerk in the finance department. From an early age Mehmed Ragıb showed himself to be a brilliant child, excelling in foreign languages and rapidly mastering the ornate and complex fasih Türkçe (eloquent Turkish), the medium of communication among his fellow court bureaucrats, with its more than 80 per cent archaic linguistic borrowings from Arabic and Persian.[19] Elsewhere ordinary Turks spoke the vernacular kaba Türkçe (rough Turkish) or one of at least two-dozen other indigenous languages in regular use throughout Ottoman-controlled territory.

---

* Since the chancery based at the 'Sublime Porte' was the leading branch of the Ottoman bureaucracy, the Christian European world used the name 'Sublime Porte' or simply 'The Porte' to mean 'the Ottoman government'. In what follows, I shall also generally follow this tradition.

Mehmed Ragıb was first appointed grand vezir on 12 January 1757 by Mustafa III's predecessor, Osman III, but continued in this position after Osman's death ten months later because – as Baron de Tott acknowledged – he was widely respected for his experience and sound judgement. Also presumably because in 1753 he had married a widowed sister of Mustafa, Saliha Sultana, thereby cementing a close and enduring friendship between the two men. As grand vezir, Mehmed Ragıb was ennobled with the highest rank after the sultan himself, a paşa of three horsetails. However, as with all the *kapikulus*, his wealth and possessions belonged to the sultan; and on his death they were appropriated by his master, Mustafa III, thereby causing financial disaster to Ignatius Mouradgea's patron and father-in-law, who had lent large sums to Ragıb Paşa.[20]

In the same year that Mustafa III became Ottoman sultan, a new ruler, Muhammad bin 'Abdallah, (r. 1757–90), commonly known as Sidi Muhammad, came to power in Morocco, the only Muslim state in the Mediterranean which had never been absorbed into the empire of the Turks. The fact that Morocco survived as a separate, independent Islamic polity was, in large part, a consequence of its topography and, to a lesser extent, its ethnic identity. It was a land segmented by the range of near-impassable Atlas Mountains running from the southwest to the northeast; an Atlantic coastline protected it from the west. Indeed, although Morocco's Mediterranean coastline is about 500 kilometres long, this is less than half that of its approximately 1,335-kilometre Atlantic coastline.

To the southeast of the Atlas range is a land of palm oases and desert gradually merging into the Sahara. It was from this frontier region, with its historic trade routes stretching as far south as West Africa's rich resources of gold and slaves, that the Alaouite forebears of Sultan Sidi Muhammad emerged to conquer and rule Morocco and its historic capital, Fez. Indeed, for centuries the rulers of Morocco had looked to West Africa rather than the Mediterranean to pursue their territorial ambitions. By the early eighteenth century their sub-Saharan possessions had been abandoned, but Morocco's rulers still referred to themselves as 'emperors'.

Although the Arabs had conquered most of Morocco and had Islamised and Arabised their peoples and language, its peoples retained their indigenous Berber culture and appearance. By the eighteenth century they often showed markedly African characteristics, the heritage of those earlier sub-Saharan conquests. Morocco's Atlas Mountains were peopled, on their lower levels, by three Berber tribal confederations, identified by the great Medieval Arab historian Ibn Khaldun (1332–1406) as the Sanhaja, the Zanata and the Masmuda. The other distinctive ethnic population of Morocco were the Moors, descendants of the Spanish Muslims who had been expelled from, or had fled, their own country in the late fifteenth and early sixteenth centuries. Fired by an intense hatred of all Christians, they settled on the Mediterranean and Atlantic coasts, where many became corsairs who preyed upon Christian merchant ships.

An estimated total of around 25 million people lived in the Ottoman Empire at the end of the eighteenth century. There do not appear to be any reliable estimates of the religious composition of this population. The first attempt at an official census (and one containing data on religious affiliation) wasn't taken until 1831, by Sultan Mahmud II (r. 1808–39). However, it was restricted to enumerating the adult male inhabitants liable to taxation and covered only the *eyalets* of Rumelia and Anatolia. In total, it showed that only two-thirds of the population were Muslims. In the Balkans, Muslims constituted 37 per cent of the total, with Greek Orthodox Christians making up 59 per cent, Roma at 2.2 per cent, Jews at 0.9 per cent and Armenians at 0.3 per cent. For Anatolia (the Turkish heartland) Muslims constituted 83 per cent, although the proportion of Greek Orthodox, living mainly in the coastal cities like Izmir (Smyrna), was a sizeable 15 per cent.[21]

The eighteenth-century Christian states of Mediterranean Europe had a geopolitical configuration very different from that of the late nineteenth and early twentieth centuries. Greece and the Greek islands were an integral part of the Ottoman Empire and would remain so until 1832. The Austrian Empire (which would become landlocked after 1918) had outlets to the Mediterranean at the port-cities of Trieste and Rijeka (Fiume) at the head of the Adriatic, dating from the inauguration of Trieste by the Habsburg Emperor Charles VI in 1719. In 1797 Austria-Hungary obtained Venice (previously captured by France) and its colony Dalmatia on the Adriatic coast, to which the ancient independent republic of Ragusa (Dubrovnik), also previously occupied by the French, was added by the Congress of Vienna in 1815. Britain, which had seized Gibraltar in 1704, also held the island of Menorca between 1798 and 1802, when it was returned to Spain.

Italy was divided into eleven individual polities of which the three largest in area were the Kingdom of Naples/Sicily, the Papal States and Venice. Two other Italian states, Tuscany and Palma, belonged to the Austrian (Habsburg) Empire. Only the Mediterranean borders of Spain and France have remained broadly unchanged since the eighteenth century.

France's population has been put at 23.8 million in 1730, rising to 28.6 million by 1789.[22] In Spain the population was around 7.6 million in 1717, rising to 10.5 million in 1797.[23] England (and Wales) – admittedly not a Mediterranean power, but with a presence in the Mediterranean – experienced a population increase from 6.2 million in 1750 to 8.21 million in 1791,[24] while the first 'modern' census of 1801 showed the population of England and Wales to be 9.4 million, including the country's armed forces. Russia, also geographically distant from the Mediterranean, would nevertheless be a player in the region's political and military affairs from the late eighteenth century onwards. Its population was around 15–17.5 million in the first half of the eighteenth century, but increased considerably towards the end of the century as a result of territorial acquisitions, especially in Poland.

Governments of the day generally felt that a large and growing population was beneficial to the state, in particular because it was a reservoir of manpower for the armed forces in an age when warfare had become almost endemic. The great French military engineer the Comte de Vauban (1633–1707) wrote that 'The greatness of Kings ... is measured in the number of their subjects'; and the Prussian military theorist Carl von Clausewitz (1780–1831) considered that superiority in military manpower was 'the most general principle of victory'.[25] With this in mind, a simple comparison of population size between the Ottoman Empire and the Mediterranean Christian states is revealing. Even if we restrict the comparison to Spain, France, the Italian states and the Austrian Empire (omitting Britain and Russia), and even if we make the comparison with the *total* population of the Ottoman Empire (including its non-Mediterranean provinces), then it is still clear that the potential human military resources of the Christian Mediterranean states were nearly three times those of the Turks' Islamic empire. And if we were to include the British and Russians then the comparison would look even more threatening to the Ottomans.

The discrepancy in military manpower was actually even greater than the figures for total populations reveal. The non-Muslim population of the

Ottoman Empire (mainly Orthodox Christians and Jews) were *dhimmi*s, protected but discriminated-against 'second class citizens'. They were allowed freedom of worship but did not serve in the army. Instead they had to pay the additional *cizye* (poll tax). As already noted, the proportion of the total population of the eighteenth-century Ottoman Empire who were non-Muslims is unknown, but from the scanty data in the 1831 religious census it would have made the Empire's effective military capacity vis-a-vis the Christian world even weaker than the total state population figures indicate.

Although other factors (recruitment problems, desertion, etc.) played a part, these basic demographic and religious considerations must have been the principal cause of the strikingly weak numbers enrolled in the Ottoman armed forces (army and navy). With only 150,000 men, in 1780 the Ottoman forces were lower than Russia (427,000), France (268,000), Austria (253,000), England (198,000) and Prussia (181,000). Only Spain (126,000) and the Dutch Republic (49,000) were smaller. In contrast, in 1700 Ottoman military manpower had been greater than any one of the major European states.[26]

Fortunately for the Ottomans, France, arguably the most powerful European state in the eighteenth century, had been a de facto ally of the Ottomans since the sixteenth, when both had begun a lengthy series of wars with the Austro-Spanish Habsburg Empire – little evidence of the so-called 'Clash of Civilisations' so recently popularised. As long as these conditions prevailed and the Ottomans did not get drawn into the Christians' wars, then the arithmetic of population size is less significant. Rivalry between the states of Christian Europe – and in the nineteenth century this meant Russia, Britain and France – would therefore be a crucial precondition for the Ottoman Empire's survival, as it was for the 'empire' of Morocco.

Urbanisation in the Islamic Mediterranean appears to have been surprisingly high.[27] In the Mediterranean Region there was a rough comparability in size between Muslim and Christian cities.* In fact, in 1800 the Near East was already more urbanised than most regions of the World, with something approaching 15 per cent of the population living in towns of over 10,000.[28]

---

* See Appendix A.

A drawing of the city of Aleppo in the early eighteenth century
Aleppo was a key trading entrepôt between the Mediterranean and the East.

Eighteenth-century Muslims and Christians were born, lived, worked, consumed, fought and ultimately died (usually at an early age) in separate Mediterranean societies. But for the moment putting on one side the most obvious difference – their religious beliefs – just how different were these two societies? For example, what were their respective levels of economic development and living standards? Their distinctive patterns of social stratification? Their degrees of economic inequality?

Perhaps surprisingly – since the period would later be seen as the major turning point in world history[29] – the years into which the average late-eighteenth-century European child was born were ones of growing economic deprivation. Indeed, this era has been called 'the crisis of mass poverty'.[30] This was true even of the countries which, so far, had been the 'economic power-houses' of the day: England and the Netherlands. Across all of Europe the output and value of goods and agricultural produce was actually increasing, but for reasons which are still not entirely clear, population was growing much faster. In short, what today we call 'National Income per Head' or its equivalent, Gross Domestic Product per capita (GDP/c), was falling.*

We know this because an ingenious economic historian has been able to establish GDP (and therefore GDP/c) estimates for a number of European countries (including Mediterranean Europe) using a mixture of reconstructed data and economic theory.[31] For example, between 1750 and 1780 it has been estimated that the GDP/c of the Italian states fell by 8 per cent; for France, it fell by over 5 per cent; and, in the case of Spain, by nearly 2 per cent. Surprisingly, while England's GDP/c was considerably higher than France's, and about the same as in the Netherlands, it too fell in the second half of the eighteenth century – by 6.5 per cent.[32]

Did the same trend occur in the Islamic Mediterranean? Unfortunately the data necessary to make the same calculations are unobtainable; and, in any case, the Ottoman Empire was so vast and varied that it would be difficult to make sense of any overall GDP/c figure even if it were possible to construct one.

However, it is possible to construct a proxy for GDP/c which allows us to compare 'living standards' between the mid-eighteenth century Christian and Islamic worlds. This 'proxy GDP/c' is a figure for real daily wages in particular cities,† the only solid information about living standards in many parts of the world before 1800.[33] However, to use this indicator effectively we need real wages from an industry that was widespread throughout the regions studied, used the same sort of technology, and produced a broadly similar output in terms of quality. The ideal such industry is construction, and the measure taken is for both skilled and unskilled workers.[34]

Using this GDP/c proxy in a study of eight cities,‡ it has been shown that

---

* GDP is the sum of all incomes (wages, profits, rent, interest) received in one year. In a modern economy it is usually calculated by an accounting equivalent which is the total expenditure of a country on goods and services. It includes all household expenditure (C), government expenditure (G) and business investment expenditure (I) plus income from exports (X) minus expenditure on imports (M). In conventional macro-economic symbols, C + G + I + (X – M).

† Money wages in oz. of silver for inter-city comparability and adjusted by the cost of a typical 'basket' of consumption goods for comparisons between time periods.

‡ London, Antwerp, Amsterdam (Northwest Europe), Paris, Vienna, Leipzig, Warsaw (mid-Europe), Valencia (Christian Mediterranean) and Istanbul (Islamic Mediterranean).

for the period 1750–1799 'Ottoman real wages *were comparable to those in most parts of Europe* [my emphasis] though about a third lower than those in north-western Europe.'[35] Two other important conclusions can be drawn from this particular study. Real wages fell in all eight cities in the study (including London, Antwerp and Amsterdam). This is the same trend as the estimates of GDP/c for six European countries referred to above, and it confirms the accuracy of using real wages for major cities as a proxy for national GDP/c and hence 'the average standard of living'. Second – and relevant for our particular interest in the Mediterranean region – in the later part of the eighteenth century, 'the average standard of living' was lower in Christian Valencia (Spain's principal port) than in Muslim Istanbul.[36]

However, if we dig around there are other indicators with which we can supplement our comparison of the European and the Ottoman standard of living in the later eighteenth-century Mediterranean World. Diet, human stature, life expectancy and material culture (possessions) can all provide us with this additional information. And all these indicators, which can be drawn from a range of different locations, suggest that, like our proxy for GDP/c, there was little difference between the Southern European and Ottoman worlds.*

In addition to such indicators of the standard of living, it would be useful to have a picture of a 'typical' Ottoman community in the mid-eighteenth century, for example the kind of small country town of the kind equally common in the Christian Mediterranean world. To date, only one such picture exists: a study of Kastamonu, a predominantly Muslim town in Anatolia comprising around 4,000 households. From the limited information about the town's occupations, Kastamonu appears to have been an administrative and commercial centre with a strong contingent of minor religious and judicial dignitaries and some retired military. It also housed a number of artisans and merchants involved in local trade networks which dealt in wool, cotton cloth and copperware.

In northwest Europe real wages of both skilled and unskilled workers were the highest. However, wages of skilled construction workers were higher in Istanbul than in Paris, Vienna, Leipzig and Valencia, and wages of unskilled workers were higher in Istanbul than in Leipzig and Valencia, roughly equal to those in Paris and Vienna but less than those in Warsaw. (See charts in Özmur and Pamuk, 202, pp. 312–13.)

*   See Appendix B (and A).

From information derived from probate registers for the years 1712–60, it seems that, although there was a disparity of wealth among the town's citizens, it was modest. Inequality was not a major issue. The richest 5 per cent of deceased householders had owned only a modest 29.7 per cent of the total wealth bequeathed.[37] Moreover, the average value of an inherited estate (749.2 *kuruş*)* at current prices would have bought 7,700 kilos of mutton, or two to three average-sized houses, five average-sized shops, thirty horses, four adult slaves or thirty silver clocks. Consequently, the authors of this study concluded, 'we can surmise that poverty was not a pressing problem for most'.[38]

However, if the concentration of wealth in a small town like Kastamonu was fairly modest, the same cannot be said of the Empire's major cities. For example, using probate data as in the study of Kastamonu, it has been calculated that, for the period 1776–98, the richest 3 per cent of Cairo's deceased accounted for 51 per cent of the total wealth bequeathed; and for Damascus (albeit somewhat earlier, around 1700) the richest 10 per cent of the population owned over 70 per cent of the total wealth.[39] Making comparisons with cities and provinces in the eighteenth-century Christian Mediterranean world is not straightforward: the various studies have used measures of wealth drawn from, for example, annual tax liability on property rather than probate data (which are probably more accurate). Nevertheless we get estimates quite similar to those of Damascus and Cairo. For example in the provinces of Apulia, Tuscany and Piedmont (representing southern, middle and northern Italy) in 1750 the richest 10 per cent of the population owned 72, 78 and 65 per cent of the total wealth respectively.[40]

Who, then, were the individuals at the top of the wealth distribution pyramid in Cairo and other Ottoman cities? We might assume that they were all *askeri*s (the tax-exempt elite). However, in the eighteenth century the link between *askeri* status and wealth (in land, urban property or specie money) was breaking down. From a study of the bequeathed estates of a group of deceased Istanbul *askeris* for the period 1750–51,[41] we can single out a certain Sheikh Abdulkerim Efendi, whose legacy (before taxes and

---

* The *kuruş* (known in the West as the *piastre*) was the most commonly used coin in the Ottoman Empire. Its value was fixed at 120 silver *akçes* (each with a metallic silver content of 0.121 grams in 1751). At mid-eighteenth century exchange rates, one £ sterling was equal to 110 *kuruş* and therefore 100 *kuruş* equalled £0.909.

administration charges) was 5,905 silver *akçes*; this was barely enough to cover his outstanding debts and funeral expenses. Similarly, one Molla Hasan, whose estate was 11,587 *akçes*, was also one of the poorest men in the group. By their titles (*effendi, molla*), both men would have been officials in the religious establishment; but the wealth they bequeathed hardly compares with that of another *askeri*, Elhac Hüseyin, described as a 'leather manufacturer', whose estate was calculated to be worth 371,607 *akçes*.* (Why a 'leather manufacturer' should have been an *askeri* may be explained by the probability that this individual was also a Janissary soldier moonlighting in trade, a common occurrence).

At the same time non-*askeris* were moving up the social pyramid, amassing wealth, and with it power. Such may have been the 'nouveaux riches' described by Baron de Tott in the 1770s.

> The riches of some persons of large property maintain, in the environment of Smyrna [Izmir], a system of independence, the progress of which increases every day. *They rely principally on the power of money and this power is irresistible.* It is likewise to be remarked that the efforts made by the Porte for some years to destroy one of these aghas has less terrified the rest than shown the weakness of the Despot. [My emphasis][42]

These newly rich individuals are often referred to in the historical literature as *ayan* (Ar. *a'yan*), or grand *ayan*.[43] Of non-*askeri* status, or men who had acquired it corruptly through their wealth, they were mainly the product of a particularly important development during the eighteenth century: the emergence of what were, in effect, private landed estates worked by landless peasants or sharecroppers, often growing cash crops for the European market. These were typically the outcome of what has been called the 'privatisation' of the taxation system: the move away from the old 'feudal' system, known as *timar*, and the emergence of 'tax-farming'. Tax farms were not all (as the name suggests) agricultural properties. For example the term might refer to the exclusive right to collect customs duties from a particular region. They were sold to the highest bidder,

---

*   The title *Elhac* (Ar. *Hajji*) indicates that the individual has made the pilgrimage to Mecca.

or group of bidders. Moreover, in some regions they became, de facto, heritable property.[44] Some such tax farms were huge, and coincided with Ottoman provincial boundaries.

So far, we have seen that in a number of important respects – national income per head, living standards, food consumption, etc. – there were many similarities between the European world and that of the Islamic Mediterranean. Only in Europe's far northwest, in England and the Netherlands, was society moving in a new direction as it became progressively more capitalistic, although even there living standards were falling.

However, there are two areas where it is usually accepted that the two societies markedly differed – the literacy rate and the development of science and technology. According to historians H. A. R. Gibb and Harold Bowen (1951), the vast majority of the population of the Islamic Mediterranean during the mid-eighteenth century 'remained entirely illiterate'.[45] A widely accepted literacy rate for the Ottoman Empire at this time is only 2 to 3 per cent.[46] Compared with estimates for a range of Mediterranean Christian countries in the mid-eighteenth century (29 per cent for France, 23 per cent for the Italian states and 8 per cent for Spain)[47] the Muslim figure is very low indeed.

But before we accept this apparently startling difference we need to understand how this Ottoman 'literacy' rate was calculated. The fact is, we don't really know. Indeed, how could we know for such a vast and highly divergent area? Moreover, it has recently been pointed out that there are gradations of literacy. For example, in early modern Europe, many of those classed as 'illiterate' (because they couldn't sign their names) could actually read: signatures did not necessarily indicate literacy.[48] Indeed, the idea that Ottoman society was strictly divided between a highly literate Ottoman-Turkish-speaking *askeri* stratum and a uniformly illiterate *reaya* of vernacular-speaking country bumpkins is extremely doubtful. Non-*askeri* traders and artisans needed considerable familiarity with the written word (in whatever script and vocabulary) if they were going to successfully defend their business interests.[49]

In addition, Islamic society was very much based on courts and legal documentation. The adjudication of trade disputes, inheritances, property transactions and family matters depended crucially on legal transactions based on the written word. Documentary evidence of ownership was required for even the smallest property transaction: deeds of ownership were often needed just to protect one's home.[50] Among the peasantry matters were probably very different; but this was also true among the peasantry of southern Europe and the Christian Mediterranean. So while we may concede that Islamic society was less literate than that of Christian Europe, it would be unwise to exaggerate the extent of the difference or place great emphasis on whether it had a critical role in that society's economic development and ultimate survival.

It has been argued that a lower literacy rate was the consequence of the much slower adoption of printing in the Ottoman Empire. It did not become established – and then only to a limited degree – until three centuries after Johannes Gutenberg invented the moveable-type press in the German city of Mainz in 1455. Until recently, the mostly widely accepted reason for this was that the Sultan Bayezid II issued a *firman* (edict) banning printing in the Arabic script in 1485,* and that the ban was repeated by his successor Selim I in 1515. It is also generally assumed that the edict remained in force until printing was approved by Sultan Ahmed III (r. 1703–30) in 1727. For example, in Bernard Lewis's *The Arabs in History* (1958) we read that 'The Ottoman sultans for long banned printing in Arabic or Turkish,'[51] a claim he reiterated in *The Emergence of Modern Turkey* (1961). It has also been generally accepted that these 'bans' emanated from pressure exerted by the religious establishment. For example, in a work published as recently as 2017, we not only find reference to the 'widely known' edicts of sultans Bayezid and Selim, but also the argument that the bans were issued because 'The Ottoman religious establishment had significant incentive to encourage the sultan to block the printing press... [i.e.] its monopoly over the transmission of religious knowledge.'[52]

That the Ottomans were very slow in adopting the printing press is undeniable. And it is quite possible that this did have an impact on the spread of literacy. But for the time being two crucial points can be made. First, the most recent scholarship demonstrates that there is no reliable historical evidence for the 'sultanic bans' (no extant Ottoman documentation of the

---

*   This also applied to Ottoman Turkish, since this was also written in a (modified) version of the Arabic script.

two *firmans*).[53] The story emanates from one unreliable French source.* Indeed, the only extant *firman* of this period relating to printing is that of Sultan Murad III in 1588 authorising the importation of European books printed in the Arabic script[54] – hardly an indication of any opposition to printing in Arabic script per se.

There is also no written evidence that the *ulema* systematically opposed printing, although, of course, individuals may have done so. Not only is there nothing in the Qur'an or the hadiths† which could be used as grounds for such an opposition, but when the first printing press was eventually established in 1727 by the Hungarian Protestant convert to Islam Ibrahim Müteferrika, religious scholars of the Ottoman Court‡ actually supported Müteferrika's press.[55] Moreover, some of those who owned printed and expensive books included religious functionaries. According to the historian Orlin Sabev, the latter is significant since it had been alleged that the religious functionaries were the traditional opponents of the printing press.[56] Clearly, then, the slowness with which the Ottoman Empire adopted a print culture must have had other causes.

With regard to the secular sciences and their related technological innovations, the writers who have emphasised the backwardness of the Ottomans are on stronger ground. Even among the educated strata there seems to have been a lack of acquaintance with, or interest in, this area of human knowledge, and consequently a wider reluctance to engage with science-based technological innovation.

The libraries of the *askeri* were still dominated by religious texts, not only the Qur'an and hadith literature but many lesser commentaries and works of exegesis. For example, a study of the libraries of forty-four deceased members of the *askeri* strata in Istanbul for 1750–51 shows that 82 per cent of the 617 manuscripts and books in their possession were

---

* The originator of the 'ban' theory was a French Franciscan priest, André Thevet (1502–1590), in a work published in Paris in 1584 (Schwartz, 2017, p. 12). In fact he claimed that the 'bans' were against 'reading' works printed in the Arabic script. Although Thevet had travelled in the Levant, he had little or no knowledge of its languages. His later works on the Americas are regarded as unreliable by anthropologists and historians.

† Reported statements and authorisations of the Prophet.

‡ For example, Şeyhulislam Yenişehirli Abdullah Efendi, Şeyhulislam Mevlana Efendi, Mevlana Esad, Sheikh of the Kasimpaşa Mevlevi (Sufi) lodge.

religious. Moreover, the situation had barely changed fifty years later: of the 1,276 manuscripts and books owned by forty-four *askeris*, 76 per cent dealt with religious topics. In contrast, only nine items on such subjects as geography, mathematics, natural sciences, astronomy and medicine were found in the libraries of those deceased in 1750–51 and only sixty-eight for those deceased in 1800–01.[57] The British orientalist Edward Lane noted the same pattern in Cairo during the 1820s. Reviewing the libraries of educated men, he notes that 'works on medicine, chemistry, the mathematics, algebra, and various other sciences, are comparatively very few'.[58] Although the printing of non-religious books in Turkish had been authorised by the *fetva* (A. *fatwa*) of 1727, only 142 such works were actually printed in the years before 1838 and these in very small print runs.[59]

In the Ottoman world there were no institutions of higher secular and scientific education,[60] and matters were actually far worse in the isolated 'empire' of Morocco. There, at the once-great centre of Islamic learning the University of Fez, the curriculum included subjects such as 'the determination by calculation of the influence of the angels, the spirits and the stars'. This 'science', as the American historian F. R. Flournoy remarked, was one 'in which few appear to have attained a high degree of proficiency'.[61] In contrast, even in some of the relatively backward aristocratic states of Italy, where the universities were generally conservative and hide-bound, 'enlightened' members of the nobility established scientific academies during the eighteenth century. And by the latter part of the century there were also state-supported academies where public lectures were given, such as the Neapolitan Academy of Science and Letters, founded in 1778, and the Genoese Society for Arts and Manufactures, established in 1786.[62] Needless to say, in England, the Netherlands and France levels of literacy, popular education and the sciences were of a different order.

It is therefore clear that by the mid-eighteenth century the Muslims had fallen behind the European Christian world in respect of non-religious knowledge and culture, not only with respect to current scientific developments but also the intellectual achievements of much earlier Islamic eras. This is strongly suggested in the account of the famous Egyptian *'alim* (religious scholar) and historian 'Abd al-Rahman al-Jabarti, in which he revealed his amazement at not only the richness and variety of the library which the French brought with them during their 1798 invasion, but also the 'wondrous' scientific equipment at their disposal. For example, he acknowledged that the French

> possess extraordinary astronomical instruments of perfect construction and instruments for measuring altitudes of wondrous, amazing and precious construction. And they have telescopes for looking at the stars and measuring their heights, conjunctions, and oppositions, and the clepsydras and clocks with gradings and minutes and seconds, all of wondrous form and very precious, and the like.[63]

And yet, during the Middle Ages, Arab and Persian scientists had demonstrated an extensive knowledge of scientific topics and methods of constructing a wide range of scientific instruments and experimental methods.[64] Why this intellectual decline occurred remains obscure and controversial. In the older literature of the 'Eastern Question', the apparent lack of interest in science and technology is directly attributed to Islam and its guardians – the *ulema*. A recent and more nuanced version of the same argument attributes Islam's 'scientific decline' to developments within the evolution of Islam: specifically to the so-called 'closing of the gates of *ijtihad*' (independent religious thinking) around the ending of the first millennium,* and to the pernicious influence of the *ulema* 'as the legitimating and propagating agents for Islamic rulers'.[65]

But before we resort to locating such major societal and cultural changes in the realms of theology, there are more fundamental factors to be explored. These are to be found in the transition of a medieval world of competing Arab caliphs and warring emirs to the vast patrimonial 'gunpowder empire' of the Ottomans. This is not to deny that, as late as the sixteenth century (and long after the 'closing of the gates of *ijtihad*'), the Ottoman world witnessed the emergence of many brilliant individual scientists, especially in the fields of mathematics, astronomy, medicine and geography.[66] But by

---

*   *Ijtihad* is the exercise of a jurist's independent thought in situations where the Qur'an and hadiths do not provide a clear decision. Its opposite is *taqlid* (tradition or precedent).

comparison with the situation in Europe, advances in scientific thought were not accompanied by a transformation of the mode of production – in technology and the economy. And it is to the nature of the Ottomans' 'statal' economy and its economic thought that we now turn.

CHAPTER 2

The Ottoman 'Economic Mind':
Technology, Innovation, Industry and Trade

During his confinement in the *kafes*, Mustafa III would have been taught that an Ottoman sultan had an obligation of great importance and antiquity. All sultans were obliged to practice *hisba*, an Islamic concept which can be loosely translated as 'accountability' or 'responsibility', a divinely sanctioned duty of the ruler to intervene in society to 'command the right and forbid the wrong', a duty enjoined by a similar phrase in the Qur'an.

One of the most important aspects of *hisba* was exemplified by the Ottoman economic system. Ottoman political economy was based on the precept that the state was responsible for maintaining a social and economic equilibrium favourable to collecting the maximum fiscal revenue, yet also subject to the continued well-being of the *reaya* (tax-paying classes) and the Empire's internal peace and security.[1] It is exemplified in the popular expression, 'A ruler can have no power without soldiers; no soldiers without money; no money without the well-being of the subjects; and no well-being without justice',[2] sometimes known as the 'circle of equity'. As such, it was a model which 'partially stifled competition (and efficiency/growth) for the sake of economic stability and a certain level of equity for those established within its boundaries'.[3] Indeed, the Turkish historian Halil İnalcık goes as far as describing the Ottoman economic system as a form of 'welfare state'.[4] It is important not to discount the extent to which the sultan's duty of *hisba* had real meaning for the urban population of large Ottoman cities. As we shall see, on the one occasion when a sultan and his entourage displayed an open disregard for social justice and the expected degree of moderation in his personal spending, Istanbul came the closest to a genuine social revolution as it would in its entire history.

The dominant mode of production in the eighteenth-century Ottoman Empire was artisanal. The everyday needs of the people were supplied by small-scale craftsmen, much as they still were in Europe. However, there was one important difference. One of the most important objectives of the Ottoman 'statal economy' was to provide a basic minimum standard of living for the mass of the ordinary people, especially that huge artisan class of Istanbul and other great Ottoman cities. This meant a far greater degree of state intervention in the market than was the case in Europe. In essence, the Ottoman economy was 'provisionist'. Both internally and externally (foreign trade) it aimed to provide the Empire's artisans with a reliable supply of affordable raw materials while at the same time requiring them to sell their own goods at 'fair' prices and in accordance with state-regulated weights and measures. There could also be selective intervention in the market: for example, from time to time *narh* (ceiling prices) would be mandated during periods of shortage. These, and other measures, were enforced by an official known as a *muhtasib* who was appointed by, and acted on behalf of, the local *kadı* (judge and administrative officer).[5] In addition, the state believed in the need to prevent 'excessive' competition, which might destabilise the artisan class in the cities and also put *hisba* in jeopardy.

The fundamental precept underlying Ottoman economic thought was social stability. Innovations, especially machinery and productivity-raising new technologies, were frowned upon if they might disrupt the equilibrium of the state by creating unemployment. This fear of a breakdown in social stability was by no means unjustified. As we know, the introduction of labour-saving machinery in the early years of Britain's industrial revolution caused massive social unrest bordering on revolution.

The example of printing, briefly referred to in the previous chapter, is highly relevant here. Printing has been seen by some historians as the crucial 'information revolution' which underpinned the later economic superiority of northwest Europe, and the slowness of the Ottomans in adopting this technology has been given as one of the main reasons for their future economic decline.[6] However, as we have also already seen, the fifteenth- and sixteenth-century sultanic 'bans' against printing appear to have been a myth.

If there had never been any actual sultanic ban on printing, what then were the principal reasons for its failure to take root in the Empire until the end of the eighteenth century? Even the installation of Ibrahim Müteferrika's press in Istanbul (it operated from 1729 to 1742) resulted in a very modest output of very expensive books (sixteen works with a total printing of 10–11,000 copies of which 30 per cent remained unsold at Müteferrika's death in 1746).[7] Various arguments have been put forward for this lacklustre performance, including the high production cost (and price) and the difficulty of printing cursive (joined-up) script, which resulted in unfavourable comparisons with the calligraphy of manuscript copies.[8] But the most likely reason was recorded by the Italian Count Luigi Fedinando Marsigli (1658–1730), who spent many years in the Ottoman Empire:

> The Turks do not print their works, but this is not because, as commonly believed, printing is banned or because their works are not worth printing. They do not want to prevent the copyists, numbering 90,000 when I was in Constantinople, from earning a living.[9]

The contrast could not be sharper between such a 'moral economy' and the *laissez-faire* which accepted the privations, misery and cruel repression of tens of thousands of hand-loom weavers in early nineteenth-century Britain. But this was the price paid by the many for Britain's industrial revolution and its subsequent economic development. Or, as the twentieth-century French historian Fernand Braudel put it, 'The English people paid very dearly for their victory.'[10]

In addition to the sultan's obligation of *hisba*, there were two further elements of the Ottoman 'moral economy': the *waqf* (religious or quasi-religious endowment)* and the *esnaf* (loosely translated as occupational guilds).

A *waqf* was an inalienable tax-exempt endowment, typically taking the form of a piece of land or some other asset whose usufruct is dedicated in perpetuity to some charitable cause. *Waqfs* pre-dated the Ottoman Empire by centuries and were not restricted to wealthy male Muslims: they could also be set up by poor people and women, and to Christians and Jews living

---

* Since this Islamic institution pre-dated the Ottoman Empire, I prefer to use the original and better-known Arabic term '*waqf*' rather than the Turkish '*vaqif*'.

in Islamic territory as *dhimmi*s (state-protected non-Muslims).* Although *waqf*s were established as private initiatives they can be seen as fulfilling the practical implementation of the sultan's general duty of *hisba*. Moreover, the cash flow from their original, protected capital funds served an even wider function than mere charity. Indeed, a broad spectrum of what we now designate as public or municipal services, e.g. welfare, education, religious services, construction and maintenance of water systems, hospitals, etc., were set up, financed and maintained almost exclusively by *waqf* endowments. Among the 'welfare' functions of the *waqf*s we can also include the provision of 'soup kitchens' for the poor in times of general economic distress and – by virtue of their large portfolios of urban buildings – the control of rents: 'It may be argued that the *waqf* provided economic stability by keeping rents low'.[11]

In the eighteenth century the *esnaf* (guilds) were prolific in almost every Ottoman town or city. For example, it has been estimated that there were at least seventy-four in Cairo.[12] Writing in the seventeenth century, the famous Ottoman traveller and commentator Evliya Çelebi (1609–1657) described a grand procession of the guilds through the capital in a carnival-like event, with their gaudy banners and floats representing their particular trades. On that occasion, Çelebi listed 735 separate guilds representing trades such as woodcutters, chalk-makers, masons, butchers, sea captains, bakers, toy-makers, firemen and so on. Some, like the guild of watchmen, were huge, with as many as 12,000 members; others belonging to more esoteric trades had only a handful of members, like the guild of map-makers with only fifteen. There was even a one-man 'guild' for the making of instruments of torture.[13]

Typically, each guild had six governing officials elected from among its master-craftsmen and headed by an executive officer, the *kethüda*. To occupy the position of *kethüda*, the individual concerned required a diploma from the sultan, since it was he who would represent the guild's members in dealings with the local *kadı* in matters pertaining to regulation, disputes and

---

* However, it should be noted that under Islamic law the usufruct of a certain class of *waqf* (known as a cash *waqf*) could also be reserved for future generations of the endower's own family, down to the last descendent, and only then would *waqf* income be used for some designated charitable purpose. Nevertheless, it seems the vast majority of *waqf*s did have a charitable objective, and in one manner or other functioned as a sort of supplementary 'welfare state'.

any malpractices. For example, he would handle complaints about 'unfair' competition from newcomers entering a particular trade.[14] However, the *kethüda*s were also the conduits through which the sultan dictated any new market regulations or prohibitions, such as the 1795 instructions concerning the height, shape, material and use of new buildings replacing those destroyed by fire.[15] As such, the close relationship between the *esnaf* and the state created forms of 'consumer protection' largely unknown in Europe.

While earlier writing on the *esnaf* emphasised state control and the means whereby the state could monitor and tightly control the output of goods deemed necessary for the satisfaction of the population,[16] a much more nuanced interpretation is required. Especially in the provinces, *esnaf* acted independently when their members required it. They negotiated with the *kadı* and other local authorities from positions of relative power. On the other hand, only very occasionally would individual *esnaf* band together in a common cause, and they showed no general sense of 'class interest'. For example, one of their main concerns was to prevent artisan outsiders coming into their cities and competing with their own existing fields of operation.

Nevertheless, *esnaf* members clearly had a deep-rooted understanding of the principles embodied in the sultan's *hisba*: a rudimentary belief in social justice and equity. That this belief could be severely put to the test was exemplified in the 'Patrona Halil' uprising of 1730. The reigning Sultan Ahmed III and his grand vezir and son-in-law Nevşehirli Damat Ibrahim Paşa had begun to introduce a number of European-influenced reforms into Ottoman society including the printing press, a fire brigade, and better water supplies. But they also indulged in ostentatious luxury – building splendid new palaces like Ahmed's own Persian-influenced Saadabad, constructing Frenchified villas for his ministers and their families along the banks of the Bosphorus, and digging up public land for use as exotic tulip plantations. These extravagances occurred at a time of additional 'non-Qur'anic' taxation, currency depreciation and a massive inflow of refugees from territory lost in unpopular wars with Persia, all of which weighed heavily on the *esnaf*.

In September 1730, learning of an Ottoman military disaster on the Persian front, the *esnaf* of Istanbul, supported by the Janissaries, rose up under the leadership of one Patrona Halil, an Albanian former soldier and second-hand clothes dealer. They rampaged through the city and destroyed most of the extravagant palaces and tulip gardens. They proceeded to force the sultan to have the grand vezir Damat Ibrahim and certain members of his family executed and then compelled him to abdicate in favour of his nephew Mahmud I (r. 1730–54). However, the revolution soon collapsed. Patrona Halil and his lieutenants became overconfident, demanded the appropriation of many of the senior positions in the Empire, and were tricked into an audience with the Sultan Mahmud I, where they were seized and executed on 24 November 1731.

The uprising has often been described as 'anti-Western' and a major setback to the first attempts at modernising the Empire. For example, it has been said that 'The Patrona Halil rebellion temporarily and in some cases completely stopped the flow of ideas, literature, ambassadors and military consultation which had begun to take place between Europe, largely France and the Porte.'[17] In fact there is little evidence for this view. Military cooperation with Europe actually increased after Mahmud I came to power. But perhaps far more significantly, that one major 'Western innovation' of the era, Müteferrika's new printing press, recently authorised by Ahmed III's *firman*, was ignored by the 'anti-Western' rebels. Indeed, not only did his printing venture survive the rampages and destruction of 1730, but under the reign of Ahmed's successor printing continued. One of Müteferrika's most important works, published in 1732, was actually dedicated to Mahmud I.*

There was, however, a good reason for the *esnaf* rebels' apparent lack of concern about this first Ottoman printing enterprise. Sultan Ahmed's *firman* had made it clear that Müteferrika's press would produce only non-religious works. Such religious works were by far the bread-and-butter of the manuscript copyists' business. In any case, Müteferrika himself was really only interested in printing secular works, geography, history, natural science (he printed a work on magnetism). So with scant threat to their livelihood, the *esnaf* of copyists and calligraphers showed little concern

---

* After Müteferrika's death in 1746 two high-ranking members of the ulema acquired his printing press, but only one further work was published (in 1756) after which it temporarily closed down, probably for economic reasons; but printing resumed under new owners in 1784 and six further works were published between then and 1794. In 1797 the reforming Sultan Selim III purchased the press for use in his newly established military school.

about the introduction of the printing press. In short, it didn't threaten their economic survival. On the other hand, 'The overthrow of Ahmed III as well as the destruction of the Saadabad palace and its tulip gardens sounded a call for a return to a moral economy in this time of need, one that would improve the welfare of Istanbul's residents at large.'[18]

Although the dominant mode of production in the Islamic Mediterranean remained artisanal throughout the eighteenth century, in a few areas we can witness the beginnings of a more advanced and capitalistic form of economic organisation; for example, the high-quality red-cloth-making industry of Ambelakia in Ottoman Greece and the *shashiya* industry of Tunisia. A form of early capitalism which historians have described as 'manufacturing' (factory-based production without any significant machinery) appears to have become well established at this time.

The *shashiya* was a conical hat or fez made from felt which was worn throughout the Mediterranean Islamic world. Due to the quantities of raw materials involved, the level of investment and production, the sophisticated division of labour, the size of some of the workplaces and the vast commercial networks created for the distribution of the product, the 'capitalist character' of the industry has been called 'indisputable'.[19] Moreover, in certain respects – total volume of production, the quality and variety of the product – the Tunisian *shashiya* industry was superior to its major competitor, the *shashiya* manufacturers of Marseille.[20]

It could be argued that the Tunisian *shashiya* industry was only in transition towards capitalist manufacturing. This is because a considerable part of the labour process, for example, the spinning of the wool, was still based on the artisanal 'putting-out' system with production carried out in individual households. Perhaps for this reason, other historians have described the industry as only 'proto-capitalist'.[21] However, whether capitalist or proto-capitalist, the Tunisian *shashiya* industry demonstrates that whatever the obstacles facing the development of capitalism in the Mediterranean Islamic world, they were not *religious*: they had little to do with Islam itself.

And if the Tunisian *shashiya* industry was indeed only proto-capitalist and there were no indications of fully fledged manufacturing capitalism in the Islamic world at this time, the same could be said for most regions of Mediterranean Christian Europe where, with a few exceptions, small-scale artisanal production remained the rule. One of the few large-scale enterprises was in Bourbon Spain. In the eighteenth century its monarchs established state-owned cloth manufacturing enterprises in the belief that they could thereby catch up with Britain and France. But these large, vertically integrated cloth-manufacturing factories produced far in excess of demand, could not compete with foreign imports in either price or quality, made continuous losses, and had almost all been shut down by the end of the century.[22] Even in eighteenth-century France where we can we see the emergence of a manufacturing economy by the 1770s,[23] it was still largely at the transitional stage, like that of Tunis. Indeed, as late as the 1830s, the great silk textile industry of Lyons was still essentially a huge putting-out operation in which a group of around 1,400 merchants and financiers advanced the raw silk on credit to some 8,000 artisans operating their own looms.

As far as trade – and its facilitator, credit – are concerned, there can be no doubt that merchant capitalism was as prolific among Mediterranean Muslims as among Mediterranean Christians (and Jews) and had been since the Middle Ages. As the great French sociologist and orientalist Maxime Rodinson pointed out,[24] it was no more difficult for a Muslim supplier of credit at interest to get around the Qur'anic prohibition against *riba* than it was for the Catholic moneylender to evade the sin of usury. The evidence of thousands of court cases in both large cities and small towns involving lenders and borrowers 'leave[s] no doubt that the use of credit, small and large, was widespread among all segments of urban and rural parts of society. It is clear that neither Islamic prohibitions against interest and usury nor the absence of formal banking institutions prevented the expansion of credit in Ottoman society.'[25]

However, when it comes to what we might call state economic policy there were significant differences between the Islamic and Christian worlds. The mercantilist concept, predominant among seventeenth- and eighteenth-century European states – that the government should aim to maximise exports and minimise imports in order to accumulate 'bullion' – was alien to the Ottoman economic mind. As already noted, the sultan's economic *hisba* was essentially provisionist. The primary function of trade was to ensure the adequate supply of goods to the *reaya,* in particular the artisanal *esnaf*, who were an important source of the tax revenues supporting the military, religious and administrative *askeri* class. This meant that the system encouraged the import of commodities which were, or might become, in short supply. At the same time it often discouraged exports – especially foodstuffs – which might create a shortage and thus rising consumer prices at home. 'The benefits of the state treasury and the needs of the internal market seemed to be the only concern of the Ottoman government.'[26]

A valuable tool for encouraging the commerce of the Empire, and in particular the provisioning of imported goods deemed necessary for the smooth functioning of Ottoman society, were the agreements known as the 'capitulations'.* First issued in 1569 and reissued in revised form five times until 1740, the capitulations established freedom of commerce between France and the Ottoman Empire, extra-territoriality for French subjects (the right to be tried in their own courts for every crime except murder), freedom of dress and worship, and freedom from Ottoman taxation except import and export tariffs.† Armed guards were also provided to ensure protection for France's consulates within the Ottoman Empire. England and Holland, opponents of the Ottomans' principal enemy (the Habsburg dynasty ruling Spain and Austria), were also granted capitulations on the French model in 1581 and 1612 respectively, and eventually others would follow.[27]

The commercial linkages between Ottoman Muslims and the nationals of states enjoying capitulations encouraged the growth of highly cosmopolitan Mediterranean ports such as Izmir, Salonika, Beirut and, later, Alexandria. Over the period 1748–89, one in every four of the ships leaving Marseilles (the Empire's single biggest trading partner) went to Izmir. Even Tunis, whose corsairs intermittently attacked and captured the shipping of Christian states, still grew into an important international trading city with settled communities of French, Italian and Jewish merchants.[28]

The commerce of the Ottoman Empire's Levantine ports engendered the adoption of *lisan al-faranji*, a lingua franca (initially largely based on

---

* Named after the chapters (capitulae) the agreement's text contained.

† And import tariffs were only 3 per cent *ad valorem* compared with 5 per cent for goods imported by Ottoman citizens.

Italian) used by both Muslims and Christians. In the words of the historian Philip Mansel, 'Its widespread use from the Middle Ages to the nineteenth century disproves the notion of two hostile worlds or that Islam had become a closed world.'[29] On the other hand, nothing equivalent to the capitulations was available to Muslim merchants who occasionally found themselves in Christian lands. In fact very few Ottomans travelled to Christian Europe; they were frightened of the persecution they suffered there, ranging from being spied on to outright assault.[30]

Although the capitulations would eventually become an Achilles' heel for the Ottoman economy, in Sultan Mustafa III's time this eventuality could not have been foreseen. As yet, there was little fear of any threat to the Ottoman economy from excessive imports from Christian Europe or declining Ottoman exports.

The opening of the Cape route to India and the East largely robbed the Muslims of the lucrative trade in spices which they had dominated in the Middle Ages. It used to be thought that this left the Empire and its Arab provinces – in Bernard Lewis's words – 'in a stagnant backwater through which the life-giving stream of world trade no longer flowed'.[31] Historians have now abandoned this view. Although it is true that after 1630 the pepper and spices bound for Europe were largely diverted to the Portuguese and Dutch-dominated Atlantic routes, the Ottoman Empire remained the source of a variety of both basic commodities and exotic and luxurious goods much in demand among western and southern Europe's aristocracies and emergent middle classes. By the eighteenth century, the trade in exotic spices had been replaced by Ottoman-sourced silk, coffee, tobacco, medicinal drugs and cotton textiles both printed and plain. The Empire also supplied Christian Europe with a substantial part of the raw materials upon which Europe's still largely artisanal manufacturing industries depended, including raw cotton, leather, hides and items used for dyes.[32]

Although British imports from the Ottoman Levant declined during the first half of the eighteenth century,[33] French imports from the region grew substantially, increasing in value from an annual average of 8,857 thousand *livres tournois* in 1711–15 to 13,401 thousand *livres* by 1750–54.[34] Raw cotton, much of it from Palestine and Egypt, accounted for by far the largest part of this increase. Over the same period, France also increased its imports of mohair yarn, saffron and artisan textile manufactures from Ottoman territories. Moreover, while some European imports were transit trade originating in Asia, the Levant and parts of North Africa were the nearest seats of production of many products which, for reasons of geography and climate, were not easily produced in Europe.

It is reckoned that by the second half of the eighteenth century the Ottoman Empire's balance of trade with Western Europe was in surplus. Although Istanbul imported three to four times what it exported, all the other major Ottoman maritime trading cities had favourable trade balances with Christian Europe.* The Europeans' trade deficits were settled in letters of credit or specie money (mainly silver) much of which went to pay for the Ottoman Empire's own trade deficit with Asia.[35] In 1783 the value of the exotic wares from the Indian sub-continent, the Indonesian archipelago and China imported to Egypt via Jeddah were worth twice Egypt's exports to those regions.[36] Unfortunately, we do not know the size of the Ottoman Empire's total trade deficit with Asia or whether it outweighed its surplus with Europe, although according to Braudel silver money was always in short supply in the Empire because much of it 'drained away in massive quantities to the Indian ocean'.[37]

However, while the Ottoman Empire's international trade – the vast majority of which was maritime – appears to have been flourishing in the mid-1700s, its significance in the Ottoman economic mind was rated fairly low in comparison with domestic trade within the Empire itself. Most of this internal economic traffic was carried overland by great caravan convoys, like those observed by the Swedish linguist and naturalist Peter Forsskål. A member of the ill-fated Danish Royal Expedition to the Yemen, he describes a caravan of several thousand camels arriving at Cairo from Mecca in 1762 carrying 'emeralds, pearls, diamonds, hyacinths, musk, civet, Indian cotton and silk garments and balm of Gilead'. A month or so later Forsskål saw the same caravan setting out on its return trip to Mecca carrying 'silks with interwoven silver and gold threads, glazed and unglazed paper, French and Venetian clothes, blue and white linen, sewing needles, knives, gunpowder and shot, syrup and sesame oil, white and brown honey, beans, peas, lentils, rice, wheat and all kinds of edible grain, not to mention, salt and ammonia'.[38]

---

*   See Appendix C.

It was the great strength of the Ottoman economy at this time that it was both huge and largely auto-sufficient, much like the US today. This gave it considerable protection against the instabilities of fluctuating flows of silver and gold arising from trading imbalances.

We can get some general idea of the Ottoman Empire's degree of auto-sufficiency in the eighteenth century from the account of the French Ambassador at Istanbul in 1759, who recorded that the total textile imports into the Empire would clothe a maximum of 800,000 inhabitants. Given that the Empire's total population was at least 25 million (and given that they all had to be clothed) this indicates that the volume of textile imports was equivalent to a mere 3 per cent of the total Ottoman demand for textile products and therefore that the remaining 97 per cent was provided by domestic producers.[39] In Braudel's words, 'the products consumed in Turkish cities mostly came from domestic producers'.[40]

A somewhat more precise idea of the relative importance of the Ottomans' internal trade compared with its international trade with Christian Europe can be gleaned from an estimate of the total value of trade (imports plus exports) for the Ottoman province of Egypt in 1776. Its commerce with 'Turkey' was worth 67.5 million *livres*, as opposed to its commerce with Europe of only around 13 million.[41] Another estimate for the whole of the Ottoman Empire at approximately the same date gives the value of the total 'internal' Ottoman maritime trade in the Mediterranean, Black Sea and Red Sea as 180-200 million *livres*, nearly double that of Ottoman trade with Christian Europe (110 million).[42]

However, there was one economic problem for the Ottomans which was increasing: the weakness of its own merchant shipping industry. In the case of its trade with Christian Europe this was largely attributable to the fact that ships carrying the Ottoman flag or the flags of its North African provinces were still almost entirely banned from the major Christian European ports like Marseille.[43] It is perhaps typical of the Ottoman economic mind that the Empire showed so little concern over this. Another factor was the preference of Ottoman merchants (not only Muslims, but also Jews and Christians) to have their goods shipped by French and other European ships for protection against the depredations of Christian corsairs operating out of Malta. Moreover, European shipping was also beginning to dominate maritime trade within the Empire itself.

Indeed, so regular were the convoys of European (mainly French) merchant ships carrying goods between the North African Regencies and the rest of the Ottoman Empire that they became known as the 'Maritime Caravans'.[44]

The supply of one particular 'commodity' to Ottoman 'consumers', largely dependent on French shipping, was that of African slaves. Although tiny in volume compared with the 80,000 African slaves per year despatched to their American colonies by the states of Christian Europe, the Muslim trade in African slaves was also an important component of the economies of the three Ottoman North African Regencies, Algiers, Tunis and Tripoli.*

Estimates of the total number of African slaves taken from sub-Saharan Africa to the entrepôts of the Maghreb (North Africa)† during the eighteenth century have tended to settle on an annual average of around 6,000–7,000 per year.[45] Within the Ottoman Empire, the largest slave market was Tripoli, which had been ruled by the semi-independent Karamanli dynasty since its founder expelled its imperial governor in 1711. According to the French consul resident in that city, between 1753 and 1756 an average of 1,413 slaves per year were arriving there from slave markets at Murzuk in the Libyan region of Fezzan and Ghadames.[46] At the North African ports the slaves were loaded into French merchant vessels. They then joined the 'maritime caravans' sailing eastward along the coast, unloading the slaves at Alexandria for the Cairo market and onward to other Ottoman ports in the Levant where other 'retail' slave markets were held. Tripoli's exports of African slaves were valued at 1,110 thousand *livres*, accounting for 88 per cent of the province's exports in 1766.[47]

This final part of the slave trade was apparently very profitable for the French shippers. Indeed, in 1767 the British consul in Tripoli, the Hon. Archibald Fraser, wrote to his superiors in London regretting the fact that the French had got control of this lucrative trade from Tripoli to the Levant.[48] Estimates of the actual profitability of the Ottoman slave

---

*   Slavery had been a pillar of Mediterranean society since antiquity, and for centuries it had been acceptable to both Christians and Muslims. The Qur'an itself simply assumes the existence of slavery and then regulates its practice (kind treatment of slaves, provision of basic necessities of life, a slave's right to marry, etc.), thereby implicitly condoning the institution (Wright, 2007, p. 4).

†   'The Maghreb' refers to the geographical region stretching from the western border of modern Egypt, through Libya, Tunisia and Algeria, to Morocco.

trade vary enormously; but for retail slave prices in the mid-eighteenth
century, we have the testimony, once again, of the Swedish traveller and
explorer Peter Forsskål. He visited the Cairo slave market in 1762, where he
witnessed a slave caravan that had just arrived directly from the sub-Saharan
Africa. According to Forsskål, young boys of about eight cost 25 *mahbub*,*
Young men from twenty to thirty years could be got for between 35 and 40
mahbub; young women cost up to 40 *mahbub* for virgins and for those who
were not virgins up to 30 *mahbub*. However, those women who knew how
to prepare and cook food cost around 60 *mahbub*.[49]

This last piece of information gives us our clue as to the principal raison
d'être of the Muslim African slave trade. On average, two-thirds of each slave
caravan were women and their primary function was domestic usage, either
in housework and cooking, or in the case of those deemed sufficiently sexually
attractive, in the harem.[50] Herein lies the basic difference between the slavery
practised in the eighteenth-century Islamic world and that practised by the
Christian states in their American colonies. In the former the slave was more
of a luxury item: a member of a household, a drudge perhaps, but also a status
symbol. And in both male and female cases it was mainly the rich – including
Jews and Ottoman Christians – would could afford slaves. Unlike in the
Americas, the labour of these black slaves did not produce any monetary
surplus value, nor did it contribute to the kind of capital accumulation
whose manifestations can still be seen in the great maritime ports of France,
Spain and above all, Britain. Karl Marx would later describe this as 'capital
developing on the basis of an alien social mode of production'.[51]

Taking an overview of the Ottoman economy in the later eighteenth
century there is little evidence that it was 'medieval' or 'at the lowest level
of competence, initiative and morality' (to quote Oxford professor Bernard
Lewis), certainly not compared with its neighbouring Christian states in the
Mediterranean region. With the exception of Britain and the Netherlands,
the evidence of the current and previous chapters (and Appendix B) show

---

* Its full name was the *zer-i mahbub*. It was a gold coin, in 1768 equal to 2 *kuruş* and 90
akçes (2.75 *kuruş*). In 1766, 8 *kuruş* = £1 (1 *kuruş* = £0.125) (Pamuk, in Inalcik & Quataert,
1994 p. 968), therefore the *mahbub* was equal to around £0.34, and a domestic female slave
who could cook, etc., would have cost around £20 (£3,500 in 2020 money). However, the
mahbub had no official exchange rate and its value was determined by the market. For
example, another source gives 1 *mahbub* = 4 *kuruş*.

levels of GDP per capita, diet and general living standards which were similar to those in Europe. The Empire had a favourable balance of trade with Europe and its auto-sufficiency protected it against externally generated economic fluctuations. According to the French Historian Daniel Panzac:

> In the eighteenth century, the Ottoman Empire still constituted a vast domestic economic entity where consumption and production were designed to satisfy and complement each other ... and this economic dimension of the empire was an essential factor to its cohesion and long life.[52]

In its towns and cities it also had a degree of social welfare provision largely unknown in Europe. As one historian has argued, 'The early-modern Ottoman economy is hard to envision today, as we are caught in a modern, neo-liberal paradigm that idealises the economy as a free and potentially ever-growing entity.'[53] But it functioned reasonable well for its era: 'The Ottomans opted for a "good enough" stable economy that protected the interests of those established in the system.'[54]

However, the comparatively small size of Ottoman–European trade in the later eighteenth century and the favourable Ottoman trade balance with Europe concealed the beginnings of what would eventually become a serious economic problem. In exchange for primary products like raw cotton, the Empire was beginning to import greater quantities of finished European goods, for example, a British fine woollen cloth appropriately known as 'londrine' which constituted about 41.4 per cent of the total import tax revenues of Izmir in 1771–72.[55] And with a growing fascination for European luxuries among the Ottoman upper classes – items such as Swiss clocks, binoculars, spectacles, coffee-bean grinders and Bohemian glass – these trends would eventually reverse the Empire's favourable trade balance with Europe. Still, the process of change was a gradual one. As yet, the development of European capitalist industry and the creation of commercial linkages with the Mediterranean had not developed sufficiently to produce an irreversible transformation of the Ottoman economy. This would have to wait until the mid-nineteenth century, especially once the flood of English manufactures arrived after the 1830s as the mechanisation of factory production began to make its mark.[56]

And there was one area where the Islamic Mediterranean was unquestionably suffering an economic weakness compared with the Europeans. Given the military burdens being placed upon them, both external and internal, neither the Ottoman nor Moroccan states could mobilise sufficient fiscal resources to cope with the financial demands they were facing. During the eighteenth century government expenditures began to outstrip fiscal revenues. And this fiscal crisis brought with it other undesirable economic consequences: currency depreciation and price inflation. Underlying this fiscal crisis was an interrelated complex of factors alluded to in the previous chapter and the Introduction: the growing power of the landowning 'grand *ayan*' in the provinces; the weakening in the coercive power of the state; the loss of territorial integrity; and – in a vicious spiral – the fiscal revenue-collection leakage siphoned off by those new provincial magnates. These are the themes of the next chapter.

CHAPTER 3

The State, Land and Taxation: The Fiscal Crisis of the Ottoman System

The latter part of the eighteenth century and the first part of the nineteenth have been rightly called the 'Age of Revolutions.'[1] But there was another revolution which preceded it – a military revolution in weaponry, tactics and tax-raising.

The first phase of this revolution, occurring in the sixteenth and early seventeenth centuries, was the realisation that bodies of infantry organised in two or three ranks, armed with matchlock firearms and firing repeated volleys (and protected by similarly disciplined units of pikemen) could be deadly against close-quarter attacks by charging cavalry.[2] In short, the cavalry were demoted to a secondary role to be used mainly after an infantry breakthrough or, in the case of light cavalry, for scouting and skirmishing. The second phase, which had occurred by the early eighteenth century, was the use of the more reliable flintlock musket; this weapon enabled quicker volley-firing and further advantaged the infantry over the cavalry. At the same time smaller, lighter and more mobile field guns replaced the extra-heavy, slow-firing cannons of earlier years; and these could be used equally in a defensive or offensive posture.

Furthermore, iron discipline and repeated drill training enabled European infantry to make complicated manoeuvres while maintaining the integrity of their formations: changing swiftly from column to line (and reverse), forming squares for greater defence against cavalry, or making the kind of attacks by echelon perfected by Frederick the Great's Prussian army. In addition, the old-style castle inherited from medieval times was replaced by the star-shaped fortress devised by the French military engineer Sébastien Le Prestre de Vauban, with its 'scarp', 'counterscarp' and 'glacis' creating deadly killing zones for attacking troops. Finally, it should be noted that by the mid-eighteenth century European armies were much larger than they had been in the previous century.[3]

European naval warfare was also revolutionised during the seventeenth and eighteenth centuries with the introduction of 'line of battle' tactics, with warships sailing in column and then manoeuvring to deliver the greatest weight of broadside shot against the enemy's own 'line'. 'Ships of the line'* were built as huge floating gun platforms with sixty to more than a hundred 12-, 24- and 32-pounder guns. Depending on the distance and elevation, the heaviest of these could batter their way through up to 2 feet 6 inches of solid oak.

Meanwhile, Ottoman military organisation and tactics remained largely fossilised in the 'pre-military revolution' era. Until the late seventeenth century the Ottomans' battlefield organisation and tactics had been superior to those of the Christian powers. Although numerically subordinate to the *sipahi* 'feudal' cavalry, the Janissary infantry, organised in *ocak*s (corps), *orta*s (regiments) and *bölük*s (companies), were the Muslim fighters most feared by their enemies.[4] By the second half of the eighteenth century their bows, crossbows and matchlock harquebuses had been largely replaced by flintlock muskets, but some still carried a fearsome array of axes and swords, in particular the deadly *yatagan*.

The typical Janissary assault would begin with the infantry advancing in groups of forty to fifty, one rank or group advancing and firing while the second rank reloaded, maintaining a steady advance regardless of losses. This was followed by a relentless charge accompanied by the deafening percussive music of drums, fifes and horns and continuous calls to God to give them victory. As they surged forward all sense of formation would collapse, and every Janissary would have been fighting heroically for individual glory. In that earlier age of ferocious, religiously inspired warfare, few Christian armies could resist such a terrifying assault.

By the mid-eighteenth century, there were around 40,000 Janissaries registered in the Istanbul army lists.[5] Tunis had a Janissary garrison of around

---

*   In the British Navy 'ships of the line' were generally 'rated' from '1st rate' to '3rd rate' according to their number of guns. In the remainder of the text I have used the term 'battleship' rather than the more cumbersome 'ship of the line'. There were also lower-rated and unrated smaller, faster vessels with fewer than 50 guns such as frigates, sloops/corvettes, gunboats, bomb vessels (firing explosive shells), etc.

8,000 and Algiers between 8,000 and 10,000.[6] There was also a Janissary regiment named the *müstahfizan* ('guardians') among the seven regiments composing the Egyptian garrison. Its size in 1797 was estimated to be 6,893.[7] There were other units conventionally known as 'Janissaries' scattered around the imperial provinces; but they were often a shadow of the original fearsome warriors whose famous name they were determined to preserve.

Janissaries of Istanbul c. 1797

| *Junior Officer* | *Ladle-Bearer* | *Subaltern* |

Note (1) The Ladle-Bearer was a high-ranking Janissary. The Ladle (representing the regiment's soup kitchen) was considered the equivalent of the European military standard.

The long period of peace between 1740 and 1768, for which Ragıb Paşa was largely responsible, was nevertheless a mixed blessing for the Ottoman state. With little actual fighting required, the Janissaries became involved in extensive moonlighting as shopkeepers and artisans.[8] The original method of *devşirme* recruitment had been abandoned, and the rules preventing the recruitment of the sons of Janissaries and ordinary Muslims were now relaxed. Thousands of men had become enrolled in the *ocaks* to corruptly

enjoy the many welfare benefits of the corps or, as in Cairo, to work as
heavies defending shopkeepers against the depredations committed
by other members of the soldiery.[9] As for Istanbul, where the Janissaries
supposedly constituted the sultan's bodyguard, this once-feared elite corps
had turned into a semi-criminal state within a state.

Nevertheless, these swaggering Janissaries still boasted of their military
prowess and their fossilised notions of how war should be fought. They
looked with contempt upon the disciplined infantry ranks of the Christian
European armies, loading and firing their muskets like automata, and the
repeated drills and manoeuvres in which they were meticulously trained.[10]
They saw no honour or bravery in the Western way of war, which they also
claimed was contrary to Islamic principles, and in this they were supported
by the both the official *ulema* and the heterodox Bektaşi Sufis* from
whom were drawn the Janissaries' 'chaplains'. Consequently, when they
did engage the enemy in battle, adherence to the old tactics of the heroic
but disorganised charge usually meant defeat by the new, modernised
armies of the two Christian states with whom they often fought during
the eighteenth century: Austria and Russia. In the words of the French
commander Marechal de Saxe, speaking of the Ottoman army in 1732, 'It
is not valour, numbers or wealth that they lack; it is order, discipline and
technique.'[11]

However, unlike the Ottoman infantry which still resisted the new ways
of warfare, its navy was more willing to adapt, and acquire the new type
of warships from friendly powers, or actively seek technology transfer in
the construction and armament of its ships.[12] While oar-powered galleys
were retained until the end of the century for some inshore uses, by 1735–40
the Ottoman Navy had acquired four battleships (1st rates with 90 guns
and over) available for service in the Mediterranean compared to Britain
with six and France and Spain with only one each.[13] By 1784 the Ottoman
navy had twenty-four battleships (mainly 3rd rates with 74 guns per ship)
and by 1790, thirty. Similarly, the number of Ottoman frigates armed with

---

*   Sufism (Dervishism) may be very broadly defined as Islam's inner, mystical dimension. Its
     adherents seek to reach direct communion with God and become fully absorbed to the
     point of becoming unaware of themselves or the objects around them. Adherents of Sufism
     would belong to particular *tariqas* (orders, literally 'the way', or true way) which were formed
     around individual *sheikhs* (Sufi masters) who established *zawiyas* (colleges).

between twenty and forty-six 12-pounder or 18-pounder guns increased from six in 1735–40 to twenty-four in 1787.[14]

The military revolution had to be paid for. New forms of warfare, more advanced weaponry and much larger armies and navies required greatly increased tax revenues. To give just one example, the construction of HMS *Victory*, launched in 1765, cost five times as much as building Ambrose Crowley's ironworks, one of the most important investments of the early industrial revolution and in its time the largest such industrial plant in Europe.[15] Everywhere, taxation was increased throughout the eighteenth century to keep up with military spending, even in a small European state like the Duchy of Savoy where its Army increased from 26,547 in 1704 to 55,000 in 1747, and taxes increased from 9.5 million lire in 1702 to 16 million in 1763.[16] A massive fiscal burden was imposed on the governments of the European 'fiscal-military' states by the new military system and the almost incessant warfare of the eighteenth century. As an example, it is worth noting that in times of war between 61 and 72 per cent of British government revenues were allocated to military expenditures.[17] Similar figures are recorded for the other major European states. In Russia expenditure on the army alone amounted to 70 per cent of net fiscal revenue in the 1770s.

While the armies of the Christian states of Europe slaughtered each other during the eighteenth century,* their relations with the Ottomans became relatively amicable. From the 1720s onward, 'normal' diplomatic links became established and, as already noted, the Ottomans were able to stabilise their frontiers through peace treaties with their historic enemies, in particular Habsburg Austria. But in spite of this, by the late 1750s Sultan Mustafa III and his Grand Vezir Ragıb Paşa cannot have had any illusions about the potential threat some of those fiscal-military states posed for the Empire.

Ragıb Paşa died before the appearance of the most profound critiques of the Empire's antiquated army and its comparative military weakness; however, he would almost certainly have been familiar with Ibrahim Müteferrika's 1730 treatise on the need for state and military reform, *Usülü'l-Hikem fi Nizami'l Ümem* (*Philosophical Principles for Organising*

---

*   The War of the Spanish Succession (1701–14), the War of the Austrian Succession (1740–48), the Seven Years War (1756–63), the American Revolutionary War (1765–83).

Nations). Müteferrika was much more than a printing entrepreneur. Having fled Hungary and converted to Islam he initially became a *sipahi* (cavalryman) in the sultan's regular corps. In 1716 he was appointed to the elite *müteferrika* corps, and between then and 1736 he carried out various diplomatic missions on behalf of the Porte. In 1738 he was appointed scribe of the Ottoman artillery and in 1744 official imperial historian. He was also a brilliant linguist. Indeed, one European historian has described him as 'a figure of the early Ottoman Enlightenment'.[18]

In his *Philosophical Principles for Organising Nations* Müteferrika recognised the virtue of incorporating the successful elements of the European way of war into the Ottoman military. He believed that, like all empires before them, infidel or Muslim, the Ottomans should learn from their enemies. While he acknowledged the bravery of the Ottoman troops, Müteferrika argued that courage needed to be harnessed and disciplined, and he gave Tsar Peter the Great of Russia as an example of how a ruler could succeed in rebuilding his army and navy by copying his enemy's organisational and tactical reforms. However, Müteferrika did not venture into recommending any detailed military innovations at the tactical level, and adherence to the strictest religious and moral precepts of the Shari'a remained his principal advice.[19]

Some attempts to reform the Ottoman military were made under Sultan Mahmud I. The Ottomans had once been pioneers in their use of artillery and explosives; but by the beginning of the eighteenth century they had fallen well behind Europe. To modernise this branch of their army, in 1731 – probably on the recommendation of Ibrahim Müteferrika – the sultan invited the experienced French officer Claude Alexandre, Comte de Bonneval (1675–1747) to take charge of the Ottoman *humbaracı* (bombardier) corps. De Bonneval had the distinction of fighting both with and against his own country, as well as the even more remarkable one of being condemned to death for insubordination in both countries, and on both occasions being reprieved. After the commutation of his second death sentence to one year's imprisonment and exile to Venice, he not only responded to the Sultan's invitation but also converted to Islam, taking the name Humbaracı Ahmed and receiving the title of paşa.

With the support of Müteferrika, with whom he became close friends, Bonneval wrote his own treatise recommending a wide range of improvements to the military and in particular better training. He succeeded in reorganising the *humbaracı* corps and modernising the imperial cannon and weapons foundries and the production of gunpowder. With the support of the sultan in 1734, he established the first school of military engineering where geometry was a part of the curriculum, and he was later appointed governor of Chios. However, for reasons which remain unclear – but may have much to do with his notorious bad temper and exceptionally quarrelsome personality – he lost favour with key members of the Porte and for a time was exiled to a location on the Black Sea. Three years after his death his school of military engineering closed, almost certainly because of opposition to his whole reform project from the Janissaries. When a second French military advisor, Baron de Tott, arrived in Istanbul many years later he reported that he had found almost all of Bonneval's work abandoned.

A lack of 'wealth' may not have been a serious problem for the Ottomans' military capacity in 1732 (when Marshal Saxe delivered his judgement) but by the second half of the eighteenth century it certainly was. The fiscal resources which the Ottomans required for the support of their existing forces, let alone their modernisation, were rapidly proving inadequate.

The central problem for the Porte was that the tax revenues which should have flowed into the imperial treasury were leaking away into the pockets of the local magnates and private landowners, the 'grand *ayan*'.[20] To comprehend adequately how this perilous weakening of the Ottoman state's fiscal resources occurred, we need to understand how the Ottomans actually collected taxes, and in particular the manner in which tax collection was related to land tenure.

By the seventeenth century the old semi-feudal *timarlı* system had already outrun its usefulness. The state required more cash revenue rather than the *sipahis*' military services. Many *timar* landholdings were therefore converted into *iltizam*s (tax farms),* awarded by auction for short periods, where the holder provided the state with an initial lump sum and agreed annual tax payment thereafter.[21] Many of the larger tax farmers (*mültezim*s) sub-let part or the whole of their 'farms' to deputies (*mütesellim*s) who might be part of their extended household or other local notables under their patronage and control.

---

* Also known as *mukataa* (Ar. *muqata'a*).

By the eighteenth century, this system had been supplemented by auctioning tax farms on a lifetime basis, an arrangement known as *malikane*. However, like the *iltizam*s, the *malikane* contract could be sub-leased, and many leases went to non-Muslims, Jews and Christians who lent the successful bidder the up-front payments required. In theory, *malikane* would provide the state with much-needed cash advances, as well as giving tax-farmers a greater incentive to raise the productivity of the land they controlled, since any investment made to improve yields would lead to greater profit.[22] But getting a piece of government tax revenue became an activity more lucrative than investing in agriculture, trade or manufacturing. And, as we shall see, the introduction of *malikane* tax-farms failed to produce the regular budget surpluses (or balanced budgets) which were its main intention.

Accompanying these changes in the tax system, two significant social and economic developments occurred. First, as a result of European population growth there was an accompanying increase in demand for food supplies from Ottoman sources. In spite of frequent official bans on the export of foodstuffs, especially grain, this provided a strong incentive for the expansion of commercial agriculture in the Ottoman Empire, especially in the lands bordering the Mediterranean, notably Palestine, and the Adriatic coast. Second, and closely related to this development, many *malikane*s were obtained by the grand *ayan* and were converted into quasi-private landed property. These lands were typically worked by various forms of labour regime, combining landless 'free' peasants, sharecroppers, and in some cases forced labour. They did not, however, combine commercial cash-crop production with better technology or improved land use, but on the intensification of surplus extraction. In other words, these *ayan* were not emulating the kind of 'gentlemen capitalists' now predominant in Britain, let alone were they a rising rural bourgeoisie.

The first and arguably the most important trait of the grand *ayan* was attachment to the land tenure and revenue collection system of the state. But they also posed a threat to the integrity of the Ottoman state and to the sultan's patrimonial order and 'moral economy'. For example, many of them were able to take the law into their own hands administering 'justice' (including capital punishment) by-passing the traditional judicial system administered by the appointed officers, the *kadı*s. This development was ominously known as *siyasa* (politics) and was little more than extra-judicial murder.[23]

In spite of the threat of potential breakaways from the Empire posed by the *ayan* – especially as they began to establish links with powerful European commercial interests – the Porte was forced to adopt a highly ambivalent attitude towards them. For while the private armies of the *ayan* (generally known as *levend*s) potentially threatened the state, it was to these same irregular militias that the Empire was having to turn for defence as the quality and quantity of its regular forces (the Janissaries) declined. By the time Mustafa III was having to defend his northern borders against the Russians in 1768 the vast majority of his army was composed of these *levend*s.[24]

Histories of the rise to power of particular members of the *ayan* vary greatly depending upon the regions and cities from which they emerged. Typically, though, a local family would acquire a tax farm in a region where the land was suitable for growing commercial crops, and proximity to the coast offered the possibility of lucrative marketing deals with European merchants. The superior profitability of this form of agriculture, which allowed the quasi-landowner to fund his own private armies, also gave him the financial resources to attack rival *ayan* and seize their lands. As one Syrian notable explained when asked how he and his neighbouring *ayan* spent the huge amounts of money they extracted from the local peasantry, 'We spend it on injuring one another.'[25]

Two regional examples illustrate the extreme to which the combined trends of growing *ayan* power, imperial disintegration and tax revenue leakage were leading during the eighteenth century: Palestine and Egypt.

By the late 1730s a local sheikh and *mültezim*, Zahir al-'Umar of the Zaydani family, had managed to build a formidable power base in Galilee from where he extended his control to the coastal city of Acre. This stronghold soon became the chief centre of trade in Palestine and its most important town, both economically and politically. Zahir established close links with the French merchants resident in Palestine with whom he formed partnerships in the rapidly expanding cotton export trade. His share of the huge profits from this trade enabled him to build up his own armed forces, and by 1742 he was able to oppose any moves by his nominal superior, the Vali of Sidon, to collect the taxes Zahir owed to the government.[26] With his income from his tax farms, his profits from the cotton trade and his acquisition of customs dues, by 1750 Zahir had become the real power in the eyalet (province) of Sidon, with its Turkish *vali* barely in control of his own capital. As for his contributions to the imperial government, in 1752 it was calculated that of the 85,000 *kuruş* due to be paid from Zahir's *iltizam*s, to date, only 15,000 had been handed over to the sultan's treasury.[27]

With the accession of Mustafa III in 1757 and the confirmation of Ragıb Paşa in his position as grand vezir, the sultan began to appreciate the threat posed by Zahir's revenue appropriation, and with a new *vali*, Uthman Paşa, installed in Damascus it appeared that at last Zahir might be deposed. But after Ragıb's death in 1763, the government backed down. In 1773 Uthman Paşa was instructed to make a deal with Zahir. He would pay the Ottoman Treasury half a million *kuruş* against past arrears and the taxes for the current year, which came to an additional quarter of a million; but, in return, Zahir would be granted the whole eyalet of Sidon as a *malikane* and the *sancak*s of Nablus, Gaza, Ramle, Jaffa and 'Ajlun as *iltizam*s. This only gave further impetus to Zahir's growing economic and political domination of the region.

While the loss of imperial revenue siphoned off by such a powerful local *ayan* was a serious problem in Palestine, it was an even greater one in Egypt, the Empire's largest and richest province, where its imperial governors had been reduced to mere figureheads.[28] No one better understood the 'Egyptian problem' than Ragıb Paşa. At the age of forty-eight and already occupying the post of *reisülküttab* (foreign minister) in 1746 he had been awarded the governorship of Egypt by the reigning Sultan Mahmud I – a poisoned chalice if ever there was one, but one he was duty-bound to accept. The problem the new *vali* faced was that Egypt was now – for the second time – the domain of the *Mamluk*s: slave-soldiers of diverse ethnicity who had long ago evolved into a powerful warrior class.*

In January 1517 the last of the medieval Mamluk sultans of Egypt, Tuman bay II, had been defeated by a huge Turkish army under Sultan Selim I; his severed head had been displayed over one of the city gates. Thereafter, Cairo was garrisoned by seven Ottoman regiments. However, Egypt's new

---

* The Mamluks were a caste of Islamised slave-soldiers, originally of Caucasian or Turkic origin, who came to rule Egypt after overthrowing their Arab masters. Although later conquered by the Ottomans, the 'Mamluk system' survived and returned to power in the eighteenth century.

Turkish rulers found it necessary to retain Mamluk cavalry to maintain order in the city and countryside and the institution of Mamluk military slavery continued. By the early eighteenth century the Mamluks had recovered much of their former strength and status. Their slave-recruits were now being drawn from a wide range of subjugated Christian and Muslim territories: Georgia, Abkhazia, Circassia and Bosnia.[29] By the year of Ragıb Paşa's appointment as governor, power in Egypt was shared more or less equally between the commanders of the seven Ottoman garrison regiments and the military households of the Mamluk grandees known as *sancak* beys.[30] The Mamluks probably numbered no more than 8,000 to 10,000 fighting men,[31] compared with an Egyptian population of about 3.9 million inhabitants; but what they lacked in numbers they made up for in brutality and ruthlessness.

Meanwhile, the boundary between the two military groups – Mamluk *sancak* beys and Ottoman garrison officers – had become permeable. The beys began to obtain officer positions within the seven garrison regiments, and senior officers in the seven regiments acquired their own retinue of newly arrived Mamluks. For example we find that, in 1740 a Mamluk bey was the *kethüda*[*] of the Müstahfizan Janissary Regiment;[32] and somewhat later, the senior officer positions of the 'Azaban Regiment had all been taken by Mamluks, who handled the lucrative administration of the customs duties on the Nile.

By the last few decades of the eighteenth century The Mamluks held all the important political positions in the province of Egypt. A divan of twenty-four Mamluk-dominated *sancak* beys formed what might be considered the aristocracy of the Egyptian state and from these were chosen the two most powerful (and financially remunerative) state functionaries – the *sheikh al-balad* (literally, 'the elder of the city'), and the *amir al-hajj*, in command of the annual caravan carrying pilgrims and gifts to Mecca and Medina.

Mamluks of the highest rank headed 'households'. They were quasi-military institutions headed by the *ustadh* ('master'), usually a bey, with a phalanx of retainers and clients most of whom were themselves Mamluks acquired as slaves from the Caucasus. In other words it was rare for a Mamluk

---

* A *kethüda* was second in command to the regimental *ağa*, but by mid-eighteenth century the *kethüda* appears to have become the de facto commander of this particular regiment. The equivalent English term would probably be colonel and the term the *kethüda* was frequently added to their name as in Mustafa Kethüda al-Qazduğlı (see below).

Mamluks c. 1797

An Egyptian   *A Mamluk*   *A Mamluk of the*
Mamluk   *bey*   *sultan's household*

household to be made up of actual family members or that command of the household was hereditary. Other household members were Turks and other nationalities drawn from the seven regiments. Some were recruited as pure mercenaries, while those euphemistically called 'servants' were little more than hired thugs and hit-men from the poorer classes.[33]

Although, collectively, the Mamluk households represented an Egyptian ruling caste, they exhibited few, if any, indications of corporate identity and loyalty, even though they tended to live in close proximity to each other in one of the more exclusive suburbs of Cairo. They frequently attacked and massacred other households to acquire the most profitable *iltizam*s and *muqata'a*s. The younger household Mamluks, who had not yet been manumitted, bonded together as *khushdashiya* (comrades) to attack and pillage the *khushdashiya* of their rivals. Gang warfare, assassinations and revenge killings abounded. By the time of Ragıb Paşa's arrival in Cairo the frenzy of political conspiracy and murders had reached new heights, given a particular impetus by the Mamluks' recent purchase of European-manufactured pistols and carbines.[34]

Foremost among the Mamluk grandees were the Qazduğliya, a household of Georgian origin founded in the seventeenth century by

Mustafa Kethüda al-Qazduğli (d. 1704). In 1732 four out of the ten most powerful Mamluk beys in Egypt were members of this household. Since then, its leading men had been flexing their muscles for a further ascent up the ladder of power with their sights set on the total control of the province and even the creation of an independent state. They were certainly not the kind of men to bow to a sultan's wishes – or those of his imperial governors.

However, sometime in 1748 the grand vezir sent Ragıb Paşa secret orders to liquidate the current head of the Qazduğliya household, Ibrahim Jawish al-Qazduğli, kethüda of the Janissaries and one of his close associates, Ridwan Kethüda al-Julfi, commander of the 'Azaban Regiment.[35] But when the plot became common knowledge and the assassin Ragıb had chosen for the job was unmasked, the leading Mamluks and regimental officers refused to accept Ragıb as vali and he was forced to leave the country.

Ragıb Paşa was replaced by another powerless imperial governor, and within a few years the Qazduğliyya Mamluks and their collaborators launched an increasingly blood-soaked campaign to become the sole centre of power in the province. This bold venture would eventually culminate in the dominance of a Qazduğli, who would defy Istanbul to the point of secession. Meanwhile the garrison regiments and Mamluk households were collectively taking control of four-fifths of the rural tax farms and 60 per cent of the customs duties. According to one source, out of 412 million *paras**of land taxes collected, only 88 million were sent to the imperial treasury.[36] According to another, during the 1750s the Mamluk beys repeatedly sent an annual tribute to Istanbul that was 10–15 million *para*s short of Egypt's tribute.[37]

One might ask, why did the Porte persist in the feeble and futile policy of sending governors periodically to Egypt only to see them ejected whenever it suited Egypt's current Mamluk strongmen? The answer may be simply that, so long as the sultan's government was unable to subdue the Mamluks by military might, continuing the charade that Egypt was still a loyal imperial province at least guaranteed *some* payment of revenue. For their part, the Mamluks complied because they were dependent on the Porte for the regular passage to Egypt of Mamluk recruits to fill the junior

---

* The *para* was another unit of Ottoman currency generally used for small change in preference to the much smaller *akçe* (one third of a para). Forty paras were equal to 1 *kuruş*.

(i.e. un-manumitted) ranks of their quasi-military households. In fact, the Mamluks were desperate for such recruits, because their households were so frequently devastated in number by both internecine warfare and the bubonic plague which regularly afflicted the province.[38]

By now, the authority of the Ottoman state was clearly crumbling, and with it the fiscal resources required to combat both internal and external enemies. For the period 1750–59 (which encompasses the first three years of Mustafa III's reign) and measured in tonnes of silver, the annual fiscal revenues of the Ottoman Empire were only 179.4 tonnes of silver. Compare that to the annual sums collected by other states with a presence in the Mediterranean: France (1,081.2 tonnes), Britain (821.1), Spain (439.3), and Austria (349.3). Only the small Republic of Venice (83.3 tonnes) had lower revenues. Clearly, the absolute size of these tax revenues to some extent reflected population size: the more inhabitants to tax, the greater the total tax received by the state. But this factor alone cannot account for the Ottomans' poor fiscal performance.

This is graphically revealed when the fiscal revenues are calculated *per head of population*: on this measure the Ottomans fall to the lowest rank. Moreover, while all the Christian states steadily increased their tax revenues over the eighteenth century, the Ottomans were the only state which experienced a decline – from an annual average of 163 tonnes in the period 1700–09 to 147.2 tonnes during 1780–89.[39]

The basic problem was that, over the course of the century, around 1,000 to 2,000 individuals, based in Istanbul, and perhaps as many as 5,000 to 10,000 living in the Empire's provinces, had taken control of the state's revenue, together with a vast army of contractors, agents and financiers.[40] And these intermediaries – men like the Palestinian Sheikh Zahir al-'Umar, the Mamluk grandee Ibrahim Jawish al-Qazduğli, and their clients and business associates – retained more than half of the gross tax receipts collected from the Empire's rural and urban *reaya*.[41] When the calculation is done in 'net' terms (after the subtraction of what were euphemistically called 'expenses') 'only one third of net receipts ended in the central treasury'.[42]

The budgetary consequences were inevitable. The response of the state was debasement of the currency: current reserves of silver in the treasury could then pay a larger number of bills. In 1740–49 the silver content of the *akçe* was 0.12 grams; by the end of the eighteenth century it had fallen to a mere 0.05 grams, and, as a result, since the mid-century consumer prices had risen by 245 per cent.[43]

There were winners and losers from this depreciation of the currency. Debtors (including of course the state) initially gained. Creditors, especially the merchant class, lost out. The peasantry, most of whose transactions and tax obligations were still paid in kind, were little affected. But it was those who were paid in fixed nominal sums, the standing army of Janissaries and the state bureaucracy, who suffered most from the decline in their purchasing power. Disaffection, especially among the former, would be the inevitable consequence.

As for the fiscal system of Morocco, it was even more dysfunctional than that of the Ottomans, as we shall observe in the next chapter.

CHAPTER 4

At the Gateway to the Mediterranean: Britain and the 'Empire' of Morocco

Three thousand kilometres west of the Ottoman capital, on 17 January 1721, a British fleet under Commodore Charles Stewart sailed into the Bay of Tetouan on an important mission. Since June 1704 England had been occupying the peninsula of Gibraltar, ceded to Britain 'in perpetuity' in 1713 by the Treaty of Utrecht which ended the long War of the Spanish Succession. But the Spanish had fortified the narrow strip of land linking Gibraltar to the mainland, and Britain's Gibraltar garrison still depended upon intermittent sea-borne food supplies.

From time to time Morocco's aged ruler, the pathologically cruel but militarily successful Sultan Mulay Isma'il Ibn Sharif (r. 1672–1727),* allowed Moroccan merchants to trade with Gibraltar. Britain's garrison had become increasingly dependent on Moroccan food supplies; however, there was as yet no treaty between Britain and Morocco which would give greater assurance to those essential provisions. Moreover, Moroccan corsair vessels sailing out of its Mediterranean port of Tetouan and its Atlantic port of Salé frequently attacked and seized British merchant ships, enslaving its passengers and crew. On his arrival on Moroccan soil, Commodore Stewart was greeted by an emissary from Sultan Isma'il, a Jewish merchant named Moses bin Attar, with whom he signed articles of peace between Britain and Morocco, after which Stewart sailed back to England for ratification of the treaty.

---

* The title *Mulay*, a word of Arabic origin meaning 'Prince of the blood' (sometimes transliterated as *Mawlay* or *Moulay*), was conventionally used by all members of the Alaouite dynasty.

In May, Stewart returned to Tetouan with the treaty ratified and set off on the long journey to Isma'il's great new palace at Meknes, not arriving there until the beginning of July. On 6 July, Stewart had his first audience with the toothless, seventy-five-year-old tyrant and was shown around his palace. After a certain amount of prevarication on the part of Isma'il (during which he took the opportunity to personally execute two of his chieftains) the sultan finally signed the treaty on 23 July 1721. Among its terms were the freeing of 296 British slaves, who had been captured by Moroccan corsairs, and the return of a number of Moroccan captives in British hands, together with a substantial supply of British gunpowder, sulphur, cloth and 13,500 specially made gun parts.[1]

The remaining terms of the treaty were remarkably favourable to Britain. For the first time British subjects were to have the right to British protection in Morocco; they might establish consulates in any towns they wished; trade was to be encouraged; British ships could sail unmolested off the Moroccan coast, their security being guaranteed by a system of passes; and peace between Britain and Morocco was to 'endure for ever by land as by sea and fresh waters'.[2]

Isma'il died in 1727. His reign was followed by a lengthy period of anarchy during which the remnants of his once 150,000-strong army of black slave soldiers, the *abid*, installed and then removed five sultans. Their ability to do this reflected the very nature of Moroccan government and society. Although both the Ottoman dynasty and its Moroccan Alaouite 'cousin' were Islamic states, in all other relevant respects they were sharply different: in their territorial integrity in the face of European aggression, in their religious practices, in the nature of their sultanic government, in the extent of that government's control over its provinces, and in the manner in which it collected (or tried to collect) taxes.

At the middle of the eighteenth century the Ottoman Empire remained at its zenith in terms of territorial domination: in only one case – the Algerian coastal town of Oran, occupied intermittently by Spain since 1509 – was Ottoman territory occupied by a European power (and would be abandoned by Spain in 1792). The situation in Morocco was very different. On its Mediterranean coastline Ceuta, Melilla and Peñón de Vélez were all Spanish enclaves (originally captured in 1415, 1497 and 1508 respectively), where they had built powerful fortresses called *presidios*; and on its Atlantic coastline Mazagan had been occupied by the Portuguese since 1502.

In religious matters Morocco's principal characteristic was the power and influence of its Sufi brotherhoods (*tariqas*). In the Ottoman Empire Sufism – the popular, mystical brand of Sunni Islam which had absorbed many unorthodox and even un-Islamic elements – was tolerated by the 'official' ulema. Some of its brotherhoods like the Bektaşis and Mevlevis (the famous 'whirling dervishes') were popular within the sultan's court, although many of the *ulema* regarded them with disdain. However, in North Africa the Sufi brotherhoods like the Qadiriyya, the Tijaniyya, the Darqawa, the Tayibiyya and the Senuisiyya, played a much more significant role in religious life.

In Morocco, isolated from the more conventional orders of Sufism by the Atlas Mountains, Sufi 'living saints' emerged who often accumulated huge wealth and power because the common people believed them to possess a 'divine' quality known as *baraka* (blessing). Particularly powerful *baraka* belonged to the sharifs, families who claimed lineal descent from the Prophet Muhammad and his daughter Fatima and son-in-law 'Ali ibn Abi Talib. The Alaouite dynasty and its predecessor (the Sa'adians) claimed this distinction. Consequently, from the sixteenth century onwards the highest political authority had been wielded by a sharif, whose exercise of power was rendered legitimate not so much by safeguarding and affirming Muslim law but by the mysterious spiritual gifts which his descent from the Prophet was supposed to have given him. While the sultan was the centre of the cult of the mysterious *baraka*, other sharifs and Sufi sheikhs formed the focus of this cult on the local level.

Consequently, 'the spokesmen of the Moroccan Muslim community were thus no longer the *ulema*, whose training in the law and the principles of its interpretation and application rendered them rational and intellectually responsible,'[3] and by the eighteenth century Moroccan Sufism had largely degenerated into a broad range of superstitious fetishes. For example, there was widespread belief that the special powers of *baraka* extended to such things as foretelling the future, the ability to be transported in an instant to distant places, to see the whole world as though it were spread out in the palm of the hand. Moreover *baraka*, it was believed, could be obtained by physical contact with a living 'saint' or even touching the hem of his garment. It could even sometimes be purloined by stealth against the will of its possessor.[4]

At the same time, some of these Sufi brotherhoods and their sharifian sheikhs had become quasi-military organisations with their own fortified strongholds. *Tariqas* such as the Tayibiyya and the Tijaniyya were becoming virtual states within a state. And some had spread their influence across the ill-defined frontier into the Ottoman regency of Algiers. More importantly they were increasingly exercising political power over large areas of Moroccan territory itself.

And they were not the only ones to do this. Like the Ottomans, the Alaouite dynasty had no succession based on primogeniture; but neither did it have the Ottoman *kafes* and the 'rule of elderness'. Succession was simply a free-for-all among the deceased sultan's relatives. Hence the anarchy which followed the death of Sultan Isma'il. However, even after the final (and sixth) accession to power of Sultan Abdallah V (r. 1729–34, 1736, 1740–41, 1741–42, 1743–47 and 1748–57) and the suppression of the rebellious *abid* soldiery, Morocco had no real government to speak of. There was nothing like the patrimonial bureaucracy and system of provincial control which – in spite of the growing threat from the provincial *ayan* – still provided a reasonably efficient linkage between the Ottoman sultan and his people.[5] Instead the Moroccan sultan ruled only through a grand vezir and an unstable and unreliable entourage of lesser officials and favourites, and their control extended only over a fluctuating band of territory known as the *bled al-makhzan*, literally 'the land of the treasury'. Outside this government-controlled land lay the anarchic realms of the *bled al-siba* (land of no authority). It was here that power lay in the hands of independent Berber *qaids* (Ar. *qa'ids*), especially in the Atlas mountains and southern deserts where they built their towering, grim, crenellated *kasbahs* and *qasrs* with their own private dungeons. Here they exercised an unchecked feudal-like power which, when it suited them, could determine the politics of the sultans' own power bases at Fez or Meknes.

The *bled al-siba* was also 'the land of no taxation'. The only way the current sultan could extract cash from the semi-feudal *qaids* of this region was by mounting what were, in effect, military expeditions into their dominions, known as *harkas*.* However, what one gathers from a

---

*   According to Gavin Maxwell (1966, p. 33), the word *harka* means 'the burning' (believed to be from the word *haraqa*), implying the extreme brutality and destruction with which they

nineteenth-century example of one of these campaigns is that much of the
plunder which was seized fell into the hands of the grand vezir, his under-
officials and the common soldiery.[6] As an instrument of fiscal policy the
harka was barely sufficient to cover its costs. It was for this reason that, from
Isma'il onwards, successive Moroccan sultans turned to customs duties,
exports and import tariffs as the only reliable source of taxation, and this
in turn meant establishing friendly trading relationships with the European
powers. Consequently, Isma'il's treaty with Britain was renewed four times,
in 1729, 1734, 1750 and 1751.[7]

Under the repeated and short-lived reigns of Abdallah V, relations
between Britain and Morocco frequently broke down. British shipping
was attacked in contravention of the treaties and their crews enslaved.
This was largely due to the refusal of British negotiators to pay the amount
of ransom demanded by the sultan for the release of previously enslaved
British sailors. It was also the result of the arrogant behaviour of some
of those British envoys who refused to accord to the sultan the degree of
respect he expected.[8] However, matters were usually settled eventually by
the payment of suitable 'presents' to the sultan or the provision of military
supplies which he demanded for his ongoing wars against the Spanish.[9]

With the accession of Abadallah's son, Sidi Muhammad (r. 1757–
90),* the treaty was once again renewed (in 1760), and relations between
Britain and Morocco settled into a prolonged equilibrium which reflected
the prevailing balance of power between the two countries. Morocco was
forced to acknowledge the growing might of Britain's navy, while Britain
had come to realise that Morocco's size and mountainous interior made
any gunboat diplomacy difficult to enforce. Moreover, Moroccan sultans
typically established their capitals well inland (as at Fez and Meknes)
where they were able to isolate themselves from the representations of
British consuls at Tetuán. Reasonably friendly relations therefore became
obligatory.

While British merchants were granted greater access to Moroccan
markets, the sultan's subjects were given the same right of entry and

---

were carried out. This is plausible, but it seems more likely that Maxwell is confusing it with
the word *haraka* (meaning 'military campaign'). To a European the pronunciation of the
two words could have seemed virtually the same.

* Muhammad III. Sidi Muhammad was his popular name.

unmolested trade in British territories. In the 1729 Treaty, Britain had granted the specific right of Moroccan Jewish and Muslim merchants to trade in Gibraltar – and for the Moroccan merchants, supplying Gibraltar with cattle and agricultural produce was the most profitable market for their goods.[10] As the treaties were renewed, Britain agreed to make substantial payments to the reigning sultan and to deliver military supplies. For example, when Sultan Sidi Muhammad renewed the Treaty in 1760, he demanded – and received – £25,000 in settlement of all outstanding disagreements, prompting the administration at Gibraltar to calculate that since 1734 the British had given the Moroccans a total of £120,000 in various settlements of this kind.[11]

For Britain, good relations with Morocco meant, above all, regular supplies of fresh meat for the Gibraltar garrison. Between 1750 and 1776, imports of cattle from Tetouan and Tangier more than doubled. In 1777, Gibraltar had a garrison of around 4,000 officers and men, and a civilian population of 3,201, 519 of whom were Britons, 1,819 'Catholics' (mainly Spanish, Portuguese and Genoese) and 863 Jews. To feed this number of inhabitants, Gibraltar imported annually from Morocco around 3,000 cattle, as well as about 3,000 sheep and 7,200 head of poultry.

However, the fact that British merchants were known to trade opportunistically at ports temporarily controlled by the Emperor's enemies – sometimes with the connivance of British consular officials – led the Moroccan ruler to diversify his maritime trading partners. Sidi Muhammad signed treaties with Spain and six other European countries during the first twelve years of his reign. Between 1766 and 1773, he also raised export duties on all types of supply to Gibraltar, in some cases by more than 100 per cent, and when it was reliably reported that his enemies in the northern Gharb region were buying arms from Gibraltar, he expelled the British consuls from Tetouan and Tangier.

Anxious to maintain good relations with Morocco, the British government's usual response to the politically dangerous opportunism of some of its merchants was to officially express dismay at their behaviour and assure Sidi Muhammad that such practices were absolutely contrary to the government's wishes or control. It was partly to mollify Sidi Muhammad's frequent outbursts of indignation about illicit British trading that, in 1774, a Moroccan delegation visiting London was offered military aid when

Sultan Sidi Muhammad bin Abdallah of Morocco

Sidi Muhammad's troops were besieging the Spanish enclave of Melilla on Morocco's Mediterranean coast.

After Sidi Muhammad's death in 1790, his son and successor, Mulay al-Yazid (r. 1790–1792), cultivated better relations with Britain. At a time when his country had descended into chaos and civil strife, he recognised the latter's growing economic and military importance. This was not least because Britain offered Morocco support against its traditional enemy, Spain, at a time when the latter was aiding one of the sultan's many enemies. So as the eighteenth century drew to a close, in 1791 this short-lived 'Emperor of Morocco' signed another treaty with Britain, becoming the first sultan to grant Britain 'most favoured nation' status.* He also reduced many of the export duties charged to the British, on cattle, wool, goat hides and ostrich feathers, while import duties on British iron, steel, cotton and opium were also reduced.[12]

The fierce religiosity of Yazid's successor Mulay Suleyman (r. 1792–1822) led him to fear increased contact with Christians and the threat to

---

*   'Most favoured nation' status guaranteed that the host country will not grant any privilege to another country without also extending it to the British.

Islamic moral values which he believed trade with Europe might involve. Nevertheless, in 1796 he reluctantly agreed to the establishment of the first Moroccan consulate in Gibraltar, a position granted to a prosperous Muslim merchant with an interest in the Morocco–Gibraltar cattle trade, named Muhammad bin 'Umar Bajja.

Subsequent hostilities between Britain and Spain led to further attempts by the Spanish to regain their lost territory, and on a number of occasions Britain's rulers seriously considered exchanging Gibraltar for some other piece of Spanish real estate – preferably in the Americas.

For a time the strategic importance of Gibraltar also appeared diminished by the decline of British Mediterranean trade with the Ottoman Empire's dominions in the Levant and Egypt. Since the Ottomans would not permit the export of gold and silver money to Europe, any favourable British trade balance with them had to be settled by the import of commodities. During the seventeenth century, silk had been the primary commodity which balanced Anglo-Ottoman trade. But as cheaper and sometimes better-quality supplies became available, mainly from Italy and Bengal, British demand for Ottoman silk declined, with a reciprocal decline in British exports to the Levant. For example, during the period 1722–24, the average annual value of British imports from the Ottoman Empire totalled £356,000; by 1752–54 this had declined to £152,000. The largest part of the decline was attributable to the fall in the value of silk imports, which fell from £274,000 to £81,000.[13]

However, these commercial doubts about the value of holding Gibraltar would soon be superseded by strategic considerations. In the closing years of the eighteenth century, Britain was once more at war with France and Spain, the latter having been coerced into an alliance with France's new republican government in 1796. In these circumstances, not only would the Gibraltar base soon be regarded as a crucial military asset, but Morocco too would increasingly become the object of particular British interest and concern. Henceforth, British officials in Morocco would follow a consistent policy of maintaining good relations with the reigning sultan while making sure that Morocco did not give offence to the other European powers (in particular France) that would give them an excuse to invade her and deny Gibraltar its crucial food supplies.

It was a policy pursued consistently throughout the following century by Britain's two brilliant consul-generals in Morocco, Edward Drummond-Hay

(1785–1845) and his son John Hay Drummond Hay (1816–1893), men who became fluent in colloquial Moroccan Arabic, established close relations with successive sultans and, above all, had a deep understanding and sympathy for the ordinary Moroccan people. It was a policy that was remarkably successful until a major realignment of the imperialist powers which began in the 1890s, and the subsequent change in British foreign policy towards both the Ottoman Empire and Morocco itself.

CHAPTER 5

The Ottoman Regencies
and the Barbary Corsairs

Let us picture a small Neapolitan merchant ship – for example, a pinque with two lateen sails, a flat bottom and a raised narrow stern – hugging the coast of southern Italy in the summer of 1752 as it rounds Cape Santa Maria di Leuca and enters the Adriatic Sea. It might be one of many smaller craft taking advantage of the light summer breezes to carry high-value goods like Parmesan cheese, juniper berries and essence of bergamot from the major Italian port city of Livorno to the maritime city-republic of Ragusa (Dubrovnik) which lies under the protection of the Ottoman Empire.

At this time of year, the sailing will be easy and the small crew are probably sunning themselves on deck. However, around midday the captain notices what appears to be a xebec under sail and coming up swiftly on the starboard bow; but, since it is flying a Spanish ensign, he feels no immediate alarm.

Diagram of lateen-rigged xebec with auxiliary oar power

However, as he watches the stranger put on more sail and close in on the small merchant vessel, the Neapolitan captain is puzzled by the absence of any crew visible on the warship's deck, except for a single helmsman in European dress. And as the much larger ship draws even closer, the man at the tiller makes vigorous gestures signalling the pinque to heave to. By now, any possibility of outrunning it is out of the question, so the captain of the Neapolitan ship has little choice but to obey.

Then, as the warship comes alongside, it quickly lowers its Spanish ensign and runs up the flag of the Regency of Tripoli – three crescent moons on a dark-green background – and at this point a crowd of bare-footed armed men wearing baggy trousers and red caps, armed with a variety of swords, boarding pikes and pistols, surges over the gunwales and onto the deck of the Neapolitan ship.

In fact the attacking warship is not a xebec with 6- or 8-pounder guns. It is a disguised British-built corvette carrying thirty-six guns including 12-pounders, commanded by the notorious renegade and corsair Antoine Sicard, originally of Marseille, and crewed by around 200 fighters, mainly Albanians.[1]

The ship itself had been sold to Sicard by the resident British Consul in Tripoli, Robert White, sometime after his taking up the post in August 1751 and during the prolonged peace between Britain and Tripoli originally signed in 1730.[2] It was a cynical piece of deal-making not untypical of the British and French consuls and businessmen, whose rival nations could deploy financial resources and naval power sufficient to protect their own shipping. It was also at the cost of their weaker fellow Christians like those of the Kingdom of Naples who would consequently lose trade to their more powerful competitors.

After the capture of the Neapolitan ship, Sicard would have demanded to see the captain's 'passport'. This was a standard document signed between Tripoli's Paşa and those Christian states with which Tripoli had signed peace treaties. Because many corsair captains were illiterate, the 'passports' were cut in half in an irregular fashion, one half being distributed to each corsair captain and one to the captain of each Christian vessel whose government was a co-signatory to the treaty. If the zig-zag tear on the Christian captain's copy exactly matched that of the corsair then it indicated that there was a treaty between the host country of the corsair and that of its captured vessel. The disappointed corsair captain would then be obliged to release his prize and its crew. By the seventeenth and eighteenth centuries this regularisation of the corsair wars in the Mediterranean was a standard procedure, accepted also by the other two regencies, Tunis and Algiers.

However, in the case of the unfortunate vessel which Sicard captured, the captain's half-'passport' was useless. This was because on 15 August 1748, Muhammad Karamanli, son and successor of the founder of Tripoli's semi-independent Ottoman autonomous province, had been persuaded by his divan to recommence corsair operations after thirty years of peace. Consequently, Karamanli revoked existing treaties with Christian states – with the exception of those with Britain and France – for fear of their ability to inflict overwhelming military and naval retribution. On that same August day, Signor Bigani, the Neapolitan consul, was summoned to Muhammad's court in Tripoli's citadel and brusquely informed that a state of war now existed between Tripoli and the Kingdom of Naples. Subsequently, Sicard's Neapolitan prize was brought into Tripoli's harbour, its captain and crew fitted with manacles, after which they were thrown into the *bagnio* – the slave prison.

The three Ottoman regencies originated in the Spanish Reconquista, the final defeat of the Arab and Berber dynasties which had ruled most of Spain since the eighth century and whose domination ended in 1492. Spurred on by the descendants of the vengeful Andalusian Muslim refugees who had been forced to flee Spain, the Muslims of North Africa began to prey upon the merchant shipping of Spain and other Christian states, and launched retaliatory raids against Christian communities on the Spanish and Italian coasts and islands. At the same time the North African Muslims sought assistance from their co-religionists in the Ottoman Empire to recapture the North African territories which had been previously lost to the Spaniards.

After a number of successes against the Spanish and the recapture of Algiers in 1529, the Ottoman Sultan Süleyman I (r. 1520–66) was offered the city in return for troops and military supplies. The Sultan agreed and despatched an *ocak* of 2,000 Janissaries to Algiers together with 4,000 Turkish volunteers, and the whole of the Maghreb region (except Morocco) was designated an Ottoman *sancak*. In 1587 it was divided into three provinces, Algiers, Tunis and Tripoli, all supplied with Janissary garrisons, and Ottoman paşas (governors) with a three-year tenure. Subsequently, the Ottomans recaptured all the fortified Spanish enclaves on the southern coast of the Mediterranean except for Oran, and Morocco's Ceuta, Melilla and Peñón de Vélez.

The Muslim corsair fleets controlled by their *ta'ifas* (councils) of sea captains soon became the scourge of Christian shipping in the Mediterranean. Estimates of Christian slaves being held by the three regencies during the sixteenth and seventeenth centuries vary considerably, but the numbers were certainly huge. For instance, in the case of Algiers, Christian sources put captured white slave numbers for the year 1683 at 35–40,000.[2]

To Mediterranean Muslims the corsairs were heroic figures practising the jihad. Acquisition of booty and slaves must have been a powerful motive for their raids; but in their own eyes, and those of their land-based supporters, these *mujahidin* were not pirates but soldiers waging war against the infidel enemy. This religious interpretation of the corsairs' activities is reflected in popular accounts of their adventures, such as the following report of a Tunisian chronicler:

> The Bey armed his ships to fight against the enemies of the
> Word of God [which] is the highest in its conformity to the
> word of the Prophet. He who fights at sea has ten times the
> virtue of he who fights on land. The blood of the martyr that
> dissolves in the waves is like that of the martyr that flows to
> the earth. God has charged the Angel of Death with taking
> possession of all souls except those who fall as martyrs at sea
> because it is God himself who takes care of them. God forgives
> all the sins of one who dies a martyr on land, except his debts;
> whereas he forgives all of the sins of one dying as a martyr at
> sea, including his debts.[3]

Those captured and enslaved by the corsairs fell into four main categories. A considerable number 'turned Turk'; they accepted Islam, were freed and became 'renegados', and some of these, like Sicard, went on to become captains of corsair ships themselves. Captured naval and military officers were reasonably well treated and enjoyed various privileges, while those from the wealthier classes were put up for ransom (which was usually paid). A third group of prisoners – usually those with some special skills

– were purchased by individual Muslims to become various types of artisan or household slave. The fourth, largest and most unfortunate group were those who were clearly poor and came from the labouring population. These were retained by the state and put to work building fortifications and undertaking other forms of arduous manual labour.

The conditions under which these 'slaves of the state' lived and worked were certainly harsh, but the Qur'an and hadiths (reputed sayings) of the Prophet contained certain strictures concerning the treatment of all slaves. These were embodied in Islamic jurisprudence. Slaves could freely practise their religion. Work, which began at dawn, should end three hours before sunset. There was to be no work at all on Fridays, the Muslim day of communal prayer and, most surprising of all, some slaves were permitted to run small shops and even 'cafés' where alcohol was sold.[4] Most historians accept that the treatment of Christian slaves in the three Ottoman regencies (but probably not in Morocco) was certainly better than the fate of Muslims captured by the Christian corsairs of Spain, Malta, Tuscany and the Papal States, the majority of whom were condemned to the living hell of life as a galley slave.[5] However, attempts to escape from Muslim captivity were not tolerated: those Christian slaves who did so (and failed) were often subjected to forms of punishment or execution equal in cruelty to those inflicted on runaway black slaves in the Americas.

During the later eighteenth century the three regencies experienced a decline in corsair activity.[6] This was partly due to the number of treaties signed with the major Christian naval powers and partly because the Christian sea-going powers had adopted many of the newer warship technologies mentioned in Chapter 3. The American consul in Algiers, Joel Barlow, recorded that between 1724 and 1796 the Regency's total naval strength declined from twenty-four to eleven ships.[7]

The official French translator at Algiers, Jean-Michel Venture de Paradis – later to be Napoleon's translator in Egypt – paints a similar picture. In 1788 Algiers's naval forces consisted of only ten warships: eight 'xebecs or barques' with between eighteen and thirty guns (typically of 6-pounder or 8-pounder calibre) together with two oar-powered, open-decked 'half-galleys'.[8] Tunisia, in 1785–87, had a total of thirty-eight ships carrying 202 guns, but these were mainly small vessels, thirty of which were open-decked, oar-powered galliots with between two and six guns each.[9] Tripoli's corsair fleet was at the time the smallest – two xebecs with ten and eighteen guns respectively and twelve galliots with between two and four guns.

Along with this decline in the corsair fleets, the number of white slaves had also fallen. In Algiers it fell from 35–40,000 in 1683 to around 7,000 towards the end of the eighteenth century. In Tunis and Tripoli combined there were as few as 2,000 white slaves in 1780.[10] Initiatives taken by the Moroccan Sultan Sidi Muhammad bin Abdallah, who used the freeing of captives as a diplomatic lever to obtain better commercial terms with the Christian powers, also reduced the total number of enslaved Europeans.

Meanwhile, a substantial change had been taking place in the ethnic and social structure of the regencies. Over the two centuries since Algiers, Tunis and Tripoli had become integrated into the Ottoman Empire, there had been a substantial growth in the number of Kuloğlus – the offspring of Turkish Janissary soldiers and local Arab women.

By the seventeenth century, the regencies' Janissary *ocak*s (military corps) had evolved into an ethnically exclusive caste. One particular aspect of this racial exclusiveness was a resurrection of the old tradition (which had died out elsewhere in the Empire) of excluding the sons of Janissaries – in this case the Kuloğlus – from entry into the Janissary ranks. This policy was partly for material reasons: to restrict access to the generous perquisites to which the Janissaries were customarily entitled. But it also had a strongly ideological basis which emphasised the racial superiority of 'pure' Turks and was reflected in a variety of discriminatory measures against both Kuloğlus and the indigenous populations of Moors, Arabs and Berbers. In short, by the seventeenth century the Turkish presence in North Africa had taken on a distinctly colonial character.

Nowhere was this racial policy implemented more rigorously than in Algiers, the largest and strongest of the regencies. To preserve their racial, cultural and military supremacy the Turkish troops maintained their distinctiveness from the Kuloğlus and indigenous population by a variety of methods. They spoke only Turkish and in matters of jurisprudence they jealously guarded their Hanafi rite.* In dress they swaggered about in elegant

---

* Contrary to much European current misunderstanding, the Shari'a is not monolithic. Over the centuries of Islamic rule since the death of Muhammad and in the context of a

clothes: elaborately embroidered cotton shirts, large cotton pantaloons usually from bright red cloth, red stockings and yellow Moroccan leather slippers. They also liked to sport voluminous cloaks, burnouses, draped over their shoulders with large hoods which hung down their backs, sometimes trailing a brightly coloured tassel.[11]

The pattern of racial dominance and segregation was also practised in the corsair fleet. By the late eighteenth century the senior officers in each ship were exclusively Turks; Kuloğlus were restricted to the position of junior officer and leading seaman, while Moors and Arabs could serve only as ordinary seamen; moreover many of these had been press-ganged into service.[12]

In order to prevent an increase in the number of Kuloğlus, Janissaries were discouraged from marrying; if they did so they lost the various perquisites to which they were entitled. The Algerian Janissaries took virtually no part in the Regency's production and trade, which was almost entirely in the hands of the Jews, and this further isolated them from the social and economic life of those they ruled. The preservation of a Turkish identity was now a pervasive and powerful ideology based on the elite's non-hereditary status. This they preserved by offsetting the natural decline in Turkish troops by enlisting 'pure' Turks from Anatolia. Recruiting officers were sent out to this region where an overpopulation of poor Turkish peasants, desperate for financial gain, offered a ready human resource with which to restock the Algerian *ocak*.

Most eighteenth-century Europeans probably thought of the regencies as little more than anarchic, piratical rabbles, but this was far from reality: in fact they were governed by quite complex bureaucracies. To take Algiers as an example once again, it was headed by a committee of seven individuals, known to the French as *les puissances* (the powers). At its apex was the *dey* (literally 'maternal uncle'), a senior military officer chosen as supreme ruler by the Turkish Janissaries.

By the mid-seventeenth century the triennial imperial *vali*s sent from Istanbul to Algiers had already lost effective power to the Janissaries' dey.

series of Islamic empires extending over three continents, schools of jurisprudence emerged which interpreted Islamic law in different ways. There emerged four principal Sunni legal interpretations known as madhhabs, named after the scholars most closely associated with each one – the Hanafi, the Maliki, the Shafi'i and the Hanbali.

For a while, they were retained as figureheads, but in 1710 the incumbent dey, 'Ali Chaouch, sent the latest candidate for the governorship back to Istanbul; henceforth all subsequent deys appropriated the role of governor and, with the acquiescence of the sultan, adopted the title of paşa.[13]

In addition to the dey, the ruling council in Algiers consisted of the *khaznaji* (chief financial officer) who was usually the dey's successor, the *ağa* of the Janissaries, the *agha al-arab* (commander of auxiliary Arab cavalry), the *wakil al-kharj* (in charge of the marine and relations with foreign powers), and the *khoja al-khayl* (the 'horse secretary') originally responsible for receiving cavalry mounts from the inland tribes but, by extension, the collector of all taxes in kind for the provisioning of the whole Regency.[14]

While it was perhaps natural for the Europeans to concern themselves only with the maritime policies of the dey and political events in Algiers itself, by the late eighteenth century the Regency as a whole encompassed a territory of approximately 140,000 square kilometres. Of this domain about 80,000 were under direct or indirect government rule, while the remainder was populated by nomadic or semi-nomadic Arab tribes, especially in the pre-Sahara, which 'usually managed to stay beyond the fiscal and military reach of the Regency system, but who could never totally ignore its presence either'.[15] As for the many Berber clans of the Grand Kabylia and other mountain ranges, they too managed to remain largely free of Turkish domination. In effect, there were two 'Regencies': the one outward facing, maritime and with links to the wider world; the other of the interior, dependent on the land and its resources and inward-looking.

For administrative purposes, outside the *dar al-sultan* – the territory ruled directly by the dey and constituted by the city of Algiers and the surrounding crescent of rich cultivated land – the Regency was divided into three provinces, each under the control of a bey (provincial governor): the Beylik of the East with its capital at the city of Constantine; in the centre, the Beylik of Titteri with its administrative centre at al-Media (Medea); and the Beylik of the West with its capital at Mascara until it moved to Oran in 1792 after the Spanish abandoned that port city. Twice each year the three beys sent out military columns to collect tribute in both cash and kind from the tribal chiefs in their province which was then delivered to the dey at Algiers in an elaborate ceremony. The ultimate source of this tribute, however, were the *reaya* – the sedentary Arab cultivators typically employed as sharecroppers who were allowed to retain only one-fifth of the harvest.

The problem facing the Turks was that, even with regular infusions of Anatolian recruits, by the end of the eighteenth century they constituted a tiny minority – at the most 10,000 – of the Regency's total population, which probably numbered around 3 million. Even in the city of Algiers itself, Turks were only a small fraction of the resident population. According to Venture de Paradis, in 1788 the population of the city numbered around 50,000, of whom only 3,000 were Turks. Outside Algiers itself, the remainder of the Turkish forces of occupation were scattered around a vast countryside in tiny urban garrisons, known as *nauba*s. For example, in the Beylik of Constantine, which had a total population of perhaps one and a half million, its eight *nauba*s contained a mere 396 troops, an average of eighteen Janissaries per garrison.[16]

In these circumstances it was inevitable that, away from the capital, the racial discrimination practised against the Kuloğlus by the Turks had to be diluted if the regency was to continue to exercise its authority and fiscal power over the tens of thousands of indigenous Arabs who worked the land. Consequently, outside Algiers and the *dar al-Sultan*, Kuloğlus were used as garrison troops to supplement the tiny number of Turks available for this duty. For example, before the French invasion of 1830 the garrison of Tlemcen in the far west of the Regency consisted of 500 Kuloğlus; at Mostaganem there were also 500 Kuloğlus and a similar number at Mazouna, an important religious centre.[17] There were even a number of Kuloğlus who were able to acquire positions of power and in some cases constituted veritable dynasties of high office, most notably in the case of Constantine, where one particular Kuloğlu family occupied the position of bey from 1756 to 1792.[18]

By the end of the eighteenth century, such eminent Kuloğlus considered themselves just as 'Ottoman' as the ethnic Turks. In public they often spoke Turkish, and like the ethnic Turks they made a point of adhering to the Hanafi rite in matters of jurisprudence. Gone were the days when the Turks could treat the Kuloğlus with disdain and even fight against them. In certain areas of the Regency the Kuloğlus had become a local aristocracy, forming their own intimate links with the Turks of the Imperial centre. At the same time, they saw themselves as racially superior to the tens of thousands of Arabs over whom they exercised power.[19]

Not all the native Arab tribes were reduced to subordination and exploitation by the Turks and Kuloğlus. Considerable numbers of Arab auxiliaries were required to control the countryside and assist their overlords in the collection of taxes and deal with outbreaks of rebellion. Certain tribes were therefore co-opted into the role of law enforcement. These were called *makhzan* (government) tribes, and in return for their services they were exempt from taxation.[20] Of these the most important were the Dawa'ir and Zmela in the Beylik of Oran, where they were known as *makhzan al-kabir* (elite *makhzan*); but there were others, too, numbering perhaps as many as 126 *makhzan* tribes.[21]

By all accounts the indigenous Jews – many of whom had an ancestry dating back to Roman times, and others who had arrived after their expulsion from Spain in 1492 – occupied the lowest rung of the status and income ladder in the regencies' cities. They held lowly positions in artisan manufacture, petty trade and labouring, and they were frequently bullied and exploited by the Muslims. But there were other Jews who had arrived, mainly from Italy, in the early eighteenth century who acquired positions of quite elevated power and wealth. These were the small number of Jewish families who excelled in finance and trade, like the Bacri and Busnach families of Algiers. They lent money to the deys, beys and other senior members of the Turkish establishment, they had shares in corsairing operations, they acted as intermediaries in the ransoming and exchange of European and Muslim slaves, they chartered shipping for the regencies' exports, and they financed both export and import trading. Although on occasion they might fall victim to the whims – and greed – of the regencies' rulers, those same rulers depended upon the skills and expertise of these upper-class Jews and their networks of fellow Jewish merchants and financiers, which extended throughout the whole Mediterranean region in cities like Livorno, Izmir, Alexandria, Marseille, Malta and Gibraltar.[22]

Within five years of the seizure of power by the Janissaries' dey in 1710, which put an end to direct imperial rule in Algiers, similar transfers of power occurred in Tripoli and Tunis. In the former, this change took place in the midst of a civil war between different Janissary factions. After a succession of murdered deys, in April 1711 a resourceful young Kuloğlu cavalryman named Ahmed Karamanli seized power. Before that his people had been forced to live outside the city of Tripoli in the *menshia* (oasis) some miles to the east. On 30 August, leading a combined force of Kuloğlus and Arabs and backed by dissident Janissaries and the *ulema** of Tripoli, Karamanli also defeated an attempt to impose an imperial appointee as governor; he declared himself supreme ruler. Further attempts were made to impose imperial governors, but by 1722 the reigning sultan acknowledged defeat and appointed Ahmed Karamanli as paşa of Tripoli. He established a dynasty which lasted until 1835.

Similarly, in Tunis, in 1705 a Turkish-speaking commander of the Arab cavalry, a man of Cretan or Genoese origin, Husayn bin 'Ali, curbed the power of the Janissary officers and allowed the Kuloğlus full participation in his state and army. Although a Turkish speaker himself, he mobilised the local Arabic *ulema*, notables and tribal leaders against the dey of the Tunisian Janissaries and established himself as ruler with the title bey. When the sultan sent a fleet to Tunis with an imperial governor in 1715 the same popular forces rejected the Ottoman appointee and compelled the sultan to recognise Husayn bin 'Ali as provincial ruler. He too established a dynasty, which would last until 1957.†

In spite of their rejection of imperial governors, all three regencies continued to profess formal allegiance to the sultans in Istanbul. They did not send tribute but, as a relic of the old system of triennial imperial paşas, every three years they sent presents to the sultan; and from time to time they despatched naval units to support the Ottoman navy during its successive wars with Spain and Russia.

The real problem in the relationship between the regencies and their sultans was a question of foreign policy: in particular the reluctance of the regencies to adhere to the current Ottoman one emanating from whatever agreements had recently been reached between the sultan and various Christian powers. For example, at the Treaty of Passarowitz in 1718, the sultan had agreed to order the North African regencies to cease their attacks on the shipping of Austria and Venice with whom he had negotiated a peace treaty. But with the Ottoman governors replaced by local deys, beys and

---

*   The Arabic *'ulama* would be correct here, but *ulema* is retained throughout the book for simplicity.

†   Although after 1881 the bey was a French puppet ruler. In 1957 a republic was proclaimed.

paşas, these new rulers conducted their own foreign policies. So agreements like that of Passarowitz were casually ignored.

However, each sultan still had a powerful lever which he could exercise against a recalcitrant regency. Like the Egyptian Mamluks with their dependence on new supplies of young Caucasian captives, all three regencies periodically needed infusions of Anatolian volunteers to strengthen their Turkish Janissary contingents. In the case of Algiers, these new recruits had to be transported across 2,000 kilometres of sea to that most distant of the sultan's realms. Without the sultan's permission and assistance, the reproduction of the Algerian *ocak* could not take place. Moreover, the Turkish forces in Algiers were exposed to the continuing threat from Christian Spain, so they feared abandonment by the Ottoman centre – just as much as the Empire had no wish to lose territory, even that of an 'autonomous' province like Algiers. And so this commonality of interests set a certain limit to the regencies' readiness to disobey their sultan. Likewise successive sultans understood the need to exercise caution in trying to impose their will on these distant provinces.

As for the practicalities of shipping the annual quota of Turks from the eastern to the western end of the Mediterranean, the Ottoman government chartered vessels from nations such as Denmark, Holland and Venice: Christian ships to protect their Muslim military passengers from the attacks of Christian corsairs.[23]

CHAPTER 6

The Russians in the Mediterranean

October 1768: Sultan Mustafa III is anxiously awaiting news from the North. For months, a large Russian army has been assembling suspiciously close to the border between Russian-occupied Polish territory and the Ottoman vassal state of Moldavia.* There have also been messages from the Tatar Khan of the Crimea, a loyal Ottoman vassal, that the Tsarina Catherine's troops are repairing fortresses and building new ones along the ill-defined northern frontier. Diplomatic notes have been exchanged, but Russian equivocation about the size of the Russian forces in Poland has not satisfied the sultan and his divan.[1]

Worse still, a messenger has arrived carrying news that Russian Cossacks, pursuing the remnants of a fleeing rebel Polish army, have actually entered Ottoman territory in southwest Ukraine and killed hundreds of Muslims in the town of Balta. Mustafa's grand vezir, Silahdar Hamza Paşa, and the French Ambassador, the Comte de Vergennes, are pressing Mustafa to declare war on Russia.[2]

The prospect of war with the sultan was by no means unattractive for Tsarina Catherine II (1729–96). Before its capture by the Turks in 1453, Istanbul, had been the holy city of Constantinople ruled by the Byzantine Christian emperors. With their inheritance from the Byzantines of both the Greek Orthodox liturgy and the Cyrillic alphabet, Russia's deeply religious rulers would always believe they had a fundamental duty to re-take Constantinople for Christianity and liberate the conquered Greek, Balkan and Levantine Christian subjects of the sultan. Almost certainly, the Tsarina shared this ambition.

---

* Moldavia and its southern neighbour Wallachia were vassal states of the Ottoman Empire, known to the Europeans as the 'Danubian principalities'. Together they were broadly equal to the modern-day state of Romania.

With war looming, precedent required that the sultan's imperial divan should decide on such a weighty matter after formal discussion. The divan was the nearest thing to a council of state in the Ottoman political system, but it functioned in a very different manner from those of the Christian states. By the eighteenth century the divan might have included as many as forty members of the Porte's bureaucracy, including the highest-ranking cleric, the şehülislam. Typically, the grand vezir would initiate discussion by calling on the şehülislam to comment on the matter in hand in the light of the Shari'a, something the latter would usually do in only the most general terms. The discussion would then have been opened up to the other members of the divan; usually, however, they would avoid speaking for fear of opposing the wishes of the grand vezir. Were he to press them for their opinions they would answer evasively, for example, saying that he was the wisest, that it was he who had the confidence of the sultan, that it was for him to command and them to obey, etc. In short, the real function of these 'consultations' was not actual decision making or any serious discussion of the pros and cons of the issue under 'debate', but rather the legitimation of controversial government action in the eyes of the populace. In short, the divan sought to insulate the sultan and grand vezir from censure.

So at this crucial moment of war or peace, the current grand vezir, Silahdar Hamza Paşa, who had been appointed only in August 1768 (and may have been insane), was urging Mustafa III that he had no real choice but to avenge the Russian atrocity at Balta.

Yet the sultan was still wavering. He could hardly have forgotten the advice of his former grand vezir, his kinsman and friend Ragıb Paşa. The vezir's death five years earlier had left Mustafa suffused with grief – a grief which he tried to assuage by composing an elegy to his old chief minister. Ragıb had repeatedly urged him to avoid, at all costs, any entanglement in the wars of the Christian states which had plagued Europe since the beginning of the century.

In the last of these European conflagrations – the Seven Years' War – Russia, Austria and France had been allies, their forces on land and sea pitted against Britain, Prussia and various minor German states. But a year before the war ended in 1763, Russia withdrew from the conflict, leaving an exhausted and financially crippled France to face defeat. Since then, an embittered French aristocracy had begun to fear that Russia, under its new sovereign the Empress Catherine, would soon replace France as the premier military power in Europe.

In November 1764 France's anxiety about growing Russian influence in Europe reached a new intensity when Catherine's protégé and former lover, Stanislaw Poniatowski – backed by the Russian Army – was placed on the throne of Poland. France's fear of Russia's intentions had also been inflamed by the knowledge that Britain, its near-permanent enemy, was building up a flourishing maritime trade with Russia, and there were rumours that the two countries might soon sign a formal alliance. Consequently, when a group of Polish nobles met at the fortress town of Bar in February 1768, formed the Confederation of Bar and launched a rebellion against the Russian-backed Polish King Poniatowski, the French government swiftly offered the rebels diplomatic support and military advisors.

Meanwhile, France's Foreign Minister since 1766, Etienne François, duc de Choiseul, a fervent Anglophobe, had become convinced that Britain was behind Russia's growing strength around the Baltic Sea and was planning to form a 'northern league' against France. To counter what he believed were Britain's evil intentions, Choiseul thought he could seriously weaken Russia by encouraging the Ottoman Empire to declare war upon her. Consequently, the French Ambassador in Istanbul, the Comte de Vergennes, had been ordered to use his influence to persuade the Porte to attack Russia in support of the Bar Confederation.[3] And now, Russian Cossacks had given Choiseul and Vergennes a powerful lever with which to push the sultan into a proxy war in furtherance of France's strategic interests.

Finally, the sultan decided. The latest news from the network of Ottoman fortresses which stretched from the Danube to the Sea of Azov all appeared to confirm the Tsarina's hostile intentions. According to Ottoman spies the Russian army was composed of nothing but half-starved serfs conscripted for life and only held together by a ferocious discipline. In 1711 the glorious army of Mustafa's father had crushed them on the River Pruth, so the sultan felt confident that his own brave warriors could now do the same. Thus, on 6 October 1768, he ordered the arrest of the Russian Ambassador and all his staff – an open declaration of war. On the same day the sultan dismissed his half-mad grand vezir, replacing him with Yağlıkçızade Mehmed Emin Paşa, who promised the sultan a swift and victorious war.

Although Choiseul was pleased by the sultan's decision, he was less confident than Sultan Mustafa that after so many years of peace the Ottoman troops had the martial prowess they would need to beat the Russians. Above all, he feared a hasty ceasefire which might follow a sudden collapse of the Ottoman armies. So he ordered the new French Ambassador at the sultan's court, the Comte de Saint-Priest (who had recently replaced Vergennes), to ensure that the Turks did not make peace or forge an armistice with the Russians without French consent.[4]

However, Choiseul's instructions to Saint-Priest, delivered on 17 July 1768, contained another intriguing element. For while the ambassador was to do nothing to undermine France's traditional friendly relations with the sultan and his ministers. Saint-Priest should also advise him on what opportunities there might be for France in the event of an Ottoman defeat, and the Empire losing control of significant parts of its territories to the various provincial *ayan* who were already threatening its integrity. And Choiseul made particular mention of Egypt 'which is already in a state of effective independence'. France must leave all options open, he believed.

In one respect the Ottomans appeared to have a considerable advantage over the Russians: there was no shortage of Muslim volunteers. Contemporary estimates of the size of the Ottoman Army mobilised for the campaign on the Bessarabian front vary enormously,* but the total, including 40–50,000 Crimean Tatars, may have reached 300,000.[5]

However, the vast majority of these troops were no longer Janissaries but *levends,* local provincial militias drawn from landless labourers, vagrants, semi-bandits and the private armies of powerful provincial *ayan.*[6] The problem was that there were simply too many men of this kind. Often without any military experience, enticed by the promise of good pay and motivated by an intense religious enthusiasm, they flocked to join the green standard of the sultan. But not only were they incapable of standing up to the disciplined regulars of the Russian Army, their presence on the march north to confront them posed enormous logistical problems for the Ottoman command.

---

*   Bessarabia was nominally (vassal) Ottoman territory in southwest Ukraine, bordered by the River Dniester in the East and the Pruth in the West. It had a coastline on the Black Sea, and to the south it bordered the Ottoman vassal state of Moldavia.

As for the Janissaries, who formed a relatively small part of the great horde which set off towards the Bessarabian front in January 1769, they numbered around 60,000 men. Yet the quality of these 'elite' full-time troops left much to be desired, as did what remained of the fief-based *sipahi* cavalry. Baron de Tott, who had returned from France to act as consul at the court of Krim-Geray, the Tatar Khan of the Crimea, observed some of the opening skirmishes of the war. According to de Tott, the 10,000 *sipahis* who had been sent in advance of the main Ottoman Army to join forces with the Tatars merely contented themselves with ravaging what was left of the town of Balta and neighbouring villages.

> Such bad and ill-disciplined troops... This cavalry accustomed
> to the sweets and inactivity of a long peace, not able to endure
> fatigue, incapable of resisting cold and too ill-clothed likewise
> to support it, was effectually useless.[7]

And sometime later de Trott spoke witheringly of the famed *serdengeçti* contingent of the Janissaries, volunteers who were reputedly the first to throw themselves upon the enemy defences. Their motto was 'conquer or die': de Tott wryly commented that 'they never perform one nor the other'.

Meanwhile, as the hundreds of anarchic and ill-officered bands of provincial *levend*s trundled northwards towards the Ottoman Army's concentration point at Bender on the right bank of the River Dniester, over two and a half thousand kilometres away to the northwest, the hardy Yorkshire fishermen of the port of Hull were witness to the strangest sight. As they cleaned their nets on the morning of 5 October 1769, a large and distinctly weather-battered vessel flying an unfamiliar white ensign with a blue diagonal cross loomed out of the sea mist cloaking the estuary of the River Humber. It drifted slowly into their harbour, followed by three similarly damaged, smaller ships. And as the vessels came closer in, it could be seen that all four carried on their bows ship names in an unrecognisable language.

The ships in question were the 66-gun battleship *Sv. Evstafi* flying the flag of the fifty-six-year-old Rear-Admiral Gregori Andreyevich Spiridov; another 66-gun battleship, the *Syevernyi Orel*; the 32-gun frigate *Nadezhda*

Blagopolutchia; and the 12-gun bomb vessel, *Grom*.* Over the next few days these Russian vessels would be joined by four more 66-gun battleships, a 22-gun pinque and a despatch boat. The first of these latecomers, the battleship *Trech Ierarchov*, was under the command of a thirty-three-year-old Scotsman, Samuel Greig.[8]

These ships were the first of two fleets of the Imperial Russian Navy ordered to sail around the Iberian Peninsula, through the straits of Gibraltar and into the Mediterranean to attack the Ottoman Empire on its weaker, southern flank.[9] The instructions from the Tsarina Catherine to Count Alexsei Orlov, the overall commander of the expedition, were to interrupt the shipping of foodstuffs from Greece to the Ottoman capital, to support an uprising of the sultan's Greek subjects in the Peloponnese and – if circumstances were favourable – to penetrate the Dardanelles, sail across the Sea of Marmara and attack the Ottoman capital itself. This was a remarkably risky, daring and ambitious military project; but given that the Russian merchant navy still had no access to the Black Sea, it was the only way in which the Russian Empire's growing maritime strength could be brought to bear upon their enemy. And, if it succeeded, the rewards would be immense.

To pave the way for the expedition, on 9 February, Count Orlov had already arrived in the Italian port of Livorno to organise naval supply and watering points in the eastern Mediterranean; and Greek-speaking Russian agents sent to the chieftains of the Peloponnese were urging them to rebel against their Turkish rulers, promising substantial Russian military assistance.

But what were the Russians ships doing in British waters and in a British port? In fact, the government of King George III was now playing a devious game. For some time, Britain had been steadily increasing its trade with Russia's Baltic region while its Mediterranean trade had been declining. For example, in the latter part of the eighteenth century an annual average of 600–700 British merchant ships went to Russia while no more than twenty-seven went to the Levant.[10] Britain was dependent, in particular, on Baltic Russia for bar iron and essential naval stores, such as sailcloth and hemp. However, negotiations over a full-blown treaty had eventually broken down on Russia's insistence on the 'Turkey Clause': that in the

---

* A bomb vessel was a small warship, broad in beam, and armed with large-calibre guns firing explosive shells. These ships were generally used for coastal bombardment.

event of an Ottoman attack upon Russia, Britain would wage war on the Ottomans in Russia's defence.

However, the handful of ministers making foreign policy now believed they had discovered a way to ingratiate themselves with the Tsarina Catherine without actually making war on the Ottomans themselves. Moreover, they considered the war a win-win opportunity. If the outcome was a stalemate, as they hoped, they would be called upon to mediate; if the Ottomans lost and had to concede territory to Russia, it would be Britain, with its great commercial experience, which would be able to make the best of the opportunities newly available.

So, Britain declared its neutrality; but it would be a 'neutrality' unilaterally defined in British terms. Britain would provide Russia with what it needed most. A month or so before the arrival of the first Russian warships at Hull, the Russian Ambassador in London, Count Ivan Chernyshov, had asked the British Foreign Secretary, Lord William Rochford, for permission to use British ports including Gibraltar and Mahon (Minorca) and receive all necessary help in refitting and repairing Russian vessels damaged at sea. Rochford agreed to the Russian request and instructed the Lords of the Admiralty to give the Russian ships, 'the most friendly treatment and every kind of assistance and succour which may be necessary for them to continue their voyage'.[11]

Meanwhile a number of British naval officers had been recruited by the Russian navy. These included Lieutenant Samuel Greig and Captain John Elphinston, who had been languishing on half pay since the end of the Seven Years' War. The former was immediately promoted to Captain and the latter to Rear-Admiral. In due course a number of additional British naval officers would join them.

However, by the spring of 1769, the Duc de Choiseul had already received intelligence of Russian naval preparations, and on 13 September he instructed his Ambassador Saint-Priest to urge the authorities in Istanbul to strengthen the defences of the capital and the Islands. The following month Choiseul and Saint-Priest began to provide the Ottoman government with detailed and accurate information about the Russians' plans and the fact that Britain was giving them assistance.

In February 1770 the Greeks of the Peloponnese launched their rebellion in anticipation of what was expected to be a major Russian expedition carrying large infantry and artillery contingents. At first they met with considerable success, seizing towns like Kalamata and Mystras. But in the course of these and other successes, and in a tragic forerunner of what would occur half a century later, Turkish men, women and children were indiscriminately killed.

With war to their north and the Greek rebellion in their rear, The Porte was perplexed and angered by Britain's behaviour. On 11 March 1770 the head of the chancery and Ottoman foreign minister, the *reisül-küttub*, urged the British to stop the advance of the Russian fleet. However, John Murray, the British Ambassador at Istanbul, replied with the disingenuous assertion that Britain was strictly neutral and it was quite impossible for the Royal Navy to block the progress of a fleet belonging to a country with which Britain was not at war.

Meanwhile, the Russian fleet arrived off the southern coast of the Peloponnese and landed some small contingents of Russian infantry and artillery, which made desultory attempts to capture Ottoman fortresses. But the uprising was already facing defeat. Although at one stage the number of Greek insurgents in the Peloponnese may have reached 50,000, apart from the island of Crete (where Russian agents had also been at work) the uprising failed to spread to other parts of Greece or the Aegean islands. The small Russian landings did nothing to improve the morale of those Greeks still fighting.

Ethnic Albanian troops in Ottoman service, heading for the Russian front, were now rushed south to crush the Greek rebels, and with their arrival the tide turned against the rebels. The small Russian infantry detachments which had been left isolated on the coast of the Peloponnese found themselves facing overwhelming odds. So on 28 May Admiral Spiridov re-embarked his troops, leaving the Greeks of the Peloponnese to a terrible fate at the hands of the vengeful Albanians.

On 27 June the Russian fleet anchored off the island of Paros in the central Aegean to put on water. It was here that Spiridov heard that the main Ottoman fleet was lying between the island of Chios and the Anatolian mainland. Weighing anchor on 1 July, the Russians continued their crossing of the Aegean, and on the morning of 5 July 1770 they rounded the northern end of Chios and saw the Ottoman fleet at anchor to leeward. The decisive naval battle was now about to commence.

The Ottoman fleet consisted of seventeen battleships, two frigates and two 50-gun caravels, together with a number of smaller craft including xebecs, galleys and galliots.[12] They were anchored a few kilometres north of the Bay of Çeşme, parallel to the coastline, in two lines where they awaited the Russian attack. The Russian line of battle included just nine battleships, three frigates and the bomb vessel *Grom*. Admiral Spiridov and Prince Orlov were in the 66-gun *Sv. Estafi* in the van of the Russian line and Elphinston was in the rear of the line commanding the 80-gun *Svyatoslav*. In terms of fire power the Ottomans had around 1,300 guns to the Russians' 710.[13]

With a NW wind behind them, the Russians came down upon the enemy under sail and then turned on the port tack to bring their ships in a line roughly parallel to that of the Ottomans. At about 11.45 a.m. the Ottoman ships opened fire and a little later the Russians replied. Spiridov's ship soon suffered serious damage to its rigging and drifted alongside the leading Turkish ship, the 84-gun *Real Mustafa*, commanded by one of the Turks' three flag officers, Cezayirli Gazi Hasan Paşa.

Spiridov and Gazi Hasan Paşa fought yard-arm to yard-arm for some time, but then, suddenly, the *Real Mustafa* caught fire. The flames spread quickly and soon both ships were ablaze. At about 1.30 pm the blazing mainmast of the *Real Mustafa* fell upon the *Sv. Estafi*. Spiridov, Orlov and Gazi Hasan Paşa all managed to escape by boat only minutes before the *Real Mustafa* blew up. From the Russian battleship only sixty-three men were rescued out of a crew of 699. The losses on the *Real Mustafa* were probably even greater. The explosion of the *Real Mustafa*, one of their most powerful battleships, demoralised the remaining Ottoman captains. They cut their cables and fled into the harbour of Çeşme – it would be a fatal step. By 2.00 p.m. this first stage of the battle was over.

Apart from the loss of the *Sv. Estafi*, Russian losses had been light. By the evening, their fleet had taken up position across the mouth of Çeşme harbour, but the narrowness of the entrance to the Bay of Çeşme meant that Orlov could send in only four battleships, two frigates and his bomb vessel. The second Russian attack began on the morning of 6 July with the Russian ships bombarding the Ottoman vessels and positions on land.

The decisive Russian attack was led by Captain Greig, now promoted to Commodore and commanding the 66-gun *Rotislav*. The Russians

Bust of Admiral Cezayirli
Gaza Hasan Paşa

concentrated on bombarding the Ottoman coastal batteries. But at about
1.30 p.m. an explosive shell from the bomb vessel *Grom* set fire to one of
the topsails of a Turkish battleship; the topmast came down and soon the
whole ship was in flames. The fire now spread, and by 2 p.m. two more
Ottoman ships had been set alight and had exploded. Commodore Greig
now sent in his fire ships to administer the *coup de grace*. The first, under a
junior British officer, Lieutenant Dugdale, was intercepted and sunk by two
Ottoman galleys; however, with great bravery and accompanied by another
British officer, Lieutenant Drysdale, Commodore Greig personally set the
match to his own fire ship, after which both men leapt overboard and swam
to their own boats.

The principal weakness of the Turkish fleet at Çeşme was not in the quality
of its ships or the bravery of its crews but in the fatal decision to anchor
its ships too close together. As the Ottoman vessels tried to manoeuvre to
escape the raging fires they collided with each other. The fire then became
general, and more and more Turkish ships exploded. By evening it was all
over. During this final phase of the battle, the Russians lost just eleven men
and suffered only light damage to their ships. The Ottomans, however, lost
eleven battleships burnt and one captured; they also lost six frigates and
eight galleys burnt and five captured. Thirty-two smaller vessels were also
destroyed by fire.[14] For the Ottomans it was a total disaster.

It wasn't the only catastrophe suffered by the Ottomans that day. On the banks of the River Larga in Moldavia a Russian army of 38,000 routed a combined army of 65,000 Crimean Tatars and 15,000 Ottoman infantry; and only a fortnight later the sultan's troops experienced an even greater military disaster on the Kagul River in southern Bessarabia, losing over 20,000 killed and captured, for the loss of only around 1,000 Russians. By late July 1770 Sultan Mustafa III was facing the possibility that his great Islamic Empire was about to collapse.

However, unaware of Russian successes on the Danube, Orlov had no clear idea of how to follow up the victory at Çeşme. In Elphinston's opinion he should have immediately sailed for the Dardanelles, forced his way through and attacked the Ottoman capital on the Bosphorus. But Orlov considered this too risky. Instead he ordered Elphinston to begin a naval blockade of the Dardanelles, through which Istanbul received most of its food supplies.

Meanwhile, Rochford and the British government had belatedly come to realise that their expectations of a stalemate in the war had been a serious mistake. Indeed, the war might even have ended with the capture of Istanbul by the Russian Empress, something that the British government had neither contemplated nor desired. On 10 July 1770 a British frigate was sent to the eastern Mediterranean to order British storage ships flying Russian colours to return home. In April 1771 Britain stopped supplying Russian ships in the Mediterranean with stores, and also made clear to the Russians that Britain rejected any suggestion that they should permanently occupy any of the Aegean islands as a naval base.[15]

At around the same time the majority of the junior British naval officers in Russian service returned home, under pressure from the Admiralty. Elphinston himself resigned his commission in the Russian navy, complaining of a lack of fighting spirit among his fellow Russian naval officers, although Samuel Greig remained in his post. He was promoted to Admiral and, in years to come, became governor of the Kronstadt naval base.

As the war between Russia and the Ottomans continued, it became clear that neither of the combatants intended to satisfy Britain's desire to be a mediator in any future peace negotiations. Indeed, Russia, was increasingly inclined to make peace at the point of the sword. Whatever Britain's disingenuous protestations to the contrary, the Ottoman government was aware that it had given crucial support to the Russian fleet. For the time being, Britain had 'thrown away the chance, such as it was, of building up at İstanbul a political influence which might seriously challenge, if not supplant, that of France'.[16]

There now occurred one of the most remarkable turnabouts in the fortunes of war. The attention of Orlov's frustrated expedition turned to Lemnos, lying only sixty kilometres from the mouth of the Dardanelles. On 31 July soldiers and marines were landed with some artillery and laid siege to its citadel, Pelari. If they had succeeded, it would have provided the Russians with a superb base from which to intensify the blockade of the Dardanelles and Istanbul, but the siege dragged on through the summer and on 4 October Orlov's troops were thrown into disarray by a totally unexpected Ottoman counter-attack.

It was led by Gazi Hasan Paşa (1713–90), one of the three Ottoman commanders at Çeşme who had escaped from his burning flagship, the *Real Mustafa*. He was better known as Cezayirli Gazi Hasan (Hasan the Algerian warrior). Originally a Georgian slave, he had been purchased by a Turkish merchant who had treated him on a par with his own sons. For a time, he had fought as an Algerian corsair (hence his sobriquet) but he returned to Istanbul where he rose through the ranks of the Ottoman navy. It was he who brought news of the Çeşme disaster to the sultan's court; yet he was praised for his bravery and would ultimately be raised to the rank of grand vezir. In 1773 he would also be responsible for establishing the first naval engineering school and shipyard on the Golden Horn.

Arriving off Lemnos with an assorted collection of twenty-three vessels, Gazi Hasan Paşa disembarked a strong body of troops, albeit weaker in numbers than those of the Russians. When he heard of the counter-attack, fearing entrapment, Orlov panicked and ordered the abandonment of the siege and the re-embarkment of his troops. Although the engagement was tiny in relation to the Russo-Turkish battles continuing elsewhere, strategically it was an Ottoman masterstroke. In effect, it removed the blockade of the Dardanelles, which was already causing near-starvation among the poorer classes of Istanbul, and it also crushed any lingering Russian hopes of seizing the Ottoman capital.

Thereafter, in spite of eventually receiving three more Russian squadrons from the Baltic, the Russian naval campaign in the Eastern Mediterranean degenerated into a series of fitful minor engagements with Turkish ships and (with one exception) brief and indecisive landings on Ottoman-held Greek islands.

Meanwhile Mustafa III begged Baron de Tott – currently French consul at the court of the Crimean Khan – to come to Istanbul to repair and reposition the Turkish artillery defending the Dardanelles. On the instructions of the French government, de Tott rushed to Istanbul and by late 1772 the work had been completed. So, even had they been willing to do so, the Russian navy would now have faced severe difficulties had they attempted to force the Straits. De Tott was also instrumental in founding a naval mathematics school in 1773 and later (in 1776) an engineering school.

The Russians enjoyed only one remaining success in the Mediterranean – and this only a temporary one. On 18 June 1772, a Russian squadron commanded by a junior naval officer arrived off the port of Beirut, landed troops and began a siege of the city and its 5,000 inhabitants. But they were unable to wear down its defenders, so the attempt was abandoned on 23 June. However, the following year the Russians returned in greater strength and again landed troops, this time beginning a full-scale siege of the city. The defence of Beirut was in the hands of a fifty-three-year-old Bosnian soldier of fortune, Ahmed al-Cezzar (the Butcher) Paşa, later to be appointed governor of the eyalet of Sidon, who had received a military education as a Mamluk in Egypt (although he wasn't himself a Mamluk).[17] We shall meet this individual again in a later chapter. For the present, suffice it to say that he would play a critical role in the affairs of Egypt and Palestine during the last three decades of the century.

Although Ahmed al-Cezzar and his small force of defenders put up a strong resistance to their Russian attackers, on 10 October 1773 Beirut's defenders were forced to surrender. The Russian occupation lasted until February 1774. It was the first mainland Muslim town in the Mediterranean to be occupied by a Christian power since the Crusades. The town itself was systematically sacked and its inhabitants forced to bow to a portrait of the Empress Catherine erected above the main gate of the city walls.[18]

With this final blow, Sultan Mustafa III, worn out physically and psychologically by the consequences of his disastrous decision to go to war, died in his Topkapı Palace on 21 January 1774. One of his last acts before his

death was to compose a poignant quatrain ruminating on the failures of the
Ottoman Empire over which he had presided for the past seventeen years.

> The world is turning upside down, with no hope for better
>   during our reign,
> Wicked fate has delivered the state into the hands of despicable
>   men,
> Our bureaucrats are villains who prowl through the streets of
>   Istanbul,
> We can do nothing but beg God for mercy.[19]

After Mustafa III's death, the sultanate passed to his younger half-brother,
Abdülhamid I (r. 1774–89). Although Abdülhamid I had been opposed to
the war, he felt that he had no choice but to continue fighting. But on 20
June 1774, another Ottoman army was decisively defeated by a numerically
smaller Russian one under the command of the famous General Suvorov at
the Battle of Kozludzha in the northeast of present-day Bulgaria. This was
the coup de grâce.

The Russians now made it clear that they neither wanted nor needed
any mediation by foreign powers, thus dashing any lingering British hopes
that they might play that role. The treaty which would now be imposed on
the Ottomans was unmistakeably one dictated at the point of the sword. Its
most important terms – signed at the Bulgarian town of Küçük Kaynarca
on 21 July 1774 – were that Russia acquired a small area of land between the
lower courses of the River Bug and River Dnieper together with the mouth
of the latter. Thus, for the first time, it gained a foothold on the Black Sea.
Moreover, Russia now acquired freedom of navigation on the Black Sea
(an exclusively Muslim 'lake' since the fifteenth century) and the right of
passage for Russia's merchant ships through the Bosphorus and Dardanelles
into the Mediterranean.

Most significant of all were two further clauses: the Crimea should be
'independent' (which most observers recognised as only the prelude to a
complete Russian takeover); and, in a clause which was to be the cause of
much diplomatic – and eventually military – conflict, Russia gained the
right to build a church of the Orthodox Christian religion in Istanbul and
to 'make representations on behalf of it and those who serve it'.[20] Partly

because of mistranslations of the treaty, this clause would eventually become interpreted as meaning that Russia could act as 'guardian' to all Orthodox Christians living in the Ottoman Empire.[21] Eighty years later it would be the proximate cause of the so-called Crimean War.

The remarkable naval second front which the Russians had established in the eastern Mediterranean undoubtedly made a significant contribution to their victory over the Ottomans; but after the destruction of the Ottoman fleet at Çeşme, Russian naval operations, lacking any safe permanent harbour and unsupported by any substantial land forces, became strategically aimless. After peace was signed the remnants of the five Russian squadrons which had eventually entered the Mediterranean were ordered to return to the Baltic. A considerable number of the ships had to be abandoned, burnt or sold because of the poor conditions into which they had fallen; and of the thirteen battleships which had sailed from the Baltic in the first three squadrons, only six eventually returned.[22]

Fighting on two fronts – the northern one in Bessarabia, the Balkans and the Crimea; and the southern one in the Mediterranean – made it almost impossible for the Ottomans to win the war. But they also had to face a third, lesser known front. Within a year of the Porte's declaration of war with Russia in 1768, a forty-one-year-old Mamluk of the Qazduğliya household named 'Ali Bey had launched a campaign to seize control of Egypt, the Empire's richest province, eliciting support from Russia. In the pages of Egyptian history he would come to be known as 'Ali Bey al-Kabir ('Ali Bey the Great).

CHAPTER 7

Ottoman Egypt:
The Empire Fraying at the Edges

We last encountered the Qazduğliya Mamluk household in the late 1740s as they shot, stabbed and poisoned their way to become the dominant element among Egypt's tiny ruling class while taking control of the two most important Ottoman garrison regiments. Ibrahim Jawish al-Qazduğli seized the position of *kethüda* in the Janissary regiment, and his ally, Ridwan Kethüda al-Julfi, became head of the 'Azaban regiment. Together with 'Abd al-Rahman al-Qazduğli, they established a triumvirate which endured until Ibrahim's death in 1754, although 'Abd al-Rahman, the only son of a Qazduğliya Mamluk and (unusually) head of the household, was more of a sleeping partner.[1]

At the mid-century, coffee imported from Jeddah in Arabia (but originating in Mocha, Yemen) was the single largest item in Egypt's trade. It afforded Egypt's rulers huge customs duties and underwrote a period of fiscal stability during which a massive programme of construction was carried out in Cairo, the biggest in the city's history.[2] Years later, the great Egyptian historian 'Abd al-Rahman al-Jabarti looked back nostalgically to the period of Ibrahim's dominance. 'Cairo was peaceful, free from strife and violence … Cairo's beauties then were brilliant, its excellences apparent, vanquishing its rivals. The poor lived at ease. Both great and small lived in abundance.'[3] All that would change during the final two decades of the century.

Among the Mamluks acquired by the de facto head of the Qazduğliya Ibrahim Jawish, was a certain Georgian (or Abkhazian) slave named 'Ali whom he later appointed a *sancak* bey *to* administer part of Ibrahim's extensive tax farms. Sometime in 1760, after eliminating a number of his rivals, 'Ali Bey seized the dominant position of *sheikh al-balad*.[4] The ruthlessness that characterised his rise to power continued as he turned his attention to potential rivals in the Qazduğliya-dominated Janissary regiment. He had its remaining senior officers killed and thereafter the regiment became little more than a legal fiction.[5]

Some years later, he himself purchased a sixteen-year-old Mamluk, Muhammad Abu al-Dhahab, a Circassian who became his closest and most trusted friend and, later, his brother-in-law. And among those whom 'Ali Bey recruited as his principal bodyguard, executioner and hit-man was the Bosnian soldier of fortune, Ahmed al-Cezzar (the Butcher) – the same Ahmed al-Cezzar who would later distinguish himself at the siege of Beirut in 1773. Reputedly, al-Cezzar won his rather ominous sobriquet after an engagement with around forty marauding Bedouin in which he and his men slaughtered the whole band. In years to come the appropriateness of Ahmed al-Cezzar's name would be underlined by an unrivalled and ferocious cruelty towards his enemies as well as his undeniable bravery in battle.

'Ali Bey initially attempted to maintain polite and civil relations with the Porte, although this may have been a clever strategic move. Whether he was sincere or not, a continued suspicion and hostility towards him on the part of Mustafa III's government resulted in a determination to strike out on his own for a greater degree of independence for Egypt than it had ever previously experienced.[6] By early 1768 he had begun to formulate a plan to gain control over neighbouring Ottoman provinces, and re-establish something like the domain of the great Mamluk sultans who had ruled before Egypt's conquest by the Ottomans in the early sixteenth century.

In September 1768 'Ali Bey turned against Ahmed al-Cezzar, his *khushdash* (bondsman) and henchman. Al-Cezzar was part of an assassination squad ordered to kill a former ally of 'Ali Bey, but the intended victim appears to have been a friend of al-Cezzar and on the occasion of the ambush al-Cezzar openly refrained from taking part in the killing.[7] It is also possible that by this time al-Cezzar had become disenchanted with 'Ali Bey's megalomania and his increasingly apparent willingness to tear Egypt away from the sultan's empire.

Certainly, for the remainder of his long life al-Cezzar remained faithful to the Ottoman state and it is possible that he had already been acting as an Ottoman government spy for a number of years. Al-Cezzar's refusal to be involved in the killing of a friend signified his open defiance of 'Ali Bey, who promptly ordered his arrest. Al-Cezzar's own murder would certainly have followed, so he fled Cairo and travelled to Istanbul where he presented the sultan and his ministers with a detailed intelligence report concerning the Egyptian political system. In it al-Cezzar inveighed against the 'tyranny' of the Mamluk beys and pointed out the opportunities which he claimed existed to return Egypt to full Ottoman control under an effective imperial governor – with a strong suggestion that the governor might be someone very much like himself.[8] He even recommended a 12,000-man invasion of Egypt to liquidate the Mamluk beys.

However, with Mustafa III's declaration of war against the Russians this was not the most opportune time to implement al-Cezzar's ambitious plan. Apparently his proposals were well received, but at the time the sultan's attention was firmly focused on the northern front. On the other hand, the outbreak of war with Russia gave 'Ali Bey just the opportunity he had been waiting for to begin to put into practice his move towards independence.

The outbreak of the Russo-Ottoman war in 1768 coincided with a growing interest among some British merchants to establish an 'overland' route to the Mediterranean from India. The precious wares of Madras, Bombay and Calcutta, together with coffee loaded en route in Yemen, would be shipped up the Red Sea to the port of Suez where – or so it was believed – they could be sold at a huge profit.[9] And from there, some would be transhipped across Egypt to Alexandria and the Mediterranean. At the same time, advised by a separate coterie of merchants headed by the Venetian ambassador at Istanbul, 'Ali Bey had also become convinced that an overland trade route to Cairo and the Mediterranean via Suez would bring his regime a huge increase in the customs revenues charged on those exceptionally profitable India trades.[10]

But there were two problems. First, the prevailing winds in the Red Sea between May and September were from the north, and this made it almost impossible for sailing ships to navigate up the Sea from the south during this season. This natural feature could seriously impact the time and cost of the journey. Second – and more seriously – so long as the Hejazi port of Jeddah and the Red Sea remained under the control of the Ottoman Empire, Christian merchants were forbidden from trading in the Red Sea, on the grounds that trade would bring Christians into dangerous proximity to the holy cities of Mecca and Medina. According to the *ulema,* if this were permitted, then Islam's most holy places would soon become 'defiled' by infidel influences and customs.

Some years earlier though, in the mid-eighteenth century, the Porte had made an important concession. A limited number of Christian merchant ships were allowed to enter the Red Sea and dock at Mocha in the southern Yemen where they could take on cargos and continue as far north as Jeddah – but no further. The reason for this exception was both fiscal and commercial. The stony and unproductive Hejaz ruled by the Sharif of Mecca was fed by Egyptian grain which was exchanged for Yemeni coffee from Mocha. So long as the Red Sea remained closed to Christian shipping above Jeddah all goods, although they may have ultimately bound for Egypt, paid customs duties on being unloaded at Jeddah. These lucrative duties were then shared between the Ottoman government and the Sharif of Mecca.[11]

However, 'Ali Bey and European merchants – including the East India Company – found they had a common interest in shipping goods directly from India to Suez, ignoring the Ottoman injunction that Christian ships should sail no further north than Jeddah. Consequently Egypt – not the Sharif of Mecca and Istanbul – would be able to appropriate all the customs duties. Moreover, by 1769 'Ali Bey had extorted sufficient cash from the European and Jewish merchant communities in Cairo to finance an army of around 25,000 troops to remove Egypt, Syria and the Hejaz from Ottoman control. With the same objective he had also taken personal control of the Ottomans' customs houses in Cairo and handed their management to Christian Syrians. He also expelled the Ottoman governor and stopped all payment of the tribute to Istanbul.

In April 1771 'Ali Bey sent his protégé and trusted personal Mamluk, Muhammad Abu al-Dhahab, out on campaign to conquer Syria in an offensive coordinated with the elderly Palestinian *ayan*, Zahir al-'Umar. On 4 June al-Dhahab ordered a general attack on Damascus, the capital of the larger of the two Syrian eyalets. Finding himself completely besieged, its *vali*, Osman Paşa, managed to slip away from the city and four days later Damascus quickly surrendered to 'Ali Bey's lieutenant.

There then occurred an event which has puzzled historians ever since. Three days after this brilliant success for 'Ali Bey's battlefield commander, Abu al-Dhahab withdrew his forces from Damascus and headed back to Cairo to attack his own mentor, friend and kinsman. To maintain the loyalty of Abu al-Dhahab's troops rumours were spread that 'Ali Bey had died. But the whole episode looks like an all-too-common example of inter-Mamluk treachery and is most likely to have been the quid-pro-quo for a substantial imperial bribe.

Meanwhile, as Abu al-Dhahab was attacking Damascus, the war between Russia and the Ottomans was reaching its climax. News of the Russian fleet in the Mediterranean and its devastating attack on the Ottoman fleet at Çeşme was spreading throughout the Empire. Faced with a growing shortage of funds and armaments for his rebellion against Mustafa III, 'Ali Bey began to make approaches to Count Orlov with a view to forming an Egyptian-Russian alliance. However, for many in Cairo and elsewhere in the Empire this was one step too far: to form an alliance with a country which was at war with Islam (and that is how it would have been viewed) seemed outright treachery.[12] So when Abu al-Dhahab returned to Cairo he found a powerful element among the *ulema* and notables who had turned against 'Ali Bey.

On hearing of Abu al-Dhahab's defection, 'Ali Bey sent an emissary to Acre in Palestine, the stronghold of Zahir al-'Umar, to reaffirm their alliance, after which 'Ali Bey left Cairo and established his headquarters at Gaza, within striking distance of his rebellious capital. But he was becoming concerned that his approaches to Count Orlov had received only a polite but non-committal reply, and he now sent one of his men to make direct contact with Orlov, carrying a letter addressed to the Tsarina Catherine herself. He also presented three richly caparisoned horses to Orlov, and in his address to the Empress proposed a commercial treaty between Egypt and Russia. In return he requested a force of 3,000 Russian troops with artillery together with a body of military engineers and military instructors.[13] Furthermore, on 18 May 1772, 'Ali Bey sent an ambassador, Zulficar Bey, overland to Russia. (Actually, he was never heard of again.)

In the event, all that 'Ali Bey received from Count Orlov were two military instructors, three artillery pieces and a fairly small quantity of cannon balls, gunpowder and musket shot. Nonetheless, the Russian commander reassured 'Ali Bey that his proposal for an alliance was being forwarded to the Empress. 'Ali Bey's problem was that he was unaware he was just a pawn in the Tsarina's diplomatic manoeuvrings to bring about a peace which would be overwhelmingly advantageous to Russia. And in this diplomatic game 'Ali Bey's value as a serious military ally was rapidly depreciating.

For 'Ali Bey the feeble Russian response to his requests for military aid was a disaster. He was already compromised in the eyes of many devout Muslims; it was now apparent that his behaviour had failed to yield any real material results. By this time he had only 6,000 men under his command. With little hope of any immediate and substantial Russian aid, and heavily outnumbered, 'Ali Bey nevertheless attacked the forces of Abu al-Dhahab near Cairo. However, in the heat of the fighting 'Ali Bey saw two of his own lieutenants, Murad Bey and Ibrahim Bey, abandon him and change sides. Defeated on the battlefield, he was killed on 8 May 1773, somewhere outside Cairo's city walls.

Abu al-Dhahab now re-established relations with the Porte, restoring the Ottoman governor and the annual tribute to the sultan – a pattern of behaviour that seems to confirm that Abu al-Dhahab's treachery towards his master was, at least in part, the consequence of suborning by imperial agents.[14] On the other hand Abu al-Dhahab soon made it clear that, as far as a rapprochement with Istanbul was concerned, this was as far as he was willing to go: he had by no means abandoned 'Ali Bey's policy of building a financially viable and militarily powerful political entity in Egypt, with a position within the sultan's empire at least as independent as those of the North African regencies.

Abu al-Dhahab's sudden death of the plague in late 1775 initially did nothing to damage this strategy. There was a relatively smooth transition to power in Egypt with Abu al-Dhahab's two Qazduğliya associates, the twenty-five-year-old Murad Bey and forty-year-old Ibrahim Bey, agreeing to share power in a duumvirate during which they successively exchanged the two post powerful positions in Egypt, the Sheikh al-Balad and the Amir al-Hajj.

Until now the British government had shown little interest in events in Egypt; nor had it responded to the supplications of the British merchants who were urging the development of the so-called overland trade from India via Egypt, because the Porte was still adamant that European ships could sail no further north than Jeddah and promised to inflict severe penalties on any nation's ships which tried to offload their cargos as far north as Suez.

Moreover, the whole diplomatic scene was about to change. It was discovered that in late 1784 the captain of a French brig, a man named Treguet, had been sent on a secret mission to the Mamluk duumvirate in Cairo. In January 1785 Treguet met with the French consul, Charles

Magallon, who had been a prominent merchant in the city for seventeen years. With the help of Magallon's wife, who had befriended Murad Bey's favourite lady of the harem, Treguet extracted a treaty not only guaranteeing France's rights to bring goods directly to Suez from Mocha and India, but also the protection of French caravans carrying their commerce overland to Cairo.[15] Informed of this diplomatic coup, the British government – in the person of its energetic young prime minister, William Pitt (1759–1806) – was shocked into action.

Britain was not unduly concerned about the commercial aspects of France's new alignment with Egypt's rulers: Britain's trade with the Levant was still tiny compared with its trade with the Americas and Northern Europe. But the French treaty carried with it the potential danger of a French-backed Egyptian breakaway from the Ottoman Empire. And this in turn might provide Britain's enemy with a military, as well as commercial, conduit to India where the two countries were competitively nibbling away at the territories of the decaying Mughal Empire. From this point onwards British policy towards Egypt began to change. Egypt was no longer seen as a rather unimportant Mediterranean trading partner but as a crucial stepping-stone to India, a stepping-stone upon which Britain now feared the French had trod the first step.

With the disastrous war with the Russians ended, the new sultan, Abdülhamid I, decided the time was right to forcibly reincorporate Egypt into his Empire. In early August 1786 the new Grand Admiral, Gazi Hasan Paşa, who had distinguished himself both at Çeşme and the relief of Lemnos, was sent to Egypt with a powerful army. His instructions were to remove Murad Bey and Ibrahim Bey, who had now followed in the footsteps of 'Ali Bey by stopping the payment of tribute to the Porte. On the arrival of Gazi Hasan's troops, the duumvirate fled to Upper Egypt and the Admiral replaced them with another Qazduğliya bey, Isma'il, who swore to acknowledge Ottoman authority. But within a year, and before the Ottoman admiral could firmly re-establish imperial rule, Gazi Hasan Paşa was recalled to Istanbul to take part in another disastrous war against the Russians.*

---

*   The war in question was the Russo-Ottoman war of 1787–92. The Ottomans suffered major
    losses of territory on the Black Sea coast.

The Ottoman invasion and reconquest, short-lived though it was, proved ruinous to the long-established French merchant community in Egypt. After his arrival in Alexandria, Gazi Hasan demanded loans from the French merchants to finance his campaign against Murad and Ibrahim, loans which would never be repaid. Moreover, when the two beys fled Cairo, the debts they had previously incurred with the French merchant community went with them, also never to be repaid.

After the withdrawal of Gazi Hasan Paşa the French consul Magallon won the friendship and support of Isma'il Bey, Egypt's new *sheikh al-balad*, but only one French cargo from India would ever reach Cairo via Suez – in March 1789. And in the vengeful world of the Mamluks, the French association with Isma'il Bey earned their Cairo merchant community the enmity of Murad and Ibrahim, the displaced duumvirate, who were still languishing in Upper Egypt.

The last two decades of the eighteenth century were calamitous for Egypt. The province experienced a number of severe famines and was swept by repeated outbreaks of plague. During one of these Isma'il Bey died and in 1791 Murad and Ibrahim returned to power in Cairo. They were determined to punish the French for their allegiance to Isma'il. Magallon and his associates suffered repeated acts of extortion (so-called 'fines') and were forced to extend loans, not only to Murad and Ibrahim but to Mamluks of all ranks. In these circumstances the overland trade via Suez, which in 1785 appeared to have fallen into French hands, looked as though it would never be profitable. Consequently there were those among the French merchant community in Cairo who were coming to the conclusion that a more forceful French policy towards Egypt's rulers was required.

CHAPTER 8

A Spanish Disaster, 1775

With news of the Muslim naval disaster at Çeşme spreading rapidly across Christian Europe, the fifty-eight-year-old Spanish monarch Carlos III decided the time was ripe to mount his own attack upon the Muslims of the western Mediterranean.

Carlos was well into the sixteenth year of his reign – having acceded to the throne after the death of his father Philip V in 1758 – when he received a letter dated 19 September 1774 from the Emperor of Morocco. In it Sidi Muhammad bin 'Abdallah informed him that, in alliance with Muhammad bin Othman, the Ottoman dey of Algiers, he had now decided that King Carlos must remove all Spain's remaining enclaves on the North African Coast from Oran to Ceuta. The Moroccan emperor gave Carlos III four months to remove his bases.

What must have been particularly infuriating about this letter to Carlos III was that Sidi Muhammad coupled his demand for this expulsion of the Spaniards with an insultingly disingenuous statement. Namely, that the Emperor felt this could be arranged without any disturbance in the regular commercial relations between Morocco and Spain. It was rather like a neighbour threatening the violent seizure of part of your garden while, at the same time, assuring you that there was no reason why a previously amicable exchange of vegetables should not continue as before. The only charitable complexion which Carlos III could put upon Sidi Muhammad's bizarre communication was that it was due to the Emperor's ignorance of the norms of European diplomatic behaviour.[1]

In 1769 Sidi Muhammad had already been successful in driving the Portuguese from their enclave at Mazagan, but Carlos III had no intention of capitulating to the Moroccan Emperor. He therefore replied to Sidi Muhammad that henceforth all peaceful relations with Morocco would end and there would be a return to the state of war which existed before the signing of the most recent treaty with the Moroccan Emperor, in 1767.

In reply, the Moroccans besieged the Spanish enclave of Melilla. Its defences were already in a very poor state since the Spanish had themselves been debating whether or not to abandon the position before the Emperor's decision to try to force them out. However, Spanish honour was now at stake and the small garrison of 700 infantry with sixteen small bronze cannons was ordered to stand firm. The troops were given some comfort by the fact that Melilla could still be supplied by sea. Meanwhile, on 9 December 1774, the Moroccans brought up a battery of 9- and 12-inch mortars and the following day began to bombard the town.[2]

The problem for the Moroccans was that, although they were able to fire around 9,000 projectiles at Melilla, they did not have the large-calibre heavy guns with which to make a breach in Melilla's old walls. They had been expecting the arrival of heavy siege guns from Britain via its base at Gibraltar. In early 1774 a Moroccan ambassadorial delegation to London was offered thirty-six such weapons along with a variety of other military supplies, specifically for a long-anticipated siege of Melilla.[3] Unfortunately for the Moroccans the ship carrying these weapons was intercepted by the Spanish en route to Gibraltar. At the same time the Spanish were able to bring six frigates and nine xebecs close in to the Moroccan siege lines and batter them with *their* heavy weapons. Faced with these problems, Sidi Muhammad decided to withdraw his army, which was suffering heavy losses, and the siege was raised on 23 March 1775.

'It had all been a misunderstanding' was the essence of the message from Sidi Muhammad carried by Morocco's ambassador to the Spanish Court – 'the result of bad intelligence'.[4] Moreover, not only did the Moroccan Emperor hurry to make peace with Spain but he went one step further. It had not gone unnoticed by the Emperor that the Dey of Algiers, his supposed ally, had failed to carry out the simultaneous attack on the Spanish enclave of Oran that had been agreed the previous year. Sidi Muhammad therefore offered King Carlos to make war on the Dey in revenge – although it seems unlikely that this was seriously intended.[5]

Nevertheless, Sidi Muhammad's proposal gave King Carlos the excuse he had been waiting for to launch his own major attack on the Dey. The expedition against Algiers had originally been proposed by Carlos III's secretary of state, the Genoese nobleman the Marqués Pablo Jerónimo Grimaldi y Pallavicini, together with two Catholic clerics, Fray Joaquín de Eleta, King Carlos's personal confessor, and Fray Alonso Cano Nieto. Both of these churchmen had been involved in the ransoming of Christian slaves from the corsair ports and therefore the invasion also had a strongly religious and philanthropic ethos.

The specific objectives of the invasion were to destroy all the North African corsair ships raiding from ports lying between Algiers to the Straits of Gibraltar, to free the estimated 18,000 Christian slaves currently held by the Algerians,* to destroy all of Algiers's fortifications, and 'to shut the port for ever'.[6] However, it was also King Carlos's fervent desire to win the glory and grateful plaudits of all the Christian powers trading in the Mediterranean. Whether the Spanish intended to retain possession of Algiers after achieving these objectives remains unclear. But given the ambitious nature of the operation – which would have involved the invasion force remaining in the city for a considerable period – it is probable that Carlos III would have been tempted to add another Spanish enclave on the North African shore to the state's existing possessions at Ceuta, Melilla and Oran.

The individual placed by Carlos III in overall command of the expedition was the fifty-three-year-old General Count Alejandro O'Reilly. Like many Irish Catholics he had entered Spanish service, initially as a sub-lieutenant in the Hibernia Regiment. Subsequently he served briefly in Germany, from where, on his return, he played an important part in reforming the Spanish Army, in particular by introducing Prussian methods of drill, discipline and manoeuvre.[7] By 1775 he had been promoted to the rank of brigadier-general. However, although he had also campaigned in Portugal and the Caribbean, his experience was more in administration and organisation than battlefield leadership. Nevertheless O'Reilly enjoyed the full confidence and friendship of King Carlos, and the Marqués Grimaldi promised to raise him to the post of Captain-General of the Royal Spanish Army if the expedition to Algiers was successful – as was confidently expected.

The Spanish invasion force was very strong. Three large naval contingents, from Ferrol, Barcelona and Cadiz, were to converge on Cartagena before

---

*   The use of the term 'Algerians' at a time when there was no such country or nationality is obviously an anachronism. However, throughout the rest of the book I have used this term to refer to the collectivity of peoples who lived within the Regency of Algiers, in preference to 'Muslims', which is far too general, and 'Algerines', which is both unfamiliar and archaic.

the attack on Algiers; each would number seven seventy-gun battleships, together with thirty-six smaller warships. In addition there were 348 transport ships carrying 18,827 infantry and 954 cavalry.[8] They were joined by three warships from Spain's allies, two frigates from the Grand Duchy of Tuscany commanded by a British officer, Captain Sir John Acton, and a single frigate from the Knights of Malta.

By 25 May the three battle fleets had joined forces at Cartagena and the process of embarking the troops, horses and equipment had begun. But there were already considerable difficulties in arranging the immense convoy in such a way that all the vessels would arrive together off the Algerian coast. Consequently the expedition did not leave Cartagena until 23 June, a month later than originally intended. O'Reilly planned two waves of landings, with the first contingent arriving in the Bay of Algiers on 30 June 1775, and the second the following day. So far, apart from the initial delay in embarking the troops and equipment, the mission appeared to be going more or less according to plan.

There are three absolutely essential conditions for success in ambitious amphibious combined operations of this kind. First, the invasion force must have a clear understanding of the nature of the terrain upon which they are landing. Second, they must also have reliable intelligence concerning the size and disposition of the enemy's forces. And third, the objectives, planning and date of embarkation of the invasion force must remain absolutely secret. In the event, none of these three preconditions was met.

With regard to the terrain upon which the invasion force was to disembark, it would soon become clear that no attempt whatsoever had been made to understand the lie of the land. Similarly, O'Reilly appears to have had no information regarding the size and composition of the enemy's forces. As to the most crucial factor of all – secrecy – a Sephardi Jewish merchant of Algiers named Moises Daninos, at the time resident in Gibraltar and, like his compatriots bitterly hostile to the Spanish, learned of the invasion plan and sent a letter to the Dey containing much of its essential detail. In spite of all these deficiencies, General O'Reilly was so confident of success that he had allowed many of his officers to bring along their wives and daughters to witness the entertainment.[9]

Having arrived in the Bay of Algiers it immediately became clear that O'Reilly had no idea as to the best place to disembark his army. He was therefore obliged to call a conference of his senior officers to resolve the issue. The resulting disagreements and prevarications, together with an unanticipated heavy swell in the waters of the bay, delayed the attack for a further eight days[10] – a respite which the Dey used to mobilise a combined force of Turks, Kuloğlus and Arabs. These were men who were frequently at each other's throats but now had no reservations about combining to crush the common Christian enemy. Among the troops that hurried in from the east was a large force of camel troops sent by the Bey of Constantine. Meanwhile the citizens of Algiers began digging entrenchments outside the city walls.[11] In this, the Jews of Algiers were particularly energetic, dreading the return of the hated Spanish Inquisition if the expedition were successful.

To make matters worse for O'Reilly's men, on 7 July, when the soldiers of the first division of the invasion force were loaded into launches and were approaching the chosen beachhead, it was suddenly decided that the location was totally unsuitable, being clearly occupied by a large number of enemy troops. So the landing craft were recalled to the ships and the unfortunate Spanish infantry had to pass the night tossed about on board the waterlogged launches.

At dawn the following day the landings recommenced, this time on a stretch of sandy beach about five miles east of Algiers. Behind the beach lay an area of shifting dunes and behind the dunes a tree-covered ridge. At about five o'clock on the morning of 8 July some 6,000 men of the invasion's first wave made a successful landing and formed up on the beach, although an element of confusion had already afflicted the operation since the troops and their equipment had been disembarked in separate companies rather than in complete regiments – a failure which would become even more apparent when the second wave arrived, somewhat later.

The first wave now moved forward to make room on the narrow beachhead for the second contingent to land and deploy. But as they began to advance they were met by a hail of musket and cannon fire from the ridge above the dunes. They were swiftly brought to a halt, and then forced to retire towards the beach. By now the second wave of the invasion force was landing and it wasn't long before its most advanced units became entangled with some of those of the first wave attempting to retreat towards the beach. As more and more launches arrived on the beach and disembarked their troops, companies from one regiment became hopelessly mixed up with companies from another, while officers lost touch with their own units and other units found themselves without any officers at all.[12]

Meanwhile the Algerians kept up a sustained rain of fire from the ridge, their marksmen concentrating on hitting the officers. Within the first hour, a number of elegantly apparelled Spanish grandees, there to enjoy the show, were picked off by Algerian snipers – the Marqués de la Romana, the Conde del Asalto, the Conde de Fernán Nuñez, Marshall Luis de Urbina and General Antonio Ricardos were either killed or seriously wounded during this first stage of the engagement. Like the men he commanded, any officer killed or seriously wounded within reach of the enemy had his head removed by the Turks, Kuloğlus and Arabs, who could expect to be duly awarded by their officers for the presentation of their trophies.

As for the Spanish field artillery, which could have made an important contribution to the attack, attempts to bring its guns into play were stymied by that almost total lack of intelligence about the nature of the landing site: the artillery pieces quickly became bogged down in the fine sand of the dunes and had to be abandoned. The Spanish commanders also soon realised that their cavalry were massively outnumbered by the 10–12,000 Arab and Kuloğlu irregular cavalry who would play a major part in the battle.

Eventually, a force composed of experienced Spanish and Walloon guards charged the ridge from where the Muslim sharpshooters were firing. Breaking through their lines and finding themselves upon the road leading towards the city of Algiers, they attempted to advance towards the city; but any further advance was blocked by the series of entrenchments and other well-prepared obstacles constructed by the citizens of Algiers and manned by growing numbers of fighters. Forced to retreat towards the beachhead, these brave men now found themselves hemmed in with the remainder of the army entrenched in a small confined area just out of range of the enemy's musket fire. However, when the Muslims brought up a 24-pounder field gun and began to bombard the disorganised rabble of Spanish troops on the beachhead, O'Reilly finally realised the scale of his defeat and gave the order to re-embark all the troops.

A complete panic now set in as men rushed into the sea, scrambling to get into any available launch.[13] Captain John Acton's two Tuscan frigates came in as close as the water depth permitted to shower the pursuing Algerians with shot and canister, but they could do little to ameliorate the scope of the disaster. As the Spanish naval officers and crews struggled to save as many of the ground troops as possible, the dimensions of the disaster were already becoming clear – around 5,000 officers and men killed and wounded.[14] Moreover, the Spanish losses included fifteen field guns and a remarkable total of 9,000 muskets, most of them jettisoned as the panicking infantry rushed into the sea to grab a place in the launches and escape the perils of capture by the men of Algiers. By 14 July what remained of the invasion force had returned to Spain to disembark at Alicante.

In spite of the disaster, war between Spain and Algiers continued intermittently. A Spanish fleet under the Catalan Admiral Antonio Barceló was despatched to bombard Algiers in August 1783; but despite the city suffering heavy damage the Dey refused to capitulate. In retaliation his privateers captured two Spanish merchant ships the following month. Moreover, with the assistance of European advisors the city's defences were strengthened with a new 50-gun fortress, and 4,000 Turkish volunteers from Anatolia were brought in to reinforce the garrison, demonstrating the close relationship between the Porte and its 'autonomous' western outpost. Barceló began a second bombardment of Algiers on 10 July 1784 supported by naval contingents from Naples-Sicily, Malta and Portugal. Once again serious damage was done; yet after eleven days the Spanish had to call off the attack because of contrary winds, combined with the fact that Algiers was receiving an abundance of all sorts of munitions from both Holland and Denmark.[15]

During these naval attacks the Algiers Janissaries kept up their spirits by singing their war songs celebrating earlier encounters, such as the following composed by a certain Seferlioğlu. The first and last verses run as follows:

> We learnt of the approach of the infidels
> And they'd sent a warning to the city of Algiers:
> We prepared for war, crying out: 'Allah, Allah',
> We drew our swords for the holy religion.
> Seferlioğlu drank the wine of holy ardour;
> Without ceasing he glorified the Supreme Warrior,
> Good luck to the Turk and the Arab;
> They drew their swords for the holy religion.[16]

Spain and Morocco had previously signed a new treaty of friendship at the peace of Aranjuez (1780). Now in 1786 Emperor Sidi Muhammad sponsored a separate peace between Spain and Algiers under which Spanish ships would be protected against Algerian corsairs and there would be an exchange of all captives. The status of Spanish-occupied Oran remained a source of tension between Spain and Algiers, but in 1792, after Oran suffered a devastating earthquake, Spain decided that the Algerian city was of little use to them while it still required a garrison of around 4,000 men. Consequently it was evacuated in 1792 and Ottoman sovereignty restored.

However, one important result of the 1786 treaty was a marked decline in corsairing in the western Mediterranean. As this began to deplete the revenues of the Algerian state, the dominant Turkish element increased their exactions from the indigenous Arabs and Moors. The unity between Turks, Kuloğlus and Arabs, which had characterised the defeat of the Spanish invasion of 1775, started to dissipate and would have serious consequences when, half a century later, another European enemy would invade this distant outpost of Ottoman rule.

CHAPTER 9

'Liberating the Egyptians':
The Origins of French Republican Imperialism

We now need to go back briefly to the return to power of the Mamluk chieftains Ibrahim Bey and Murad Bey after the end of the Russo-Ottoman War of 1768 to 1774. For the French government it was a time both tumultuous and threatening.

When the restoration of the Mamluk duumvirate led to ill treatment of the French merchant community in Cairo, the already-growing concern in France increased. There were fears for the future of its old ally the Ottoman Empire, and the security and prosperity of its trade with the Empire's Egyptian province. If the Empire actually collapsed – and the possibility of that occurring within the next few years was now being taken seriously – the ensuing chaos could deal a serious blow to the French economy.

According to France's ambassador to the Porte at that time (the Comte de Saint-Priest), the French had two – and only two – options in responding to this challenge. They could either throw France's military and diplomatic support fully behind the sultan and prevent the feared Ottoman collapse from occurring, or abandon the Ottomans to their fate while simultaneously picking up that part of the debris which would be most advantageous to France – Egypt.

The wisdom of the second option was not without its opponents. The Comte de Vergennes – Saint-Priest's predecessor at Istanbul and since the accession of King Louis XVI in 1774, France's foreign minister – was basically hostile to the idea of invading the territory of France's oldest friend and ally, a relationship that had lasted since the sixteenth century. He had always believed that the Ottoman Empire could be saved if it looked for 'the instruction it needs and ... obtain educated men from abroad until the nation is educated'.[1] It was, therefore, with considerable reluctance that he agreed to send the Hungarian military officer in French service, Francois Baron de Tott, on a new mission to the Levant in May 1777. He was sent, officially, as 'Inspector' of all the French trading posts in the Ottoman Empire, but unofficially to examine the state of Egypt's defences and formulate a plan for a successful conquest of the province if that eventually became necessary.[2]

A year later Baron de Tott submitted his report to the Minister of the Marine. It contained the proposals that, if an occupation of Egypt were considered expedient, the invasion force should comprise 20,000 infantry, 5,000 foot dragoons, six companies of artillery with forty field guns, ten howitzers and thirty heavy-calibre siege guns. To transport the army to Egypt would require eighty troopships, accompanied by five battleships and seven frigates, together with three xebecs and six half-galleys for service on the Nile.

In the event, this particular plan was never implemented. By the time de Tott's report was presented, France was at war with Britain in support of the American Revolution; so it was decided that this was not the time for a massive deployment of military power in the eastern Mediterranean. But at the end of the century General Napoleon Bonaparte would retrieve a dusty copy of de Tott's work from the former Royal Library and find its contents of considerable value in preparing his own plans for invading Ottoman Egypt.

Baron de Tott was not the only Frenchman who travelled extensively in the Ottoman Empire during the second half of the eighteenth century. Comte Constantin François de Chasseboeuf, who wrote under the pseudonym M. de Volney, was a French nobleman, philosopher, historian and politician who travelled to the Ottoman-governed Levant in 1783, first to Egypt, where he spent seven months, and afterwards to Syria where he studied Arabic for two years. Volney was very much a man of the Enlightenment, moreover a republican and a convinced atheist. On his return to France in 1785 he wrote two highly influential works: *Voyage en Egypte et en Syrie*, published in 1787, and *Considérations sur la Guerre des Turcs et de la Russie*, published the following year.

Volney shared the opinions of those other Enlightenment travellers in the Ottoman Empire, like De Tott, who viewed the Ottoman system of government through the prism of 'oriental despotism'. In Volney's opinion it was the Muslim religion and its fatalistic quiescence in the face of despotic power which also accounted for the many defects which he identified in Islamic society – but then, as a confirmed atheist, Volney was antagonistic

towards *all* religions, including Christianity. He had little confidence in
the longevity of the Ottoman Empire and looked forward to the time
when it would be overthrown by its subject peoples (especially the Arabs).
Consequently, he was opposed to a continuation of France's traditional
policy of protecting and sustaining the Ottoman Empire. He also thought
that possession of Egypt would undoubtedly be advantageous to France
from an economic standpoint.

Volney also took a very dim view of the military capacity of the Ottoman
forces supposedly defending Egypt against any such invasion. Referring to
the much-vaunted 'seven regiments' ostensibly guarding the province, he
expressed the opinion that:

> Today the Janissaries, the 'Azaban and the five other regiments
> are nothing but a bunch of artisans, boors and vagabonds who
> guard the doorways of whoever will pay them and who tremble
> before the Mamluks like the rest of the Cairo population.
> Truly, it is only the Mamluks who constitute Egypt's military
> capacity.[3]

In his hugely influential work *Orientalism*, Edward Said portrays Volney
as one of the principal intellectual advocates of colonialism. 'He eyed the
Near-Orient as a likely place for the realisation of French colonial ambition',
and 'his work constituted a handbook for attenuating the human shock a
European might feel as he directly experienced the Orient'.[4] However, as
the British Arabist Robert Irwin has pointed out, in spite of his hostility to
the Ottoman Empire in his *Considérations sur la Guerre Actuelle des Turcs*,
Volney actually opposed an invasion and occupation of Egypt of the kind
being advocated by de Tott.[5] He had lived in Egypt and Syria for two and
a half years. He knew the environment, its climate and diseases. He knew
the people, their religious passions and cultural principles and prejudices,
and he was realistic about the dangerous political consequences for France
in Europe if such a project went ahead. In what must be one of the most
prescient judgements in history, he warned that a French invasion of Egypt
would involve the country in three separate wars: against the Turks, the
British and the indigenous Arabs,[6] although it seems he never imagined
that these enemies would have to be fought simultaneously.

At the very end of *La Guerre Actuelle des Turcs*, Volney wrote of the disastrous consequences of a French invasion of Egypt for both the inhabitants and the conquerors – but also of the evils of colonialism in general.

> But suppose the Mamluks were exterminated and the people subdued, we would still have only overcome the lesser obstacles; it would be necessary to rule these men: and we don't even know their language, nor their customs and mores: misunderstandings would arise at every instant causing trouble and disorder... We would end up like the Spanish in the Americas, like England in Bengal, the Dutch in the Moluccas and the Russians in the Kiril Islands: we would exterminate the whole people... To keep Egypt we would need 25,000 troops ... and for what advantages? To enrich a few individuals who had been favoured by being in charge and would use their power to amass scandalous fortunes.[7]

Nevertheless, in spite of Volney's wise words, the outbreak of the great French Revolution in 1789 set in motion a train of events which, within a decade, would lead to a situation where a French Army of nearly 50,000 would become bogged down in a disastrous and cruel war and counter-insurgency operation, from which less than half of its men would ever return to France.[*]

Meanwhile, as different revolutionary factions struggled for power in Paris, the authority and influence of the French state was crumbling away both at home and abroad. In 1791 the great slave revolt began in the French plantation colony of Haiti,[†] while in Egypt revolution spread to

---

[*] Sadly for Volney's future reputation, he later abrogated these anti-colonialist views. See Chapter 10.

[†] Haiti, the economic 'jewel in the crown' of France's Caribbean slave plantation system, would become independent in 1804 in the wake of the great slave revolt that began in 1791. Although the French Bourbon government threatened re-occupation in 1825 and forced Haiti to pay a crippling indemnity in return for French acknowledgement of Haiti's sovereignty, it never recovered its former great slave state. However, French slave-trading with its Caribbean colonies resumed, averaging 137,000 slaves per year during the period 1821–30, virtually the same as during the late eighteenth century.

the crews of the French merchant vessels at Alexandria where a number of mutinies took place. At the same time the return to power of the Mamluk duumvirate, Murad and Ibrahim, gave free reign to all the Mamluks to pile more 'fines' and forced loans upon the unfortunate French merchants. So in 1791 consul Charles Magallon returned to Paris in what was very much a last-ditch attempt to rescue French commercial interests, not only in Egypt but in the Levant generally.

As the Revolution began to accelerate towards the Terror, 'Citizen' Magallon lobbied the Ministry of Marine, the National Assembly and the President of the Committee of Commerce to elicit protection for his sixty-one fellow merchants currently being despoiled of their wealth in Egypt. It was hardly the best time to be making demands on the struggling French Republic, but he did obtain one significant achievement. In 1777, the French consulate-general in Egypt had moved from Cairo to Alexandria. For the past four years the post had stood vacant, since the previous incumbent had gone on indefinite leave. Magallon believed that it was essential to return the consulate to Cairo where there was still some hope of influencing the ruling duumvirate. The re-establishment of a consulate-general in Cairo would, he believed, restore the prestige of the French merchant community. He also argued that he should be the new consul-general. His requests were granted and, on 30 January 1793, the authorities decreed that 'the citizen Magallon, by virtue of his public spirit, his zeal and his ability' was to be appointed consul-general in Egypt with a stipend of 16,000 *livres*, on the understanding that he would move the consulate back to Cairo.[8]

But that was all. Indeed, at this particular moment, the interests of the French merchants in Egypt were of little concern to the Committee of Public Safety, by now the most powerful Republican institution. The Committee was seeking a military alliance with the Ottomans against the infant Republic's principal enemies, Russia and Austria; and with this objective, on 19 January 1793, they had despatched to Istanbul Citizen Marie Louis Descorches, formerly the Marquis Descorches, as a special envoy, but as yet without ambassadorial status. Persuading the sultan to intervene in Egypt in the interests of a small group of French merchants was no part of Descorches's instructions.

To take up his new post as consul-general, Magallon left Paris on 5

February and, travelling in a French barque, he arrived in Cairo in April 1793. His first objective was to try to re-establish amicable relations with Egypt's rulers, Murad and Ibrahim. Accompanied by two other French merchants he sought an interview with the duumvirate in an attempt to enlist their support in curbing the rapacious appetites of the lesser Mamluks. A 'present' of 35,000 *livres* ensured the deputation a friendly welcome; but if Consul-General Magallon had any expectations that this would result in an amelioration of the French merchant community's situation, he was soon to be disappointed. Far from improving, the situation got worse. By now, the Mamluk Beys had abrogated the ancient capitulations which protected French citizens in Ottoman territory; indeed, the plundering of the French merchants' wealth was now backed by threats of violence. And far from offering their protection it soon became clear that Murad and Ibrahim were themselves not averse to joining in the plundering. In April 1794, Ibrahim Bey extorted the sum of 14,000 *pataques** from the merchants while Murad demanded and received a 'gift' of luxurious bed linen.[9]

By July Magallon's patience was at an end. He consulted the members of the French community as to whether they should abandon Cairo and return to the relative safety of Alexandria, where they would be under the protection of French warships. After some disagreements, the merchant community voted unanimously to move. But the Beys would not let them. In effect, they were now prisoners of Murad and Ibrahim. It took all Magallon's efforts of persuasion and another hefty bribe before they were allowed to go on their way in December 1794.

In spite of the retreat to Alexandria, Magallon was still convinced that it was only in Cairo that the French could effectively conduct their business. He now began a tireless campaign to persuade the republican authorities in Paris to intervene more energetically, both in their representations to the sultan and – if it eventually became unavoidable – to use military force in Egypt itself. Meanwhile Sultan Selim III (r. 1789–1807), unwilling to abandon his Empire's traditionally friendly relations with France, had reluctantly reconciled himself to the execution of his fellow monarch Louis XVI; so when Descorches was replaced by another republican envoy,

---

*   *Pataque*: a French unit of account used in the East. In the late eighteenth century the *pataque* was worth 90 *paras* or 2.25 *kuruş*, assuming £1 = 11 *kuruş* in 1794, 1 *pataque* = £0.205.

Raymond Verninac, he was formally accredited as ambassador to the Ottoman court.

On 17 June 1795, Magallon sent a long letter to Verninac, copied to the Commission for Foreign Relations in Paris, stating it was now pointless asking the sultan to provide assistance to the French merchant community in Egypt, since the sultan's own authority there had simply withered away. Instead, Magallon now proposed that France should seriously consider a military invasion and occupation.[10]

To broaden the appeal of this project to Verninac and the Foreign Relations Commission, Magallon not only repeated his demands on behalf of the embattled French merchant community but also emphasised the great commercial advantages of occupying Egypt, adding his views on the broader strategic advantages to the Republic of an invasion. 'I repeat, Citizen, if we become masters of the Red Sea, it won't be long before we can lay the law down to the English and chase them out of India.'[11]

Magallon followed this up with two further letters, sent on 1 and 3 October 1795: the first to the Head of the Commission for Foreign relations, Jean-Victor Colchen; the second (partly a reiteration of the first) to the Committee of Public Safety itself. Taken together these letters adopted a perceptibly colonialist tone. In addition to emphasising the enormous trading possibilities which the geographical position of Egypt would afford, Magallon pointed out to Colchen 'the advantages there would be for us from liberating three million hard-working men [i.e. the Egyptian peasantry] placed in a country where the land, as yet only lightly cultivated, could be incredibly productive'. And among the many crops whose cultivation could be expanded, Magallon made special mention of wheat, 'which could be a great resource for France during years of poor [French] harvests'. At the same time, as Egypt grew richer it would be 'in a state to consume substantial amounts of our manufactures'.[12]

With regard to those 'three million hard-working men' 'pulled out of the debasement into which tyranny has plunged them', they would be left 'to enjoy, as is only just, the fruits of their labour', and they would be subjected to what Magallon described as only 'modest taxation'. Precisely what was intended by the reference to enjoying 'the fruits of their labour' was not stated, but it is clear from the context that it would be the French merchants who would acquire and sell the 'hard-working' cultivators' produce. As to the mention of 'modest taxation', 'liberation' for the downtrodden Arab *fellahin** would obviously have to come at a price.

By the time these letters arrived in Paris in November 1795 the Committee of Public Safety had been replaced by the more conservative five-man 'Directory', and Charles-François Delacroix had been appointed Foreign Minister, replacing Colchen (who had carried out this role). Now, for the first time, Magallon's radical solution to the 'Egyptian problem' began to be taken seriously. The Foreign Ministry decided to conduct research, ordering the collection of all documents relating to Egypt which the government possessed, and 'which could enable us to make a judgement about the merits of the proposition indicated'.

Meanwhile, before its demise in February 1795, the Committee of Public Safety had finally agreed that Ambassador Verninac in Istanbul should send one of his entourage to Cairo. This person would be charged with trying to persuade the ruling Beys to restore the rights of the French merchant community under the capitulations and recover for the merchants the forced loans which the Mamluks had extracted from them. To the envoy Verninac selected to carry out this task – a certain Dubois-Thainville – it was also suggested that, while his discussions with the Beys should be conducted in a thoroughly diplomatic and amicable tone, he should also impress upon them the growing strength and military power of the Republic, which, by now, had scored a number of major victories over its European enemies.

On 29 October 1795 Dubois-Thainville arrived at Alexandria, where he met with Magallon and the remainder of the French merchants. They expressed their unhappiness at the Republic's efforts so far and urged him to exert maximum pressure. This was their last chance, they told the visiting envoy, and if he failed they would all leave Egypt. Subsequently, on 26 January 1796, Thainville, Magallon and two other merchants had an audience with the resident (but impotent) Ottoman Paşa in the Cairo Citadel, followed by another with Murad and Ibrahim, the real rulers of Egypt. Once again the duumvirate received the delegation politely, stressing their friendship and goodwill towards the French Republic; as to the question of the reimbursement of the merchants' financial loss, the

---

*   The peasantry, the 'common man'.

Beys indicated that they were perfectly willing to come to a satisfactory arrangement on this thorny matter.

But weeks passed and it gradually became clear that neither Murad nor Ibrahim had any intentions of complying with Dubois-Thainville's requests. Prevarication followed prevarication and, after four months of fruitless wrangling, Thainville abandoned his mission in Egypt.

However, the tide of war in Europe was now turning. Using the huge reserves of manpower generated by the *levée en masse*, French armies crushed the Royalist uprising in the Vendée, surged into the German states and Switzerland, and, most importantly, invaded Italy where the young general Bonaparte won a series of striking victories over the Austrians. Prussia had already made peace with the Republic in 1795, and in October 1797, under the terms of the Treaty of Campo Formio, Austria also made peace, losing its former possessions in Italy and the Netherlands in the process. And with these startling military successes came a new confidence and willingness to deal with the Mamluk Beys, although it would be another year before the exact manner by which this would be achieved was finally resolved.

It fell to a forty-seven-year-old former bishop, Charles Maurice de Talleyrand-Périgord, to provide the political analysis which would begin the process of reconciling France's still-resonant republican ideals – *Liberté, Fraternité, Égalité* – with the acquisition of colonies. He had studied theology with the expectation that his aristocratic family's connections would provide him with a bishopric, and in 1789 their influence resulted in his appointment as Bishop of Autun. However, when the Revolution began Talleyrand quickly saw that his best interests lay elsewhere, and opportunistically adopted an anti-clerical position. His education fitted him for a diplomatic role, and in 1792 he was sent on two unsuccessful missions to Britain in an attempt to achieve a peace agreement. But with the beginning of the revolutionary Terror and its indiscriminate executions of suspected 'counter-revolutionaries', he remained in England, later travelling to America.

In 1796, after the Terror had ended, he was allowed to return to France. Talleyrand believed that the loss of France's colonial plantations in the West Indies, as a result of the great slave rebellion in Haiti, had dealt a severe blow to an economy that was already suffering from poor harvests and financial collapse. He doubted whether these colonial possessions could be recovered and concluded that, for the Republic to survive, France would have to replace them with colonies elsewhere. On 3 July 1797 he gave a public lecture titled 'An Essay on the Advantages of Getting New Colonies in the Present Circumstances'. On 16 July he was appointed Foreign Minister.

Around this time, Talleyrand also recalled Magallon to Paris. The Consul-General left his nephew in charge of consular duties in Alexandria and arrived in the capital at the end of 1797. The Directory was then planning an invasion of England; but, having returned from his victories in northern Italy, General Bonaparte had become influenced by the ideas of Talleyrand and Magallon about colonies. Indeed, under the terms of the Treaty of Campo Formio in October 1797, France had already gained a strong foothold in the eastern Mediterranean, acquiring the Ionian Islands – Corfu, Cephalonia, Zante and Lefkas – formerly possessions of the Venetian Republic. The idea of adding Egypt to these new French colonies now appeared more attractive and feasible than an invasion of England. 'The day is not far off,' Bonaparte wrote to the Directorate, 'when we shall appreciate the necessity, in order really to destroy England, to seize Egypt,' adding, 'The vast Ottoman Empire, which is dying day by day, obliges us to think, while there is still time, of the measures we must take to preserve our trade with the Levant.'[13]

It was a few months later, on 9 February 1798, that Magallon wrote his most important report to Talleyrand, which furnished the Foreign Minister with the arguments he would present to the Directorate five days later. In this *Memoire sur Egypte*, Magallon reiterated the grievances of the French merchants in Egypt and the severe damage which this was doing to the whole of French commerce in the Levant. He also reiterated the great economic advantages which France would enjoy if it conquered Egypt and 'liberated' its people from the Mamluk 'tyrants'. Fairer treatment of the indigenous population, he explained, would lead to an increase in agricultural production; and 'moderate' taxation raised on this bounty would pay for a French garrison installed in the country.

He continued by considering the military requirements of a successful invasion and occupation. Since, according to his estimation, there were only about 8,000 Mamluks equipped and ready to fight, the French would require no more than 20,000 troops, accompanied by four or five battleships and six frigates to guard the convoy of transports from Toulon to Alexandria.

Finally, Magallon framed the proposed invasion in the context of France's worldwide struggle with Britain for colonial possessions. The British, he pointed out, had only 15–20,000 men in India to control such a vast area. If 15,000 French troops – perhaps supported by those of Britain's current enemy in southern India, Sultan Tipu Sahib of Mysore – were sent to India from a French-occupied Egypt, it would suffice to drive them out, provided the French operation was conducted in great secrecy before the British could bring in reinforcements. But Magallon also emphasised that Egypt itself was vulnerable to an attack from India by the same army of 15,000 British-officered sepoys supported by 5,000 or 6,000 'European' troops. The clear implication was that France must invade and occupy Egypt to pre-empt any such move.[14]

During the remainder of February 1798 the Directory was still wrestling with the military, logistical and financial problems which an invasion of England would involve. In a lengthy session on 1 and 2 March, its members accepted Bonaparte's opposition to the project: he feared the British naval strength in the Channel. Consequently, in principle, the Directory agreed to an expedition to occupy Egypt. Three days later, Bonaparte submitted a detailed note itemising all the military and material requirements for the Egyptian invasion, which had now emerged from the realms of intelligent speculation to enter the first stage of actual realisation.

On 12 April the Directorate ordered the formation of an 'Army of the Orient', and named the twenty-six-year-old Bonaparte as commander-in-chief and the former Royalist naval officer, Vice-Admiral François-Paul Brueys d'Aigalliers, as naval commander. The objectives of the mission, communicated to Bonaparte by the Directory in great secrecy on the same day, were grandiose and suitably vague. The Army of the Orient was to seize both Malta and Egypt, dislodge the British from their establishments in the East, 'pierce the Isthmus of Suez' if this were feasible, and establish a new route to India by gaining control of the Red Sea. His orders also included instructions to improve the lot of the Egyptian people and maintain good relations with the Ottoman government.[15]

With the latter in mind, the invasion was to be portrayed as actually being on behalf of the sultan – an intervention to protect the Ottoman Empire from the 'tyranny' and disloyalty of the Mamluk Beys. It was also decided that, as foreign minister, Talleyrand should leave for Istanbul to 'explain' these benevolent intentions to Selim III.[16]. Finally, the date on which the expeditionary force should sail from Toulon was fixed for 19 April.

Yet among those who broadly favoured an invasion of Egypt, there were some who still remained troubled by the ideological implications of the project. Surely Republicans – free men who had liberated their own country – could not subjugate and dominate other human beings? And colonial status would, on the surface, seem to imply such a relationship. Reflecting this kind of concern, a prominent Republican, Charles-Guillaume Theremin, wrote a report for the Foreign Affairs Ministry in February 1798 in which he envisaged a French conquest establishing only 'armed trading posts' at Alexandria, Rosetta and Cairo to protect French commerce and block British communications with India, 'since the Republic cannot have subjects and since conquest will not make the Egyptians into French citizens'.[17]

In the same report the author insisted that, whatever the scope of the invasion, the invaders must 'gain the respect of the population for the name of France, ensuring that they continue to be governed by their own laws, but with a form of government more sensitive and less absolute than that of the beys and Mamluks'.[18] The author appears to have believed that such a remedy would obviate any question of French Republicans denying Egyptians the 'liberty' which they themselves enjoyed. However, a year later, with the invasion in full swing, another, anonymous, report was considering the likelihood of the French in Egypt making use of large numbers of Arab (and Greek) auxiliaries to form the majority of the French garrison and bear most of any future fighting. 'This is how the European powers conduct themselves in India in regard to the sepoys in their pay,'[19] it added. In other words, France's new possession could follow the same sort of general *modus operandi* that Britain was using to dominate India.

By the date of the Armée d'Orient's embarkation for Egypt, yet another conceptualisation of the French Republic's colonial mission had emerged. Henceforth this new outlook would become France's 'official' ideology, as the Republic sought to expand its territory both within and outside Europe. The recently acquired Ionian Islands had been 'liberated' in a very specific way: they had simply become French *départements*, integral provinces of what would now become La Grande Nation. Similarly, in Egypt and elsewhere, the new 'citizens' of France, the 'Great Nation', would absorb all the blessings of republican virtue – cultural, scientific and economic. In other words, indigenous republican revolutions were no longer necessary for a country's 'liberation'. In fact such local movements could actually be a source of irritation to their French 'liberators', as had already occurred in Italy.[20] From now on, only complete integration into the original temple of liberty – the French state – would count as genuine freedom. Thus, the idea of the 'Great Nation' served to reconcile the idea of liberating other peoples from tyranny with the Republic's new colonialist objectives.

CHAPTER 10

The French in Egypt:
From Military Victory to Colonial Failure

Louis-François Lejeune's painting *The Battle of the Pyramids* – first exhibited in 1806 – is among the most brilliant pieces of war art ever created. As the title to the painting indicates, its subject matter is the decisive victory of Napoleon Bonaparte and the invading troops of the young French Republic over the Egyptian Mamluks.

The battle took place on 21 July 1798 and soon became the subject matter for a number of great painters in oils. One can understand why: the exotic scenery and vegetation, the pyramids themselves and, above all, the crushing victory. Artists like Antoine-Jean Gros (1771–1835) and François-Louis-Joseph Watteau (1758–1823) painted grandiose views that were largely imaginary in terms of the fighting, the location of the pyramids and the role of the twenty-six-year-old Bonaparte. Lejeune's panoramic view of the battle, however, is almost photographic in its accuracy, while at the same time demonstrating a masterly use of light, texture and perspective.[1] Indeed, when this and other military paintings by Lejeune were exhibited to the British public in the 'Egyptian Hall' in Piccadilly in 1828, barriers had to be erected to protect his works from the thousands of admiring visitors.

The reason why Lejeune's *Battle of the Pyramids* is so impressive is almost certainly because he was a soldier as well as a great painter. Louis-François Lejeune (1775–1848) was born in Strasbourg and in his youth studied oil painting before volunteering for the French Republican Army in 1792, at a critical moment when the Revolution was threatened by all the other major European powers. During his long and turbulent career as a soldier-artist, during which he rose through the ranks to become a senior officer, Lejeune painted many of the key battles of the Napoleonic Wars; but his 'Battle of Pyramids' remains the most striking and innovative. Although he wasn't present at the battle, as a soldier he would easily have learnt of the details of the engagement from the survivors who had eventually returned

to France. Therefore, he was able to portray the overall 'shape' of the battle
– its topography, the military formations adopted, the tactics employed,
the weaponry brought into play – in a manner which makes the observer
feel almost drawn directly into the smoke and violence.

Imagine we are viewing the painting in a gallery. The artist places you
and me – the battlefield observers – on rising ground, looking down on
the fighting as it enfolds. Below, and to the right, some 300–400 metres
from this vantage point, we see one of five great French infantry squares,
each composed of around 5,000 men, advancing in oblique order towards
the left (western) bank of the Nile. This is the square commanded by the
experienced, forty-year-old General Louis André Bon. Its deployment is in
the textbook formation for protection against cavalry charges, although its
size, and those of the remaining four squares, is unusually large.

Sheltering inside this huge square (actually a rectangle) with its blue-
coated infantry in ranks six to ten deep, are the general's staff, transport
and a small cavalry contingent. Somewhat closer to our observation post,
a company of what appear to be grenadiers of an infantry demi-brigade,*
in red-plumed bearskins, has moved outside the square and is pouring
volleys of musketry into a group of richly dressed Mamluks, some on white
horses, who are fleeing towards the river; and on each corner of the French
infantry square artillerymen have moved outside its protective anti-cavalry
shield and are firing deadly case shot at the retreating Mamluks and their
Arab levies. Behind General Bon's square and further into the distance
we can just make out the divisional square of General Honoré Vial, partly
shrouded in clouds of musketry smoke; and behind that, barely visible,
General Charles-François-Joseph Dugua's square, as the whole force of
25,000 battle-hardened troops move forward to the attack. Only then is
our eye drawn to the three pyramids of Giza on the distant horizon.

Great art as it is, Lejeune's painting is also the celebration of the victory
of 'modern' European arms, organisation and military science over a
'backward' and disorganised oriental horde, as are almost all the artworks
that emerged from Napoleon's expedition to conquer Egypt. And therein

---

* A demi-brigade was the earliest form of military organisation under the Republic. It
originally consisted of two battalions, one of regulars from the old army, one of volunteers.
By the time of the Egyptian campaign, demi-brigades usually contained three battalions,
one of which was light infantry.

lies the paradox of Lejeune's great painting: in reality the whole campaign was actually a major strategic defeat, a great military calamity for European arms, albeit one which would have an impact upon the Mediterranean world of enormous magnitude.

The French expedition weighed anchor at Toulon on 19 May under the command of Admiral Brueys with 335 ships of various sizes: its formation covered an area of over ten square kilometres. Of this huge fleet, fifty-five were battleships, the biggest being the huge flagship *L'Orient* with 1,026 guns. In the centre of the convoy, protected by the warships, were 130 merchant ships carrying supplies and guns and 150 transport ships carrying the Army of the Orient.

According to the account of Pierre-Dominique Martin published in 1815, the fleet carried fourteen infantry demi-brigades, a total 30,800 men. In addition the convoy carried seven light cavalry regiments totalling 2,800 horsemen. There were also Bonaparte's 500 personal mounted bodyguards, known as the Guides, and artillerymen and military engineers, numbering about 2,400 men.[2]

Aside from the military, there were about 900 physicians, pharmacists and nurses, and 167 specially selected *savants* (civilian engineers, scientists, artists and writers) who would study and document the human and economic geography of Egypt, its natural history and its pharaonic monuments. Together with an assortment of bureaucrats, merchants and various hangers-on the expedition numbered around 54,000 men, women and boys, about the same as a fair-sized city at the time.[3]

On 12 June, the French captured the strategically situated island of Malta where its defenders, the 1,500 Knights of Malta, surrendered after a short military engagement. To encourage the idea that his expedition was friendly to the Muslim states of North Africa, Bonaparte informed their rulers that he was releasing the island's 2,000 Arab and Turkish slaves and asked them to reciprocate by liberating any Christians who might be found on their galleys or elsewhere. On 18 June, Bonaparte ordered his fleet to raise anchor and sail eastwards; and it was around this time that information on his final destination began to leak out and circulate around the sailors and troops. Many of his officers and men, including Bonaparte's second in command General Jean-Baptiste Kléber, were far from happy about this wild venture, which was taking them from their homes on a campaign that seemed to have little to do with the objectives for which they had previously been fighting in Europe.

Meanwhile, probably on 15 June, Admiral Horatio Nelson, commanding a British Fleet which had been sent out to intercept the French expeditionary force, realised that Brueys was heading for Alexandria. Nelson raced off in pursuit of the French. But during the night of 22–23 June, in foggy conditions, the opposing fleets crossed each other's paths and Nelson overtook Brueys, arriving off Alexandria on 28 June. A frigate was sent into the port to warn the Egyptians that a French expeditionary force was at sea, probably heading for Egypt. Its captain also asked for water and other supplies, but the city's suspicious Mamluk *kashif* (local governor) refused to offer any assistance and regarded the warning as some kind of Christian trick.

Nelson now concluded that the French must be planning to disembark elsewhere and he impetuously left Alexandria and went off on a wild goose chase towards Crete. Less than a day later, French scouting ships arrived off Alexandria.

The local French consul, Magallon's nephew, came on board the battleship *L'Orient* and informed Bonaparte that Nelson had been there only two days before and might reappear at any time. Bonaparte ordered an immediate disembarkation. So around 9 p.m. on 1 July 1798, the first units of the French invasion force began to land on Egyptian soil at a place named Marabout Bay, about four hours' march from Alexandria.[4]

Before and after the capture of Alexandria, Bonaparte issued two proclamations which illustrate the contradictions of this war, and all colonial wars. In the first he tried to educate his men about the population his expedition was intended to 'liberate'. He briefly described their religion, and urged 'respect for their Muftis and their Imams', saying 'tolerance must be shown to their ceremonies which are governed by the Qur'an and to their mosques ... You will find here many customs different to those in Europe and you must learn to accept them'.[5] Bonaparte appears to have genuinely believed that by insisting on good conduct from his troops (he specifically warned against rape and plundering) amicable relations could be established with the indigenous population, but this was wishful thinking.

The second proclamation was composed in Arabic by Bonaparte's personal interpreter, the sixty-year-old Jean-Michel Venture de Paradis, and disseminated to the Egyptian population. Its central theme had already been decided by Talleyrand and Bonaparte before the despatch of the invasion force. The official propaganda was that the French had arrived to remove the 'tyrannical' Mamluks who had exploited the Egyptian people for centuries and, by so doing, to respect the wishes of their sultan, Selim III. Napoleon also announced that 'I worship God more than the Mamluks do; and that I respect his prophet Muhammad and the admirable Koran.'[6] Years later Napoleon would freely admitted that this was a piece of egregious 'charlatanry'.

The same proclamation then listed orders about how the population should behave towards their new rulers. Villages within three miles of the route of the French army must send deputations to the commanding general declaring their obedience and promising to fly the tricolour and the flag of the Ottoman sultan. All sheikhs, *kadis* and imams should remain in their posts and continue to exercise their functions. In every locality the properties of the Mamluks should be sealed so that nothing could be removed (the French wanted to get their hands on as much Mamluk wealth as possible for themselves). Any acts of disobedience to these and other commands would be met with severe retribution: 'All villages that take up arms against the army will be burned to the ground.'[7] And so, in due course, they were: demonstrating from the outset the futility of attempting to implant a European colonial administration among a people with a vastly different culture and long memories of the misdeeds of European Christian crusaders.

After the capture of Alexandria, where Napoleon left a strong garrison, his army began its advance on Cairo. The main body of the army was ordered to follow the line of the old, largely dried-up canal linking Alexandria with the Nile, a route which was mainly across desert. Meanwhile one division under General Dugua was sent east along the coast to Rosetta from where the men were to advance down the Nile to the planned concentration point of El Rahmaniya, a town on the Nile about seventy kilometres from Alexandria.

The seventy-two-hour march of the main army across the desert was a near disaster. In his haste to win a glorious knockout blow, Napoleon had not bothered to issue his troops with canteens (water bottles), and their heavy European uniforms proved totally unsuitable for the conditions at that time of year. Napoleon had simply assumed that there would be suitable wells or other sources of water on the route chosen, but there were none to speak of. The men suffered grievously from the heat, thirst and from attacks by marauding Bedouin. Around 500 died as a result. On the other hand, General Dugua's route to El Rahmaniya proved relatively easy.

During the advance of the main army towards Cairo, the French troops, who had already become demoralised by the conditions of their march, ransacked entire villages, pillaging anything they could get their hands on and killing anyone who resisted. On one such occasion, on 19 July, the troops who had been sent to seize food and other supplies from an Arab village named Shum met strong resistance from its 1,800 armed inhabitants, who began firing on the French. When two demi-brigades of infantry attacked the Arab villagers, 900 of the defenders were killed and an indeterminate number of women and children were burned to death when the troops set fire to their houses. According to a French sergeant who took part in the action, 'we finished burning the rest of the houses, or rather huts, so as to provide a terrible object lesson to these half-savage and barbarous people'.[8] The irony of French peasants killing Egyptian peasants in the name of 'liberty' was no doubt lost on them.[9]

At last the French Army was in sight of Cairo, and its first major confrontation with the Mamluk-Arab forces occurred on 21 July. In spite of the grandiose title accorded to it by Napoleon – the 'Battle of the Pyramids' – the fighting actually took place near a village on the Nile called Imbaba: those ancient monuments to pharaonic grandeur were actually twenty-four kilometres away and would have only just been visible to Bonaparte and his troops.

According to the previously quoted contemporary French historian Martin, after leaving a garrison of 4,000 men in Malta, one of 1,800 in Alexandria and another at Rosetta of 200, the total French army which took part in the battle amounted to around 30,000 troops.[10] This figure has generally been accepted by both French and Egyptian historians.

But how great was the Muslim army which opposed them? We know that in 1797 the actual enrolment numbers for the 'seven regiments' who garrisoned Egypt totalled 18,309. Of these the Janissary regiment (the *mustahfizan*) had 6,893 officers and men and the *'azaban* 3,274, both being infantry units, while the five regiments of cavalry – the *müteferrika*, the *çavuşan*, the *gönullüyan*, the *tüfenkçiyan* and the *çherakise* – amounted to 8,142 horsemen.[11] But a decade earlier, Volney had described the men of the seven garrison regiments as being militarily useless 'artisans, boors and vagabonds'.

It seems certain that by 1798 the seven regiments had disintegrated almost entirely and virtually disappeared as an effective fighting force, as Volney recorded. The only unit which seems to have survived reasonably intact was the *mustahfizan*; but from the manner in which these men were later utilised under the French occupation it seems their role had already become little more than a local police force.

The problem therefore arises as to who exactly – and how many – were those 'Mamluk' troops whom the French refer to as their principal enemy at Imbaba and who are so beautifully portrayed in Lejeune's painting? Had they, in some way, taken-over or merged with the five Ottoman cavalry units among the seven regiments? Or had they completely replaced them? It seems the latter is the most likely. As to their numbers, both Consul Magallon and Martin agree that there were little more than 8,000 Mamluks in the whole of Egypt. Only half of the Mamluk troops at Imbaba were on the left bank of the Nile, facing Napoleon, under the command of Murad Bey.* It is therefore clear that Napoleon's later claim that he was facing a total of 78,000 enemy at the 'Battle of the Pyramids' is nonsense. In reality his forces were not only massively superior in weaponry, organisation and tactics, but they also vastly outnumbered the Mamluks and the small number of native Egyptians who fought with them.

Murad Bey and his fellow Mamluks had never encountered the discipline and experience in manoeuvre of European troops: their ability to move rapidly from one formation to another, from column to square, from loose skirmishing formation to solid, bayonet- and artillery-defended line. As a result, the Mamluks could only ride round and around the great French infantry squares or make futile charges against the wall of bayonets which met them when they tried to break the serried ranks of French infantry.

---

* The other half, under Ibrahim, had remained on the right bank of the Nile, anticipating an attack from that side.

Murad Bey: Commander
of the Mamluks at the Battle
of the Pyramids

In a little over two hours the Mamluks had given up any hope of victory and left the ragged, under-armed *fellahin* and townsmen accompanying them to be slaughtered. Most of the Mamluks under Murad Bey managed to cross the Nile to join up with Ibrahim Bey's contingent on the right bank. Then Murad Bey and his men fled north with their commander towards Upper Egypt while Ibrahim Bey retreated to Cairo. From there, with a small entourage, he escaped eastwards towards Sinai and Palestine.

It was certainly an important French victory, but it was no great battle like those Napoleon would win in later years like Austerlitz or Borodino, as the casualty figures indicate: probably not more than 1,000 dead on the Egyptian side and a mere twenty-nine dead together with 260 badly wounded among the French.[12]

Nevertheless, when news of the 'Battle of the Pyramids' reached Europe, people were electrified. To his immense discredit and damage to his future reputation Volney now abrogated his previous opposition to colonialism and, completely taken in by the nationalist rhetoric drip-fed from Bonaparte's propaganda machine, began to write hagiographical articles in the official bulletin, the *Moniteur*. In these he imagined that Bonaparte was actually creating some new Arab nation which had thrown off the 'Turkish yoke'.

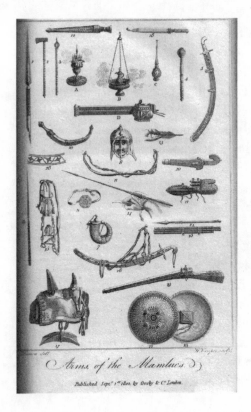

Mamluk Arms,
c. 1798

On the day after the battle the sheikhs and *ulema* of Cairo assembled in the great mosque of al-Azhar. They could see no point in future resistance and sent a deputation to Bonaparte asking for terms. After further negotiations Bonaparte sent five senior officers accompanied by two companies of infantry into the city to take possession; and on 24 July 1798 he himself entered Cairo. On the same day Bonaparte reported to the Directory his general impression of Egypt: 'It would be difficult to find a richer land and a more wretched, ignorant and brutish people.'[13]

Meanwhile, unbeknown to Bonaparte, Nelson's fleet had returned to Egypt. On the evening of 1 August they found Admiral Brueys's fleet in Aboukir Bay where it had remained since the beginning of the invasion, awaiting further orders from Bonaparte, and with 20 to 30 per cent of its seamen and marines on shore, off-loading supplies. As dusk fell

Nelson attacked. The broadsides from the British ships overwhelmed the predominantly young and inexperienced French sailors; and the devastating explosion and complete destruction of Brueys's flagship L'Orient marked the beginning of the end for the French fleet. Only two French battleships and two frigates escaped. And while the British lost 218 dead and 677 wounded, the French lost one admiral (Brueys), three captains and 1,700 men killed, while their wounded numbered one admiral, six captains and 1,500 men.[14] Thereafter three British battleships under Commander Samuel Hood and three lately arrived frigates were despatched to cruise between Damietta and Alexandria, thereby imposing an almost complete blockade of Bonaparte's army.

This disaster was a devastating blow to the morale of the whole French Army in Egypt; but Bonaparte quickly overcame his initial despondency. The loss of the fleet confirmed him in the belief that Egypt must now become an outright French colony. His plan was that he and his men would now take full control of the country's wealth and land. They would build up an army of native mercenaries, as the British had done in India, and crush the remaining Mamluks and any Ottoman forces sent against them. He also expected that, in due course, France – a better and faster shipbuilder

An Orientalist view of Egyptian Life, c. 1800

than Britain – would send another fleet to re-establish contact between the mother country and his army.

Among those who recorded the French entry into Cairo (although perhaps not himself an eye witness) was the highly respected 'alim (Muslim scholar) 'Abd al-Rahman al-Jabarti. In the vast majority of episodes of European imperialism and colonialism the narrative has been provided by the conquerors: typically, the voices of the 'natives' are silent and we look in vain for their reactions to the trauma of foreign occupation. The great value of al-Jabarti's work, therefore, is that it allows us to see the French invasion through the eyes of a contemporary, highly perceptive and remarkably open-minded member of the Egyptian intellectual elite. Al-Jabarti was later to gain the reputation of being 'one of the greatest historians of the Muslim world and by far the greatest historian of the Arab world in modern times'.[15]

Al-Jabarti was born in 1753, the only child who reached puberty out of the forty infants born to a wealthy merchant Hasan al-Jabarti. Hasan was himself a famous 'alim, a master of both Persian and Turkish and an expert in mathematics and astronomy, as well as a great calligraphist. We know that he was visited by Ragıb Paşa during the latter's abortive term of office as Egyptian governor; and he corresponded with Sultan Mustafa III, especially on their shared interest in the Hanafi branch of Islamic jurisprudence.[16]

An Egyptian Lady,
c. 1800

Al-Jabarti wrote three separate accounts of the French invasion. The first, *Tarikh muddat al-Faransis bi Misr* (The History of the Period of the French in Egypt), covers only the first six months of the occupation and was composed as early as 1798; it offers the reader an immediacy of experience and a feeling for the cultural shock felt by a man who later became unwillingly drawn into the structures of French domination.

The chronicle begins with the arrival of the British frigate at Alexandria, warning of a possible attack by the French but rebuffed by the city's Mamluk commander. It continues by describing the arrival of the French and their capture of Alexandria. Al-Jabarti is bitterly critical of the Mamluk beys who, he states, had recklessly failed to spend money on constructing modern fortifications at Alexandria and elsewhere.[17] Al-Jabarti then provides his reader with a remarkably perceptive explanation of the French republican form of government, but he continues with a denunciation of the personal habits and social mores of the French invaders. To some extent his account echoes the traditional unfavourable views about 'Christians' common among Muslims, but includes some elements which may well have been true of the common soldiery and their women at this time.[18]

Typical of these are his remarks about French women 'who do not veil themselves and have no modesty; they do not care whether they uncover their private parts'. As for the men,

> Whenever a Frenchman has to perform an act of nature he does so wherever he happens to be, even in full view of people and he goes away as he is, without washing his private parts after defecation. If he is a man of taste and refinement he wipes himself with whatever he finds, even with a paper with writing on it, otherwise he remains as he is.[19]

However, elsewhere he declares his admiration for French military prowess and organisation. And in another passage (from which we quoted in Chapter 1) he expresses his high regard for the scientific and technical advances which the French had achieved – 'such things which baffle the mind'. Al-Jabarti was also impressed by the French system of elected councils drawing on local Arab notables, whose decision-making processes were based on secret ballots. At the same time, he was not averse to recording some acts of egregious cruelty perpetrated by the Mamluks and Arabs upon unfortunate captured French soldiers.

As for Bonaparte's propagandist declaration, which he had issued on 2 July, al-Jabarti easily saw through it. He dismissed Bonaparte's pretensions that his invasion was in some way in defence of 'true Muslims' and sanctioned by the sultan. For the deeply religious al-Jabarti, the French were simply 'materialists' and atheists. Al-Jabarti also had few illusions about Bonaparte's plans for Egypt. He furthermore seems to have gained a fairly clear understanding of European power politics and the great rivalry between France and Britain. It was al-Jabarti's view that Egypt's role under French rule was to form some kind of launching pad from which the French could attack the British in India, an insight that reflected the actual objectives shared by Bonaparte and the Directorate.[20]

The remainder of al-Jabarti's chronicle contains a month-by-month account of the occupation in which he records in detail the depredations of the army, and the appointment of 'unworthy' persons to positions of authority. One example was the vicious Greek artilleryman and shopkeeper Barthelemy Serra, who was chosen to be *kethüda* of the Janissaries. In particular, he detailed the manner in which the French usurped the income flows from *iltizam*s, *muqata'a*s and even private *waqf*s. The revenues raised from taking over *iltizam*s and other fiscal instruments were crucial to sustaining the occupation, and by this method the French were reportedly able to raise around 1 million francs per month.[21]

Meanwhile, in Istanbul the twenty-eight-year-old Sultan Selim III was struggling to understand how the French could have so deceitfully stabbed him in the back. Although never a formal ally, France had for centuries been considered a friend. Selim's reign had begun at a particularly low point in the history of the Ottoman Empire. In 1787 his predecessor, Abdülhamid I, had launched a futile attempt to regain territory lost to the Tsarina Catherine during the reign of Mustafa III. The war had turned into another Ottoman disaster. Its nadir came on the night of 6 December 1788 when the Russian army under Prince Grigori Potemkin and General A. V. Suvorov stormed the besieged fortress-city of Ochakov on the Black Sea, putting the whole garrison and civilian population to the sword. Hearing the news, Abdülhamid had died of a seizure and Selim III, as the most senior male relative, was released from the *kafes* and girded with the sword of Osman. The young sultan felt he had an obligation to continue the war, but the Ottomans' fortunes went from bad to worse; in January 1792, at the Treaty of Jassy, they were forced to recognise Russia's annexation of the Crimea and its control of Ochakov and Odessa.

After understandable prevarication, in September 1798 Sultan Selim declared jihad against the French. His decision was all the more difficult given that it now placed him, by default, in an alliance with the Ottomans' historic enemy, Russia – apart from Britain, the only other state currently at war with the French Republic. As a consequence of this unlikely alliance Selim was obliged to let a Russian Black Sea fleet under Admiral Dmitry Senyavin pass through the Turkish Straits to join British ships in the Mediterranean. Once there, they recaptured the French-occupied Ionian Islands which now became the 'Septinsular Republic' under joint Russo-Ottoman protection.

However, Selim was fortunate in that the beginning of his reign coincided with the growing influence of sections of the scribal bureaucracy and army leadership. These were people who saw the need for modernisation and the adoption of European military methods capable of resisting the attacks of the Christian world from whatever direction they came.[22]

So, in 1792 Selim had started to build a new, reformed army separate from the largely useless Janissaries and provincial *levend*s. These troops were known as the *Nizam-ı Cedid* (the New Organisation) and their training and equipment were based on the European model. Secrecy was necessary because of the fierce opposition to any such new army, not only from the Janissaries but also among reactionary elements of the *ulema* and even members of Selim's own divan. Training by European officers took place in locations far afield and well away from the barracks of the traditional Ottoman troops. In these secret camps the recruits were issued with new uniforms, equipped with muskets carrying bayonets, and drilled in the sort of manoeuvres which were normal practice among European armies. They were paid more than the Janissaries but, in exchange, had to accept a much stricter European-style discipline.

By 1794 a single regiment of 1,602 infantrymen had been established consisting of two battalions, each of 800 men divided into twelve companies. Each company was given five cannons manned by eight artillerymen and an artillery officer. The troops wore blue 'berets' and red jackets and breeches while their officers, headed by a *binbashi* (colonel) carried swords and identifying buttons sewn above the pockets of their jackets.[23] In 1799 a second regiment was created which contained both infantry and cavalry and whose uniforms were light blue in colour, to distinguish its men from the first regiment.

Selim had hoped that the Nizam-i Cedid troops would number around 12,000 by 1798, but difficulties in the recruitment and training of largely inexperienced men meant that at the time of Bonaparte's invasion of Egypt the two regiments were composed of only 4,317 men and thirty officers. Nevertheless, Selim was now able to despatch a contingent of 700 Nizam-i Cedid troops to Acre in Palestine, where they were expected to form the backbone of an army of resistance being mobilised to confront the French.[24]

Meanwhile Selim's declaration of jihad triggered a massive and totally unexpected uprising in Cairo beginning on 21 October. Its history constitutes probably the most dramatic part of al-Jabarti's narrative of the French invasion, from which much of our knowledge of the event derives.

As well as the declaration of jihad, the uprising was also provoked by an accumulation of grievances against the occupiers, in particular the excessive taxation which the French were squeezing out of both rural and urban Egyptians. Al-Jabarti himself was strongly critical of the Cairo uprising, which was accompanied by the widespread murder of individual French soldiers and those civilians and Christian Arabs believed to be sympathetic to the occupation. He feared the brutal retribution that would inevitably follow if the rebellion were crushed (as he believed it would be). Moreover, in his patrician mindset, the uprising largely involved 'riff-raff' and 'vagabonds' from the lowest social strata.[25]

As al-Jabarti correctly anticipated, once the French authorities recovered from their initial shock and disarray, they were able to crush the rising with their superior weaponry and discipline. Bonaparte ordered that all Egyptians captured with arms in their hands should be beheaded and their corpses thrown into the Nile. In addition hundreds of those believed to be involved in some lesser degree were rounded up and tortured by the sadistic Barthelemy Serra and his Janissary police, to extract further information on other participants. Those whose names were divulged were taken to the Citadel and other locations and executed by beheading or bayoneting.

An infantryman of the Nizam-1 Cedid,
c. 1797 (Second Regiment)

Al-Jabarti lists the names of some of those killed. But even he seems to have been unaware of the exact scale of these reprisals, only commenting that 'so many people died that their number cannot be determined'.[26] French reports of the number of summary executions vary from 300 to 2,000 people, including a number of senior *ulema*.[27]

Eventually, Bonaparte put a stop to the executions after Cairo was returned to some kind of normality, and he issued a general amnesty to the population of Cairo. However, in the wake of the rebellion, he learnt of another threat to his Egyptian colony. The fugitive Mamluk Ibrahim Bey was reported to be forming an army to oust the French invaders, in an alliance with the governor of the Palestinian city of Acre, Ahmad al-Cezzar.

Since we last met him, al-Cezzar 'the Butcher' had won the admiration of the sultan, and been appointed *vali* of the *eyalet* of Sidon, with the coastal fortress of Acre as its main stronghold. It had previously been the capital of the Arab ayan Zahir al-'Umar; but in 1775 Sultan Abdülhamid had grown tired of Zahir's refusal to pay his required quota of taxes. So he had sent his admiral, the redoubtable Gazi Hasan Paşa, with 3,000 troops to put an end to Zahir's control over Palestine. The admiral's troops were able to storm Zahir's stronghold, against little resistance, and kill the eighty-five-year-old

Arab ruler. In his place the sultan appointed al-Cezzar.[28] He would rule Palestine with an iron fist until his death in 1804.

Like his predecessor al-Cezzar promoted the cotton trade and turned Palestine into the most important source of French imports. But he soon realised he could obtain a bigger share of the income from cotton production by sidelining the French merchants and monopolising the sale of this commodity. His income from cotton exports, together with customs duties and increased taxes levied upon the Palestinian peasantry, enabled him to build up a personal army of around 25,000 North African, Albanian, Bosnian and Arab mercenaries which could, if necessary, challenge the weak and disorganised Ottoman troops based in Palestine.[29] Although al-Cezzar sometimes held back payment of taxes to the reigning sultan he was still at pains to maintain as far as possible a semblance of legality and correctness in his dealings with the Ottoman treasury.

This was the man to whom Bonaparte sent an ultimatum on 19 November 1798 claiming that he did not want to be his enemy, but if al-Cezzar continued to give asylum to Ibrahim Bey, 'I shall regard this as an act of war and shall march on Acre.'[30]

Meanwhile, General Louis Desaix had been ordered to pursue Murad Bey into Upper Egypt. On the night of 25 August 1798, and armed with only 2,861 infantry and two field guns, Desaix's small force set off up the Nile in one of the most remarkable campaigns in military history. Over the next few months his pursuit of Murad Bey up and down the middle and higher reaches of the Nile would involve his ragged, half-starved men, many suffering from ophthalmia, marching and counter-marching a total distance of over 2,000 kilometres.

By the time Desaix's weary troops finally returned to Cairo in July 1799, Murad Bey was still at large and posing a threat to French control over a large swathe of territory bordering the middle and upper reaches of the Nile. Moreover, the campaign had done nothing to reduce the French soldiers' fear and loathing of the merciless nature of the colonial warfare in which they were now involved. As al-Jabarti recorded with respect to one particular day in October 1798:

> On that same day boats arrived from Upper Egypt bearing wounded, mutilated and blinded soldiers. It was said that

they had fought once again with Murad Bey and after they
had been defeated some were captured. 'Ali Paşa al-Tarabulsi
[an associate of Murad who had fought at the Battle of the
Pyramids] ordered that they were not to be killed. Instead
they gouged out their eyes and mutilated them, leaving them
in this state as a warning to others and a cause of grief.[31]

And over the coming months the horrors of this colonial war were to
escalate without bounds.

By the end of 1798, Napoleon had given up any hope of winning the
acquiescence of the Porte for his Egyptian invasion, and he also feared
an attack from Palestine by Ibrahim Bey, al-Cezzar and his army of
mercenaries. Napoleon decided to take the offensive against them by
setting out to invade Palestine, crush al-Cezzar, deny the English a supply
base for their frigates cruising in the Eastern Mediterranean, and compel
the Porte to open negotiations. Most of Bonaparte's officers were opposed
to the plan, yet none was willing to challenge him. So in early February
1799 an expedition of around 13,000 troops, including a newly established
camel corps of eighty-eight specially trained men, began the advance into
southern Palestine.

At first the advance met with little resistance. On the night of 14
February the coastal border town of El Arish, the gateway to the Sinai
Peninsula, was captured and, on 24 February, Gaza was taken and
looted. The French troops marched quickly northward along Palestine's
Mediterranean coastline, and on 3 March the city of Jaffa was besieged.
After only three days it was stormed and captured; around 2,000 Turks
who were attempting to surrender were bayoneted and all the women and
children killed. There remained a further 1,500 Turkish, North African and
Egyptian troops in the citadel. These also offered to surrender provided
their lives were spared, to which Bonaparte agreed, guaranteeing them safe
conduct. However, their surrender presented him with a serious problem:
he did not have sufficient troops to leave behind to guard these prisoners,
and if they were simply released it was feared that they would return to
attack his army in the rear. The decision was therefore taken to kill them all.

In the eighteenth and early nineteenth centuries the slaughter of
surrendering enemy troops and even civilians during the actual storming of

a fortress was broadly accepted as a regrettable but inevitable occurrence: in the heat and fury of battle, after suffering heavy losses, the vengeful attacking soldiers simply could not be controlled and atrocities were frequently committed.* But the cold-blooded murder of those troops whose surrender had actually been accepted was almost unheard of. Just one day after the capture of Jaffa the massacre commenced and around 800 of the prisoners were bayoneted to death. The following day a further 600 were killed in the same manner and on 10 March 1,041 were either bayoneted or shot.[32] An especially pitiable sight was the futile attempt to escape death by those who had fled into the sea: as they were cut down by musket fire they began building barricades of the bodies of their dead comrades, behind which they attempted to shelter.

But as well as arguably having an military reason for the massacre, Bonaparte clearly intended it as a warning to al-Cezzar and the 8,000 men defending the strategic city of Acre. If so, Bonaparte had misread al-Cezzar's character. Terror tactics could have absolutely no impact on 'the Butcher', and a few weeks later al-Cezzar demonstrated his own brand of terror by killing several hundred Christian Arabs resident in Acre whom he regarded as a potential 'fifth column'.

On 20 March 1799 Bonaparte's 11,500 French troops arrived outside Acre and began constructing the earthworks required to surround and besiege al-Cezzar's troops. But by now the French learnt that they had suffered another disaster at sea. Two days' earlier, a British naval squadron had ambushed a convoy of French transports carrying the heavy artillery needed to batter down Acre's elderly city walls, and captured six of its nine vessels. The victorious British ships were part of the squadron blockading Alexandria, now under a flamboyant new commander, the thirty-four-year-old Sir Sydney Smith, from his station on the 80-gun battleship HMS *Tigre*.

Once the siege began, Smith sent the battleship HMS *Theseus* into Acre's port, followed by his own ship, and the two warships dropped anchor in the harbour so that their broadsides could help the defence. Smith also supplied al-Cezzar with additional cannon manned by sailors and marines

---

* For example, during the Peninsular War, this was the fate of the innocent Spanish and French civilians in the aftermath of the storming of the city of Badajoz by the British troops in 1812.

and assisted him in organising the repair of those parts of the old city's walls
which were most in need of additional fortification. Later, Smith would
greatly exaggerate his role in the defence of Acre. In reality, it was al-Cezzar
and his personal army, reinforced by the 700 European-trained Nizam-1
Cedid troops which Sultan Selim had despatched to his aid, which would
defeat Bonaparte's army.

Time and time again the French troops, led by elite grenadier
companies, hurled themselves at the city's walls, clambering over fallen
debris and climbing wooden ladders, only to be thrown back by al-Cezzar's
men. Al-Cezzar himself was in the front line, alternately haranguing and
threatening his men to stand fast against the infidels. By 10 May, after
thirteen separate assaults, the French troops themselves were nearing a state
of mutiny. Bonaparte, facing undisguised antagonism from his divisional
generals – especially Kléber – finally accepted defeat.

However, the suffering of his troops had not ended. The retreat back to
Egypt was a terrible ordeal. Disease, including outbreaks of plague, caused
hundreds of deaths, almost equalling the losses in battle. By the time the
retreating army reached the outskirts of Cairo, the campaign had resulted
in around 1,200 killed in action, 1,000 deaths from disease and about 2,500
ill or seriously wounded: a total casualty rate of about 36 per cent. Among
the dead were two generals and Bonaparte's personal interpreter, Venture
de Paradis.

Nevertheless, Bonaparte still had a powerful and experienced army at his
command in Lower Egypt; and when a Turkish army of 15,000, transported
by British ships, landed at Aboukir on 25 July it was utterly defeated. This
was in part the result of a magnificent charge by the French cavalry under
the flamboyant General Joachim Murat. The Turks may have suffered as
many as 8,000 casualties – most of them killed – compared with total
French losses of about 1,000.

It was at this point that Bonaparte decided to return to Paris, having
received news that the French Republican armies had suffered some serious
defeats at the hands of the Austrians and Russians, and convinced that he
was needed to restore morale and lead the counterattack. But he also had
personal reasons. Although his Palestinian campaign had failed miserably,
the crushing defeat of the Turks at Aboukir meant that he could return on
the back of 'great victory'. On 2 August, accompanied only by four of his

generals and three of the *savants*,* he left Cairo in great secrecy and went aboard a French frigate which had slipped through the British blockading squadron. Arriving in France on 9 October, Bonaparte went straight to Paris where his propaganda machine hailed him as the conquering hero of Egypt. There, on 9 November 1799, he and his supporters staged a coup against the Directorate, making him the 'First Consul' of the Republic – in effect France's dictator.

The only instructions Bonaparte left to his beleaguered army were that Kléber should take over as commander-in-chief and that General Desaix should follow Bonaparte to France as soon as he was able. Kléber was furious. As far as he was concerned Bonaparte had deserted his army and abandoned his men, 'shitting in his pants'. The new commander-in-chief was aware that with a few exceptions (notably General Jacques-François Menou) the army was desperate to return to France. So he immediately began to make plans to extricate his men from what had now become a detested mission. On 17 September he wrote to the sixty-six-year-old, one-eyed grand vezir Yusuf Ziyaüddin Paşa, asking for negotiations under which Egypt would be restored to the sultan.

Although an Ottoman army of 80,000 under Yusuf Paşa was now advancing from Palestine, it was suffering grievously from illness, starvation and thirst, and on 1 November the French crushed another attempt at a large Turkish seaborne attack near Damietta. Sir Sydney Smith appears to have decided that he could now act as peacemaker. It was largely through his intervention that, on 24 January 1800, Kléber and Smith (believing he had the support of the Porte) agreed the 'Convention of El Arish', according to which the French would withdraw their forces from certain key strong points, and one month later from Cairo. All French troops would then retire to Alexandria, Aboukir and Rosetta (Rashid) and the Turks would provide the ships to transport them back to France with all their arms and personal effects. In the meantime, the Porte would provide the French with 2 million francs to sustain them for the duration of their remaining months in Egypt.

However, the British government under its Tory prime minister, William Pitt, was having none of it. As a mere commodore, Smith had no jurisdiction

---

* *Savants*: one of which was the famous Vivant Denon (1747–1825), artist, writer and archaeologist.

to determine British foreign policy. Strongly supported by Nelson and Admiral Keith, the naval commander-in-chief in the Mediterranean, the government refused to accept the peace terms agreed at El Arish. The Porte also acknowledged that the sultan couldn't make peace without the agreement of his British and Russian allies. So on 18 March 1800 Keith sent an insultingly worded letter to Kléber stating categorically that the British government would only accept his complete and unconditional surrender. Meanwhile Yusuf Paşa's rag-tag army was moving closer to Cairo.

Kléber now realised that for the time being he and his army were condemned to remain stuck in Egypt, but he was able to rouse his troops out of their despondency following Bonaparte's departure. On 20 March he led them to inflict a crushing defeat on a Turkish force four times as great as his own at the battle of Heliopolis, driving Grand Vezir Yusuf Paşa and most of his army out of Egypt. After this resounding victory Kléber began negotiations to put an end to the struggle against the Mamluks under Murad Bey. In April negotiations were concluded whereby Murad would make peace with the French and in return be acknowledged as governor of Upper Egypt.

But then, on 14 June, General Kléber was stabbed and killed by a Syrian religious student from Aleppo, named Sulayman. The command of the army fell to the pot-bellied, former Royalist officer, forty-eight-year-old Jacques-François Menou. Much to the derision of the troops, Menou had converted to Islam in order to marry an attractive Egyptian lady, although he had prevailed upon the tame *ulema* of Cairo to grant him dispensation from the rite of circumcision. 'Abdullah' Menou (as he now called himself) swiftly convened a military court, headed by himself, which condemned to death Sulayman and three Cairo notables who were his alleged fellow-conspirators. The tragic irony was that Kléber's killer, presumably intending to strike a symbolic blow against the continuing French occupation, killed the very French commander who was most determined to end that same occupation.

The three Cairo conspirators were duly decapitated, but a far worse fate awaited the actual assassin. The hand which committed the act was to be burned off following which Sulayman was to be impaled alive at the hands of the notoriously sadistic police chief Barthelemy Serra. His torture and execution took place on 17 June in front of a large contingent of the French Army. His agonising death throes lasted four hours until he died of his internal injuries.[33] Apparently no voices were raised against this appalling exhibition. The French claimed that they had come to Egypt to bring its inhabitants the benefits of civilisation and progress. But the brutalities of colonial war had changed all that. Instead these 'children of the Enlightenment' had now reverted to the kind of sadistically cruel punishments of the *ancien régime* which their own revolution had stamped out only a decade or so earlier.

And so, the occupation would continue. Menou had opposed Kléber's efforts to extricate the army from Egypt. He was one of the very few officers who still believed that France should hold on to its colony – in spite of the fact that the French position in the Mediterranean had been weakened further by the capitulation of the French garrison at Malta to the British and Maltese insurgents on 5 September 1800.

By now, all Britain's European allies had either been beaten into submission or withdrawn from the fighting for other reasons. It looked increasingly likely that Britain would have to make peace itself within a year or so. But the possibility that peace would leave a powerful French army in Egypt filled the government with horror. The war minister Henry Dundas insisted that Britain could survive only if it protected its colonial wealth and ocean trade which, in his opinion, were 'the sinews of war'. If the French army in Egypt were allowed to remain there it would be a standing threat to Britain's rich East India trade and the revenue which flowed from its colonies in Bengal and elsewhere.

Consequently in October 1800 the cabinet agreed a plan to expel the French from Egypt. Admiral Keith was to assemble a fleet of ships to carry 17,000 British troops under General Sir Ralph Abercrombie to make a landing at Aboukir. It would be supported by the landing of Ottoman troops under the command of the Grand Admiral, Küçük Hüseyin Paşa. Another force of 3,000 Indian sepoys, together with a further 2,000 British troops picked up at its colony at the Cape of Good Hope, would be despatched to Kosseir on the Red Sea. From there they would attack French troops in Upper Egypt and then move north to join up with Abercrombie's men. In addition a British delegation under General Sir John Moore would be sent to Jaffa to coordinate these British operations with the remnants of the grand vezir's army, which would once again advance into Egypt across the Sinai desert.

The campaign, the outcome of which was anticipated with much trepidation by both the British government and its naval and military commanders, was remarkably successful. Although General Abercrombie was killed during the first major battle after his men had made a successful landing at Aboukir bay on 8 March 1801, over the next four months the near-mutinous French troops were overwhelmed by the forces closing in upon them. They were forced to split into two isolated positions, at Cairo under General Belliard and at Alexandria under Menou. Offered terms for an 'honourable' capitulation, Belliard surrendered at the end of June. Menou hung on in Alexandria until he too surrendered on 27 August. By the end of September 1801 all the surviving French troops had arrived back in France, accompanied by a number of Christian Arabs, who had compromised themselves by working for the occupation, together with some of the officers' Arab wives and mistresses and a few Mamluks.

For the French public, recent successes in the European war clouded any understanding of the extent of the disaster which had befallen Bonaparte's Egyptian expedition. Out of a total of around 50,000 men who had sailed from France in 1798, only a little over 23,000 (of whom 3,000 were invalids) returned to their homeland.[34] The campaign had resulted in the death of four of Bonaparte's most experienced generals – Kléber, Bon, Dommartin and Cafarelli – together with Admiral Brueys and Bonaparte's chief interpreter, Venture de Paradis. As for Egypt's Arab population, their sufferings during the French occupation are beyond any estimation.

CHAPTER 11

The Troubled Beginnings
of Britain's 'Blue-Water Empire'

Should Britain become a Mediterranean power? That was the question which the ministers in Henry Addington's Tory government wrestled with after the signing of the Treaty of Amiens on 23 March 1802. The Treaty brought peace between Britain and France, but one of its clauses was proving particularly troublesome. According to Clause 10, the island of Malta, which the French surrendered to Britain on 5 September 1800, was to be handed back to the Knights Hospitallers, evicted by Bonaparte in 1798. The island was strategically positioned mid-way between southern Europe and North Africa; moreover, its capital, Valetta, had the best harbour in the whole Mediterranean Sea. In London there was a growing feeling that the peace was working to Napoleon's advantage; and the ministers had begun to listen to the strident voices of their own parliamentarians, urging them to hold on to Malta whatever the Treaty had agreed and whatever the consequences for the peace.

There was also anxiety about the situation in Egypt which the government now found thrown into its hands. The ministers were desperate to find some accommodation between the Porte and the Mamluk beys which would re-establish the sultan's sovereignty over the province. They had sent General John Stuart to Istanbul to try to mediate between the two parties but, so far, to no avail.

To make matters worse, the French had clearly not abandoned their objective of controlling the country. As soon as the Treaty had been signed, Napoleon appointed a new consul-general in Cairo, Mathieu de Lesseps, and, in addition, sent a cavalry officer, General Horace Sébastiani, to Egypt as his 'Middle East Envoy'. Sébastiani's official task was to enquire why the final evacuation of British troops (required by the Treaty of Amiens) was taking so long. General Stuart was determined to maintain a token British force at Alexandria until a final settlement of the Mamluk-Ottoman quarrel.

But now de Lesseps and Sébastiani were making the task all the more difficult by attempting to restore French influence over the contestants squabbling for power.

In fact, Consul-General de Lesseps had arrived in Cairo with secret orders from Napoleon 'to seek out a person, bold intelligent and trustworthy' capable of mastering the Mamluks and creating a strong state, independent of Istanbul and hostile to Britain.¹ So, while intriguing with the pro-French Mamluks, de Lesseps had also begun to ingratiate himself with a certain Mehmed Ali,* a thirty-five-year-old Albanian officer, son of a tobacco merchant of Kavala in Macedonia and second in command of the Kavala Volunteer Contingent in the Ottoman Army that had been sent to Egypt after the French Army withdrew.

For the British ministers matters came to a head on 30 January 1803 when the official French journal, *Le Moniteur Universel*, published a report by General Sébastiani which argued that France could re-establish control over Egypt with a mere 6,000 troops.² On 11 March General Stuart decided that the negotiations in Istanbul were going nowhere and ordered the withdrawal of the last British troops from Egypt to Malta. Finally, Addington's government decided to hold on to Malta and, anticipating Napoleon's reaction at this breach of the Amiens Treaty, Britain declared war on France on 18 May 1803.

Meanwhile, in Egypt anarchy was heaped upon chaos. Fighting between Mamluks and Ottoman troops repeatedly erupted, usually to the advantage of the former. But soon, separate power struggles broke within the ranks of both the Ottoman soldiery and the Mamluk beys. Having received no pay for months, the Albanian contingent of the Ottoman army mutinied and fought running battles with Turkish troops throughout the streets of Cairo. At the same time fighting broke out between two of the principal Mamluk households, the one headed by Muhammad Bey al-Alfi and the other by Osman Bey Bardisi.

With the end of the old duumvirate – Murad Bey had died and Ibrahim Bey was now in Upper Egypt – the Mamluks reverted to their customary internecine slaughter. But the second outbreak of war between Britain and

---

*   In much of the historical literature 'Mehmed' is written in the Arabic form, 'Muhammad'. However, given his origins it seems more appropriate to use the colloquial Turkish version.

France gave the fighting an international dimension. With brutal daily encounters between the *khushdash* of Muhammad Bey al-Alfi and those of Osman Bey Bardisi, the two chieftains let it be known that they were 'pro-British' and 'pro-French' respectively.

After General Stuart ordered the withdrawal of the last British forces in Egypt he left his military secretary, a certain Major Edward Missett, to remain in Alexandria as consul. Missett was described by a brother officer as 'clever, vain, impatient and busy with schemes for re-establishing British influence but his cleverness included no power of judgement and did not exclude a large element of credulity'.[3] To this weakness of character was added a further characteristic which made Missett unsuitable for this important position: he apparently suffered from some serious physical disability which made him almost totally dependent upon 'intelligence' provided by unreliable local agents. To make matters worse he took to meddling in the murky and violent politics of the Mamluk households.

Misset was as yet unaware that de Lesseps was patronising the Albanian commander Mehmed Ali as a more promising pro-French ruler than any Mamluk bey. He became convinced that Britain must cultivate a Mamluk chieftain for that position: the obvious choice, he reported, was Muhammad Bey al-Alfi. Misset arranged for him to travel to London, where he was lavishly entertained and even presented to King George III. Having been expensively primed as Egypt's new pro-British ruler, he was then returned to the country on 10 February 1804, with his baggage containing a copious supply of a brandy-laced alcoholic beverage with the innocuous name of 'milk punch'. According to the Edwardian military historian Sir John Fortescue, the beverage in question appeared to be 'the most solid result of his visit to the West'.[4]

Unfortunately for both al-Alfi and his handler, Major Missett, on his arrival the Bey and his entourage were attacked by the pro-French Mamluks under Osman Bey Bardisi, and were forced to flee into the desert. Eighteen months later Muhammad Bey al-Alfi died, allegedly poisoned by one of his harem concubines.[5] Coincidentally, the pro-French Mamluk chieftain Osman Bey Bardisi also died suddenly at around the same time. The death of these two powerful men left Mehmed Ali the undisputed de facto ruler of Egypt. Consequently, in early 1805, Sultan Selim, with no means of bringing Mehmed Ali to heel, was forced to confirm him as Vali of Egypt with the latter's agreement that he would pay an annual tribute of 2,500 *kis* (purses).*

However, unaware of al-Alfi's death, and on the basis of dubious information from his 'intelligence agents', Missett continued to report to his superiors that there remained a powerful 'pro-British' element among the Mamluks which could wrest power from Mehmed Ali.

While these events were taking place, Selim III had been greatly impressed by Napoleon's sweeping victories over the Austrians and Russians at the battle of Austerlitz on 2 December 1805. General Sébastiani had been sent to Istanbul as French ambassador on 10 August 1806, and under his strong influence the sultan's francophile tendencies re-emerged from the hiatus of Napoleon's Egyptian adventure. Moreover, for some time Selim had suspected that the Russians – with whom he was still officially tied in an anti-French alliance together with Britain – were meddling in the politics of the two nominally Ottoman Danubian principalities of Wallachia and Moldavia. Napoleon's military successes, and the apparent weakness of the Russians in the face of Napoleon's continuing advance eastwards, convinced Selim that the time was ripe to confront the Tsar over Russian subversion in his Danubian vassal states. Within four days of the French Ambassador's arrival in Istanbul, Selim dismissed the Greek notables appointed to rule Wallachia and Moldavia on his behalf and who he now suspected were conspiring with the Russians to detach these territories from his Empire.

Sébastiani's increasing influence over the sultan, and Selim's growing admiration for Napoleon – reinforced by the French Emperor's stunning victory over the Prussians at the Battle of Jena on 14 October 1806 – was now a matter of acute anxiety to the British ambassador, Charles Arbuthnot. He was convinced that, without some forceful intervention by his own government, Selim would change sides and declare war on Britain's Russian ally.

---

*   The value of the *kis* (purse) in the early 1800s is uncertain. At its original issue in the seventeenth century it was worth 25,000 *paras* = 625 *kuruş*. However, by 1833 its value had fallen to 500 *kuruş* (Issawi, 1966, p. 521). With 1 *kuruş* = £0.010 in 1833 the *kis* would have been worth £5. This calculation is broadly confirmed by Edward Lane, who lived in Egypt in the 1820s and 1830s, and who states that 6,000 purses (*kis*) were worth £40,000, i.e. 1 *kis* = £6.66. (Lane, 1846, p.129),

Following the death of William Pitt in January 1806, a coalition had been formed between Britain's two rival aristocratic parties, the Tories and the Whigs.* The Whig prime minister, William Wyndham Grenville (Lord Grenville), informed the Porte that it intended to remain neutral in the escalating dispute between the Porte and the Tsar, its only two remaining allies.[6] However, by the autumn, the Tsar was urging Britain to take action to deter the sultan from falling further into the grasp of the French. The Russians feared that French pressure would lead the Ottomans to close the Straits to Russian ships and trap the Russian fleet currently operating in the Mediterranean. The British were all too aware that this could lead to outright war between its two allies.

In response, the new British government decided on two courses of action. First, on 14 November 1806 the British Foreign Secretary, Lord Howick, sent instructions to Ambassador Arbuthnot at Istanbul that he should demand the expulsion of General Sébastiani, informing the ambassador that a fleet was being sent through the Turkish Straits to ensure that the Porte complied with the British government's wishes.[7] If it refused, then Admiral Sir John Duckworth was under orders to bombard Istanbul until Selim agreed to meet Britain's demands.

Second, Major Missett's repeated warnings about Mehmed Ali's pro-French sympathies were heeded, as were his claims that there existed a powerful pro-British faction among the Mamluks ready to support any British army sent to Egypt from its bases in Sicily. Therefore orders were also sent to General Henry Fox, the British Commander-in-Chief at Messina, to hold 5,000 troops in readiness for an expedition to Alexandria, should this become necessary.

Circumstances were now propelling the Ottomans and the Russians towards open conflict. On 21 November 1806, the sultan refused Arbuthnot's demand that Sébastiani be dismissed. By the end of the month, the Russians had sent an army of 40,000 into Wallachia and Moldavia, and on 16 December the sultan's divan resolved on war with Russia.[8] Shortly afterwards the Straits were closed to Russian ships.

---

* The Tories were strong supporters of the Crown and the established Church of England. The Whigs were strongly supportive of parliamentary rule and the ascendency of Protestantism, and were tolerant of the many 'dissenting' Protestant churches.

Unfortunately for Admiral Duckworth, when his fleet arrived off the Dardanelles in February 1807 it was prevented from entering the Straits by a fierce northerly gale. After a week's delay the fleet finally passed into Sea of Marmara, but once again it was held back by the weather and was unable to enter the Bosphorus.

Strong winds continued to blow down the Bosphorus until the end of February, making it impossible for his fleet to move closer to the Ottoman capital. Meanwhile, urged on by Sébastiani, the citizens of Istanbul were building extensive earthworks to defend their city against an attack from the sea, and hundreds of cannons had been moved into position, both at Istanbul and along each side of the Dardanelles. Meanwhile, realising his diplomatic efforts had been in vain, Arbuthnot made his escape from Istanbul on the sole British frigate which had managed to reach Istanbul before the adverse weather set in.

Finally, on 1 March, Duckworth wrote to his superior, Admiral Collingwood, that he believed it was his 'positive duty, however wounded in pride and ambition', to abandon the attack on Istanbul. Two days later he ordered his captains to return to the Aegean.[9] But matters were not so simple. As his ships began to pass through the Dardanelles they came under heavy fire from the Ottoman artillery on either side of the Straits. Masts and rigging were shot away, the mainmast of one of his ships, the *Windsor Castle*, being more than three-quarters cut through by an immense granite cannon ball of two-and-a-half tons.[10] During the whole sorry venture, 137 seamen and marines were killed and 412 wounded before the British squadron reached Tenedos in the Aegean.[11]

On 8 March, Duckworth's fleet was joined by Admiral Senyavin's squadron, which was now blockading the Dardanelles. The two admirals considered another attempt to force the Straits and bombard Istanbul. But they decided that it wasn't worth the risk to their ships, and in any case they had no troops with which to strike a militarily decisive blow. Consequently, on 13 March, Duckworth sailed off into the Aegean leaving Senyavin to continue the blockade.[12]

Meanwhile, on 18 February 1807, 6,000 troops were embarked from Sicily under the command of General Alexander Mackenzie Fraser. They were to be transported to Alexandria where it was expected that they would be joined by the 'pro-British' Mamluks who Major Missett claimed were waiting to support them. Unfortunately, the purpose of the expedition was never really made clear. General Fraser was instructed to capture Alexandria and hold it, but not to extend his operations outside the city. What exactly was to happen afterwards, and what was to be the longer-term purpose of this 'base' at Alexandria, does not appear to have been seriously considered by the British government or relayed to the expedition's commander. Major Missett, however, had very clear ideas about what should follow and he had already taken it upon himself to tell various 'pro-British' Mamluks that Britain intended to restore the government of the country to them.[13] By implication this suggested that the British troops would somehow assist in ejecting Mehmed Ali and his 12,000 Albanians from the country, together with the remaining small number of Turkish troops.

The expedition which sailed out of Messina numbered 5,672 troops and 242 officers.[14] As was not uncommon at this time, the troops had been allowed to bring their families. The army was, therefore, accompanied by 364 women and 323 children. General Fraser was an experienced and popular commander, 'a frank, straightforward and honourable gentleman of good plain sense', but he was also 'without the slightest knowledge of the higher branches of political or military science'.[15] His second in command was Major-General Patrick Wauchope, 'a brave and excellent officer within the narrow range of regimental duty, but unequal to greater things and therefore unable to supplement the defects of his chief'.[16]

Because of storms which separated nineteen of the thirty-three troop transports, and difficult landing conditions due to the surf, General Fraser was not able to disembark all his men and position them around Alexandria until 20 March. However, two days later, Admiral Duckworth's squadron arrived in Aboukir Bay from the Aegean to provide greater security for the operation.

So far, General Fraser had accomplished his mission with very small loss of life, and he now awaited the arrival of the large body of 'pro-British' Mamluks. His commander-in-chief in Sicily, General Henry Fox, had explicitly assured him of their presence before Fraser's departure. He was therefore considerably surprised when Major Missett, who had only recently learned of the death of al-Alfi Bey, informed the general of this unfortunate development. However, Missett assured him that messages had been sent to a number of other Mamluk beys who – so he claimed – had rallied to the British side.

A second piece of information conveyed to the General by Missett was of much greater concern: according to the Consul, there was very little food in Alexandria, indeed its inhabitants were on the verge of starvation. Unless certain steps were taken, for the foreseeable future the Army would have to live on whatever ships' biscuit and dried meat could be spared by the Navy.

Missett then outlined the steps that would have to be taken to avoid this crisis. The General was to send troops to occupy the town of Rosetta, about 64 km to the northeast, on the left bank of the Rosetta branch of the Nile, and to El Rahmaniya about 48 km down river. If this were accomplished, he would be able to obtain supplies of wheat from the former and cattle from the latter in quantities sufficient to feed both his army and the city's population for as long as required.

Fraser was now in a quandary. His orders were to restrict his operations to Alexandria and to move no further; but if Missett was correct – and Fraser had no reason to disbelieve him – it would soon become impossible to remain in possession of Alexandria without extending his operations much further afield.

Finally, the General made up his mind, and on 29 March he despatched a column to capture Rosetta consisting of 1,600 officers and men, commanded by Major-General Wauchope. The principal features of the terrain between Alexandria and Rosetta were three great lakes. From west to east these were Lake Mareotis, Lake Mahedia and Lake Edko, whose shallow waters merged into the Rosetta branch of the Nile just south of the town. Between these lakes and the sea was a narrow strip of land following the curve of Aboukir Bay until it broadened out at the small village of Edko, from where the land turned into desert stretching up to some hills overlooking Rosetta itself.

The little column advanced along the track between the lakes and the sea and across the desert, reaching the heights overlooking Rosetta the following day. The town appeared perfectly still, the gates were wide open and there was no sign of any defending troops. So Wauchope marched his men into the town, through its narrow streets and into the market place where his men were allowed to rest and consume their rations.

Meanwhile, Mehmed Ali had taken a strong contingent of his Albanians into Upper Egypt in pursuit of a large force of Mamluks; but he left his second-in-command, an Egyptian Arab named 'Umar Makram, in the

Delta with a mixed force of Albanians, Turks and local Arabs. Unbeknown to the British, on learning of the despatch of Wauchope's column, Makram had sent a part of his force into Rosetta where they distributed arms to the local population. At the same time the Muslim fighters were ordered to conceal themselves in the lattice-windowed upper rooms of the houses.

Only a short while after their arrival, the British troops were suddenly subjected to a fusillade of musketry from these concealed positions. Major-General Wauchope was shot through the head and his troops only managed to escape the ambush with great difficulty, losing three other officers and 181 men dead and carrying with them the wounded – nineteen other officers and 263 men.[17] Fortunately, they were not pursued as they withdrew from the town, or their losses might have been even greater. In celebration, Rosetta's defenders decapitated many of the British dead and despatched ninety of their heads to Cairo, where they were placed on spikes along the road from the upper-class district of Ezbekiya to the city centre.[18]

By now, Mehmed Ali had heard of the fighting at Rosetta. Having fought an indecisive action against Ibrahim Bey's Mamluks at Assiut, he came to an agreement with him. The combined force of Albanians and Mamluks then marched south on opposite sides of the Nile and reached Cairo on 13 April. At the same time Mehmed sent 4,000 Albanian infantry and 1,500 Turkish and Mamluk cavalry down the left bank of the Nile to reinforce Makram's Arab troops defending Rosetta.[19]

While Mehmed Ali was organising these counter-measures, Major Missett continued to believe his agents' reports that a large body of Mamluks were moving south to join the British. Consequently, Fraser decided to make another attempt to capture Rosetta. So, on 3 April a force of 2,500 men with eleven cannons and howitzers of various sizes, commanded by Brigadiers William Stewart and John Oswald, marched out of Alexandria along the same track taken by General Wauchope. In addition to the artillerymen the column consisted of the 20th Light Dragoons, the 1st Battalion of the 35th Regiment, the 2nd Battalion of the 78th (Highlanders) Regiment, De Roll's Regiment, a composite light infantry battalion made up of all the light companies in Fraser's army, and 200 seamen under the command of the captain of HMS *Tigre*.[20]

On 5 April reconnaissance showed that a party of Albanians had occupied a village named al-Hamad, about four miles southeast of Rosetta and lying on a neck of land between the Nile and Lake Edko. These were quickly driven off by 300 men of de Roll's Regiment who proceeded to occupy the village. Meanwhile Brigadier Stewart, who concluded that his force wasn't large enough to mount a proper siege of Rosetta, ordered an intense bombardment of the town.

Two letters from Brigadier Stewart to General Mackenzie Fraser dated 18 and 25 April 1807 give an account of the ensuing battle – the outcome of which Stewart describes with considerable understatement as being 'of a peculiar nature and the result has been peculiarly unfortunate'.[21]

In his first letter, from the 'Rosetta Lines', the brigadier reports how his bombardment of the town, although heavy, was having no impact. The defenders of Rosetta's walls showed no willingness to surrender.[22] Attempts to approach the town under a flag of truce had been fired on and the brigadier records that 'it was only by means of a great reward that a common Arab could be induced to be the bearer of any communication with such enemies'. This message to Rosetta's defenders contained Stewart's expectation that his troops were soon to be joined by a strong body of Mamluks. His letter to General Fraser then adds, rather pointedly, that this was after 'having been informed by you of the cooperation which was likely to exist between us and the Mamluk beys'. Stewart then goes on to say that he has heard nothing more of his message to the defenders of Rosetta and that he had 'reason to apprehend that the unfortunate Arab has been beheaded'.[23]

Stewart then reports that from 12 to 15 April, 'nothing extraordinary occurred', but once again notes that he is 'relying on the approach of the Mamluks'. At the end of the report Stewart repeats that 'our success will depend on the arrival of the Mamluks' and that in the meantime he had placed more troops in the village of al-Hamad which had become of greater value since 'our friends [i.e. the 'pro-British Mamluks'] are expected to approach it'.[24]

The second report from Stewart to General Fraser, dated 25 April, was written at the eastern approaches to Alexandria and therefore after the retreat of his column from Rosetta. It begins with yet another mention of his 'expectation of the junction with the Mamluks' which had 'chiefly induced me to persevere with the attack on Rosetta'. He goes on to give an account in some detail of this small but sorry episode in British military history.[25]

On 19 April strong reinforcements of Turkish cavalry arrived in the vicinity of al-Hamad, while the defenders of Rosetta had begun to make sorties from the town against Stewart's main position. Further British troops were detached to reinforce the position at al-Hamad. On the night of 20 April – by which time the brigadier was becoming increasingly worried about the security of this outpost – Stewart briefly visited it himself, leaving orders that it should be held stoutly if there were a fair chance of success. Otherwise these men should retreat towards the shores of Lake Edko to cover the flank of his own forces.

Yet as Stewart left al-Hamad at two o'clock in the morning of the 21st, he found the plain surrounding the village swarming with Turkish cavalry, from which he escaped only through the speed of his horse. Not long afterwards information reached him that a large fleet of native boats were coming down the Nile loaded with enemy reinforcements. He immediately ordered a general retreat across the desert plain after destroying his heavy guns and forming his men into squares as protection against the enemy cavalry. But 'to my surprise, not an individual from the al-Hamad detachment joined us in this march nor could firing be heard in that direction'.

By the time the main body of the column reached the promontory on which sits the Aboukir castle, Stewart had received 'no certain intelligence ... respecting the fate of the detachment [at al-Hamad]'. In fact, the thirty-six officers and 780 men at al-Hamad had been completely overwhelmed by the combined army of Albanians and Turks, losing twelve officers and 280 men killed and the remainder taken prisoner.[26] Those who survived their wounds were subsequently taken to Cairo, where Mehmed Ali had them march past the severed heads of their comrades who had fallen in the first attempt to take Rosetta.

After bringing the remnants of the second attempt on Rosetta into Alexandria, and, having lost a third of his men, General Fraser now found himself besieged by the Albanian and Turkish troops under Mehmed Ali's command. He remained extremely anxious about the fate of the prisoners whom he feared would be sold into slavery. However, he soon received news that Mehmed Ali, advised by the new French consul-general, Bernardino Drovetti,* had decided that the approximately 500 British prisoners in his

---

* Bernardino Drovetti (1776–1852) is best known as the highly successful but notoriously

hands would be well treated as prisoners of war. He had apparently realised that they were more use to him as a bargaining chip than being sold off as slaves.

Fraser was less pleased with a remarkable admission by Consul Missett that he had now discovered that the city was not, after all, on the verge of starvation. In fact, ample supplies of rice had been found, and quantities of wheat and meat could be purchased from the local Arabs. Given that Missett had also been the source of the spurious tale of the 'pro-British' Mamluks eagerly awaiting the British arrival, it is hardly surprising that the revelation about the true state of Alexandria's food supplies – in the very restrained words of the historian Sir John Fortescue – 'led to unpleasant passages between Missett and Fraser'.[27]

Fortunately, by the end of May 1807, the Alexandria garrison had received victualling ships from Malta together with two battalions of infantry reinforcements. Now General Fraser was feeling a good deal more relaxed. He had also entered into discussions with Mehmed Ali aimed at recovering the prisoners.

In Britain, the ineffective coalition government of Lord Grenville had been replaced on 31 March 1807 by a Tory administration in which the fiercely anti-French but experienced Viscount Castlereagh was appointed Secretary of State for War. A few months later, the geopolitical situation in Europe underwent a dramatic transformation. On 14 June Napoleon attacked the Russians at Friedland near present-day Kaliningrad, decisively defeating them. The following month, on 7 July, Napoleon and Tsar Alexander made peace in the Treaty of Tilsit. This allowed Russia to refocus its war effort on defeating the Ottomans; but it also meant that Britain no longer had any military or diplomatic obligations towards Russia. Hence its own war with the Ottoman Empire in support of the Tsar had become pointless. At the same time France's peace with Russia meant that its troops were released to present a greater threat to Britain and its allies in the Mediterranean.

Castlereagh realised that military manpower shortages meant that retaining Alexandria would force Britain to abandon Sicily. Since the latter was regarded as being both politically more important and most at danger

---

unscrupulous excavator and seller of Egyptian antiquities. His work greatly contributed to the rapid growth of European interest in Ancient Egypt

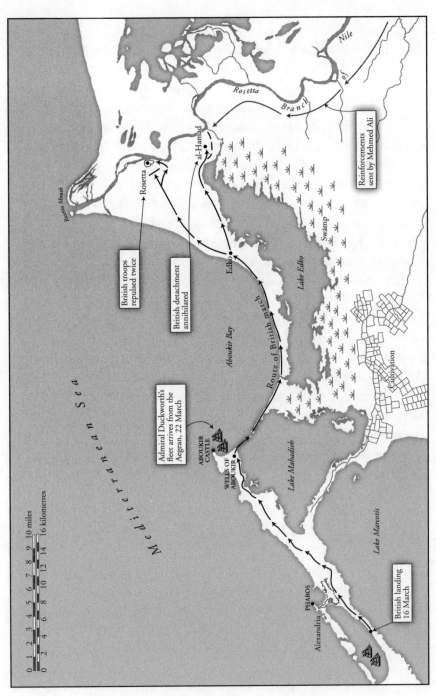

Nile

Rosetta

Branch

Reinforcements sent by Mehmed Ali

al-Hamad

Rosetta

Rosetta Mouth

British troops repulsed twice

British detachment annihilated

Edko

Swamp

Lake Edko

Aboukir Bay

Route of British march

Mediterranean Sea

Admiral Duckworth's fleet arrives from the Aegean, 22 March

Cultivation

ABOUKIR CASTLE

WELLS OF ABOUKIR

Lake Mahadieh

0 1 2 3 4 5 6 7 8 9 10 miles
0 2 4 6 8 10 12 14 16 kilometres

Lake Mareotis

PHAROS

British landing 16 March

Alexandria

THE FAILED BRITISH EXPEDITION TO ALEXANDRIA 1807:
TERRAIN AND TROOP MOVEMENTS

from French attack, on 3 September 1807, General Fraser was informed that his troops were to be withdrawn from Egypt, subject to satisfactory negotiations with Mehmed Ali for the release of the British prisoners. In fact, the vast majority of these, who had been held in the Citadel, had already been freed, except for around fifty who had been seized and enslaved by Mamluks.

These unfortunate individuals have disappeared from history – except one. Seven years after the military disaster at the tiny village of al-Hamad, the great Swiss explorer Jean Louis Burckhardt (1784–1817) acquired a Muslim slave named Osman. Exactly when and how he acquired him is uncertain, but Burckhardt must have been surprised – to say the least – when Osman spoke to him in a broad highland Scottish.

Burckhardt's new acquisition turned out to be a young man named Donald Donald. He had been a young drummer boy, captured by a Mamluk at al-Hamad and offered execution or conversion to Islam (including circumcision). Donald was obviously a sensible boy and he chose the latter. He was later acquired as a slave by Mehmed Ali, became fluent in Arabic, married a girl of Mehmed's harem and fought with him against the Wahhabis of Arabia. After his sale to Burckhardt he became his loyal servant and friend during his adventurous journeys; and when Burckhardt returned to Cairo, Osman was freed and became a permanent member of the great explorer's household, until Burckhardt died of dysentery on 15 October 1817. It was Osman who supervised Burckhardt's funeral which, according to the explorer's own wishes, was according to the Islamic rite. Osman Donald Donald subsequently became the principal dragoman (translator) attached to the British Consulate in Cairo, a position he held until his own death.[28]

After the departure of the British from Egypt, on 16 April, Mehmed Ali staged a triumphal entry into Alexandria to the accompaniment of celebratory artillery salutes. By 19 September the troops of the disastrous Alexandria expedition, including most of the surviving prisoners, were all returned to Sicily. It was not until 5 January 1809 that peace between Britain and the Ottoman Empire was finally agreed with the Treaty of the Dardanelles. The treaty restored various British commercial and legal privileges within the Ottoman Empire, and Britain committed itself to protecting the Empire against any threat from the French. However, the most important clause was agreement on the principle that no warships of any power should enter the Turkish Straits while the Ottoman Empire was at peace.

Despite the debacle in Egypt, by the end of the Napoleonic Wars the foundations of a British maritime empire in the Mediterranean had been laid. In reality, Britain's war with the Ottomans had been an aberration: for all except those twenty-two months of hostilities, the years spanning the French Revolutionary and Napoleonic Wars, 1793–1815, had been years of alliance between successive British governments and the Porte. On the back of Britain's great naval victories at Aboukir Bay and Cape Trafalgar, Britain had driven the French out of the Mediterranean; it had retained its strategically important bases at Gibraltar and Malta; by removing the 17,000 troops which had been tied down in Sicily it had rid itself of its troublesome military commitment to its despised and devious 'ally', the Kingdom of Naples; and it had gained a new base in the Ionian Islands where first Zante, and then Cephalonia and the remainder of the smaller islands, were captured from the French in 1809. Corfu and its formidable fortress finally surrendered at the general peace of 1815, and on 5 November 1815, all the Ionian Islands passed by treaty under British control as a 'protectorate'.[29]

Commercial supremacy followed in the wake of naval supremacy. The Revolutionary and Napoleonic wars destroyed the eighteenth-century status quo whereby France had held a near-monopoly of trading rights in the Levant. Malta in particular benefited. In 1806, there were only twenty British businesses on the island; by 1811 there were sixty and in that mere five years the value of merchandise shipped from Britain to Malta multiplied twentyfold.[30] As a result of Napoleon's inability to force his sanctions against British goods upon the Ottoman Empire, 'it was largely as a vent into Turkey and back into Europe through many circuitous but profitable channels that a new Mediterranean emporium for British industrial output took shape'.[31]

French trade with the eastern Mediterranean did not entirely collapse, but it seriously declined. While French exports to the Levant had reached an average annual value of £1,280,000 in the years before 1791, by 1816–17 they had fallen to £440,000.* British exports continued to increase rapidly after

---

*   Converted at 25 francs = £1 sterling.

the end of the Napoleonic Wars. In 1814 they were valued at £153,903 and by 1815–19 had reached an annual average of £460,661, overtaking France, and rising to £566,315 for the years 1820–24. Approximately three-quarters of the value of British exports to the Levant in these years was contributed by cotton cloths, which were lighter, cheaper and more brightly coloured than those of their competitors and found a ready market in the Islamic lands of the Mediterranean.[32]

At the same time, rapidly expanding trade between Britain and Egypt erased any lingering hostility arising from the events of 1807. In 1810 Mehmed Ali welcomed the re-establishment of a British consulate in Alexandria, and Egypt became the major source of wheat exports to the British outposts in the Mediterranean. Britain's own exports to Egypt also increased rapidly – such that, by 1812, Egyptian warehouses were said to be 'stuffed with British goods'. By the 1820s, Egypt's exports to Britain included large quantities of high-value long-staple raw cotton.* In 1821–25, the average annual exports of Egyptian cotton amounted to 124,252 *cantar*s;† by 1835–39, they had reached 228,939.[33] Most of this was fed into the new British factories whose output of cotton manufactures was beginning to find overseas markets not only throughout the Mediterranean, but the whole world. But what Britain's rulers ignored was that the wealth flowing into Egypt from its cotton exports would help Mehmed Ali consolidate his rule over Egypt: and with continuing French support Mehmed Ali would come to pose a serious threat to Britain's strategic interests in the eastern Mediterranean.

---

*   Long-staple cotton, a chance discovery of which was found in a Cairo garden, is cotton with fibres of 1.75 inches: before 1820 Egyptian cotton was of short or medium staple. See Owen (2009, p. 66n).

†   A *cantar* was approximately 94 lb in weight.

PART TWO
C. 1815 - C. 1870

We maintain the integrity and independence of Turkey not for the love and affection for the Turks, but because we prefer the existing state of things there to any other state of things which at present would be humanly possible, and because the interest political and commercial of England and Europe would be dangerously injured by the destruction of that integrity and independence.

LORD PALMERSTON
(1853)

CHAPTER 12

The Beginning of the End for the Ottoman Regencies

The Congress of Vienna took place between September 1814 and June 1815. It was attended by the British foreign minister Viscount Castlereagh, Prince Klemens von Metternich, foreign minister of the Austrian Empire, the Tsar Alexander I of Russia, the Chancellor of Prussia and Charles-Maurice Talleyrand, formerly Napoleon's foreign minister, but now the representative of the recently installed royalist government of Louis XVIII. It would later be joined by representatives of most of the other European states in a series of additional conferences and treaties lasting until 1822. But the Ottoman Empire – which was at least partly European in its geographical dimensions, was equally conservative, and had generally supported the anti-French coalition in the Napoleonic wars – was excluded. Officially, this was because it wouldn't agree to make territorial concessions to Russia, but in reality it was because the members making up the 'Concert' – the power balance that evolved from the Congress – could not contemplate a Muslim member of their 'European' and 'Christian' club.

The main agreements of the 1815 Congress and the diplomatic process of the Concert were intended to establish the mechanisms which would prevent any future Europe-wide war; to return the frontiers of the old European empires to their pre-revolutionary state; and to crush any liberal, revolutionary or republican movements which might threaten the status quo (movements which the Congress's deeply conservative participants believed were the main cause of the calamity they had experienced over the preceding twenty-two years). They also resolved to eliminate the 'white slavery' of the Muslim North African corsairs. The British Parliament resisted the 'anti-liberal' part of the Concert and gradually Britain fell away from supporting European interventions to crush nationalist and liberal movements. Nevertheless, all successive British governments held firm to the principal objective of the Vienna Congress – to prevent the re-occurrence of another general, European-wide war.

We have seen in the Introduction how Britain perceived that the efficient extraction of revenue for India was vital to it economic prosperity. Consequently, 'The future security of India required British control of the Mediterranean and political domination of the Ottoman Empire whose territories now became a vast *glacis* defending India's western frontiers.'[1]

To men like Britain's Foreign Secretary Lord Palmerston (1774–1865) the geo-strategic policy which followed was clear: 'domination of the Ottoman Empire' meant maintaining its territorial integrity: but on the understanding that the Empire would do Britain's bidding. The objective – although this was never really achieved – was that the Ottomans should become part of Britain's 'informal empire'.[2] In return for protection by the Royal Navy, the Ottomans would be 'encouraged' to follow the advice of Britain's powerful ambassadors in Istanbul and its numerous consular agents now installed throughout most of the Ottoman Empire. Of special importance were the requirements of Britain's expanding textile exports and therefore the incorporation of the Ottoman Empire into its growing network of free trade.

For the time being therefore, Britain had little interest in acquiring any further possessions in the Mediterranean other those it already held; but it did have two crucial *defensive* strategic objectives, both of which focused on the protection of the overland route to India. First, to shore up British India's defensive 'glacis', the Ottoman state – in particular by countering any Russian attempt to seize the Turkish Straits, a move which could bring a Russian fleet into the Mediterranean. And second, to block any French advance eastwards along the North African coast and the re-establishment of French power in Egypt, which would also threaten the overland route.

In 1957, Henry Kissinger, later to become US Secretary of State for Presidents Nixon and Ford, published an influential book, *A World Restored*,[3] in which he characteristically attacked the 'liberal' nineteenth-century critics of the Congress of Vienna and defended, at least implicitly, its reactionary clauses. Some historians had called the Congress a failure because it didn't prevent some future wars such as the Crimean War (1853–56), the German-Danish War (1864), the Austro-Prussian War (1866), and the Franco-Prussian War (1870–71). But as Kissinger himself pointed out, these were disputes which could be mediated by the neutral members of the Concert without them spreading to Europe as a whole; to which he might have added that the casualties involved were tiny in comparison with the Napoleonic wars, and largely limited to the military.

So, for Kissinger, the Congress of Vienna and what followed was a success. 'What is surprising about it is not how imperfect was the settlement that emerged, but how sane, how balanced ... a period of peace lasting almost a hundred years.'⁴ But that hundred years of relative 'stability' pertained only to Europe.

What Kissinger ignored was that, while the Congress of Vienna may arguably have produced 'a period of peace and stability' in Christian Europe from 1815 to 1914, it also led to a new and lengthy era of European expansionism – one which would deny 'peace and stability' to the inhabitants of the territories south and east of the new Christian Europe. To a large extent the frontiers of those great powers were now largely firmly established *within Europe*; so their aristocratic rulers, financiers, merchants and unemployed military switched their attentions elsewhere. And what was more convenient than to look to the Ottoman Empire and especially its semi-independent 'regencies', along the Mediterranean's southern coast, as well as to the 'empire' of Alaouite Morocco? Here lay an old Islamic world which was becoming increasingly vulnerable to the better-organised, better-financed and better-armed states that had emerged out of the wars between France and its enemies between 1793 and 1815.

*

Sixteenth February 1804, around 7 p.m. Under the dim light of a waxing crescent moon, a small open-decked lateen-rigged vessel with a long protruding prow edges its way along the channel between the reefs which guard the entrance to Regency of Tripoli's harbour. By the time the ship has passed through this channel, night has fallen. And when a guard boat approaches and hails the stranger, only the figure of its Maltese-dressed pilot can be seen. In the lingua franca of the coast, the pilot replies that his vessel has come from Malta to collect a cargo of bullocks. Unsuspicious, the guards let the 'Maltese' vessel pass and it creeps into the harbour, approaching a heavy frigate anchored within the harbour walls. Another guard boat comes alongside and the pilot is told to sheer away from the frigate; but having explained that he has lost his anchor during bad weather he is given permission to tie up to the frigate's hull.[5]

In fact, the small 'Maltese' ship is actually the USS *Intrepid*, formerly the Turkish ketch *Mastico*, found to be carrying troops from Tripoli and captured by the Americans on 23 December 1803. The *Mastico* had previously taken part in a successful attack on the 36-gun US frigate *Philadelphia* – the very same frigate that is now being held captive in Tripoli's harbour.

Twenty-seven years earlier the Moroccan Sultan Sidi Muhammad bin 'Abdallah had been the first head of state to recognise the newly independent United States of America, and in 1786 a 'Treaty of Peace and Friendship' between the two countries had allowed US merchant ships to pass through the Straits of Gibraltar and break into the European-dominated Mediterranean trade without attack by Moroccan corsairs. But now that lucrative trade was threatened by the Regency of Tripoli. The *Philadelphia* had been blockading Tripoli's harbour in response to the declaration of war against the US by Tripoli's Paşa, Yusuf Karamanli, in May 1801 and the capture of a number of American merchant ships. Yusuf had been demanding a steep increase in the tribute payments originally agreed in the first peace treaty between his state and the US in 1796. But by now the Americans had constructed a force of heavy frigates capable of protecting their merchantmen in the Mediterranean, and they were no longer willing to submit to extortionate 'peace treaty' demands by the regencies' rulers.

Philadelphia had been part of an American squadron of three frigates and a brig sent out to deal with the Tripolitanian corsairs. On 31 October 1803 it had been chasing a vessel running for Tripoli's harbour when it grounded on one of its hidden reefs. After enemy gunboats bombarded its masts and rigging for four hours from positions to which the *Philadelphia* could not reply, its captain was forced to scuttle the ship and go into captivity along with his 304 crew. To make matters worse, the weather had later permitted the Tripolitanians to float the American frigate off the reef and had repaired its damaged hull. Such a powerful warship would have made a dangerous addition to Tripoli's corsair fleet.

But now the Americans are about to respond in what Britain's Admiral Horatio Nelson would describe as 'the most bold and daring act of the age'.

The *Intrepid*, commanded by the twenty-five-year-old Lieutenant Stephen Decatur and filled with sixty American sailors and marines armed with cutlasses and boarding pikes, are crouching beneath the vessel's makeshift deck awaiting Decatur's orders. At the command 'Board!' they swarm up the gunwales of the frigate, surprising the scratch crew on board and killing them or chasing them over the side.

Decatur's original orders from Commodore Edward Preble, who was based at Syracuse in Sicily, were to attempt a 'cutting-out' operation – to take control of the frigate and tow it out of the harbour into the bay assisted by the boats of the sixteen-gun brig USS *Siren*, which was waiting in support further out. But finding this impossible Decatur followed Preble's back-up plan and set fire to the frigate, after which he and his men escaped into the bay. Then, after seeing the *Philadelphia* completely aflame – the conflagration fuelled by exploding gunpowder – they sailed-off to Syracuse and a heroes' welcome.[6]

Decatur's splendid action was followed by a further act of heroism by Decatur during a subsequent attack on Tripoli by Commodore Preble's entire squadron in August 1804. But this and two other attacks on the city by the American squadron had only mediocre results, and Tripolitanian gunboats retaliated in spite of suffering losses. Consequently, the Americans resorted to a political-military diversion.

Lieutenant William Eaton, the former American consul in Tunis, had for some time been urging American support for Hamet Karamanli, Yusuf's brother, who had been overthrown by Yusuf in 1795 and forced to take refuge in Egypt. Eaton recruited a small army in Alexandria and gave himself the title of 'General and Commander'. Assisted by Lieutenant Presley O'Bannon of the US Marine Corps and a handful of marines, and accompanied by Hamet, he marched his little force across 600 miles of desert and on 27 April 1805 he captured the coastal town of Derna. Although Yusuf's troops mounted counter-attacks on the town, they were driven off.

Now Eaton threatened to march on to Tripoli itself. But the Paşa had tired of the continuing and costly struggle with the Americans, and on 10 June 1805 he signed a peace treaty with the US Consul-General for North Africa, whereby hostilities ended. All American prisoners in Tripoli were released and Yusuf received the original cash payment only.

The US-Tripoli 'Barbary War' of 1801–05* came in response to a general upsurge in activity by the corsairs of the three regencies, which had begun in 1793. The outbreak of the great struggle between the French Republic and its enemies, and the lengthy war for supremacy between Napoleon and the rest of Europe, shattered the maritime status quo in the whole Mediterranean region.

Taking advantage of France's protracted commercial decline during the war with Britain, the merchants of smaller nations, both within and outside the Mediterranean, saw the chance of grabbing a share of the profitable opportunities previously denied them by the overwhelming French presence. They were mainly the north European countries – the Netherlands, Denmark, Sweden, the Hanseatic city-states, Bremen, Lübeck and Hamburg – but also the young United States of America. These states had previously held only a small share of Mediterranean trade. Now they believed great commercial opportunities had opened up for them.

However, from the perspective of the Barbary regencies the great European war opened up quite different opportunities. In the years before the outbreak of war the ships of their corsair fleets had been mainly languishing in dock; but now came the opportunity of preying on these relatively weak new entrants into Mediterranean trade.

The corsairs were greatly assisted by the traditional short-sightedness of the major European states (and the Americans) – a short-sightedness based on the cynical assumption that providing assistance to the Barbary states' shipping industries would be most likely to harm their smaller European commercial rivals. Between 1785 and 1804 Spain, France, Britain and the US all supplied the regencies with modern warships and even the smaller European powers sold them naval supplies. As one historian concluded, a typical clash with corsairs in the Mediterranean was one where 'Barbary frigates and xebecs chased Danish ships with Dutch canvas and fired Swedish cannons with Venetian powder at Neapolitan merchant ships.'[7]

---

* The term 'Barbary' was the European colloquial word for the geographical term 'Maghreb' (of Arabic origin). It derives from the original predominance of the Berber people inhabiting large parts of North Africa from Libya to Morocco. During the eighteenth century the term became commonly attached to other words as in 'Barbary Coast' and 'Barbary corsairs'.

Two other developments helped the corsairs. First, the capture of Malta by the French in 1798, and its permanent seizure by the British in 1801, put an end to the Maltese Christian corsairs who had posed a major threat to the Muslim vessels engaged in the same profession. Second, as a result of the onslaught of the French armies and the treaties which followed their victories, some of the old states of Christian Europe fell under the control of different national rulers. This gave the corsairs the opportunity to play fast and loose with the customary 'passport' system. For example, although Venice became Austrian territory at the peace of Campo Formio in 1797, Venetian ships now flying the Austrian flag were still seized by corsairs, even though Austria was at peace with the regencies, since the corsairs claimed that they had not been officially notified of the transfer of sovereignty.

Profitable though it could certainly be, just *how* profitable was corsair activity, and what contribution did it make to the economies of the regency states? First it is important to note how variable this income was. Corsairing was a gamble and the risks considerable. The corsair's *reis* (captain) might do well and seize a rich merchant ship loaded with valuable cargo and eminently ransomable passengers; he would return to port a hero and a very rich man, as would each member of his crew, albeit in lesser degree. On the other hand, another might fail to find a single merchant vessel; or if he did, it might be one whose captain held a 'passport' ensuring it was inviolable as the result of a recently signed peace treaty. Then again, the prize might simply be of small value; or if it wasn't and its riches were a cornucopia of opulence, the corsair might lose his prize in a storm or suffer shipwreck. And there was also the possibility of the corsair vessel being captured by a more powerful European man-of-war, although the chances of this happening diminished significantly during the wars of 1793–1815.

Some figures available for Algiers illustrate the great variability, from year to year, in the value of the prizes seized. In 1801 just five Algerian corsairs were at sea and they captured only four prizes, a total value of 333,853 francs. Therefore the value per corsair ship averaged 66,771 francs. By 1805 Algiers's corsair fleet had risen to ten ships and they captured eight prizes; however, their total worth was only 133,159 francs and the value obtained per corsair ship was only 13,316 francs.[8]

Given this great variability in annual prize money its contribution to both a regency's state apparatus, and its economy as a whole, must also have fluctuated wildly. In Algiers, its contribution to the Dey's income ranged between a maximum of 26 per cent during the years 1798–99 to a minimum of five per cent in the period 1804–10.[9] Corsairing may have provided a useful bonus for the regency's ruler, useful, among other things, for providing cash to his restive soldiery. But income from corsairing was far less important to the head of state than rents extracted from the peasants who worked his estates, or the 'presents' obtained as part of treaty settlements with foreign powers.

However, piracy was not the only maritime activity practised by the 'Barbary states'. Even while corsairing was in full spate, normal commercial relations between the regencies and those Christian states with whom they had concluded peace treaties had always continued. However, the regencies' trade was almost always carried by French shipping.

But now war and the British blockade of French ports meant the virtual disappearance of French merchant shipping from the Mediterranean. The opportunities which this offered were quickly seized by the merchants and ship owners of the regencies, as well as Morocco. The switch from corsairing to merchant shipping was most noticeable after the short-lived Peace of Amiens. In 1802, out of seventy-three ships delivering cargos from the regencies to Marseilles, thirty-one were flying the French flag and only two from the regencies. But by 1806 the French ships had disappeared altogether while the regencies' ships had increased to thirteen.

The replacement of European ships by those of the regencies during the Napoleonic wars must have been a serious culture shock for the merchants and sea captains of Marseilles. The most striking example of this trend occurred on 5 November 1809. The arrival of a single ship passing through the British blockade was always the talk of the town, but on this particular November morning it was not a single ship but a convoy of six that hove into view. Even more astounding to the merchants, seamen and ordinary citizens of Marseilles was the fact that the ships in question were all flying the blue-, red- and green-striped flag of Tunis. The first of these ships was the former corsair *Gamba*, captained by Reis Muhammad Morali. It was a large xebec armed with thirty-eight guns and a crew of 200, carrying a cargo of barilla, a type of soda used for making soap. The remaining five ships carried more barilla, pistachios, osier, wool, sponges, soap and olive oil, and the final ship to enter Marseilles carried twenty-one passengers including the French Consul in Tunis and his family.

The rise in merchant shipping is also illustrated in the list of Muslim North African vessels arriving at the British-controlled port of Malta. In 1801, twenty such vessels called in at the port of which nine were corsairs and five were merchantmen. By 1806 another twenty ships from the Maghreb arrived, but seventeen of these were merchantmen and only three corsairs. By 1809, the year in which the maximum number of North African-flagged vessels docked at Malta – eighty ships in total – seventy-five (94 per cent) were merchant ships and only five were corsairs.[10]

Although corsair attacks still continued during the Napoleonic wars, for just a few years it looked as though the regencies might be able to turn away from the infamous activity they had practised for over three centuries; but it was not to be. The Europeans – even the French who, for a time, had benefited from the North African blockade-runners – were unwilling to receive the Muslim ships and their captains back into the fold of normal commercial relations. In spite of the contribution the visiting North African ships made to France's wartime economy, French port officials and customs officers at Marseille and Livorno were not averse to swindling and mistreating the captains and crews. They often sequestered their goods, imposed vexatious delays and charged exorbitant port charges, much to the disgust of the French consuls in North Africa who bitterly complained of 'this gratuitous harshness which in no way belongs to the Emperor's policy'.[11]

Moreover, when the war in the Mediterranean ended in 1814, with Napoleon imprisoned on Elba, the obstacles in the way of North African commercial shipping became so great that this trade came to an abrupt end. Between 1805 and 1807 nearly half the ships arriving at Marseilles were from North African ports; between 1811 and 1813, the proportion increased to nearly two-thirds; but between 1814 and 1816 and the years thereafter, not a single North African ship entered the port. And as North African commercial shipping was frozen out of Mediterranean trade, the Muslim merchants who supplied the goods and were often the ship owners also suffered, and much of their business was taken over by Europeans.

In reaction to the hostile attitude which the Europeans displayed towards their commercial trading activities, the regencies returned to corsairing; and by now their fleets contained much larger and heavier-gunned ships than before the French wars had begun. Tunisian ships embarking on corsair campaigns in 1812 and 1813 totalled only thirteen; but in the single year 1815 this figure increased to forty-one. Over the same interval, the number of Tripolitanian corsair campaigns increased from nineteen to fifty-three.

However, by now the attitude of the major European powers towards corsairing had changed. Their rulers who met at the Congress of Vienna were no longer willing to accept these activities. They had finally realised that the 'beggar-my-neighbour' treaties previously signed with the deys, beys and paşas were in no one's interest.

Nevertheless, it was the Americans who struck the first blow. After their war with Britain ended* their heavy frigates were free to re-enter the Mediterranean. Faced with a demand for an increased 'gift' and a number of attacks on American shipping, on 23 February 1815 the US declared war on Algiers. A squadron commanded by the redoubtable Stephen Decatur discovered an Algerian squadron of three frigates and several smaller vessels, commanded by the notorious corsair chief Reis Hamidou, cruising off the Spanish coast near Malaga. In the action that followed Hamidou's own ship was attacked by the American frigates *Constellation* and *Guerrière* and forced to surrender, with the loss of thirty dead, including Hamidou. After another Algerian warship was captured, Decatur sailed into Algiers and compelled the Dey to sign a new treaty abolishing any tribute payment and arranging an exchange of prisoners.

The Americans' peace treaty with Algiers was the last of those bilateral arrangements which had been customary in relations between the regencies and the European states during the eighteenth century. From now on, the European powers were resolved on a combined approach towards those small but troublesome North African Muslim states. However, for the time being the Europeans looked to Britain as the major naval power in the region capable of bringing about a comprehensive solution to the Barbary corsair problem. Britain had been embarrassed by the Americans' recent military success against the Algerian corsairs, and the Royal Navy was still

---

* The war of 1812 to 1814: it was caused largely by the Royal Navy's practice of stopping American merchant ships and seizing American sailors to help man British warships. The Americans failed in their invasion of Canada and the British lost the Battle of New Orleans.

smarting after its defeats in a number of frigate-to-frigate engagements during the recent war with the US. The Royal Navy was therefore more than happy to take upon itself the task of eliminating the threat posed by the corsairs, and thus restoring the Navy's honour.

The Royal Navy's first attempt to put an end to the corsairing and slaving activities of the regencies was a rather feeble affair. In September 1815 the fifty-eight-year-old veteran of the French wars Admiral Edward Pellew, recently ennobled as Lord Exmouth, was given secret orders to take a fleet of five battleships and seven frigates and sloops into the Mediterranean and visit Algiers, Tunis and Tripoli. There, he was to impose new peace treaties upon them which would achieve the Europeans' objectives. The precise details of his instructions are unknown and it seems he was allowed considerable freedom of action with regard to the specific demands and chastisements he should make upon the regencies' rulers. Exmouth sailed for Algiers on 4 March 1816, arriving in the Bay of Algiers on 1 April.

Exmouth was no skilled negotiator, and in addition he appears to have been charmed by a very courteous reception from the then-incumbent dey, 'Umar bin Muhammad. The only concession Exmouth extracted was that the Dey agreed to free 357 out of 1,000 Sicilian slaves, albeit at the exorbitant price of 1,000 dollars per head. But no general agreement to cease enslaving corsairs' captives was reached.[12] After these very modest achievements Exmouth sailed on to Tunis and Tripoli where negotiations achieved better results. Both regencies agreed to end enslavement and most of the existing slaves were redeemed at a much lower price than in Algiers.

Setting sail for home, Exmouth received news of his government's extreme displeasure at the meagre results of his visit to Algiers. Exmouth therefore felt obliged to return to the Regency to make some tougher demands on the Dey. But once again the Admiral allowed himself to be persuaded of 'Umar's good intentions. The Dey would comply with Exmouth's demands, he assured him, but it would take time, it needed the permission of the sultan in İstanbul (completely false), and he would have to persuade his divan, etc.

That the Dey 'Umar was able to exercise some considerable degree of charm over Lord Exmouth was attested by the sympathetic description of him by William Shaler, the US's consul in Algiers from 1815 to 1828. According to Shaler:

His manner was always dignified, sometimes cordial and friendly, and he was never known to lose the equilibrium of his temper on any occasion ... Omar was a man of strong natural good sense, quick perception and great dignity of character ... in private life he is said to have been of exemplary moderation and strict moral values according to the rules of the faith which he professed. ... after he rose to power he was noted for several acts of friendship and gratitude and I have not heard him accused of any instance of private injustice.

In the belief that he had accomplished his mission to the best of his ability, Exmouth set sail, returning to Britain on 3 June 1816. But to his evident surprise and discomfort, on his return he was subjected to intense criticism in the British press. It was widely agreed that he had been fooled by the rulers of the regencies. He was also accused of paying excessive amounts to redeem only a few of their enslaved prisoners. To make matters worse for the Admiral, comparisons were made with the more virile approach of the Americans.

The government decided that the fleet would have to return to Algiers yet again; and if the Dey refused to agree to abandon Christian slavery once and for all, the Navy must bombard the city into submission. Nothing less would silence the attacks from both their own supporters in Parliament and the opposition. Therefore, on 1 July 1816, Lord Exmouth was appointed to command yet another expedition to Algiers. He was to demand the release of the British Consul, his family and twenty officers and men of the Royal Navy corvette *Prometheus*, who had been seized and imprisoned by the Algerians on 31 July when making a failed attempt to smuggle the consul's family out of the city. He was also ordered to demand the release of all Christian slaves being held in the Regency, to repay the money previously paid for the small number of slaves redeemed during Exmouth's first visit to Algiers, and to require the Dey to sign a treaty renouncing all future enslavement of Christians. The Dey would be given an hour to accept these conditions or the British fleet would begin to bombard his city.

Exmouth may have been considerably out of his depth when trying to negotiate with the rulers of the regencies: diplomacy was not his forte; but he was a brave and experienced naval commander and he began to make meticulous plans to deal with the many hazards his expedition would face.

His chief problem was the one facing all naval officers ordered to attack fortified positions on land. It was a well-established precept of naval operations that in a gun battle between a fleet at sea and a heavily fortified position on land, the advantage generally lay with the land-based fortifications. The bombarding ships were protected only by wood – at best oak, but often weaker woods like pine – while the gun positions on land would normally be situated in stone embrasures. In addition, while the land batteries were positioned on a firm, absolutely static base, the guns of the attacking ships would be subjected to the weather and the natural movements of the sea which could adversely affect their aim. The problem could be considerably alleviated by bringing the attacking ships in as close as possible to the shore batteries, although this carried its own risks if not carried out surreptitiously.

On 28 July 1816, Exmouth's fleet weighed anchor at Plymouth and sailed to Gibraltar. The flotilla he had assembled consisted of two three-decker battleships, the 104-gun HMS *Queen Charlotte*, and the ninety-eight-gun HMS *Impregnable*, three two-decker battleships each with seventy-four guns, three heavy frigates with between fifty and fifty-eight guns, and twelve smaller vessels. The principal weapons of the battleships and heavy frigates were 24-pounder cannons with smaller vessels carrying 18- or 12-pounder guns. However, all the ships also carried 32- or 42-pounder carronades, short-barrelled guns with a very heavy projectile which could pulverise the enemy at short distance. The sailors aptly called them 'smashers'. In addition, the planned bombardment by the warships was to be supplemented by an attack from specially strengthened gunboats carrying a new 'terror weapon' – the Congreve rocket – which could fire a 32-pounder explosive shell a maximum curved distance of about two miles. The rockets were not terribly accurate, but fired in large numbers they could wreak havoc among the shipping which might try to escape Algiers's harbour, or the gunboats which might try to come out and attack the British warships.

At Gibraltar the British fleet was reinforced by a Dutch squadron of five frigates and a corvette which had recently arrived in the port. And on 27 August the combined fleets arrived off Algiers. Exmouth sent his ultimatum to the Dey. But after what seemed deliberately lengthy prevarication on the part of the Dey, and with no satisfactory answer received, at 2.50 p.m.

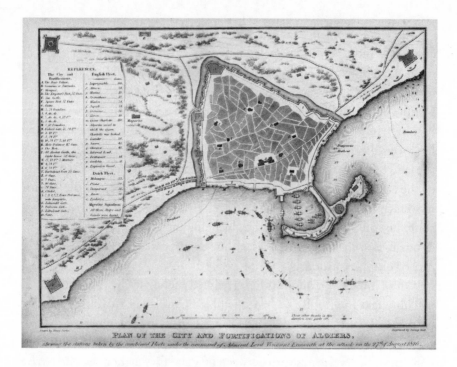

REFERENCES.

PLAN OF THE CITY AND FORTIFICATIONS OF ALGIERS,
showing the stations taken by the combined Fleets under the command of Admiral Lord Viscount Exmouth at the attack on the 27th of August 1816.

Diagram of the Bombardment of Algiers by the British and Dutch fleet, 1816

Exmouth's flagship, *Queen Charlotte* – which had meanwhile edged to within fifty metres from the mole of Algiers harbour – opened fire. His other ships followed suit, and a tremendous weight of shot from 24-pounder carronades and 18-pounder long guns smashed into the Algerian gun emplacements.

The bombardment immediately became general, with battleships and frigates firing broadside after broadside into their allotted targets. At the same time Exmouth's heavily armed gunboats and barges launched hundreds of mortar shells and rockets into the city and the Algerian shipping anchored closely together in the harbour. But in spite of the ferocity of the initial bombardment and the terrible destruction unleashed by the fleet, many of the Algerians managed to man their guns and return fire from the gun emplacements which had escaped the first onslaught. The Dey himself came out on the battlements, waving his scimitar in defiance and urging his men to keep up the fight.

Both sides bombarded each other ferociously and, as the afternoon wore on, at 4.30 p.m. the British battleship *Impregnable* was hit by a plunging mortar shell which burst within her main gun deck, killing and wounding 150 men and officers. Then, as night fell, a massive hail of Congreve rockets hit the shipping in the harbour and within minutes all the Algerian vessels were ablaze. For a time the relentless bombardment and counter-fire continued. It was as though 'two bare-knuckle prize-fighters ... had fought themselves to a standstill: they had exhausted their strength and were unable to continue this brutal slogging match'.[13] By 10 p.m. the ships' munitions stores were running low. Fortunately the firing from the city was weakening. At 11 p.m., satisfied that the resistance of the city's defenders was almost over, Exmouth ordered the fleet to cut its cables and withdraw to seaward. By 1 a.m. on the 28th all the guns fell silent, and both the Dey and Lord Exmouth began to assess the damage they had suffered and the numbers killed and wounded.

The material losses on either side were vastly disproportionate. On the Algerian side, most of their gun emplacements had been destroyed and large areas of the city were in ruins. Almost all their fleet was sunk or destroyed by fire. The British and Dutch ships suffered some damage to their hulls and masts and the *Impregnable* had been badly damaged by the exploding mortar shell, but no ships were lost. However, as for the human casualties, according to the US Consul William Shaler (the only recorded eye witness actually located in the city), the Algerians' 'killed and wounded did not exceed about 600. Indeed nothing after the battle indicated a great loss of life.'[14] The British dead numbered 128 and the Dutch, thirteen. The wounded, many of whom would later die, were, respectively, 690 and fifty-two.[15] It is worth noting that the total British and Dutch dead and wounded – 883 – were nearly as many as the British casualties at the Battle of the Nile – 895.

As dawn broke on the morning after the battle, Exmouth was now fully aware that the fleet did not have sufficient munitions to recommence the bombardment on anything but a largely symbolic scale; and, as yet, there was no sign from the Algerians that they had capitulated. Nevertheless, he was determined to press home his advantage even if it involved a strong element of bluff. At 11 a.m., he sent his four bomb vessels close in to the city walls and his flag lieutenant and a translator into the harbour under a flag of truce. The lieutenant carried a letter to the Dey, demanding his submission within three hours. Unaware of Exmouth's lack of ammunition and assuming the presence of the bomb vessels indicated another major attack, the Dey and his divan accepted defeat. It was all over.

On the following day the British Consul was released from his dungeon and went aboard the *Queen Charlotte*. On 30 August a peace treaty was signed in which the Dey conceded all the British and Dutch demands. In any future war between Algiers and a European power, prisoners would not be enslaved but treated with all humanity as prisoners of war. Condemning any Christians to slavery was to be renounced for ever. All slaves within the Regency were to be immediately released. All moneys paid by the Italian states as tribute since the beginning of the year were to be repaid, and a substantial financial compensation was to be made to the British Consul in recognition of the ill treatment he had suffered. Finally, new treaties of peace were to be made with Britain, Holland and the Italian states. On 3 September the British and Dutch fleets began their journey home. Lord Exmouth arrived at Portsmouth on 6 October to a hero's welcome.

There can be no doubt that the British and Dutch demonstration of overwhelming power at Algiers had a salutary effect on all three regencies; but this was not the end of the Barbary corsairs, although it was the beginning of the end. According to Consul Shaler, by the end of the year the fortifications at Algiers had been replaced 'in as perfect a state of defence as they were previously to the battle'.[16] The Algerians had also refloated and recovered some of their larger warships which, with considerable foresight, they had deliberately sunk in the harbour before the bombardment began. Indeed, by 1825, Consul Shaler reported that the Algerians could still put to sea a fleet of three frigates with between forty and sixty-two guns, two corvettes with forty-six and thirty-six guns, and several smaller vessels.[17] So corsairing continued, albeit on a reduced scale.

In autumn 1818 the Concert of Europe met at Aix-la-Chapelle. It agreed on two important new resolutions: the new, reliably conservative France was to be admitted to the Concert, and Britain and France were given the responsibility of informing the regencies that they must cease corsairing once and for all, or else face reprisals from a 'European League'. Subsequently, in September 1819, a combined British and French fleet visited Algiers, Tunis and Tripoli to convey to them this decision. The Paşa of Tripoli agreed to the Europeans' injunction, but the Dey of Algiers and Bey of Tunis rejected it.[18] It was now becoming clear that naval bombardments, like that of 1816, no matter how spectacular, were insufficient on their own to put an end to the Barbary states. Only a full-scale invasion – a combined operation of naval and ground troops – could accomplish this objective.

As if to prepare the ground for a final assault on one or more of the regencies, fortune now favoured the Europeans. Over the next two decades both Algiers and Tunis were racked by a combination of political, economic and natural calamities which hastened their declining military strength. In Algiers, in spite of Dey 'Umar's energetic defence of the city against Exmouth's bombardment, he fell victim to a Janissary faction and was murdered in September 1817. His successor, 'Ali Khuja, then took the precaution of isolating himself from this unruly Janissary corps by abandoning the Janina Palace, the traditional residence of the deys, and withdrawing to the fortress-like Kasbah. He took along with him the contents of the treasury and a bodyguard of 2,000 Berber Zouaves (light infantry) and 6,000 Kuloğlus.[19] From that point on, 'Ali Khuja and his successors ruled more like monarchs than representatives of the *ocak*. There followed a succession of Janissary revolts, inter-Janissary conflicts and murders. 'Ali Khuja also launched raids to plunder Tunis by land and sea, only ended on March 1821 by the intervention of the sultan. Meanwhile, in Tunis itself, and also in Tripoli, similarly disruptive struggles for power occurred, motivated by dynastic quarrels within the ruling Husaynid and Karamanli families.

In addition to these internal power struggles, between 1816 and 1824 North Africa was ravaged by a series of natural disasters. Over these years the Regency of Algiers suffered seven outbreaks of plague, four periods of serious food shortages, three attacks of locusts and two earthquakes. Tunis experienced five plagues, four periods of food shortages and an epidemic of smallpox, while Tripoli also suffered three outbreaks of plague. The most serious plague epidemic occurred in Algiers between 21 June and 6 September 1817, when at least a third of the population of the city perished.

As the four horsemen of the apocalypse stampeded through the region, demographic collapse inevitably followed and, with it, a decline in the area of cultivation. Traditional exports to Europe of wheat, olive oil and other primary products declined. At the same time, imports of European manufactured goods, prized by the regencies' ruling elites, increased considerably. The economic consequence was the emergence of balance of payments deficits. For 1800 it is estimated that the value of Algiers's exports amounted to 2.6 million francs and their imports 2.2 million;[20] but by 1822 the corresponding figures were 1.5 million francs for exports and 5.8 million for imports. The deficit had to be settled out of the Regency's gold and silver reserves.[21]

Tunis's trade balance also deteriorated, from a surplus of 0.7 million francs in 1816 to an average deficit of 2 million francs for the years 1828–30. A particularly significant indicator of Tunis's economic difficulties at this time was the decline of the Regency's key industry – the manufacture of fezzes. In the 1780s the Regency sold around 1,200,000 units; by the 1820s production problems and competition from France and Tuscany had reduced this figure to around 800,000.

As the regencies' economies declined after 1815, so the financial pressures on their rulers increased; and this was exacerbated by the gradual disappearance of the state's income from corsairing. The elites responded by monetary depreciation and levying additional taxes on a rural population that was already suffering from disease and falling agricultural production. By the late 1820s fiscal shortfalls meant that both the Bey of Tunis and the Paşa of Tripoli were compelled to borrow large sums from European financiers to meet their needs.

Meanwhile, the European governments, especially those smaller states whose citizens had been the victims of the Barbary corsairs, were emboldened by the weakness of the regencies. They began to treat their rulers and envoys with disdain. For example, they refused to continue the old custom whereby their consuls kissed the hand of the ruler in formal audience. But it was France, which had traditionally been on friendly terms with the regencies and their principal trading partner, which made the first move to take advantage of the shifting balance of power in the Mediterranean.

During the years when the French Republic was engaged in a life-and-death struggle with its enemies, the Jewish firm of Bushnaq and Bacri, in the Regency of Algiers, supplied France and its armies with huge amounts of wheat. In one year alone 240,000 sacks of wheat were exported to France from the beylik of Constantine.[22] Since the French did not have the financial resources to pay for the wheat it was supplied on credit; by the end of the Napoleonic wars payment for the wheat – by now amounting to a debt of between 7 and 8 million francs – had still not been made. In the following years repeated requests to settle the debt were ignored by the royal Bourbon government, who were inclined to ignore a debt acquired by their Republican and Napoleonic predecessors. But by the mid-1820s Bacri himself owed a considerable sum to the Algerian state and he convinced the standing dey, Husayn bin Hasan, that he was unable to settle his own debt until the French settled their debt with him.[23]

The matter came to a head on 29 April 1827 when the French Consul, Pierre Deval, went to pay his respects to the Dey on the occasion of the *'id al-fitr*, the end of Ramadan. When asked by Husayn why the King of France had repeatedly declined to answer his letters requesting settlement of the debt, Deval replied in an insulting manner that King Charles X did not stoop to correspond with a mere dey. At this point an infuriated Husayn is said to have struck the consul three times with his peacock-feather flywhisk.

The altercation now spiralled out of control. In the second week of June the French sent a fleet to Algiers to demand a public apology and the raising of the Bourbon flag of France, the Fleur-de-Lys, over the kasbah. When the Dey refused, Consul Deval boarded a French warship and the fleet began a blockade of Algiers.

This first attempt at subduing the Dey was not particularly effective, and it damaged the profitable trade with Algiers which was mainly in the hands of the merchants of Marseilles. Consequently, in May 1828 the deputy of Marseilles in the Chamber of Deputies began a campaign in favour of the conquest of Algiers.[24] While the stand-off continued throughout 1828 and the merchants' fortunes suffered, the government of Charles X lost power in elections to the Chamber. Nevertheless in 1829 the arrogant ruler imposed the ultra-royalist Prince Jules de Polignac as foreign minister and president of the council (equivalent to prime minister).

By February 1830, Charles X had become increasingly unpopular, and Polignac and the King sought to bolster their prestige by launching what they believed would be a magnificent demonstration of French arms. On 2 March the King announced to the deputies gathered at the inaugural session of parliament that he could 'no longer allow to go unpunished the grave

insult to my flag'. Preparations would therefore begin for an expedition to
Algiers to inflict the required punishment.[25] However, the planned invasion
of Algiers was something more than a mere insult to the Bourbon flag of
France.

During the eighteenth century the immense slave plantation economy
of Saint-Domingue (Haiti) had been of enormous economic importance
to the French economy – so much so that in 1802, after the success of the
great slave rebellion, Napoleon had attempted (unsuccessfully) to invade
Haiti and re-impose slavery. In 1825 the Bourbon monarch Charles X sent
a fleet to Haiti threatening reoccupation unless an enormous indemnity
was paid to compensate the former plantation owners' 'losses'. The
reoccupation never took place because the Haitian government agreed
to pay the crippling indemnity. In the same year the arch-conservative
Bourbon government began to cast its eyes on alternative colonial targets
to compensate for the loss of Saint-Domingue. A report by the Direction
du Commerce Extérieur at the Ministry of the Interior envisaged the
creation of a colonial regime in the Regency of Algiers where there was a
large area of uncultivated land and where the inhabitants 'could easily be
encouraged to work'.[26] The humiliation of the French Consul by the Dey
of Algiers in 1827 was therefore 'a pretext rather than a proximate cause of
the seizure of Algiers'.[27]

Once the preparations for the French military operation got underway
and came to the notice of the British government, led by the ageing Duke
of Wellington, its suspicions about French motives gathered pace. Since
the end of the Napoleonic wars the British government had regarded the
Mediterranean as very much a 'British Sea'. Not only did Britain, with its
bases at Gibraltar, Malta and the Ionian Islands, command the sea itself,
but this strategic dominance was accompanied by a rapidly expanding trade
with the states and provinces around the Mediterranean's shores, notably
with the Ottoman Empire and its provinces. Consequently, three days
after the French King's announcement, Lord Aberdeen, the British Foreign
Secretary, wrote to Britain's ambassador in Paris, Sir Charles Stuart (Baron
de Rothesay), of his concern that the size of the French expedition seemed
to indicate that something more than mere punishment of the Barbary
state might be intended and that:

This probable change in the condition of a territory so important from its geographical position cannot be regarded by His Majesty's Government without much interest and it renders some explanation on the part of the French Government the more desirable.

Nevertheless, he added that 'The intimate union and concert' existing between Britain and France should mean that its government would surely provide a full account of the objectives of their expedition concerning 'a matter which may be ... productive of the most important effects upon the commercial and political relations of the Mediterranean States'.[28]

Consequently, the British ambassador asked the French government, in the person of the Prince de Polignac, for further clarification about the size and composition of the planned Algiers expedition. But Polignac's response on 12 March went no further than stating that the expedition's objectives were simply to punish the Dey's dishonour to the French flag. French interests, he explained, were to achieve 'the definitive destruction of piracy, the abolition of Christian slavery, and the suppression of the tribute paid to the Regency by the Christian powers', and that, after the military task was completed, France would discuss with her allies what further action should be taken.

Lord Aberdeen did not find Polignac's reply satisfactory and on 23 March he wrote again to Ambassador Stuart pointing out that 'The character of the expedition is of no ordinary description', and that it looked suspiciously like 'a project which may possibly lead to a war of extermination'. The British foreign minister also pointed out that 'the entire silence respecting the rights and interests of The Porte has been observed with some surprise'.

Most important of all, Aberdeen emphasised that:

> Whatever may be the means which shall be found necessary to secure the objects of the expedition, the French Government ought at least to have no difficulty in renouncing all views of territorial possession or aggrandisement.[29]

The problem was, however, that the French government *did* have such a difficulty, as becomes clear from the correspondence between Aberdeen and Stuart over the next three months as the French preparations for the attack on Algiers proceeded.

Polignac gave only verbal assurances to the British ambassador that France had no territorial ambitions in North Africa – but he was unwilling to put this in an official written despatch. Understandably this frustrated Aberdeen and by 21 April he was writing to Ambassador Stuart in stronger terms. 'Let us be candid; the war carried by France against Algiers is of another character and a different end is proposed ... the utter destruction and annihilation of the State itself.' The planned invasion involved 'a French army, the most numerous it is believed which in modern times has ever crossed the sea' and one which 'is about to undertake the conquest of a territory which, from its geographical position, has always been considered as of the highest importance'. It was a matter 'deeply affecting the interests of British commerce as well as the political relations of the Mediterranean States'.

Again, on 24 April, Aberdeen requested the written assurance that 'the Court of France entertains no project of conquest or acquisition of territory on the coast of Africa'. But when Stuart wrote on 30 April it was to report that Polignac had politely, but in so many words, refused to do so.[30]

By 4 May, and with news of the build-up of the French invasion force suggesting its imminent departure, Aberdeen told Stuart that the British government was puzzled about why it was receiving no assurances, and that 'the affair, in truth begins to wear a sinister appearance'. When Polignac did eventually provide the official 'assurances' concerning the attack on Algiers in written form, Aberdeen considered that they contained 'manifest contradictions' which certainly did not satisfy the British government. However, by now, the French expeditionary force was fully assembled and its army was about to embark for the shores of North Africa.

Statistical information from contemporary sources about the Regency of Algiers on the eve of its invasion is scanty and sometimes contradictory; for example, the US Consul William Shaler reckoned that the total population of the Regency was about 1 million,[31] whereas the Regency's former registrar, Hamdan Khoja, claimed it was ten times greater.[32] (The modern-day estimate is about 3 million).[33]

Of the total population figure, Shaler enumerates 4,000 Turks, 20,000 Kuloğlus and 30,000 Jews, offering no information on the Moors, Arabs and Berbers who made up the remainder of his total. Clearly, neither Shaler nor Hamdan Khoja had any idea of the size of the nomadic and semi-nomadic rural Arab population nor the sedentary Berber cultivators in their mountain fastness. Modern sources have estimated that the former constituted around 45 per cent of the total population and the latter as much as 50 per cent.[34]

With regard to the urban population, that of Algiers Shaler estimated at around 50,000,[35] the same as the figure recorded by Venture de Paradis in 1788. Of these, the Turkish Janissary garrison numbered between 1,500 and 2,000 while the Jews numbered around 5,000. As with the total Regency population, Shaler does not enumerate the Moors and Arabs of Algiers. Constantine, he estimated at around 25,000 inhabitants; Oran about 8,000 and al-Media, 8–10,000. Shaler reckoned the Regency's army numbered 15,000, with Turks and Kuloğlus serving as infantry and the Arabs as cavalry.[36] This number seems quite small, however; a modern source puts the total of Turks and Kuloğlus who could be 'mobilised for war' in this period at 10–12,000, broadly consistent with Shaler's estimate.

On 25 May 1830, the French fleet of 635 assorted vessels set sail for Algiers. The Minister of War, the Count de Bourmont, had put himself in charge of the invading force, which consisted of eighteen infantry regiments, three cavalry squadrons and a number of artillery and engineer units totalling 34,184 troops together with 3,389 non-combatants. Perceval Barton Lord, an enthusiastic British supporter of the French invasion and a surgeon with the East India Company, published a an account of the French invasion in 1835 based on a number of different French sources, and commented that the size of the army was calculated such that:

> It would not only be sufficient to overcome all opposition which might be encountered but to enable the French to reduce the kingdom to a province and retain it in subjection for any length of time which might be considered advisable.[37]

And with this objective in mind the non-combatants included 'a section of engineer-geographers whose business was to survey and map the country as it was conquered'. The supplies accompanying the invading force were 'of the completest kind and in great abundance' and included 'a balloon with two aeronauts to reconnoitre the enemy's position' and a hospital train. The latter was provided with 'thirty wooden legs and 200 crutches for the relief of the unfortunate heroes'.[38]

Unlike the King of Spain's abortive attack on Algiers in 1775, the French were in possession of detailed intelligence regarding the best point at which to mount the landing of their troops. In 1808 Napoleon had contemplated a second landing on the shores of North Africa and his minister of marine had sent Chef de Bataillon Vincent-Yves Boutin as a secret agent to the Regency, justifying his presence through his being a 'close relative' of the resident French Consul. At considerable risk, Boutin had carried out an extensive survey of the coastline in the vicinity of Algiers and the fortifications of the city on both the seaward and landward sides. His conclusion was that the most suitable location for an invading army to land was the peninsula of Sidi Feruj, to the west of Algiers, where there was an excellent sandy beach, undefended by any fortifications and only about thirty kilometres from the city. Boutin's report was filed away in the Ministry of Marine. And in just the same way that Baron de Tott's 1778 report on Egypt's defences was utilised twenty years later by Napoleon, so Boutin's 1808 report on Algiers provided the crucial information which guided the French invasion force in 1830.

The disembarkation began on 14 June and, following Boutin's advice, took place at Sidi Feruj. The troops committed to the ensuing battle amounted to 21,000 infantry, while the Muslim army was somewhere between 43,000 and 49,000 including both infantry and cavalry.[39] In spite of the Muslims' numerical superiority they were seriously handicapped by the historical hostilities and rivalries between the different ethnic contingents and, in particular, the fact that many of the Arab tribal contingents, some of whom deserted before the fighting began, owed little or no loyalty to the Turkish Dey. In the words or one French historian, the composition of the Muslim army 'already revealed the weakness of the Turkish state [i.e. the Regency]... This disparate army was the complete opposite of a national army'.[40]

The battle took place on the plateau of Staouéli on the western approaches to Algiers; within a few hours the Muslims were routed. The city itself surrendered on 5 July. The terms of the surrender appeared generous: the wealth and property of its inhabitants would be protected and their religion and religious institutions respected. In fact, these promises were worthless and would soon be cynically abandoned.

The capitulation of Algiers was followed by the visit of French warships to Tunis and Tripoli. The document defining the status of France's new Algerian colony was drawn up in Tunis on 8 August by Mathieu de Lesseps, who had recently been withdrawn from Egypt and appointed Tunis's consul-general in 1827. In the second week of August 1830, the Bey of Tunis and the Paşa of Tripoli were forced to sign new treaties with France.[41] In addition to the prohibitions on corsairing and Christian slavery, various economic clauses were added, all of which favoured European commercial interests. In particular the Bey and the Paşa were forbidden to establish any form of economic monopoly in their regencies and European merchants would be free to import or export any type of merchandise without hindrance. In the words of the French historian Daniel Panzac:

> The treaties of 1830 were the first of the lopsided treaties that the European powers – thanks to their naval power – would impose on the states of Africa and Asia right throughout the nineteenth century.[42]

In the mid-eighteenth century Muslims could still hold to the old belief that the Mediterranean Sea was theirs and that the Christian Europeans made use of it only with their consent and on their terms. By 1830 this was clearly no longer the case. Henceforth the Great Sea would be dominated by the Europeans. Moreover, as the infidels' merchants and soldiers began to probe deeper into the North African hinterlands it was also clear that Islam's Mediterranean shore was no longer a barrier to European penetration.

CHAPTER 13

The Multiple Crises of Mahmud II

News of the capture of Algiers by the French in July 1830 was just one more heavy blow to Sultan Mahmud II. The cousin of the reforming Sultan Selim III, Mahmud had acceded to the sultanate during one of the most turbulent and bloody episodes in the history of the Ottoman Empire. To put matters in perspective we need to go back to the beginning of these rapid and violent upheavals. Much of this chapter will therefore be a whirlwind of political strife and deadly action.

Although consigned to the *kafes* in the customary manner, both Mahmud and his elder brother Mustafa had been well treated by Selim III during the latter's reign, which had commenced in 1789. Mahmud had reciprocated by becoming a strong supporter of the sultan's reforms – in particular the military reforms. Indeed, by 1806, Selim's Europeanised army, the Nizam-1 Cedid, had been built up to 22,685 men and 1,590 officers.[1] But it was the very success of this military reform which prompted the determination of the Janissaries and their reactionary supporters among the *ulema* to put a stop to these 'un-Islamic' innovations.

The military old guard took advantage of a series of major crises which afflicted the Empire in 1806–07 – the destruction of the revered shrines of Mecca and Medina by Muhammad bin Sa'ud's fanatical Wahhabis of Arabia, which had made a mockery of Selim's title 'Guardian of the Two Holy Places'; the Russian Admiral Dmitry Senyavin's blockade of the Dardanelles since 6 March 1807, which caused near-starvation in the imperial city; and the defeat of an Ottoman fleet by Senyavin on 11 May 1807. The Janissaries blamed all these calamities on Selim III, claiming they were divine retribution for his introduction of 'un-Islamic practices'.

The Janissaries and their deeply conservative supporters seized the opportunity to launch a ferocious attack on Selim's 'European' regiments, hunting down and killing hundreds of its officers and NCOs. On 29 May, they compelled the sultan to abdicate after he completely lost his nerve and handed over some of his reforming ministers to be hacked to death by the mob.

For a year following Selim's overthrow, Istanbul was racked by civil war between the Janissaries and troops returning from the Russian front who were still loyal to Selim. Meanwhile, the Janissaries placed Mahmud's older, half-mad brother on the imperial throne as Mustafa IV. The new sultan promptly had Selim III murdered and ordered the killing of Mahmud; but Mahmud managed to escape the executioners. As fighting between the rebel Janissaries and loyalists continued and Istanbul descended into anarchy and chaos, the Empire appeared to be nearing the point of total collapse which had long been the prediction of European observers. In the words of the London *Gentleman's Magazine and Historical Chronicle* of November 1807: 'The dethroning of that monarch [Selim] has hastened the great catastrophe; and Mustafa is probably the last Ottoman sovereign who will reign over the provinces of the ... Empire.'[2]

But then Mustafa IV was himself deposed by loyalist troops in favour of Mahmud, who acceded to the sultanate on 28 July 1808. Mahmud II ordered the execution of his half-brother on 17 November 1808. Even then, the chaos in Istanbul was not brought to an end until the intervention of the *ulema*, who stopped the fighting but left the Janissaries still a powerful force to be reckoned with.

Realising the strength of the conservative forces still surrounding him, Mahmud advanced only very cautiously with his own modernisation project. He began to place his own reforming supporters in positions of power in the state bureaucracy; and he successfully removed or killed many of the rebellious regional *ayan* who had stood in the way of the re-centralisation of the Empire, crucial to its survival[3] – notably the Albanian warlord 'Ali Paşa of Tepelene, who was killed by Mahmud's agents in January 1822. But the problem of the unruly and militarily useless Janissaries remained as Mahmud faced his next major crisis.

In 1821, the Greeks of the Peloponnese launched a second rebellion against their Ottoman rulers. The rebels swiftly captured a number of Turkish-controlled towns, notably Kalamata and Kalavrita, where the defenders were slaughtered when they surrendered. Tripolitsa, the principal Turkish town in the Peloponnese, was stormed on 23 September 1821. The rebels killed around 8,000 of its defenders, including most of the town's

Portrait of Sultan Mahmud II (r. 1808–39), before his adoption of European dress

Jewish community, after which a further 2,000 half-starved Turkish civilians, mainly women and children who were being held at the Greeks' main camp, were taken to a nearby gorge and murdered in cold blood.

In response to this rebellion in which 'the Greeks treated Turkish civilians as animals to be exterminated',[4] the following year the Turks responded in kind. When a party of Greeks from the island of Samos landed on the nearby peaceful and prosperous island of Chios and attacked its Turkish garrison in March 1822, its inhabitants made it clear that they had no desire to be dragged into the insurrection. But this didn't save them from Mahmud's vengeance. He ordered his Kapudan Paşa (Admiral), Kara 'Ali, to attack the island with 15,000 troops and a horde of Anatolian volunteers. The Turkish attack on Chios began on 22 April and continued well into May, during which its overwhelmingly loyal and peaceful Greek population were massacred and around 45,000, mainly women and children, were taken into slavery.

Nevertheless, in the Peloponnese the Turkish and Albanian troops sent to suppress the revolt met defeat after defeat. By February 1825, Mahmud realised that his only hope was to appeal to his Egyptian *vali* for military assistance. That was Mehmed Ali, the former Albanian soldier whom Selim III had reluctantly appointed to this position during the chaos in Egypt after the British left in 1803. The now-powerfully independent ruler of Egypt responded by sending his son Ibrahim to the Peloponnese with a substantial army – although this gesture of support came with certain conditions attached.

The Egyptian army of 10,000 infantry and 1,000 cavalry which disembarked at Methoni on 24 February 1825 was something new in the annals of Islamic warfare. Mehmed Ali had witnessed years of fighting during which, like Sultan Selim III, he had become convinced of the superiority of the disciplined European military methods and the regular, professional armies that the Europeans could put into the field. Only the Mamluk beys and their antiquated mode of warfare stood in his way.

In 1811 Mehmed Ali's opportunity arrived. Sultan Mahmud had ordered him to destroy the Wahhabis of Najd who had seized control of Mecca. Mehmed chose one of his sons, Tusun, to lead the expedition and also invited the Mamluk beys to join his campaign. On 1 March 1811, the beys and a substantial number of their own Mamluks and servants were invited to a feast at the Citadel to celebrate the inauguration of what was expected to be a triumphant march into Arabia. But as the beys entered the great courtyard of the Citadel its gates were closed behind them and hundreds of Mehmed Ali's Albanian infantry stationed on the surrounding walls poured volley after volley into the defenceless Mamluk chieftains. Once the massacre of the beys – around 450 in total – was complete, Mehmed Ali's troops roamed the streets of Cairo hunting down and killing about 1,000 more.[5]

With the Mamluk beys destroyed, in 1812 Mehmed Ali proceeded to confiscate all their tax farms in Upper Egypt, completing the seizures in Lower Egypt in 1814. The country now became one great state farm, owned and controlled by the *vali*. Together with his personal monopolisation of the international trade in wheat, rice, sugar and eventually cotton, Mehmed acquired the resources that allowed him to begin the creation of a conscript army, equipped and drilled along European lines – precisely the type of army that his imperial masters, Selim III and Mahmud II, had so far been unable to establish.

His first step was to create an officer corps. The recruits were initially drawn from Mehmed's personal Mamluk servants and those of his sons (who had been excluded from the massacre of the Mamluk beys); but soon, attracted by generous pay, these were supplemented by Turks drawn from all quarters of the Ottoman Empire. To instruct them he hired European soldiers, mainly former Napoleonic Army junior officers – notably the self-styled 'Colonel' Joseph Sève, who converted to Islam, and took the name Sulayman. By 1819, one thousand of these new officers had graduated from the special barracks which had been set up at Aswan. Moreover, unlike Sultan Selim, Mehmed had no qualms about placing Europeans in command positions within his army rather than restricting them to training functions. 'Sulayman' soon became Sulayman Paşa, a senior officer and later second in command of the whole army, and he was joined by other Frenchmen – a M. Planet, who became director of the staff college, Colonel Seguera, head of the artillery school, Antoine Clot, director of the military medical establishment. And in 1823 the French Consul-General, Bernardino Drovetti, recommended a former officer in Napoleon's Egyptian campaign, General Pièrre Boyer, to Mehmed Ali. Boyer arrived in Egypt as the head of a French military mission.

To man the ranks of his infantry, Mehmed Ali first used black slaves, who had been seized during the invasion of the Sudan by his son Isma'il in 1820; but they soon fell victim to the many virulent diseases they encountered in the Nile valley. To replace them he conscripted the *fellahin* – the long-suffering Egyptian Arab peasantry. Beginning in 1822, thousands of these unfortunates were dragged from their homes and villages, housed in isolated barracks, rigidly drilled and brutally disciplined, although they did receive regular pay, adequate food and medical attention. Although thousands deserted, the number of trained infantry and cavalry increased from 4,000 in 1822 to around 30,000 in 1825, and by the mid-1830s would reach 130,000 men.[6]

Unlike the troops of Selim's Nizam-ı Cedid, which had been organised in hybrid 'regiments' combining all three arms, Mehmed Ali's army was structured on conventional European lines with separate regiments for infantry, cavalry and artillery. In the case of the infantry, each regiment (*alay*) of 3,264 men and officers was composed of four battalions (*ortas*) with 816 men each.[7] In spite of the fact that all field officer positions were restricted to Turkish speakers (later, Arabs were permitted to rise to the rank of captain – but no further) the ordinary soldiers were taught to obey all the essential commands given in Turkish by demonstration without needing to understand the actual meaning of the words. Given the relatively small number of battlefield commands required, the system appears to have worked quite well.

What was particularly distinctive about Mehmed's new army was that it was supported by an efficient supply and logistics organisation with a bureaucracy of thousands of scribes and clerks to sustain it. To this extent, it was even superior to most of Napoleon's armies, which had to plunder their way across conquered territory, living off the land. In contrast, Mehmed's troops were forbidden to plunder or seize booty and, as far as possible, they were fed by an efficient commissariat. To provide the clothing and military equipment for his new army Mehmed Ali established state-run factories for which machinery and skilled workers were acquired from Europe. He established his first cotton-spinning and weaving factory for the production of uniforms in 1816 and, in the same year, a large arsenal within the Cairo citadel was built to turn out high-quality muskets as well as cannons, swords and munitions. Shipbuilding yards appeared at Alexandria, and in 1825 a factory for making the 'Tunisian' fez, a distinctive element in the uniform of his soldiers, was established at Fouah on the Nile.[8]

So, by 1825 Mehmed had a well-trained and well-equipped conscript army, commanded by his son, Ibrahim.[9] Its official name was 'the Jihadi Army of Egypt' and its banner, like the Ottoman flag, was red with a white crescent – except whereas the latter carried just one five-pointed star, the Egyptian flag carried three.[10] By early 1826, Ibrahim's Egyptian army had largely crushed the Greeks of the Peloponnese and were besieging their last major stronghold at Mesolongi on the northern side of the Gulf of Corinth.

It was now that Sultan Mahmud realised he would have to accelerate his own long-planned reforms of his own army. He carefully prepared the ground to emulate Mehmed Ali's destruction of the Mamluks by an onslaught against the militarily ineffectual Janissaries. However, in emulating Mehmed Ali, Mahmud faced a more difficult task: the Janissaries were far more numerous than the Mamluk beys and they retained a certain amount of support among the *ulema* and the Istanbul populace. But the sultan had learnt the lessons of his predecessor's failure. Over the years he had carefully placed supporters of his plans for military reform in key positions, crucially that of the Şehülislam (chief cleric), which was given to the energetic and loyal Mehmed Tahir Efendi in November 1825. Mahmud also ensured that reformers were given the senior officer positions in the Janissary corps itself without alerting the rank and file. In particular the rank of *ağa*, the Janissaries' commanding officer, was given to Hüseyin Mehmed Paşa, a covert 'reformer'. By early 1826, the sultan also knew that in any showdown with the Janissaries he could count on support from his bombardier corps, the artillery and the navy.

In April 1826 Mahmud heard that his Egyptian allies had finally captured Mesolongi, and he felt ready to strike against his domestic enemies. On 28 May, he announced that henceforth the Janissaries would be transformed into a modern army with 'European-style' uniforms, drill and discipline. It was also announced that the *ulema* were now unanimous that Muslims had a religious duty to acquire the modern military sciences.[11] On 5 June, Mahmud proclaimed his intention to review the Janissaries in their new uniforms on 18 June.

The proclamation triggered the open defiance of the junior officers and rank and file of Istanbul's five Janissary *orta*s, as it was probably intended to do, and four days before the planned review they came out in open rebellion. They assembled at their Istanbul barracks awaiting the anticipated revocation of the sultan's pronouncement, but instead they were suddenly attacked by loyal bombardiers and artillerymen. Within minutes, hundreds were blasted to pieces by case shot fired by the sultan's loyal gunners. The remainder, unprepared for such an eventuality, were taken prisoner but then executed. Meanwhile those who escaped were systematically hunted down and killed over the next few days. Henceforth these bloody events would be known as 'The Auspicious Occasion'.

Mahmud now signalled that the transformation of Ottoman society would begin. On 16 June he appeared at Friday prayers wearing a distinctly 'European-style' uniform; and instead of the traditional escort of Janissaries he was guarded by loyal bombardiers and artillerymen armed with muskets and bayonets arranged in European order and performing the new forms of military drill.

Portrait of Sultan Mahmud II in European-style uniform, c. 1826

On 17 June, the Janissary corps was formally abolished along with the Bektaşi Sufi order which had provided their 'chaplains'. Throughout the remainder of June, eight executioners were kept fully employed finishing off what remained of the once all-powerful military institution. In total, around 6,000 Janissaries were eliminated in Istanbul during June 1826.[12] The sultan's onslaught against the Janissaries had been overwhelmingly successful. Nevertheless, he was careful to dress his military and other reforms in the language of religion. The new army which he set out to build would be called the *Muallem Asakir-i Mansure-i Muhammediye* (the Trained Victorious Army of Muhammad) with Hüseyin Paşa, the reformist ağa of the Janissaries, as its first *serasker* (commander-in-chief).[13]

Still, the war against the Greeks continued in a desultory fashion. Initially the European powers had displayed a distinctly hostile attitude towards the Greek uprising. Their leaders viewed it as a threat to the conservative status quo that had been established with the final overthrow of Napoleon and the creation of the 'Concert of Europe'. In July 1822, the British foreign secretary, Viscount Castlereagh, condemned it: in his opinion, it was another symptom of 'that organised spirit of insurrection which is systematically propagating itself throughout Europe'.[14] The Austrian chancellor, Klemens von Metternich, went further, and openly supported the Turks. Even Tsar Alexander I, who was sympathetic towards his Greek co-religionists, made it clear that he could not support a revolutionary movement against a legitimate fellow ruler.

However, by 1825 the British and French middle classes – who knew nothing of the Greek atrocities at Tripolitsa and elsewhere – were being bombarded with tales of Turkish barbarity, promulgated by the various philhellene organisations that were springing up. By the early nineteenth century governments in Britain and France were no longer completely immune to the influence of public opinion. News of the Chios massacre was circulating through Europe, as were reports that Ibrahim had plans to expel or kill all the Greek inhabitants of the Peloponnese and replace them with Egyptian settlers. Britain's new foreign secretary, George Canning, was forced to write to his prime minister, Lord Liverpool: 'I begin to think that the time approaches when *something* must be done.'[15]

The eventual outcome of this change of heart was the signing of an Anglo-Russian protocol on 4 April 1826, whereby both countries would seek an end to hostilities in the Greek war, and grant a limited autonomy to the Greeks, similar to that prevailing in the Danubian Principalities. But Mahmud II, his spirits buoyed up by the recent Ottoman-Egyptian victories, was not in the mood for even the most limited concessions to the Greeks, so he rejected the protocol out of hand.

Meanwhile he was having to deal with a quite separate dispute with Russia. It had arisen out of serious disagreements over the implementation of the terms of the Treaty of Bucharest, which had put an end to the Turko-Russian War of 1806–12. Mahmud was dragging his feet over the restoration to the Danubian Principalities of their autonomous status and the withdrawal of Ottoman troops from these territories. He also disagreed over the passage through the Straits of Russian and Greek merchant ships (the latter flying the Ottoman flag). These vessels typically carried Russian wheat supplies to the Mediterranean Christian states, but also to the Greek rebels. On 17 March 1826, the Russian government sent an ultimatum to the Porte that these disputes must be settled (in Russia's favour); if not, hostilities between the two contending parties would recommence. In the circumstances, with the Empire recovering from the violent events of the 'Auspicious Occasion', Mahmud felt he had no choice but to concede most of the Russian demands. So on 7 October 1826, at the Convention of Akkerman, the sultan accepted the right of merchant ships flying the Russian flag to have the freedom of navigation in all domestic waterways of the Ottoman Empire.[16]

The Convention of Akkerman made no reference to the Greek uprising, which by now had degenerated into little more than a sporadic guerrilla war against Ibrahim's Egyptian army of occupation. However, with the death of the cautious and conservative Tsar Alexander, his successor Nicholas I (r. 1825–55), was willing to take a much stronger line in support of the Greeks; and a similar mood now inclined the British and French to take a more active role.

Therefore, on 6 July 1827, the three European powers agreed the Treaty of London, the essence of which was that the sultan must accept an armistice in the Greek war leading to the creation of a Greek autonomous political entity. At the same time they accepted that such a polity should remain within the Ottoman Empire with a status similar to that of the Danubian Principalities. But if either belligerent refused an armistice, the three powers would 'jointly exert all their efforts to accomplish the objective of such an armistice'.[17] Under Russian pressure the British and French governments ordered their naval commanders in the Mediterranean to cut off all military supplies entering the Greek war zone from Egypt. They also authorised the blockade of Dardanelles if the Porte refused to accept these terms. In the meantime, a Greek government had finally emerged from a foolish and futile civil war among the rebels during the previous two years. It accepted these terms, but Mahmud stubbornly rejected them.

Consequently the British and French fleets under the command of Admiral Sir Edward Codrington, a veteran of Trafalgar, began a blockade of the Peloponnese to prevent further Egyptian reinforcements and supplies. The British government was reluctant to see the Ottoman Empire fatally wounded, so Codrington's instructions were suitably vague and stopped short of ordering him to use force against Turkish and Egyptian warships. However, there followed a sequence of events which would inevitably lead to precisely such an outcome, indeed one which was far more devastating than any of the European powers had foreseen.

On 8 September 1827, a large Egyptian fleet arrived at the port of Navarino, Ibrahim's main supply point on the Peloponnese. Two days later Codrington's fleet arrived in Navarino Bay and found seventy-seven

Turkish and Egyptian vessels, four warships from the Regency of Tunis and six from Algiers anchored in the harbour. On the 21st Codrington was joined by a French naval squadron, and on 10 October a Russian squadron arrived from the Baltic; in all, a total of twenty-four warships. Just after midday on 20 October, a blazing fire ship from the Muslim fleet was seen bearing down on the allied squadron. In response, Codrington ordered an immediate attack. Within three hours two-thirds of the Muslim fleet was sunk with the loss of 8,000 lives. It was a naval disaster for the Ottomans greater even than that of Çeşme in 1770.[18] Among the Muslim losses were the whole of the Algerian squadron and most of Tunisian contingent sent by Tunis's ruler Husayn Bey II.

Despite this catastrophe, Mahmud still refused to give way. On 31 November 1827 he repudiated the Convention of Akkerman, and on the same day all the European ambassadors to the Porte swiftly left Istanbul to escape incarceration. On 18 December, a defiant sultan declared a holy war against Russia, and in April the following year the Straits were closed to all the allied warships. Consequently, in June, the Russians declared war on the Ottoman Empire. On 9 July 1828 the British government, presided over by a reluctant Duke of Wellington, agreed that French troops should be sent to the Peloponnese, in effect to support the Greeks. Facing the reality of defeat, Mehmed Ali ordered his son, Ibrahim, to abandon the sultan. On 4 October Ibrahim's remaining troops, devastated by disease and losses in battle, were shipped back to Alexandria. The allies had never welcomed the Greek rebellion, but had been forced to support it as a result of a combination of public opinion at home and futile stubbornness on the part of the sultan. It had succeeded against all expectations.

As yet, however, there was still no indication that the realities on the Greek battleground were acknowledged by the sultan; nor was it clear where the frontier of any putative Greek State would lie. To address this issue, on 12 December the ambassadors of the allied states initially recommended a line drawn west–east from Arta in southern Epirus to Volos on the coast of southern Thessaly, 326 kilometres north of Athens. This proposed area would include the island of Evia, although Greece would remain an autonomous state under Ottoman suzerainty.*

---

* Suzerainty is the relationship between two states where the more powerful allows the

However, on 22 March 1829, fearing that such a northerly frontier would never be accepted by the sultan and that it was far too generous to the Greeks, the three allied governments decided on a frontier including little more than the Peloponnese.[19] Meanwhile, the Russian army had broken through into the Ottoman heartland and captured the major city of Edirne (Adrianople); and by 7 September some Russian cavalry units had even reached the Aegean. Mahmud now had little option but to sue for peace, and on 14 September 1829 the Treaty of Adrianople ended the Russo-Turkish War. Tsar Nicholas and his clever foreign minister Count Karl Nesselrode agreed that to seize Istanbul and deliver a death blow to the Ottoman Empire would create a dangerous schism in the status quo of aristocratic conservatism, which had been carefully nurtured since the overthrow of Napoleon. As a result they settled for quite moderate Ottoman concessions. Serbian autonomy was guaranteed; Russia gained access to the mouths of the Danube; the Turkish Straits were opened to all commercial shipping; and a large Ottoman indemnity was to be paid, during which the Russians were to occupy Moldavia and Wallachia until it was fully settled. But it could have been worse.

In addition, two separate but important agreements were made at the conclusion of the 1828–29 Russo-Ottoman War which introduced an element of humanity into the conduct of future military confrontation between the two empires. The enslavement of war captives would end[20] and Sultan Mahmud decreed that the mutilation of the enemy dead and wounded by using 'ear counts' and the like would cease.[21]

Mahmud was now compelled to accept the existence of a Greek state, albeit one still under the suzerainty of the Ottoman Empire and with its frontiers still not agreed. On 26 October 1829 the last battle in the Greek war was fought at Petra, near Thebes. Thereafter the Turkish army in Greece gave up any attempt to reconquer territory lost to the rebels; and on 3 February 1830 the allies resolved to establish a fully independent Greek state with a king chosen from one of the ruling European families.

So when, in late July, Mahmud received news of the French invasion and capture of Algiers, there was nothing he could do to assist the Regency's

---

less powerful autonomy in its internal affairs but controls its foreign policy and external relations.

embattled Muslim forces. With its regular infusion of Anatolian recruits, Algiers had always been the Regency most closely linked to the sultan and the Porte. But now Mahmud no longer had a navy with which to carry a relief force to the western Mediterranean, even if he had been able to withstand the recent Russian onslaught. And worse was to come – this time, from Egypt. Sultan Mahmud II was about to face his third major crisis.

The military assistance that Mehmed Ali provided to the sultan in Greece had come at a price: Mahmud had promised Mehmed Ali the governorship of Syria. However, by mid-1830 Mahmud was showing little willingness to honour any such agreement.

Consequently, on 2 November 1831, Mehmed Ali ordered his son Ibrahim to invade Syrian Palestine with four infantry regiments and four of cavalry, together with forty field guns and siege artillery. He also dispatched a newly built fleet of sixteen warships and seventeen transport vessels with French officers along the coast parallel to the advancing Egyptian army. Ibrahim's force of around 30,000 men swiftly captured Jaffa, Haifa, Sidon, Tyre, Beirut, Latakia and Jerusalem, and laid siege to Acre.

In response Sultan Mahmud obtained a *fetva* from his *ulema* 'excommunicating' Mehmed Ali and appointing his elderly commander-in-chief Hüseyin Mehmed Paşa as Vali of Egypt. Yet this imperial edict had little effect on the ground. After a long siege, Acre was captured on 27 May 1832 and Ibrahim's troops stormed through Syria, occupying Damascus on 16 June and defeating a poorly led Ottoman Army south of the town of Homs on 8 July.

Meanwhile, on 7 May, Britain, France, Russia and Bavaria signed a convention establishing Greece as an independent country with the unlikely personage of Prince Otto of Bavaria as its king. (Nobody else appeared to want it.) Moreover, it was agreed that Greece's frontier would be the 'generous' Arta-Volos line originally proposed by the allied ambassadors in 1828. Even so, the new state would have a population of only around 800,000, compared with the two and a half million Greeks living in the rest of the Ottoman Empire, most of whom were content to remain within it.

Mahmud was still unable to reconcile himself to the loss of those 800,000 former Ottoman citizens; but as the Egyptian army continued its advance and the Empire's military crisis accelerated, the British Ambassador to the Porte, Stratford Canning, used the opportunity to encourage the sultan to make a final peace settlement with the Greeks. Canning hinted at possible British intervention to help the sultan against Ibrahim who, by now, had defeated another Ottoman army of 45,000 men under Hüseyin Paşa, and crossed the Taurus Mountains into Anatolia. In the peace agreement orchestrated by the British, Mahmud had to acknowledge the existence of an independent Greek state and accept that its frontier with Ottoman-controlled territory would be the Arta-Volos line. Nevertheless, after Stratford Canning returned to London in August, nothing more was heard of any British support for Mahmud against Ibrahim's approaching Egyptian army. In London it was expected that the Ottoman Empire was rapidly approaching the long-anticipated moment of its disintegration.[22]

Ibrahim's modern army was now advancing into the Turkish heartlands. Antioch was captured on 28 July and on 31 July Ibrahim's army captured the city of Adana. Mahmud now ordered the mobilisation of a new army drawn from all parts of the Empire, and by October the sultan had 80,000 men under arms. On 21 December 1832 the two armies met at Konya on the central Anatolian plateau. In a seventeen-hour battle Ibrahim's 15,000 Egyptian troops routed an Ottoman army of 53,000, killing 3,000, taking 10,000 prisoners, and capturing ninety-two field guns. The way to Istanbul now lay open and largely undefended.

A desperate Ottoman government appealed to Britain for help, but the cabinet ignored the request. Later, the British foreign secretary, Lord Palmerston, wrote that 'no British Cabinet at any period of the history of England ever made so great a mistake in regard to foreign affairs.'[23] Consequently, on 2 February 1833, Sultan Mahmud did the unthinkable: he requested military aid in the form of an army of 30,000 troops from the Christian Tsar to defend his capital against an army of fellow Sunni Muslims.

On 16 February Mehmed Ali offered peace terms: to halt Ibrahim's advance he demanded the whole of Syria and the southern Anatolian province of Adana. Four days later a Russian naval squadron entered the Bosphorus and, backed by his new and unlikely ally, the sultan rejected Mehmed Ali's demands outright. As yet, however, the Russians were unable to bring the Russian troops from Odessa to defend Istanbul; Ibrahim and his father's Egyptian army were preparing for a fresh advance. Mahmud finally realised that he would have to give in to at least some of Mehmed

Ali's demands. On 30 March a Turkish envoy was sent to Ibrahim's camp to invest his father with the governorship of the three *paşaliks* which constituted the region of greater Syria. Although 5,000 Russian troops landed on the Bosphorus a few miles north of Istanbul on 5 April, Ibrahim persisted with his demand for Adana, which had rich timber resources of great value to the Egyptians. In early May, as a face-saving device, the Porte appointed Ibrahim as the *muhassil* (tax-collector) for Adana. But in reality it meant that all Mehmed Ali's demands had been met.

The arrival of Russian troops so close to the Ottoman capital naturally aroused great discontent among its population, especially among the *ulema*. In these circumstances, a weaker sultan than Mahmud might have found himself consigned to the *kafes* – or worse. But over the years Mahmud had shown himself to be ruthless with dissent: those he believed had failed him or were known to harbour opinions contrary to his own had met with death by strangulation, including one of his grand vezirs. So the sultan was able to ride roughshod over the dismay of those who were appalled at the acceptance of help from unbelievers against fellow Muslims. On 8 July 1833, in the Treaty of Hünkar İskelesi, the Porte agreed an eight-year defensive pact with Russia.

Both Britain and France protested against the Treaty, which appeared to have given Russia a special position in the Ottoman Empire. Of particular concern was the article specifying that, in the case of Russia being at war with another country, 'the Sublime Porte ... will confine its action to closing the strait of the Dardanelles, that is to say, to not allowing any foreign vessels of war to enter therein under any pretext whatsoever'. It was feared that Russian leverage over the Porte now meant that her fleet would be able to dash into the Mediterranean, attack an enemy and return to the Black Sea in safety before any other state could react.[24] In short, it was felt that the Empire was in danger of becoming a Russian protectorate – and certainly this was how the recent events were viewed by Russia's foreign minister, Nesselrode.[25]

Mehmed Ali's rebellion against Sultan Mahmud II and the battlefield victories of his modern Egyptian army under his son Ibrahim had prompted the near collapse of the Ottoman state. This opened a fissure among European states hitherto united in preserving a post-Napoleonic status quo based on the twin pillars of peace between nations and stubborn resistance to reform and social change. Britain was already concerned about the recrudescence of French influence in Egypt; now both Britain and France were becoming fearful of Russia's influence in Istanbul and possible control over the Straits. In the years to come these fissures would widen and the Mediterranean would increasingly become a major sphere of inter-imperialist rivalry. But that same rivalry between Britain, France and Russia would offer a considerable degree of protection for an ageing Islamic empire which, only recently, had been considered on the verge of extinction.

CHAPTER 14

The French Invasion of Algiers and the Growth of the Resistance, 1830–36

When news of the capture of Algiers reached France, it was received with widespread approval, especially among the country's middle classes; but it was of little assistance to the increasingly authoritarian King Charles X. While French troops were consolidating their position in Algiers, on 26 July 1830 he made an attempt to crush the rising tide of opposition to his rule by dissolving the newly elected Chamber of Deputies, shackling the press and excluding the middle classes from future elections. This sparked a three-day revolution in Paris. The Tuileries Palace was sacked and most public buildings fell under the control of the civilian rebels. The army failed to intervene.

On 2 August Charles X was forced to abdicate and flee to England. On 9 August, Louis-Philippe, the Duke of Orléans, was sworn in as 'King of the French', a title signifying his liberal political tendencies and sympathy for the interests of the rising French bourgeoisie. Subsequently the Bourbon minister of war was replaced by the sixty-one-year old Jean-de-Dieu Soult, and on 2 September General de Bourmont was replaced as Marshal of France by his second-in-command in Algiers, the fifty-eight-year-old Bertrand, Comte de Clauzel.

Meanwhile, officers and men alike of the invading French army completely ignored the terms agreed at the capitulation of Algiers. The houses of Algerian citizens who had fled before the French entry into the city were ransacked and plundered, mosques were desecrated and the public treasury was extensively looted. It is estimated that in 1830 over 100 million francs was transferred to France, obtained from the Dey's treasure trove and private and *waqf* sources. Only about half this amount arrived in the French Treasury, the remainder being pocketed by French officers and other ranks.[1]

In 1830 the French had given the British government vague undertakings about consulting with France's allies regarding the future of the Algiers Regency after its capture; these were now entirely ignored. This was partly because, in November 1830, the Tory government of the Duke of Wellington was replaced by a Whig ministry. Their members – in particular the new foreign secretary, Lord Palmerston – were sympathetic to the July Revolution and the monarchy of Louis-Philippe, which they believed represented the emergence of a sort of moderate representational government which they themselves favoured. Palmerston also doubted that France would continue aspiring to 'territorial aggrandisement', the motive which Lord Aberdeen had attributed to the previous French regime. He felt they would be satisfied by France's success in eradicating corsairing, white slavery and the demanding of tribute. But as future events would demonstrate, in the words of one of Palmerston's biographers, 'Palmerston did not yet appreciate French policy in North Africa.'[2]

In fact, Palmerston was not alone in this misconception. In the autumn of 1830 most knowledgeable observers considered the evacuation of Algiers to be imminent. They were wrong. For the next four years the new French government temporised over what to do with its new possession; but in the absence of any clear official policy, facts were being created on the ground by the military.[3]

The most striking feature of the military occupation of the Algiers Regency, after its initial conquest, is the extent to which its commanders were middle-aged former Napoleonic officers – like the War Minister Soult, General Clauzel, General Jean-Marie René Savary and General Pièrre Boyer. These were men who had already served in some of Napoleon's most brutal colonialist campaigns including Egypt, Haiti, Spain and Portugal, and were now embarking on another.* Until the overthrow of Charles X and his replacement by Louis-Philippe, Soult and his comrades had been proscribed by the royalist government of arch-reactionaries and far-right Catholics; some had even been forced to flee the country. However, the new 'bourgeois' government readmitted them to high military office; and the invasion of Algiers opened up tempting vistas of military glory and personal enrichment.

---

* Jean-de-Dieu Soult (1769–1851) commanded an army in Spain and Portugal. Bertrand Clauzel (1772–1842) fought in Haiti, Spain and Portugal. Jean-Marie René Savary (1774–1833) fought in Egypt and later became Napoleon's minister of police. Pierre Boyer (1772–1851) fought in Egypt, Haiti, Portugal and Spain and later became military advisor to Mehmed Ali.

The Dey's capitulation led to the removal of the Turkish troops and many of the Regency's functionaries, who were shipped off to Izmir having been compelled to abandon all their wealth and property. In their stead the French installed some rich Moorish and Jewish merchants in positions the Turks had vacated, but the mass of the city's population, Arabs, poorer Moors, Jews and Berbers, refused to collaborate and retreated in fear to their homes.[4]

During the remainder of 1830 al-Media, the administrative capital of the Beylik of Titteri, eighty-three kilometres south of the capital, was occupied. So was Blida, sixty kilometres to the southwest on the southern edge of the Mitidja plain. When the inhabitants of Blida tried to resist the occupation of their town, troops led by General Clauzel responded with a series of random executions. After leaving a small French force to garrison the town, Clauzel returned to Algiers. But when, a few weeks later, the townspeople of Blida rose up against the French garrison, Clauzel sent a French column to punish the insurgents. Consequently, on 17 November almost the whole population of Blida, around 800 men, women and children, were slaughtered, and most of the town left in flames. However, with Blida now reduced almost to ruins and nowhere to billet the French troops, some days later Clauzel's men had to be withdrawn.[5]

For the present, Clauzel controlled only the city of Algiers and its immediate hinterland, and struggled to find a way to extend French control of the interior. Without it, his troops were dependent upon mainland France for supplies of food, fuel and other necessities. His first attempt (without any authorisation from the new French government) was to try to win over the three provincial beys, who would then continue their functions as rural tax collectors, while transferring to their new French masters their former allegiance to the Dey. To the west, Hasan Bey of Oran initially accepted this proposal, but then fled to Alexandria on 4 January 1831, after which the French entered the city. In the beylik of Titteri, Mustafa Bou Mezrag also initially agreed to continue to serve as bey; but he renounced the agreement when he became aware that the French were ruthlessly ignoring the terms of the Dey's capitulation. To the east, the Bey of Constantine, Hajj Ahmed bin Muhammad (1784–1851), rejected Clauzel's proposal out of hand.

Having failed to co-opt the three provincial beys, Clauzel decided to offer the two most important beyliks, Oran and Constantine, to Husayn, the Bey of Tunis. There was no love lost between the deys of Algiers and the Husaynid dynasty which had ruled Tunis for the past 100 years. Indeed, since the beginning of the nineteenth century there had been a number of outbreaks of conflict between the two regencies, the most recent having been in 1820.

In Tunis the veteran French consul-general, Mathieu de Lesseps, had been assiduously working to bring the Bey, Husayn II, into the French sphere of influence, as he had done previously with Mehmed Ali in Egypt. It was de Lesseps who encouraged Husayn to accept Clauzel's initiative. So on 18 December 1830 a treaty was signed between Tunis's first minister and Clauzel, according to which the beylik of Constantine would be given to Husayn Bey's brother, Sidi Mustafa Bey, and that of Oran to Mustafa's son, Ahmed. In return, Husayn Bey would pay 800,000 francs to the French government in 1831 and 1,000,000 francs in each of the succeeding years.[6]

The French were given to believe that a Tunisian army would march into the neighbouring beylik of Constantine in March 1831, but that never took place. Husayn II changed his mind. The Bey of Tunis rejected Clauzel's idea of governing Constantine (and Oran) via Tunisian princes when he realised that his appointees would be little more than French puppets. Worse still, Clauzel had never troubled to discuss his plan with the French government. When he heard about it, King Louis-Philippe refused to ratify the treaty which Clauzel had signed with the Tunisians.[7] Consequently Clauzel felt obliged to ask for his remission, and in February 1831 the position of commander-in-chief was given to General Pièrre Berthezène, another Napoleonic veteran, but one who had little enthusiasm for the whole Algerian operation. Berthezène would not countenance brutal measures against the population like the massacre at Blida. However, his views were strongly opposed by many French officers and he retained the post for only nine months before being replaced by General Savary in December 1831.

By the spring of 1832, the strategic situation of the French army remained precarious. Outside Algiers and the adjoining Mitidja plain, they were still pinned down in small, coastal enclaves: in the beylik of the west (Oran) the flag of France was flown by only the city-port of Oran together with the neighbouring ports of Arzew and Mostaganem; and in the east, 'Annaba, the main port of the beylik of Constantine, was captured by French marines only in March 1832, after changing hands a number of times.

To complicate matters the tribes of the western beylik, who had long enjoyed close trading relations with those across the undefined border with Morocco, had called upon the Sultan of Morocco, 'Abd al-Rahman (r. 1822–59), to support them against the French. On 7 November 1830 the sultan sent Mulay 'Ali, his fifteen-year-old cousin and brother-in-law, with 500 Moroccan troops to seize the border town of Tlemcen. However, Mulay 'Ali was unable to dislodge the garrison of Turks and Kuloğlus holed up in the ancient, but immensely strong, citadel of Tlemcen, the Meshwar, and proved himself such an incompetent and rapacious commander that 'Abd al-Rahman was forced to withdraw him.

Fortunately for the French, the very topography of the Regency militated against any combined and effective resistance movement, at least for the time being. The country is segmented by a series of five mountain ranges running roughly parallel to the coast, with peaks ranging from 500 to about 2,500 metres in height. These are cut by a number of gaps and passes through which most of the trade with the Sahara and beyond was conducted. This segmentation of the topography made communications between the different Algerian communities slow and difficult, and hindered any unified resistance to the French.

Drawing a line from the greatest of the gaps in the mountain chains, the Hodna depression, through the town of Miliana to the sea, marks the geographers' rough distinction between 'eastern' and 'western' Algeria. The former, at least approaching the Mediterranean coast, benefits from more rain and is therefore suitable for cultivation. It includes the Grand Kabylia mountain range to the east of Algiers and close to the coast. This region is occupied almost entirely by Berber tribes with their distinctive social organisation of independent and frequently feuding village communes. Further east and inland lies the great plain of Constantine. Here the land was divided into large estates cultivating arable crops, in particular cereals, worked by sharecroppers or landless labourers in what can best be described as a 'semi-feudal' system.

In contrast, the land to the west of the geographers' dividing line has only about half the precipitation of the east. While the great valley of the River Shelif (Chelif) was mainly one of peasant agriculture, further west the drier lands of rolling hills and valleys were more hospitable to pastoralists than farmers. Historically, this was the region of nomadic and semi-nomadic Arab tribes. Criss-crossing this topographical segmentation lay the ethnic and cultural divisions – Arabs, Berbers, Kuloğlus and some remaining Turks.

Consequently, the various groups among the Algerians reacted in different ways to the French invasion. Without any unifying leadership they remained in disarray as to how to respond to the shock of an invasion which – unlike many European Christian attacks over the centuries – appeared unwilling to withdraw back across the sea. Sporadic episodes of Algerian resistance were breaking out, but the 300-year legacy of Ottoman rule had never created anything remotely resembling a 'national' consciousness in the Regency. Once the Turkish state apparatus was stripped away, what remained was a fractured, heterogeneous population with little but religion to hold it together – and even this was undermined by the proliferation of rival Sufi *tariqa*s (brotherhoods).[8] However, the most serious cleavage was between those who continued to believe in an umbilical cord which held them to the Ottoman Empire, and those who had no desire to retain any links with the sultan. The latter party looked instead to one or other of the Sufi *tariqa*s to convert the Regency into an independent Arab state.

The leader of the former tendency, and the first to declare his unconditional opposition to the French, was the forty-seven-year-old Hajj Ahmed bin Muhammad, Bey of Constantine. A Kuloğlu notable and great landholder, he had been appointed Bey in 1826. He considered himself a loyal servant of the Ottoman Empire; now that the Dey had abandoned the Regency, he believed that his loyalty reverted directly to the sultan in Istanbul. In a letter of October 1831 to Mahmud II, Ahmed Bey expressed this loyalty with absolute clarity: 'I have administered my affairs and led the country to which I have been assigned by the representatives of the Sublime Porte without ever exceeding the Imperial orders.'[9]

After the defeat of the Muslim army at the Battle of Staouéli, Ahmed Bey had gathered together around 2,000 of the vanquished troops and marched them back to the city of Constantine, 322 kilometres east of Algiers. This walled stronghold, which dates back to pre-Roman times, is situated in an almost impregnable position on a huge rocky outcrop, 2,000 feet above sea level and surrounded on three sides by a deep gorge. In some places the gorge is no more than 200 feet across, but it plunges down over 1,000 feet into the River Rummel.

The beylik was the largest and richest in the Regency with a population of around 1.1 million accounting for 40 per cent of the Regency's total population.[10] Its wealth came mainly from its trade with Tunis and – before the port of 'Annaba was captured by the French – its exports of wax, honey, olive oil, butter, wheat, barley and livestock via that port to Marseille.

On his return to Constantine, Ahmed Bey's first task was to follow in the footsteps of his sultan and eliminate the unruly and militarily useless Janissaries. After they were slaughtered he began to build an army composed of Arabs and Kabyle Berbers. By the mid-1830s the garrison of the city had been raised to 12,000 infantry and 12,000 cavalry, including the Bey's personal bodyguard of 2,000 Berber Zouaves.[11] Although a Kuloğlu with a strong attachment to the Ottoman Empire, the Bey recognised the necessity of eliminating the many offensive trappings of Turkish domination. In its stead he created a new, distinctly Arab state, albeit one which remained loyal to the sultan.

From now on, in a move to solidify opposition to the French, Arabic was made the beylik's official language. This was in spite of the Kuloğlu Ahmed Bey personally regarding all Arabs as an 'inferior race'.[12] All taxes on the population which did not have a Qur'anic basis were abolished and an eleven-man council was established, including both Hanafi and Maliki jurists, to advise the Bey in all civil and military matters. By all accounts this was no subservient talking shop, and Ahmed Bey participated in the council's discussion as simply one among equals. Furthermore Ahmed declared himself Paşa of the whole Algerian Regency and minted a new coinage stamped with the head of the sultan to emphasise Ottoman sovereignty over his new regime. He now called upon the other great Kuloğlu and Arab landowners of the Beylik to rally to his standard in preparation for war with the French, a war in which he expected to receive substantial military aid from Istanbul.

In the west, resistance against the French was slower to emerge and was complicated by a second Moroccan intervention on 16 August 1831 under the governor of Tetouan, Muhammad bin al-Himari. Al-Himari made two unsuccessful attacks on Oran and briefly occupied the town of Mascara, but after failing to win much support from the local Arab tribes he returned to Morocco in April 1832.

Nevertheless, this second Moroccan intervention served as a catalyst to rouse the Arabs of the western beylik against the French and those remaining Turks and Kuloğlus who had sided with the invaders. As a face-saving gesture for his royal master, before returning to Morocco, al-Himari named the revered seventy-five-year-old Muhyi al-Din – the leader of the Algerian section of the Qadiriyya Sufi *tariqa* – as the Moroccan sultan's *khalifa* and governor of Oran. In response, Muhyi al-Din decided to raise a jihad against the French. However, unlike Ahmed Bey of Constantine, Muhyi al-Din and his twenty-five-year-old second son, 'Abd al-Qadir, had long been hostile towards the Turks, whom they considered oppressors of the Arabs. And they rejected any identification with the Ottoman Empire.[13]

On 3 May 1832, Muhyi al-Din, leading a small force drawn from tribes of the West, launched his first attack on the French. Three days later, with an army that had now swelled to 12,000 men from thirty-two tribes, he began a blockade of the city of Oran.[14] It was at this point that the tribes called upon Muhyi al-Din to be their sultan and unify the resistance. But when the chiefs of the seven major tribes around the plain of Ghriss* came to the old man with this petition, he declined, offering instead his son who had already distinguished himself skirmishing with the French. So, on 21 and 22 November at Mascara, the old capital of the beylik of the West, a vast crowd of tribesmen acknowledged Muhyi's son 'Abd al-Qadir as the leader of the jihad. They witnessed his exchange of the black burnouse of the Beni Hashim tribal confederation for the crimson cloak of leadership.[15]

However, 'Abd al-Qadir also refused to accept the title of sultan out of respect for the one to whom he believed he owed his ultimate religious and political loyalty – not the Ottoman sultan in distant Istanbul, but 'Abd al-Rahman, the Alaouite sultan of Morocco. Instead he initially accepted only the title of Emir, but later chose the much more religiously significant *amir al-mu'minin* – Prince of the Believers. Following his investiture 'Abd al-Qadir sent the following letter to the chiefs of all the tribes in the Oran beylik:

---

* The plain of Ghriss is situated in the semi-arid region surrounding the town of Mascara at an altitude of around 585 metres, and covers an area of approximately 1,366 square kilometres.

Praise be to God.

To the Tribe of .....

Especially to its *ashraf* [nobles], religious leaders and distinguished men. Truly, the people of Mascara and the eastern and western Ghriss and their neighbours and allies have unanimously acknowledged me as their Emir and promised me to hear and obey in both good times and bad. [...] I have acknowledged their pledge and their obedience. As for myself, I have accepted this position against my own inclination, but hoping for the unity of the Muslims and the removal of infighting and quarrelling among them, and for the security of the traveller, the prevention of behaviour which contradicts the immaculate Qur'an, for the protection of our lands from the enemy, and for the enforcement of the law equally towards the strong and the weak. Be it known that my ultimate objective is the unity of the righteous community and the establishment of the most commendable religious practices. In all that my trust is in God so attend us and make clear your submission, render your allegiance and may God favour you and guide you. By order of the Defender of the Faith,

'Abd al-Qadir bin Muhyi al-Din
Mascara, 27 November 1832[16]

Although some of the biographies of 'Abd al-Qadir verge on hagiography, there can be no doubt that the young man was a remarkable individual. In his early years, he had been educated at the famous *zawiya* (college) of the Sufi Qadiriyya at El Guetna (Guittena), some sixteen kilometres southwest of Mascara. There, and also at another *zawiya* in Oran, he had studied widely, not only the traditional religious literature but also mathematics, geography, history and philosophy including the Greek masters, Plato and Aristotle. He also excelled in the military arts and especially in horsemanship, in which he was a master.

As to his appearance, he was small and slightly built, a little over five feet tall, but he was physically strong and could ride for days living on the most meagre rations. His pale skin, prominent forehead and aquiline nose were framed by a small, neatly trimmed black beard; and the colour of his eyes, depending on different accounts, was either black, grey or hazel.[17] According to General Thomas Bugeaud, who would later meet him, his face reminded the French officer of the conventional pictures of Jesus, an impression which is easy to understand if the portrait of him, attributable to Horace Vernet, is anything to go by.

However, by the beginning of 1833 only three of the seven tribes to whom 'Abd al-Qadir addressed his appeal had acknowledged the Emir's authority to lead the jihad against the French: the eastern and western (Gharaba) sections of the Beni Hashim and the Beni Amar. The chiefs of the former elite *makhzan* tribes, the Dawa'ir and Zmala, looked down upon the tribes they had previously policed on behalf of the Turks. While both their chieftains, Mustafa bin Isma'il and his nephew Muhammad bin Isma'il al-Mazari, came to Mascara and offered their submission, they ignored 'Abd al-Qadir's request that they move their tribes away from their lands in close proximity to Oran.[18]

Nevertheless, by 18 May 1833, 'Abd al-Qadir was able to assemble a total of 8,000 tribal cavalry and 1,000 infantry on the plain of Ersibia, near Mascara, where the Emir unfurled his banner, a white flag in which was displayed the image of an open hand.[19]

With the forces available to him, in July 1833 'Abd al-Qadir was able to take partial control of Tlemcen where he placed his own governor, a Berber of the Ouhassas tribe named Bou Hamedi.[20] 'Abd al-Qadir faced a challenge, however, because Tlemcen's Turks and Kuloğlus who had sided with the French* still occupied the town's ancient citadel which could hold up to 5,000 troops.[21] On 4 July the Emir's forces also captured the coastal town of Arzew, thirty-six kilometres east of Oran on the gulf of the same name, and on 29 they took Mostaganem.

While 'Abd al-Qadir consolidated his power in the beylik of Oran, two changes of leadership occurred among the French: on 29 April 1833 General Savary, who had become ill, was replaced as commander-in-chief by General Théophile Voirol. At the same time General Boyer, whose cruelty had become notorious even in France, was replaced as commander

---

* The attitude of the Kuloğlus and remaining Turks towards the French appears to have varied depending very much on local circumstances.

of the French troops in Oran by the fifty-one-year-old General Louis-Alexis Desmichels (1779–1845), yet another Napoleonic veteran and a renowned cavalry officer.

It was around this time that 'Abd al-Qadir began to record his ideas about how the struggle against the French should be fought and how modern European methods of military organisation and tactics could be combined with a movement for religious *tajdid* (renewal) and *islah* (reform). He saw both of these elements as necessary if the French were to be defeated.

Until now, his forces were almost entirely made up of tribal cavalry. Their traditional tactics were aptly known as *al-karr wa al-farr* (charge and retreat).[22] However, against disciplined European infantry the method was hopelessly ineffective, and so far 'Abd al-Qadir had only been able to hold his own against the French by weight of numbers. But during his pilgrimage to Mecca as a young man, 'Abd al-Qadir must have witnessed Mehmed Ali's new model army as he passed through Egypt, and it may have been this which prompted him to adopt the European military paradigm.

Sometime in 1833 he won the support of his eleven-man *shura* (advisory) council to create such a 'European' army, and he wrote a manual of military principles which would eventually be disseminated among his commanders and troops. It carried the flowery title *wushah al-kata'ib wa zaynat al-jaysh al-muhammadi al-ghalib* (The sword-belt of the battalions and the adornment of the conquering Muhammadian soldiers), and it contained a preface and twenty-four regulations.[23] However, in one respect the *wushah* departed from the type of army created by Mehmed Ali. In the Emir's new army there was to be no conscription; although the recruit would be expected to submit to rigorous drill exercises and strict military discipline, enlistment would be entirely voluntary.[24] Religious devotion was expected to be the potential recruit's primary motivation.

So great was the reverence for 'Abd al-Qadir's person and that of his father that he faced none of the religious opposition to his plans for a European-style army that Sultan Selim III had encountered. However, as a precaution the Emir took great pains to stress the Islamic identity of his new army, and the preface to the *wushah* invokes the Qur'anic verse *Sura* 64.1, titled 'The Battle Array', where Muhammad instructs his troops to fight 'as if they were buildings tightly packed together'.[25] Similarly, in his later recruitment proclamation to the tribes, he called upon volunteers to enrol 'under the banner of Muhammad' (*taht al-liwa al-muhammadi*) and always referred to his army as 'the army of Muhammad' (*al-jaysh al-muhammadi*).[26] In addition, the insignia of rank on his officers' shoulders, chests, etc. were to be strictly Islamic, such as the *shahada* evocation (No god but Allah and Muhammad is the Messenger of Allah) or the titles of the four Sunni juridical mathhabs (schools of law).[27]

According to the *wushah* manual there should be a clear functional separation of the three arms – infantry, cavalry and artillery. The infantry were to be organised in battalions of a 1,000 men commanded by an *agha* (colonel, Tur. *ağa*) with each divided into ten companies of 100 men under a *qa'id* (captain).[28] The organisational structure was clearly meant to be on the European model. His 'European' cavalry were to be organised in regiments of 1,000 divided into squadrons of fifty men and the artillery in teams of twelve men per cannon plus a commander. All the 'European' troops were to receive regular wages and rations according to their rank, and medical services provided by doctors and nurses; and if they were injured or killed in action their families would continue to receive the soldier's wages as a pension. There was also to be a corps of scribes to deal with all administrative matters, under the command of two officers with the rank of *bash katib* (senior scribe), one of whom was also tasked with ensuring the troops had access to places of prayer and clean water for their religious ablutions.[29]

However, despite this detail about organisational structure and the size of each military unit, 'Abd al-Qadir's *wushah* was more a theoretical schema than a project that could be rapidly implemented. Indeed, as late as January 1835 the Emir's 'European' troops consisted of just one battalion of 800 to 1,000 men and an artillery corps with only four cannons.[30] In the meantime he had to rely on his irregular forces and their traditional mode of combat.

French officers could not move very far from their coastal enclaves, yet that did not stop them from seizing prime agricultural property on their periphery, especially in the fertile Mitidja plain to the south of Algiers. At the same time, a small but steady stream of French, Spanish and Italian colonists were beginning to arrive with the intention of grabbing their own pieces of rural property. These land seizures inevitably involved further violence against the indigenous population, much of it committed under the rule of the Commander-in-Chief, General Savary, and General Boyer, his deputy in Oran, whose rationale was that 'to bring civilisation sometimes it is necessary to use uncivilised methods'.[31] It was probably Boyer who began the practice of collective punishments and reprisals for armed resistance. However, in the second major atrocity of the occupation, General Savary ordered the killing of the whole Arab tribe of al-'Ouffia, southeast of Algiers in October 1832. He also tyrannised the population of Algiers itself and executed a number of sheikhs who were not involved in any acts of resistance.[32]

Meanwhile, a few members of the old Ottoman Regency had remained in the city, one of whom was Hamdan ben Othman Khoja. Fifty-eight years old in 1830, he was the son of the first secretary of the Dey of Algiers and an Arab woman, and hence a Kuloğlu. The Kuloğlus had, by now, come to occupy a social and economic status virtually equivalent to that of full-blooded Turk, and in time Khoja became advisor to the Dey as well as being a great landowner on the Mitidja plain. He was also one of Algiers's principal merchants, a professor of Islamic law and not only bilingual in Arabic and Turkish but also a competent speaker of French and English, which he learnt during various missions to Europe with his father. Consequently, he was well versed in the affairs of Europe, European science and the political literature of the French enlightenment. He was also father-in-law to Hajj Ahmed Bey of Constantine.

Having observed the behaviour of the French occupation forces at first hand he decided to write an account of these events, which he took with him to Paris in early 1833. His original account, written in Arabic, has been lost: but the French translation was published in Paris in October 1833, titled *Le Miroir: Aperçu historique et statistique sur la régence d'Alger.*[33] It appears to have been written specifically for a French audience, partly as ammunition for the anti-imperialist members of the Chamber of Deputies which was currently debating the invasion, and partly to persuade a wider French audience that the actions of the French army in Algiers flagrantly violated the moral sentiments upon which – so he believed – the French state was founded.

The first and lengthy part of the *Miroir* deals with the history, geography and ethnology of the Regency of Algiers. It was intended to provide a general background for the French reader who had little idea of the complexity of Algerian society and its peoples other than the conventional horror stories of the 'Barbary pirates'. It is at the beginning of the second part that we get a clearer picture of the author. In spite of his Kuloğlu background, Hamdan

Khoja is the first Algerian voice to articulate the concept of the Regency of Algiers as a state, equivalent to any European state, as he makes clear in the following statement.

> When I examine ... the *other states* which surround us not one of them seems to me condemned to suffer consequences comparable to those which is our destiny. I see Greece, free and solidly established having been extracted from the Ottoman Empire. I see the people of Belgium separated from Holland because of their different religions. I see all the free peoples concerned about the Poles and re-establishing their independence ...and when I turn my eyes back to *the country of Algiers [le pays d'Alger]*, I see its miserable inhabitants placed under the yoke of arbitrary rule, of extermination and all the scourges of war, and all these horrors committed in the name of Free France. [My emphasis.][34]

As well as expressing his shock and disillusionment at the French invaders' behaviour he argues that the invasion threatens to destroy France's reputation for morality, culture and modern civilisation. He laments:

> this terrible war which has been a calamity for all Algerians [and] will unfailingly damage the French in the opinion of posterity for having allowed, not to say committed, all the horrors of which Algiers has become the theatre.

And then he continues in this poignant sentence:

> In the nineteenth century we might have thought that all narrow ideas of fanaticism have been forgotten, that the era of the emancipation of the peoples had arrived, and that all mankind that live on the surface of the globe should only be considered as forming one and the same family.[35]

Khoja does not deny the foolishness and incompetence of the old rulers of Algiers in dealing with the initial breakdown of the previously good relations with France. Yet most of the second part of the *Miroir* documents the series of French illegalities and cruelties in breach of the treaty which had ended the initial hostilities, for example, the 1830 massacre at Blida.[36] In spite of such events, it seems that Hamdan Khoja retained some hopes that the French would soon realise the futility of trying to subdue an indigenous population which he believed (incorrectly) amounted to 10 million.[37]

Using those sections of the Parisian press which were sympathetic, Khoja tirelessly publicised the grievances of his countrymen and sent requests to both King Philippe and his war minister, Marshal Soult, for a committee of enquiry to be sent to Algiers to investigate the abuses committed by the army of occupation. In July his request was granted. The report of the investigatory committee published in 1834 was devastating and included the following damning words:

> We have sent to their deaths on simple suspicion and without trial people whose guilt was always doubtful and then despoiled their heirs. We massacred people carrying our safe conducts, slaughtered on suspicion entire populations subsequently found to be innocent; we have put on trial men considered saints in the country, men revered because they had enough courage to expose themselves to our fury so that they could intervene on behalf of their unfortunate compatriots.[38]

The report prompted six tumultuous months of debate in the Chamber of Deputies which pitted colonialists against republican and socialist anticolonialists. But the legislature found itself unable to either accept or reject its recommendations. Ultimately matters were settled by Soult, the war minister, who persuaded King Louis-Philippe to sign an ordinance on 22 July 1834, ignoring the investigatory committee's report and establishing a military colony in Algeria with the title 'Les Possessions Françaises dans le Nord de l'Afrique'. The former Regency would now be headed by a governor invested with both civil and military powers. As such, this and further ordinances 'conferred upon Algeria a regime of legislation by executive decree totally at odds with French public law'.[39]

Meanwhile the French government had adopted a measure to boost its troop numbers in Algiers where disease, desertion and the hit-and-run tactics of the Muslim resistance were making continued service in the new colony unattractive. On 9 March 1831 a royal ordinance announced the formation of a 'Foreign Legion' for service only outside French continental territory. Another ordinance on 18 March excluded French and Swiss citizens from enlisting in the new unit, although in practice this would frequently be circumvented by French local authorities who contrived to empty their undesirables from jails and workhouses into the Legion.[40]

The Legion was organised along the same lines as regular French infantry, with battalions composed of eight companies each of 112 men. As far as possible each battalion was composed of men speaking the same language. The first three battalions created consisted of ex-soldiers from disbanded Swiss and German regiments; the fourth was largely Spanish; the fifth, Italians and Sardinians; and the sixth, Dutch and Belgians. The regular French troops and their officers initially regarded them as little more than an unreliable rabble; but under a tough Swiss officer, Colonel Stoffel, and fierce disciplinary measures the new legionaries were moulded into a reasonably effective fighting force.[41] By January 1832 the 1st, 2nd, 3rd and 5th battalions were installed in camps around Algiers and the 4th battalion was based at Oran. In 1834 a 6th battalion of Poles was created. In due course the Foreign Legion would become the spearhead of French imperialism throughout North Africa and beyond.

In spite of winning some local skirmishes against 'Abd al Qadir's men, the newly appointed French commander, General Desmichels, was still facing considerable difficulties. France had only three enclaves on the coast, which were being blockaded by the Arabs; and in the largest of these, Oran, Desmichels had only 2,500 troops under his command, many of whom were now suffering from typhus.

Desmichels's difficulties were well known to 'Abd al-Qadir because he had wisely continued to allow some limited trading with the French by a key group of Jewish merchants, in particular Judas Ben Duran and Mordecai Amar. With their extensive network of agents in both Algiers and France itself, these traders were able to supply him with up-to-date intelligence. They became, in effect, the Emir's 'foreign office', and it was Mordecai Amar who was chosen to conduct diplomatic relations with the French in Oran over the coming months.

*French Infantry
in Algeria c. 1832*
Note the Napoleonic-era uniforms
still in use.

Desmichels concluded that, with no reinforcements likely in the foreseeable future, the only way to remove the blockade of his enclaves and pacify the interior was to make peace with 'Abd al-Qadir, in the expectation that the Emir would become an ally of France and not its unrelenting enemy. He therefore sent a document containing a number of peace proposals to the Emir. These included the pledge that 'the religion and uses of the Muslims would be respected', the Emir would 'give up all French prisoners', 'The markets shall be free', 'French deserters would be given up by the Arabs', and 'every Christian travelling in the interior shall be furnished with a passport carrying the seal of 'Abd al-Qadir and that of the General'.[42]

'Abd al-Qadir indicated that he agreed with these terms by appending his seal to Desmichels's document. On 25 February 1834 he sent Mordecai Amar to Oran with the signed document – but adding some additional conditions of his own: that 'the Arabs shall be at liberty to buy and sell powder, arms, sulphur; in a word everything necessary for war' and that "Abd al-Qadir should have a monopoly over Arab trade with the French which could only be carried out through the port of Azreu'.[43] By now Desmichels's situation was becoming desperate and he accepted these additional terms. The wording of what became known as the Desmichels Treaty was finalised on 26 February 1834, but it now included yet another clause favourable to the Arabs: 'to avoid collisions between the French and the Arabs, representatives on the part of the Emir shall reside at Oran, Mostaganem and Azreu', and 'French officers shall reside at Mascara.'[44] This was equivalent to agreeing to an exchange of consuls, and implicitly recognised 'Abd al-Qadir's sovereignty over the whole beylik of Oran outside its three French coastal enclaves.

The Desmichels Treaty was rather typical of the way French commanders operated during the first years of the invasion. They behaved as though their commands were matters of private enterprise. Desmichels did not immediately inform his superior in Algiers, General Voirol, of his pact with 'Abd al-Qadir and, when he did, he presented it as his achieving 'the submission of the province of Oran, the largest and most belligerent of the whole Regency'.[45] Voirol and many of the other French commanders did not see it that way. Nevertheless the Treaty was later approved by King Louis-Philippe. Eventually, however, knowledge of the precise details of the Treaty became widely known and there was a wave of vociferous criticism of both the Treaty and Desmichels himself in the French press and parliament. As a result, in February 1835, he was removed from his position at Oran and replaced by General Camille Alphonse Trézel (1780–1860), who rejected Desmichels's whole strategy of controlling the interior through a strong, respected Arab leader.

Matters soon came to a head over the Dawa'ir and Zmala *makhzan* tribes. By now the agha of the Dawa'ir, Mustafa bin Isma'il, had come out openly against 'Abd al-Qadir and had fled to Tlemcen where he joined the Kuloğlus and Turks occupying its citadel. At the same time, the Dawa'ir and Zmala tribes began trading independently with the French, contrary to the Emir's orders. When 'Abd al-Qadir ordered the Dawa'ir and Zmala to stop, they offered their submission to General Trézel. On 16 June 1835 Trézel signed a treaty with the two *makhzan* tribes under which they became allies of the French. Two years later, on 29 July 1837, the French awarded Mustafa bin Isma'il the rank of Brigadier General.

'Abd al-Qadir complained that this favouring of the *makhzan* tribes contradicted the Desmichels Treaty, which stated that the French would not harbour Arab deserters: this, he not unreasonably argued, included whole tribes, not just individuals. In response, he withdrew his consuls from Oran, Mostaganem and Azreu, and expelled the French consul from Mascara. It was a return to war.

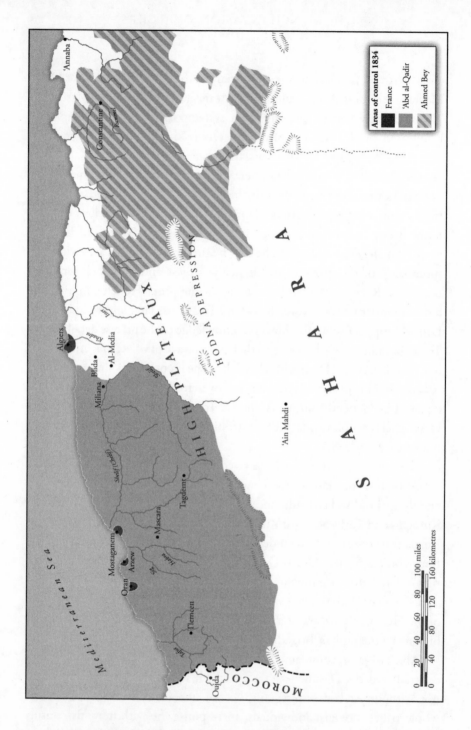

THE FORMER REGENCY OF ALGIERS, SHOWING TERRITORY CEDED
TO ʿABD AL-QADIR UNDER THE 1834 DESMICHELS TREATY, AND
AREAS CONTROLLED BY THE FRENCH AND AHMED BEY

The territory of the Dawa'ir and Zmala lay about 60 miles southwest of Oran. 'Abd al-Qadir decided to remove their warriors and their families into the interior by force, far from Oran and towards Tlemcen. To protect his new allies, on 26 June Trézel marched on Mascara with 2,500 infantry – including two battalions of the newly formed Foreign Legion, the 4th Battalion (Poles) and the 5th Battalion (Italians).[46] The column was also made up of a cavalry regiment, the Chasseurs d'Afrique, four pieces of artillery and a mobile hospital.[47]

The Emir learnt that Trézel was allowing his cavalry to cut down all the crops on the lands of 'Abd al-Qadir's own tribe, the Beni Hashim, and use them for forage. The Emir's main army lay somewhat to the west of Trézel's line of march; he despatched 2,000 cavalry and 800 infantry towards the Sig River where the tribal lands were situated. Learning of their approach, Trézel decided to attack them before they were reinforced by the Arabs' main army. Marching towards what Trézel believed would be the Arabs' line of approach, on the 27th the French and Legionary troops entered a forested area known as Mulay Isma'il. Before the General realised it, he had collided with the advanced guard of the Emir's army of around 8,000 cavalry and 4,000 infantry. Fired on from all sides by Arab sharpshooters hidden in the dense, undulating woodland, Trézel's men panicked and began to flee, but somehow he managed to restore order and avoid a complete rout of his inexperienced soldiers.

As night drew in, the French enjoyed a respite from the fighting; but by now 'Abd al Qadir was approaching with his main force. The following day Trézel decided he had to return to Oran with his wounded, after which he might be able to renew the offensive, but he found his way blocked by the Emir's forces. Instead, he turned towards Azreu. This meant marching his men through the defile of the Habra River which later merges with the Sig before it changes its name to the Macta on its final journey to the Gulf of Azreu.[48] About midday the French entered the defile of the Habra only to find that on either side it was bristling with Arab infantry. Their foes had been rushed to the gorge, each soldier having been carried by one of al-Qadir's cavalry. Then the remainder of the Emir's cavalry fell upon Trézel's men who fled, abandoning all their wagons, their guns and hundreds of muskets in the salt marshes where the Sig and Habra meet.[49]

In the Battle of Macta, as it was later known, the French lost 362 dead and 308 wounded.[50] These casualties would have been much heavier had not the Arabs halted to pillage the French baggage train and kill the wounded, most of whom were decapitated along with those who had already been killed. It was a practice which disgusted 'Abd al-Qadir and henceforth he decreed that, while cutting off the heads of the enemy in the heat of battle was acceptable, the killing and decapitating of the wounded was contrary to Islam and would be severely punished.[51] Trézel, who had acted with considerable bravery during the debacle, accepted full responsibility for the defeat, but was removed from his command and replaced by another officer.

Unfortunately for 'Abd al-Qadir, his victory at the Battle of Macta only provoked the colonialist elements in the French government to redouble their efforts to crush the Emir and his forces. In the Chamber of Deputies the fiercely nationalistic French interior minister, Adolphe Thiers, raged against those who advocated a limited, small-scale occupation. He engineered the appointment of General Bertrand Clauzel as governor-general; Clauzel returned to Algiers for a second time on 8 July 1835. On 21 November 1835, the Governor-General set sail for Algiers, accompanied by the royal heir apparent, the Duke of Orleans, 10,000 reinforcements and an order from the King to demolish 'Abd al-Qadir's capital, Mascara. In early December the French advanced on Mascara with around 15,000 men and swept aside 'Abd al-Qadir's troops. The French entered the town on 6 December and set fire to many of its buildings. The Emir retreated six miles south of the town to his family's tribal lands, but with every intention of keeping up the struggle, in spite of the demoralised flight of some of his tribal allies. As the British journal the *Annual Register* commented, 'The Amir has been chastened inasmuch as the destruction of his capital is concerned; but the destruction of an African town does not dry-up the resources of an Arab chief.'[52]

Indeed, having largely destroyed Mascara, Clauzel had little choice but to return to Oran with his army, as they were depleted by illness and desertion. However, he had undoubtedly scored a victory of sorts, and he followed it up by marching on Tlemcen where, on 13 January 1836, he relieved the Kuloğlus besieged in the citadel. Meanwhile most of the town's Arab population fled towards the Moroccan border. On 23 January, determined to retain the town and its surrounding area as a communications link with the mouth of the Tafna River, Clauzel engaged 'Abd al-Qadir's troops in what turned out to be a straggling, ten-day battle. Weakened by constant guerrilla attacks, he was forced to retreat to Tlemcen where he left a small French garrison. He then returned to Algiers where he announced, 'The war is over! 'Abd al-Qadir has fled to the Sahara to lick his wounds.'[53] In fact the Emir had simply slipped across the border into Morocco.

Meanwhile, Marshall Soult had chosen Brigadier-General Thomas Bugeaud (1774–1849), another Napoleonic veteran, to continue the campaign in Oran. On 6 June 1836, Bugeaud commanded three freshly arrived regiments numbering 4,500 men, and landed at the mouth of the River Tafna. He then marched on Tlemcen where he rescued the small, beleaguered French garrison which Clauzel had left there. In response, 'Abd al-Qadir mobilised his forces and on 7 July 1835 he attacked Bugeaud on the Sikkak River, north of Tlemcen. But 'Abd al-Qadir's army was decisively defeated in the pitched battle which followed, losing over 1,200 men killed, 130 taken prisoners, and 700 precious muskets.

The Emir retreated with the remainder of his army to a new base he was constructing at the old ruined town of Tagdempt, 130 kilometres southeast of Oran. It was in the interior and thus out of reach of any lumbering French columns with their supply trains and other impedimenta. Similar strongpoints were also being prepared at Sayda, south of Tlemcen; Taza, south of Mascara; Boghar, south of Miliana; and Bel Kherout, south of al-Media.[54] It was at Tagdempt that he established a mint issuing coins with, on one side, the inscription 'It is the will of God: I have appointed him my agent', and on the other 'Struck at Tagdemt by Sultan 'Abd al-Qadir'. Clearly the Emir now saw his role as the founder of a new state, not just an agglomeration of tribes.

Bugeaud's successes at Tlemcen and Sikkak were rewarded by his promotion to lieutenant-general, and for the time being he returned on leave to his estate in the Dordogne where he was also a deputy in the Chamber of Deputies. Meanwhile Clauzel, who remained flushed with his own 'success' at Mascara, began to plan a much more ambitious campaign: to advance into the former beylik of Constantine, 322 kilometres east of Algiers, and besiege and destroy its capital and ruler, Hajj Ahmed Bey.

For the previous four years, successive French commanders had attempted to get Hajj Ahmed Bey to submit. The terms were always the same: he would retain the beylik of Constantine, but in return acknowledge the sovereignty of France and pay the French the tribute he had formerly paid to the Dey of Algiers. But Ahmed Bey repeatedly refused the offers and, on 29 September 1833 he began a campaign of all-out war against the French and their tribal allies in the province. By November he had extended his control as far west as al-Media in the former beylik of Titteri, although later he was later forced to evacuate it, having first ordered the execution of 100 of the town's notables who had previously pledged their loyalty to the French.[55]

By January 1834, Ahmed Bey felt he had achieved enough to expect military support from Sultan Mahmud to further prosecute his war against the French. But no such support was forthcoming. Desperate for European help against Mehmed Ali, Mahmud merely instructed his grand vezir to reply on his behalf: 'There is no doubt I would like to support you. But at this moment I am at peace with all the Christian powers [including France] and I cannot break with them without the most serious motive.'[56]

There was another reason why Sultan Mahmud and the Porte showed such comparatively little interest in any involvement in the affairs of the Algiers Regency at this time, except via desultory diplomatic activity in Paris: political events in Tripoli suddenly offered the possibility of fully re-absorbing this most independent of the regencies into the Ottoman Empire.

In 1832, Tripoli was still ruled by the sixty-five-year-old Yusuf Karamanli, who had held the *paşalik* since 1795. The ailing Yusuf had nominated his son by a white concubine, Prince 'Ali Karamanli, as his successor, but Muhammad Karamanli, Yusuf's grandson by a different concubine, challenged the decision. On 12 August 1832, the Paşa abdicated in favour of Prince 'Ali; and the supporters of the rival, Muhammad, began a civil war against 'Ali. In 1834, 'Ali received the *firman* (decree) of Sultan Mahmud confirming his legitimacy as paşa, and his rival, Muhammad, committed suicide. Even so, the struggle between Muhammad's supporters and the new Paşa continued.

Then, on 20 May 1835, a Turkish brig arrived in Tripoli's harbour. It carried a despatch from the grand vezir announcing that the sultan was sending troops to help 'Ali restore order, since he was deeply concerned by the continuing power struggle in the Regency. In reality, Mahmud had become increasingly worried about growing French influence over 'Ali, at a time when he was also confronting the menace of Mehmed Ali's French-trained army.

Five days later, Tripoli's harbour received a Turkish squadron of ten warships and ten troop transports. Courtesy visits were exchanged between the ships and the shore, after which 5,000 Turkish troops disembarked. On 28 May, the Turkish commander, Nejib Paşa, invited 'Ali Paşa and his chief minister aboard his flagship. It was a clever ruse. The two men were kidnapped and Nejib Paşa arrived onshore with the declaration that Tripoli had now returned to the full control of the Ottoman Empire.[57] After 135 years of virtual independence, the Regency of Tripoli disappeared. It was the most successful of Mahmud II's efforts to recentralise the Empire; and Tripoli would remain an integral part of that Empire until 1911.

Encouraged by this success and aware that negotiations in Paris over the fate of Algiers were making no progress, Sultan Mahmud began to reconsider his previously negative attitude to Hajj Ahmed's appeal for help. In early 1836 the Porte sent an emissary, Kamil Bey, to Constantine to evaluate the political and military situation in the beylik. At the same time Tahir Paşa, minister of marine, was instructed to take the Ottoman fleet to Tunis with the objective of reasserting full imperial control over that Regency, as had occurred in Tripoli.

On his arrival in Constantine, Kamil Bey was given a joyful reception. Hajj Ahmed had convened a large gathering of city notables and loyal tribal sheikhs to receive the emissary's message. They heard Kamil Bey convey the sultan's praises for their continued allegiance. While Kamil Bey urged them keep up their spirits, he also announced that the sultan still believed it was necessary to continue negotiations with the French in Paris: in a few days' time a successful outcome was anticipated – but if not, then 'the decision would be taken to come to your aid with substantial forces'.[58]

Kamil Bey returned to Istanbul with a highly positive view of Hajj Ahmed and his endeavours. But by now the Porte was under heavy pressure from the French ambassador, Admiral Roussin, to abandon any attempts, either directly or indirectly, to recover even a part of the Regency of Algiers. Meanwhile Tahir Paşa's fleet was approaching Tunisian waters. Placing Tunis under Ottoman control would remove French influence and enable arms and men to flow over the border into Hajj Ahmed's territory.

The French government recognised the danger. A fleet was immediately despatched to Tunis and the French government informed the Porte that it would not tolerate any attempt to replicate what had occurred in Tripoli the previous year. Mahmud contemplated the likely destruction of his navy, and capitulated. Tahir Paşa received orders not to enter Tunisian waters. It was clear that from now on Hajj Ahmed Bey and his men would be on their own.

Clauzel believed the time was now ripe to inflict a crushing defeat on Hajj Ahmed Bey. His first term of duty in Algiers had been less than successful and this second chance since his demission in 1831 gave him the opportunity to return to France in glory. He had always been one of the most enthusiastic supporters of colonisation and he believed that the greatest opportunities lay in the former beylik of Constantine – provided the power of Ahmed Bey could be broken. And that meant the capture of the city of Constantine.

War Minister Marshal Soult was sceptical. Did his new governor-general really understand the nature of the terrain, the state of the roads and the likely response of the tribes in that part of the Regency? Would he have enough troops to mount an effective siege of Constantine? Given that a campaign could not be launched until the autumn, was there not a risk of adverse weather? And, if so, were troops sufficiently well equipped and supplied to meet any such contingencies? But none of these considerations seemed to trouble Clauzel, because he had received intelligence, which he believed to be accurate, that the inhabitants of the city of Constantine so hated Ahmed Bey that as soon as the French arrived outside the city its gates would be thrown open to welcome them. So with the roughly 8,700 troops under his command Clauzel believed the campaign would be a 'promenade'. Soult was not convinced; but in the curiously laissez-faire attitude which had, so far, characterised the whole occupation, the war minister shrugged his shoulders and allowed Clauzel to proceed at his own risk.

Clauzel arrived at 'Annaba on 31 October 1836 and issued his orders for the campaign. His 8,000 infantry were organised in four brigades; one brigade formed the advance guard under General de Rigny; and, of the remaining three, one was commanded by General Trézel. They were supported by 780 engineers and sappers commanded by a Colonel Lemercier, and by an artillery train of six field guns and ten mountain howitzers. However, the number of effective French troops was considerably lower than these figures would suggest. Many of the men were suffering from malaria: for example, of the engineers and sappers only 464 were fit for service. Colonel Lemercier himself was already ill.

The advance guard left 'Annaba on 8 November heading for the small town of Guelma, 60 kilometres south-south-west of 'Annaba and about halfway between that town and Constantine. En route the engineers constructed bridges and ramps across the Seybouse River to help the heavy wagon trains which would have to cross. Clauzel and the main army left 'Annaba on the 13th in fine weather, but later that day a thunderstorm broke and some parts of the wagon train got bogged down in the mud. Only with great difficulty did the engineers manage to recover them. The rain continued until 9 a.m. on the 14th and the terrain became so waterlogged and ploughed up that they had to abandon quantities of forage and twenty-one heavy scaling ladders, to lighten the wagons' load.[59]

Between 15 November and the 19th the army struggled into the mountains over difficult territory, and on the night of the 19th the heavy rains returned, continuing the following day. On the 21st all night the rain fell in torrents mixed with hail and snow. By the morning seventeen soldiers had frozen to death; many others had their feet frozen.[60]

By the evening of the 21st the whole army reached the plateau of Mansoura on the eastern side of Constantine. They faced one of the precipitous gorges, carved out by the River Rummel, which surround the city on three sides. From this vantage point the only access to the city was on the northeast corner of the city, over El Kantara, the ancient Roman bridge, eighty metres long but only two-and-a-half metres wide. It spanned an impassable chasm hundreds of metres deep. At the far end of the bridge two heavy gates, strengthened by iron bars, blocked entrance to the city. The only easily accessible approach to Constantine lay to the south on a kind of isthmus from the neighbouring tableland, known as Koudiat Aty; but even on this side the city was defended by substantially built walls, and to reach the plain of Koudiat Aty the French troops would have to cross the dangerous waters of the Rummel.

Meanwhile, Ahmed Bey had known for some days about the French expedition approaching his stronghold. So he placed his principal commander, Bin 'Aissa, in charge of the city with 1,000 experienced soldiers, backed up by around 1,000 volunteers. Ahmed Bey planned to take the cavalry out of the city to harass the French when the opportunity arose. He didn't have to wait long.

Clauzel ordered his artillery, positioned about 600 metres from the city gates of the Kantara, to try to make a breach so that his infantry could storm across the Roman bridge. At the same time he sent his advance guard to cross the Rummel and take up positions on Koudiat Aty. His troops managed to accomplish this manoeuvre only by fording the river up to their waists in freezing waters.

The principal French baggage train, loaded with essential supplies of food and ammunition, was still struggling to ascend the heights, and straggled six kilometres behind the rest of the army. Since the men and horses were exhausted, the officer in charge, Colonel Lemercier, ordered a halt to bivouac, a bivouac which the French troops soon called 'the camp of mud'. By the 22nd, snow was falling. It seemed impossible to make any further progress with the wagon train, so it was decided to abandon some of the heavy carts. The food they were carrying was distributed to the wagoneers, engineers and men of the 62nd Regiment of Infantry who were guarding the column. But at this point discipline collapsed; weary troops broke into brandy casks and many of them became hopelessly drunk. Unbeknown to the column, Hajj 'Ahmed's cavalry had for some time been shadowing them. Now the Arab forces seized this opportunity to attack. Many of the French were slaughtered before discipline could be restored and the march resumed, but a total of nine wagons carrying food supplies were lost, together with two ammunition carts. [61]

During the night of the 22nd the French artillery continued to hammer away at the at the city gates on El Kantara, but two attempts to scale the city walls, made the following day, failed. As a result of the catastrophic loss of the baggage train, Clauzel now had ammunition and food supplies for only three days. Unless he could break into the city very soon, he would have to abandon the whole campaign and retreat to 'Annaba. With great bravery, sappers from the engineering corps and the elite companies of the 63rd infantry made further attempts to break into the city. But when these failed, Clauzel was forced to admit defeat.

The retreat from Constantine was a terrible experience for the demoralised French army, comparable to Napoleon's retreat from the siege of Acre. Harried by Ahmed Bey's cavalry, alternately drenched with rain and frozen by heavy snowfalls, what was left of the expedition managed to get back to 'Annaba by 1 December 1836. The army had lost between 3,000 and 4,500 men dead and wounded, mostly during the retreat.[62] It was the worst military defeat suffered by the French army since the beginning of the occupation. As a result Clauzel was relieved of his position as governor-general on 12 February 1837 and replaced by General Charles-Marie Denys, Comte de Damrémont – yet another former Napoleonic officer.

This battle marked the high point of the resistance to the occupation. In spite of some setbacks, in the west 'Abd al-Qadir's forces controlled virtually the whole of the former beylik of Oran; in the east Hajj Ahmed Bey had driven the French from most of the beylik of Constantine. After nearly six years of occupation the French were still largely confined to Algiers, its immediate hinterland and a few coastal enclaves. Only 14,561 European settlers had arrived, mostly confined to the city of Algiers, and they had to be protected by 29,897 French troops.[63] And these forces were still in disarray with regard to the purpose and value of the invasion. If 'Abd al Qadir and Hajj Ahmed Bey had united their forces, as the perceptive Hamdan Khoja was now advocating, they might have convinced the French to abandon what was proving to be a terrible drain on manpower and resources. But it was not to be.

CHAPTER 15

Saving the Sultans:
The Emergence of Inter-Imperialist Rivalry

If Britain was showing scant concern over France's imperialist project in Algeria – a project which was currently looking pointlessly wasteful of both money and men – it was because Britain's ruling class of aristocratic financiers and commercial landowners, together with its junior partner of prosperous manufacturers, was busy pursuing a very different form of imperialism: an 'imperialism of free trade'.[1]

By the 1830s, Britain had made the crucial leap from simple manufacturing to steam-powered mechanisation. The Industrial Revolution had truly begun, spearheaded by great improvements in the productivity of the cotton goods industry and resulting in huge falls in costs and prices. As a result, Britain virtually destroyed competition from the Indian artisan cotton cloth industry. In the years 1810–19 British exports of cotton cloth totalled 227 million yards; by 1830–39 this figure had almost doubled to 553 million. By the same comparison exports of cotton thread and yarn increased six-fold, from 14 million lb to 87 million.[2] Dragged along by the beginnings of the railway-building boom in 1832, production of iron also soared and iron exports – a consequence of British railway construction in Europe – increased from 47,000 tons in 1810–19 to 180,000 in 1830–39. The British merchant navy expanded along with this surge in exports. The average tonnage per year carried by shipping registered in the UK during the decade 1790–99 was 1.443 million tons; by 1830–39 this had risen to 2.278 million per year of which 52,000 was carried by steam ships.[3]

In response to this flood of British exports into their countries many of Britain's trading partners throughout the world were beginning to raise tariffs or establish trading monopolies to protect their own infant industries. It was therefore very important for Britain to persuade these countries – ideally by peaceful diplomacy but if not, by more virile methods – of the error of their ways in ignoring one of the main precepts of the new 'science' of political economy. Namely, that by removing those 'obstacles to trade' they would ultimately prosper too. It was a policy cleverly designed to reduce foreign protection against British exports once Britain had successfully used tariff protection to support its own infant industries. And it would soon have a bearing on events in the Mediterranean basin.

Very much at the helm of this 'free trade imperialism' was Britain's foreign secretary, Lord Palmerston. Henry John Temple, 3rd Viscount Palmerston, hailed from a family of minor Irish aristocrats. He was forty-nine in 1833. While he had been involved in government and political life for twenty-seven of those years – the greater part of them as secretary at war* – he had not obtained high political office until 1830, when he switched his allegiance from the Tory party to the Whigs. Perhaps surprisingly, given his earlier, conservative political allegiance, it was the 'liberal' wing of the Whigs to which Palmerston gravitated, although it should be stressed that the word 'liberal' did not have the same connotations as it does today. For Palmerston to be a 'liberal' was simply to favour greater representation in Parliament for the middle classes, and energetically promote free trade.

Palmerston was tall, handsome, strong (he engaged in the popular sport of pugilism) and an inveterate womaniser, characteristics which won him the affection of many of those who slaved in his country's 'dark satanic mills'. For his part, he despised them: were they enfranchised, he argued, those 'men who murder their children to get £9 to be spent on drink' would only 'sell their vote for whatever they can get for it'.[4]

He is often described as an imperialist, an impression associated with his occasional resort to gunboat diplomacy. The 'imperialism of free trade' which Palmerston favoured had only a secondary interest in acquiring formal colonies, as the French were currently attempting. It was generally only when and where informal political means failed to provide the framework of security for British enterprise that the question of establishing formal empire arose.[5] Occasionally this became necessary, as when the Chinese attempted to block imports of British opium in 1842 and were then severely

---

* The secretary at war was responsible for the financial affairs of the British Army. Palmerston held this office from 1809 to 1828.

punished by the Royal Navy, compelling the Chinese to surrender to Britain the commercially useful island of Hong Kong. But such acquisitions were not the primary objective of Palmerston's brand of imperialism.

The Ottoman Empire was a particular focus of Palmerston's attention. With French trade in the Mediterranean severely weakened after the Napoleonic Wars, by the early 1830s the sultan's dominions appeared to offer rich opportunities for Britain's manufactured exports. They also held attraction as a convenient source of raw materials. However, the sultan's empire was recalcitrant and had thrown obstacles in the way of Britain's economic penetration. Moreover, for the time being, Palmerston's plans to bring the Ottoman Empire into the fold of 'free trade' had to be subordinated to his concern for the actual survival of the sultan and his government.

In 1833, Lord (John) Ponsonby, who had been appointed Ambassador to the Sublime Porte the previous year, was tasked by Palmerston with three principal objectives. First, to win back for Britain the influence and prestige it had lost to the Russians when it failed to come to the aid of Sultan Mahmud after his Syrian provinces were seized by Mehmed Ali's Egyptian army. Second, Ponsonby was to do everything he could to prevent the sultan from launching a premature counter-attack on Ibrahim's forces. Such an attack, Palmerston believed, might end in military disaster; if so, it could give the Russians – currently in alliance with the Porte – an excuse to bring more troops and warships to the Straits and strengthen their grip on the Ottoman Empire. Third, Palmerston was well aware that British merchants were currently unable to trade profitably with the Ottoman Empire as a result of its trade monopolies and customs duties (principally its internal tariffs). Ponsonby was therefore to prevail upon the Porte to sign an agreement that would remedy these obstacles to free trade. This reflected Palmerston's favourite epithet: 'It is the business of government to open and secure the roads for the merchant.'[6]

However, the immediate priority was the actual survival of the Empire. So Palmerston wrote to Ponsonby in December, stressing that:

> Our great aim should be to try to place the Porte in a state of internal organisation compatible with independence and to urge the government to recruit their army and their finances

and to put their navy into some order ... The army ought to be their first object.[7]

Although Palmerston had no particular desire to expand Britain's formal empire, nonetheless he was keeping a watchful eye on other European powers which might seize parts of the Ottoman Empire where Britain had strong commercial interests. Such an event, he believed, could lead to the outbreak of another major European war. It was with this possibility in mind that Palmerston became, in effect, the protector of the Ottoman Empire and the opponent of any forces – inside or outside that Empire – which might lead to its dissolution.

However, it encouraged Palmerston somewhat that, since the destruction of the Janissaries, Mahmud had been taking cautious steps to modernise not only the army but the Ottoman state as a whole. The beginnings of a modern war ministry had been established, and in 1827 an army medical school was created. In 1831 the last remnants of the semi-feudal *timar* system of landholding were abolished. In the same year the first Ottoman newspaper (in Turkish) was published, although it was a purely official one. In 1834 the Porte authorised a School of Military Sciences. Efforts were also made to increase the small number of educated Turks with knowledge of European languages, and to establish Ottoman embassies in European capitals; these had previously existed for only a short time under Sultan Selim. In addition, something was being done to weaken the power of the *ulema* by bringing religious foundations under state control.[8]

But one legacy of the old regime seemed intractable – the question of Ottoman 'finances'. In his December 1833 letter to Ambassador Ponsonby, Palmerston had mentioned this issue only in passing, yet fiscal problems remained the Achilles' heel of the Empire. The expenses incurred during the wars fought by Mahmud and his predecessor, Selim, combined with the costs of building Mahmud's new 'European' army, continued to outstrip the revenues collected by the central government. These revenues were continuously being drained away by the army of intermediaries embedded in the tax-collection system. Although Ottoman official budget documents do not exist from the 1780s to the end of the 1830s, there is no doubt that budget deficits soared during this period.[9] The indirect evidence of this can be seen in the repeated debasement of the Ottoman currency as the government sought to balance its books by paying its bills in currency containing a diminishing proportion of silver. Between 1808 and 1839, the silver content of the *kuruş* declined by 80 per cent; and the exchange rate of the *kuruş* against the British pound sterling declined from 18 in 1808 to 110 in 1844. The inevitable consequence was inflation: consumer prices increased more than five-fold during the same period.[10]

By the mid-1830s the British merchant community in Istanbul was vociferously demanding 'free trade' in its commercial dealings with the Porte, and Palmerston could not ignore these people. According to the long-standing capitulations system, European merchants paid an *ad valorem* of a mere 3 per cent on goods imported into the Empire. In reality the merchants paid far more than this. To the duties paid at the point of importation were added numerous other taxes charged as the goods were moved inland. These inland duties greatly exceeded those stipulated in the capitulations. According to a British official in Istanbul advising Ponsonby on obtaining a new trade convention, 'our imports were taxed, forty, fifty, sixty per cent and Turkish exports sixty, seventy and a hundred'.[11] This was probably an exaggeration, but it was certainly true that, in addition to the 3 per cent import and export tariffs, both foreign and Ottoman merchants paid at least a further 8 per cent duty on all commodities transported within the Empire.[12]

The problem for Palmerston was that, by the mid-1830s, these additional 'internal' charges, together with the import and export duties and the sale of monopolies, had become an important part of Ottoman revenues. Hence, they made a significant contribution to the fiscal improvements which Palmerston was so strongly urging via his ambassador, Ponsonby. The dilemma was that it was precisely these duties that the British wanted to abolish in the interests of 'free trade'.

Meanwhile, an ailing Sultan Mahmud, his body weakened by excessive consumption of alcohol and narcotics, was still determined to drive Mehmed Ali's Egyptian army out of Syria. So, in order to sideline the influence of Russia, Ponsonby was forced to hold out to Mahmud the hope that Britain might support the sultan militarily should the threat from the Egyptian army intensify.

However, at this particular conjuncture, Palmerston was distracted by a civil war in Spain, where Britain was supporting the legitimate Queen against the rebellion of the fanatically Catholic contender, Don Carlos.

So he was reluctant to intervene further in Ottoman affairs at this time unless Ibrahim launched a major offensive against the sultan and directly threatened Istanbul.

Nevertheless, in spring 1838 Palmerston was forced to turn his attention back to the Mediterranean. Hitherto Mehmed Ali had been willing to keep up the pretence of being merely a *vali* of the Ottoman Empire; but, on 25 May, he announced his intention to establish an independent state, one which would incorporate not only Egypt, Crete, Sudan, Arabia and Syria but also part of the Turkish heartland in southern Anatolia.

Palmerston and Ponsonby now seized the opportunity to get Sultan Mahmud to agree to the commercial treaty on free trade and the abolition of monopolies which Britain's merchants had been demanding for so long.[13] According to the principal terms of the commercial Treaty of Balta Limani, signed between Britain and the Ottoman Empire on 16 August 1838, the tariffs on British imports and exports would remain the same as under the capitulations, at just 3 per cent; and all 'internal' customs duties applied by the governors of the different provinces, which averaged around 8 per cent, would be prohibited. In addition all Ottoman state monopolies, primarily in the purchasing of agricultural commodities, were abolished. In other words British merchants were permitted to purchase these either for domestic or export trade without hindrance at the prevailing market price.

However, the provisions of the Treaty that removed all the internal customs duties would have inevitably damaged the sultan's tax revenues. The Porte therefore insisted on some compensatory increase in the existing external (import and export) duties. As a result, the outcome of the negotiations on tariffs in 1838 was something of a compromise.

There was no immediate 'free trade' for Ottoman wheat exports to Britain as British landlords were protected by the infamous Corn Laws until 1846. Meanwhile the export of British manufactures to the Ottoman Empire rose steeply. By 1850 there was an eleven-fold increase, making it one of Britain's most valuable export markets (surpassed only by the Hanseatic towns and the Netherlands).

One article of the Commercial Treaty of Balti Limani carried significant political implications. Article Six stipulated that the provisions of the Treaty would apply to all parts of the Empire, including Egypt, and would come into force in one year. If implemented in Egypt, the Treaty would deny Mehmed Ali the huge profits from his agricultural monopolies which he relied upon to finance his army. This system had started with the wheat and rice markets in 1812 and had been extended to all commercial crops. It functioned like a modern marketing board whereby the state purchased agricultural exports from the peasants at very low prices and then sold them on world markets at far higher prices – a policy like an export tax, but one far higher than the 12 per cent stipulated in the Balti Limana Treaty.[14]

However, Article Six also held out the possibility that, if Mehmed refused to accept its requirements, the British might be compelled to turn their vague promises of support for the sultan into reality and send a fleet to compel Mehmed's agreement. And if he resisted further, the full weight of the British Empire would fall upon him, so removing Mehmed Ali's threat to the sultanate once and for all.

But Mahmud was in such seriously bad health that he believed he simply did not have time enough to wait one year in order to see whether Mehmed would ignore Article Six and face possible British military intervention. He was convinced his life was draining away. In June 1839, enraged at Mehmed's continuing challenge to his imperial power, he did precisely what Palmerston had feared: the sultan declared war upon his Egyptian vassal.

Both Ottoman and Egyptian armies were now organised on European lines, but Mahmud's army suffered serious deficiencies compared with that of Mehmed Ali. Some years later, Karl Marx's lifelong friend and colleague Frederick Engels, a perceptive military analyst, summarised the difficulties in creating a 'military revolution' in a non-European context:

> The main point and at the same time the main difficulty is the creation of a body of officers and sergeants educated on the modern European system ... A sultan or shah is but too apt to consider his army equal to anything as soon as the men can defile in parade, wheel, deploy and form columns without getting into hopeless disorder.[15]

In fact, it seems the new 'European' Ottoman army was unable to achieve even this minimal requirement of military efficiency. France's Marshal Auguste de Marmont attested to observing Ottoman troops still 'incapable of manoeuvring and whose invariable practice it is to either await the advantage of their enemy or to rush forward to attack without either system or order'.[16]

In sharp contrast to the perfectly disciplined troops of Mehmed Ali and his son, the Ottomans lacked competent senior officers and had ineffectual junior ones. The ostensibly modern army of the sultan still drew its officers from the ranks of courtiers, state functionaries and even the favoured household slaves of these traditional elites, men with little or no military education.[17] In addition, where European officers were employed they were paid considerably less than those in Mehmed's army, and in combat their Ottoman fellow officers frequently obstructed and overruled them. Sometimes they were even overruled by members of the *ulema*.

As for the junior officers in the sultan's army, the subalterns and NCOs were drawn from the same lowly social strata as the men they commanded. They received no special training, shared the same living quarters as their men, and even wore uniforms which did not appreciably differ from the rank and file. As a result, European observers commonly remarked upon the lack of sufficient respect and subordination on the part of the common soldiers, factors which were crucial in the heat of battle.[18] All this was in sharp contrast to the Arab junior officers of Mehmed Ali, whose fully militarised state provided them with education in special schools, including literacy classes when required. They possessed a distinct esprit de corps and higher status such that the conscripted *fellahin* they commanded dared not treat them with familiarity or challenge or disobey their commands.

On 24 June, the Ottoman and Egyptian armies met in battle at Nezib in south–eastern Anatolia, a few kilometres north of the present Syrian border. Both armies fielded more than 30,000 troops with the sultan's army probably the larger of the two. As usual, Ibrahim Paşa was in command of the Egyptian army with Colonel Sèves as his second in command. Mahmud's army was led by Hafiz Osman Paşa, the commander of the sultan's troops in Anatolia, accompanied by the German military advisor, Captain Helmuth von Moltke (later chief of staff of the Prussian Army). Von Moltke counselled the Ottoman commander to keep his troops in a defensive position and await the Egyptian attack, but he was overruled by the attendant *ulema*. The Ottoman advance towards the Egyptian lines met a hail of bullets and canister fire and quickly fell into disorder. Within a few minutes the sultan's army collapsed and was routed, suffering huge casualties and losing over 10,000 prisoners and all their guns.[19] Mahmud did not live to witness the military disaster. He had died seven days earlier and was succeeded by his sixteen-year-old son, Abdülmecid (r. 1839–61). And then, to add insult to injury, on 1 July the young heir was deserted by the Ottoman fleet, which sailed off to join Mehmed Ali at Alexandria.

Now the road to Istanbul lay open and undefended to Mehmed Ali's forces. In panic, on 5 July 1839, the Porte offered Mehmed hereditary rule over Egypt; in response, he insisted that such hereditary rule should include Syria. Palmerston now foresaw the possibility that, if Ibrahim's army marched northwards towards Istanbul, the young Sultan Abdülmecid would activate the terms of the Treaty of Hünkar İskelesi and call upon the Russians to protect him. As a precaution, Palmerston instructed Ponsonby to summon the British Mediterranean fleet to the Dardanelles if a Russian fleet entered the Bosphorus. However, on 27 July the Porte's resistance to Mehmed Ali's demands simply collapsed: to halt any further advance by Ibrahim's troops, Mehmed Ali was given what he had continuously been demanding: independent hereditary rule over both Egypt and Syria.

By now, Palmerston had managed to persuade all the five Great Powers, including not only Prussia and Austria but also France and Russia, that it was in their collective interest to protect the sultanate and abstain from any attempt to exploit its current weakness for their own interests. It was tacitly acknowledged that any such move might lead to another European war. So, on the very same day that the Porte succumbed to Mehmed Ali's demands, the five European powers sent Abdülmecid a collective note informing him that they were now in agreement as to how to deal with 'the Question of the East'. In effect, they were instructing him to take no further action whatsoever with respect to Mehmed Ali. The five European powers stood ready to deal with him on the sultan's behalf. After some deliberation, on 22 August the Porte agreed, stipulating merely that any settlement should not involve the cession of Syria.[20]

But just as it appeared that Palmerston had achieved a diplomatic coup in getting all five members of the Concert of Europe to agree to a collective approach, a breach was opening between Britain and France. With Mehmed Ali's reliance on French officers and experts, the French government had come to see him as a potential client ruler, one who would assist the growth of French imperialism in North Africa. Indeed, in the words of one French historian, with France's existing foothold in Algeria, its growing influence in Egypt and Tunis, and its long historical connections with the Christian Maronite population in Syria's Mount Lebanon, 'one could truly say that the whole Mediterranean was on the way to becoming a French lake'.[21]

For his part, the young Sultan Abdülmecid recognised that he could secure the support of the European powers against Mehmed Ali only if he responded to Britain's pressure to introduce major internal reforms. Consequently, on 3 November 1839, before an audience of state dignitaries, senior *ulema* and foreign dignitaries, Mustafa Reşid Paşa (1800–1858), the Ottoman foreign minister, read out the first 'reforming' imperial decree – the *Hatt-ı Şerif* of Gulhane (The Rose Chamber Edict). It did not carry the status of legislation but it announced the intention to carry out a series of changes. Although their purpose was not immediately apparent, they were intended to reinforce the process of centralisation begun by Mahmud II, to bring the Ottoman Empire into the fold of the Concert of Europe, and to create a government which would reshape and rebuild the Empire into a modern state. It was the beginning of what would later be called the *tanzimat* (reorganisation).

The Edict promised new laws which would include the guarantee of life and property rights, the prohibition of bribery, the abolition of tax farming, the creation of clear rules for the conscription of soldiers into the 'European' army, the outlawing of execution without trial, and the confiscation of property. Although the Edict was accompanied by various references to the Shari'a and criticism of the people's neglect of the Qur'an, its most radical feature was that the reforms would apply to all Ottoman subjects, Muslims and non-Muslims alike.[22] The assembled foreign dignitaries were duly impressed. Two days later the British ambassador, Lord Ponsonby, wrote to Palmerston, 'A victorious answer to those who say that this empire cannot be saved by its ancient government'. The Foreign Secretary replied that the Hatti-ı Şherif had been an event 'fraught with incalculable advantage'.[23]

However, for the time being Abdülmecid's main concern was not implementing European-directed reforms but defeating Mehmed Ali. Moreover, Palmerston, who had never been entirely convinced that the *entente* with post-Napoleonic France would last, now became increasingly suspicious of French motives. In December 1839, writing to the then British ambassador to France, he expressed the opinion that the virtual empire which Mehmed was creating was 'to be placed under the protection and be subject to the influence of France.'[24] He was also disturbed by the rapid increase of the French naval establishment in the Mediterranean, especially after France rebuffed his attempt to reach an agreement to limit a naval arms race in the region.

As if to confirm his suspicions, both King Louis-Philippe and his prime minister, Soult, refused to listen to any suggestion that force should be used to drive Ibrahim's army out of Syria.[25] However, precisely at this juncture, a quite unprecedented rapprochement between Britain and Russia occurred. The Tsar was deeply troubled by family affairs and the country's financial position and decided that Russia simply could not afford to respond to any request by the Porte for military aid against Mehmed Ali. Furthermore, Russia's ambassador to Great Britain informed Palmerston that his country did not intend to renew the Treaty of Hünkar İskelesi when it expired in 1841. The Tsar also agreed with Britain that Ibrahim's army should be driven out of Syria by force if necessary. Subsequently, on 5 January 1840, Palmerston told the French ambassador in London that Britain and Russia agreed that Mehmed Ali's rule should be confined to Egypt and that on this point they also had the agreement of Austria and Prussia.[26]

This was a powerful and unexpected challenge to France's new prime minister, Adolphe Thiers, who had replaced Marshal Soult on 1 March 1840. Thiers was not only a fierce supporter of France's colonialist policy in Algeria but he was also determined to do all he could to protect Mehmed Ali, whom he saw as a French protégé, one who would advance French interests throughout North Africa and the Middle East. In fact, Thiers's views represented the opinions of a great many of his countrymen, who envisaged Egypt as a potentially independent Muslim state which could be brought into existence under French auspices and would eventually fall under French control.[27] Thiers's popular support for his colonialist objectives lay in the fact that he controlled a considerable part of the French press, including the *Siècle*, which had a larger circulation than any other French newspaper.[28]

Palmerston was all the more opposed to Thiers and his ambitions because, apart from Britain's genuine desire to keep the 'Concert of Europe' united, Mehmed Ali threatened Britain's own imperial interests on a much wider scale than just the eastern Mediterranean. By now Mehmed Ali had created his own substantial empire encompassing Egypt, Sudan, Syria and most of the Arabian Peninsula, including the Hejaz with its two holy cities, Mecca and Medina, and the coast of Yemen, which his troops had seized in 1833 to take control of the lucrative coffee trade from Mocha.

Meanwhile a major technological advance in navigation had made the so-called 'overland' route to and from India of great commercial utility, something previously of only of marginal concern to the British government. In 1830, the small British paddle steamer the *Hugh Lindsay* completed the journey from Bombay to Suez in just one month, making possible the transport of mail, official despatches and passengers between Britain and India in only fifty-nine days. The steam-powered vessel had overcome the old problem facing sailing ships on the Red Sea: the prevailing northerly winds between May and September.

By 1834 the House of Commons had approved the idea of a permanent system of navigation in the Red Sea, both to and from India, with the use of steam-powered ships. And enterprising British merchants and sea captains now envisaged the profitable transportation of not only despatches and passengers but also goods. In 1837, their evidence to a House of Commons Select Committee persuaded its members to give further support to steam-powered navigation in the Red Sea by recommending a permanent coaling station at the Egyptian controlled port of Mocha.[29]

But by 1839 concerns were raised that Mehmed could soon establish a stranglehold over this route to India. He might also be in a position to invade Mesopotamia (modern Iraq) and with French help extend his influence to the Arabian Gulf either from Syria or Arabia. Indeed, in 1839 Mehmed despatched one of his senior officers, Kurshid Ali, on an expedition across central Arabia to the Arabian Gulf where Mehmed had announced his intention to seize the island of Bahrain.[30] Fearing this possibility, Palmerston opined that 'the mistress of India cannot permit France to be mistress directly or indirectly of the road to her Indian dominions.'[31] Consequently, an East India Company expeditionary force from Bombay was despatched to seize the strategic port of Aden at the entry to Red Sea to pre-empt its occupation by Egyptian troops.[32]

The crisis now intensified. On 7 April 1840, the Porte presented a note to the European powers requesting them to protect Ottoman interests and inform Mehmed Ali that he would be given the hereditary possession of

Mehmed Ali c. 1830

Egypt – but only if he surrendered all his other captured territories and returned the Ottoman fleet to Istanbul. Thiers alone refused to accept the note, insisting that Mehmed must be allowed hereditary control of Syria. On 15 July 1840, Britain, Russia, Austria and Prussia and a representative of the Porte signed the Convention of London 'for the regulation of Near East affairs'. Thiers declined.

According to the Convention, Mehmed Ali would only be offered the hereditary tenure of Egypt and the lifetime tenure of the *paşalik* of Acre. All the laws of the Ottoman Empire would apply to Egypt (including the one abolishing monopolies). In short, Egypt would remain a province of the Ottoman Empire, even if ruled by Mehmed and his descendants. Mehmed was given ten days to accept these terms, but after twenty days the sultan could withdraw this offer.[33] In such a case, the four powers agreed that military action could be taken.

Mehmed rejected the ultimatum, and on 17 July Thiers issued a statement to the diplomatic representatives of the other major European powers announcing that his government intended to support its Egyptian protégé. However, on the urgings of Palmerston, the other powers had already agreed that military pressure was to be applied straight away, even before the Convention was ratified.

On 5 August Palmerston sent instructions to Admiral Robert Stopford commanding the British Mediterranean fleet to commence naval and military action against Mehmed and Ibrahim's forces. At the same time orders were issued to Palmerston's 'special agent' in Syria, Richard Wood, the Arabic-speaking son of the British Embassy's translator in Istanbul. He was instructed to support and arm the guerrillas who had formed bands in Mount Lebanon to resist Ibrahim's conscription of both its Christian Maronite and Druze inhabitants.

In France, there was a storm of angry protest orchestrated by the press. Threats were made against Britain's control of Malta, and King Louis-Philippe – although deeply troubled by the then-current spirit of war mongering – was forced to agree to a range of bellicose measures. These included increasing the size of the navy (with nine new steam-powered warships among the additions) and a huge project to encircle Paris with fortifications in case of a land-based attack by Prussia, Austria and Russia.

Palmerston received news of these developments with equanimity. By 11 August, Britain had fifteen ships of the line and six steam-powered warships in the eastern Mediterranean, while most of France's army was tied down in Algeria. In Istanbul, Ponsonby exercised all his formidable diplomatic powers to get the sultan and his foreign minister, Reşid Paşa, to mobilise the Ottoman forces required for the campaign against Ibrahim. In a quite remarkable move, the sultan and his *ulema* were persuaded to appoint a British naval officer, Captain Baldwin Blake Walker, to command what remained of the Ottoman navy, and even placed him in charge of the 5,500 Turkish troops embarking for the Syrian coast. Such a departure from tradition may well have been sanctioned because the *ulema* were so deeply offended by Mehmed Ali's recent claim to be the 'Protector of Islam'.[34]

Once it became clear that Mehmed Ali had no intention of accepting the terms of the London Convention, the sultan deposed him from the *paşalik* of Egypt and named his successor. By now a squadron of the British Mediterranean fleet under Commodore Charles Napier was cruising off the Lebanese coast, while in Paris the crescendo of Gallic pride appeared to herald a naval war with Britain. At the very least, the French Mediterranean fleet was expected to sail out from its current base at Salamis and shadow Napier's squadron. But although they had raised the passions of the French bourgeoisie, it now dawned upon Thiers and King Louis-Philippe just how vulnerable they were to British sea power: so the French fleet was ordered to remain at Salamis.

Ibrahim still had a formidable army spread out over the Levant: thirty-eight infantry regiments, around 10,000 cavalry and a well-trained artillery corps. In August, Napier's squadron appeared off Beirut and ordered Colonel Sèves to remove his Egyptian troops from the town. He refused, but on 11 September Napier's squadron was joined by the whole British fleet and Turkish transports. Admiral Stopford, commander of the fleet, intended to commence negotiations with Colonel Sèves; but after his flag of truce was fired on he began an intense bombardment of the city which killed many civilians, as well as hundreds of Beirut's Egyptian occupiers. On the 26th Napier's squadron mounted a land and sea attack on Egyptian-occupied Sidon, which surrendered after a two-day assault. On 10 October, Commodore Napier, in what must be one of the very few major combats in which the infantry were commanded by a naval officer, led a combined force of Turkish troops and British marines and sailors against a demoralised Egyptian army at the Battle of Boharsef, where they inflicted a serious defeat upon Ibrahim's troops.

An Infantryman of Mehmed Ali's conscript army

By the end of October, Acre was the only Syrian coastal fortress still under Ibrahim's control. On 3 November the British fleet, supported by a squadron of Austrian and Turkish warships, moved into position to attack the town. The British flotilla included four of the new steam-powered paddle-wheel sloops, *Phoenix*, *Gorgon*, *Vesuvius* and *Stromboli*, which could manoeuvre independently of the prevailing winds. After a three-hour bombardment by the battleships, an explosive shell fired by HMS *Gorgon* hit the fortress's powder magazine, causing a huge explosion killing over a thousand of the defenders. Shortly afterwards, all resistance ended and the town was occupied by British troops.[35]

With Ibrahim's army defeated and isolated in the Syrian interior, Admiral Stopford ordered Commodore Napier to sail to Alexandria where he arrived on 25 November and imposed a blockade of the city. Meanwhile, on 21 October, the French King, under attack in the press for what had clearly become a major political debacle, forced Thiers's resignation as first minister and brought back Marshall Soult.

Charles Napier was notoriously eccentric and self-willed. The fifty-four-year-old, fourteen-stone Scot was a veteran of the Napoleonic wars, and his actual rank in the Royal Navy was only that of captain (the rank of 'commodore' being a temporary appointment related to a specific campaign). Nevertheless, without awaiting the arrival of his superior, Admiral Stopford, he took it upon himself to go on shore. There he engaged with Mehmed Ali in what appears to have been a very amicable meeting, and signed a peace treaty with the Paşa.

Its terms specified that, in return for Mehmed abandoning all claims to Syria, acknowledging the sultan as his sovereign and returning the Ottoman fleet, the British navy would help evacuate Ibrahim's beleaguered army from Syria. Meanwhile Mehmed and his heirs would remain in possession of Egypt. This final clause was quite contrary to the wishes of both the sultan and Ambassador Ponsonby and was immediately repudiated by Admiral Stopford. Within the Admiralty there were calls for Napier's court martial; but Palmerston was privately quite happy with Napier's 'treaty'. The terms of the formal peace treaty, eventually signed on 26 November 1840, were virtually identical to those in Napier's original agreement with Mehmed Ali. Consequently, the following year Sultan Abdülmecid issued a *firman* proclaiming Mehmed

Ali hereditary Viceroy of Egypt and the Sudan, but also limiting his army to 18,000 men.

The French government now found itself forced to agree to a settlement in the Levant on British terms. The final stage of Palmerston's great diplomatic victory was the agreement of all the major European powers to the Straits Convention of 13 July 1841. The agreement, signed in London, denied passage through the Straits to all warships while the Ottoman Empire was at peace. This protected Russia against foreign navies forcing their way through the Dardanelles and Bosphorus and attacking her in the Black Sea. Equally, it denied Russia the opportunity to attack in the opposite direction. Istanbul was now, in theory, under the protection of *all* the powers. Nevertheless, Palmerston insisted that, in an emergency, the sultan had the right to summon the Royal Navy – and the Royal Navy alone – to Istanbul.[36]

With Syria freed from Egyptian control, Sultan Abdülmecid sent 15,000 troops under Mehmed Izzet Paşa, his commander-in-chief, to disembark at Beirut. There they were met by Richard Wood, to whom Palmerston had given the momentous task of trying to establish an interim Ottoman regime that would be satisfactory to all Syria's various religious communities in the recaptured areas, in particular the Christians and Muslims of Mount Lebanon. It would prove to be a hopeless mission.

Some Egyptian historians have interpreted Britain's attack on Mehmed Ali and the terms imposed upon him – the severe reduction in the size of his army and the subsequent destruction of his 'statist' economic model via the abolition of his monopolies – as the crushing of an early attempt to build a modern, independent Egyptian nation. But Mehmed Ali's state, his army and his economy were never in any real sense 'Egyptian'. The institutions he created were only 'Egyptian' in the sense that the cannon fodder for his army, the toiling peasants on his fields and the sweated labourers in his factories, were all Arabic-speaking Egyptians. What he created was an exclusively Turko-Circassian* dynastic empire with its own distinctly

---

* The term 'Turko-Circassian' reflects the fact that, after the conquest of their Caucasian homeland by the Russians, many Circassian leaders migrated to Syria, Palestine and especially Egypt, where they became officers in Mehmed Ali's new army. Some also intermarried with Turkish women. In this manner they became part of a new colonial ruling class dominating the indigenous Arabs (see Chapter 22).

colonial apparatus of power and control, not dissimilar to the eighteenth-century European 'fiscal-military' states. Perhaps the most revealing remark on this subject was made by the Paşa himself. 'I have not done in Egypt except what the British are doing in India; they have an army composed of Indians and ruled by British officers, and I have an army composed of Arabs ruled by Turkish officers.'[37] Well-drilled, well-officered, well-armed and well-supplied, the army of Mehmed Ali was essentially a colonial, not a national army.

Meanwhile Britain had become the undisputed master of the Mediterranean. At the Straits of Gibraltar, and the Dardanelles, Britain controlled both entrances to what was then a closed body of water of increasing commercial and military importance. Its powerful navy was based at Gibraltar, and it had become an established principle that there should be permanent garrisons of 1,000 men at Gibraltar, 3,000 at Malta and 3,000 at the Ionian Islands. As for Palmerston, his experience of dealing with the French during the 1830s had made him increasingly doubtful about their sincerity in adhering to the *entente* which had supposedly characterised the relationship between the two countries since the end of the Napoleonic wars. And by now he had belatedly realised that the French were digging their feet deeper into one key area of the Mediterranean: Algeria.

CHAPTER 16

Algérie Française

The defeat of the French at Constantine in 1836 left the Parisian government and deputies in a state of confusion as to what to do next. They simply could not agree on what they wanted, or the amount of resources France should commit to its occupation of Algiers, or even whether to abandon the whole enterprise. By default, the policy of 'limited occupation' continued. Consequently General Bugeaud, the victor of the Battle of Sikkak a few months before the disaster at Constantine, was sent back to Oran on 7 April 1837 to negotiate a new peace treaty with 'Abd al-Qadir.

However, certain conditions were deemed essential. Bugeaud's orders were to extract from 'Abd al-Qadir an acknowledgement of France's sovereignty over the whole former Regency; in recognition of this, an annual tribute would have to be paid to France and the Emir's jurisdiction was to be limited to the tribes of the former beylik of Oran. Specifically, that meant the land to the west of the great River Shelif which drains into the Mediterranean a few kilometres northeast of Mostaganem.

The subsequent Treaty of Tafna between Bugeaud and 'Abd al-Qadir was negotiated by the latter's Jewish Counsellor, Judas Ben Duran, and finalised on 20 May 1837. However, to the shock of most of Bugeaud's fellow officers, including Governor-General Damrémont and the pro-colonisation politicians in Paris, the resultant document almost entirely ignored the restrictive conditions that Paris demanded.

The Treaty was largely a re-run of the earlier Desmichels Treaty of 1834. Indeed, on the face of it, Tafna was even more favourable to 'Abd al-Qadir. In particular, it was agreed that the territory over which the Emir was to have control would stretch inland as far as the Khadra River, which empties into the Mediterranean about thirty kilometres east of Algiers. In effect, this meant conceding to the Emir not only most of the former beylik of Oran but also that of Titteri where the tribes had recently pledged him their allegiance, and even part of the fertile Mitidja Plain. Essentially, all that was left to the French was part of the beylik of Constantine, Algiers, and the coastal strip westwards to the border with Morocco and eastwards to the Khadra.

In addition it was agreed that the chiefs of the *makhzan* tribes, including Mustafa bin Isma'il, would be deported; the Arabs could continue to import weaponry and ammunition through the French ports; and Tlemcen, which had changed hands so many times, was to be finally handed over to 'Abd al-Qadir. Moreover, in the final compilation of the Treaty, while the French version included the Emir's acknowledgement of French sovereignty over the former Regency, the Arabic version – the only one which 'Abd al-Qadir actually signed – did not. As for the question of tribute to the French, this was limited to the 'gifts' of a one-time payment of 30,000 measures of wheat and barley and the delivery of 5,000 head of cattle.[1]

By signing the treaty with France 'Abd al-Qadir was now able to turn his attention to crushing those Arab chieftains who rejected his authority and refused to pay the *ma'una* (special war tax). The Emir believed this non-Qur'anic tax was necessary – even in times of peace – to build up his 'European' army and establish factories to produce muskets and other weaponry with which to equip his men.

Meanwhile, Hamdan Khoja was still hoping to persuade Mahmud to intervene militarily.* He was now virtually penniless, since General Clauzel had seized all his lands and possessions in Algiers and the Mitidja; in 1836 he had been forced to leave Paris and settle in the Ottoman capital as a pensioner of the sultan. He warned Sultan Mahmud that 'the French will not accept this defeat [at Constantine] and Hajj Ahmed Bey will never be their equivalent in military might, as a result it is certain that they are going to occupy Constantine; then they will infiltrate Tunisia'.[2] It was therefore essential that Mahmud provided military aid to the resistance, including both Ahmed Bey of Constantine and 'Abd al-Qadir. But in spite of Hamdan Khoja's appeals for unity in the struggle against the French, Hajj Ahmed Bey stood by his opinion that he didn't need or want assistance from 'Abd al Qadir, who wasn't 'born of a race which can provide princes'.[3]

---

*   Hamdan Khoja eventually died in Istanbul, probably in 1842.

As Hamdan Khoja had foreseen, on 1 October 1837 20,000 French troops, strengthened by a contingent withdrawn from Oran and commanded by Governor-General Denys de Damrémont, set out from their camp at Guelma to attack Hajj Ahmed's stronghold. This time the expedition was well planned and well supplied. Sixty pieces of artillery, including heavy siege guns, formed part of the column, and along the route strongpoints were constructed, with food supplies which would be needed for the return march.

By 6 October the French army reached the plateau of Mansoura, having suffered few losses, and decided to launch the principal attack from the isthmus of Koudiat Aty. Meanwhile a diversionary bombardment would be made upon the side of the city protected by the gorge. On 11 October, the French siege guns on Koudiat Aty breached the city walls and the following day widened the breach and prevented the defenders from repairing it. At 9 a.m. General Damrémont was shot dead while inspecting the damaged wall, but by now the breach was wide enough to allow a major infantry attack. General Damrémont's replacement was General Sylvain Charles, Comte Valée, commander of the artillery; he decided the assault would take place the following morning.

At 7 a.m. on 13 October, the first assault column went into the breach. There followed a vicious struggle inside the city with the defenders fighting street by street and house by house. But by the end of the day the city was captured, although Hajj Ahmed Bey escaped. While he would never return to his city, for many years he would keep up a guerrilla struggle among the Berbers of the Aurès Mountains.

Meanwhile, Bugeaud was recalled to France where he was heavily criticised for the terms of the Treaty of Tafna. But he was able to defend himself against attacks in the Chamber of Deputies by essentially using the same argument that Desmichels had used.

> We have to negotiate with the Arabs or exterminate them. To negotiate it is necessary to have a chief ... where do we find one? Abd-el-Kader [sic] is the only Arab who has acquired control over his coreligionists; his power already existed, it wasn't created by the Treaty of Tafna.[4]

But Bugeaud was playing a clever political game. In effect, he was saying to the French government and the Chamber of Deputies: if you want only a limited occupation, then Tafna, and all that it involves, is all you can expect. On the other hand if you really want total domination and successful colonisation then you will have to change course. And although Bugeaud wasn't seriously suggesting that the alternative to 'negotiation' was 'extermination', some among his audience were already thinking that perhaps something close to it would have to be the next step.

There were those in Paris who still aspired to a vision of France's presence in North Africa much grander than the status quo of 'limited occupation'. The most important of them was the austere Protestant politician François Guizot, who would become foreign minister in October 1840. Guizot belonged to the moderate wing of the Conservative Party. He had originally been opposed to the occupation, but by 1838 his views had totally changed, as the proceedings in the Chamber of Deputies, published in the *Revue des Deux Mondes*, recorded.

> In Africa France must dominate absolutely, and not be reduced
> to some commercial trading posts. The victors of Algiers and
> Constantine cannot tomorrow just become merchants. France
> must not abandon the idea of conquest, but it must be done
> in stages and systematically. In a word, M. Guizot believes in
> French Africa.[5]

And, in spite of the criticism which had been heaped upon him as a result of the Treaty of Tafna, it was General Bugeaud whom Guizot had in mind when he contemplated a conquest which would be 'done in stages and systematically'. Significantly, in the same year another Royal Ordinance changed the name of the 'French Possessions in North Africa' to 'Algeria'; and, more ominously, the government declared that 'Henceforth and forever it will be a French province.'[6] Preparations – including the drafting of thousands more conscripts – would now be made for the creation of Algérie Française.

Moreover, from now on the war against 'Abd al-Qadir would be a very different kind of conflict. As Bugeaud explained to the Chamber of Deputies:

The Arabs are like birds ... they fly away as we approach.
The Arab villages are the camps to which they fly off, twelve
to fifteen leagues from our columns. ... With artillery we
are exposed so that the Arabs know in advance the points
where our columns are forced to pass and which provide
opportunities for ambush. We can't abandon our baggage
trains and equipment. It is necessary to halt and defend them
and during this time the Arabs harass our flanks and decimate
us. Without guns and baggage trains, on the contrary, we can
take the offensive, and a fight which would previously last a
whole day is over in little more than three-quarters of an hour.[7]

What Bugeaud did not say to the assembled deputies was that henceforth
it would be a war against those Arab villages to which the Arabs 'fly away
like birds'. It would be a war of small, highly mobile columns in which the
civilians, their houses, their crops and their very lives would be the principal
targets.

By December 1838 'Abd al-Qadir's dominion over around two-thirds
of the former Regency of Algiers was completed with the surrender of
the fortress of 'Ain Mahdi on the edge of the Sahara Desert. This was
the stronghold of Sidi Muhammad al-Tijani, head of the Tijaniyya Sufi
brotherhood, who had rejected the Emir's leadership. And even the Berber
'petty republics' of the Grand Kabylia, who had always felt secure in their
mountain fastness, fell under the sway of the Emir for a time.

'Abd al-Qadir also continued to build his modern army. According to
one recently published Arabic source, in 1839 there were 63,000 young
men who signed up for training.[8] This may be true, but from contemporary
sources we know that at any one time the actual number of effective troops
was only a fraction of this figure. This is perhaps because many recruits were
considered unsuitable. However, it is more likely that the Emir simply did
not have the weapons, munitions and, above all, experienced European
officers to train them.

The Emir made considerable efforts to manufacture his own military
equipment in his fortified towns. There was a cannon factory at Tlemcen,
managed by a Spaniard, which was constructing brass 4-pounder and
6-pounder field guns with the aid of French prisoners of war; and a French

engineer was supervising a factory at Tagdemt producing muskets, although the production rate was rather modest – an average of eight per day.[9] For a time there was also an iron foundry established by a French mineralogist at Miliana. But the problem faced by 'Abd al-Qadir was that most of these foreign technicians remained with him for only a short time, and most of the Emir's military supplies had to be acquired from Gibraltar-based merchants and delivered via Morocco.

Bugeaud now confidently awaited the call to return to 'finish the job' in Algeria. His opportunity came in late 1839. During the Tafna peace both sides had broken its terms on a number of occasions, but with Damrémont's successor, the Comte Valée, acting as governor-general, the French were behaving in a deliberately provocative way. On the basis of a mistranslation of a phrase in the Tafna Treaty, French columns began passing through territory allotted to 'Abd al-Qadir forming a land bridge between Algiers and Constantine. The most serious of these passages occurred in late October 1839 when the Emir learnt that French troops led by King Philippe's son, the Duc d'Orléans, had passed through the narrow defile in the Biban Mountains, known as the 'Iron Gates'. This was a direct challenge to 'Abd al-Qadir's authority and he immediately consulted his shura council as to whether it justified renewing hostilities.

The shura council were divided. The Emir's Jewish counsellor, Judas Ben Duran, warned him of the growing numerical strength of the French army and advised against initiating hostilities. But 'Abd al-Qadir sought religious opinion from the leading *ulema* of Fez. Finally, on their advice, the Emir declared jihad on 18 November. And after warning the Comte Valée of his intentions and advising that all French colonists and travellers should take whatever precautions they deemed necessary, he ordered his three *khalifas* (regional commanders) whose provinces were nearest to Algiers to launch their attacks.[10] Arab irregulars now descended upon the Mitidja plain, killing European settlers, looting their property and driving the terrified settlers back into Algiers. On 21 November 1839 as many as 108 colonists were killed.[11]

By now, General Valée had received substantial reinforcements and in April 1840 he began an advance down the River Shelif into the heart of 'Abd al-Qadir's territory. The Emir decided the time had come to confront the French head on with his 'European' troops, and at a point on the river known as the Gorges of Mouzaïa he prepared a line of defence including a substantial redoubt and five of his new infantry regimets.[12]

The outcome of the battle was a disaster for the Algerians. The 'European' troops were unable to withstand the furious French attacks and fled the field. According to the British officer Colonel Henry Churchill, who would later write the first English-language biography of 'Abd al-Qadir:

> It was the fate of 'Abd al-Qadir to discover now that in attempting to realise the theorem of European military science in the open field and on open ground, with the levies under his command, the elements he wielded were below the requirement of his genius.[13]

'Colonel' James Scott gives us some idea of what those 'elements' amounted to and how 'Abd al-Qadir organised his territory and marshalled the state of his 'European' army. The writer was a British soldier of fortune, and once a lieutenant in the British Legion that fought for the 'liberals' in the Carlist Spanish Civil War (1833–40). He arrived in Tetouan, Morocco, in February 1841 and eventually made his way to 'Abd al-Qadir's court where he offered his services as 'chief of staff' to the Emir. 'Abd al Qadir clearly made a very good impression on him. Scott describes him as 'a youthful hero':

> possessing a noble and generous mind: one who is incapable of treachery and whose liberal policy and government, were he only on the throne of Algiers, would render that country, in a short time, the most enlightened under the Muslim sway.[14]

Scott records that it was during the Tafna peace, in 1837, that 'Abd al-Qadir 'proceeded to establish everything in his Kingdom upon the European system'. He describes how the Emir divided his territory into seven provinces, each one under a *khalifa*, which Scott interprets as a 'Lieutenant General'. He goes on to state that each *khalifa* appointed a certain number of aghas (colonels) and village mayors. In 1837 each of the seven *khalifa*s had a regiment of 'regular' infantry of between 1,200 and 1,300 men together with a company of European renegades, mainly French deserters. Some such units were as large as 200 men. Scott further testifies that, while he was in Algeria, forty Spanish troops from the Foreign Legion had come over to 'Abd al Qadir, 'having shot their officers'.[15] In addition each *khalifa* had 400 to 500 'regular' cavalry.[16] In other words the total size of 'Abd al-Qadir's 'European' army at this time, including the renegades, was probably around 12,600.*

Scott also gives us a description of one of the Emir's modernised infantry units, the Tagdemt Regiment. In 1841 it consisted of 800 men, uniformed in blue jackets 'buttoned up' and loose 'Turkish' trousers. Each infantryman wore a waist belt which Scott describes as being like the ones in which Spanish troops carried their ammunition. The regimental commander, the company captains and the NCOs all wore red uniforms with distinctive decorations, those of the commander being 'three stripes of gold or silver on his cuffs'. Perhaps most interesting of all is Scott's observation that the regiment's drummers were all French deserters, and consequently the unit marched to French tunes.[17] However, when he observed the regiment carrying out field manoeuvres, Scott was not particularly impressed, commenting that 'their field day did not consist of many evolutions'. Overall, we get the impression that, in both strength and performance 'Abd al-Qadir's 'European' troops still fell a long way short of the idealised modern army he had described in his *wushah* manual in 1833.

In spite of his victory over 'Abd al-Qadir's troops at the Gorges of Mouzaïa, on 29 December Soult removed Valée from office and named Bugeaud as his successor. He arrived in Algiers on 22 February 1841 and immediately made it clear that from now on there would be no 'limited' occupation. With 72,000 troops under his command, most of them conscripts, he issued a number of instructions announcing the beginning of total war against the Arabs. Any tribe which refused peace terms would be prohibited from trading with the French; individual defections to the French would not be permitted: they would have to bring with them their whole tribe; and all Arabs circulating in French-controlled areas would be required to wear a badge with the words 'submitted Arab'.

While 'Abd al-Qadir was slowly constructing his modern army, concentrating mainly on organised battlefield formations, Bugeaud

---

*   Based on the mid-points for the three units: 1,250 for the infantry regiments, 450 for cavalry
      and 100 for the renegades, multiplied by seven.

had adopted a strategy which, to a considerable extent, made the Emir's 'European' project irrelevant. From now on he would fight a counter-insurgency war where set-piece confrontations with disciplined ranks of infantry exchanging musketry volleys and artillery duels would occur only when he deemed it necessary.

Bugeaud's new strategy was based on the 'razzia' – a corruption of the Arab word *ghazu* (raid). It involved small mobile columns surrounding rebel Arab villages, killing all the men, young and old, and taking the women and children into prison camps where they were given the bare minimum of subsistence. All the tribe's animals would be seized, their crops would be destroyed and their precious fruit and olive trees destroyed.[18] At the same time larger units would attack and seize those key towns, like Tagdemt, which 'Abd al-Qadir had fortified and where his embryo weapons-manufacturing facilities had been built. It was indeed a system of total war.

To implement this strategy, the French infantryman would no longer be encumbered by a uniform that had, until then, changed little since the Napoleonic wars. Shakos and stiff collars were replaced by smaller casquettes and soft collars; on the march, packs were lightened to carry just four days' supplies for a twenty-day campaign (anything more would be seized from Arab villages). Most importantly, the heavy impedimenta of the earlier campaigns were abolished: from now on there would be no artillery except small 'mountain guns', no baggage trains, and everything essential would be carried by mules, including the wounded when necessary. As to the true nature of the Bugeaud's 'war of the razzia', we have the testimony of one of his senior officers. General Armand-Jacques Leroy de Saint-Arnaud.

> I shall leave not a single tree standing in their orchards, not a
> head on the shoulders of these wretched Arabs ... These are the
> orders I have received ... and they will be punctually executed.
> I shall burn everything, kill everyone.[19]

To justify this kind of war-making, Bugeaud circulated propaganda sheets to his troops in which the Arabs were portrayed as 'animals' who tortured their prisoners and therefore had to be treated accordingly. At a time when 'Abd al-Qadir was punishing any of his men who decapitated wounded prisoners, Bugeaud and his officers were deliberately turning a blind eye to the mutilations and decapitations perpetrated by their own men, even to the point of ignoring their troops' practice of parading Arab heads on their bayonets.

The General's strategy met with almost continuous success. It began with the capture or destruction of 'Abd al-Qadir's principal towns. In May 1841 the French army occupied Mascara and Tagdemt. In February 1842 Tlemcen was recaptured. 'Abd al-Qadir decided that he would have to establish a 'mobile armoured city' known as a *smala*. It would serve as his headquarters, treasury, principal army corps and refuge for the thousands of civilians who were fleeing the dreaded razzias. It was a huge tent city of over 30,000 occupants which included mosques, shops, markets and all the paraphernalia of an actual town. It also served as the base for guerrilla raids into enemy territory; and at the approach of French columns the *smala* could pack up its horses and camels, round up its sheep and goats, and slip away into new, less accessible territory.

The *smala* worked well for a time but, to a large extent, it was a response to defeat. Meanwhile Bugeaud's men were put to work building roads and bridges and generally bringing more and more of the wild and previously inaccessible land under the grip of French Army.

Then, on 16 May 1843, disaster struck the *smala*. While 'Abd al-Qadir was away on one of his raids into enemy territory, a 600-strong cavalry column under the command of the nineteen-year-old fifth son of King Louis-Philippe, the Duc d'Aumale, located the Emir's mobile camp. In a surprise attack headed by the Chasseurs d'Afrique they won a remarkable victory. The battalion of 'European' regulars guarding the *smala* fired one musketry volley and then fled; and as confusion and panic spread throughout the host of non-civilians, the Emir's treasury was seized, his great library destroyed, tens of thousands of sheep and other livestock were captured, and around 3,000 prisoners taken. Three days later, a further 2,500 captives were taken.

For 'Abd al-Qadir it was the end of the war – or rather, it was the beginning of the end. He spent a few months operating along the ill-defined border with Morocco, accompanied by only a few hundred loyal horsemen, but in November he retreated into Morocco. Over there he knew he could not only count on supporters but, when the time was right, he could launch guerrilla raids back into Algeria: at least, that was his hope and expectation.

Morocco's Sultan, 'Abd al-Rahman, did not receive news of the arrival of 'Abd al-Qadir on his soil in November 1843 with any great enthusiasm. He was already in a serious dispute with Spain over a small area of land outside its enclave of Ceuta, which had been seized by local tribesmen. Moreover, for some time, the French in Algeria had warned Morocco that unless it stemmed the sale of arms to 'Abd al-Qadir, transited through Moroccan territory, the French would take military action. The appearance of French warships off Morocco's few ports only added to the atmosphere of fear, loathing and bellicosity among 'Abd al-Rahman's subjects. In 1843 they were calling for a jihad against all Europeans, making it virtually impossible for the few who resided in the country to leave the safety of their homes.

The crisis was of particular concern to Britain. By the 1830s British merchants based in Gibraltar controlled about 75 per cent of Morocco's foreign trade.[20] But, at the same time, Gibraltar remained heavily dependent on Moroccan supplies shipped across the narrow Straits. These strategic interests would be seriously threatened were a foreign power to take control of the northern coast of Morocco.

For Palmerston it was clear who that 'foreign power' would be. Out of office since the fall of the Whig government in 1841, Palmerston had begun to study the historical background of France's occupation of Algeria and must have regretted his earlier, relaxed attitude to that episode.[21] Indeed, he was now convinced that, for a number of years, France had been making 'systematic endeavours to undermine British interests in every quarter of the globe'.

But the British had no desire to go to war with France. While he had been foreign minister, Palmerston had repeatedly issued instructions to Britain's consul-general at Tangier, Edward Drummond-Hay, as to how to respond if serious disputes arose between Morocco and any other European country: he was to prevail upon the sultan to swiftly offer amends and compensation, to avoid giving the offended country any excuse to intervene militarily. So far, the Moroccan sultan had reluctantly followed this advice.

However, when 'Abd al-Rahman and his ministers learned that, on occasion, the British had privately issued strongly worded warnings to France against even fairly limited intervention in Morocco, they drew an unwarranted conclusion – that Britain was not just a friend of Morocco but that, whatever the circumstances, it stood ready to intervene militarily against her enemies if Morocco were ever attacked.[22]

The arrival of 'Abd al-Qadir on Moroccan soil placed the new British Tory government and its prime minister, Sir Robert Peel, in a difficult situation. The presence of the heroic Emir, and his stated intention to continue his war of resistance across the border into Algeria, was a direct challenge to Franco-Moroccan relations. In 1842 Bugeaud had already proposed an invasion of Morocco to put an end to its support for the Emir. He was restrained only by the French foreign minister, Guizot, who feared Britain's reaction. In fact the British government was just as much concerned about the possibility of 'Abd al-Qadir's operations triggering a French invasion of Morocco and a possible occupation.

In May 1842, Consul-General Drummond-Hay was instructed to make a special visit to the sultan's camp at Rabat to urge him to deny 'Abd al-Qadir any further assistance. At the same time the British government prohibited any further export of arms to the Emir from Gibraltar. In response to Drummond-Hay's entreaties, 'Abd al-Rahman took steps to discourage his Moroccan subjects from supporting the Emir. For a time relations between France and Morocco improved somewhat but, as a result, the sultan's authority – already virtually non-existent in large parts of his realm – suffered a further blow, and popular demands for a jihad against all Europeans increased.

The final breach between France and Morocco came in spring 1844. Bugeaud began to construct a fortress at Oujda on the site of an old Muslim shrine, outside territory which had been traditionally claimed by the Dey of Algiers. On two occasions Moroccan tribal forces attacked the French camp. On 12 June the French sent an ultimatum to the sultan. It required the immediate dispersal of all the Moroccan troops on the border; that the tribal chiefs responsible for the attacks on the French should be punished; that 'Abd al-Qadir be handed over to the French; and that the boundary between France and Morocco be settled once and for all.[23] To support this ultimatum, a French fleet was sent to Tangier and Bugeaud's army was reinforced.

In response to the French ultimatum, 'Abd al-Rahman's vezir, Ben Driss, replied that Morocco would never accept a single one of their demands. This haughty intransigence was based on the sultan's assumption that, in the event of war, 'that she-devil whom the English consul calls the Queen' would send her forces to support him.²⁴ He was seriously mistaken.

On 6 August 1844 a French fleet commanded by the Prince de Joinville, composed of three ships of the line, three frigates, four brigs, three steam-powered paddle-wheel corvettes and two smaller vessels, bombarded the city of Tangier. Eight days later a French army of 11,000 under Bugeaud himself entered Moroccan-claimed territory at a point on the River Isly and encountered a Moroccan force of around 20,000 cavalry commanded by the sultan's son, Sidi Muhammad. The Moroccan troops, fighting in the traditional method of 'charge and retreat', were utterly destroyed by the musketry volleys of the French infantry. Then, on 15 August, the same French fleet which had attacked Tangier sailed back through the Straits of Gibraltar and began a bombardment of Morocco's main Atlantic port, Mogador (today Essaouira). In the three-day operation French troops destroyed all Mogador's defences, landed on the island of Mogador and briefly entered the town itself. When they withdrew, Mogador was in ruins.

The war was a disaster for 'Abd al-Rahman. He was compelled to sign the Treaty of Tangier on 10 September 1844, in which he agreed to implement all the requirements of France's June ultimatum: withdrawing support for 'Abd al-Qadir, reducing Moroccan frontier garrisons and shifting the Moroccan-Algerian border further west, closer to the Moulouya River. Such a demeaning capitulation only further weakened the sultan's authority and sparked outbreaks of rebellion in various parts of his 'Empire'. Moreover, many tribes began to look to the popular 'Abd al-Qadir as a suitable replacement for a sultan who appeared to have lost all the *baraka* (divine status), and dignity, of a sharif. For his part, 'Abd al-Rahman now considered 'Abd al-Qadir his enemy.

Faced with the choice of waging a defensive war against the Moroccan sultan, or returning to fight the French, 'Abd al-Qadir decided to launch another campaign. It would prove to be his last.

'Abd al-Qadir advanced into the valley of the Tafna with 6,000 horsemen. Bugeaud had previously returned to France to receive the accolades for his victory at the Battle of Isly. But now, learning of the Emir's arrival on Algerian soil, he was forced to return to Algeria. By the time he arrived on 15 October 1845, 'Abd al-Qadir was roaming the country, sometimes only a few kilometres ahead of his French pursuers, trying to encourage the tribes who had supported him for many years to return to the struggle. But with their women and children under continuous threat from the French razzias, few agreed to re-join the war. And so on 18 July 1846 a despondent 'Abd al-Qadir returned to his Moroccan camp in the eastern Riff.

On 9 December, the Emir defeated a Moroccan army led by the sultan's nephew Mulay Hasan, and then moved his camp to Agueddin on the left bank of the river Moulouya. Here he was again attacked, this time by a Moroccan army of 50,000. With only 1,200 cavalry and the 800 remnants of his 'European' infantry, 'Abd al-Qadir inflicted another crushing defeat on the Moroccans. However, the end of his great struggle was fast approaching: he was running short of ammunition, and knew that most of his *khalifas* and their tribes had given up the fight. Meanwhile his loyal *khalifa* Bou Hamedi was sent to try to make peace with the Moroccan Sultan but 'Abd al-Rahman simply demanded his surrender.[25] And now the French army was approaching the Moulouya's right bank. Realising that he faced being trapped between his two enemies, the French and the Moroccans, 'Abd al-Qadir finally accepted defeat.

He decided it was better to surrender to his old enemy, the French, than to the Moroccan sultan whom he regarded as a coward and a traitor. On 21 December, General Christophe de Lamoricière, one of Bugeaud's most experienced commanders, learnt that the Emir, his family and his small remaining body of troops had entered French-controlled territory. The following day 'Abd al-Qadir made an offer of surrender to a Berber officer of French cavalry who carried it to Lamoricière. The Emir proposed to hand himself over to the general provided he and his entourage could travel either to Acre or to Alexandria en route for Mecca, where he intended to remain for the rest of his life. Lamoricière gave him his word that these terms would be accepted. The surrender took place on 23 December 1847 and two days later 'Abd al-Qadir, his family and followers were carried by frigate to Toulon.

To their shock, on their arrival at Toulon the Emir and his entourage were seized and imprisoned. At a time when the French royal family were becoming increasingly unpopular with the French bourgeoisie, they were divided about the question of what to do with the Emir, and they hesitated to fulfil the agreement made with General Lamoricière. Moreover, Guizot, now President of the Royal Council, argued that a general could not tie the hands of the King's government.

The following year King Louis-Philippe was overthrown in France's third revolution. Had the socialist forces triumphed it is probable that 'Abd al-Qadir and his entourage would have been released. But after one of Bugeaud's senior officers, General Louis-Eugène Cavaignac, crushed the uprising of the Parisian workers in June 1848, the angry voices of the right-wing pro-colonial lobby reasserted themselves. They demanded the Emir's continued imprisonment on the grounds that in April 1847 one of his lieutenants had killed a large number of French prisoners, something which had occurred without 'Abd al-Qadir's knowledge or agreement.

It was not until 1852, after the seizure of absolute power by Napoleon's nephew Louis Bonaparte, that France's new ruler 'magnanimously' decided to release 'Abd al-Qadir and his dwindling entourage. The self-proclaimed 'Emperor' Louis Napoleon III felt that his own prestige would be greatly enhanced by such a highly publicised demonstration of 'French honour'. On 21 December 1852 'Abd al-Qadir, his remaining family and followers were allowed to sail from Marseille to Istanbul, en route to Bursa, his first place of exile.

Six months after 'Abd al-Qadir surrendered to the French, on 5 June 1848, Ahmed Bey of Constantine also gave himself up. After the capture of his city he had continued a sporadic guerrilla war against the French; but, to the end, he had arrogantly refused any cooperation with the Emir. As with 'Abd al-Qadir, initial promises of exile in another Muslim country were revoked, and he was kept under house arrest in Algiers until his death in 1850.[26]

The defeat of 'Abd al-Qadir and Ahmed Bey did nothing to end the violence of the French occupation of Algeria. Nor did these victories alleviate the sufferings of the French soldiers and their high mortality, mainly from lack of medical care and protection against disease. For example, between 1830 and 1851, 87,325 French troops in Algeria died. Of these, only 4,750 were 'deaths in combat'; 'deaths in hospital' were 82,585.[27]

But French losses were nothing compared with the sufferings of the Algerian population. It has been estimated that, during the period of total war, between 1840 and 1848 it declined by around 300,000 – about 10 per cent of the total.[28] And as French columns pushed south into the Sahara, French atrocities – and occasional reciprocal revenge attacks on European colonists – continued until the final conquest of the Algerian Sahara in 1902.[29] Indeed, almost every year following the surrender of 'Abd al-Qadir and Ahmad Bey witnessed a desperate but futile uprising somewhere in 'Algérie Française', culminating in a great Berber rebellion in the Grand Kabylia in 1871.

And what of for France's ambition to build a self-sustaining European colony in Algeria which would develop a thriving agricultural economy? After 1831 the number of settlers increased from 3,228 to 99,800 in 1845; but the vast majority of these settled in Algiers and other towns. In the countryside, the growth of small independent peasant colonists was sluggish, and large tracts of Arab land were taken over by European joint stock companies, turning landless Arabs and Berbers into a rural proletariat. And with the total number of French troops in Algeria reaching 95,000 in 1845,[30] the occupation required nearly one soldier to protect one settler. It would be many decades before Algeria was sufficiently 'pacified' for European colonists to arrive in large numbers.

Subjugated Arabs of the province of Oran c. 1850

Although the subjects are drawn in what may be a deliberately demeaning and subordinate posture, the drawing is interesting because it shows Arab costume in a specific province of Algeria.

CHAPTER 17

Inter-Imperialist Rivalry:
Proxy War and Real War

With the expulsion of Mehmed Ali's forces from Greater Syria, Britain was determined to challenge France's political dominance in the province, although it was facing an uphill struggle. By 1828, France already had consuls in Aleppo, Damascus, Beirut, Latakia and Acre, whereas Britain had only one, in Beirut, to which Damascus was added in 1830. While Ibrahim's army dominated Syria, until 1840 British citizens could enter the province only with French passports, and vessels carrying British goods could sail into Syrian ports only under the French flag[1] – although by 1836 British exports constituted 43 per cent of all the commodities flowing into the ports of Latakia, Tarsus, Alexandretta and Tripoli.

In 1840 Greater Syria had around 1 million inhabitants. It also had the most diverse religious and sectarian population in the Ottoman Empire. Only 49 per cent of its inhabitants were Muslims, even if we include in that category all the 'heretic' groups such as the Druze and Shi'i Isma'ilis, as well as the roughly 100,000 nomads. Christians constituted around 48 per cent; but they too were fractured into fiercely competing sects, with the Greek Orthodox, at 240,000, slightly out-numbering Catholic Maronites (180,000–200,000), a smaller number of 'Greek' Catholics* and a tiny proportion of Protestant converts, among whom American missionaries were busy at work.[2] This heterodox religious population was to prove a critical problem for the Ottoman authorities in Syria as they introduced the reforms demanded by Britain and other European states.

Syria's major cities were Damascus, with around 100,000 inhabitants of all faiths, and Aleppo with 70,000, but the coastal town of Beirut and its environs had recently grown to around 15,000. It was also fast becoming

---

* Greek Catholics followed the Byzantine (Greek) liturgy but were in full communion with the Pope and Rome.

a major trading port, with total exports from Beirut increasing from 3.2 million francs in 1825–27 to 16.1 million in 1841–43.[3] The increase in exports was largely due to the expansion of raw silk production and silkworm cocoons destined for France's silk-cloth industry at Lyons. The bulk of these came from the Mount Lebanon region whose population in the early 1840s accounted for about one third of the Syrian total.[4]

The topography of the Mount Lebanon range is very distinctive. It runs north–south, parallel to the Mediterranean coast of the present-day state of Lebanon, reaching an average height of 2,500 metres within only thirty-seven to fifty-two kilometres of the coastline. Humidity, sweeping eastwards from the sea, produces precipitations which turn to snow on the high limestone peaks, which melts during the dry season and descends through the porous strata until it is forced to the surface near outcrops of basaltic and sandstone layers at around 900 to 1,200 metres. These natural springs feed a number of streams and rivers which provide irrigation for an agriculture based on terracing and the cultivation of mainly arboraceous crops like olives, vines, fruit trees, and the cultivation of mulberry trees for the collection of silkworm cocoons destined for the production of raw silk.

The political history of Mount Lebanon is also highly individual. Unable to subdue its inhabitants by military might, the Ottoman sultans came to accept this mountain fastness as having a special status. Since the late sixteenth century Mount Lebanon had enjoyed a unique political regime known as *al-imara* (the Emirate). The Emir al-Hakim of Mount Lebanon – known to the Europeans as the 'Prince-Emir' – was its supreme tax-farmer, and was chosen by his own feudatories, not by the Porte. Today historians of the Middle East generally shy away from the use of social categories drawn from Europe's historical development. Even so, it seems appropriate to describe the land tenure system of *al-imara* – a system generally known as *iqta'* – as a type of feudalism.[5]

The feudal chiefs of Mount Lebanon controlled twenty-four exceptionally large tax farms (*muqata'as*). They themselves were known as *muqata'jis*. However, unlike the *muqata'as* and *iltizam*s which we have already come across elsewhere, the tenure of these tax farms was not only for life but also usually hereditary.[6] Most *muqata'jis* were the heads of extended, clan-like families, a social structure fostered by the custom of cousin-marriage. The heads of each family within the clans were known as sheikhs, who would own the whole or particular sections of the total *muqata'a*. The *muqata'jis* or sheikhs collected the Empire's taxes – mainly the *'ushr* – from their peasants, a part of which was taken by the Amir Hakim. He, in turn, paid a part to the Vali of Sa'ida, who then paid his quota to the Porte. The *muqata'jis* also had military obligations towards the Emir al-Hakim and responsibility for law and order in the regions comprising their tax farms.

The peasants of Mount Lebanon worked for their *muqata'jis* or sheikhs as sharecroppers. They had certain serf-like obligations of personal fealty towards their sheikhs; for example, a number of days unpaid labour on the sheikh's private land and the giving of 'presents' to the sheikh on the occasion of a sheikhly marriage.[7] However, until the early nineteenth century, the social mores of the Mount Lebanon Imara also dictated that the *muqata'ji* was expected to look after his tenants and support them and their families in times of financial difficulty or illness.

Like Greater Syria itself, Mount Lebanon was distinguished by its religious heterogeneity. During the Middle Ages it had provided sanctuary to various religious minorities, in particular the Maronites and the Druze, who were escaping persecution by both the Byzantine and Sunni Muslim empires. The former are a Christian sect which had united with the Roman Catholic Church; and since the sixteenth-century capitulations they also enjoyed the official protection of France along with that nation's merchants. For many years they had been receiving French Catholic missions which established schools in their principal towns.

The Maronites predominated in the northern and central parts of Mount Lebanon. Unlike the arrangements applying to the heads of the other Ottoman religious millets (communities), the Maronite Patriarch was chosen by his own clergy, not appointment by the Porte. Monks of the denomination controlled a number of wealthy estates with privileges and duties similar to those of Muslim *waqfs*.

Second only to the Maronites in social and political importance were the Druze, a secretive, heterodox breakaway from Shi'i Islam whose religion incorporates Hellenistic, Iranian and other pre-Islamic traditions and believes in reincarnation and the transmigration of souls. At the end of the eighteenth century they were most numerous in the southern part of Mount Lebanon, especially in the region known as the Shuf. However, following an internecine struggle between Druze *muqata'jis*, many Druze migrated to the

Hauran, a great basaltic mountain stronghold in southwestern Syria, where they grew to be a powerful military and political force in Syrian politics.

Quantifying the relative size of the Christian and Muslim populations in Mount Lebanon in the early nineteenth century is problematic.[8] However, in 1846 the French consul in Beirut estimated that 83 per cent were Christians (Maronites, Greek Catholics, Greek Orthodox) and 16 per cent were Muslims (the 'heretical' Druze, plus Sunni and Shi'i). Of particular significance, the feudal nature of Mount Lebanon was the same regardless of a community's religion. Moreover, it was by no means uncommon for a Druze lord to have Christian peasants and visa-versa. In the many areas where both Druze and Maronites settled as sericulture expanded, until the beginning of the nineteenth century 'a liberal and mutually tolerant atmosphere prevailed in the resultant mixed communities'.[9]

From 1711, the family which furnished successive Prince-Emirs of Mount Lebanon were the Shihab, originally Sunni Muslims, although some had converted to Maronite Christianity. These included Bashir Shihab II, who gained the emirate in 1789 and would rule for a further fifty-one years – albeit with numerous intermissions. Although baptised into the Maronite church, Bashir's notion of Christianity fell considerably short of the precepts of his Saviour: for example, in 1807 he arrested the sons of a rival who threatened his claim to the emirate, blinded them, cut out their tongues, and placed them under life-long house arrest.[10]

It was during Bashir's lengthy reign that relations between France's Catholic Church and the Lebanese Maronites became more firmly entrenched. French clergy established schools in Mount Lebanon and some Maronite chiefs adopted elements of French culture, including learning the French language.

In 1806 he built for himself a beautiful palace at Bayt al-Din, close by the prosperous Christian town of Dayr al-Qamar. From there Prince-Emir Bashir II ruled as an 'enlightened despot'. He built roads and bridges, supported the construction of both churches and mosques, promoted the arts and generally established a greater degree of law and order in his virtual kingdom. Although a Maronite (a fact which he largely concealed) Bashir 'rooted out every intrigue liable to sow the seeds of discord between Druze and Maronites'.[11] But he remained a ruthless and cruel enemy to those who opposed him. A painting of him, probably dating from the 1830s, shows an elderly man (by now he would have been in his mid-sixties) with thick eyebrows bushing out above small piercing dark eyes and a huge white beard stretching to his waist: the appearance of a rather malevolent Santa Claus.

Until the 1830s Bashir carefully abstained from any involvement in political affairs outside his realm. For example, during Napoleon's invasion of Palestine in 1799 he had politely refused the requests of both Napoleon and Cezzar Paşa to support them; and he had given every facility to the grand vezir's Ottoman army as it trundled through Syria to attack the French in 1801. However, as Ibrahim's Egyptian army advanced into Syria in 1831, Bashir decided to throw in his lot with Mehmed Ali's rebellion against the Ottomans. From the beginning of the Egyptian invasion of Syria by Mehmed Ali's son, Ibrahim, Bashir began to openly surround himself with Maronite officials and acolytes. He also became increasingly suspicious of certain Druze emirs whom he suspected of conspiring against both himself and the Egyptian occupation. He drove these emirs from Mount Lebanon and confiscated their property.

In 1834 Ibrahim, operating on instructions from his father, ordered the disarmament of both Christian and Druze and the conscription of their young men into his European-style army. This policy provoked a mass flight of Druze to join their co-religionists in the Hauran. Consequently, in 1837–38 Ibrahim sent a number of military expeditions against the Hauran Druze, including 4,000 Maronites commanded by Bashir's son. These were all defeated, but the fighting inevitably exacerbated the growing hostility between Maronites and Druze in Mount Lebanon, which had been sown by Bashir's collaboration with the Egyptians.[12] Indeed, in the view of one Lebanese historian, 'For the Amir to send his own son to fight the Druze with Christian troops meant the final alienation of the Druze.'[13]

By mid-1840, with the retreat of Egyptian forces, Bashir realised his days as Prince-Emir were numbered. On 3 September 1840, Sultan Abdülmecid dismissed him and, on the advice of the British, replaced him with his cousin Bashir al-Qasim (who became Bashir III). Bashir II surrendered to the Royal Navy and was shipped off to Malta.

The decision to appoint Bashir al-Qasim was a serious mistake. He showed no inclination or ability to reconcile the Maronites and Druzes and he antagonised the Druze feudal lords. The principal Druze *muqata'jis* – the Junblat, the Abu Nakad, the 'Imad and others – had lost their lands because they opposed Bashir II's fiscal exactions. Now, returning to Mount Lebanon, they expected the return of their confiscated estates and restitution of their feudal rights. But those who had Christian tenants found their claims resisted, and Bashir III refused to help the Druze nobility. To make matters worse, the Maronite Patriarch, Yusuf Hubaysh, issued an inflammatory instruction to all Maronite villages in Druze *muqata'a*s, urging them to appoint their own representatives to assume all the local political rights previously held by the Druze lords. Learning of this provocative action, Colonel Hugh Rose, commander of the British military contingent in Syria and later consul-general, immediately sent a despatch to the British government in which he warned, with tragic prescience: 'The Maronite clergy show a determination to uphold their supremacy in the mountains at the risk of a civil war.'[14]

Meanwhile, in the void that followed the British and Ottoman expulsion of the Egyptian army from Syria, the Porte started negotiations with the European powers to return Mount Lebanon to Ottoman control. However, Britain, France and Russia were all seeking to extend their political influence in Syria, not only in Mount Lebanon but also in the Palestinian 'Holy Land'.

With this objective, they began fishing in the deep and poisonous waters of religious sectarianism. Each foreign power sponsored a separate community: the British supporting the aspirations of the Druze, the French those of the Maronites, and the Russians those of the Greek Orthodox. Over the next ten years Mount Lebanon witnessed three civil wars, in 1841, 1845 and 1860. The wars began as mainly Maronite-Druze conflicts but by 1860 they had degenerated into a general Christian-Muslim struggle, with the undermanned and underpaid Turkish Ottoman troops standing on the sidelines. During this roughly twenty-year period the British and French governments and their local consular agents in Mount Lebanon and Syria supported their respective clients in a struggle which became a proxy war between the two European powers.[15]

The French moved first. On 1 January 1841 the Maronite patriarch requested the French consul in Beirut, Nicolas Bourée, to urge the French government to give more active support to their cause. France hoped to win back some of the prestige it had lost after the expulsion of Mehmed Ali's troops. So it seized this opportunity by raising both public and official subscriptions equivalent in value to £5,000 (around £525,000 in 2020 sterling) and sent this money to the Maronites.[16] The British consul in Beirut was Nevin Moore, a man who 'saw a French plot behind every move that did not comport with his likings'.[17] On 22 March, he wrote to Palmerston arguing that, if Britain was unable to counter the French with similar outlays to help win over one of the other religious sects, then British warships should be sent to the Lebanese coast 'to show the Syrians that they are within the reach and observation of the British government'.[18] Moore was nevertheless accurate when he drew Palmerston's attention to the growing activities of French agents among the Maronite clergy. Meanwhile, as Tsar Nicholas I became obsessed with extending the influence of the Orthodox Church, the Russians were playing the same game with the Greek Orthodox clergy.

A suitable beneficiary for British largesse had already appeared. Sometime in 1839, a Druze notable, Sheikh Mirza of Suwaydah, from the Hauran, informed an American Protestant missionary that his people wanted English schools for their children and protection. It also appears that this request was 'sweetened' by suggesting an interest in conversion to Protestantism. The information was duly passed on to the British, although for the time being there was no official British response.

Then, after another group of Druze leaders let it be known that they were seeking both schools *and* protection from a suitable foreign power, on 2 July Consul Moore reported to Palmerston that Druze emirs had formally opened negotiations at the British consulate. In these talks the Druze requested that they 'be permitted to look to England as their protector against wrong or oppression from whatever quarter it may be attempted',[19] a clear reference to the Maronites. On 15 July, Palmerston responded to the Druze requests with considerable enthusiasm, although in his message to their emirs he stressed that any such relationship with Britain must in no degree interfere with or weaken their loyalty to their sovereign, the sultan.

Subsequently, on 26 July – and as a blow to the American missionaries in Syria, who cherished their own opportunity to 'convert the Druze' – Colonel Rose recommended to Palmerston that a missionary of the Anglican Church (doubling as a government agent) be sent to Syria to establish a British foothold among the Druze. Palmerston agreed. While arrangements were being made for sending this individual to Druze-controlled territory, on 9 August and at the urging of Colonel Rose, Palmerston also agreed that Isma'il, the younger brother of the Druzes' chief spokesman, Nu'man Junblat, should be brought to England for his education. Palmerston duly instructed Rose to make arrangements for Isma'il to be carried in a British warship.[20] Meanwhile British consular agents in Syria were instructed to work with representatives of the Anglican Church Mission Society to cement ties with the Druze. For their part, the Maronite clergy absolutely forbade any Protestant evangelising in Mount Lebanon, including areas which were in Druze *muqata'a*s.

No administration in Mount Lebanon could be effective without financial support, and this meant the collection of taxes, including those remaining unpaid from previous years. But the Maronite clergy were now deliberately encouraging the Maronite tenants of Druze lords to refuse to hand over to them the *'ushr* (tithe) or its urban equivalent. A particular flashpoint in this respect was the predominantly Christian town of Deir al-Qamar: it lay within the *muqata'a* of Manasif, whose lords were the great Druze family of Abu Nakad. The tax question now became an additional source of anger between Christians and Druze.

France wanted the Porte to engineer the return from exile of the old Prince-Emir Bashir II, and the local French representative counselled civil war as a means of achieving this objective. Writing to Guizot, the French foreign minister, Consul Bourée advised that 'the only real assurance for a system convenient to our interests here is one in which the Christians win and the Druze lose'.[21] In fact, French agents in Sidon had already begun funnelling arms and gunpowder to Maronite militia, knowing full well they would be used against the Druze.[22]

On 14 September 1841 the first serious outbreaks of sectarian violence commenced, with fighting around Dayr al-Qamar, whose inhabitants called for support from other Maronite areas, while militant clerics drew up battle plans with the assistance of French agents.[23] As if to signal direct French military support for the Maronites, on 20 September a French naval squadron arrived off the Lebanese coast, but in the event took no further action. Fighting took place over the next five weeks in those *muqata'a*s with mixed populations. The number of Christian (predominantly Maronite) adults capable of bearing arms outnumbered the Druze by more than three to one. Yet the better-disciplined and militarily experienced Druze fighters drove the poorly organised Maronites from their villages and looted their property. A number of killings occurred after they forced the defenders of Dayr al-Qamar to surrender. However, the Druze attack on the predominantly Greek Catholic town of Zahle in the fertile Biqaʻ Valley failed.

On balance, the Druze won this short 'war', but they suffered the greater number of casualties. Another casualty of the growing violence was the current Prince-Emir himself. The incompetent Bashir III was unceremoniously removed from his position by the Porte in January 1842 and replaced by an Ottoman governor, Omar Paşa, a Croatian renegade from the Austrian army who had converted to Islam and would later command Ottoman troops in the so-called 'Crimean War'.

Although the British officials in Syria made some offers to mediate between the two sides, the Maronites, encouraged by the French, rejected them, alleging that the British were actively supporting the Druze. Even though the Maronite claims were not strictly true, ever since 1840 the British had grown highly antagonistic towards the Maronites and their clergy. For example, Colonel Charles Henry Churchill, a fellow officer in Rose's regiment and one-time vice-consul at Damascus, recorded that, 'In the late civil war' – referring to the sectarian violence of 1841 – 'the [Maronite] fanatics of Dayr al-Qamar' were intent upon the 'general cause of Druze extermination'. In a later work, Churchill states

> The French consular authorities in Beirut exercise a direct and almost sovereign power over the Maronite clergy, who, on their part, make no scruple of boasting of their allegiance to France and of declaring the Maronites to be the French of the East. [24]

In Istanbul, the European powers and the Porte met to try to establish a form of government for Mount Lebanon which would put an end to the sectarian conflict. But there were deep divisions within the European camp. The 'Papal powers', France and Austria, backed the Maronites' demand for an emirate covering the whole of Mount Lebanon, while the Protestant Britain and Prussia, supported by Russia, favoured Druze demands to retain their own independent feudal power bases. Unfortunately, the eventual compromise resolution between the European powers on a new political structure for Mount Lebanon – proposed by the Austrian chancellor Prince Klemens Von Metternich and ratified by the Porte – was almost designed to intensify sectarian divisions.

In January 1843, Mount Lebanon was split into two political entities, each under a *qa'imaqam* (lieutenant-governor). This 'dual *qa'imaqamate*' was established by drawing a line running horizontally along the Beirut-Damascus road, and designating the northern and southern halves as, respectively, Christian and Druze *qa'imaqamate*s. However, the Russian consul in Beirut challenged the dividing line imposed by the European powers as it meant that 43 per cent of the families in the southern, Druze *qa'imaqamate* would be Christian.[25] In fact the number of Christians then resident in the Druze sector (164,940) was greater than the number living in the Christian sector (127,300).[26] Sure enough, civil war broke out once again in 1845 after Maronite leaders insisted that the jurisdiction of the Christian *qa'imaqam* and his agents should be extended to the numerous Christian enclaves in the Druze sector.

For some time the Maronites in the religiously mixed *muqata'a*s under Druze control had been forming militias; and with the help of agents under the direction of the French consul-general, Eugène Poujade, they had been acquiring arms. While the Maronite feudal lords stood aside, sections of the Maronite clergy led by Tubiya 'Awn, Bishop of Beirut, encouraged their peasant flock to mount a 'holy war' against the Druze feudal lords. Their primary political objectives were to compel the Druze to relinquish their jurisdiction of the Maronite peasants and to restore the Shihab Emirate over the whole of Mount Lebanon, either in the person of the exiled Bashir II or one of the numerous Shihabi 'princes' of his extensive household. [27]

The second civil war began with Maronite bands attacking and burning neighbouring Druze villages. Many of these militia bands carried French flags supplied by Consul-General Poujade; they apparently expected to receive direct French military assistance. However, not only did this French military aid fail to materialise, but appeals for help sent to the Maronites living in the northern, Christian *qa'imaqate* fell on deaf ears. Moreover, in some areas of fighting the Greek Orthodox Christians sided with the Druze.[28] At the end of May, the Maronites had again been defeated and the Druze remained in full control of their administrative areas. Deaths on both sides were estimated at between 1,500 and 3,000.[29]

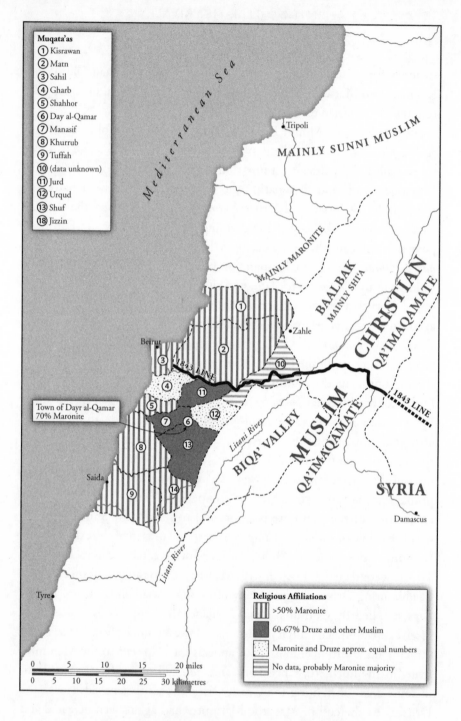

Muqata'as
1. Kisrawan
2. Matn
3. Sahil
4. Gharb
5. Shahhor
6. Day al-Qamar
7. Manasif
8. Khurrub
9. Tuffah
10. (data unknown)
11. Jurd
12. Urqud
13. Shuf
18. Jizzin

Mediterranean Sea

MAINLY SUNNI MUSLIM

Tripoli

MAINLY MARONITE

BAALBAK
MAINLY SHIYA

CHRISTIAN QA'IMAQAMATE

Zahle

1843 LINE

Beirut

Town of Dayr al-Qamar
70% Maronite

MUSLIM QA'IMAQAMATE

1843 LINE

BIQA' VALLEY

Litani River

SYRIA

Saida

Damascus

Litani River

Tyre

Religious Affiliations

>50% Maronite

60-67% Druze and other Muslim

Maronite and Druze approx. equal numbers

No data, probably Maronite majority

| 0 | 5 | 10 | 15 | 20 miles |
| 0 | 5 | 10 | 15 | 20 | 25 | 30 kilometres |

THE MUQATA'AS OF MOUNT LEBANON, SHOWING THE 1843
DIVIDING LINE BETWEEN CHRISTIAN (MAINLY MARONITE)
AND MUSLIM (MAINLY DRUZE) QA'IMAQAMATES

With the defeat of the Maronites the proxy war between Britain and France fizzled out. It was followed by a dramatic – if short-lived – realignment of the imperialist powers and one which, for a time, created a major schism in the 'Concert of Europe'.

On Good Friday 1846 an unseemly quarrel took place in Jerusalem between Catholic and Greek Orthodox priests. It was about who had the first right to carry out Good Friday rituals on the altar of Calvary inside Jerusalem's Church of the Holy Sepulchre. It soon developed into a virtual battle that rival monks and pilgrims joined in. By the time the no-doubt mystified Turkish guards brought the fighting to an end, more than forty people lay dead. The following year another violent squabble between Catholics and Greek Orthodox occurred in Bethlehem. Yet another outbreak of sectarian violence had broken out in Greater Syria – but this time between rival Christians, enflaming religious passions between their respective sponsors, France and Russia.

For Sultan Abdülmecid and the Porte the status quo was that the Orthodox rite had pride of place in the maintenance and rituals of the 'Holy Places' and, in fact, by far the largest number of pilgrims travelling to the 'Holy Land' – around 15,000 each year – were Russian. Indeed, one Russian theologian of the day claimed, 'Palestine is our native land, in which we do not recognise ourselves as foreigners.'[30] But with the coming to power of Emperor Louis-Napoleon, France's new ruler felt the need to rally the Catholic Church behind his precarious regime. Consequently, in May he sent the zealously Catholic Charles, Marquis de Valette, as ambassador to İstanbul to demand a reversal of Ottoman policy. First came the threat of an attack by the French Mediterranean fleet if the Ottomans did not concede the prior right of the Catholics in Palestine's Christian rituals. Then, in November 1852, the Porte issued a new ruling granting the Catholics the right to hold a key to the Church of the Nativity in Bethlehem which had previously been in the sole hands of the Orthodox.

This, even partial, concession to France and the Palestinian Catholics infuriated the ageing Tsar Nicolas I. It at last gave him the excuse to pursue his long-desired objective: a 'crusade' to bring the ancient Byzantine Christian empire of the Greeks under Russian control and 'to take on the whole world in accordance with what he believed was his holy mission to extend his empire of the Orthodox as far as Constantinople and Jerusalem.'[31]

Fed on a diet of Florence Nightingale, the Charge of the Light Brigade, 'The Thin Red Line' and bungling generals, some British readers might be excused from concluding that the 'Crimean War' was a pointless and incomprehensible conflict, and the violent squabbles about access to the 'Holy Places' were a mere laughing-matter. But in reality it was a far more significant struggle; and while the British have persisted in referring to it as the 'Crimean War', the Russians have used the far more appropriate name 'The Eastern War'.

It would be a war which pitted France, Britain and the Ottomans* against Tsarist Russia. By the early 1850s both Britain and France had important economic interests in the Ottoman Empire and its appendages. Since 1840 British trade with the Empire had grown rapidly, and Britain had earned consistent surpluses on its trade balances. Investors in both Britain and France had become major creditors to the Empire. In 1854 both British and French governments encouraged investors to subscribe to the first foreign loan floated by the Ottoman government. Common economic interests were bringing these two old rivals together in the face of the Russian threat.[32]

To realise his grand ambition the Tsar planned a massive military campaign, through the Principalities and the Balkans, capturing Istanbul and the Turkish Straits and allowing his Black Sea fleet to sail out to dominate the Eastern Mediterranean. It was indeed to be another 'crusade', one to replace Ottoman Islam with Russian Orthodox Christianity as the dominant force in those regions of coastal Syria that had once been under the domination of the original crusading kingdoms.

On 27 December 1852 the Tsar ordered the mobilisation of 37,000 troops in Bessarabia in preparation for a lightning strike on Istanbul and 91,000 for a simultaneous invasion of the Principalities and the rest of the Balkans.[33] For the time being he held back his planned assault and in February 1853 sent an envoy to Istanbul, ostensibly with the intention of demanding the Porte restore to the Orthodox Church its original 'rights' to the Holy Places, but in reality to pursue his much more ambitious objective by forcing the sultan into war. By now he had 140,000 troops stationed on

---

*   The Ottomans also received contingents from Egypt and Tunisia, and later in the war the
     Kingdom of Sardinia joined the alliance.

the frontier of the Principalities and was prepared to use them, together with the Russian Black Sea fleet, to seize Istanbul should that be needed to force the sultan into submission.[34]

The envoy chosen was the sixty-five-year-old Prince Alexander Menshikov, a notoriously brutal general who, only four years previously, had crushed a liberal and nationalist uprising in Hungary at the request of the Emperor of Austria, Franz Joseph, and had executed Hungarian nationalists en masse. He presented the Porte with the most outrageous demands deliberately calculated to elicit a furious response from Sultan Abdülmecid and his ministers. Making use of a highly disputable interpretation of the Treaty of Küçük Kaynarca which had ended the war of 1768–74,* Menshikov demanded a new treaty. In the words of Orlando Figes, it 'would reassert [Russia's] rights of protection over the Greek Church throughout the Ottoman Empire ... without any control by the Porte. European Turkey would become a Russian protectorate and the Ottoman Empire would in practical terms become a dependency of Russia, always threatened by her military might.'[35] In other words, the Ottomans would have to accept the extension of Russian military power well beyond 'European Turkey' and deep into the Eastern Mediterranean.

The Tsar's objective was clearly understood by Napoleon III, who had his own long-term objectives in the Mediterranean. In a speech to the Senate and Legislative Assembly on 4 March 1854 he provided a powerful rationale for a war to curb Tsar Nicholas's grandiose plan.

> [For the Russians] to reign at Constantinople means to reign over the Mediterranean ... Why are we going to Constantinople? We are going there with England to defend the sultan's cause, and no less the right of the Christians [i.e. the Catholics], we are going there to protect the freedom of the seas, *and our rightful influence in the Mediterranean*. [My emphasis.][36]

---

* One clause of the Treaty of Küçük Kaynarca gave the Russians the right to build an Orthodox Christian church in Istanbul and to make representations on behalf of it 'and those who serve it'. The Treaty was promulgated in various languages which differed considerably, and the Russian version was written in such a way that it appeared to give Russia the right to act as protector of all Orthodox Christians living in the Ottoman Empire.

Fearing that the Russians were about to seize the Dardanelles, Colonel Hugh Rose, who had been transferred from Syria to act as chargé d'affaires in the temporary absence of Ambassador Stratford Canning, sent a note to Vice-Admiral Richard Dundas in Malta calling upon him to bring up a squadron to Izmir as a precautionary measure in the event of any Russian move. However, when the request was passed on to the government, the cabinet still decided that the crisis could be settled peacefully once Stratford Canning returned to Istanbul. Once the cabinet's reticence was reported back to the Tsar it encouraged him in the belief that the British would acquiesce in his planned attack on the Ottoman Empire.

This was partly because in 1844 Tsar Nicholas had made a state visit to England where he had been warmly received by the Queen and aristocracy. This misled the Tsar into believing that Britain would either support his planned campaign or stay neutral. What the Tsar was unaware of was the growth of Russophobia among the remainder of British society, largely as a result of Russia's well-publicised brutal suppression of the Hungarian patriots in 1849. And riding the tide of this wave of Russophobia was a powerful and popular politician – Lord Palmerston, once again Britain's foreign secretary.

When the sultan predictably rejected Menshikov's demands, Tsar Nicholas sent 80,000 troops to occupy the Danubian Principalities. Britain and France sent fleets to the mouth of the Dardanelles, but for the moment they took no further action. However, in April 1853 Stratford Canning, convinced that Russia posed a massive threat to Britain's economic interests in the East, urged the sultan to resist Russia's action and on 4 October the Ottomans declared war on Russia. In response, on 30 November the Russian Black Sea fleet aimed a devastating blow against Sinope, the Ottoman naval base on the northern coast of Anatolia, destroying the Ottoman fleet and killing many civilians in the town.

On 5 December 1853 the Concert of Europe, with Russia absent, met in Vienna and presented peace terms to both the Russians and Ottomans. However, the Porte considered the terms far too favourable to Russia and called upon Britain and France to come to their aid. At the same time, Sultan Abdülmecid announced a jihad and both Egypt and Tunisia sent troops to join the Ottoman army marching to reinforce its line of defence on the Danube.

By now the British press were urging a war against the 'Russian despot'. Palmerston in the Foreign Office successfully orchestrated the clamour for war, winning over a divided cabinet. Consequently, on 27 and 28 March 1854 France and Britain respectively declared war on Russia. It was the beginning of a conflict which had had originated in the Mediterranean (the 'Holy Land'), and had become a war for control of the Mediterranean – but a war which would be fought hundreds and even thousands of miles from the Great Sea.

By the spring of 1854 the Tsar's great plan was faltering. The initial Russian military objective was to capture the Ottoman fortresses guarding the southern bank of the Danube and then storm through the Balkans and seize Istanbul. Of these fortresses the most important was Silistria on Wallachia's southern border. However, by the 1850s the Ottoman army was far better organised, equipped and provisioned than it had been in the war against Mehmed Ali. The Ottoman commander-in-chief, the renegade Croatian officer Omar Paşa, recognised that his troops must play to their strength: avoid futile assaults and fight a defensive battle. Consequently when the Russians began their spring campaign in 1854 they were soon delayed in the Danubian Basin by determined Ottoman resistance from forts and defensive earthworks. Although the Russians were eventually able to break through the Ottoman defence line and reach Bucharest, a series of assaults on the besieged fortress of Silistria – garrisoned mainly by Egyptian and Albanian troops – repeatedly failed.

Meanwhile the ill-provisioned Russian serf-soldiers were beginning to die in their thousands in their typhus-infected camps. News reached the Tsar that Austria was threatening to move 100,000 troops into the Principalities unless Russia withdrew, and that British and French troops had disembarked from their troopships and were concentrating at Varna (in modern Bulgaria); on 28 March 1854 he issued orders to withdraw from Walachia and abandon the siege of Silistria. The Ottomans began a determined counter-attack, pursuing the Russians north, but Austrian troops moved in, blocked Omar Paşa's advance and, for the rest of the war, occupied both the Principalities.

To all extent and purposes the war was now over. The Russians had failed to make their breakthrough. Apart from the Russian capture of the great Ottoman fortress of Kars in eastern Anatolia, the Ottomans had won the 'war for the Mediterranean'.

The British and French governments were now in a quandary. The principal objective of the war – to prevent a Russian capture of Istanbul and the Turkish Straits – had already been achieved without their men firing a shot in anger; and by now there were around 50,000 allied troops camped around Varna with thousands succumbing to disease. Public opinion at home demanded 'something more' should be done, so the allied commanders decided that a suitably ambitious objective would be to destroy the large Russian naval base at Sevastopol on the Crimean peninsula.

The military operations and battles in the Crimea are too well known to require repetition. Suffice it to say that Sevastopol eventually capitulated on 9 September 1855 after an eleven-month siege during which thousands died on both sides, mainly as a result of disease and frostbite during the terrible frozen winter of 1854–55. Meanwhile the British prime minister, Lord Aberdeen, resigned in January 1855 amid growing scandals over the conduct of the war, and was replaced by Palmerston. Two months later, a dejected Tsar Nicholas died of pneumonia, being superseded by his son Alexander II (r. 1855–81) who was forced to continue the defence of Sevastopol.

In the spring of 1855 the Austrians sponsored a conference of the powers in Vienna with the aim of ending the war on the basis of the four main points the allies had agreed would be their minimum terms: Russia to abandon its claim to a protectorate over the Danubian Principalities; the abandonment of its claim to 'protect' Orthodox Christians throughout the Ottoman Empire; the demilitarisation of the Black Sea; and the opening of the Danube to all foreign commerce.

France was initially inclined to support Austria's peace move, but Britain was not. Palmerston was determined to crush Russian power once and for all by pursuing and extending the war on all fronts. So, even after the capture and destruction of Sevastopol, the war dragged on.

The troops of both Britain and France now faced another freezing Crimean winter. But France, which had committed the most troops to the war and had played the leading part in the capture of Sevastopol, was tiring of the struggle.* There were signs of impending mutiny among the

---

* Total combatants in the war were as follows: France, 309,268; Ottomans, 165,000; Britain,

French troops if they were ordered to spend another winter under canvas in the snow and ice. Napoleon III had other imperial objectives and his propaganda machine disseminated the idea that France had already 'won the war'. Together with Austria, peace proposals based on the 'Four Points' were put before the Russians and Tsar Alexander's ministers persuaded him to accept the Austrian terms. On 16 January 1856 the Austrians received a note to this effect from Alexander's foreign minister, and on 30 March the 'Crimean War' came to an end with the signing of the Treaty of Paris. The terms of the peace settlement were broadly the same as the 'Four Points'.

As far as territory was concerned not a lot changed. In return for a small area of Bessarabia Austria agreed to remove its troops from the Principalities. The latter remained as nominally Ottoman vassals, but with privileges which amounted to near independence. Russia retained the Crimea and made some gains in the Caucasus, but the fortress of Kars was returned to the Porte. Russia relinquished its claim to a protectorate over all the Orthodox Christians in the Ottoman Empire; but as far as the original cause of the war – the 'rights' of the contending Christian sects in the 'Holy places' – the status quo was reinstated, giving the Orthodox the predominant position.

The most important territorial issue was the agreement that the Black Sea would be demilitarised: neither the Russians nor the Ottomans would be permitted to have war fleets in the Sea, nor build naval bases and similar coastline fortifications. On balance this favoured the Ottomans.

Neither Britain nor France gained anything from the war, but France's success in bringing it to a relatively early conclusion, against the wishes of Britain, reopened the old Anglo-French antagonism which their wartime alliance had briefly suppressed. However, the 'Crimean War' and the manner in which it was brought to an end by the great powers had consequences which were ultimately detrimental to the long-term survival of the Ottoman Empire.

Before the signing of the Treaty, on 18 February Sultan Abdülmecid had been informed that, as a quid pro quo for their support, the European powers expected him to accelerate the internal reforms that had been

---

107,864; Piedmont-Sardinia 21,000; Russia, 324,476 (888,000 deployed). Total casualties including death later from wounds and death from disease etc., were: Russia, 530,125; France, 135,485; Britain, 40,462; Piedmont-Sardinia, 2,166.

promised in his original *tanzimat* declaration of 1839, the *Hatt-ı Şherif* of Gulhane. Consequently he was prevailed upon to proclaim the *Hatt-ı Hümayun* (Reform Decree) of 1856. Once again, tax farming was 'officially' abolished and would be replaced by salaried tax collectors.* But, more significantly, the proclamation committed the Empire to abolishing all the old distinctions of rank and privilege enjoyed by the Empire's Muslims and create a new 'national' identity.

The old distinction between the *askeri* and *reaya* had long since faded away, but the reforms of the *Hatt-ı Hümayun* had far greater implications. They abolished the religiously ordained, second-class *dhimmi* status of Christians and Jews, along with the whole millet system under which they enjoyed a measure of self-government. One particular consequence was that the old *cizye* tax on non-Muslims was abolished and replaced by a simple military service tax, the *bedel-i askeri*, imposed on all non-Muslims who were liable for conscription.

From now on, the law would recognise only 'Ottomans'. However, to abolish – at a stroke – the whole structure of centuries-old tradition was bound to provoke opposition. It was a profound shock to ordinary Muslims accustomed to considering the Jews and Christians as inferiors. And in the longer term it would provoke the violence between Muslims and Christians which would provide ample opportunities for further European intervention.

Moreover, the war had wrecked the Empire's finances. For the first time in 1854 and again in 1855, the Porte was forced to go to the European capital markets to acquire funds. From now on the Ottomans would become dependent on foreign loans to compensate for their fiscal inadequacy, with dire consequences for their Empire's long-term economic and political autonomy.

---

* As with the proclaimed abolition of tax farming in 1839, it proved impossible to abolish it without a heavy loss of tax revenue; and in most parts of the Empire, even as late as the early twentieth century, tax farming accounted for 95 per cent of all the miri (tithe) taxes collected from the peasants (Quataert in Inalcik and Quataert [eds] 1994, p. 855).

CHAPTER 18

The Second French Expedition to the Eastern Mediterranean

While the Crimean War raged, an uneasy calm settled over Mount Lebanon. Ottoman *vali*s and *qa'imaqam*s came and went. In 1848, Consul-General Rose was sent as chargé d'affaires to Istanbul. Nevin Moore replaced him as consul-general and in 1855 Richard Wood, who had been awarded the consulship of Damascus in 1846, was sent as consul-general to Tunis.

The promulgation of the *Hatt-ı Hümuyan* reforms occurred at a time when the tentacles of European capitalism were reaching deeper into the semi-feudal world of Mount Lebanon. The great French silk cloth industry of Lyons was increasing its links with the region's Christian and Druze feudal lords and encouraging the rapid expansion of the French industry's raw materials, raw silk thread and silkworm cocoons. By 1860, France's production of fine silk textiles had doubled in a mere ten years, with sales in 1859–60 valued at 600 million francs, of which 400 million were exports.[1]

Between 1850 and 1856 the value of raw silk exports from Beirut increased from 2.4 million francs to 10.1 million, falling only slightly in 1857 to 9.8 million; and over roughly the same period the price of an *okka** of silkworm cocoons rose from 12 *piastre*s in 1848 to 45 *piastre*s in 1857.[2] Although part of the increase in the value of silk exports from Mount Lebanon can be attributed to price increases, production and exports were also rising, and cultivation of the mulberry was extending into new, fallow areas or replacing other crops. It would be an exaggeration to talk of 'monoculture', but the *muqata'ji*s and peasants of Mount Lebanon were being drawn deeper into dependence on a crop whose production could be extremely profitable but whose price could be extremely volatile. At the same time

---

*   One okka = 1.28 grams.

European, predominantly French, companies were establishing their own steam-operated silk-reeling factories in Mount Lebanon, replacing the old-fashioned plant owned by the *muqata'jis*.

As the traditional society of Mount Lebanon found itself penetrated by these capitalistic forces, the *muqata'jis*, sheikhs and peasants all fell under the whip hand of commercial pressure and the uncertainties of the European silk market. As a result, the peasantry increasingly found the old feudal obligations unjust and unwarranted, especially since the reciprocal feudal obligations of *himaya* (caring for and protecting tenants) were fast disappearing. According to Colonel Charles Henry Churchill, the British consul in Damascus, the peasant of Mount Lebanon nowadays 'has to shift for himself ... his landlord neither extends the hand of charity nor consoles him by the voice of inquiry and consolation'. Consequently, the peasant's traditional feudal dues owed to the *muqata'ji* were regarded as just an additional kind of tax and, in Churchill's view, 'In the Lebanon no ... ground exists for sympathy between the tenant and the proprietor.'[3]

Consequently, when the Christian peasants of Mount Lebanon heard news of the 1856 Imperial Edict which guaranteed equal status to all citizens of the Empire, large numbers of young men began to demand the abolition of the feudal privileges of *all* the *muqata'jis* and sheikhs, Christian and Druze alike. This agitation was most fierce in the Christian *muqata'a* of Kisrawan which lay just north of the dividing line between the Christian and Druze *qa'imaqates* and had long been under the sway of the Christian Khazin *muqata'ji* clan.

In 1857 Mount Lebanon experienced a severe winter and an economic crisis linked to the general European depression of that year, exacerbated by the disruption of the silk trade by the Crimean War:[4] Production of raw silk fell by 50 per cent.[5] This left both the Khazin sheikhs and their Christian peasants owing huge debts to the Lebanese and European money-lenders of Beirut who had advanced the credit upon which their production depended. In an attempt to reduce their debts, the Khazin sheikhs intensified the feudal burdens on their peasants, reintroducing old ones which had fallen into disuse and imposing newly invented special taxes upon them. Gangs of hired thugs were employed to extract the required sums.

Beginning in October 1858, the peasants of a number of Kisrawan villages began to confront the Khazin sheikhs. The peasant movement grew and became increasingly violent, especially after the emergence of a charismatic leader, Tanyus Shahin. What gave the movement a special impetus was the backing it received from most of the Maronite clergy, many of whom were themselves the sons of peasants. By the middle of 1859, the Kisrawan peasants had driven the Khazin sheikhs from their properties, plundering their goods and killing some of those who had resisted.

So far, the peasant movement was restricted to Maronite territory; but at the end of May 1859 Tanyus Shanin's men crossed the Christian-Druze border of the *qa'imaqate*s and entered the Druze *muqata'a* of al-Matn, roaming south of Beirut in an attempt to raise the Christian peasants of this religiously mixed area against their Druze lords.

With long memories of the Maronite threats of the 1840s to drive the Druze from Mount Lebanon – threats which were now repeated by a small number of fanatical Maronite clergy like Bishop 'Awn of Beirut – the Druze *muqata'ji*s were able to win the support of their own Druze peasants in an anti-Maronite reaction. Soon, sectarian tit-for-tat killings were breaking out in all parts of Mount Lebanon. By the end of May 1860, what had begun as a Maronite class conflict had degenerated into a deadly general war between Christians and Muslims.

Although the Druze were again seriously outnumbered, in six weeks fighting their ferocious martial capability repeatedly overwhelmed the Maronites, while other Muslims, including the Shi'is of the Biqa' valley, to the east and south of Lebanon, joined them in assaulting Christian-controlled towns. A terrible massacre occurred at Deir al-Qamar deep in Druze territory, and at many Christian villages, with the Druze militias killing all male Christians, including children. During the fighting the garrisons of Turkish troops, who the European consuls had been led to believe would intervene and bring an end to the slaughter, did nothing. In some cases they openly supported their fellow Muslims. On 19 June the strategic Christian town of Zahle in the Biqa' fell to the Muslims. By now, those like Bishop 'Awn who had encouraged the Maronites to invade Druze territory realised that their hopes of driving the Druze from Mount Lebanon had terribly backfired. However, the Druze feudal lords, whose peasants, both Christian and Druze, had suffered most in the war, were anxious for peace.[6] It was therefore possible for the European consuls and the Ottoman authorities to bring both sides to a peace agreement at the beginning of July.

It has been estimated that in the civil war at least 5,000 people were killed, of which perhaps 3,800 were Christians and 1,200 were Druzes. However, whereas the majority of the latter were killed in combat, most of the Christians were killed in cold blood after they had surrendered and had given up their arms in the expectation that they would be protected by Turkish troops. Two-hundred Christian villages were burned and destroyed, and perhaps as many as 100,000 people were displaced as a result of the 'ethnic cleansing' which accompanied the fighting.[7] But, just as the war in Mount Lebanon ended, the carnage spread to the city of Damascus.

Here, Sultan Abdülmecid's 1856 edict, which required an end to all forms of discrimination suffered by Christians and Jews, was received with a general fury among the Muslims. This was especially true among the poor who had daily observed the growing wealth of Damascus's large Christian community with its well-established trading links to Beirut and Christian Europe. This anger was intensified by daily provocative celebrations of the sultan's edict by Damascus's Christians.

The proximate cause of the catastrophe which was about to fall upon the Christians lay in widespread reports that they were refusing to pay the *bedl-i askeri*, the tax which had replaced the old *cizje* in Abdülmecid's second great reform. Probably another was the Muslims' recent capture of Zahle in the Mount Lebanon war. However, in any case, it appears that certain local Muslim leaders in Damascus had begun planning a pogrom against their Christian neighbours with the complicity of at least some of the city's Turkish authorities.

For three days following 9 July 1860, mobs of local Muslims – supported by Druze and Sunni Muslim militias and marauding Bedouin and Kurds who poured into the city – slaughtered thousands of men, women and children belonging to all the Christian sects, and looted their houses, churches and property. The American and Dutch consuls were killed, as was an English missionary. As in the Mount Lebanon civil war, estimates of the total killed vary greatly, some being as high as 8,500. A French report put the figure at 4,000. The most objective historian of these events has concluded that the 'most likely' number is 3,000.[8]

'Abd al-Qadir as pensioner of the French government, 1865

The deaths would have been even greater had it not been for the intervention of the Emir 'Abd al-Qadir. After his release by Napoleon III he had been living as a French pensioner on his estate on the outskirts of Damascus, together with his former *khalifa* for the Grand Kabyle, Ben Smela, and a growing number of Berbers who had migrated to work on their lands. As a conservative Muslim 'Abd al-Qadir opposed the reforms of the *Hatt-ı Hümayun*; but he also believed that the killing of innocent, unarmed 'people of the book' was totally contrary to the teachings of the Qur'an. Once the massacre started many of those escaping the mob were taken to his estate and protected by his armed Berbers while others were lodged in Damascus's citadel, also under the protection of his men. Exactly how many Christians were saved is debatable, but it may have been as many as 12,000.[9]

When news of the killings of Christians in the civil war and the massacre at Damascus reached the European governments they all reacted with horror – although, predictably, British officialdom was quick to see its old and recent enemies as the underlying cause of the disaster. Writing to the British foreign secretary from Istanbul on 17 July 1860, British Ambassador Sir Henry Bulwer opined that 'the reasons for the calamities and misfortunes' could be traced back to Mehmed 'Ali and 'the intrigues between the Maronites and French agents, and in addition the intrigues of the Russian Government'.[10] To which the historian 'Usama Kamil Abu Shuqran comments, 'However, whatever the effect of Russian interference on these regrettable events, it was much less than that of the involvement of France or Britain.'[11]

Nevertheless, the publicity these terrible events attracted in the press made it impossible for any European government not to take action. The French moved first.

On 17 July Napoleon III and his Foreign Minister decided on armed intervention. Two days later they proposed to the other European powers a plan to send an expeditionary force to Syria, the majority of which would be supplied by France. The British were deeply suspicious of the proposal and it was not until 3 August that the European powers agreed a protocol for the despatch of 12,000 troops to Syria to restore law and order, half of which would initially be provided by France. It was also agreed that the intervention would last for only six months; no state was to make any territorial or other gains from it; and an International Commission composed of delegates from the major European powers and the Porte would be set up to investigate the causes of the tragic events. Its remit was extended to deciding how governmental institutions could be created in Mount Lebanon to prevent any such sectarian conflicts reoccurring.

In reality, only France had the military capacity to mount such an operation and at such short notice. After its well-publicised and widely derided deficiencies in the Crimean War, the British army was in no state to carry out the task. So on 16 August a French army commanded by General Charles-Marie-Napoléon de Beaufort d'Hautpoul – who had previously been chief of staff in Mehmed Ali's Egyptian army – was disembarked at Beirut.

In what looked suspiciously like an attempt to emulate his illustrious uncle, Napoleon III appointed the 'savant' Ernest Renan, an expert on Semitic languages, to accompany the expedition; and a number of skilled cartographers were included to draw the first map of Mount Lebanon, almost certainly intended for future military purposes.[12] These echoes of Bonaparte's invasion of Egypt cannot have reassured the Porte as to the expedition's true purpose. Indeed, that the French were contemplating a reprise of Napoleon's invasion must have seemed a serious possibility when, on their arrival at Beirut, the French troops sang the old Napoleonic-era anthem 'Partant pour la Syrie', written in 1807.

Meanwhile, in fear of what might otherwise turn out to be a permanent European occupation, and to demonstrate its willingness to punish the guilty, the Porte despatched its foreign minister, Fuad Paşa, as 'Extraordinary Commissioner' to Damascus with 3,000 regular troops. He arrived on 29 July, and over the next twenty days 3,000 of those suspected (or denounced) for having taken part in the killing and looting were arrested, by which time a further 4,000 Turkish Ottoman troops had arrived in the city. After summary trials 167 Muslims were found guilty, most of whom were hanged or shot; eighty-three were condemned to death in absentia; 139 to lifetime service in the galleys; fourteen were exiled; 186 sentenced to hard labour and the galleys; and 3,000 Damascene youths were immediately drafted into the army; the condemned included leading notables and *ulema*.[13] This was Muslim justice in retribution for Muslim crimes against Christians on a scale which had never happened before. Furthermore, on 7 September a military tribunal presided over by Fuad Paşa himself found the hapless Damascus governor, Ahmad Paşa, and three other senior Turkish officers, guilty of negligence, complacency and inaction in failing to protect the Christians. All four were shot.

Napoleon III had announced that his military expedition to Syria was 'in the name of humanity'. But the British were not disarmed by this declaration. As events unfolded and the French showed reluctance to leave, it became apparent that Napoleon's aim was to encourage a government that would promote French interests and policies.[14]

In order to better understand the complex motives behind the French expedition to Syria – motives which did not exclude humanitarian concerns – it is necessary to sketch the particular conjuncture of French economic and political ambitions in the eastern Mediterranean and its hinterland, which set the context for the expedition and especially the surprising reappearance in our narrative of the Emir 'Abd al-Qadir.

One consideration was the long-held French dream of building a Suez Canal. In 1799, Bonaparte's chief engineer calculated that the difference in the levels of the Red Sea and the Mediterranean would make the construction of a canal between them virtually impossible. By the mid-1840s, however, the consensus among European engineers and scientists was that this conclusion was seriously in error. In reality, there was little difference in the levels of the Red Sea and the Mediterranean. The canal project was perfectly feasible.

The individual whose ceaseless efforts over six years brought the canal project to fruition was Ferdinand, the son of Mathieu de Lesseps. In 1802, he had accompanied his father to Egypt when Napoleon appointed him consul; in 1832 Ferdinand had been appointed vice-consul at Alexandria, and the following year consul at Cairo. During these periods of service he became close friends with Sa'id, Mehmed Ali's youngest son. By 1854, he had retired from diplomatic service and was living on his estate in French-occupied Algeria when he became fascinated by the new scientific knowledge concerning the possibility of piercing the Isthmus of Suez. But any notion of building a canal evaporated when Mehmed Ali died in 1849, with his son Ibrahim predeceasing him by a few months. Under the traditional Ottoman rules of succession, Mehmed was followed by his oldest living male relative, his grandson Abbas Hilmi, rather than his youngest son, Sa'id. Abbas, a staunch conservative and religious bigot, had no interest in the canal project. However, when Abbas was assassinated by one of his slaves in 1854, the portly thirty-two-year-old Sa'id, with a fondness for all things French, acceded to the Viceroyalty.

Ferdinand de Lesseps sailed immediately to Egypt, renewed his old friendship with Sa'id, and on 30 November 1854 Sa'id Paşa signed a concession agreement with de Lesseps to build a ship canal from Port Sa'id to Suez. When, shortly afterwards, Napoleon III invested Sa'id Paşa with the insignia of the Legion of Honour, he clearly intended to demonstrate that France itself was enthusiastically backing the project.

The contract was distinctly unfavourable to the Egyptians. First, construction of the canal would mean their government would lose considerable income from the transit of mails and passengers crossing Egypt from Alexandria to Suez. Second, another canal would be built from the Nile to the Isthmus for irrigation purposes, but all the land it cultivated would belong to the company, as would lands adjacent to the maritime canal. Third, 20,000 Egyptian forced labourers would be provided to carry out the actual work. And fourth the Egyptian government would contribute to the financing of the whole project (which would cost an estimated 200 million francs) by purchasing 64,000 of the initial share issue of 400,000 shares, each valued at 500 francs. The financial viability of the canal was based on the claim that, at a charge of ten francs per ton, at least 3 million tons of goods would pass through it each year.[15] The only financial benefit Egypt was to receive from the contract was 15 per cent of the net profits – profits based entirely on the assumption of a heavy traffic flow through the canal.

Palmerston, who had become prime minister in February 1855, was not particularly concerned about the iniquities of the contract; but he immediately identified the canal as representing a threat to British interests. Not only was a British company already building a railway from Alexandria to Suez via Cairo, but a French-controlled canal would pose a major risk to Britain's communications with India. Moreover, the considerable areas of land granted to the company adjacent to the maritime and sweet water canals could easily become the basis for French colonisation and the beginning of a permanent French presence in Egypt.[16]

Therefore, with the assistance of Ambassador Stratford Canning (now Viscount Stratford de Redcliffe, and at the height of his powers), Britain put pressure on Sultan Abdülmecid – Sa'id's nominal sovereign – to put a stop to the canal project. Although the British government's hostility to the canal was not without its opponents, especially among British ship-owners, over the next two years British opposition to the project intensified, accompanied by a further deterioration in Anglo-French relations. Consequently in January 1858, Britain's foreign secretary, Lord Clarendon, warned Reshid Paşa, the incumbent grand vezir, that if the sultan gave his assent to the project he could no longer expect Britain to continue in its traditional role as guarantor of the Ottoman Empire's integrity.[17]

Although the company established to develop the canal was manifestly a French project, de Lesseps named it the Compagnie Universelle du Canal Maritime de Suez, with much propaganda about it being in the interests of all countries. It was also agreed with Sa'id Paşa that no more than 51 per cent of the 400,000 shares would be allocated to French investors. The remaining shares were allocated to other countries depending on the interest shown by their potential investors. But when the results of the flotation were announced on 30 November 1858, while the French allocation had been fully subscribed, only a minuscule number of shares which had been set aside for Austria, Britain, Russia and the US had been purchased (85,506), and subscriptions from other countries fell well short of what had been expected. The flotation looked doomed. Sa'id Paşa had previously promised de Lesseps that his government would purchase any shares not sold, imagining that this would be only a handful. In the event he was forced to buy a further 113,000 shares, thus making the Egyptian government's total contribution 177,000 shares at a cost of 88 million francs, an amount greater than a whole year of Egypt's tax revenues.[18]

On 25 April 1859, work started at Port Sa'id. However, Sa'id Paşa soon learned from the Porte that the sultan was opposed to the canal project, so on 1 June he ordered de Lesseps to stop the work. Faced with economic disaster, in October de Lesseps appealed directly and in person to Napoleon III. The Emperor now made his position absolutely clear. He was intent on giving the canal project his full support – and 'protection'. To the British government this public declaration made it even clearer that the canal was part of a grander French plan to re-establish the influence it had enjoyed in Egypt during the reign of Mehmed Ali. Its view was reinforced when Sa'id, impressed by the French Emperor's declaration that he was personally behind the project, swiftly reversed course, ignored the instructions of the Porte, and permitted the work on the canal to recommence.[19]

Therefore, when, in August 1860, a French army arrived to fulfil its 'humanitarian mission' in Syria its intention was – at least in part – 'to force the sultan to abandon his opposition to the Suez Canal'.[20] But that was by no means the only motive behind the French 'humanitarian' expedition. Indeed, it was not long before the conduct of General d'Hautpoul, the French expedition's commander, lent substance to the suspicions held by all the other European powers alike, namely 'that France had undertaken the expedition ... to pave the way for an eventual occupation of the country'.[21]

The first of the expedition's ulterior motives was economic. During the 1850s, the French silk industry faced an almost insatiable demand for its luxury products, but its raw material, raw silk, was in short supply and expensive. The Lyons capitalists had established their own mulberry tree plantations for the cultivation of silkworms in the Rhône Valley, but in 1853–54 and again in 1856 they were hit by a devastating silkworm disease. Three Lyons silk companies had mulberry plantations in Mount Lebanon and five of its nine silk-reeling factories were French-owned.[22] The French were now increasingly dependent on Mount Lebanon for raw silk supplies from these facilities.

Consequently the agrarian unrest in Mount Lebanon in 1858 and the subsequent civil war in 1860 was a serious blow to the industry. The prospect of a French expedition to Syria offered the French industrialists the opportunity to recover their Lebanese property, repair the damage which they had suffered, and get their labourers back to work.[23] Indeed, not long after his arrival in Syria, the French minister of war thanked General d'Hautpoul for sending an infantry battalion to Mount Lebanon to protect and, where possible, restore the French silk-reeling factories.[24]

But France had a wider political agenda: a suitable candidate was required to rule Mount Lebanon and, if possible, the wider Syria, one who would firmly re-establish French influence in the region. But who might serve these ends?

During the events leading up to the tragedy of 1860, 'Abd al-Qadir's French pension, which had initially been set at the huge amount of 100,000 francs per year [25] (compared to the French consul's 5,000 per year) was raised to 200,000 and eventually to 300,000 francs per year.[26] With these resources he had become a man of great property, with a large town house in Damascus, various farms and estates – one of which extended as far west as the Sea of Galilee – and investment in a new road linking Beirut with Damascus.[27] At the same time his recruitment of Algerian Berbers was well underway; some of them were clearly intended to provide him with a sort of praetorian guard. 'Abd al-Qadir now enjoyed complete control over his Syrian 'mini-state', absolutely free of Ottoman jurisdiction.

The Emir's French 'minder', Georges Bullad, had the task of trying to detect whether 'Abd al-Qadir had any plans to return to Algeria and lead another jihad. Yet now Bullad was forced to concede to his superiors that the Emir was a devout loyalist towards France and to Emperor Louis Napoleon.[28] Meanwhile 'Abd al-Qadir and an up-and-coming young Maronite leader from the northern *muqata'a* of Bshirri, named Yusuf Karam, began a lengthy correspondence which established 'a close personal and political relationship'. The historian who discovered this adds that both 'enjoyed the warm and active support of certain French religious and diplomatic circles', and that while Karam was being groomed as the future governor of a Christian Lebanon, "Abd al-Qadir was promoted as a resplendent monarch of a Syrian or Arabic kingdom'.[29] But who exactly was doing the 'promoting'? And what, if any, evidence points to 'Abd al-Qadir's compliance?

The steady flow of Algerian migrants to 'Abd al-Qadir's territory (ostensibly they were making the hajj to Mecca) greatly concerned the military authorities in Algiers. However, when the governor general of Algeria discovered that the emigrations had been sanctioned by France's war minister Marshall Jacques Louis Randon, he speculated whether some strategy, to which he was not party, was underway; he asked the Minister: 'Is it among the Emperor's intentions that 'Abd al-Qadir might play a role in the East?'[30]

It appears most likely that Louis Bonaparte did have such 'intentions'; and the French expedition to Syria gave him the opportunity to realise them. On 22 September, Marshall Randon wrote to General d'Hautpoul asking the expedition's commander, 'Do you think that 'Abd al-Qadir could govern Syria?'[31] D'Hautpoul answered that he thought it would be impossible to place a Muslim in control of Mount Lebanon, but the *paşalik* of Damascus, or Acre, or Judaea would be another matter.[32] The following month Randon wrote to d'Hautpoul acknowledging that it would be best to place a Christian in the governorship of Mount Lebanon, but that 'if 'Abd al-Qadir can take hold of the Arab tribes currently left to their own ends we would find him a powerful agent'.[33]

Meanwhile, d'Hautpoul demanded the extension of the six-month time-limit originally placed on the French expedition. On 19 February 1861 Edouard Thouvenel, the French foreign minister, in conference with the representatives of the other powers, claimed there was a risk of further massacres if the French troops departed on schedule; the delegates reluctantly agreed to an extension of two months beyond the original termination date.[34]

For the time being the question of 'Abd al-Qadir's future role in Syria was left in abeyance; but on 30 April 1860 M. de Vallette, the French ambassador at Istanbul, sent a dispatch to General Auguste-Alexandre Ducrot, commander of the French expedition's infantry brigade, which set out in considerable detail what he understood to be Napoleon III's ambitions for a great pro-French Arab enclave within Ottoman territory. The list of objectives included:

> The constitution of an Arab empire formed from the various
> states and principalities of the peninsula [Arabia?] both those
> in submission and independent, grouped under the sceptre

of 'Abd al-Qadir; ...with civil and political guarantees for all the peoples, as much as for the Arabs as for the others; ...the adoption of a code consistent with the Code Napoleon and with the decimal system and the separation of the spiritual and the temporal; with its political capital at Baghdad and Mecca its spiritual centre; the immediate opening of the Isthmus of Suez with liberty of passage for all nations...[35]

Virtually the same objectives had already been published in an anonymous pamphlet widely circulated in Paris the previous year and titled 'Abd el-Kader, Emperor of Arabia'.[36] However, if the pamphlet and de Valette's letter (which may have been deliberately leaked) were meant to put the frighteners on the sultan and persuade him to abandon his opposition to the Suez Canal project, it clearly failed. For his part, Sa'id Paşa continued to support the Canal until his untimely death in January 1863.

The question remains, however, to what extent 'Abd al-Qadir's own ambitions favoured the role that Napoleon III appeared to be planning for him. We know that Louis Bonaparte and the Emir held each other in high regard – indeed 'friendship' might be a better word. We also know from 'Abd al-Qadir's experience in Algeria that he had no love for the Turks or the Ottoman Empire; he had been obliged to fight them on some occasions where the remaining Turks had sided with the French. The only other evidence is that in August 1860, coinciding with the arrival of the French expeditionary force, 'Abd al-Qadir is reported to have written to a French nun, a certain Sister Luce, saying 'Here is the moment to display our gratitude to France. It is French bread which we eat.'[37] Nevertheless, such second-hand and cryptic evidence can hardly be considered conclusive. As far as we know, during the ten months of the French military presence, the Emir never made any public statement about his intentions; only after their withdrawal from Syria did he declare that he no longer had any interest in politics. Had he simply been waiting to see 'which way the wind blew'? It seems we shall never know.

D'Hautpoul had meanwhile formed his own plan for maintaining French influence over Mount Lebanon. He spent substantial sums bribing Maronite notables to support his favoured candidate for another Shihabi Emirate, Majid Shihab, and petitioned the international commission on Majid Shihab's behalf. But with the extension of his army's presence in Syria coming to an end and Napoleon III's interest in the whole affair waning, the general admitted defeat. To save face he proclaimed that he had always said he would not leave Syria until the administration of Mount Lebanon was settled – and an international agreement on such a settlement now appeared certain. D'Hautpoul had no choice but to order his commanders to prepare to leave Syria.

On 9 June, the representatives of the European powers and the Porte met in conference at Pera, Istanbul's 'European' suburb, to agree a final settlement of the Mount Lebanon problem. It was known as the *Règlement Définitif* and was formalised in one of the last edicts of Sultan Abdülmecid, who died on 25 June 1861.

The disastrous dual *qa'imaqate* was abolished along with the whole neo-feudal system of *muqata'a*s, although many of the old *muqata'ji* families were allowed to retain large estates. Henceforth Mount Lebanon was to be governed by a non-native Christian, named by the sultan and removable by the Porte. The appointment was to last for three years and the governor, with the rank of *mutasarrif*, was to have a police force of no fewer than 1,500, with authority to call upon Turkish regulars if required. While the Porte was thus assured central control over the whole region, the individual religious sects were given local autonomy with the right to appoint their own local leaders, to be known as *mudur*s.[38] It was an outcome deeply pleasing to Britain's prime minister, Lord Palmerston, who had championed the maintenance of the integrity of the Ottoman Empire for so many years.

The first *mutasarrif* was a learned Armenian Catholic, Karabid Efendi Davidian, formerly the director of the Istanbul telegraph office. His appointment was welcomed by all the sects except the Maronites; he ruled wisely. His term of office was later extended to five years; and in spite of repeated disruption and upheavals in the Maronite districts, over the next decade Mount Lebanon enjoyed a period of prosperity and economic growth. A significant increase in silk production – with output of cocoons increasing from 960,000 in 1861 to 3,400,000 in 1866 – must have made a significant contribution to this economic revival.[39]

Comparing Louis Bonaparte's coup d'état of 1852 with that of his illustrious uncle in 1801, Karl Marx famously observed that when historic facts and personages appear twice they do so 'the first time as tragedy, the second time as farce'.[40] Something very similar could be said of the second

'Napoleonic' French foray into the eastern Mediterranean. After ten months of relative inaction, the troops who had set out for glorious exploits with the war cry '*Partant pour la Syrie*', left silently and without the display that had marked their arrival. 'It was a poor fizzling-out of an ambitious scheme hatched to regain the influence lost by the exclusion of France from the shaping of Near Eastern destinies in 1839.'[41]

As for the Suez Canal which Napoleon III had championed, neither Egypt's ruler, Sa'id, who had part-financed it, nor Britain's Prime Minister Palmerston, who had continuously opposed it, would live to see its completion on schedule in November 1869.* Sa'id's successor, and Mehmed Ali's grandson, Isma'il (r. 1863–79), had meanwhile put a stop to the use of forced labour, one of the conditions demanded by the Porte. Instead, work continued using steam-powered machinery (greatly adding to its costs). After various other financial matters had been settled, largely in favour of the Suez Company, on 19 March 1866 the new Sultan Abdülaziz (r. 1861–76) issued a *firman* authorising the completion of the canal. In the meantime, realising that the canal project could now prove a success after all, the British government began to consider ways and means whereby the new waterway could serve its imperial needs.[42]

In a lavish ceremony commencing on 17 November 1869, the canal was officially opened by the newly titled Khedive Isma'il.† Napoleon III's consort, the Empress Eugénie, headed the list of six thousand guests. But what might have been the crowning glory of the Second French Empire was blotted out the following year on the battlefield of Sedan, where the Emperor's army went down in total defeat before the disciplined ranks of Prussian infantry.‡ Louis Bonaparte – no longer Napoleon III – retired into exile in Britain. And only a few years later a new British prime minister, the mercurial and unlikely Conservative, Benjamin Disraeli (1804–1881), would wrest financial control of the canal from both Isma'il and the French shareholders.

---

* Sa'id died in 1863 and Palmerston in October 1865.

† In 1867 Isma'il Paşa had persuaded Sultan 'Abd al-'Aziz to award him the title khedive, an obscure word of Persian origin, replacing the old title of vali, in return for an increase in the annual tribute paid to Istanbul from £376,000 to £720,000. In a second firman Abdülaziz was persuaded by Isma'il to replace the old Ottoman 'rule of elderness' by that of primogeniture, giving his direct descendants permanent rule over Egypt (and its 'colony', Sudan).

‡ The Franco-Prussian War, 1870–71.

CHAPTER 19

The Industrialised
and the Non-Industrialised

To fully understand how European industrialisation would bring about a cataclysmic transformation of the Mediterranean's Islamic world, we must first briefly return to the last years of the eighteenth century.

In 1780, the Greek merchants and artisan manufacturers of the town of Ambelakia in Ottoman Thessaly formed an association to produce red yarn, whose bright colour and high quality was much in demand, especially in Austria and the German states.[1] The description of the association given by the French consul Félix de Beaujour in 1800 suggests that the organisation and scope of its yarn industry was probably very similar to that of the Tunisian *shashiya* industry, described earlier. According to Beaujour's account, the association was certainly a type of capitalist enterprise in which the town's families held shares, appointed directors to manage the business and had marketing agents who established commercial houses in Buda, Vienna, Leipzig, Dresden, Bayreuth, Salonika, Izmir and Istanbul. Little is known about the exact production process except that in the 1790s there were twenty-four separate 'factories' and it was certainly based on a quite advanced division of labour. It was also highly profitable. According to Beaujour:

> The greatest harmony long reigned in the association ... The company profits increased every day on a capital which had rapidly become immense; each investment realised a profit of from sixty to one hundred per cent, all of which was distributed in just proportion to the capitalists [sic] and workmen .... The shares increased tenfold.[2]

However, when the British economist and traveller David Urquart visited Ambelakia in 1831, he found the company had completely disappeared and the town itself was deserted. Apparently there had been disagreements regarding the distribution of the profits and the association had fractured into a number of separate companies. These no longer had the marketing power of the original association. But Urquart adds that 'the revolution in commerce that English cotton yarn was beginning to effect' was probably the main cause of the association's downfall:[3]

> It would be very unjust to attribute its fall to its internal troubles ... these, and its losses, might soon have been repaired had the industry not been outstripped by that of Manchester.[4]

Since the introduction of machinery into British textile production did not become widespread until the 1820s and 30s, Ambelakia must have been one of the earliest victims of cheap British cloth exports. However, with the steady replacement of water power by steam power, the impact of the new mode of production was soon felt worldwide.

Between the late 1840s and the mid-1870s the steam-power capacity driving Britain's Industrial Revolution increased from 1,290 thousand horse-power (HP) to 7,600 thousand HP. This industrial revolution soon spread throughout Europe. In the states which constituted the new unified German Empire, over the same time span, steam power (again, measured in 000s HP) increased from 92 to 5,120; in France from 370 to 3,070; and even in Russia, from 70 to 1,700.[5] Most of this new energy source was dedicated to textile production and ironworks.

Coinciding with the spread of industrialisation from Britain to the other major European countries (and the US), around the mid-1840s there commenced a remarkable worldwide economic boom. During the first four decades after 1800, the rate of growth of per capita national income in the major European nations had been around 0.5 per cent per year; but from 1840 to 1870, it increased to an unprecedented annual rate of 1.2 per cent.[6] The population of major European cities grew enormously, and with it grew the demand for imported foodstuffs, raw materials and consumer goods. International trade flourished as never before.

As the Ottoman Empire was drawn into this rapidly expanding capitalist world economy its imports, almost entirely of European manufactured goods, increased enormously. From 1830–32 the value of Ottoman imports from Britain, France, the German states and Austria amounted to an annual average of £2.4 million; by 1870–72 this had become £15.9 million. Of this total Britain's share increased from 39 per cent to 42 per cent.[7]

Even before the 1838 commercial Treaty of Balta Limani, the Ottoman Empire was importing increasing quantities of European manufactures. However, the 94 per cent increase in British exports to the 'Eastern Mediterranean'* between 1836–39 and 1850 – most of which was cotton goods – certainly suggests that the Treaty, together with the abolition of Ottoman monopolies, was a major factor in this trend.[8]

To what extent did this flood of British and other European manufactures result in the de-industrialisation of the Islamic Mediterranean world? The issue is a controversial one.[9] The traditional answer, based largely on the example of Ambelakia and reports of contemporary consuls and travellers, is that local industry withered, and imports were a significant factor; and this conclusion has been echoed by a good number of historians. But was this the fate of *all* manufacturing in the Islamic Mediterranean? More recently, a much more nuanced view has emerged.

The inflow of cheap industrialised cotton goods certainly had a damaging effect upon artisan textile production in the regions affected. The impact was most strongly marked in the cotton-spinning sector. For example, it has been calculated that in the Ottoman Empire the number of domestic spinners (measured in full-time equivalents) fell from 215,000 in 1820–22 to 50,000 by 1870–72.[10] By the 1840s, hand spinning of cotton yarn was nowhere to be found in some areas.[11]

On the other hand, in the case of handicraft weaving, some of the contemporary reports of catastrophic decline have been questioned. The same methodology which calculated the fall in the numbers of domestic spinners cited above suggests that the number of cotton textile weavers fell by a relatively undramatic amount, from 65,250 to 53,750 by 1870–72.[12]

Among the reasons for the survival of a significant part of the Ottoman artisanal weaving industry is the fact that the domestic weavers maintained

---

*   The data include 'Turkey' (probably Istanbul and Anatolia), Egypt and Syria/Palestine.

their incomes in the face of falling woven cloth prices by taking advantage of the lower prices of imported yarn. In addition, large sectors of the domestic weaving industry, especially in Anatolia, were for a considerable time out of reach of competition from low-priced imports which mainly impacted coastal regions. Moreover, artisan manufacturers proved exceptionally adaptable to changing economic circumstances. Often they would switch to different product lines to take advantage of changing styles and tastes, and they found niche markets where there was no competition from European imports. By and large, Ottoman artisan manufacturing proved surprisingly resilient.[13]

Nevertheless, to point to the resilience of handicraft production gives us no idea as to whether or not this artisan activity could ever have developed into industrialised capitalist production – even without the fierce competition from British and other European imports. While the Islamic Mediterranean had a host of merchants and traders, at this time the political, legal and economic conditions for the emergence of a truly capitalist class were largely absent: for example there were no banks,* nor was there a legal framework sufficiently established to further the accumulation of capital by proto-capitalists. In these circumstances, capital formation sufficient to create a national industrial base was virtually impossible and short-termism was the rule. Those who had wealth to invest found the most lucrative short-term investment in purchasing shares in tax farms. And increasingly, as time went on, they bought the short-term floating debt that their rulers were beginning to rely upon to cover their fiscal deficits.

There remained a few proto-capitalist enterprises like the Tunisian *shashiya* industry, described in chapter two. The industry was apparently still flourishing in the first decade of the nineteenth century and, according to one British observer, causing 'a great circulation of wealth within the state'.[14] *Shashiya* merchants are mentioned as playing an important role in a 'Commercial Council' set up during the rule of Tunisia's modernising ruler Ahmad ibn Mustafa Bey (r. 1837–55).[15] Nonetheless the industry declined because it never mechanised, especially after a competing Ottoman state fez

---

*   The first incorporated banks did not appear until the 1850s and '60s: the Bank of Egypt (1855), the Ottoman Bank (1856), the Anglo-Egyptian Bank (1864), the London and Baghdad Association (1864). They were all European-owned.

factory was established in Istanbul in 1835. The continuing competition from European manufacturers almost certainly added to this downward path.

In the European provinces of the Ottoman Empire, proto-capitalist enterprises, where merchants used artisan labour in the 'putting-out' system, survived into the early twentieth century. But few if any evolved into modern factories, let alone fully mechanised, steam- or water-powered enterprises. Even where they did, as in Salonika, factory owners placed much of their profits in non-industrial enterprises and the capital being amassed spent on other endeavours.[16] So, if there was no indigenous capitalist bourgeoisie to face the threat of European industrialisation, there were only two alternatives: the state and foreign capital.

Initially it would be the state which took up the challenge. The rulers of Mediterranean Islam were by no means ignorant of the economic and technological advantages of industrialisation and the factory. They soon saw the need to follow Britain and the Europeans; and, in an Islamic world that was beginning to fall behind in the development of the means of production, they saw the role of the state as one of kick starting the industrialisation of their own economies. Although their efforts to emulate the advances of the Europeans were made in very different circumstances and in different degrees, for a time, Turkish and Egyptian rulers made considerable progress.

Sultan Selim III, whose reign more or less coincided with the birth of the British Industrial Revolution, correctly saw that factory production fitted well with his other key objective: military modernisation. His 'European' army and modern navy required large-scale production of weaponry, uniforms and other military and naval equipment. With the aid of hired European experts and technicians he set about the systematic establishment of an Ottoman industrial base which could support his military objectives.[17] Selim hired French military engineers to help him re-equip and expand a number of factories and foundries which had been established earlier under the guidance of Baron de Tott. Selim also introduced modern European processes into the production of artillery, muskets, mines and gunpowder and in 1804 he initiated the construction of factory buildings to house a woollen mill for uniforms and a paper factory near the Bosphorus at Hünkar İskelesi.[18]

Some of these endeavours survived Selim's abdication and murder, until Sultan Mahmud II recommended Selim's incipient industrialisation campaign in the 1830s. His first steps taken to revive Selim III's factory-building programme were undertaken after his destruction of the Janissaries. Mahmud's initiatives included a spinning mill built in Istanbul in 1827, the conversion of Selim III's paper mill at Hünkar İskelesi to cloth manufacturing, a fez-manufacturing plant for his 'European' army in 1835, a wool spinning and weaving mill at Islimiye, south of the Balkan Mountains in 1836, a saw mill and copper sheet-rolling mill near Tophane also in 1836; and in the late 1830s the old Tophane cannon foundry and Dolmabahçe musket works were converted from animal to steam power.[19]

Mehmed Ali's Egypt witnessed a more sustained drive towards industrialisation during the 1830s. The Paşa established a considerable number of factories to provide clothing and military equipment for his army, but his industrial policy went much further and constituted a general programme of 'import substitution'. At its height, the total industrial workforce in all his factories may have been 30–40,000, many of them women and children.[20] In a world ranking of machine cotton spinning for the year 1834, Egypt had 400 thousand spindles, more than Belgium and two-thirds that of the German states. And in the number of spindles per 1,000 population it ranked fifth, only one place below France.[21] However, whether his 'statist' model of early industrialisation would have ever come to full fruition – regardless of the undoubted restrictions placed upon it by the implementation of the Balta Limani Treaty after 1840 – is called into question by the observations of European visitors.

For example, the British traveller and writer James Augustus St John, who visited a number of Mehmed's factories in 1833, informs us that in 1819 Mehmed Ali, 'was led by the advice of Europeans to attempt the introduction of the manufacturing system ... being persuaded with the aid of certain French and Swiss adventurers it was possible to render Cairo a second Manchester'.[22] He lists a wide range of factories in various stages of operation, whose machinery – at that time powered only by bullocks – had been bought in Europe, and according to St John, with no expense spared. In addition to the existence of twenty-three cotton cloth factories, some of which employed 600 to 800 workers, St John lists twenty-five other types of factory. However, the factory workers were entirely forced labour. And 'although they generally arrive at the factories in good health...':

The insalubrious nature of the employment, imprisonment, their scanty wages, the insufficiency of their food ... in a short time render them diseased and despicable. Inattention or mismanagement is followed by chastisement ... Such being their treatment, it is not at all surprising that the operatives eagerly avail themselves of the first opportunity which presents itself for making their escape.[23]

St John then proceeds to give a number of examples of the inefficiency, wastefulness and unprofitability of the cotton factories. He also refers to the Paşa's intention to acquire a number of steam engines (apparently in 1833 none had yet been obtained); but St John doubted they would survive very long in an atmosphere where the prevalence of fine siliceous dust quickly damaged the machinery, especially since there was little emphasis on the kind of regular maintenance which was normal practice in Britain. As for the European 'technicians' who were appointed to manage the new factories, St John considered them 'for the most part unprincipled adventurers'. But above all, he stresses the futility of trying to build a modern industrial economy on the basis of forced labour.

A second glimpse of Mehmed Ali's industrialisation project, from a somewhat later date, is provided by an Irish traveller, the novelist Eliot Warburton, who visited a sugar plantation and refinery at the village of Rhoda (Rawda) on the Nile in 1839, or perhaps 1840.

According to Warburton:

Its superintendent is an intelligent and hospitable Irishman, a Mr McPherson, who left the West Indies on the emancipation of the slaves and who has been here ever since. The West Indian sugar cane thrives here; its juice is expressed by two English steam engines ... This is one of the Pasha's monopolies; it occupies 300 labourers who are all conscripts; they nominally receive a piastre a day (about two pence half-penny) for their labour; but this is always a year in arrear and, when paid, is paid half in kind.[24]

Warburton's mention of two steam engines is evidence that Egypt's manufacturing technology had moved on to a more advanced stage by this later date. Some sources suggest there may have been at least seven or eight steam engines functioning at this time. However, by the late 1840s Mehmed Ali seems to have concluded that his objective of making Cairo 'a new Manchester' had failed. Four steam-powered cotton cloth factories continued into the 1850s under his successor, Abbas, but then disappeared. According to the census carried out shortly before Mehmed Ali's death in 1848, around 11 per cent of the economically active male population of Cairo worked in the 'modern' sector (i.e. industrial manufacturing); by the next census, carried out in 1868, the proportion had fallen to 2.8 per cent.[25]

A number of reasons have been suggested for the failure of Mehmed Ali's industrialisation programme, especially the application of the terms of the Balta Limani Treaty, enforced by the British, and the return to a regime of free trade and laissez-faire. A further weakness may have been the over-centralised 'command and control' system of management, whereby all local decisions had to be referred to the Paşa himself, together with his inability or unwillingness to foster a cadre of educated and independent native managers and technicians. But it is likely that a key factor, in St John's words, was 'the difficulty of procuring workpeople for the factories',[26] and the consequent compulsion of the peasantry under conditions in which, as industrial workers, 'they can never excel'. In short, for the development of a truly capitalist industrialised economy, a landless proletariat had to emerge in the countryside as it had in Britain. In early nineteenth-century Egypt this had not yet happened.

Under Sultan Abdülmecid (r. 1839–61), the industrialisation drive begun by his predecessor intensified. In 1842 a massive new industrial park was established at Zeytinburnu, west of Istanbul in an area between Edirne and the Sea of Marmara. According to Charles MacFarlane, a British visitor to this new manufacturing centre in 1848, it contained a foundry and machine works:

> Not only penknives, razors, calicoes, cotton stockings, cannon, ploughshares, iron railing, iron pipes, castings, bits and stirrups, lance-heads, swords, locks, and padlocks, etc.,

etc., [were] to be made here, but iron and steel and all the tools to be used were to be produced on the spot, instead of being bought as heretofore in England and Germany. Every thing was to be done at home, sur la place![27]

At Zeytinburnu the steam engines were built on site by European engineers. Although MacFarlane scoffed at the futility of the Ottomans trying to create 'a Turkish Manchester and Leeds, a Turkish Birmingham and Sheffield',[28] he was forced to admit that the Ottoman industrialisation plans were 'certainly very bold and ambitious'.[29]

Abdülmecid's industrial complex employed around 5,000 workers, predominantly men but with some women and children. Unlike Mehmed Ali's industrialisation programme, the workforce was recruited without forced labour, drawing upon the reservoir of landless poor living outside Istanbul's old city walls, swelled by numbers of Crimean and Circassian refugees.

Another part of the Zeytinburnu industrial complex was built to produce cloth and cloth stockings. Later a second industrial park was established further to the west which included a factory to spin, weave and print cotton cloth, another iron works with two forges, a steam-powered

Sultan Abdülmecid I
(r. 1839–61)

machine shop and a boatyard to construct small steamships. Overlooking the Sea of Marmara near Izmit another factory was established using the most modern machinery whose products were second to none in Europe. In an attempt to create a truly effective Ottoman industrial independence, a crash programme of obtaining local raw materials was initiated: by 1845 iron ore was being extracted from the Princes' Islands in the Sea of Marmara, and a few years later coal was mined at seams near Ereğli on the Anatolian coast of the Black Sea,[30] albeit in very small quantities. In spite of this promising start, by the early 1850s many of the factories had fallen into disuse, although a few of them lingered on until the First World War.

In 1861 the Porte persuaded its European trading partners to allow an increase in Ottoman import tariffs from 5 to 8 per cent to give domestic production more protection.[31] Despite this, the Ottoman attempt at state-run industrialisation failed. Nevertheless, in the opinion of one modern historian, the Ottoman industrial experiment 'was not beyond the Empire's technical capacities'; and although it would never have become the basis of an Ottoman industrial revolution, it might have developed 'in such a way as to have reduced the necessity of importing such large quantities of equipment'.[32]

If the state was unable to launch an Islamic industrial revolution, European capital investment was also unequal to taking up the task. Only in very specific regions and very particular industries was there a concentration of European-developed steam- or water-powered industrial production. The most important of these was the silk-reeling industry of Bursa.[33] The first foreign-owned factory for reeling silk appeared there in 1838 and was followed by another European-owned steam-powered factory in 1845. These were followed by further, mainly Italian-owned factories until in 1851 there were eight such enterprises.[34] By 1859, 80 per cent of Bursa's raw silk production was factory made. Bursa continued as an industrial sector where foreign capital played a significant part throughout the remainder of the nineteenth century, but it never provided the basis for any kind of take-off to an industrial revolution. Much the same could be said for those other sectors – in particular railway construction – where foreign capital played a leading role.

A whole range of factors have been identified as impediments to the development of industrialisation in the Islamic Mediterranean: the ever-increasing cost of machinery repairs; the cost of imported raw materials when local supplies proved inadequate; a generally declining interest on the part of the region's rulers; the exceptionally high wages being paid to the European technicians and supervisors upon whom the programme had become increasingly dependent; and the absence of a landless proletariat.

However, there remains one factor which would always have made the industrialisation of the Islamic Mediterranean problematic. In our Introduction we mentioned three key deficiencies suffered by the region in comparison with Christian Europe: men, money and materials. Men and money we have dealt with. It is time to turn to raw materials and natural resources.

The Ottoman Empire was quite well endowed with metallic minerals: some of these, like iron, copper and lead, were very important raw materials used in industry. However, mining methods were primitive and restricted extraction to the minimum. According to an Austrian mining engineer describing the situation in the 1830s:

> The mines of Asia Minor [Anatolia] are run with no consideration for practical extraction of the ore or for drainage. The machines which we in Europe for centuries have found indispensable to help in these matters are completely lacking here. There are neither shafts nor tunnels, just a labyrinth of clay-bed burrows, in which it is impossible for a man with a fully loaded wheelbarrow to work and in which a machine for extracting the ore could be built only with great difficulty.[35]

The problems confronting the availability and use of energy resources required for modern factory production were more numerous and varied.

In 1772 the first machinery producing pure cotton cloth, Arkwright's Mill at Cromford in Derbyshire, was powered by a fast-flowing and constant supply of water. Thereafter watermills spread throughout Britain and then to Germany and the US. Water power remained the prime mover in the early mechanised factories until it was overtaken by steam power in the first decades of the nineteenth century.

The Ottoman Empire was not short of rivers, but they were of the 'wrong' kind. Rivers like the Nile, the Euphrates and the Tigris were suitable for irrigation but their slow and seasonally intermittent flow made them unsuitable for use in driving machinery. There were a few exceptions where some water-powered cotton cloth production was feasible; but for most of the Ottoman world this was not a practicable option.[36] And as the nineteenth century entered the world of electric power it would also become clear that the geological structure of the Ottoman Empire's mountain ranges made the building of dams and the provision of hydroelectricity far more difficult than in Europe.*

The Empire was better favoured in its forests, the wood from which could be used for steam raising. There were extensive forests in Ottoman Thessaly, Macedonia, Anatolia and especially in Syria. One of the reasons for Mehmed Ali's conquest of Syria was, at least in part, to obtain wood supplies for his newly acquired steam engines.[37] The problem with wood as an energy source is, not surprisingly, its very low and variable calorific value, less than half that of hard coal. This would probably have been sufficient for some industries such as the processing of silkworm cocoons in the Bursa silk factories, but in general would have been very inefficient for steam-powered machinery. As for Mehmed Ali's supplies of Syrian wood, these were lost when his control of the province ended in 1840.

Once steam raising by coal became the standard method of powering machinery, the deficiency of this fuel source in both Mehmed Ali's Egypt and the Ottoman Empire became critical. During the former's control of Syria, Egypt was able to obtain modest supplies from deposits in Lebanon, which are believed to have yielded around 4,000 tons per year; but, as with wood fuel, this small energy resource was lost along with his control of the province. According to one source, Mehmed Ali's Egypt imported some cargos of coal for its steam engines, but data on quantities are unavailable. Since the only likely source is Britain, and British coal exports didn't commence until the 1840s – and then in very small quantities – it seems unlikely that these supplies could have been sufficient to make much of an impact on Mehmed's industrialisation programme.

---

*   In sharp contrast, the new nation of Italy established in 1859 found itself extremely well endowed with just the kind of mountain ranges suitable for the rapid development of hydro-electricity and the basis for a remarkably rapid creation of an industrial base.

The Ottoman Empire did have some indigenous sources of coal, and some of these were suitable for steam raising. Hard (bituminous) coal is found in a number of small separate fields along the Black Sea coast of the vilayet of Kastamonu. According to the official story, the coal was found at Ereğli in 1822, after Sultan Mahmud II reputedly offered money to anyone who could discover the coal required for his early industrialisation efforts; but it is more likely that the local population had known about these outcrops of coal for hundreds of years.

A more reputable account of Mahmud's initiative is David Urquart's 1833 report on the economic capacity of the Ottoman Empire, in which he records that 'the Sultan [Mahmud] at one time took a personal interest in the working of mines. I visited the supposed coal measures in Thrace which were anxiously hoped would be suitable for his steam engines.'[38] In fact, the coal measures in question were low-calorific lignite. According to Urquart, Mahmud agreed that samples should be sent to England for technical evaluation, but the court officials to whom they were entrusted never sent them.

It wasn't until 1849 that a group of English financiers and palace officials began a mining enterprise at Ereğli. A number of problems faced the mining company, problems which were to last throughout the remainder of the Ottoman era, and beyond. First, the coal seams were found in highly faulted strata which had been violently twisted by tectonic forces.[39] Most of the 'mines' were little more than pits or short drifts into the hillside. A second problem was transportation: only small quantities of coal could be carried by mules to the Black Sea coast and from there in small boats to Istanbul. The third and major problem was labour. The peasant population of the Black Sea coast had little appetite for the dirty and dangerous work in the mines and there was a chronic labour shortage until draconian measures were introduced in the 1860s.

As in most coal-producing countries (except Britain and the US), all sub-soil resources belonged to the monarch, and were either operated directly by the state or leased to a private operator. During the Crimean War, a second English company took-over the Ereğli mines, which were worked to supply coal for the boilers of the British and French steamships cruising in the Black Sea. The company's coal output never exceeded 30,000 tons per year.[40] At the end of the war the company ceased production.

In 1852 Sultan Abdülmecid ordered a registry of the coal seams to be carried out, and from 1853 to 1865 the English company was permitted to renew its operations at Ereğli. Annual production barely increased, to only 35–40,000 tons between 1861 and 1865, although by now around 300 villages were providing labour for around 100 different mines.[41]

Then, in 1865, with the increased demand from Sultan Abdülaziz's new steam-powered ironclads, a major change occurred in the management of the coalmines. The Ministry of Marine took charge of the industry. Two years later the villages adjacent to the coalfield were converted into a unique, militarised district and regulations were decreed installing a system of forced labour.

The state was faced with a major problem in attempting to recruit labour for its coal mines. It was the same problem which had faced Mehmed Ali's factories in Egypt. There had been no prior 'agricultural revolution': there was no 'free', landless rural proletariat with no other opportunities except wage labour. Instead there was a peasantry which was tied to the land by both economic and emotional considerations, a peasantry which had no desire to risk life and limb in the notoriously dangerous mines.

Skilled underground workers – the coal-face hewers, the mechanics, foremen etc. – these were exempt from coercion and attracted by relatively high wages. But the thousands of men needed to perform the unskilled work of carrying the coal in 40–50 kg baskets, both underground and on the surface, were subject to a brutal regime of compulsion. With the aid of village headmen, and often by violent military force, males aged between thirteen and fifty were compelled to work one half of the month in the mines on a rotational basis. They were paid a wage (out of which they still had to pay their taxes) and were exempted from military service, but in all other respects, 'the Ottoman state adopted a 'pre-capitalist form of labour to exploit coal, that most capitalist of commodities'.[42]

The Ottoman state's pre-capitalist methods failed to result in any significant increase in production. In 1865 annual output was 61,000 tons; by 1870 it had only increased to 64,000; by 1875 there was a marked increase to 142,000; but by 1880 it had fallen back to 56,000 and by 1882 still only stood at 65,000 tons.[43]* In short, and given the almost incessant

* As a point of comparison, in 1856 Britain was already producing more than 65 million tons

military threat from Russia, there was a total failure of the state to achieve
its most basic goal in coal mining – the assurance of adequate coal supplies
in wartime.[44]

Moreover, the very fact that the management of the Ereğli mines was in
the hands of the Ministry of Marine suggests that the Ereğli coal deposits
were never seriously considered as being sufficient for industrialisation on
a major scale. The simple fact is that the Ottoman Empire just didn't have
enough coal, a problem which could never have been solved by imposing
a regime of forced labour. There was a significant improvement in coal
output after 1896 when control of the coalfield was handed over to a private
company, financed largely by French capital, called the Ottoman Ereğli
Company. By the end of the century production had increased to 258,000
tons per year. Even so, when a number of studies of world coal production
and resources were published during the First World War, none of them
even bothered to include the Ottoman Empire.[45]

With the failure of state-sponsored industrialisation and insufficient
foreign investment in manufacturing, by the 1870s the Islamic world of
the Mediterranean had become a region of agricultural and raw material
exports, driven by European demand and the great world capitalist boom.
To further intensify that switch to primary product exports, between 1840
and roughly 1870 the terms of trade* for the agricultural exports of the
Middle East underwent a secular increase,[46] continuing a trend that had
begun around 1800, and making cultivation and export more profitable. As
a corollary, the same period saw Middle-Eastern handicrafts dwindling.[47]

To give just two examples from different regions of this general drive
to agricultural specialisation and increased exports: the value of Ottoman
sea-borne exports from Izmir (mainly cotton, wool and dried fruits)
increased from an annual average of 34.4 million francs in the period
1850–54 to 108.1 million in 1870–74;[48] and the value of Egypt's raw cotton
exports increased from £0.9 million in 1850–54 to £10.8 million in 1865–
69, almost all of it exported from the rapidly expanding Mediterranean
port of Alexandria.[49]

---

per year.

* The 'terms of trade' between one region A and another B is the ratio of the weighted average
  price of A's exports to those of B. In this case A would be the Ottoman Empire including
  Egypt and B is Britain, the usual comparator.

From now on the Islamic Mediterranean became integrated into the world capitalist system in a subordinate role. Lacking an industrial base it would have to import almost every item of heavy machinery, every item of advanced weaponry and even the machinery required for the semi-processing of the agricultural exports upon which its economy was increasingly dependent. In the words of Fernand Braudel, 'It was the industrial revolution which in the end got the better of an empire whose undoubted vigour was nevertheless insufficient to haul it out of its archaic ways and the legacy of the past.'[50]

For the time being world economic conditions concealed the dangers inherent in this subordinate 'model' of economic growth. But it would not be long before they became apparent.

PART THREE
C. 1870 - C. 1895

There is no doubt that in the present age, distress, misfortune and weakness besiege all classes of Muslims from all sides.

SAYYID JAMAL AL-DIN, 'AL-AFGHANI'
(C. 1881)

CHAPTER 20

The Age of the Rentiers

Between 1870 and 1900 the human geography of the world experienced a seismic shift unequalled by anything since the end of the Roman Empire. It was an era when Europeans, or peoples of European origin, came to dominate almost all the non-European peoples living on this planet Earth. According to the liberal economist and first serious analyst of imperialism, John Atkinson Hobson, in his 1902 work *Imperialism: A Study*, 'for convenience, the year 1870 has been taken as indicative of the beginning of a conscious policy of Imperialism'.[1]

Hobson calculated that, by 1900, European countries with a total surface area of 13.4 million km^2 controlled colonial territory of 49 million km^2, while a population of 440 million Europeans dominated a colonial population of 490 million.[2] By the year 1914, Lenin added to this total of colonised peoples those occupied by smaller European imperialists (Belgium, Holland, etc.). These amounted to a further 45.3 million colonial inhabitants, and together with 361 million inhabitants of 'semi-colonial countries' (in which he included 'Turkey') they made a total of roughly 900 million non-Europeans directly or indirectly dominated by around 500 million Europeans.[3]

Many of the conquered territories and their inhabitants had already been acquired in the eighteenth and early nineteenth centuries, but what distinguished this late 'Age of Imperialism' was the sheer pace of the European acquisitions. According to historian Eric Hobsbawm, between 1876 and 1915 'about one quarter of the globe's land surface was distributed or redistributed as colonies among a half-dozen states'.[4] Britain acquired some 4 million square miles; France about 3.5 million; Germany more than 1 million; Belgium and Italy just under 1 million each; Portugal around 300,000; and the US about 100,000.[5]

Historians have given varied accounts of the precise chronology of this 'Age of Imperialism'. For some historians the period extends from 1875 to

1914;[6] others 1876–1912;[7] or 1880–1914,[8] depending on their particular focus; but as to the starting point, I prefer to follow Hobson's 1870 date.

To trace the origins of 'late nineteenth century' imperialism we need to return briefly to the great worldwide economic boom which commenced around 1850. The crushing of the working-class and nationalist revolutions of 1848–50 soon witnessed the splintering of the forces which had led those uprisings. The alliance between the workers and the middle classes in the great European cities broke apart and the bourgeoisie threw itself into the arms of the aristocracy, a stratum which was now merging into a ruling class of 'modern' landowners, financiers and nouveaux-riches manufacturers.

With capitalism broken free of the fear of working-class revolution, financiers and industrialists were able to expand their operations, and the economic boom spread throughout Europe. As industrial production and trade expanded, so did the 'services' sector, especially in the British economy. Indeed, as early as 1841 the services sector accounted for 26.3 per cent of total employment in England, and in the greater metropolitan region of the South East the figure had reached 35.8 per cent.[9] 'Services' included a vast range of occupations, for example, banking, shipping, insurance, stockbroking, export and import trade, government service, the law and so on. At the same time, the services sector was already playing a key role in sustaining a favourable balance of payments for the country.*

As this sector of the economy expanded it created a middle class of the newly wealthy. Wealth trickled down into the pockets of ship-owners, bank employees, insurance agents, national and local state employees, merchants, solicitors and even clergymen. It afforded them the wherewithal to acquire more desirable residences and beautify their homes. But it also opened up the possibility of acquiring financial assets whose steady stream of income would ensure they lived in comfort during their declining years or even took early retirement. In short, the boundaries of the existing rentier class of aristocratic landowners and rich financiers expanded downwards to reach a much larger section of the population.

---

* In spite of claims that nineteenth-century Britain was the 'workshop of the world', in reality throughout the century (and beyond) the UK had a perpetual deficit in its balance of trade. It was only because of its earnings from services (mainly shipping), and income from interest and dividends remitted from UK foreign investments, that Britain maintained a favourable current account surplus. (See Mathias 1983, 277–80.)

In Britain and France in particular, these new middle classes found a ready outlet for their investible funds in the appearance of new financial institutions – like the Crédit Mobiliers, first founded in 1852 – which aggregated the savings of small and medium-sized investors and lent them both in Europe and abroad.[10] Hitherto government bonds had been the safe haven for the smaller rentier, but with returns on British government 'gilt edged' stock often as low as 3 per cent, the higher-yielding bonds of foreign governments, railways and utilities, traded by investment banks like Rothschild and Barings, began to look increasingly attractive.

By chance, the appearance of these new European middle-class rentiers coincided with a new demand for loans among three independent or semi-independent Islamic governments of the Mediterranean. Although the fiscal regimes of Tunis, Egypt and the Ottoman Empire were fragile, their rulers were currently luxuriating in a boom in the demand for raw materials and foodstuffs. This was the mirror image of the industrial boom occurring to the north of the Great Sea.

The rulers of Tunis, Egypt and the Ottoman Empire saw surging demand for these commodities reflected in prices. Between 1854 and 1864 the composite price of a typical 'basket' of raw materials exported by the Ottoman Empire to Europe increased by 35.4 per cent, while the composite price of foodstuff exports (excluding cereals) increased by 17.5 per cent.[11] However, it was the price of one particular raw material – cotton – which showed the most dramatic increase during the boom years; and its chief beneficiary was the Viceroyship of Egypt. In 1850 the price of Egyptian cotton at Alexandria was just $US 8.75 per *qantar*.* It then began a steady increase. With the outbreak of the US Civil War and the Northern States' blockade of exports from the cotton plantations of the South, Egyptian cotton prices soared, reaching US$45.00 per qantar in 1863.[12]

The increase in raw material prices during the worldwide boom of the 1850s and 1860s convinced the rulers of the Islamic Mediterranean that this was no brief windfall but was here to stay. They embarked upon a general spending spree on their military, their own luxury and to a lesser extent on infrastructure, mortgaged on the higher rents they expected from the peasants who produced those same raw material and foodstuff exports.

----

* 1 qantar = 45 kg. (Arab), 56.449 kg. (Ottoman standard).

Ottoman Ironclad Avnillah *(Divine Assistance), c. 1870*

Under Abdülmecid's successor, Abdülaziz (r. 1861–76), military expenditure increased enormously, much of it to pay for the Sultan's pet project – a massive navy which could protect the Ottoman Empire's territory in both the Mediterranean and the Black Sea. With little industrial capacity of its own, between 1861 and 1874 the Empire placed twenty-two orders for modern steam-powered ironclads of which thirteen were placed with British companies, eight with French and one with an Italian company. By 1875 the Ottoman Navy was the third largest in the world with twenty-two ironclads of different types and eighty other steam-powered warships.[13]

In Tunis, a succession of beys, Ahmad ibn Mustafa (r. 1837–55), Muhammad II ibn al-Husayn (1855–59) and Muhammad III al-Sadiq (1859–82) spent huge sums on their attempts to build a 'European' army, on major public works and luxurious palaces. But it was in Egypt during the Viceroyship of Isma'il Paşa that the boom in raw material exports encouraged the most profligate spending.

Isma'il's grandfather, Mehmed Ali, believed that the firm establishment of his dynasty depended upon a policy of European-type reforms, as did

Mehmed's fourth son, Sa'id; but on his accession to the viceroyship in 1863, Isma'il was determined to go one step further: he 'wanted to make Egypt a part of Europe'.[14] To this end he began a massive building project to Europeanise Cairo and Alexandria with splendid new public buildings designed and decorated to emulate those of the European rulers – in particular Napoleon III – whose trappings he so much admired. All this seemed perfectly feasible during Egypt's great cotton boom.

Isma'il supported this great construction boom with generous government grants. In Cairo a new European-style quarter, named Isma'iliya, sprang up between the Ezbekiya Gardens and the Nile. South-west of Ezbekiya a vast new palace, Abdin, was built as Isma'il's official residence followed by two other palaces: Qasr al-Nil, on the banks of the river, and Gezira, on the island of Zamalek. An opera house on the French style was built and a European-style 'spa', in the desert, twenty miles south of Cairo and linked to the capital by a railway. And in Alexandria, rapidly becoming a major Mediterranean city on the basis of its cotton exports, a new garden suburb sprang up at Ramle, east of the city, inhabited mainly by European cotton magnates.[15]

Isma'il's extravagance was not simply spent on beautifying his two main cities to impress their European residents and the visitors who were beginning to arrive as tourists. In addition to continuing expenditures on the Suez Canal, he brought an additional 1.25 million acres under cultivation. Linked to this expansion of agriculture, 112 new canals, totalling 13,500 kilometres, were constructed, bringing water supplies to cities and providing better water transportation. Four-hundred bridges were constructed, including the famous Qasr al-Nil bridge. Eight-thousand kilometres of telegraph lines were erected, and by 1870 Isma'il had increased the railway mileage from 805 to 1,287 kilometres.

Finally, Isma'il was convinced that, to be a truly European state, Egypt needed its own empire. His grandfather had failed to acquire one in Syria and his military expeditions in the Sudan had been little more than slave-hunting raids. Isma'il wanted much more, and during his reign Egyptian troops – commanded mainly by former American Confederate State officers – conquered territory as far south as present-day Uganda.

While the general increase in prices for agricultural and raw materials during the boom of the 1850s and 60s undoubtedly benefited the economies of the Islamic Mediterranean – especially its landowning classes – it did not have a commensurate beneficial impact upon the fiscal revenues of their governments.

In the Ottoman Empire the centralising reforms of the *tanzimat*, and the accompanying elimination of most of the grand *ayan* in the provinces, had certainly improved revenue collection, but it was still insufficient to provide the imperial treasury with consistently balanced books. For the years 1860/1 to 1871/2, seven Ottoman statements of revenue and expenditure are available. In these the figures for expenditures are given only as 'estimates', and in fact are likely to be underestimates. Nevertheless, over this period there was a total deficit of 400 million *kuruş*.[16] Against such a fiscal background (and the situation was worse in Egypt and Tunisia), the extraordinary expenditures of the rulers was financed by government borrowing – and there was no shortage of European rentiers eager to invest their savings in the highly attractive bonds which were being placed on the money markets of London and Paris.

The first Ottoman loan had been raised in 1854 as the Porte struggled to finance its expenditures in the Crimean War. Its face value was 3.3 million Turkish pounds* with a coupon (nominal interest rate) of 6 per cent; but the bonds were eventually offered for sale at only 79 (79 per cent of their face value) to attract lenders concerned about their security, so the amount actually received by the Porte was reduced to £T 2.6 million. And after further deductions for fees and commissions, it reduced even further to only £T 2.5 million.[17]

Moreover, because the 6 per cent nominal interest rate was attached to the face value of the loan, the *effective rate* of interest which the Porte had to pay on the reduced amount it actually received was no longer 6 per cent but nearly 8 per cent.[†]

The following year another loan was required as the fiscal deficit caused by the Porte's wartime expenditure threatened its continuing participation in the Crimean War; but on this occasion the loan was underwritten by the British government. This time the effective interest rate was only 3.9 per

---

* One Turkish pound (Ottoman Lira) (£T) = £0.909 sterling. It was introduced in the currency reform of 1844 and remained the principal unit of account until 1923. The kuruş remained as a denomination of the lira with 100 kuruş = 1 lira.

† For a more detailed explanation, see Appendix D.

cent, almost the same as the nominal rate. But it would be the one and only occasion when such official support was given to an Ottoman loan.*

By the early 1860s, Ottoman finances were beginning to deteriorate. The general weakness in the Ottoman fiscal regime meant that the increased tax revenues which had been expected to flow from the raw materials boom were less than anticipated. The effective interest rates on Ottoman loans reached an all-time high in 1869 when the government was paying a massive 11.5 per cent. By 1873 interest and repayments of the national debt were 651 million *piastres*, more than 30 per cent of total government spending.[18]

For the time being, foreign capital inflows to finance Ottoman military expenditure and the construction of infrastructure (mainly railways) exceeded outgoing payments of interest and capital to the foreign bondholders. But it was a trend which would soon come to an end.

Tunisia and Egypt were also obliged to seek foreign loans. Under Muhammad al-Sadiq Bey (r. 1859–82) Tunisia's expenditure on its army and various public works exceeded tax revenues, as it had done under his predecessors. To meet these deficits, by 1862 the Tunisian state had already borrowed 28 million francs locally; but the following year the Bey's corrupt prime minister, the former slave and Mamluk Mustafa Khaznadar, organised, via a Lebanese protégé, a loan of 65 million francs, repayable in five years. The financier who raised the loan was the Parisian banker Frédéric d'Erlanger – 'that evil genius of Tunis' as one historian has described him.[19] The terms of the loan and the various deductions of 'commissions' (in which d'Erlanger, Khaznadar and their corrupt associates participated) meant that Tunisia received only 37.8 million francs.[20] Further extortionate and corruptly arranged loans followed in 1865 and 1867.

Egypt, too, was forced to borrow abroad. On his death in 1863, the Viceroy Sa'id bequeathed to Isma'il a total external debt of £3 million state debt and £7 million personal debt.[21] In the same year, government expenditure exceeded revenues by 8,300,000 Egyptian pounds. Egypt's financial situation had been untenable even before Isma'il's great spending spree. The new ruler concluded that only a very large foreign loan could relieve the financial pressure until some respite was offered by the expected continuation of the great cotton boom. However, Egypt was still tributary

---

* See also Appendix D.

to the Ottoman Empire, and any separate Egyptian foreign loan would require the sultan's permission.

With a great deal of bribery paid to Ottoman officials, the sultan granted his approval, and in 1864 Isma'il's first public loan was floated by the German-Jewish Sal. Oppenheim Bank. Its face value was £5.7 million at a nominal interest rate of 7 per cent. Discounting to encourage investors was relatively modest and only reduced the loan's value to £5.3 million; but the actual amount Egypt received was just £4.8 million after the 'fees' of £440,072 charged by the Oppenheims. After other fees were deducted the effective interest rate on the amount borrowed was 8.2 per cent. Further loans continued every year, with an enormous loan of £32 million in 1873 at an effective interest rate of 11 per cent.[22]

In his attempt to solve the underlying fiscal problem, Isma'il had been squeezing greater and greater amounts of revenue out of the peasantry, with the proceeds of the land tax increasing from £E 2.88 million in 1862 to £E 4.86 in 1872. But by now something like 70 per cent of annual state revenue was required simply to service the combined foreign and internal debt, including that owed on the Suez Canal. Such a degree of indebtedness was unsustainable.

Meanwhile, as the 1870s dawned, the great international boom which had begun in the early 1850s was reaching its zenith. Never was there such a great euphoria among European capitalists and would-be capitalists. The most crazy – and fraudulent – companies were floated. 'It was an era in which companies were founded to win mass sales of boot polish to the natives of the South Sea Islands,' claims Hobsbawm.[23] It all ended in a worldwide stock market crash, first in Vienna in May 1873, followed by New York in September and then affecting most of the capitalist world in varying degrees; for example the value of German shares fell by 60 per cent between the height of the boom and 1877. The financial collapse also brought with it the closure of vast stretches of productive activity, such as the shutdown of almost half the blast furnaces in the major iron-producing countries of the world.[24] The crisis lasted from 1873 to 1879 and, although output in Europe and the US recovered and national incomes returned to growth, the recovery in prices and profits from their initial falls proved far more protracted.

It was perhaps inevitable that the end of the worldwide economic boom in 1873 would have disastrous financial implications for the debtor states of the Islamic Mediterranean. In these circumstances the European rentiers were willing to lend only at even higher effective interest rates. The first casualty was the Porte.

When the boom ended and the financial crisis struck, the Austrian banks trading in Istanbul – which provided the Porte with short-term finance – collapsed and were refused aid by the Hapsburg government in Vienna. Most of the small private Ottoman banks were also swallowed up in the wash of the sinking Austrian banks.[25] In 1874 a record loan of £T 41.0 million at a nominal 5 per cent interest floated by the Porte had to be discounted to £T 16.6. This left the Porte paying an effective interest rate of 12.3 per cent on the money it actually received.[26] And, by now, 60 per cent of total government expenditure had to be disbursed in interest payments and amortisation (repayment) on the foreign debt.

In spite of an attempt to raise more revenue by imposing a significant increase in taxes, on 6 October 1875 an İstanbul newspaper announced that, in the light of a budget deficit of £T5 million, the government had decided to pay only half of the money required to service its foreign debt in cash. The remainder would be settled by a new issue of bonds. It was tantamount to a formal statement of bankruptcy and was taken as such by the Empire's creditors. A full sovereign default was announced on 30 October. However, as we shall see in the next chapter, before any steps could be taken to satisfy the creditors, the Ottoman Empire's Balkan region exploded in peasant revolt, interethnic atrocities, state repression and war.

One month later, the sultan's nominal vassal, the Khedive Isma'il, was forced to abandon his dynasty's one great asset. The financial prospects of the Suez Canal Company, in which Isma'il and his predecessor had invested so heavily, were grim. The project had cost 453,645,000 francs, more than double the original estimate. In its first year of operation fewer than 500 ships passed through it, carrying only 436,000 tons of merchandise, compared with the expected 1 million for that first year. During 1870 the company had been unable to pay a dividend. The following year tonnage increased to 761,000, but this was still below expectations. Expenditures on the canal exceeded income. Not only did Isma'il receive no profits but he and the other shareholders had been compelled to pump more cash into the struggling company, which was soon facing bankruptcy.[27] In 1875 Isma'il believed he could hold off his creditors only by selling Egypt's shares in the Canal.

Fearing that the French would acquire Isma'il's 177,000 shares, Benjamin Disraeli, heading a newly elected Tory government, won the approval of the cabinet – and the Queen – to pre-empt any such possibility. On behalf of the government, Disraeli contracted a loan with James Rothschild of £4 million, at 5 per cent interest, to buy the shares. The transaction went ahead smoothly and by the end of November 1875 Britain held 44 per cent of Suez's capital, thus becoming the largest single shareholder and effectively in control of the company.[28]

Although there was some criticism of the deal in Parliament and parts of the press, the overall reaction in the country was aptly summed up on 27 November in the *Manchester Guardian*. The decision, the *Guardian* declared, 'has been an act of self-preservation' and had been 'centred in the urgent necessity of maintaining our communication with India'. It added rather coyly that the purchase had been made because 'one of our neighbours' sought to profit by the Viceroy's sale. Indeed, the *Guardian* went further, stating that it had become known that 'somebody in the interests of a great state, desired to benefit by the Khedive's condition, and get, if not control, at least a large interest in the Suez Canal'.[29] Of course, virtually everybody in England could guess the identity of that 'neighbouring' and 'great' state. Britain had outmanoeuvred France and had successfully established a foothold – albeit indirectly – on the southern shore of the Mediterranean.

For Isma'il, however, the sale of Egypt's shares came too little and too late. With nothing of any real value remaining to sell, and no way to pay the next instalment of interest, the Khedive was borrowing at rates of around 30 per cent at a time when most European governments could borrow at five. On 8 April 1876 payment on Egypt's treasury bills was suspended. Under intense pressure from European governments, Isma'il was forced to issue two Khedival decrees. The first on 2 May established the Caisse de la Dette Publique ('The Public Debt Receiver'), usually referred to simply as 'The Caisse'.

The Tory foreign secretary, Lord Derby, didn't believe government should intervene in a strictly private financial matter, so the initial composition of the Caisse included only representatives from the French, Italian and Austrian governments.[30] They were empowered to receive the land taxes from Egypt's richest provinces, along with the property taxes from Cairo and Alexandria, the taxes on salt and tobacco, and the customs duties. These resources were then earmarked for repaying the bondholders. The Khedive's second decree, of 7 May 1876, required by the representatives of the Caisse, brought about the unification of the entire indebtedness of Egypt, which stood at £91 million.[31]

However, the bondholders considered these measures insufficient and despatched two of their members, G. J. Goschen and R. Joubert, to Egypt where, by a further decree of 18 November, they secured from Isma'il the appointment of two controllers-general. One official (British) was to supervise the revenues and the other (French) the expenditures of the state. The institution was known simply as the 'Dual Control' and the bondholders nominated Major Evelyn Baring as Britain's first controller-general. By the end of 1877, 60 per cent of all Egyptian revenue was being paid into the Caisse for serving its national debt.[32]

Furthermore, on 28 August 1878, Isma'il was compelled to surrender his own private property for debt service and accept the formation of the country's first executive cabinet to administer its affairs. Sir Charles Rivers Wilson, governor-director of the Suez Canal Company and a man 'entirely unsympathetic to the Egyptians',[33] was appointed finance minister, while the Comte de Blignières became minister of public works. The cabinet was headed by an Egyptian-Armenian Christian, Nubar Paşa. The outcome was 'the complete loss of fiscal sovereignty and opened the way for the loss of political sovereignty'.[34]

With over half the bonds of the Egyptian Funded Debt in British hands, Wilson, the finance minister, 'actively took part in the ruthless exploitation of the country'.[35] For example, at the end of 1878 Wilson insisted on the full collection of arrears of taxes from three provinces in Upper Egypt whose peasants were already suffering from a terrible famine in which 10,000 died.[36]

The *kurbash*, a buffalo-hide whip, was found to be a very effective method for extracting money from the suffering peasants. In 1879 some apparent reluctance to use it on the part of the Egyptian authorities prompted the British consul-general, Sir Edward Malet, to complain to the British foreign secretary, Lord Salisbury, that the Egyptian prime minister was regrettably showing himself unwilling to use the 'violent measures' which were 'not yet dispensable' in collecting arrears of tax.[37] That Egyptians of all classes would continue to accept this ruthless and cruel exploitation indefinitely was highly unlikely.

CHAPTER 21

The 'Great Eastern Crisis', 1875–1878

So far, the great 'crash' of 1873, its accompanying wave of depressed prices and profits, and the inability of both the Porte and Egypt to pay their creditors, had not resulted in the sort of military intervention by the creditor nations as had happened in Mexico twelve years earlier.* Their territory appeared secure. The corpulent giant Sultan Abdülaziz remained ensconced in the beautiful waterside Dolmabahçe Palace, the seat of the Ottoman government since 1856. There he could admire his huge fleet of ironclad warships – twenty battleships, four ships of the line, five frigates, seven corvettes and forty-three transport ships – whose cost weighed so heavily upon the peasants who paid for them with their taxes. And in Cairo, his viceroy Isma'il continued to entertain rich European guests in oriental splendour in his Abdin Palace, built between 1863 and 1873 at a cost of 2,700,000 Egyptian pounds. But within five years Abdülaziz and Isma'il would be swept away, and the Ottoman Empire would lose 8 per cent of its richest and most fertile territory and 20 per cent of its population. This series of events was described by contemporary European observers as the 'Great Eastern Crisis'. Four years later, it would be followed by the loss of the Empire's two vassal states: Tunis and Egypt would become European protectorates.

This tumultuous sequence began with a small peasant uprising in Nevesinje in the Ottoman province of Herzegovina in July 1875. It wasn't only in Egypt where paying the bondholders meant increasing the taxation of the peasantry. The same draconian methods were deemed necessary in most parts of the Ottoman Empire. These exactions fell equally on Christian and Muslim peasants.

---

* The refusal of the nationalist leader Benito Juarez to pay the debts accumulated by his predecessors resulted in the sending of three European fleets (from France, Germany and Italy) to Mexico, and the intervention by Napoleon III's army which became a full-blown attempt at colonisation. It failed.

Like most of the other Ottoman vilayets in the southern Balkans, the vilayet of Bosnia (which included the southern *sancak*s of Herzegovina) had a mixed ethno-religious composition. According to an 1879 census Bosnia-Herzegovina had a total population of 1,158,440, of which 42.88 per cent were Eastern Orthodox Christians, 38.75 per cent were Muslims, 18.08 per cent were Catholics, and 0.3 per cent Jews. In general, the Muslims and Jews were concentrated in the urban centres while both categories of Christians dwelt mainly in the countryside.

However, in the predominantly Christian region of Herzegovina there existed a particularly inflammatory fault line where the tax farmers were Muslim notables (known as *ağa*s or beys) and the taxpaying peasants were exclusively Christians, Croatian Catholics and Orthodox Christian Serbs.

To increase the inflammatory nature of this fault line, the 1858 Ottoman Land Law, proclaimed under the *tanzimat* – intended to modernise the landholding regime by creating a system of private property – had turned the old state lands in Herzegovina into the private property of the Muslim beys. This bitterly disappointed the hopes of their Christian serfs, who had expected to obtain their own private land.[1] According to the British consul in Sarajevo, William Holmes, under the prevailing tax-farming regime, the Ottoman government was now 'urging the sale of taxes at yearly increasing and really exorbitant prices'.[2] This meant the tax-collecting beys had to squeeze their Christian peasant taxpayers even further. The beys now began to act as ruthless tithe collectors.

Across the border with Austrian-controlled Dalmatia the Catholic peasantry enjoyed far better conditions than did the Catholic peasantry of Herzegovina. Moreover, in April and May 1875 the Emperor Franz Joseph made a long-awaited visit where 'he received Catholics from Herzegovina and listened compassionately to their grievances'. This very public Austrian intervention in the affairs of Bosnia-Herzegovina may have been one of the principal factors that sparked the initial revolt against Ottoman rule.

Consul Holmes reported the first outbreak occurring on 5 July, near the predominantly Serb town of Nevesinje, where 'disaffected peasants robbed a caravan and decapitated five innocent Turkish merchants'. Another band seized the bridge over the Krupa River, cutting the road between Mostar and Metkovic. The perpetrators of this 'band' were all Catholic peasants.[3] Catholic agrarian unrest now spread to Orthodox Christian villages in Herzegovina. As in Mount Lebanon, an originally agrarian class conflict became transformed into a tragic ethno-religious bloodbath between Christians and Muslims.

The following year, the revolt reached neighbouring Bulgaria. In the first round of atrocities in early 1876, around 1,000 Muslim civilians were killed. In reprisal, Ottoman troops and Muslim irregulars, many of them refugees from the Crimea and Circassia, killed around 12,000 Bulgarian Christians, men women and children. These were publicised widely in Europe as the 'Bulgarian Atrocities', especially by the British opposition Liberal Party leader William Gladstone. But as in similar events before and after, no mention was made of Christian atrocities committed against Muslims.

In Istanbul, Sultan Abdülaziz was openly blamed for both the collapse of law and order in the Balkans and for the extravagant spending on his prized navy and other prestige projects, widely believed to be the main cause of the 1875 financial default. On 30 May 1876 the sultan's ministers, supported by units of the army and sections of the populace of Istanbul, staged a coup, deposed him and incarcerated him in particularly grim conditions. On 4 June its was announced that he had committed suicide, mysteriously doing himself to death with a pair of scissors. But his successor, Murad V, soon began to show signs of paranoia and he too was deposed. Finally, on 31 August the thirty-three-year-old nephew of Abdülaziz, Abdülhamid, became sultan, a candidate who, it was widely (but erroneously) believed, held moderately progressive views on constitutional matters.

However, Abdülhamid II inherited a state in continuing political turmoil. On 30 June 1876 the semi-independent principality of Serbia, intending to assert its full sovereignty, declared war on the Porte and was joined by the tiny principality of Montenegro. But the war did not go well for the Serbs and by autumn their troops were facing defeat. Pressure was now mounting in Russia to support the struggles of its 'fellow Slavs', and in October Tsar Alexander II issued an ultimatum ordering the Porte to cease hostilities. The new Sultan Abdülhamid reluctantly complied, and on 11 December a conference of representatives of the European powers met in Istanbul (to which the Porte was not invited) in an attempt to defuse the crisis by urging the sultan to grant limited autonomy to Bulgaria and Bosnia-Herzegovina.

The Porte refused to accept the conclusions of a conference from which they had been excluded. On 23 December 1876, in what was clearly an attempt to outmanoeuvre the European powers, Sultan Abdülhamid announced the promulgation of a constitution with equal rights for all the Empire's minorities. On 19 March 1877 he opened the first session of an elected Ottoman parliament.[4]

Alexander II, who had become Tsar in 1855 after the death of his father towards the end of the Crimean War, had not given up on Nicolas I's grand objective of seizing Istanbul, the Turkish Straits and the gateway to the Mediterranean. The Tsar decided that this was the time to strike, before any of the other European powers became too sympathetic to the seemingly new 'reforming' sultan.

On 24 April 1877 Russian troops crossed into the united principalities of Romania (Moldavia and Wallachia), which immediately declared complete independence. Alexander's army then continued its advance into Ottoman territory, supported by Romanian troops. On 4 January 1878 it entered Sofia and, advancing through Bulgaria, Russian troops systematically destroyed Muslim villages, killing civilians. Around half a million Muslim refugees were forced to pour into Istanbul and the surrounding areas.[5] On the 20th they took the ancient city of Edirne (Adrianople), only about 200 kilometres from the Ottoman capital. A desperate Abdülhamid called a meeting of parliamentarians to discuss what could be done to prevent disaster; but when his conduct of the war was strongly criticised the following day the sultan dissolved parliament, suspended the constitution and had a number of deputies arrested.[6] From then on, until 1908, Abdülhamid II would rule as a despot. Meanwhile, with the Russians virtually at the gates of Istanbul, on 31 February 1878 the Porte was forced to sign an armistice on Russian terms.

After much hesitation, Disraeli's government decided to send the fleet to Istanbul to prevent its capture. By 13 February the ships had passed the Dardanelles and entered the Sea of Marmara. However, the British action was unable to prevent Russia imposing draconian terms on the Ottomans in the Treaty of San Stefano, signed on 3 March 1878. Among these conditions was the establishment of a huge Russophile Bulgarian state with a frontier reaching to the shores of the Aegean Sea.

But by now splits had opened up within the Russian government: splits which were partly caused by a significant weakening of Russian finances resulting from the huge expenses incurred during the war. Moreover, divisions had also opened up between Russia's allies – Serbs, Romanians,

Bulgarians and Montenegrins – concerning their respective shares of the spoils to be taken from the Ottomans.

Consequently, Russia reluctantly agreed to accept the call made by the German chancellor, Count Otto von Bismarck, for a Congress of the Concert of Europe. The Chancellor had previously proclaimed that he was 'disinterested' in Balkan affairs, but he had his own agenda for the forthcoming Congress, to which the Porte was invited for the first time, in effect, finally making it a member of the Concert of Europe. But its presence was largely neutralised by the invitation of delegations from Bulgaria, Serbia, Romania and Greece, and the stated purpose of the Congress was to discuss the partition of the Ottoman Balkans, albeit while maintaining the territorial integrity of the remainder of the Ottoman Empire. The Congress opened on 13 June 1878 in Berlin under Bismarck's imperious direction.[7]

The primary objective of Britain, France and Austria-Hungary was to replace the terms of the San Stefano treaty with ones that would remove the threat of a huge Russian-influenced Bulgaria being established. As envisaged, the new Russian client state with its outlet to the Aegean would pose a direct threat to both Istanbul and the Straits. However, Russia's opponents also had plans to use the opportunity of the Congress to acquire parts of the deeply wounded Ottoman Empire themselves and, even before the Congress commenced, secret discussions on this subject began in the chambers and anterooms of the Chancellery building, the former Radziwill Palace.

Britain's prime minister, Benjamin Disraeli, now ennobled as Lord Beaconsfield, attended the Congress in person, along with his new foreign secretary, Lord Salisbury (1830–1903). The Ottomans' financial collapse in 1875, followed by their crushing military defeat, had brought into question Britain's long-standing policy of reforming and strengthening the Ottoman Empire in order to establish a barrier to Russian expansion. Britain feared Russia not only penetrating into the Mediterranean, but encroaching upon the whole Asian landmass where its influence in Persia and Afghanistan already seemed a threat to Britain's Indian empire. With the Ottomans apparently no longer able to fulfil their traditional role of defensive 'glacis' for British interests, Disraeli and Salisbury concluded that Britain required an insurance policy: a military base in the eastern Mediterranean which could guard its strategic interests in Egypt and the recently acquired Suez Canal. It could also serve as a strongpoint from which troops and ships could be despatched to intervene in the increasingly fragile Ottoman state, should this become necessary. Malta was just too far away, so Disraeli and his admirals began to look elsewhere.

The choice fell upon Ottoman Cyprus. Although the island did not have a good port it had several wide bays, one of which, Famagusta, the Royal Navy acknowledged 'could be made capable of sheltering more ironclads than the Grand Harbour of Malta'. So, on 4 June 1878, in a secret convention, Lord Salisbury prevailed upon a reluctant Sultan Abdülhamid to allow Britain to occupy Cyprus in return for continuing protection from the Royal Navy, with the proviso that the island remained under the suzerainty of the Ottoman Empire.

Salisbury and the Austro-Hungarian foreign minister, Gyula Andrássy, also conducted parallel negotiations before the start of the Congress. On 6 June it was agreed that Austria would support Britain's occupation of Cyprus in return for Britain's support for Austria-Hungary's demand to 'administer' Ottoman Bosnia-Herzegovina. This marked the first step in Austria's own plans for a more 'forward' policy in the southern Balkans to counter Russian influence, although, the vague concept of 'administration' implied that Bosnia-Herzegovina would remain under Ottoman suzerainty. Austria-Hungary would also be allowed to station troops in the *sancak* of Novi Pazar, a small piece of territory pointing south from Bosnia and adjoining Ottoman Macedonia.* An Austrian military presence in Novi Pazar would separate the newly independent Serbia from its ethnic cousins in Montenegro, thereby preventing the creation of a Greater Serbia with an outlet to the Adriatic.

After one month of deliberation the Congress concluded by confirming the independence of Serbia, Montenegro and Romania; but it also forced a war-weary and financially weakened Russia to abandon much of the Balkan territory it had captured in 1878 and accept the redrawing of the frontiers of the 'Greater Bulgaria' created by the war. The new map, agreed as a compromise between the British and Russian delegations, pushed its southern boundary far to the north, returning its conquered Macedonia to Ottoman rule and denying Bulgaria access to the Aegean. It was also divided into two halves, with the southern sector, named 'Eastern Rumelia'

---

* Macedonia comprised the three vilayets (provinces) of Kosovo, Salonika and Monastir.

established as an autonomous province of the Ottoman Empire, but with a Russian governor-general.*

However, before the Congress ended, the French government heard about Britain's Cyprus convention with the Porte, and there now began an unseemly wrangling over what was euphemistically called 'compensation'. Faced with violent outbursts about British 'duplicity' in the French press, Lord Salisbury offered France an important sweetener. The news soon broke that he had told the French foreign minister – in what he would later claim was only a 'private and confidential' conversation – 'Do at Tunis what you think proper ... England will not oppose you and will respect your decisions.'[8] When this became common knowledge, Bismarck made it clear that he, too, thought France should get 'compensation'. This satisfied his own agenda that France should focus its attention on extending its colonial territory in the Mediterranean and elsewhere instead of obsessing about the recovery of the provinces of Alsace and Lorraine, which France had lost to Bismarck's new German Empire in the war of 1870–71.

But now a further complication arose in this unseemly trading of Ottoman territory. When the Italians became aware of Salisbury's offer of 'compensation' to France, trading Tunis for Cyprus, they too demanded 'compensation'. So, to pacify Italy, both Salisbury and the French privately suggested to the Italians that they too could be 'compensated', by seizing the *vilayet* of Tripoli (western Libya). This was reiterated in September 1880, when the French prime minister, Charles Freycinet, asked the Italian Ambassador, 'Why will you persist in thinking of Tunis ...Why not turn your attention to Tripoli where you would have neither ourselves nor anyone else to contend with?'[9] But since 1835 Tripoli had been an integral part of the Ottoman Empire, and this secret proposal to Italy flew in the face of one of the conclusions of the Congress of Berlin, which was ostensibly intended to protect the Empire from any further encroachments.

It was only after these military and territorial issues were settled that, in October 1881, the seven nations representing the Ottoman bondholders (Britain, France, Holland, Germany, Austro-Hungary, Italy and local Ottoman) turned to the interests of the Ottoman Empire's creditors and

---

* 'Eastern Rumelia' actually had its own flag and issued its own postage stamps, but in 1885 it was reunited with northern Bulgaria.

agreed to the establishment of an Ottoman Public Debt Administration (OPDA). Its primary purpose, like that of the Egyptian 'Caisse', was to ensure that the Empire met its interest payments and some of the principal on the foreign debt. To guarantee that these payments were made, the OPDA took control of the taxes on tobacco, salt, stamps, spirits, fisheries and silk, together with some of the tribute revenues (mainly from Egypt). The council of the OPDA was composed of representatives of the bondholders from the seven creditor countries, with its presidency rotating between Britain and France; the Porte was allowed to attend its meetings but only with a 'watching brief' and without a vote.

However, the OPDA was also used by its members to obtain lucrative concessions – in particular railway construction. The Administration of the OPDA threatened the Ottomans that they would obtain future financial support only if they accepted European demands. Equally galling for the Turks was the sheer size of the OPDA's extremely well-paid staff, which the Ottoman state had to pay for. By 1886 it employed 3,040 functionaries, whose numbers would continue to grow until 1912/13 when they reached 5,500, more than the Ottoman Ministry of Finance itself.[10]

Over the five year period 1882/3–1886/7 the revenues ceded to the OPDA by the Ottoman government averaged £T 1.95 million per annum, and these increased to £T 2.16 million by 1892/3–1896/7.[11] This outflow of funds would have a devastating impact on the Empire's economy, especially when combined with a deficit on direct foreign investment between 1881 and 1887 (remittances of profit and interest exceeded new capital inflows), and a decline in the value of Ottoman exports arising from the worldwide depression. One of the principal casualties of this economic malaise was the great ironclad navy, built up on the back of Sultan Abdülaziz's borrowing. For lack of funds, it was simply left in port, to rust and rot. From now on, the Ottomans would be unable to defend their remaining presence in the Eastern Mediterranean, with dire consequences.

CHAPTER 22

Tunisia and Egypt 1881–82:
The Bailiffs Arrive

France now began manoeuvring to seize Tunisia. As the chances of its being able to repay its debts became increasingly unlikely, in 1867 the Emperor Napoleon III issued a decree authorising a landing on the Tunisian coast by 8,000 troops.[1] In the event, the invasion was called off because France was reminded of an earlier warning from Britain that it wouldn't tolerate any such move. So far, an actual default (as in Istanbul and Cairo), had been held-off by Britain's formidable Consul-General Richard Wood, who had been appointed to the Tunisian post in 1855 after serving Britain well during his consulship in Syria. In 1869 he proposed an international financial commission to control Tunisia's revenue and expenditure and to organise repayment of the country's debt. France, Britain and Italy were represented on the commission, which was accorded a decisive voice in fiscal affairs of the Tunisian government.[2] Although constituting claims totalling 275 million francs, the debt was finally consolidated at 125 million and converted into treasury bills bearing a 5 per cent interest rate. But for their redemption the Bey had to reserve 6.5 million francs – about half the revenue of the Tunisian state. It was a harsh economic blow which could do nothing to assist the already weakened Tunisian economy.[3]

It was also a major loss of sovereignty. Tunis had now become an informal European colony, comparable to some Latin American countries in the early and mid-nineteenth century; but here there was a big difference. There were three contenders to exercise that informal power – France, Britain and Italy – and over the next twenty years Tunis was to become a fulcrum of inter-imperialist rivalry. In the words of one English historian, 'a diplomatic battleground of the nations'.[4] Moreover the nations in question now included a new power with imperialist ambitions in the Mediterranean: the Kingdom of Italy.*

---

* Italy had become an independent state in 1859–60, although Venice wasn't included until its capture in the Italian Third War of Independence (1866).

There were two objectives driving France's interest in acquiring Tunisia. First, with the French occupation of Algeria now largely completed, the French Army, its ruling authority, saw neighbouring Tunisia as an obvious target for territorial expansion. Second, the French navy also had its own designs on Tunisia. The Regency had what was believed to be the best deep-water harbour in the Mediterranean, Bizerte. France saw its occupation of Tunisia as an opportunity for the construction of a naval base superior to its existing one at Toulon.

In 1872 French ambitions in Tunisia came to an abrupt halt when Napoleon abdicated and fled to London after his defeat and capture by the Prussians at the Battle of Sedan. For the time being the new Third Republic, under the veteran politician Thiers, was forced to withdraw from the contest to control the Regency. Nevertheless, French imperialist ambitions towards Tunisia continued to smoulder, especially because it was believed – in the words of the French politician and historian Gabriel Hanotaux – that any major power occupying Tunisia could 'seize the Mediterranean by the throat'.[5]

Given Tunisia's proximity to Sicily such considerations made the Regency a natural focus of interest to the newly established Italian state, especially since the original founders of that state contained men like Francesco Crispi (1818–1901) and Camillo Benso, Count of Cavour (1810–1861) who were expressed colonialists. Moreover Italy had, by far, the largest number of colonists who had settled in Tunisia, around 7,000. Taking advantage of France's weakness after its defeat in the Franco-Prussia war, in 1871 the Kingdom of Italy demanded special privileges for its colonists. When the Bey rejected Italy's demands, an invasion fleet was prepared. However, faced with the strongest opposition from a combination of Britain, France and the Porte, the Italians were forced to back down and the Italian expedition was compelled 'to stay chafing in its home port'.[6]

Britain's current policy with respect to Tunisia echoed its Ottoman one: to preserve the status quo and prevent any one major European power seizing its territory. The policy was firmly in the hands of Consul-General Wood. He was convinced that Tunisia's best chance of evading an invasion by either France or Italy was to reaffirm that Tunisia remained part of the Ottoman Empire. The Bey accepted Wood's advice, and on 24 October 1864 Sultan Abdülaziz issued a *firman* confirming Muhammad al-Sadiq

Bey as the Vali of Tunisia. In return the new vali would acknowledge the sultan as suzerain, pay an annual tribute and offer provision of troops when the sultan was at war with other countries.

Wood was also successful in his second objective. In July 1875 an Anglo-Tunisian trade convention was signed whose terms included the maximum freedom of trade, the limitation of import duties to 8 per cent *ad valorem*, and the abolition of most monopolies. It was also agreed that British nationals could obtain and own land and other property in the country.

Meanwhile, in 1873 Tunisia's prime minister, the crooked Mustafa Khaznadar, was removed from office following the revelation of his swindles; he was replaced by a reforming general, Khair al-Din et-Tunisi. The abuses of tax collectors were stopped and the country enjoyed two good harvests. The European members of the Financial Commission were satisfied, and on the international money markets the value of Tunisian treasury bills increased.

But in the following year a new French consul, Théodore Roustan, launched a carefully calculated campaign to eliminate British influence and get rid of Khair al-Din. The Tunisian prime minister had blocked an attempt to link together a French railway company's Algerian and Tunisian lines, a project with transparent military possibilities. Meanwhile the elderly Muhammad al-Sadiq Bey had become infatuated with a twenty-seven-year-old Adonis called Mustafa bin Isma'il, a close friend of the French. The Bey's new favourite persuaded him to demand Khair al-Din's resignation in July 1877. After a nonentity briefly held the post, the beloved Adonis was appointed as prime minister in August 1878.

With the young favourite in power, Tunisia reverted to tyranny, corruption and extortion. The tax collectors enriched themselves and the prime minister built himself a luxurious palace in Tunis and acquired various large estates and scores of villas. By the following year the country's finances were again in ruin and the government was unable to meet its obligations to the Financial Commission.[7] Tunisia's creditors became restive.

Meanwhile, Consul Wood learnt of Britain's shady deal at the Congress of Berlin. This 'compensated' France for Britain's acquisition of Cyprus by giving it the go-ahead for an eventual take-over of Tunisia. Wood was horrified. Since his appointment as consul-general he had spent years trying to ensure that Tunis remained under the protection of both Britain and the Porte. But, it now became obvious to him that his own employer – the Foreign Office – was content to sacrifice both himself, Tunis and all that work just because Britain and France were currently enjoying something of a diplomatic rapprochement. In fact, the Foreign Office had decided that Wood had outlived his usefulness and was beginning to become an embarrassment. Consequently, in 1879 Wood was recalled following a conveniently arranged 'reorganisation' of the consular service.

With the removal of Wood, the struggle for influence in Tunis degenerated into an unseemly squabble over concessions between Roustan and his acolytes, and those of the Italian consul, Licurgo Maccio. Roustan also began to put pressure on the ageing Bey to agree that Tunisia should become a French 'protectorate'. Muhammad al-Sadiq was assured that there would be no annexation, as had occurred in Algeria. Instead, he and his descendants would be permitted to remain in place as nominal rulers. France would take responsibility for guaranteeing the security of the Bey and his state. A French 'resident' would be installed to deal with any matters arising between the Bey and the French government, but France would not involve itself in any matters of internal administration. However, the Bey and his ministers would not be able to make any international agreements without first informing and then obtaining the approval of the French government.[8]

Elderly though he was, Muhammad al-Sadiq was not senile. He could foresee that such a 'protectorate' might easily develop into something more like a simple colony. So he resisted any such agreement. Moreover, the French prime minister, Jules Ferry, was wary of any more 'forward' colonial policy. He was a moderate republican, soon facing elections. He knew full well the reluctance of French public opinion to become involved in foreign adventures of the type which had characterised the rule of Napoleon III.

But some in Ferry's Foreign Office and the French navy – notably the Foreign Office's director of political affairs, the forty-six-year-old nationalistic aristocrat Baron Alphonse de Courcel – were determined to take advantage of the seemingly favourable British and German attitude towards a French occupation of Tunis. All that was needed to win over a reluctant Chamber of Deputies was some kind of 'incident'. It wasn't long before such a convenient 'incident' occurred.

On 4 April 1881, Ferry announced that on 30 March a Berber tribe called the Krumirs, living in the region of al-Kaf on the border with Algeria, were on the rampage. Nobody seemed to know much about these 'Krumirs' or exactly what they were doing. Indeed, there was much ribaldry in the Parisian and foreign press about the 'threat' posed by these unknown marauders. Although the Bey offered to deal with the Krumirs himself his offer was refused and the French Chamber of Deputies, egged on by the holders of Tunisian bonds, was whipped up into a state of outrage. On 7 April 5 million francs were voted for to send a force to Tunisia to punish the Krumirs, protect the poor old Bey from the depredations of these fearsome warriors, and remove the 'threat' they posed to French property and persons in both Algeria and Tunisia.[9]

On 25 April 1881 a French army of 28,000 under General Forgemol de Bostquénard crossed the Tunisian frontier from Algeria; and on 1 May another force of 8,000 under General Jules Aimé Bréart seized the port of Bizerte.[10] With no sign of any Krumirs, the two columns marched directly on Tunis. The first units of Bréart's men arrived outside the city in early May while the Bey was frantically begging the other European powers and the Porte to come to his aid. Both Italy and the Porte urged Britain to intervene. On 6 May the British Foreign Office, belatedly concerned about the future of the strategically positioned Mediterranean port of Bizerte, debated this possibility, but in the end only offered mediation. Consequently, on 12 May General Bréart, accompanied by the consul Théodore Roustan and a body of French troops, entered the Bey's palace and forced Muhammad al-Sadiq to sign the Treaty of Bardo. This new pact converted Tunisia into a protectorate overnight. Roustan became the first 'resident'.

However, this was not the end of the story. In late June, just as the French command was re-embarking its troops, a coalition of Arab tribes launched a surprise insurrection in central and southern Tunisia. Their sheikhs were enraged at the 'treachery' of their Turkish-speaking ruler. Simultaneously the cities of Sfax and Gabes burst into revolt. The French commanders were compelled to remain to fight a summer campaign and call upon 50,000 reinforcements. It was not until November that the revolt was crushed with considerable bloodshed on both sides; and by now Arab unrest had spread into the Algerian Sahara. Faced with this unexpected development, fierce opposition to the Tunisian adventure now sprang up in both the French press and the Chamber of Deputies. Jules Ferry was forced to resign, but France retained the former Regency. With the death of the old Bey in 1882 debate continued about precisely what to do with France's new acquisition, until Ferry was returned to power in February 1883.

The following June the matter was settled. Tunisia would remain a protectorate, separate from France's Algerian colony. But when the Convention of Marsa was signed in on 8 June, it contained a number of changes from and additions to the Bardo treaty. One crucial new clause stated that 'the Regency's finances should be organised on such bases as would ensure the servicing of the Public Debt and guarantee the rights of Tunisia's creditors.'[11] It was 'the end of the protectorate in any real sense. Internal sovereignty was no longer to be respected. The Bey's autonomy, of which much had been made, became henceforth no more than a sham.'[12]

As might have been anticipated, there was a serious diplomatic fall-out from France's seizure of Tunisia. In May 1882, enraged at France's occupation of a territory which had long since been a target for Italy's own colonialist ambitions, the youthful would-be imperialist state agreed a treaty with its old enemy Austria-Hungary and Austria-Hungary's ally, Bismarck's Germany. This 'Triple Alliance' against France would be renewed in 1887 and would last until the outbreak of the First World War. Meanwhile, with Tunis in French hands, it began to dawn on the British government that perhaps Egypt's profligate ruler could be the next French target.

Between the era of Mehmed Ali's rule and the European take-over of Egypt's finances in 1876, Egypt had experienced a number of major demographic, social, political and religious transformations. With the virtual disappearance of plague after 1835 and the substantial decline in outbreaks of cholera, the total Egyptian population increased from 4.3 million in 1840 to 7.1 million in 1876.[13] The fastest growth occurred in its two largest cities, Cairo and Alexandria. But while Cairo's population increased by 42 per cent over this period, reaching 349,137, that of Alexandria swelled from around 60,000 in 1840 to 212,048 in 1872, an increase of 253 per cent.[14] This enormous population growth was almost entirely related to the great increase in the exports of raw cotton. By the early 1870s Alexandria was the fourth largest Mediterranean port after Istanbul, Marseille and Genoa.

Along with this huge expansion of the cotton export business there was a commensurate increase in European immigration. European immigrants increased from a few thousands in 1860 to more than 100,000 in 1876, and it was in Alexandria that they constituted the largest proportion of the population. According to the 1848 census, 'Europeans and protégés' constituted 4.6 per cent of Alexandria's population; but by 1882 this proportion had risen to 21.5 per cent. 'Alexandria was a colonial city before Egypt was a colony.'[15]

In both Alexandria and Cairo the majority of these 'Europeans' were Mediterraneans, mainly from Greece, Italy and Malta. Here they constituted a *petite bourgeoisie*, with employment in retail, food processing and skilled crafts. In both in Cairo and Alexandria Europeans of all classes lived in segregated housing zones, including consuls, prosperous merchants, bankers and European senior employees of the Egyptian government. For example Alexandria already had the exclusive European-dominated Manshiya district along the eastern harbour; to this was added the suburb of al-Raml, some miles to the east of the city, which had become a virtual European enclave, with large homes, expensive shops, hotels, flower gardens and numerous Christian churches.[16] In Cairo, west of 'Ataba Square, foreigners outnumbered Egyptians by about three to one. All Europeans enjoyed the privileges granted in the age-old capitulations, including exemption from paying any taxes and the protection of their own courts. For example, an Egyptian plaintiff against a French citizen, or French protégé, had to have his case heard in a French court where any appeal against its judgement had to be heard in Aix-la-Provence.

The second major change that had occurred since the mid-nineteenth century was the first step towards representative government and away from the Khedive's absolutism. In 1866 Isma'il permitted the formation of a 'Consultative Assembly' (also known as the 'Assembly of Notables') composed of seventy-five members. They were mostly large landowners, elected only by the village sheikhs, and enjoying a term of office of three years. The Assembly first met on 25 November 1866.[17] Initially its role was entirely consultative and its limitations made it a far cry from a democratic government. However, it would soon be forced to exercise a much more active role.

Sayyid Jamal al-Din al-Afghani

Major changes had also been taking place within the Egyptian army. During the rule of Mehmed Ali's son Sa'id, Egyptians had been permitted to enter officer ranks. Sa'id sympathised with Egyptian aspirations to enter a military career in an army still dominated by Turko-Circassians, many of them descendants of the Mamluks who had escaped Muhammad Ali's massacre of their Beys. Under Sa'id at least two Egyptians reached the rank of colonel.

One of these was Ahmed 'Urabi, born in a village in the Delta in 1841, the son of a village headman. However, although he had been promoted to colonel in about 1860, he received no further promotion until the summer of 1879 when he was made brigadier. The continuing exclusion of native Egyptians from higher army ranks was a major grievance which would play a significant part in the growing unrest against the rule of the Turko-Circassian elite.[18]

A final important development in Egyptian life, one which had emerged since the beginning of Isma'il's rule, was a deepening of religious sentiment. Many new mosques were built and the people found refuge from the growing oppression of the Turko-Circassian elite and their European protectors in the tenants of Islam.

This tendency was considerably enhanced by the arrival in Egypt in 1871 of the famous peripatetic Muslim scholar and political activist Jamal al-Din al-Afghani. Al-Afghani (who, in spite of his name, was probably of Iranian Shi'i origin) was an advocate of political unity between Shi'is and Sunnis in the struggle against European imperialism, which he saw as posing an existential threat to the Islamic world. He didn't adhere to any of the different schools of Islamic jurisprudence and was more interested in stimulating resistance to European domination. Al-Afghani was no fundamentalist and even became involved in the Masonic movement; above all, he strongly believed that, for Muslims to resist and overcome the oppression they suffered, they should welcome and absorb European science and technology.

For example, in a lecture he would give later in Calcutta, he spoke of how strange it was:

> that our ulema these days have divided science into two parts. One they call Muslim and one European science. Because of this they forbid others to teach some of the useful sciences. They have not understood that science is that noble thing that has no connection to any nation... How very strange it is that the Muslims study those sciences that are ascribed to Aristotle with the greatest delight, as if Aristotle were one of the pillars of the Muslims. However if the discussion relates to Galileo, Newton or Kepler they consider them infidels. The father and mother of science is proof, and proof is neither Aristotle nor Galileo.[19]

In Egypt his writings criticising European financial domination, and British imperialism in particular, were widely circulated and reported on in the newly established independent Arabic-language press, especially in the magazines *Misr* ('Egypt') and *Al-Tijara* ('Trade') whose first editions appeared in 1877. For the time being his presence in Egypt was tolerated, although two years later that situation would change.

With the imposition of what quickly became labelled as Nubar Paşa's 'European cabinet' in August 1878, the indigenous Assembly of Notables – which had been little more than a toothless talking shop since its creation in 1866 – began to exert itself. When it met on 2 January 1879, its members demanded greater control of finances, a reduction in taxation, and accountability of the Assembly of the European ministers in Nubar Paşa's government.[20] But it was in the army that the greatest disaffection with the semi-colonial regime manifested itself.

After pay cuts and delays in pay had already antagonised the army's Egyptian officers, it was learnt that 2,500 of them were going to be discharged. On 18 February 1879 a large body of officers, including Colonel Ahmed 'Urabi, ambushed the carriages of Charles Rivers Wilson and Nubar Paşa as they were heading for the finance ministry; they roughed up the dignitaries and chased them into the building where they were imprisoned in some discomfort. Isma'il then appeared on the scene with his palace guard and theatrically appealed to the officers to release their captives. After they showed no willingness to do so, he ordered his guards to fire over their heads. The officers duly dispersed and Isma'il was praised by the foreign consuls for his steadfastness – even though it was widely rumoured that he had staged the whole thing.

The Khedive certainly took advantage of the affair. On 9 March he dismissed Nubar (whom he personally hated) and informed the European consuls that he could no longer tolerate the humiliating role of constitutional monarch which had been imposed upon him the previous year. He announced that he would now personally take the post of prime minister. When the European powers swiftly blocked his decision he placed his son, Tewfiq, in that position instead. For the time being, Wilson and the Comte de Blignières were retained in the government as minister of finance and minister of public works respectively.

On 29 March 1879, the Assembly presented the Khedive with a petition protesting against Wilson's first finance bill, which included a formal declaration of insolvency. They also demanded the revocation of the *muqabala* decree which Isma'il had introduced as a desperate cash-raising measure in 1871.* In addition, they insisted on a purely Egyptian government, without European ministers, and proposed their own financial plan for dealing with the debt problem.

---

* The *muqabala* decree had invited – and later required – landowners to pay six times the annual land tax in advance in exchange (*muqabala*) for a perpetual reduction of one half of the tax. Having already paid out the advance, the landowners naturally opposed revocation of the decree which reimbursed only half of the amount paid in advance and required them to return to paying the full annual amount.

Isma'il now took his hostility to European control one step further. On 6 and 7 April, he informed the foreign consuls that he supported the Assembly in rejecting Wilson's financial plan. He removed from his government Wilson (who retired to London for the time being) as well as de Blignières, and he replaced Tewfiq as prime minister. The new premier was Muhammad Sharif Paşa, a former foreign minister who held 'constitutionalist' views. The Anglo-French 'Dual Control' ended, but the Khedive pledged to respect Egypt's obligations to its European creditors.

The European powers acted swiftly to this challenge by calling on Sultan Abdülhamid to depose Isma'il. The sultan had just survived the Russo-Turkish war and was himself almost entirely dependent on European financial support, as well as the prompt payment of the Egyptian tribute. On 26 June 1879, the sultan's *firman* was announced. Isma'il meekly accepted it and sailed off into a luxurious retirement, after which the sultan appointed Tewfiq as the new Khedive.

In September 1879 Tewfiq dissolved Sharif Paşa's government and replaced it with one led by the Circassian Riyad Paşa, the former interior minister, while another Circassian, Osman Rifki Paşa, was appointed as war minister. Meanwhile, in August, the Muslim writer and activist al-Afghani was expelled from the country. And by now Britain controlled and administered the Egyptian railways, telegraph, post office, the port of Alexandria, and the Khedive's private estate. More than that, Britain now also held Egypt's 'colony' of the Sudan where Colonel Charles Gordon had recently been installed as the 'Egyptian' governor.

Over the remainder of 1879 and throughout 1880, the European powers and their puppet Khedive appeared to have brought matters under control. On 15th November 1879, the Anglo-French 'Dual Control' was re-established with Major Evelyn Baring (later Lord Cromer) as controller of revenues and France's Comte de Blignières controller of expenditures. Both were now (unlike previously) official representatives of their respective governments. In January 1880, Charles Rivers Wilson's financial plan was implemented by Khedival decree. The cash-raising *muqabala* decree was abolished, but all other taxes on both landlords and peasants were increased. Wilson himself returned to Egypt on 10 April.

On 20 May, the native-born Egyptian army officers presented a petition to the new Turko-Circassian war minister Osman Rifki, protesting against non-payment of salaries. They also demanded an end to the use of the troops on demeaning corvée-type (forced labour) duties, including work on the Khedival estates. Rifki simply ignored their petition and, in a deliberate show of disdain for these 'fellah' officers, he ostentatiously promoted a number of Circassians to high military positions.

Two months later, the 'European cabinet' decreed the Law of Liquidation according to which the floating debt (in which French banks had heavily invested) was incorporated in the total to be fully repaid by the Egyptians. The new legislation thereby rescued the semi-secure creditors from their difficulties while guaranteeing the long-term interests of the bondholders.[21]

One clause of the Law, the work of Wilson, was draconian. It allocated two-thirds of the expected tax revenues, and any surplus above it, to servicing and reducing the national debt, leaving a totally inadequate sum for the government of the country.[22] And by now there were over 1,300 British officials and businessmen in Egypt whose excessive salaries had to be paid by Tewfiq's puppet government. Nor is the term 'puppet' inappropriate: the Khedive was even prevented from leaving Cairo without the permission of the British Foreign Office.[23]

In April 1880, the British Conservative government under Disraeli fell from power and was replaced by the Liberals under William Ewart Gladstone. But any expectation that the reputedly 'anti-colonialist' Gladstone would respond differently to the non-violent resistance movement of the Egyptians would soon be swept aside.

Meanwhile a powerful nationalist movement was building among the Egyptian-born officers of the army; one in which Colonel Ahmed 'Urabi was steadily gaining support as its natural leader. As 'Urabi's popularity grew, in July 1880 War Minister Osman Rifki began a vast scheme of promotions, transfers and replacements explicitly aimed at weakening or dispersing the officers of Egyptian birth. On 17 January 1881, 'Urabi, Colonel of the 4th Regiment and two fellow officers, Colonel 'Abd al-Al of the 'Black' Regiment and Colonel 'Ali Fahmi of the 1st (Khedive's) Guard's Regiment, demanded the replacement of Osman Rifki with their own candidate, Mahmud Sami al-Barudi.

It was now that the government decided to arrest 'Urabi and his two senior military allies. The details were handed over to Rifki and, with the connivance of the Khedive, on 31 January a plot was hatched. The following day the three colonels were requested to attend the War Ministry for discussions about the arrangements for the forthcoming marriage of Tewfiq's sister.[24] But on arrival they were confronted by a group of Turkish and Circassian officers; they were arrested, abused and thrown into prison.

The plot failed. When news of the arrests reached Bimbashi (Major) Muhammad 'Ubayd of the 1st Regiment, he brought up his troops, stormed the ministry building and released his commander, Colonel 'Ali Fahmi, together with Colonel 'Urabi and Colonel 'Abd al-Al.[25] The troops then marched to the Abdin Square where they were met by crowds of jubilant civilians. Soon news of the event spread throughout the country. According to 'Urabi's biographer, the rebellion of the Egyptian troops against the clique of Turkish and Circassian senior officers 'was the beginning of a new page in the history of Egypt ... the campaign changed from a purely military one to a movement of the whole people. Its slogan was Egypt for the Egyptians.'[26] Meanwhile, a bedraggled Osman Rifki had managed to escape the fury of Bimbashi 'Ubayd's furious men by escaping out of one of the War Ministry's windows – only to find that a panicking Tewfiq had felt compelled to replace him with Sami al-Barudi.

But the will of the European consuls was not to be challenged so easily, even by these dramatic events. Osman Rifki was considered expendable, but Tewfiq was ordered to retain Riyad Paşa as prime minister along with the rest of his 'European' government. Moreover, in July, some unrelated disturbances among troops at Alexandria played into the hands of Tewfiq, enabling him to dismiss Mahmud Sami al-Barudi. In August he installed as war minister his brother-in-law, Daud Paşa Yeken, 'a certain Circassian general of the worst reactionary type'.[27]

Nevertheless, by now news of the French invasion of Tunisia was circulating throughout Egypt. Fear of a similar fate spread throughout all classes of native Egyptians and boosted support for those elements in both the army and the Assembly, who were seeking to get rid of the reactionary Riyad government and its European backers. Colonel 'Urabi's reputation as defender of the rights of his fellow *fellahin* grew rapidly among the peasantry. They were soon referring to him as 'al-Wahhid' (The Only One) i.e. the only one who might liberate them from Turko-Circassian despotism and, indirectly, European domination.[28]

By now the British government and public were being regularly regaled by spurious tales about the growing Egyptian resistance movement. These were the work of certain self-described 'men-on-the-spot', who not only began a campaign to denigrate 'Urabi and his fellow officers, but were voicing their fears about the growing unity of purpose between the military 'Urabists' and those members of the Assembly of Notables demanding a transition to full parliamentary rule.

First among these 'men-on-the-spot' was the Calcutta-born former 'collector' of the Indian revenue service, Sir Auckland Colvin. In July 1880, when Major Evelyn Baring moved to India as the government's finance member, Colvin was appointed Britain's controller-general for revenue collection in the 'Dual Control'. But Colvin was also the Egyptian correspondent of the *Pall Mall Gazette*, reputedly the only newspaper which Prime Minister Gladstone read attentively, and he soon began to feed fiercely anti-nationalist and anti-'Urabi stories to the *Gazette*.

The second of these 'men-on the spot' was Charles Rivers Wilson, whom we have already met. In April 1880 he returned to Egypt and was appointed president of the bondholders' Caisse. Given his roughing up during the officers' demonstration in February the previous year, it is hardly surprising that his views about the rising tide of Egyptian nationalism differed little from those of Colvin.

A third important opinion-former was C. F. Moberly Bell, a merchant in Alexandria where his father was a partner in a large cotton-exporting firm. Moberly Bell was the Egyptian correspondent of *The Times* and he, too, used this opportunity to denigrate 'Urabi and the nationalists, and prepare British public opinion for a possible military intervention.

Finally there was Sir Edward Malet, consul-general since October 1879. According to one who knew him well, the Consul-General 'was a man of fairly ordinary abilities ... Imagination, however, Malet had none, nor initiative, nor any power of dealing on his own responsibility with occasions requiring strong actions and prompt decisions.'[29] Malet initially professed sympathies for those Egyptians demanding a greater degree of control over their own political and financial affairs. But he would later fall under the influence of Colvin and add his voice to the other three men who had continuously argued for Britain to take a hard line against the nationalists – and in the new foreign secretary, Lord Granville, they had a willing listener.

Over the next eighteen months it would be this small group of individuals who were the most influential in determining the actions of the reputedly anti-imperialist Liberal leader Gladstone and his ministers.

However, there was one British individual resident in Egypt who viewed its nationalist and constitutionalist movement in a very different light from that favoured by those 'men-on-the-spot'. Wilfrid Scawen Blunt was a forty-year-old wealthy Tory squire who had spent some years travelling in the Middle East in the company of his wife (the granddaughter of Lord Byron). During these travels he had taken the trouble to learn something of the Arabic language and gained a deep affection for the Arab people. Returning to Egypt in November 1880, he became an unofficial advisor to Consul-General Malet. And after a personal meeting with 'Urabi in December 1881 he tried to influence Malet – and through him, the British government – with a perspective on the Egyptian nationalist movement that was totally at odds with that being portrayed by Colvin, Wilson and Moberly Bell. For Blunt, it was essentially a movement for constitutional change against the despotic rule of Tewfiq and his Turko-Circassian caste – precisely the kind of political development which seemed in tune with the professed values of Gladstone and his Liberal government. But he would soon discover that, while aspirations for freedom were welcomed when occurring among the subdued Christian peoples of the Ottoman Empire, different principles applied for subdued Muslim peoples under 'Christian' rule.

As the nationalist movement in Egypt continued to grow in strength, on 8 September the war minister Daud Paşa moved against its military leaders. He ordered the removal of the troops loyal to the nationalist officers out of Cairo. 'Urabi and his associates, fearing this could be part of another plan to kill them, moved decisively against the government. The next day troops loyal to the three colonels besieged Tewfiq in the Khedive's Abdin Palace, where they demanded the dismissal of Riyad Paşa, as well as the redress of a number military and political grievances. 'Urabi, declaring himself 'delegate of the people', also insisted that the Khedive call a Constituent Assembly and that the army be increased to its full complement of 18,000 men as agreed in 1841.[30] Tewfiq caved in and Sharif Paşa was returned as prime minister to head a new administration in which Sami al-Barudi was restored as war minister, with 'Urabi as his deputy. The Khedive also agreed to recall the Assembly of Notables, to meet on 23 December. In response, prompted by Colvin, *The Times* in its editions of 23 and 27 September 1881 called for military intervention, a demand repeated in its pages on 19 October and 4 November.[31]

When the Assembly met on 23 December it set about drawing up a real constitution, one that would impose limits on Khedival autocracy, guarantee civil liberties, and rule that the portion of tax revenues not set aside for payment of interest on the debt would be subject to the jurisdiction of the Assembly. The members also called for the dismissal of the European employees of the Egyptian government who were receiving huge salaries.

These were relatively modest demands, but they infuriated Controller-General Colvin. On 26 December he informed Lord Granville at the Foreign Office that, if this movement were not stopped immediately, Egypt would free itself from European control and repudiate its financial obligations – notwithstanding the fact that the Assembly had promised to do no such thing. Both Colvin and his French counterpart recommended to their respective governments that they should not tolerate this threat to their interests.[32] Malet was less hostile, at least initially. He wrote to Sir Charles Dilke, under-secretary at the Foreign Office, that he could 'manage' 'Urabi and his associates.[33] But the possibility of any such 'management' by a British official was now fading fast.

Furthermore, on 14 November 1881, Léon Gambetta became France's prime minister, a politician surrounded by a 'spider's web of financial intrigue' whose cronies included international bankers like d'Erlanger and Rothschild.[34] He was convinced that political events in Egypt were yet another phase in an organised pan-Islamic, anti-European movement. So on 6 January 1882 he sent what became known as the 'Joint Note' to Tewfiq and the European consuls. In essence, it stated that both Britain and France were united in giving their fullest support to the Khedive as an absolute monarch and would not tolerate any changes to the system of Dual Control and the financial powers which it exercised.

When 'Urabi read the 'Note' on the 8th he concluded that it was tantamount to a threat of invasion and war if the nationalist movement did not capitulate. Colvin, Wilson and Moberly Bell, on the other hand, were jubilant. But Consul-General Malet was still wavering: on 23 January he admitted to 'a repugnance' at what he revealingly admitted might be 'a war on behalf of bondholders'.[35] However, under pressure from Colvin he was now drifting towards a more bellicose position. As for the Egyptians, their response to the Joint Note was to compel Tewfiq to form a much more strongly nationalist government; and on 3 February Sami al-Barudi was appointed prime minister and Colonel 'Urabi minister of war.

But events in France now began to open up a fissure between the British and French approaches to the Egyptian crisis. On 30 January 1882 political events in France threw Gambetta from power after he lost a vote on electoral reform in the Chamber of Deputies. His successor, Charles de Freycinet, broadly supported his predecessor's imperialist objectives. Yet he was aware that both the French press and public were losing their enthusiasm for further colonial-type adventures after the problems they had encountered in subduing Tunisia. It would be some time before this reluctance became evident to Gladstone's government, but, in any case, from now on it would be the British who forced the pace as events moved towards a tragic and violent conclusion.

For the time being, some semblance of Anglo-French unity survived. On 15 May a combined squadron of two ironclads, HMS *Invincible* and *La Galissonnière*, together with four gunboats, entered Alexandria's harbour. The British contingent was commanded by Admiral Beauchamp Seymour, who would come to play an important – and malevolent – part in the ensuing developments. Ostensibly, the warships had arrived to offer protection to their nationals in the event of 'Muslim violence'; its real intention was to try to frighten the Egyptian government and its supporters into capitulation. But when the two fleets took up their positions in Alexandria's harbour, their presence had the opposite effect. With memories of Tunisia still fresh, Egyptians of all classes saw it as the first step in an invasion and rallied to 'Urabi and his fellow officers in a surge of patriotic emotion. Meanwhile, Gladstone had allowed the drip-feed of hostile and erroneous information flowing from the 'men-on-the-spot' to convince him that he must support the Khedive.

With the presence of the British and French warships failing to have the desired effect, on 25 May Tewfiq and the British and French consuls issued an ultimatum demanding the resignation of the al-Barudi government and the banishment of 'Urabi. The following day the cabinet accepted Tewfiq's order, but the Assembly rejected it. With widespread public disorder threatening the country, the Khedive was compelled to rescind his order

– but not before having offered the post of minister of war to a jealous rival of 'Urabi's, a certain 'Umar Lufti Paşa. Then, on 31 May, Tewfiq left Cairo for the safety of his palace near Alexandria, at which the Assembly petitioned Sultan Abdülhamid to dismiss him from the position of Khedive.

Meanwhile, as public pressure against military intervention increased, on 1 June Freycinet finally decided that no French troops should be landed on Egyptian soil, prompting Lord Granville to send the revealing message to Consul Malet that 'Freycinet's fatal indecision has nearly ruined us.'[36] For his part, Gladstone praised Tewfiq's 'honour and courage' – this, of the individual whose own father had previously described him as having 'no head, no heart and no courage'.[37]

Ten days later the long-anticipated 'incident' occurred which would play directly into the hands of the 'men-on-the-spot' and the bondholders. In the early afternoon of 11 June 1882, an Arab donkey boy named El Ajjan became involved in a dispute with his Maltese passenger about a fare, during which the Maltese drew a knife and stabbed the Arab boy. Within minutes other Arabs came to El Ajjan's assistance and crowds of Greeks, Italians and Maltese joined in the affray. A Greek was killed by an Arab, and before long the violence became general. Shots were fired by some Europeans and, as the violence escalated, individual Europeans were attacked and battered to death. There were only six British among the fifty or more Europeans killed, but three of these were from Admiral Seymour's flagship HMS *Invincible*, and one was Seymour's manservant. For some reason the Admiral and his men had foolishly gone on shore without taking any precautions, and Seymour himself only narrowly escaped back to his flagship.

'Urabi was in Cairo when the disturbances erupted. But it wasn't until around 5 p.m. that he first learnt of the affair He immediately sent 12,000 troops to Alexandria, commanded by Colonel Sulayman Sami, who managed to impose calm on the city by 7 p.m. Perhaps as many as 120 Egyptians were killed along with the Europeans. Despite this, it wasn't long before the British 'men-on-the-spot', the news media and the British government itself were describing the events of 11 June as a 'massacre' of Europeans by bloodthirsty Muslim fanatics, moreover a 'massacre' which had been instigated by 'Urabi himself.[38]

Modern historians are unanimous in seeing the initial outbreak of the rioting and killing as spontaneous – although fuelled by two decades of socioeconomic friction generated by the influx of southern Europeans, while Egyptians of the middling sort were marginalised in the new economic structure, and 'by the salient feature of European life ... its segregation from that of the Muslim inhabitants'.[39]

But there was also a particularly sinister aspect to the 'massacre'. The municipal *mustahfizan* (gendarmerie) under the control of Tewfiq's favourite, 'Umar Lufti Paşa, made no effort to intervene and stop the violence. Indeed, many of the *mustahfizan* reportedly joined in the fighting against the Europeans. On one occasion 'Umar Lufti himself refused a request from a European resident to intervene to protect those being attacked.

As the violence in Alexandria escalated, uncertain as to what action to take, the local army commander awaited orders from his commander-in-chief in Cairo, Colonel 'Urabi; but time passed and no orders came. Tewfiq, ensconced in his Alexandrian palace, was informed of the violence by 'Umar Lufti soon after it broke out in the early afternoon. But it was at least two or three hours later, at around 5 p.m., that Tewfiq told 'Urabi in Cairo about the violence occurring in Alexandria.

There can be no doubt as to who had the most to lose from the Alexandria 'massacre' – 'Urabi, the man with a national responsibility for 'law and order' – while both Tewfiq and 'Umar Lufti Paşa had much to gain from it. (Indeed, after 'Urabi's overthow, Tewfiq would make 'Umar Lufti Paşa war minister.) Suffice it to say that the British historian who carried out the most balanced and forensic study of the 'massacre' of 11 June 1882 concluded that the Khedive Tewfiq was 'very possibly the real villain of that black Sunday'.[40]

By now Admiral Seymour was only too eager to be let off the leash and wreak revenge on the Arab population of Alexandria for the deaths of his three crew members, a motive he openly admitted some months later. He informed the Admiralty that the heavily reinforced British fleet was directly threatened by the defences of Alexandria, whose forts had been strengthened since the arrival of Seymour's ships in May. He further claimed that 'Urabi was set upon launching a 'holy war' against all Christians,[41] a 'holy war' which Seymour assured the Admiralty was inspired by the Prophet Muhammad himself, with whom 'Urabi communicated nightly.[42] He therefore requested the government for permission to send an ultimatum to 'Urabi to dismantle the guns in the forts defending Alexandria, or face a bombardment. The cabinet gave him its support – including Gladstone, who had previously opposed any bombardment but now had convinced himself that hostilities against Egypt were 'an upright war, a Christian War'.[43]

Wilfrid Blunt, having returned to Britain, made a final attempt to halt the onrush of violence against his nationalist Egyptian friends. On 23 June *The Times* (presumably with some reluctance) published a letter Blunt had sent to Gladstone on the 21st explaining in great detail the true trajectory and motives of the Egyptian national movement. These, he said, were entirely consistent with 'Liberal' principles and encompassed only a desire to establish a parliamentary regime in the country.[44] But by now Gladstone had convinced himself that Blunt was just a troublemaker, and on 26 June the foreign secretary, Lord Granville, boasted in the House of Lords: 'Those views [Blunt's] did not produce any impression on me.' What almost certainly had made an impression, two days earlier, was the front-page article in Gladstone's favourite newspaper, the *Pall Mall Gazette*, warning of 'The Effect of a Collapse in Egyptian Bonds'. [45]

On 3 July the government gave instructions to Admiral Seymour to issue his ultimatum; and on the same day a new threat to British interests was intoned. For the first time the *Pall Mall Gazette* stated that Britain had a primary responsibility for 'the free passage of the [Suez] Canal' which was now threatened by 'Urabi and the nationalists. The main function of this argument appears to have been to win over the few remaining opponents of military action in the cabinet, and whip up the press and public with what sounded like a genuine reason for action. On 7 July Gladstone himself informed Lord Granville that Britain was bound to protect the canal.[46]

The only problem with this particular justification was that, five years earlier, countering an editorial in the *Observer* that events in Egypt justified an invasion *to protect the canal* against its seizure by the Russians, Gladstone himself had categorically denied that the security of the canal could be a justification for military action.[47] Blocking the canal would only delay the transfer of troops to India by three weeks, and in any case the Admiralty still preferred the sea route to India via the Cape of Good Hope. Likewise, on 12 May when Lord Granville asked Consul-General Malet what dangers he feared for the safety of the canal, he admitted that expert advice had already informed him that, although it might be blocked for a short time, it was impossible for the Egyptians to cause any permanent damage.[48]

By now, the French government had recalled its consul-general from Egypt; and on 5 July it decided not to join the British in any bombardment. Soon the French fleet was withdrawn from the positions it held near the British, although it remained in Egyptian waters.[49]

On 7 July Khedive Tewfiq secretly begged Seymour to bombard Alexandria. By now Seymour had a fleet of nine ironclad battleships, five gunboats, one torpedo boat and one steamer anchored off the city. Four days later the Admiral issued his ultimatum – but escalated it by demanding the *surrender* of all Alexandria's forts. When the Egyptians ignored the ultimatum, at 7 a.m. on 11 July the 11-inch heavy muzzleloaders of Seymour's capital ships began a ten-and-a-half-hour bombardment. Although the

The Bombardment of Alexandria, July 1882

Egyptian gunners remained bravely at their guns – some of which dated from the time of Mehmed Ali – their forts were slowly battered into submission. This was not before large parts of the city itself had been set on fire, in particular the area predominantly occupied by the Europeans (most of whom had, by now, fled the city). The bombardment continued the following day, after the British rejected an Egyptian attempt to arrange a ceasefire.

It wasn't until the 13th that Egyptian resistance finally collapsed. Two days later British marines entered the city. As a result of the bombardment, fire and devastation had cause enormous damage to the city. Around 600 Egyptians were killed compared with British losses of six killed and twenty-seven wounded. However, the bombardment and landing of British troops resulted in hundreds more innocent Europeans being slaughtered by vengeful Arabs throughout Egypt.

Only a handful of opposing voices were raised in the House of Commons during debates on the Egyptian crisis. On 25 July the Welsh MP and Congregational minister the Rev. Henry Richard described Britain's action at Alexandria as follows:

> I find a man prowling about my house with obviously felonious purposes. I hasten to get locks and bars and to barricade my windows. He says, that is an insult and threat to him, and he batters down my doors and declares that he does so only as an act of strict self-defence.[50]

A more apt metaphor cannot be imagined, but it cut no ice with the increasingly jingoistic parliamentarians. On 27 July Gladstone called upon the House of Commons to vote a war credit to pay for a full invasion. The expedition was to cost £2.3 million, to be financed by an increase in income tax of one penny (nearly 10 per cent). The plan was to send an army to Egypt under Lieutenant-General Garnet Wolseley, a self-professed 'jingo', who would command 15,000 British troops from Malta and Cyprus together with 10,000 mainly sepoys despatched from India.[51] Only a handful of MPs voted against the motion.

Wolseley decided to mount his main attack from the Suez Canal itself, and on 20 August seized Isma'iliya without resistance. 'Urabi had meanwhile assembled a force of around 15,000 and sixty guns, but most his new recruits were inexperienced *fellahin*. He positioned his army in a huge fortified camp with trenches and redoubts at Tel el-Kebir, north of the railway which linked Isma'iliya to Cairo; but no attempt was made to man outposts in front of the main defences.

At dawn on 13 September Wolseley's troops mounted a brilliant attack upon the Egyptian troops, most of whom were still sleeping. In barely an hour, the semi-trained Egyptian conscripts were overwhelmed and put to flight. What followed was more of a massacre than a battle, with the Egyptians losing around 2,000 killed out of a force of 15,000. Many of the wounded were shot or bayoneted as they begged for water.[52] The following day Wolseley marched into Cairo where he received the surrender of 'Urabi and his fellow officers.

When news of the victory reached Britain, Gladstone bathed in the adulation of an overwhelmingly delighted press and public. The whole Egyptian affair was now cast as a great victory over brutal Muslims. On 18 September, Consul-General Malet wrote to Lord Granville congratulating him and his government. 'It has been a struggle between civilisation and barbarism,' he declared, 'You have fought the battle of all Christianity and history will acknowledge it.'[53]

Queen Victoria and General Wolseley wanted 'Urabi hanged. But when a show trial was established in the Khedive Tewfiq's court, Wilfrid Blunt and a small band of 'Urabi supporters, including the unlikely figure of Lord Randolph Churchill, ensured that he was supported by a British defence counsel. 'Urabi was accused of having organised the 11 June massacre. Yet the evidence against him was so slim that eventually, on pleading guilty to the lesser 'crime' of political rebellion, he was merely sent into exile in Ceylon. His associates were not so lucky: Colonel Sulayman Sami, who was instrumental in swiftly putting a stop to the killing in Alexandria, was hanged in public on 11 June, an act which Lord Randolph Churchill denounced as 'judicial murder'.

While the 'anti-imperialist' Gladstone rejoiced along with his new-found jingoist friends, he had another very personal reason for jubilation. Since the early 1870s the prime minister had held a large amount of Egyptian bonds, valued at £40,567 in December 1881 (over £4 million at today's purchasing power) and constituting around 37 per cent of his private financial portfolio – an extraordinarily high exposure to risk on one particular asset.[54] In 1881 Gladstone's Egyptian bonds stood at 62.* But by June 1882, before the 'massacre', they had fallen back to 57 and, as the *Pall Mall Gazette* was warning, a further fall was possible.

But with Wolseley victorious at Tel el-Kebir, the bonds soared to 82. So over the period of the Egyptian crisis, between December 1881 and September 1882, Gladstone made a profit of £7,500 (£922,500 at 2020 purchasing power) on his Egyptian government bonds. Of course, it is impossible to know the extent to which pecuniary interests determined Gladstone's behaviour during 1881–82.[55] But it would be naïve to claim they had no influence on his decisions.

Whether or not Gladstone's decision to invade Egypt and crush the nationalists was motivated by anxiety over the value of his bonds, his was just a single example of an underlying structural feature of mid-Victorian capitalism. By the mid-nineteenth century, Britain was a country of rentier capitalists. As one British historian describes so precisely, 'Egypt experienced a crisis which was a direct external manifestation of the particular course taken by the development of the British economy during the previous half century.'[56]

All that remained was to decide the manner in which Egypt was to be administered in the coming years. On 28 July the cabinet informed the Porte that Britain would now have to take a more prominent role in the running of Egyptian affairs than it had previously anticipated. And this, they argued, required measures to restore the Khedive's authority and establish 'order'. It soon became clear that these measures went considerably further than those which the other European states – especially France – desired.

First, Malet, acting entirely without his French consular colleague, established a new puppet Ministry under Sharif Paşa (who had defected from the nationalists). The new constitution written by the Chamber of Notables would now be abandoned and the Chamber would lose all rights in relation to the budget and the initiation of new legislation. Egypt had to pay all the interest on its debt before it paid what was due as salaries to its government and military officials. And a new gendarmerie and army were to be formed, both commanded by British officers. Most importantly, the

---

* That is, 62 per cent over their face value on flotation.

Anglo-French 'Dual Control' was abolished. All these measures were, in Gladstone's words, required so that Britain could shoulder the burden of 'preparing Egypt for a self-governing future'.[57]

Initially the French were still broadly content with Britain's declared plans for Egypt, especially after Evelyn Baring (ennobled as Lord Cromer in 1901) was installed as Consul-General in September 1883. The French were appeased by the way he had managed the country's finances in a manner broadly favourable to all the bondholders. Baring considered himself a Liberal, and at first shared Gladstone's view that Egypt should be 'reformed' and then handed over to a 'responsible' Egyptian government. In the meantime, British rule took the form of a 'veiled protectorate' whereby the Khedive Tewfiq remained as nominal head of state under the myth of Ottoman suzerainty. In reality, Egyptian ministers were controlled by British 'advisors'.

However, on 3 November 1883 a ramshackle Egyptian army – composed largely of Egyptian troops freed after the battle of Tel el-Kebir, and commanded by British officer Hicks Paşa (William Hicks) – was totally destroyed by Sudanese tribesmen led by Muhammad Ahmad (the 'Mahdi') near the town of El Obeid, about 200 miles southwest of Khartoum. This military catastrophe, followed by the death of General Gordon when the Mahdists captured Khartoum itself on 26 January 1885, precipitated the electoral defeat of Gladstone and brought the Conservatives back to power under Lord Salisbury as prime minister. With the Mahdists now in control of the Sudan, it was decided that any precipitate British evacuation from Egypt – even after the 'reforms' had been completed – was now out of the question.

Before long, Baring's plans for Egypt began to depart from his original remit. By 1885 he was devising a justification for Britain's continuing presence on the grounds that additional 'good works' by the Egyptians were required. By 1887 he concluded that no precise date for withdrawal should be fixed, since the scope for improvements was infinite. This suited Salisbury, but by now the French had become deeply suspicious of Britain's motives. It looked as though Britain's manoeuvrings had finally cheated France out of the role which it had enjoyed in Egyptian affairs since the time of Mehmed Ali. By 1890 this opinion was confirmed by Baring himself when he acknowledged that he had changed his mind about an eventual evacuation: he opined that the inferiority of Egypt's 'oriental races' and the debilitating influence of Islam made the country permanently unfit for self-government.

France's exclusion from any role in Egypt's future enraged its politicians, and the degree of Anglo-French *entente* which had briefly characterised the early 1870s disappeared. By the late 1880s a diplomatic chasm had reopened between the two countries, and it contributed to the emergence of the first major fault-line within the Concert of Europe. It was a fault-line concerning colonies; it was also a fault-line concerning the Mediterranean and the Ottoman Empire.

Not only were Britain and France bitterly divided over the control of Egypt, but Italy was also enraged over the French occupation of Tunisia. Meanwhile Austria-Hungary, which increasingly saw its future as a major power in the southern Balkans, was fearful of a renewed Russian drive towards the Turkish Straits and the Aegean. Since Britain was also deeply concerned about the latter, a diplomatic alignment with Austria-Hungary emerged. And since both Italy and Austria-Hungary were allied with Germany (the Triple Alliance), this made closer Anglo-German relations inevitable.

These Anglo-Austrian-Italian pacts (which Spain later joined), aimed at both France and Russia, were formalised in the aptly named 'Mediterranean Agreements' made in 1887. There followed a series of secret treaties: signed on 12 February between Britain and Italy; on 24 March between Britain and Austria-Hungary; and with Spain joining on 4 May. Throughout the negotiations Bismarck's Germany gave them its backing. Further diplomatic notes were exchanged between Britain, Austria-Hungary and Italy in December.

The essence of the agreements was the preservation of the status quo in the Mediterranean region. The Agreement, made between the British prime minister, Lord Salisbury, and Crispi, his Italian counterpart, was that the territorial status quo in the Mediterranean including the Adriatic and the Aegean, together with the Black Sea, should be maintained as far as possible. Italy was to support Britain's objectives in Egypt, and Britain would support Italy if there were any French moves to seize territory in the Ottoman vilayets of Tripoli and Cyrenaica (Libya).

Austria-Hungary was brought into the 'Mediterranean Agreement' between Britain and Italy, with Britain expressing in rather vague terms its willingness to join with Austria-Hungary in preventing Russian encroachment upon the Turkish Straits and the Aegean. Finally Spain, which had anxieties about French interference in Morocco, agreed not to join with France in any treaty or other political arrangement regarding the North African territories that was aimed against Italy, Austria or Germany.

The significance of the Anglo-Austrian Agreement was that Britain had now moved close to the Austrian-Italian-German Triple Alliance. Its weakness was its Article 7, whose language (in French, the diplomatic language of the day) was vague about precisely what military means would be used – and by whom – if either France or Russia caused them to be activated. The Austrians incorrectly inferred that a Russian threat to Istanbul would be met, in the first instance, by Britain taking the lead in defending the Ottoman Empire by sending its powerful fleet to the Turkish Straits. Eight years later this Austrian misinterpretation would lead to a major crisis in Anglo-Austrian relations. Nevertheless, for the time being, imperialist rivalry in the Mediterranean had returned to its 'traditional' *modus vivendi*. By the 1890s Britain, once again, viewed France and Russia as its principal opponents.

CHAPTER 23

The Slow Death of the 'Empire' of Morocco

According to Eric Hobsbawm, 'Nobody in the 1890s would have denied that the division of the globe had an economic dimension.'[1] But unlike the earlier wave of imperialism this political climate was based on wider economic considerations than the interests of rentier bondholders. By the late 1880s the face of European (and American) capitalism was beginning to change. No longer was this exclusively a world of small family firms competing in a regime of free trade. Competition had too frequently led to massive overproduction, business failures and major slumps. The response to these crises was industry concentration, and eventually the creation of large firms where control was in the hands of managers, with the owners (now shareholders) playing a largely passive role; and, as a response to the 'Long Depression' (1873–96), the erection of high tariff barriers.

These changes in industrial capitalism had implication for the nature of imperialism. The large companies which now dominated the European economies had the capital to invest in a wide range of new technologies and products. For this they required raw materials, many of which, for reasons of geology or climate, simply did not exist in Europe: rubber, tin, oil, copper and range of other non-ferrous and precious metals. At the same time, population growth and increased working-class real incomes (as a result of falling prices) created a greater demand for the old 'colonial' consumption goods – sugar, tea, cocoa, coffee.

To ensure sufficient supplies the obvious way ahead was to seize control of the regions where such commodities were in relative abundance – both raw materials and foodstuffs. As often as not, though, colonial territories were simply grabbed in the *expectation* of future raw material discoveries, or just to put down a marker to prevent economic rivals making a pre-emptive strike. This imperialist tactic was a not-uncommon feature of the so-called 'scramble for Africa'. For example, in a speech made in 1893, the

British Liberal Party politician Lord Rosebery (Archibald Primrose) stated – appropriately, in the terminology of mining concessions – that 'We are engaged in "pegging out claims for the future". We have to consider not what we want now, but what we shall want in the future.'[2] Morocco was such a case. Little was known about its natural resources until the early 1900s, but this did not prevent a creeping intervention in the country by the European powers on the look-out for future economic opportunities. The partition of sub-Saharan Africa was largely settled between the rival claimants 'by the traditional means of adjusting their interests and by barter agreements;'[3] but this was to prove far more difficult in the case of Morocco where inter-imperialist rivalry would continue unabated until virtually the eve of the First World War.

Economic factors in this later stage of imperialism were now increasingly reflected in ideology: in the emergence of a fierce nationalism, militarism and racism. As industrialisation spread throughout Europe it was accompanied by an expansion of the middle classes and a great increase in literacy – even in 'backward' states like Russia and Italy. Along with these developments there emerged a popular press; but it was a press that – like Alfred Harmsworth's massively popular *Daily Mail*, whose first edition appeared in 1896 – was often controlled, or at least strongly influenced, by imperialist lobbyists. Notions such as Europe's 'civilising mission', and the 'white man's burden', became planted in the minds of the rapidly growing middle class, as well as some sections of the working class.[4] A particularly extreme example of this ideological and racist imperialism appears in a travel book about Morocco published in London in 1894, priced at a level which would accommodate the middle-class reader and titled *Among the Moors: Sketches of Oriental Life*:

> The Maghreb ... is the crucible in which have been cast the bestiality of the negro, the ferocity of the Arab, the cunning of the Moor, the violence of the Berber, the knavery of the Jew and the baseness of a handful of renegades, the scum of Europe giving as a result a Moroccan, a compound of all these vices.[5]

So even where politicians had their doubts about this or that particular colonial acquisition, they now found it difficult to ignore the jingoism and racism which was spreading throughout the major European states and in many cases bringing them into conflict with one another as they all struggled for a place in the sun. To Britain's prime minister, Lord Salisbury, a very cautious and selective imperialist, it was like 'having a huge lunatic asylum at one's back'.[6]

By the end of the nineteenth century, the Ottoman Empire had largely survived the late imperialist onslaught. It still had a functioning state machinery and a reformed and powerful army. Not so Morocco: in spite of the efforts of Britain's local agents to sustain the decrepit sultanate, other powers had begun to encroach upon Morocco's isolated and long-decaying Islamic world, to the horror and disgust of its fiercely independent and deeply religious people.

John Drummond Hay, Britain's consul-general at Tangier since 1845, had been promoted to Minister Resident in 1860 and latterly Envoy Extraordinary at the Court of Morocco; on 1 July 1886 he finally retired after forty years' service. During his remarkable period of service for the British government he had steadfastly followed in the footsteps of his father, Edward, the former consul-general. Like his father, he had pursued the policy objectives towards Morocco which had originally been laid down by Palmerston: protect the integrity of the 'Empire' of Morocco; dissuade each sultan from engaging in any provocative acts against European powers which might give them pretexts for invasion or territorial seizure; promote the interests of British trade; and – as far as possible – encourage the sultan to introduce reforms in government administration and criminal justice. In all but the last of these Drummond Hay had largely succeeded.

But there was one further objective in which Hay acknowledged he had failed. This was the reform and regulation of the protégé system, whereby Moroccan citizens could be 'adopted' by a European country's diplomatic representatives and enjoy all the privileges of the protection provided by treaty to the Europeans themselves. These included freedom from taxation and access to exclusively European justice. The system paralleled that of the Ottoman capitulations, but in Morocco all the abuses which 'protection' had encouraged in Ottoman lands had become magnified. The passage of the years had seen an enormous increase in the number of Moroccans who were 'protected persons'. For example, after Morocco lost the war with Spain of 1859–60, the number of Spanish protégés increased from ninety in

1859 to over 1,000 in 1861;[7] and Spain was by no means the worst culprit in this respect.

Sultan Hasan I, who had acceded to the throne in 1873, considered the protégé system abhorrent and insulting: it denied his treasury much-needed tax revenue and it progressively impinged upon the sovereignty of his state. Drummond Hay fully agreed. In his opinion the system was now completely out of hand, exacerbated by the open buying and selling of 'protection' by local European (and American) consular officials.

With Britain's support Sultan Hasan therefore organised a conference in Madrid in 1880 to try to get the European states with 'protected persons' to abolish the system. It was attended by the envoys extraordinary and ministers plenipotentiary of the US, Germany, Austria-Hungary, Belgium, Spain, France, the United Kingdom, Italy, Morocco, the Netherlands, Portugal and Sweden.

The conference was a failure. Its only positive outcome was to require protected persons to pay taxes under a uniform scheme Hasan had promulgated in order to raise money for the new, 'European' army which he was belatedly trying to build. On the other hand, the conference restated the much-abused extension of protection to Moroccan 'brokers' employed by Europeans to manage their export and import trades, which had been agreed in 1863. Even worse, the conference extended protégé status to 'cases ... in which it may be desired to reward signal services rendered by a native of Morocco to a foreign power, or for other exceptional reasons', thereby opening the door to further unlimited 'protection'.* The failure of the conference was largely due to the French, backed by Bismarck's Germany, whose then-friendly relations with France were intended to direct its old enemy away from thoughts of recovering Alsace and Loraine.

In January 1882 France appointed a new consul-general at Tangier. His name was Ladislas-Symphorien-Joseph Ordega, and although of Polish origin he was determined to show himself more French than the French. He had no knowledge of Morocco, its people or its language; but as soon as he arrived the forty-year-old Ordega began to throw his weight about through

---

*   See the copy of the 1880 Convention, in US Department of State Bulletin, Right of Protection in Morocco; extraterritorial jurisdiction in Morocco relinquished by the United States, October 6 1956.

condescending behaviour when presenting his credentials to the Moroccan court. He seized every opportunity to bully and insult local Moorish officials. It was his absolute determination, he claimed, 'to re-establish in Morocco, respect for the name French'.[8] With this objective in mind, he began to inform the French government that the quietly cautious and diplomatic Drummond Hay was a monster of perfidy, craftily preparing a British take-over of Morocco. More than that, and without informing his superiors, he himself began to do exactly the same thing. This was despite Jules Ferry – the French prime (and foreign) minister since November 1883 and himself an ardent colonialist – having explicitly told Ordega that he should for the time being adhere strictly to a policy of maintaining Moroccan independence.

The particular tool Ordega planned to use for his scheme was the revered holy man Hajj 'Abd al-Salim, the grand sharif of Wazan and head of the Tayibiyya Sufi *tariqa*. Although worshipped by his numerous followers in northern Morocco, the Sharif was not actually very 'holy'. He had travelled in Europe and had developed a particular interest in modern guns, European women and alcohol. His regular consumption of champagne was explained to his devout disciples as permissible, since once it had entered his holy mouth it immediately turned to milk.[9]

One important consequence of the Sharif's self-indulgent and spendthrift behaviour was that the Sufi Tayibiyya fraternity of which he was the head had become bankrupt. The Sharif was therefore highly amenable to any scheme which would replenish his own – and the Tayibiyyas' – financial resources.

Ordega's first move in his plan to overthrow the reigning Sultan Hasan I was to propose the Sharif as a 'protected person'. Knowing little of the individual in question, on 16 January 1884 the French Foreign Office acceded to Ordega's request.[10] Two months later the Sharif began his rebellion against Sultan Hasan and soon gathered around him a number of tribes claiming the right to collective 'protection'. On 29 April, Ordega returned to France from where he gave every impression that his country was ready to launch an invasion and overthrow the sultan. Hasan responded by gathering together what he could of his loyal *makhzan* troops and appealing to the other European powers for military and financial assistance.

Their response was far from what he had expected. Although Drummond Hay wrote to Lord Granville, Britain's foreign minister, stressing the seriousness of the crisis, Granville showed little interest. This was probably because he was still attempting (unsuccessfully) to soothe France's ill feelings over the outcome of Britain's occupation of Egypt, which had largely eliminated France's political stake in that country. In fact only Spain and Italy indicated a willingness to confront France.

In the event, it was France itself which calmed the crisis. Ferry had no wish to rush into a 'forward' policy on Morocco. The French foreign minister preferred a more gradual, piecemeal and primarily diplomatic strategy in pursuit of dominating Morocco. Moreover, Ferry had now come to realise that Ordega had been systematically ignoring the Ministry's instructions ever since he had arrived in Morocco, and was also lining his own pockets. So, in December Ordega found himself 'promoted' to a new diplomatic post – Bucharest, to where he departed in February 1885, a posting which didn't last long once the Ministry discovered the full extent of Ordega's financial misdeeds in Morocco.

Meanwhile Sultan Hasan began punitive measures against the rebel tribes involved in the Sharif's rebellion, which subsequently fizzled out. For his part the Sharif of Wazan remained safely ensconced in his hilltop Tayibiyya stronghold, where he continued to present a threat to Hasan's sultanate. So, in this less than satisfactory manner, the first of what would be a series of international crises over Morocco came to an end.

Nevertheless, the crisis had resurrected the long-running dispute about the uncontrolled growth in the number of 'protected persons' in Morocco. It was Spain which now intervened in an attempt to reform the system. The Spanish foreign minister, Segismundo Moret, had become convinced that, if unchecked, France would continue to use the 'protected persons' tactic as a political weapon to seize the whole of Morocco for itself. Consequently, his representative in Morocco was sent to the sultan's court where he persuaded Hasan to request a recall of the 1880 conference, to be held in Madrid.[11]

At first none of the powers showed much interest. Britain, for example, thought another conference worthwhile only if it included outstanding commercial issues. However, when it became known that French forces in southern Algeria were nibbling away at large areas of the huge Saharan region over which Morocco claimed sovereignty, Lord Salisbury began to see another international conference as a forum for reaffirming the Powers' commitment to Morocco's territorial integrity. And when the sultan himself proposed that the conference members would be asked to respect his government's declaration of Morocco's 'neutrality', Salisbury adopted the idea himself and confirmed Britain's attendance at Madrid, provided the conference 'must be with a wide reference'.[12]

On 1 December 1887 the Spanish Cortes announced that a second Madrid conference would soon take place to discuss the wishes of the sultan of Morocco on the subject of 'protection'. But in the fear that the international conference would become a forum with a far wider remit, possibly including France's wider objectives in Morocco, in January 1888 France insisted that it would attend only if the agenda were strictly limited to 'protection'. The French also insisted that there should be a preliminary 'entente' agreed between France and Spain to satisfy Spain that, in any future carve-up of Morocco, it would get an appropriate share. This signalled the end of any prospect of another conference involving all the European powers. Consequently, in October 1888, Sultan Hasan, 'convinced that God had not wished it', felt obliged to withdraw his request for a second conference.[13]

Meanwhile, the colonialist lobby in France was beginning to gain considerable ground. Initially the lobby was far from monolithic and had no formal structure. Its most vocal leader was Eugène Etienne, born in Algeria and a deputy for the province of Oran in the French Chamber of Deputies. He would eventually become the Chamber's long-serving vice president. His general philosophy was that 'Every colonial enterprise is a business' and one which 'must be prudently and practically conducted'.[14] In 1890 the Comité de l'Afrique Française was founded; the following year it had 942 members, including substantial backing from the Rothschild group in the person of Baron Alphonse de Rothschild.[15] At first its activities spanned French colonial operations worldwide, especially in Asia and Africa; but in February 1904 it spawned a 'subsidiary', the Comité du Maroc, and from then on it was the Moroccan question that dominated the interests of the French colonialists.[16]

The years between 1890 and 1910 are of particular interest. This was a period when Britain, France, Spain (and later Germany) were jockeying for influence in Morocco. It was also a time when, for the first time, large numbers of European journalists -- mainly British -- descended on the still-independent country. Its proximity to Europe and the relative ease of travelling there made it a magnet for both official correspondents and a host of occasional contributors to popular magazines and journals, as well as independent travellers, writers and illustrators. Many of these journalists and travel writers pandered to the growing racism of the era: 'degenerate race' was a not untypical description of the 'Moors' common in this sort of reportage; and European colonisation was widely seen as the only way to redeem them. But there was one, with deeper roots in Morocco, whose writing showed a clear sympathy for its people, while despairing of its sultanic government.

His name was Walter Burton Harris, the second son of a prosperous English shipping and insurance broker. In 1877, at the age of nineteen, he accompanied a British diplomatic mission to Morocco and, enraptured by the country, he soon settled in Tangier where he built a fine villa. He continued to live there for most of his life.

Openly homosexual, with a preference for very young men, he found the social milieu of Tangier eminently suitable for his particular proclivities. It was perhaps through his many 'friendships' with Arab boys that he soon became fluent in speaking and understanding *darija*, the colloquial Arabic of Morocco (although it appears that he never learnt to read or write standard Arabic). Although a man of independent means, he became the special correspondent of *The Times*, as well as unpaid informant to the Foreign Office. And with his knowledge of spoken Moroccan Arabic, and his ability to disguise himself convincingly as a poor Arab traveller, he was able to penetrate the interior of Morocco, make friends and allies with local dignitaries, and become a confidant of three successive sultans.

In 1921, after retiring from his work in Morocco, he wrote an account of his life and adventures titled *Morocco that Was*.[17] Although doubts have been raised about the veracity of some of the book's anecdotes (in which Harris himself usually features), James Chandler, who wrote an afterword to the modern edition of the book, concludes that 'there were careful men [e.g. the Moroccan court physician, Dr Verdon] who maintained that everything he wrote about ... was based on fact'.[18] So, it is partly through the eyes of Walter Harris that we witness the decline of Morocco into debt, dismemberment and foreign domination in the final years of the nineteenth century.

Harris's account begins with his invitation from Sir William Kirby Green (Drummond Hay's successor) to accompany him in presenting his credentials to Mulay Hasan (Sultan Hasan I) who was then at Marrakesh and at the 'zenith of his power'. Harris then describes Sultan Hasan's last great *harka* (revenue-collecting campaign), made in 1893. On its departure from the capital, Fez, it would take the sultan hundreds of miles to the south, across the High Atlas to arrive at the great Saharan oasis of Tafilalt, from where the sultan's dynasty had originally sprung. Its purpose was primarily tax collection, but it also served the purpose of 'showing the flag', demonstrating that the country Sultan Hasan traversed was unquestionably part of the *bled al-makhzan*. His tour also gave his subjects – most of whom would never have seen him before – a glimpse of his magnificence and his sharifian sanctity. Moreover, this expedition of Sultan Hasan was exceptional both in the distance it was intended to cover – a round trip of over 1,000 miles – and in the size of its retinue.

Accompanying the sultan as his 'military advisor' was a curious, tubby little individual known as Kaid Maclean.* His real name was Sir Harry Maclean and he had once been a British officer of the Gibraltar garrison. He had been seconded to the sultan's court as an artillery instructor and, having won the sultan's affection, he was appointed to supreme command of his army. As an artilleryman he had charge of an ageing 77-mm bronze Krupp artillery piece which the sultan had insisted be dragged along on his arduous journey to impress any recalcitrant non-tax-payers. Kaid Maclean habitually wore a white turban, highly polished British hunting boots, and a traditional hooded Berber burnoose made of his clan tartan.[19] Unfortunately his ability to reform, command and control the Moroccan army appears to have been negligible.

By the time Sultan Hasan left Tafilalt on his return journey he was already a dying man, and he never reached Marrakesh. To re-cross the High Atlas with the tattered remnants of his expedition, he chose the pass of Tizi-n-Telouet, where he and his men were rescued from their frozen and starving predicament by the leader of the Berber Glaoua tribe, Madani al-Glaoui. In Madani's mountain fortress, Hasan and his men were lavishly

---

*   The title Kaid is the usual English transliteration of the Moroccan colloquial *qaid* (Ar. *qa'id*) meaning 'leader'.

fed and provided with warm clothing. On their departure, Sultan Hasan promoted Madani to the position of *khalifa*, governor of the vast stretch of territory from the southern Atlas to the Sahara. Hasan also left Madani the old Krupp artillery piece and a considerable number of modern rifles.[20] This was the Glaoua tribe's first step on a road to power, one which would eventually see Madani and his brother T'hami become de facto rulers of Morocco under the French 'protectorate'.

Hasan died in June 1894. His chamberlain, Bu Ahmed – the ruthless and cruel son of a slave, who had risen to this position of great influence – engineered the accession to the Sultanate of Hasan's second son, the thirteen-year-old 'Abd al-Aziz. Bu Ahmed cast himself as regent, thereby preventing the accession of 'Abd al-Aziz's older brother, Mulay Hafid. The son of a slave now became Morocco's ruler, holding the country together and brutally crushing a number of tribal rebellions until his death in 1900. At that point the twenty-year-old 'Abd al-Aziz took up the reins of power – such as they were.

In the summer of the following year Walter Harris had his first private audience with 'Abd al-Aziz, and found the young man to be 'courteous, pleasant and intelligent'. Thereafter Harris became the sultan's unofficial advisor; and in his numerous contributions to *The Times*, he continuously advocated what was still Britain's official policy of protecting the independence and territorial integrity of Morocco.

However, 'by the end of 1902', writes Harris, 'Moulay 'Abd al-Aziz had returned to Fez [the capital], desirous of introducing reforms and recklessly extravagant'.[21] The sultan was fascinated by what the British press enthusiastically described as 'evidences of Christian civilisation' at his court.

'Of what did these "evidences of Christian civilisation" consist?' Harris asks:

> Grand pianos and kitchen ranges; automobiles and immense cases of corsets; wild animals in cages, and boxes of strange theatrical uniforms; barrel organs and handsome cabs; a passenger lift capable of rising to dizzy altitudes destined for a one-storeyed palace; false hair... [22]

And the crazy list goes on, culminating in a gorgeous state coach which was
left parked in the sultan's boggy menagerie, where it became an object of
great interest to its curious occupants, including – according to Harris – an
emu, a wapiti (with the mange) some zebras, Hindu cattle, apes, gazelles
and llamas.

By 1903 the young sultan's fascination with imported European consumer
goods, his extravagance and his well-known association with foreigners (of
which Harris, it must be acknowledged, was one) made him vulnerable
to attacks that he was 'abandoning Islam', 'a friend of the Christians', etc.
According to Harris, 'The Court had lost its prestige. The sultan was openly
scoffed at and despised and anarchy reigned on every side.'[23]

The feelings of one educated Moroccan can be gleaned from the record of
a lengthy discussion between 'a grave and personable Moor of middle age' and
the Jewish journalist and author Samuel Levy Bensusan, in 1904.[24] The elderly
Moroccan is simply referred to as 'the Hajj', reflecting a previous pilgrimage to
Mecca, but he apparently had some function at the sultan's court.

The Hajj begins by reminiscing over the times of Sultan Muhammad IV
(r. 1859–73) when he received as 'bashador' (ambassador) John Drummond
Hay, to whom the sultan had 'opened his heart' in thanks for Britain's
diplomatic support of Morocco at the end of the Spanish-Moroccan war
of 1859–60.

> A strong man was our master the sultan and he listened
> carefully to all your Bashador said, but still, knowing in his
> heart that this country is not as the land of the Nazarenes
> [Christians] and could not be made like it in haste.

But, as the Hajj perceptively observed of the reigning sultan:

> 'My lord ['Abd al-Aziz] sought to change that which had gone
> before, to make a new land ... and the land grew confused. It
> was no more the Maghreb but it assuredly was not as the lands
> of the west.'[25]

The Hajj's lament continues with a litany of how the country was being
milked by exploitative loans and the depredations of hordes of crooked

The Sultan of Morocco 'Abd al-Aziz in European clothes

European salesmen, 'entrepreneurs' with expensive projects of dubious value, and even European governments. (The Italians, for instance, had persuaded the sultan to order a modern cruiser from them when he had no sailors or naval officers.) The Hajj's testimony epitomises the tragic perception of a world which had belatedly realised that its culture, its values and its traditions (no matter how abhorrent to the Christian world) were gradually coming to an end.

By 1898, in the southeast of Morocco's far Sahara, French troops were beginning the penetration of the country's interior. The following year they occupied the key oasis of Tuat and began further incursions into Morocco territory. Meanwhile, in the northern Rif, a Moroccan fraudster named Jilali bin Idris al-Zarhuni, better known as Bu Himara, declared himself to be Mulay Muhammad, first-born son of the late Sultan Hasan and the rightful ruler of the country. Bu Himara succeeded in recruiting an army of tribesmen, announcing his intention to overthrow the 'Christian' 'Abd al-Aziz. When the sultan sent an army commanded by his teenage brother to attack the pretender's forces at Taza, it was soundly beaten. Elsewhere, the sultan's 'European' troops, in their scarlet 'zouave' jackets and blue trousers, were more engaged in plundering their countrymen than fighting a tribal rebellion.[26] And in the northwestern Rif, Ahmad al-Raysuli, a sharif of the Bani 'Arus tribe, who had begun his career as a cattle-rustler and bandit,[27] also began a rebellion. He defeated soldiers of the Makhzan and in due course was named 'governor' of the region by the pretender, Bu Himara.

In September 1902, Kaid Maclean arrived in Britain (presumably having doffed his clan tartan burnouse) and requested a loan of £300,000 and official British protection for Morocco, in return for further reforms and large railway concessions. A shrewd bargainer with only limited patriotism, he threatened to offer railway concessions to the Germans if Britain did not respond. The request for protection was rejected by the foreign secretary, Lord Lansdowne, although a government loan was forthcoming. So was another loan later obtained from a consortium of French banks: its nominal value was 62.5 million francs, yet this was reduced to 50 million after the usual deductions for 'commissions' and 'services'.[28] An independent Morocco was now coming towards the end of what Walter Harris aptly called 'the Road to Ruin'.

PART FOUR
C. 1895 - C. 1918

The main theme in the history of international relations in this period is the clash of imperialisms.

WILLIAM L. LANGER
(1951)

CHAPTER 24

Imperialist Realignments, Colonialist Deals, New Imperialists

Throughout most of the nineteenth century imperialist rivalry in the Mediterranean had taken the form of a three-sided contest between Britain, France and Russia. The new state of unified Italy made a brief appearance in its struggle over Tunisia, but was outmanoeuvred by France, leaving the kingdom in a smouldering but otherwise impotent state of antagonism against its European neighbour. In the 1880s Italy had yet to overcome its economic and military weakness before it could evolve into a state powerful enough to constitute a fully fledged imperialist power.

However, between 1894 and 1907 that three-sided equilibrium of power in the Mediterranean was shattered by a series of diplomatic realignments and colonialist deals. This dramatic diplomatic upheaval reflected the uneven development of capitalism occurring in Europe, with the emergence of three newly industrialised states seeking to expand their territorial influence either by formal or informal methods. Moreover, it was a time 'when it was taken for granted that the world was marked out by Providence for exploitation by the European white man'; a time when there existed 'nothing but a few virile nations and a large number of dying nations [and] the problem of international relations was who should cut up the victims.'[1] By 1890 it was clear which were the choicest remaining 'dying nations' – Morocco and what was left of the Ottoman Empire, including its sole remaining North African possession, Libya.

But before we examine this dramatic realignment of colonial ambitions in the Mediterranean, we must briefly turn our attention to the Concert of Europe and the network of treaties and *ententes* which had emerged before the critical year of 1890. We also need to understand why 1890 was 'the great dividing line in the history of diplomacy during the years that separated the Franco-Prussian War [1870–71] from the great conflict of 1914.'[2]

In the 1880s three secret agreements had been made between the great powers; all three were orchestrated by that towering political figure, the German chancellor Count Otto Von Bismarck: the Triple Alliance (Germany, Austria-Hungary and Italy, 1882), the Mutual Reinsurance Treaty (Germany and Russia, 1887),* and the Mediterranean Agreements (Britain, Italy, Austria-Hungary and Spain, 1887). These overlapping treaties meant that five of the European powers had some kind of treaty obligations towards each other and, for a time, created a degree of stability within the European power system. The one exception was France, which remained permanently hostile to Germany after its seizure of Alsace-Lorraine. Bitterly opposed to Britain as a result of its permanent occupation of Egypt, it was also mired in a trade war with Italy following its occupation of Tunisia.

The semblance of stability which the three secret treaties established was shattered in 1890 when the young German Emperor, Kaiser Wilhelm II (r. 1888–1918) dismissed Bismarck and, under the influence of his new chancellor, General Leo von Caprivi, recklessly rejected Russia's request to renew the Mutual Reinsurance Treaty between the two nations. This left Russia facing an antagonistic Austria-Hungary in the Balkans; a 'cold war' with Britain in Central Asia† (as well as the latter's threat to Russia's expansionary aims at Istanbul and the Turkish Straits); and, now, a potential German enemy.

In the circumstances it now faced, Russia had only one possible country to turn to for an ally – the French Republic. But the reigning Tsar, Alexander III, hesitated. At the bottom of his heart he found an alliance with an 'atheistic, radical republic' repulsive. However, a rapid sequence of events spurred both powers towards an unprecedented and unlikely alliance.

In early 1890 Britain and Germany signed a treaty whereby the tiny, British-occupied island of Heligoland in the North Sea was exchanged for certain German possessions in East Africa and the agreement that Britain should occupy Zanzibar as a protectorate. This decision was viewed by both France and Russia as signifying a growing *entente* between Britain and

---

* The Mutual Reinsurance Treaty (Germany and Russia, 1887) provided that each party would remain neutral if the other became involved in a war with a third great power, but that this would not apply if Germany attacked France or if Russia attacked Austria.

† The 'Great Game' along the frontiers of Britain's Indian Empire: in Afghanistan, Persia and Tibet.

Germany – as indeed it was. Then, on 17 May 1891, Italy, Austria-Hungary and Germany renewed the Triple Alliance. It now became public knowledge that Britain had treaty obligations to Italy as a result of one of the 1887 Mediterranean Agreements; this fired wild speculation in the European press that Britain might soon become a full member of the Triple Alliance. The final dose of fuel thrown on the smouldering embers of Franco-Russian anxiety was the visit of Kaiser Wilhelm to London on 4 July 1891, where 'the reception accorded him was almost unparalleled in its enthusiasm, cordiality and heartiness'. During his stay the German Emperor announced his 'determination to preserve the historic friendship between the two nations'.[3]

In response to these developments, and to feel out the possible success of an approach to the Tsar for an *entente*, a French squadron visited the Russian naval stronghold of Kronstadt on 24 July. To the delight of the French, it was received by enthusiastic crowds of ordinary Russians. The Tsar was now persuaded by his foreign minister, Nicolay Giers, that an alliance with France was essential to the security of both nations, although the formalities could wait a little longer.

It was therefore a profound shock to the rest of the European powers – especially Britain – when a Russian squadron from the Baltic fleet entered the Mediterranean for the first time since 1770. On 13 October 1893 a squadron of five warships under the command of Admiral Theodor Avellan sailed into the French naval base of Toulon to a rapturous applause from its citizens. There were wild celebrations at this evidence of an end to the old rivalry and animosity between the French Republic and the Tsarist Empire. In fact, it had already been decided by both governments that this close relationship should be brought to its logical conclusion. On 4 January 1894 Russia and France agreed a formal alliance, and it was also decided that the Russian squadron should remain in the Mediterranean.[4]

The reaction of the British government to the Russian naval visit, and the realisation that there could now be a permanent Russian naval presence in the Mediterranean, was one of consternation. The Russians had long since abrogated the terms of the Treaty of Paris (1856) and built a powerful navy in the Black Sea, based at Sevastopol. Britain's total fleet was only slightly greater than the combined fleets of France and Russia, and the French Mediterranean fleet was slightly larger than the British squadron stationed there.[5] As viewed from London, the Russo-French alliance meant that the French had put their fleet at the disposal of the Russians. Nothing could stop their Black Sea Fleet passing through the Turkish Straits and joining the French Fleet. In the circumstances Britain would be forced to abandon the Mediterranean.[6]

The British reaction was to accept that a substantial increase in naval power was urgently required. When the cabinet of the Liberal Party government discussed the necessary financial appropriations, only Prime Minister Gladstone and the chancellor of the Exchequer opposed the demands of the naval authorities. And in March 1894 Gladstone resigned and was replaced by the imperialist Lord Rosebery, who was in full sympathy with the naval chiefs. An additional appropriation of £3 million was made, providing for the construction of seven new battleships, six cruisers and a number of smaller vessels.[7] The first great European naval race had begun: not with the Germans in mind, but with Britain against the French and Russians – and the likely zone of hostilities was the Mediterranean.

In spite of Britain's more friendly relationship with Germany and the Triple Alliance the government still kept its distance. And that distance was soon widened by a second major realignment of the great powers in 1897, one precipitated by the ill-considered action of the Polish-born Austro-Hungarian foreign minister, Count Agenor Goluchowski.

The Mediterranean Agreements of 1887 enshrined a number of separate elements, but all were based on the principle that the status quo in the Mediterranean must be preserved: this, in turn, meant the protection of the Ottoman Empire and its territorial integrity.

For Britain the Agreements were aimed at stopping Russia seizing Istanbul and the Straits, while for Austria-Hungary the overwhelming problem they faced during the last quarter of the nineteenth century was the threat of Russian predominance in the Balkans,[8] so they shared Britain's fear of another Russian swoop upon the Ottoman capital through the newly independent Balkan states. At the same time, the Agreements committed Britain to defending Italy against French aggression; and both countries were determined to halt France's advance along the North African shore, which was steadily encroaching on the *vilayet* of Tripoli (western Libya), a territory Italy believed was rightfully hers. Any such French acquisition would also threaten Britain's dominant position in Egypt.

However, in 1895 a crisis arose over the renewal of the Agreements planned for the following year. Returning to power as Conservative prime minister in June of that year, Lord Salisbury was anxious to reaffirm them. With the French now in alliance with the Russians the old equilibrium between the three imperialists had broken down. Moreover, Salisbury was keen to secure the support of the Triple Alliance because Britain was facing hostility from both Russia and France in many parts of the globe.[9] However, Article 7 of the second, Anglo-Austrian Agreement was ambiguous. The Austrians interpreted it as requiring Britain to send a fleet to the Dardanelles if Russia threated Istanbul and the Turkish Straits. The British did not see it that way. If the Agreements were to be renewed, as Salisbury desired, then Count Goluchowski was determined to get this firm commitment from Britain.

Unfortunately for Salisbury, by 1895 'Turkophobia' had now replaced 'Russophobia' as the dominant theme in the British popular press. This was the result of a series of dreadful pogroms by Turks and Kurds against the various Armenian communities scattered across Anatolia and even in Istanbul itself, massacres which Sultan Abdülhamid was doing nothing to halt. These appalling events had been triggered by a number of terrorist attacks by a tiny group of Armenian fanatics. Their cynical strategy was to force the hitherto passive Armenian population into a nationalist uprising by means of a predictable Turkish retaliation.[10] In the event, the retaliation knew no bounds, and the Armenians were too scattered throughout Anatolia to unite in any coordinated defence, let alone an uprising. As a not-untypical example of this 'revolutionary strategy', in mid-June 1896, the British vice-consul in the eastern city of Van reported that there were around forty Armenian terrorists operating in the city. They had recently killed a large number of innocent Kurds as a consequence of which there had been a retaliatory massacre of the local Armenian population.

The Armenian pogrom put Salisbury under intense pressure to do the impossible: reaffirm to the Austrians that he stood firmly by the basis of the Mediterranean Agreements; to maintain the status quo and protect the Ottoman Empire from an attack by Russia; while at the same time demonstrating to a violently anti-Turk British public opinion – egged-on by the opposition Liberal Party – that he was determined to do whatever was necessary to compel the sultan to implement major reforms to protect the lives and property of the Armenians.

It was against this background that Goluchowski demanded an amendment to Article 7 of the Agreements, which would ensure that Britain sent a fleet to the Turkish Straits to protect the territorial integrity of the Ottoman Empire. This was because there was now a strong possibility that the Russians would exploit the bloodshed and anarchy raging in Istanbul and Anatolia, land troops on the Bosphorus, and thereby dominate Istanbul. These fears were realistic because, in 1895, a part of the Russian establishment was already seriously considering such a coup, at the urgings of their ambassador to the Porte, Aleksandr Nelidov.[11]

On 20 October 1896 Salisbury did his best to square the circle of what had now become his own political dilemma, at home and abroad. He sent a circular to all the great powers calling for a meeting of their ambassadors to formulate a coordinated action plan: one which would compel the sultan to protect the Armenians while reiterating the commitment of the great powers to maintaining the territorial integrity of the Ottoman Empire. However, the circular also proposed that, should the sultan fail to fulfil his obligations, the powers would collectively intervene militarily – provided they were all agreed to this action. In reality the circular was well-meaning but futile. It was doomed if only one of the powers rejected this last step. Unsurprisingly, while the Russian government expressed its general sympathy with the aims of the circular, it declared that it could never countenance a military intervention – and France, Russia's new ally, followed suit.

Salisbury's efforts had failed and he explained to Goluchowski with absolute frankness that Parliament would never agree to Britain acting alone to protect the Ottoman Empire. Therefore he could not agree to any amendment to Article 7 of the Mediterranean Agreements which would require Britain to send its Mediterranean forces into the Dardanelles. Consequently, in the British government's official response to the request for a strengthening of Article 7, Salisbury expressed nothing more than a strong desire to preserve Britain's *entente* with Austria-Hungary. Goluchowski furiously refused to renew the Agreements. 'The thread that had bound Britain and Austria-Hungary had been irrevocably cut.'[12]

In the words of one British historian:

> Viewed against the wider problem of the regrouping of
> the powers from 1887 to 1914, the shift in Anglo-Austrian

relations which occurred in the years 1895 to 1897 is of great importance. It played a part in the momentous change in British foreign policy: the transfer of British support for the Triple Alliance to the Dual Alliance [France and Russia].[13]

The third major realignment among the European powers occurred three years later. In retaliation for France's occupation of Tunisia, in 1887 Francesco Crispi's government had launched a tariff war against the French. At the same time Crispi sought to recover Italy's prestige by acquiring a colonial presence in the Red Sea, with Italian troops occupying the area around present-day Asmara. The following year, two independent sultanates in present-day Somalia were persuaded to come under Italian protection, while Italy's expanding Red Sea territory was declared a colony with the name Eritrea.

The ruler of neighbouring Ethiopia, the Emperor Menelik, subsequently agreed to the Italians setting up a 'protectorate' over his country. But in January 1895 a misunderstanding over what that term meant led to an Italian attempt to coerce Ethiopia into submission. On 1 March 1896, an Italian army sent to accomplish this task was completely destroyed at the Battle of Adwa in which the would-be imperialists suffered around 5,000 dead and 2,000 prisoners. A devastated Crispi resigned eight days later. In October the Italians were forced to make peace, leaving them in possession of only their Eritrean and Somali territories.

Italy's new government was forced to return to domestic matters. The tariff war with France, which had lasted for nearly ten years, had been an economic disaster for Italy, costing the country 2,000 million lire in lost exports. Italy's foreign minister, Emilio Visconti Venosta, was determined to bring it to an end and, by chance, he had a willing French accomplice in the French ambassador to Rome, Pierre-Eugène-Camille Barrère. Barrère had his own objective: he wanted to wean Italy away from the Triple Alliance with Austria-Hungary, and especially from Germany. He saw a new commercial treaty with Italy as the first stage in that plan. Consequently in October 1898 the Franco-Italian tariff war came to an end.[14]

Barrère now moved to the next stage in his strategy. French troops were continuing to move across the Sahara and infiltrate the southernmost regions of both Tripoli and Cyrenaica, where serious fighting was already taking place between the French and the local Sanusi Arab tribesmen. Barrère saw an opportunity to further his planned rapprochement between his country and Italy. With the authorisation of the French foreign minister, Théophile Delcassé, in an exchange of notes between Barrère and Visconti Venosta a secret imperialist deal was done.

In an exchange of letters dated 14 and 16 December 1900, the French offered to put an end to their encroachment on the two Ottoman *vilayets* long coveted by Italy, in return for the latter's acceptance of French control of Morocco. The language of the exchange was guarded but implicit. Visconti replied that Italy 'recognised the right of France to extend her influence in Morocco, with the reservation that if such action modified the political or territorial integrity of the Cherifian Empire in Morocco, Italy was entitled to the development of her influence in Tripoli (a diplomatic euphemism for colonisation)'.[15] This secret agreement was later amplified in the bilateral declaration of 24 May 1902, in which both parties affirmed that each could 'develop its sphere of influence' in Morocco and Tripoli respectively, 'at the moment it judges opportune, without the action of one of them being necessarily subordinated to that of the other'.[16] Twenty years of antagonism over North African colonies had come to an end – at least, for the time being.

In fact, by now, France's 'development of its sphere of influence' in Morocco had rubbed up against the fact that Spain was beginning to develop its own 'sphere of interest' in the north. Spanish imperialist interest in the country was originally fostered by the formation of a number of intellectual and commercial societies which combined a proclaimed dedication to the 'scientific' investigation of Morocco's geography with clear colonialist objectives.[17] Foremost of these was the Sociedad Geográfica de Madrid established in 1876, which spawned the Asociación Española para la Exploración del Africa (1877), the Sociedad Española de Africanistas y Colonistas (1883), the Sociedad Española de Geografía Comercial (1885) and many others.[18] The loss of what remained of its old colonial empire – Cuba, Puerto Rico and the Philippines – in its 1898 war with the US provided a major impetus for Spain to seek new colonies elsewhere, and the proximity of Morocco made it the obvious choice.

France was increasing its presence in Morocco to facilitate its links between Algeria and the Atlantic and its sub-Saharan possessions. In

1902 it proposed a secret agreement with Spain to establish each country's territorial shares of influence. Discussions took place between the French foreign minister, Théophile Delcassé, and his Spanish counterpart the Duke of Almodóvar del Río. The area of 'influence' proposed for Spain was very large, about twice the size that was finally settled ten years later, comprising the two major cities of Fez and Taza. However, the agreement was never signed. This was a time when Britain still considered France to be its principal imperialist rival and even its potential enemy in a war which might also involve France's new ally, Russia.

Indeed, in the same year that the secret agreement was proposed, the British government led by Prime Minister Arthur Balfour and his foreign secretary, Lord Lansdowne, convened a meeting of the Committee for Imperial Defence (CID), to discuss the relative strength of Britain's two potential enemies. It was decided that France was the stronger but was also the most vulnerable. A pre-emptive attack could be made against France's widespread colonies, but the main blow would be in the Mediterranean, against France's naval base at Bizerte in Tunisia. The CID was of the opinion that seizing Bizerte would provoke a Muslim revolution throughout Tunisia and Algeria and force France to divert its forces to protect the *colons*. This would quickly put an end to the war.[19]

The Spanish government had been a signatory to the Mediterranean Agreements on preserving the status quo in the Mediterranean, and was keenly aware of Britain's current determination to maintain this principle regarding Morocco. Consequently it declined to make an agreement whose contents might have come to light, and would give the impression that Spain and France were now allies. In addition, Spain was still very wary of appearing to covet a territory whose proximity to Gibraltar made it of special concern to Britain. However, two years later these considerations would suddenly evaporate.

By now Britain's relationship with Germany was rapidly deteriorating, and in 1903 Joseph Chamberlain, the member of the Conservative government who had most favoured a continuation of the 'semi-entente' with Germany, resigned as head of the Colonial Office. Many in the government feared that Britain's isolation from all the European powers was unsustainable and its security required entry into a new alliance system. It so happened that in France the powerful colonialist faction in the Chamber of Deputies was beginning to favour a rapprochement with France's old imperialist rival in order to free its hands in Morocco.[20] The most forceful proponent of this radical change in France's foreign policy was Eugène Etienne.

In a carefully calculated move, Etienne wrote an article in the English *National Review* praising Britain's colonialist record and suggesting ways in which outstanding colonial disagreements could be settled. In June 1903 Delcassé, the French foreign minister, arranged for Etienne to go to London to confer with Lord Lansdowne. During their dinner on 2 July Lansdowne broached the subject of Morocco and, to the surprise and delight of Etienne, told him that 'it had been decided that France should have a free hand to settle the situation'.[21]

The way was now clear for a more formal military *entente*, which was signed between Delcassé and Lord Lansdowne in the Entente Cordiale of 8 April 1904. The core of the agreement lay in the Mediterranean. France agreed to relinquish her rights and interests in Egypt in return for Britain's acceptance of a future French take-over of most of Morocco. In the same agreement both countries acknowledged Spain's right to a zone of control in northern Morocco, facing the Straits of Gibraltar. Britain had no difficulties with this since Spain's military power – and hence any threat to Britain's Gibraltar base – had recently been destroyed by Spain's crushing defeat in its 1898 war with the US. Subsequently Spain and France signed an agreement confirming the former's control over a strip of territory in northern Morocco, albeit one much smaller than the one France had proposed in 1902.[22]

The final major realignment of the powers took place in 1907. Two years earlier, Russia had been decisively defeated in a disastrous war against Japan resulting from colonialist rivalry in the Far East. The war began in February 1904, and on 15 October a Russian fleet was sent on an 18,000-mile journey from the Baltic to help relieve the Japanese siege of Port Arthur in Manchuria. On 28 May 1905 it was totally destroyed by the Japanese navy at the Battle of Tsushima, and the following September Tsar Nicholas II, whose reign had begun in 1894, was forced to accept the ignominy of total defeat. Meanwhile, in January 1905 a major revolution by workers, peasants and mutinous soldiers and sailors broke out, lasting intermittently until it eventually collapsed in June 1907.

Taking advantage of this Russian catastrophe, in Britain the new Liberal Party government elected in 1906 decided that the time was ripe to put an end to the 'Great Game' in the borderlands between the Russian and Indian empires: in Persia, Afghanistan and Tibet. Of these the most important area of imperialist rivalry was Persia (Iran).

On 31 August, Britain and Russia agreed to divide Persia into three separate 'zones of influence'. The northern zone, containing the major cities of Tehran and Isfahan, was allocated to Russia, which was free to negotiate exclusive 'concessions' there with the weak and eminently bribable Shah Muzaffar al-Din. The southern region, with comparable rights and privileges for its concession-hunters, contained the 'Arabian Gulf' and Baluchistan, the province directly adjacent to Britain's Indian Empire.

A central 'neutral region' was left open to the acquisition of concessions by either party. This suited Britain, since in 1901 a small British company had signed a concession agreement with the nomadic Bakhtiari tribesmen giving it the right to drill for oil in a highly prospective region. A year later, on 25 May 1908, oil was discovered in huge quantities at Masjid i-Sulayman.

However, there was an unofficial codicil to the Anglo-Russian convention. Prior to its signing, Sir Edward Grey, the new British foreign minister, met with Count Alexander Benckendorff, the Russian ambassador to London, and informed him that Britain would 'not make difficulties in the future over their access to the Straits'.[23] 'Access to the Straits' inevitably meant not only access to the waterways between the Black Sea and the Mediterranean, but implicitly to the great city which overlooked and guarded them: Istanbul.

Precisely what was intended by Grey's comment is unclear, but it was an indication of Britain's waning economic interest in the Ottoman Empire. Britain remained the Empire's principal commercial partner, but her share of Ottoman imports (mainly textiles) had fallen from a high point of 45 per cent in 1880–82 to around 24 per cent. It was also becoming more difficult to coax British capital investment into the region. In fact the trend was towards disinvestment, with investors selling their holdings to French and German companies. As Grey himself observed in 1908, regarding British political influence, 'We shall make no progress till British capital of a high class takes energetic interest in Turkey.'[24]

Meanwhile, the precarious balance of imperialism in the Mediterranean between Britain, France and Russia – which had prevailed since 1815 – was thrown into further disarray by the accelerated industrialisation and economic growth of the three members of the Triple Alliance. This impressive economic achievement encouraged Italy, Austria-Hungary and Germany to play a more interventionist role in the affairs of the southern Balkans and the Eastern Mediterranean.

Between 1896 and 1908 the value of Italy's industrial production increased from 11.2 billion lira to 20.6 billion (in 1938 prices).[25] Underpinning this rapid economic development was the geography and geology of Italy's Alpine Valleys, which supported large-scale dams and hydroelectric plants. In 1898 Italy already had 50,000 kw of hydroelectric capacity. By 1911 that figure had increased tenfold.[26]

Austria-Hungary also experienced a belated industrial revolution. Between 1870 and 1913 its gross domestic product per capita grew roughly 1.76% per year, a rate of growth exceeding that of Britain (1.0%), France (1.06%) and even Germany (1.51%). It also created the fourth biggest machine-building industry in the world after the US, Germany and Britain, while its Mediterranean port, Trieste, became a major centre for steel-making and shipbuilding.

However, it was Germany that underwent the most intense industrial transformation in the late nineteenth century. Between 1880 and 1900 its output of coal increased by 153 per cent, its output of pig iron by 206 per cent, and its output of crude steel increased fivefold, reaching 6.461 million tonnes in 1900, greater than the UK's annual output of 4.980 million tonnes.[27] Meanwhile Germany's population grew from 45 to 56 million over the same period.

However, this great increase in industrial output and population in the Kaiser's Germany required a commensurate increase in raw materials and foodstuffs and necessitated the acquisition of additional sources of supply to supplement its indigenous production. Under Bismarck, Germany had largely turned its back on the sort of worldwide expansion pursued by Britain and France. The concentration was on building up its industrial might. By 1900 British colonial territory extended over 11.6 million square miles, France, 3.7 million, but Germany only a little over 1 million.*

* In 1884 Germany annexed Togo, Cameroon and South–West Africa (Namibia), and the

But from now on, Germany would have to become a global trading power like Britain. Lacking economically useful colonies, and still largely dependent on British shipping for the international transport of its imports, Germany began a major expansion of its merchant marine, providing shipping services all over the world, while its powerful banking industry provided trade-related insurance. And if Germany had a major merchant marine, it was logical that it should also have a major navy to protect it. This coincided with the views of Admiral Alfred von Tirpitz, who saw a much larger German battle fleet as a crucial diplomatic as well as trade-related asset. Consequently in 1898 and 1900 the German Reichstag was persuaded to make huge appropriations to create a 'Home Fleet', which by 1907 would expand to become the German High Seas Fleet.

This made rivalry between Britain and Germany inevitable. Over the period 1896–1900 the UK had a deficit of £160.6 million on its trade in goods. It achieved a surplus on its balance of payments only through a surplus of £100.7 million from 'services' (shipping charges, insurance, world-wide banking, etc.) and the remittance of dividends and interest from abroad worth £100.2 million.[28] Global dominance was therefore essential to Britain's economic survival. In the eyes of Britain's politicians, Germany's plans for global expansion threatened that survival.

Germany focused on extending its global influence over what remained of the non-European world. Only one area remained which offered the possibility of acquiring great resources of both industrial raw materials and foodstuffs, as well as markets for German manufactures – the 'Asian' provinces of the Ottoman Empire, Anatolia, Syria and, ultimately, Mesopotamia (Iraq). This meant that Germany would now become another major player in Mediterranean great power politics.

To fill such a role the Kaiser and his new advisors developed a plan for Germany and its Austro-Hungarian ally called 'Drang nach Osten' (Drive to the East). In the words of an American analyst writing in 1917:

> Nothing was more natural than the German and Austro-Hungarian conception of a *Drang nach Osten* through the

---

following year established a protectorate over Tanganyika (Tanzania), Burundi and Rwanda. These possessions were largely worthless from an economic point of view.

Balkan Peninsula, over the bridge of Constantinople, into the
markets of Asia. The geographical position of these Central
European states made as inevitable a penetration policy into the
Balkans and Turkey as the geographical position of England
made inevitable the development of an overseas empire.[29]

The first step was a massive programme of railway construction in the
Balkans, mostly paid for and executed by German or Austro-Hungarian
companies. By the 1890s this railway network was largely complete,
including a major branch line linking Vienna with the port of Salonika.

The next stage in the penetration of the Ottoman Empire's eastern
provinces was conceived on a grand scale. It was expected that the sultan's
Asian provinces should become a zone of strategic influence, as well
as offering great economic and commercial opportunities to German
business.[30] Encouraged by Marshal Freiherr von der Golz, who had been
training the Ottoman Army and equipping it with German-made arms
and equipment since 1883, the Kaiser planned a German-controlled Berlin
to Baghdad Railway, through Anatolia and Syria, and ultimately to the
Arabian Gulf. There it would break Britain's stranglehold of trade with those
great Asian markets. 'In the Near East the Baghdad Railway was the most
effective motive force and the most important instrument of imperialism ...
Its continuation on Asian soil became ... the idea of forming a large empire
between Berlin and Baghdad.'[31]

Railway construction certainly seemed the most effective method
of penetrating the Ottoman Empire's East Mediterranean and Arabian
territories. In 1916 Lenin made the following point about the huge extension
of railways during the preceding quarter of a century:

> The building of railways seems to be a simple, natural,
> democratic, cultural and civilising enterprise... But as a matter
> of fact the capitalist threads, which in thousands of different
> intercrossings bind these enterprises with private property in
> the means of production in general, have converted this work
> of construction into an instrument for oppressing a thousand
> million people (in the colonies and semi-colonies), that is,
> more than half the population of the globe.[32]

However, railway construction in Ottoman territory had a more nuanced aspect than Lenin allowed for. Although largely in the hands of European financiers and bondholders, the sultan and the Porte retained a good deal of political independence. They were determined to gain the 'civilising' benefits of railway construction without allowing any one European power to have control of the Empire's infrastructure.

Sultan Abdülhamid had no doubts about the economic advantages which would follow the extension of railways into his eastern provinces. In particular, the Kaiser's great railway project would encourage an increase in agricultural production, as Anatolian peasants – previously isolated from foreign trade – would gain new markets and their greater incomes would furnish the sultan with higher tax revenues. In addition, a railway linking Abdülhamid's eastern provinces to Istanbul would enable the rapid redeployment of his Arab divisions to the Balkans where the Empire faced a continuing Russian threat.

However, Abdülhamid could see the advantages of offering railway concessions to rival European states. French interests already controlled the 168-km Izmir-Cassaba line and concessions had been agreed for French companies to construct the important 420-km Damascus-Homs-Aleppo railway, the 247-km Beirut to Damascus railway and the 87-km Jaffa to Jerusalem railway. British companies owned the 270-km Izmir (Smyrna) to Aydin line and the short but valuable 67-km Mersin to Adana line in Cilicia. At the time German capitalists owned only the 91-km Haidar Pasha to Ismid line. However, in October 1888, a German syndicate controlled by the powerful Deutsche Bank took over the Haydar Pasha to Ismit line and was awarded a concession to extend it to Ankara. The company was called the Anatolian Railway Company and its formation marked the beginning of the 'Berlin to Baghdad' railway project.[33]

The following year the Kaiser made the first of two ceremonial visits to the sultan's court, at the end of which a trade convention was signed between Germany and the Ottoman Empire. Over the next seven years construction of the Anatolian Railway Company made excellent progress. Having reached Ankara in 1892, the company was awarded another concession to continue the line to Konya in southern Anatolia, which it reached in 1896, a distance of 1,020 kilometres from its original starting point. Suddenly, the region was of significant economic importance to Germany.

Two years later, the Kaiser made a second official visit to the Ottoman Empire. From now on, his ambitious scheme of *Drang nach Osten* was to be cloaked in propagandist declarations designed to align Germany with the anti-colonial aspirations of the world's Muslims. His plan was to generally ingratiate himself with the sultan and use this to ensure that German interests prevailed in the expected concession for the continuation of the railway through Syria and Iraq to the port of Basra, where the confluence of the rivers Tigris and Euphrates creates a ship-going outlet into the 'Persian' Gulf.

After the elaborate courtesies of his meeting with Sultan Abdülhamid, the Kaiser made a spectacular entry to Jerusalem where he prayed on his knees before the holy city. 'Then adroitly changing his ground and his costume he entered the Moslem city of Damascus, where, arrayed in a turban, he paid homage at Saladin's tomb.'[34] He then announced his declaration: the eternal protection of all 300 million of the sultan-caliph's Muslim subjects. Ludicrous though this may now sound, the declaration had a special resonance in the Mediterranean where most of its southern shore now lay under British and French colonial rule.

The outcome of the Kaiser's pro-Islamic posturing was the concession for the continuation of the railway to Basra, which was awarded to the Baghdad Railway Company in 1902. In its final version, agreed the following year, the company was to be German-Ottoman in its majority ownership; but investors were invited to participate from all European countries, including Britain. French investors joined the project, together with those from Austria-Hungary, Switzerland and Italy.* The concession was particularly generous to the company's shareholders since its profits were underwritten by the Ottoman state.[35] For each kilometre of line completed the company would receive Ottoman bonds to the value of 275,000 francs secured by a mortgage on the railway and its properties. In addition, the state guaranteed the company an operating profit of 4,500 francs annually for each kilometre of line open to traffic. If the profits fell

---

*   The ownership structure of the Baghdad Railway Company was finally settled as follows: the Ottoman government 10 per cent; the Deutsche Bank-controlled Anatolian Railway Company 10 per cent; and the remaining 80 per cent a syndicate led by the Deutsche Bank. Of the twenty-seven directors of the company, eight were German, and a further three Germans were from the Anatolian Railway Company. The remainder were four Ottoman, eight French, two Swiss, one Austrian and one Italian (Earle 1923, p. 93).

below this amount the state would make up the difference (although any surplus would return to the state).

In spite of these attractive terms for investors, Britain refused to participate in the German-dominated project. The concession was met by overwhelming hostility from the British press and a large number of its parliamentarians. It was recognised that if the railway reached the Arabian Gulf it would pose a serious threat to Britain's existing domination of trade in the region. Coming at a time when Germany was building up its High Seas Fleet, British hostility to the Berlin to Baghdad railway was especially fierce.

There was also growing British concern that German banking interests were now penetrating territory which had once been exclusively Britain's. By 1908 the German-owned Banque d'Orient, the Deutsche Orientbank, and the great Deutsche Bank itself had branches in all the main cities of the Ottoman Empire.[36] In 1910 Britain signalled its continuing antagonism towards the railway project by blocking an Ottoman loan to be raised in Britain, intended to support the continuation of the railway into northern Syria. It also opposed an increase of 4 per cent in Ottoman customs duties whose proceeds were also intended to support the railway's construction.[37]

However, much of the British opposition to the railway was overdone. The bondholders controlling the Ottoman Public Debt Administration (OPDA) broadly welcomed it, since it offered better tax receipts, and therefore more secure interest payments and higher bond prices. The French did not obstruct private investors taking a part of the company's equity. Indeed, the chairman of the OPDA was French and served on the railway's board of directors.[38]

Moreover, the Germans didn't overreach themselves. Their long-term objectives were almost certainly the creation of a German protectorate in Anatolia, Syria and Iraq, but for the time being they didn't behave as such. There was no attempt to convert Abdülhamid into a puppet, like the unfortunate Bey of Tunis. In fact, for the time being, the Germans regarded Abdülhamid's empire more as a potential military ally than a potential protectorate. For his part, Abdülhamid studiously avoided any impression that he was handing over the country to the Germans, and he continued to encourage rivalry by seeking French, and even British, investment in his East Mediterranean and Arabian territories.

So far, Germany's successful penetration of the Ottoman Empire was largely commercial. Figures for European investment in the Empire show that in 1888 only 1 per cent of the capital stock of direct investment in the Ottoman Empire was German; but by 1913 Germany had increased the value of its capital stock to 27.5 per cent. France's share had also increased, from 31.7 per cent to 50.3 per cent. But the most significant figure is that of Britain: in 1888 its share of direct investment was a massive 56.2 per cent, but by 1913 it had fallen to just 15.3 per cent.[39] Over the first decade of the twentieth century British economic involvement – and political influence – in the Ottoman Empire had virtually collapsed, while Germany's had shown a remarkable acceleration.

Meanwhile, Italy's economic regeneration and rapid industrialisation between the 1890s and early 1900s had given it the possibility to construct a powerful battle fleet with which to pursue its colonial objectives in the Mediterranean, particularly important since its secret agreement with France in 1900 had laid the foundations for an eventual take-over of Ottoman Libya. By 1904, with its main naval base at Venice, Italy had constructed the third largest fleet in the Mediterranean with a total tonnage of 153,412 and a broadside throw-weight of 44,092 lb.* This figure made it considerably more powerful than the French and not far short of the British.[40] In 1905 Italian naval spending continued, increasing from £5 million to £7.8 million in 1911, as newer, more modern battleships and heavy-armoured cruisers were built.

However, by the mid-1900s it was the Austro-Hungarian Empire that had become the most important new imperialist power in the Mediterranean region. We are not accustomed to thinking of Austria as a major Mediterranean power, but this is what occurred between the nineteenth and the first decade of the twentieth century, further disturbing the old power equilibrium of Britain, France and Russia.

Austria had been able to use its port of Trieste at the head of the Adriatic Sea since its opening in 1719 by the Habsburg Emperor Charles VI; but it was not until 1833 that the Austrians began to develop a serious interest in

---

* A fleet's broadside throw-weight is the total weight of shells which can be fired in one salvo by a battleship (or heavy cruiser), multiplied by the number of ships able to put to sea. However, it is only a crude measure of a fleet's capacity since it doesn't include any reference to such matters as accuracy, speed of repeat firing and ships' armour (defensive capacity).

the Mediterranean and Mediterranean trade. In 1836 the Austrian Lloyd shipping company was established and began the construction of six steam ships at Trieste. By the 1840s the Austrian Lloyd had become a significant shipper along the Levantine coast, and during the course of the nineteenth century Trieste became a major shipbuilding and nautical engineering centre. In 1904 31 per cent of Austria-Hungary's sea-borne trade was in the Mediterranean and, of this, 44 per cent was trade with the Ottoman Empire, Greece and Egypt.[41]

To protect this maritime trade and its control of the Istrian peninsula and the Dalmatian coast,* Austria-Hungary began to build a Mediterranean battle fleet. In a short war with Italy in 1866, Austria-Hungary had demonstrated the superiority of its naval engineering capacity when a smaller but more heavily armoured Austrian ironclad fleet defeated a larger Italian fleet at the Battle of Lissa. During the remainder of the nineteenth century the Austro-Hungarian navy was relegated to a mainly coastal protection role, but it also took an interest in the development of new naval weaponry. For example, it was at its naval base at Fiume (Rijeka) that it pioneered the use of torpedoes and the fast torpedo boat.

In 1904, Count Rudolf Montecuccoli became navy commander and for the next seven years brought about the largest modernisation and expansion of Austria's navy in its history.[42] According to one naval historian:

> A powerful Mediterranean-capable navy would influence the decisions of the Ottoman Empire, giving the Austrians more influence in the Sublime Porte. It could better protect the Austrian trade with the Levantine coastline, and support Austrian interests in the Ottoman Empire.[43]

These interests were focused on the port of Salonika. By the 1900s Vienna was connected directly with Salonika via a spur from the main Paris-Istanbul railway, and the Austrians were investing in new port facilities in the city. In January 1908 Austria announced plans for a railway through Macedonia

---

* Although Italy was allied to Austria-Hungary in the Triple Alliance, there were strong irredentist forces in Italy which would have liked to 'recover' the old Venetian territory on the eastern side of the Adriatic. Consequently, Austria-Hungary had always to bear in mind the possibility of an attack by Italy.

to link up with the Ottoman rail network. Germany had already suggested to the Austrians that, if the Russians moved to occupy the Turkish Straits, Austria-Hungary should seize Salonika. Such a scenario was by no means out of the question because the press and popular opinion in Russia were now strongly agitating for the occupation of the Straits and even Istanbul itself. Therefore, 'a powerful fleet would allow the Austrians to act against the Russian Black Sea Fleet ... Finally, should the worst happen and Ottoman power finally collapse, a strong fleet capable of offensive operations in the Mediterranean would let Austria stake their claim to a large piece of the pie and a strong position at the settlement conference.'[44]

In 1904 Austria-Hungary's 41,121 tonnes amounted to only 7.75 per cent of the total combined tonnage of the four Mediterranean battle fleets (Britain, France, Italy and Austria). In terms of broadside throw-weight (6,468 lb), its situation was even worse at 5 per cent of the total. However, over the next ten years Austria's navy underwent a massive expansion. By 1909 its tonnage had increased to 86,187 and its throw-weight to 14,312 lb.[45] This occurred against a background of growing rivalry and tension between Austria-Hungary and Russia and its small Balkan allies.

In the nineteenth century Austria-Hungary had refrained from the 'scramble' to obtain colonies outside its historic borders, burdened, as it was, by its own many and fractious nationalities. However, at the Congress of Berlin in 1878 Austria-Hungary was granted the 'administration' of Ottoman Bosnia-Herzegovina as well as the right to station troops in the adjoining *sancak* of Novi Pazar, although both remained under the suzerainty of the Ottoman Empire. Austria's main objective in Novi Pazar was to block any attempt by Serbia – whose complete independence from Ottoman rule had also been confirmed at the Berlin Congress – from seizing Bosnia-Herzegovina itself. However, the Bosnian Serbs never accepted the Austro-Hungarian military presence in those nominally Ottoman provinces. Their allegiance remained to the neighbouring Russian-backed Kingdom of Serbia and they continuously agitated for union with their fellow Serbs, fired by a common adherence to the Orthodox Church and the ideology of pan-Slavism.

By the 1900s, Bosnia-Herzegovina's status – still, nominally, a part of the Ottoman Empire, but in reality a responsibility of Vienna – was highly unsatisfactory for the Austrian government. Its geographical position formed a great wedge between Austria's largely Croatian population in the north and its possessions along the Adriatic coast. Moreover, a full annexation of Bosnia-Herzegovina would allow the Austrians to establish another Adriatic naval base further to the south by opening inland routes to support it,'[46] an increasingly important consideration as the expansion of the Austro-Hungarian navy gathered pace.

It only needed an international crisis to emerge for the Austrians to 'solve' the problem of Bosnia-Herzegovina by the complete annexation of the troublesome and expensive 'administered' province.

That moment was fast approaching. By the mid-1900s a group of younger Austrian officials and military men were demanding a more assertive foreign policy; foremost among them were the aristocratic and deeply conservative foreign minister, Baron Alois von Aehrenthal, and the army's belligerent chief of staff, Conrad von Hötzendorf. The Austro-Hungarian government was now deeply concerned about developments on its southern doorstep in the Balkans. It continued to fear that a Russian-backed Serbia might seize Bosnia-Herzegovina and threaten Austria-Hungary's Adriatic possessions along the Dalmatian coast.[47] The Austrians' worst nightmare was a Russian occupation of Istanbul.

CHAPTER 25

Imperialism on the Northern Shore:
Austria-Hungary and Bosnia-Herzegovina

In the aftermath of Russia's catastrophic defeat by Japan in 1905 and the on-going workers' and peasants' uprising, Tsar Nicholas II was forced to introduce some measures of liberalisation to his autocratic rule. In April 1906 a quasi-representative parliament, the State Duma, was established along with a multi-party system and some limited press freedoms. It was in this spirit of limited reform that Alexander Izvolsky was appointed Foreign Minister in May 1906.

Izvolsky was a career diplomat who had married into a family of wealthy nobility. After the disasters of 1904–06 he was determined to give Russia a decade of peace. In Russian terms he was a 'liberal' and he believed that it was in Russia's interest to disengage from the conundrum of European politics and to concentrate on internal reforms. But he was also regarded as snobbish, self-centred and over-concerned about his public image, and he was carelessly dismissive of the 'pan-Slav' sentiments of many of his countrymen.

However, in line with overwhelmingly predominant Russian thinking, Izvolsky wanted to remove the Ottoman stranglehold over the only exit from the Black Sea and its warm-water ports into the Mediterranean. He was also determined to achieve a revision of the old Straits Convention of 1841, confirmed again in 1878 at the Treaty of Berlin, which prevented Russian warships passing through the Turkish Straits when the Ottoman Empire was at peace.

But at the same time he wanted to avoid any conflict with Austria-Hungary at a time when he believed that the status quo in the Ottoman Empire, and in particular its remaining Balkan dependencies, was unlikely to persist. He was also fully aware of Austria-Hungary's desire to convert its highly unsatisfactory situation 'administering' Bosnia-Herzegovina into an internationally recognised annexation; and with these considerations in mind, in September 1907 he paid a visit to Vienna where he met with Austria's foreign minister, Baron Alois Aehrenthal.

Aehrenthal was of a very different character to Izvolsky. He was an arch-conservative, very dismissive of 'liberal' opinion and determined to pursue his vision of Austria-Hungary dominating the Balkans. In particular he saw Serbia and the restive Serbs in Bosnia-Herzegovina as a major blockage to achieving that objective. In 1895 he had been consulted by Count Agenor Goluchowski about how to deal with Salisbury's initial request to renew the Mediterranean Agreements. Aehrenthal had sent Goluchowski a radically brutal memorandum in which he proposed abandoning the Anglo-Austrian *entente* and allowing the Russians to seize Istanbul, in return for which Austria-Hungary would simply annex the independent state of Serbia. Goluchowski had rejected it out of hand. But this was the kind of man Izvolsky was now dealing with.

At the meeting of the two foreign ministers Izvolsky was very open with Aehrenthal – perhaps too open – about Russia's great hopes to see a revision of the international law which restricted Russia's naval access to the Straits. Aehrenthal took note; and afterwards he immediately informed his German counterpart. Meanwhile, he had already decided that Austria-Hungary should proceed with the annexation of Bosnia-Herzegovina as soon as possible. This would greatly facilitate his other Balkan ambitions.

In February 1908, without forewarning Izvolsky, Aehrenthal announced to the assembled parliamentary delegates from Austria and Hungary that Austria-Hungary should build a new railway. Running southwards through the *sancak* of Novi Pazar, it would enter Macedonia and link up with the Ottoman railway system running down to the Aegean or Istanbul. The project, according to one historian, 'was part of an imperialistic policy of economic penetration of the Balkan Peninsular to secure a predominant position'.[1] It would attach the Balkan states to the Habsburg monarchy 'as a market for Austro-Hungarian industrial goods and as a source of raw materials'. And the railway was also conceived, more generally, as part of 'an independent and expansive program of imperialism which placed the acquisition by Austria-Hungary of concrete military, political and economic advantages above all other considerations'.[2] Aehrenthal reckoned that, after the Russian defeat in its war with Japan and the revolution which had accompanied it, there was little chance of any serious Russian reaction to his objectives – and he was correct.

Conscious of Russia's current weakness, Izvolsky believed that peace with Austria-Hungary was essential in order for Russia to recover from its recent disasters. So, on 2 July 1908 Izvolsky sent a memo to Aehrenthal offering a deal which he believed would meet the needs of both the Austro-Hungarian and Russian empires. He proposed an agreement whereby Russia would support Austria-Hungary's annexation of Bosnia-Herzegovina in return for which Austria-Hungary would support Russia's right to move its warships through the Turkish Straits.[3]

Three weeks later there came the strongest possible confirmation of Izvolsky's expectation that the status quo in the Balkans was doomed – a truly dramatic and unexpected turn of events. For a number of years a group of opponents to Abdülhamid's autocratic rule, banded together under the name 'Young Turks', had been planning revolution. Most influential among them were members of a secret political party, the Committee of Union and Progress (CUP). In June 1908 it became known that King Edward VII and the Tsar had met at Reval (Tallinn, in Estonia) and had discussed plans for a European intervention in Ottoman Macedonia, ostensibly to protect its Christian inhabitants from Muslim attacks.

In fact it wasn't just 'Christians' who were suffering in Macedonia. This huge Ottoman province consisting of the three *vilayet*s, Kosovo, Monastir and Salonika, was being torn apart by a brutal struggle between Muslim peasants and Bulgarian and Greek *komitadji*s (irregulars). The latter two parties were killing each other's peasants as well as Muslims in an attempt to incorporate Macedonia into their own kingdoms.[4] In the midst of this chaos the Ottoman 3rd Army was attempting, ineffectually, to protect the Muslims and generally restore law and order.

The Young Turks feared that Abdülhamid might acquiesce to the suspected foreign 'reform plan' for Macedonia. To forestall this, on 3 July 1908 a CUP member, Adjutant-Major Ahmed Niyazi Bey, with only a handful of supporters, launched a rebellion calling for the reinstatement of the 1876 Ottoman Constitution and the recall of the parliament. He was joined by Major Enver Paşa, who was already conducting a guerrilla campaign against the sultan's government in the area north of Salonika, having been denounced as a rebel and traitor.

Unexpectedly, the rebellion spread to other units in the 3rd Army and many civilians. After the gathering CUP forces had threatened to march on Istanbul, on 24 July Abdülhamid panicked and agreed to the CUP's demands.[5] Throughout Istanbul great crowds of all religious groups gathered, ecstatically welcoming the event. Unfortunately, the CUP had no clear idea of how to proceed with its 'revolution'. The CUP leaders were mainly junior officers and low-ranking bureaucrats and lacked the confidence to make any major changes in the running of the Empire. So, it was decided it would be best to leave Abdülhamid as sultan with the current grand vezir, Said Paşa, and his cabinet in office while the new parliament was being assembled.

Meanwhile, Izvolsky was increasingly confident that the other great powers would accept the agreement he was proposing to Aehrenthal. As we saw in chapter 24, on 31 August, Britain's foreign secretary informed the Russian ambassador in London that Britain would 'not make difficulties' over access to the Straits. Izvolsky believed that this would now become official British policy.

Aehrenthal saw the possibility of taking advantage of the European-wide shock caused by the Ottoman Revolution to achieve the annexation of Bosnia-Herzegovina. On 16 September 1908 he met secretly with Izvolsky in the mansion of the Austrian ambassador in Petersburg, where he accepted the deal Izvolsky had proposed on 2 July. Crucially, no timetable for the annexation was discussed, although it appears that Aehrenthal promised that Austria would make no move until Russia was in a stronger military condition to enforce its demands with respect to the Straits. In addition, both parties agreed there should be a conference to get the other powers to accept the arrangement, as well as to recognise the new Ottoman government. No formal minutes were taken at this meeting and, later, each party would give different versions of what exactly had been agreed. But according to one British historian, 'The result of this meeting was to be catastrophic, wrecking Russo-Austrian relations to a degree that cast a shadow down to 1914.'[6]

Then, suddenly, on 5 October 1908, Bulgaria announced its rejection of Ottoman suzerainty and declared full independence under its Germanic Prince, Ferdinand of the House of Saxe-Coburg and Gotha-Koháry. Taking opportunity of this *démarche*, the following day, without informing

Izvolsky, Austria-Hungary announced its immediate annexation of Bosnia-Herzegovina, and, therefore, the full incorporation of the Bosnian Serbs into the Austrian Empire.[7]

To Izvolsky's dismay, while Italy, France and even Britain opposed the Austrian annexation, they also announced that they would not accept any alteration to the 1841 Straits Convention. Without their agreement there would be no quid pro quo for Russia. Consequently, when his secret 'deal' with Aehrenthal became public knowledge, the Tsar, the Duma and general public opinion were horrified by what was seen as a secret arrangement to 'betray' the Bosnian Serbs. Izvolsky was abused and denigrated in the press. It was claimed that he had 'given away' their 'Slav brothers' in Bosnia-Herzegovina and got nothing in return.

The great strategic advantage to Austria from the annexation of Bosnia-Herzegovina was that it strengthened it as a Mediterranean power. Austria's presence was strong in the northern Adriatic; but as it stretched south along the Dalmatian coast, Austrian territory became a narrower and narrower strip, endangering the lines of communication with the new naval installations it was building. At the very south of that narrow strip of territory the great new naval base of Kotor (Cattaro) was particularly vulnerable, as it was overlooked by artillery positions in neighbouring Montenegro. The addition of Bosnia to Austria's Dalmatian territory gave it a great new Mediterranean hinterland through which it could create safe new supply routes to its Adriatic naval and military bases.

Following the CUP-instigated revolution, the first election, held in December 1908, resulted in a sweeping victory for the Unionists (CUP-supporters) and the rout of their rivals, the Liberal Party. But by early 1909 opposition in Istanbul to the CUP and the Unionist parliamentarians had grown considerably, as thousands of petty government employees and spies (of which there were probably thousands) lost their jobs. In addition, large numbers of soldiers rejected the new 'Prussian' discipline that the CUP's young officers were imposing. Meanwhile, many of the ill-educated religious students feared for their future and the Shari'a.

On the night of 12–13 April 1909, a mutiny by the Istanbul garrison erupted, supported by some of the *ulema*, most of the religious students, and probably instigated by a number of Liberal Party politicians. They soon carried out a counter-revolution demanding the removal of the grand vezir, the ministers of war and navy, the replacement of the Unionist president of the parliament and the reinstatement of the Shari'a (actually it hadn't been abolished). However, CUP loyalists in Macedonia, supported by the 3rd Army, marched on Istanbul. On 24 April they took control of Istanbul against little opposition and imposed martial law. A number of rebels were executed and the Ottoman parliament was reconvened. Three days later the legislature voted to depose Abdülhamid and replace him with his compliant younger brother, Mehmed V.[8]

In June 1909, any Russian hopes that the Ottomans would reject Bosnia's annexation by Austria were dashed. That month the Ottomans' Unionist-dominated government, beset by major financial problems and despairing of any real chance of restoring its rule in Bosnia-Herzegovina, agreed to accept the annexation in return for substantial financial compensation from Austria.[9] Meanwhile the Serbs insisted that a conference on the crisis, which had been jointly proposed by Britain and France, must go ahead, and the Serbian press made bellicose attacks on Austria.

Relations between Russia and the Austro-German alliance now became virulent. Throughout the winter of 1908–09, the Russian war ministry had been warning of a build-up of Austrian troops on the Serbian border. By March 1909 the German and Austrian military – knowing of Russia's military weakness as it was still recovering after its defeat by Japan – agreed that the time was ideal for an invasion of Serbia.[10]

Berlin and Vienna knew that Britain and France were willing to show diplomatic support for Serbia, but not much more. So they now intensified their pressure on Russia to get the Serbs to stop their diplomatic campaign demanding that Austria abandon its annexation of Bosnia. At the same time Austria and Germany refused to countenance Serbian demands that Austria give up its military occupation of Novi Pazar, which separated Serbia from Montenegro. For their part, the Serbs looked to Russia for unconditional support.

However, Russia was not in a position to use arms in the Balkans, or anywhere else for that matter. On 19 March 1909 Nicholas II called a full meeting of the Council of Ministers to discuss the crisis. After much fruitless debate, the war minister, General Aleksandr Roediger, was asked to give his honest opinion of the state of Russia's armed forces if it were forced to go to war with Austria-Hungary, and perhaps Germany too. His answer was that war would be disastrous for Russia: it lacked 'troops, guns and fortresses'.[11]

Four days later, the German foreign minister, Bernhard von Bülow, issued an ultimatum: Russia must abandon its opposition to the annexation of Bosnia-Herzegovina and cease its support for an international conference on the issue. The Tsar admitted that Russia had no choice but to back down. On 27 March Austria-Hungary began mobilisation and, knowing it had lost Russia's support, Serbia was forced to accede to all of Austria's demands, including a reduction in its armaments.

Subsequently, in April 1909, with the agreement of the original signatories, the Treaty of Berlin of 1878 was amended to legitimise the Austro-Hungarian annexation of Bosnia-Herzegovina. For the first time, a great European power had won full control of a province of the Ottoman Empire on the Mediterranean's northern shore.

But even more significantly, for the Tsar and his entourage the whole episode was one of deep humiliation at the hands of a deceitful Austria-Hungary. It was an experience they swore would never happen again.

CHAPTER 26

The French and Spanish take Morocco,
1909–1911

Kaiser Wilhelm II's declaration at Damascus in 1896 had pledged eternal German protection of all 300 million of the sultan-caliph's Muslim subjects. This may have been received with derision by the French and British rulers of colonial North Africa but, in Morocco, still independent, the Kaiser's words were taken seriously. When news of his declaration spread among the ordinary people, it created a giant wave of pro-German sentiment.

In March 1905 the Kaiser decided to make a dramatic demonstration of his opposition to any further French penetration of Morocco. In reality this piece of 'gesture politics' reflected German anger at the way the French were obstructing Germany's efforts to achieve an open door to their investment in Morocco. On 31 March the Kaiser made a much-publicised visit to Tangier, during which he and his entourage paraded through the streets. They were thronged by cheering Moors who believed that Germany was now coming to their aid against the French.

A newly self-confident Sultan 'Abd al-Aziz responded by calling for an international conference on Morocco, and Germany saw this as a useful opportunity to drive a wedge between France and Britain following their recent *entente*. Moreover, Germany's chancellor, Prince Bernhard von Bülow, felt sure that the US would strongly support the joint demand of his country and Morocco for guarantees of the latter's independence. Washington was also advocating an open door to Moroccan trade and investment, something which would be inconsistent with French dominance over the country. Von Bülow believed that Britain would wish to avoid the risk of offending America by supporting French objectives.[1]

Meanwhile, further French intervention in Morocco was being delayed by a serious disagreement between France's foreign secretary, Théophile Delcassé, and those among the colonialist party who wanted to pursue a more aggressive policy. Delcassé believed that France's acquisition of

Morocco should be achieved by building upon the *entente* with Britain and following a gradualist, diplomatic path towards that objective. Opposing him was the leader of the Algerian colonists, Eugène Etienne, now vice president of the Chamber. He was a strong supporter of Colonel Hubert Lyautey and his Foreign Legion troops, currently nibbling away at Morocco's Saharan region in his semi-private war against the tribes on its southern border. Lyautey had already seized the key oasis of Ras al-'Ain, and by early 1905 he and his small army were positioned for an advance further into southern Morocco.

Beset by accusations that he was dragging his feet over Morocco, Delcassé felt obliged to reject 'Abd al-Aziz's demand for a conference, and this stance sparked an immediate international crisis. Ironically, the Kaiser believed that Delcassé was the arch-colonialist instigating an aggressive policy of annexation in Morocco, and demanded his removal. In reality, Delcassé, with his conviction it was best to move gradually, had now completely lost the confidence of the colonialist party.[2]

Having lost that support in the Chamber, in April 1905 Delcassé fell from power. In June the prime minister, Maurice Rouvier, took over the foreign minister's portfolio himself. Although the Moroccan crisis rumbled on throughout June, with France cancelling all military leave and Germany threatening to sign a defensive treaty with Morocco, in July Rouvier agreed to 'Abd al-Aziz's demand for the international conference.

It opened on 16 January 1906 at the Spanish town of Algeciras, attended by representatives of thirteen countries. Unfortunately for both Germany and Morocco, Chancellor Von Bülow's belief that Germany's position would be supported by the US turned out to be mistaken. The Americans made it clear that they had 'little interest in the future status of Morocco'.[3] Consequently, the outcome of the conference did nothing to satisfy either Germany or 'Abd al-Aziz.

Instead the conference, which culminated in the Act of Algeciras of 7 April, merely called for a series of 'reforms', including the creation of a new Moroccan police force to be led by French and Spanish officers. The Act also called for the establishment of a Moroccan state bank financed by the European powers, with France providing a third of its capital, by virtue of which it obtained a controlling interest.[4] The Act represented a significant reduction in sovereignty for Morocco, although it also established the principle that what sovereignty remained would be collectively guarded by all the European powers. Even so, it delayed France's complete take-over for only a few more years.[5]

While Colonel Lyautey's penetration of southern Morocco steadily progressed, the colonialist party were on the lookout for a convenient 'incident' to justify a more dramatic French intervention. It came on 19 March 1907 when a French doctor, Emile Mauchamp, was murdered by a mob in Marrakesh. Mauchamp was a very able doctor with a sound knowledge of modern medical procedures. But he was arrogant, self-aggrandising, reckless and an incorrigible racist.[6] Moreover, his medical mission was financed by the French government and represented an important act of propaganda to reinforce the idea that France was only conducting a *mission civilisatrice* in Morocco. The circumstances of Mauchamp's death are unclear, but it seems the Governor of Marrakesh, whom Mauchamp had alienated, may have spread rumours that the doctor was also a French spy.

At the end of July nine Europeans, including three Frenchmen, working on a new port at Casablanca, were killed by an excited mob. Coming on top of Mauchamp's murder, this meant the French now had the 'incidents' they were waiting for. They acted immediately. French troops crossed the northern border and seized the town of Oujda. At the same time, Casablanca was bombarded by a French battleship, two French cruisers and a Spanish gunboat; and in August 3,000 French colonial troops, mainly Senegalese and Algerians, together with 500 Spanish troops, landed and seized the city. In the attack they took no prisoners. 'All captives – pathetically armed and often little more than children – were roped together and shot in the back... the Moors' first view of a Christian civilisation in armed action.'[7]

In the same month the sultan's older brother, Mulay Hafid, began a rebellion with the support of the powerful Berber clan of the Glaoua, whose towering fortress at Telouet in the southern Atlas dominated a large part of southern Morocco. In November 1908 Mulay Hafid's army marched on Fez with 40,000 mounted warriors of Berber tribesmen led by Madani al-Glaoui. When the sultan's troops were sent out to meet them they promptly deserted to the other side.

Fearing for his life, 'Abd al-Aziz fled from Fez to the port of Rabat, where he placed himself under French protection. In July 1908 he relinquished the sultanate and went to live in Tangier. Mulay Hafid accepted the terms of the Treaty of Algeciras and the French and Spanish recognised him as sultan. For the time being the French were content to leave the affairs of the country in his cruel and incompetent hands.*

Meanwhile, Spain's loss of Cuba, Puerto Rico and the Philippines in its 1898 war with the US had made the Spanish military and the country's colonialist lobby determined to replace these territories with a new colonial empire in North Africa.[8] Consequently, in 1909, Spanish forces began expanding the territory around their existing enclaves, Ceuta and Melilla, killing local Arabs and burning their villages – but facing growing tribal resistance in the Rif mountains.[9] At the same time, in the Moroccan Sahara, Lyautey's troops occupied oasis after oasis. Often French tactics involved simply purchasing the loyalty of the local tribal chieftain.[10] In 1910 Mulay Hafid agreed to place Moroccan government troops under the command of French and Spanish officers; and when rebellious tribes marched on Fez in April and besieged the sultan in his palace, the French sent a flying column which easily defeated the rebels. Mulay Hafid continued to rule, his status as a French puppet ever more transparent.

However, on 1 July 1911, on the orders of the Kaiser, the German gunboat *Panther* arrived at the Moroccan port of Agadir, followed a few days later by the light cruiser *Berlin*. Officially, the visit was to protect German civilians resident on that part of Morocco's Atlantic coast (actually there was only one such individual, who was living seventy miles away).

This decision to employ gunboat diplomacy was on the advice of Germany's new foreign secretary, Alfred von Kiderlen-Wächter, a Prussian of the German Right, reluctantly backed by the German chancellor Theobald von Bethmann Hollweg. It represented a direct challenge to France's domination of Morocco.[11] In fact Germany had a good case against France in Morocco. Had it managed things better it could have gained some sympathy and support from the other powers that had signed the Treaty of Algeciras in 1906. 'French governments and officials ... had flouted both

---

* As an example of Mulay Hafid's despotic French-backed rule and his sadistic cruelty, see the description of the sultan's torture of a prominent sheikh of a Sufi zawiya by Lawrence Harris, the *Times*'s correspondent in Morocco. Harris, Lawrence, *With Mulai Hafid at Fez: Behind the Scenes in Morocco*, Smith Elder & Co., London, 1909, pp. 144–45.

the Treaty's spirit and its provisions by trying to establish political and economic dominance over the country and its feckless sultan.'[12] In addition, German business interests in Morocco had been obstructed or even blocked completely. For example, a French agreement for Germany to build railways in Morocco had been broken.

However, Germany conducted the whole affair with lack of attention to detail and a propensity to put itself in the wrong. At the outset, the German foreign ministry informed the other powers with an interest in Morocco only after the fact, which inevitably inflamed matters and contributed to the sense of crisis which was amplified by the bellicose outcries of the press in many of the other European powers. As one perceptive critic among the German military put it, 'There was no understanding whatsoever of what might arise from it and how all these possibilities were to be dealt with.'[13]

The Kaiser and his ministers were determined not to repeat the experience of the German diplomatic defeat over Morocco in 1905–06. However, Britain now had a much closer friendship with France and was increasingly concerned about what it saw as a growing threat to its worldwide economic and military interests from Germany's construction of a powerful battle fleet. In both France and Britain, the press fanned war fever over Germany's demand for colonial 'compensation'. The British foreign secretary, Sir Edward Grey, made it clear that if war *did* break out, Britain would have to support France.

Once the press furore calmed down the matter was settled in November 1911. Germany accepted a French protectorate over Morocco in return for receiving 275,000 square kilometres of central Africa, which eventually became part of the German colony of Cameroon. Subsequently, on 30 March 1912, Mulay Hafid signed the Treaty of Fez establishing a French protectorate; and on 28 April General Lyautey was appointed resident-general. In the same year Spain began a full military occupation of the northern sector of Morocco, finally agreed with France.

Mulay Hafid was soon forced to abdicate, and another son of Hasan I was installed as the puppet Sultan Yusuf I. Resident General Lyautey established his notion of a 'veiled' protectorate. He would proceed to rule, but via the 'Great Kaids': the three Berber Lords of the Atlas, the M'tougga, the Goundafa, but above all, the Glaoua headed by the brothers Madani and T'hami. In the words of the British writer Gavin Maxwell, by their

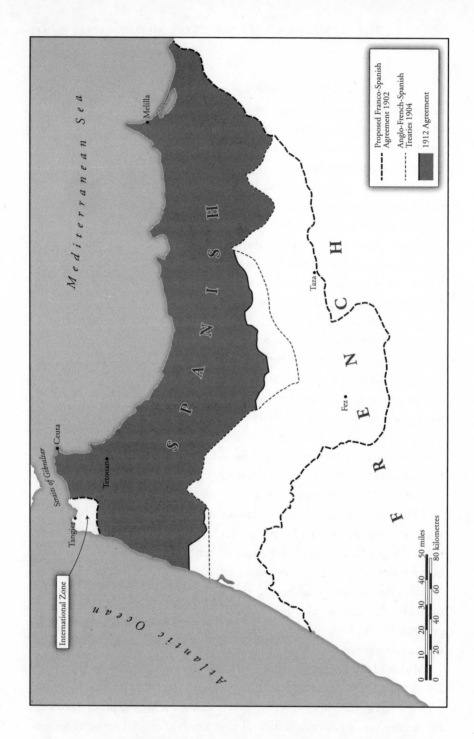

PROPOSED AND FINALISED DIVISIONS OF MOROCCAN
TERRITORY BETWEEN FRANCE AND SPAIN, 1902, 1904 AND 1912

licensed brutality and cruelty against the Moroccan population for many years to come, 'the Glaoui, the M'touggi and the Goundafi were in no sense trying to perpetuate a mediaeval feudal state; they were trying to create one ... but it was the French who assured them of their success.'[14]

In the aftermath of the affair, France's right-wing press trumpeted that France had defeated 'German bullying', and a surge of nationalism carried the right-of-centre Republican Party to victory in the elections of January 1912. The strongly anti-German Raymond Poincaré was elected prime minister. From now on France sought to solidify its relationship with Russia and generally support its interests in the Balkans.[15] Eighteen months later Poincaré would lead France into the First World War.

The Introduction to *Sea of Troubles* referred to the 'chain reaction of violence which exploded in the Mediterranean between 1911 and 1913' and – triggered by the assassination of the Austrian Archduke Franz Ferdinand the following year – sparked the beginning of the First World War. This chain reaction began with an egregious act of imperialism in the Mediterranean: the Franco-Spanish occupation of Morocco between 1909 and 1911. The next step on this tragic transmission belt would now follow: the Italian invasion of Libya in 1911 and its war against the Ottoman Empire.

CHAPTER 27

The Forgotten War:
The Italian Invasion of Libya, 1911–1912

The war between the Kingdom of Italy and the Ottoman Empire which occurred between October 1911 and October 1912 was the first European war of the twentieth century. In its geographical extension it covered the whole of the eastern Mediterranean, and beyond. It ranged from the Adriatic Sea to the deserts of North Africa; from the coast of Lebanon to the Dardanelles; from the Dodecanese Islands to the Red Sea. A major land battle took place; guerrilla warfare raged and lasted well beyond the official end of the war; it witnessed the first naval engagements in the Mediterranean since 1866; and, for the first time, aircraft and zeppelins were used to bomb land forces.

And yet, with one notable exception,[1] recent historians have almost entirely ignored the Italo-Ottoman War. For example, in what is probably the most comprehensive and well-respected history of the Ottoman Empire, the subject receives half a page.[2] In the most recent history of the Ottomans, the war is mentioned in only two sentences.[3]

If we are to provide a corrective to this historical hiatus we must begin on the Mediterranean Sea itself. Much had changed since the last decade of the nineteenth century, when the British Mediterranean Fleet of eleven great ironclads could routinely carry out its summer manoeuvres as far east as the coast of Lebanon. Then – and during the first few years of the twentieth century – the British still had the largest Mediterranean Fleet: in 1904 a tonnage of 232,480 (including the Atlantic Fleet based at Gibraltar) compared with its nearest rival, France, at 153,412 tonnes.[4] During the first few years of the twentieth century, the British were still concerned about the possibility that the Russian Black Sea Fleet, escorting troop carriers, might break out through the Turkish Straits and attack the British presence in Egypt.[5] So, there were even proposals for a major reinforcement of Britain's naval presence in the Mediterranean.

But by 1905 – with better naval intelligence downgrading the capabilities of the Russian Black Sea Fleet, the disastrous Russian defeat in its war against Japan, and a growing naval armaments race with Germany in the North Sea – Britain's strategic priorities had changed. As a result its dominance of the Mediterranean was lessening.[6] The first sign of this was the decision taken by the Admiralty to change the traditional pattern of rotating its new and most modern battleships. Hitherto these had been first stationed with the Mediterranean Fleet. From now on they would serve in the Atlantic and Home Fleets before eventually being redeployed to the Mediterranean. This meant that the Mediterranean Fleet would progressively be made up of older and less powerful warships.

As time went on and the Admiralty's perception of the threat from the expanding German navy in the North Sea intensified, the Admiralty was forced to increasingly deploy its most modern and powerful ships to counter the Germans in that region and progressively reduce the number and fire power of its Mediterranean battle fleet. And by now both the Italian and Austro-Hungarian fleets presented a formidable threat.

This was because between 1907 and 1910 a naval 'cold war' had existed between Italy and Austria-Hungary in the Mediterranean.[*] It had resulted in a fierce naval arms race between the two ostensibly allied powers. Between 1906 and 1910 the combined tonnages of the Italian and Austrian battle lines increased from 164,671 tonnes to 203,068,[7] although it was Austria-Hungary which had most aggressively enlarged its Mediterranean fleet with its battle-line tonnage increasing from 54,771 tonnes in 1906 to 86,187 in 1910, and the construction of a string of new or enhanced naval bases and supply points down its Adriatic coastline from Pula to Cattaro (Kotor).

However, in 1910–11 this 'cold war' came to an end; and with this reaffirmation of the Triple Alliance in the Mediterranean the naval authorities in both countries commenced discussions on combined operations against the British and French fleets in a future war. In this new Mediterranean geo-strategic configuration Italy had a much stronger naval capability in the central and eastern Mediterranean. By 1910 its battleship

---

[*] It had broken out as a result of a sudden revival of irredentist pressure in Italy to 'recover' the Italian-speaking territory in Croatia and Dalmatia still controlled by Austria-Hungary (see Hendrickson, 2014, pp. 63–81.

The Italian torpedo cruiser Monzambano, *soon after its completion on 11 August 1889*

numbers had increased from six to twelve, its destroyers from six to forty and its torpedo boats from seventeen to ninety.[8]

So, by 1911 one thing was certain. Although the Admiralty still had a formidable fleet of thirteen battleships and two cruiser squadrons available for service in the Mediterranean,* as far as the Great Sea was concerned, Britain no longer 'ruled the waves'. Within a couple of years it would have to rely on the French Mediterranean Fleet to protect its strategic interests in that region.

And one other thing was now clear. The rapprochement between Italy and Austria-Hungary meant that it had no need to fear intervention by the naval forces of Austria-Hungary when it moved against Ottoman Libya.

As regards the Ottoman Navy, most of Sultan Abdülaziz's great foreign-built ironclads had now become rusting hulks, and his successor Abdülhamid had done nothing to remedy this dire situation. What remained of the Ottoman battle fleet, stationed at Istanbul, was actually

---

* The combined Mediterranean and Gibraltar-based Atlantic Fleets.

forbidden to train or conduct operations, and not once were fleet units allowed to venture outside the Dardanelles.[9] Until 1909 and the reinstitution of parliamentary oversight under the CUP, the naval budget had been entirely at the discretion of the sultan. Over the financial years 1896/7 to 1910/11 the expenditure of the Navy Ministry was only 4 per cent of total government expenditure and only 11 per cent of total military expenditure.[10]

When an inspection of the Ottoman fleet had been carried out by the German Vice-Admiral Eugene Kalau von Hofe and the British Admiral Henry Woods in April 1897 it had revealed a catalogue of dismal failures. For example, the guns on the refitted *Osmaniye* class of ironclads were useless, with runners on the heavy Armstrong-built guns immovable and the hydraulic pistons on the Krupp quick-firing guns bent; some ships did not have the complete armament installed upon handover from the original builder. As a further example, there were no breaches for the 9.4-inch guns on the *Aziziye* ironclad – they were still lying in the arsenal at Istanbul. And the training of gun crews had been so neglected that it took them over two hours to load, train, fire and reload main armament.[11]

By 1910 the abject failure of the navy in the Ottoman-Greece War of 1897 (compared with the successes of the Ottoman army), together with the recent purchase of a modern heavy cruiser by Greece, prompted the CUP government to embark on a major naval rearmament programme. A British mission arrived in Istanbul in September 1908 to advise. Headed by Admiral Sir Douglas Gamble, it proposed the acquisition of major naval assets including two battleships, three cruisers and ten destroyers (although the order of acquisition was not dictated). The Porte wanted the big ships first. Negotiations with the British shipbuilder Armstrong to build the two capital ships began, but eventually fell through over the price. Nevertheless, the Porte's conviction that the navy's priority was to acquire 'line-of battle' capital ships continued. This was a serious strategic error, as an American naval historian explained:

> The Ottomans used naval programs drawn up by the British mission... the frenzy of shipbuilding indicative of the early twentieth century drove naval plans to include large capital ships. The ownership and use of capital ships was the driving

force behind *empire building*. ... the true problem the
Ottoman Empire confronted was that of *empire protecting*.
The Ottomans were not into empire building or seizing but
holding on to what was theirs.[12] [My emphasis.]

Such a strategic necessity required not large capital ships but much smaller,
faster warships that could dash out and attack the enemy under the clouds
of dense smoke typical of naval engagements at that time. As such they
could deter heavy warships from coming close to shore to bombard an
Ottoman coastal city or town. Moreover, they could be stationed in the
many tiny ports, islands and inlets which dotted the Empire's 10,000 miles
of coastline. And such vessels now existed.

   At the end of the nineteenth century the 'torpedo boat' arrived. It was
different from the torpedo boat familiar to us from the Second World War
in that it was considerably larger (30 to 50 metres), and, of course, steam-
powered. With its torpedo tubes mounted either in a fixed broadside
position (the earlier versions) or swivel-mounted on deck, and with a
speed of 20 to 30 knots, this comparatively cheap naval asset could wreak
devastation on an enemy capital ship. This made it the wonder weapon of
the early twentieth century. Indeed, as late as 1916, Britain's Admiral John
Jellicoe was in great fear of an attack by German torpedo boats at the Battle
of Jutland. A somewhat later adaptation was the 'torpedo boat destroyer'
(swiftly renamed simply 'destroyer'), which was larger and carried both
torpedoes and a forward armoured turret with (typically) a 4-inch calibre
gun. In most respects it was simply a better armed and protected form of
the torpedo boat and was used in the same manner.

   The Ottomans did have a small number of torpedo boats and destroyers,
but showed little interest in adding more. It was capital ships they wanted.
In the event, they acquired two from the Germans. On 5 August 1910
the contract was signed for the Ottomans to buy two pre-dreadnought
battleships of the Brandenburg class, SMS *Kurfürst Friedrich Wilhelm*
and SMS *Weissenburg*. On 1 September they were officially transferred to
the Porte and renamed the *Barbaros Hayreddin* (Admiral Barbaros) and
Torgud Reis (Admiral Torgud).

   Carrying six 11-inch Krupp guns supplemented by six 4-inch, these were
certainly large, powerful ships, comparable to those in the Italian fleet.

Ottoman battleship Barbaros Hayreddin *(ex-SMS* Kurfürst Friedrich Wilhelm*)*

Unfortunately, the CUP government didn't have the experienced officers and men to crew them adequately, as would become obvious in the wars which were to follow. And since the Treasury did not have the funds to pay for them, the money had to be raised largely from public subscription supplemented by funds belonging to the ex-Sultan Abdülhamid, which were banked in Berlin.

The Ottoman fleet was still heavily outnumbered and outclassed by the Italian navy, which was being prepared for the planned invasion of Libya. The Ottomans had two battleships, the Italians had fourteen; the Ottomans had three cruisers, the Italians had twenty; the Ottomans had eight destroyers, the Italians, forty-one. Most serious of all, the Ottomans had only nine torpedo boats, the Italians had ten times that number.[13] The remainder of the active Ottoman fleet consisted of just three, obsolete, ironclad battleships stationed as guard-ships at the main ports of Salonika, Izmir and Beirut, and a number of seagoing gunboats.

This was the naval situation in early 1911 at the moment when the French and Spanish were carving up Morocco, and Italy's politicians decided that the conjuncture was ripe for their own, long-awaited colonial strike in North Africa. 'If the Italians acted promptly they could stake their claim while the world was focused on Morocco.'[14]

For some years the ground had already been well prepared. In 1906 the Istituto Coloniale Italiano had been established and the following year it had called for a 'peaceful penetration' of Tripoli, one of the Ottoman Empire's two Libyan *vilayet*s. After much lobbying, it persuaded the Porte to agree to the Vatican-controlled Bank of Rome opening a branch in Tripoli.[15] Over the next four years the bank expanded to become a major financial and shipping business; but it also financed the Catholic newspaper *Corriere d'Italia*, which consistently argued for the invasion of Libya.[16]

According to the 1900 agreement between France and Italy, Italy 'recognised the right of France to extend her influence in Morocco, with the reservation that if such action modified the political or territorial integrity of the Cherifian Empire in Morocco Italy was entitled to the development of her influence in Tripoli'. For the Italians, it seemed France's actions in Morocco between 1909 and 1911 were a clear example of 'modifying' Morocco's 'political or territorial integrity'. As for Italy's consequent right to 'develop her influence' in Tripoli, this had never been clarified; but, by now, all the European powers acknowledged it would mean colonial conquest. This included Britain's Liberal Party government.

When the Young Turks' Revolution occurred in July 1908 and promised constitutional and representative government, Britain's relationship with the Porte initially recovered from the distinctly frosty one which had prevailed under Lord Salisbury. The Foreign Office under Sir Edward Grey 'received the revolution with great sympathy and pleasure'.[17] But from the outset that 'sympathy' was already qualified. In a letter dated 11 August to Sir Gerard Lowther, British ambassador to the Porte, Grey states:

> What has happened already in Turkey [sic] is so marvellous that I suppose its is not impossible that she will establish a Constitution, but it may well be that the habit of vicious and corrupt government will be too strong for reform and that

animosities of race and religion will again produce violence and disorder.

He goes on to concede that 'for the moment good influences seem to be uppermost' and that 'rejoicing at the upset of the old and the prospect of a new regime is genuine', but he concludes with the following words:

> We must welcome this prospect as long as it continues but we must be careful not to give Russia the impression that we are reverting to the old policy of supporting Turkey as a barrier against her and should continue to show willingness to work with Russia when possible.[18]

So, in spite of the fact that the Revolution promised to bring about the outcome that Lord Palmerston had always hoped for and indeed, predicted – that the Ottomans would eventually become a 'normal' constitutional European state – Palmerston's 'old policy' was now to be abandoned. This was hardly surprising, since the previous year Grey had made it clear to the Russians that Britain wouldn't 'make difficulties' over their access to the Turkish Straits, access that would inevitably involve removing the Ottoman 'barrier'.

However, for the time being Britain signalled its friendly support by offering the Porte the British naval mission commanded by Sir Douglas Gamble which, in effect, placed a British officer in charge of the Ottoman navy. So, in response to Britain's seemingly enthusiastic response to the Young Turk revolution, the new Ottoman government became distinctly pro-British.

Meanwhile, relations between the CUP-backed Ottoman government and Italy had become decidedly fraught. In October 1910 a new governor, Ibrahim Paşa, was sent to Tripoli. His instructions were to prohibit foreign companies from owning land in both Tripolitania and Cyrenaica. In November an Ottoman commission visited the two provinces and specifically recommended that the sale of land to Italians ceased. In the following months the Italian community in Tripoli never hesitated to pick quarrels with the Ottoman authorities over minor infringements of their 'rights', behaviour which was reported in the Italian press as 'threats' or 'exactions'. The ground was being prepared for a less than 'peaceful' penetration.

By mid-September 1911 Italy was mobilising troops in preparation for the invasion. Fearing such an attack, the Ottoman government despatched a transport ship, the *Derna*, to Tripoli, flying a German flag, with a cargo of 12,000 rifles and ammunition. On 25 September the Italian chargé d'affaires in Istanbul delivered a note to the Porte claiming that Italian citizens in Tripoli were being threatened by the activities of the CUP, and that the sending of arms would be considered an unfriendly act. When the *Derna* arrived in Tripoli, the Italians claimed this 'incident' was a *casus belli*. At 2.30 p.m. on 28 September Rome delivered an ultimatum to the Porte, warning that despatching 'military transports' to Libya would be 'attended by serious consequences'. Furthermore, the Ottoman authorities were instructed to order their forces in Libya to offer no opposition if Italian troops arrived. Unless such assurances were given within twenty-four hours, Italy would declare war on the Ottoman Empire. The Ottoman government immediately replied in a highly conciliatory manner, stating that there was absolutely no need for Italy to send its forces to Tripoli because it was perfectly ready to give firm guarantees for the economic expansion Italy required in the provinces of both Tripoli and Cyrenaica.[19]

But by now, the Italian government had already committed itself to war, and the Italian press was whipping up the middle classes and sections of the working class in a fervour of nationalism in preparation for hostilities. In his diary for 28 September 1911, the twenty-seven-year-old second-lieutenant Giovanni Messe of the 84th Regiment of Infantry, about to embark for Libya, recorded that 'in every Italian city great demonstrations in favour of the enterprise have taken place'.[20]

The Italian justification for the invasion threat was preposterous. The movement of weapons between two parts of a single sovereign state was perfectly legitimate. Nevertheless, at 3 p.m. on 29 September 1911 the Italian government, headed by Prime Minister Giovanni Giolitti, and with the support of its king, Victor Emmanuel III (r. 1900–46), issued a final ultimatum to the Porte, demanding the entry of Italian troops to restore law and order; and, an hour later, it declared war on the Ottoman Empire. There was no 'law and order' requiring restoration. As Commodore William Beehler of the US Navy observed in 1913, 'Italy declared war against Turkey

[sic] for commercial reasons and to provide a neighboring colony for her surplus population.'[21]

Prior to the invasion, the Italian foreign minister, Antonio di San Giuliano, had reassured all the other European powers that his government's intention was solely to detach Libya from the Ottoman Empire. The declaration of war against the Empire itself would therefore be more of a formality, and there was no intention of engaging in hostilities with any other part of its dominions or threatening its capital.[22] Consequently all the European powers, including Britain, declared their neutrality.

The day after Italy declared war, the Ottoman Grand Vezir Mehmed Said Paşa sent a communiqué to Britain via the Ottoman ambassador to London, Tewfiq Paşa. In it he pointed out that Italy had already been informed on 28 September that the Ottoman government was willing to make major concessions to avoid war. But it went on:

> Without replying to this conciliatory offer, the Italian Government, at the same time that it sent its fleet to Tripoli and made an attack on one of our torpedo boats in the waters of the Adriatic, sent us a formal declaration of war... Painfully surprised by this hostility which, given our attitude with regard to Italy, is far from being justified, we want to believe that it is still possible, given our conciliatory intentions, to avert the terrible results of a war without any real cause.[23]

And the grand vezir concluded by appealing to the 'friendship of the British Government to intervene with Italy and convince her of our sincere desire to negotiate with her to prevent a useless effusion of blood'.[24]

However, it is clear that the government had already decided to reject the grand vezir's appeal, since a note from a Foreign Office official attached to his letter states that 'we have already made clear to the Turkish Embassy our attitude regarding intervention'. There would be no intervention.

A month later, Said Paşa proposed a formal alliance with Britain whose only condition was that Britain should intervene and induce Italy to accept an arrangement on the basis of recognition of the sovereign rights of the sultan over Libya.

The proposal was declined. On 2 November Grey replied that Britain's policy of strict neutrality in the war between Italy and the Ottoman Empire meant that it was:

> Precluded from entering on any negotiations which the Imperial Ottoman Government may wish to initiate for the purpose of investing with a more formal and binding character and of extending to a wider scope the friendly relations happily existing between the Ottoman Empire and this country.[25]

Friendly indeed!

As we have already seen, Grey had now decided that Britain must not revert to the 'old policy'. In practice, this meant that anything which might cause a break in Britain's anti-German *entente* with Russia had to be avoided. Showing any support for the Porte – so he appears to have believed – might well risk such a breakdown.

An additional reason for Britain's refusal to support the Ottoman government was its anxiety not to alienate Italy and, if possible, to wean her away from the Triple Alliance. Grey was determined that British policy should avoid throwing Italy into the arms of Germany and Austria-Hungary. Although Grey doesn't mention it, it must now have been clear that the changing balance of naval power in the Mediterranean – with Britain having to keep most of its assets in the North Sea – was moving in favour of the Triple Alliance. On current trends, the tonnage and fire power (broadside throw-weight) of the combined Italian-Austrian fleet would soon equal or even exceed those of the combined Franco-British fleet.*

There had also been disagreements with the Porte as the result of Britain's attempts to gain commercial advantages in Ottoman territory, especially in Mesopotamia (Iraq) where 'concession hunting' intensified. A particular source of friction was Britain's demand for 55 per cent ownership and control of the southern section of the Berlin to Baghdad railway, planned to

---

* By 1913 the tonnage of the Austro-Italian combination (351,047 tonnes) was close to that of the Franco-British combination (389,811), and by 1914 it exceeded it (437,223 tonnes compared with 402,143 tonnes).

reach the Arabian Gulf. The Porte offered only 20 per cent, suspecting that it presaged a greater British political penetration and possible partition.[26]

But in abandoning the Ottoman Empire, Grey gave little thought to the way in which the September 1911 Italian declaration of war on the Ottomans might affect matters in the Balkans.

There, Nikolai Hartwig and Alexandr Nelidov, Russia's ambassadors in Serbia and Bulgaria, were busy forming a 'pan-Slav' Serbo-Bulgarian alliance. Russia's foreign minister, Sergei Sazonov, who had replaced Alexander Izvolsky in the autumn of 1910, was determined to stop any further Austrian advance southwards, towards the Straits, after its annexation of Bosnia-Herzegovina. He believed that a treaty between Serbia and Bulgaria, made under Russian auspices, would create a solid block to Austria's ambitions in the Balkans. That the considerable military power of a Serb-Bulgar alliance might be used not as a block against Austria-Hungary, but aggressively against the Ottomans, had not yet occurred to Sazanov. Too late, Sazanov discovered that he had played the role of sorcerer's apprentice.

Meanwhile, Germany was in a particularly difficult position over the Italian invasion of Libya. Together with Austria-Hungary it had previously accepted Italy's right to eventually occupy the territory. Germany's secretary of state, Alfred von Kiderlen-Wächter, was keen to uphold this policy in the interests of preserving the Triple Alliance, due to be renewed the following year. However, the German ambassador at the Porte, Adolf Marschall von Bieberstein, was much less enthusiastic.[27] Since 1898 the Kaiser had been posing as the European 'friend of Islam'. To condone an attack upon an integral part of the Ottoman Empire seemed to him to run completely counter to the Kaiser's own position. Marschall himself had played a key role in facilitating the substantial investments Germany had made in the Ottoman Empire and he was anxious to protect them. For some time a war of words took place between the two men, but eventually Kiderlen-Wächter was able to inform the Italians that Germany was content with the invasion of Tripolitania, provided the hostilities were localised to the North African coast.[28]

However, it seems both the German chancellor and the Kaiser were kept out of the loop in these diplomatic exchanges over the outbreak of the Italian war. The Kaiser himself expressed his concerns about the impending war, and, in an unusually prescient observation, he predicted that more countries would take advantage of the Ottoman Empire's weakness. This predicament, he argued, would reopen the issue of control of the Straits and territorial conflict in the Balkans. It was an act which the Kaiser feared could be 'the beginning of a world war with all its terrors'.[29] As for the other member of the Triple Alliance, the Habsburg Emperor Franz Joseph of Austria-Hungary also made it clear that he, personally, did not approve of the approaching Italo-Ottoman hostilities, fearing that a successful Italy might extend its imperialist objectives to Albania.[30]

The Ottoman regular forces in Libya were very weak. According to the US observer Commodore Beehler, the troops of the Ottoman 42nd Division responsible for its defences consisted of the Tripoli garrison with six infantry battalions (3,600 men), a battalion of chasseurs (600 men), four squadrons of cavalry (400 men), six field-gun batteries and two companies of fortress artillery: in total around 5,000 men. But in reality only 3,000 of these were fully trained, the remainder being raw recruits. In Cyrenaica the province's principal city had a garrison of only 400 and at Derna only seventy. Elsewhere there were small detachments at Tobruq (thirty), Solum (twenty-five) and Cyrene (twenty).[31]

On the other hand, the Italian army had two full divisions allocated to the invasion (though not initially utilised). It also had an attachment of three squadrons of cavalry and six field-gun batteries; and there was a separate division under the command of the expedition's commander which contained two regiments of elite Bersaglieri troops (infantry), a battalion of engineers, and several field-gun batteries: in total, around 40,000 men.[32]

Avnillah-class ironclad Muin-ı Zafer. *Guardship at Izmir*

With the Italian declaration of war on 29 September 1911 hostilities broke out immediately. Four Ottoman torpedo boats stationed at Preveza in Epirus were ordered to sail north into the Adriatic to the naval base at Shëngjin in Albania. Off the small Greek town of Kanali the torpedo boats *Antalya* and *Tokad* were attacked by four modern Soldato-class Italian destroyers. With only their unprotected 37-mm quick-firing gun as their main deck armament they were easily overwhelmed by the more heavily armed destroyers with their 3-inch (76-mm) guns. *Tokad* was badly damaged with the loss of a third of its crew killed, but managed to flee north and escape to Shëngjin. *Antalya* escaped back to Preveza. However, Italian warships then attacked Preveza itself and the crew of *Antalya* were forced to scuttle the ship. The following day the torpedo boats *Hamidiye* and *Alpagot*, which were still sailing north, were attacked by the Italian destroyers off the Greek town of Igoumenitsa and were sunk.[33] The Italians later referred to these events as the 'Battle of Preveza'.

Meanwhile, the main Ottoman battle fleet – consisting of the two ex-German battleships, *Barbaros Hayreddin* and *Torgud Reis*, the old ironclad *Mesudiye*, four destroyers and the torpedo boat *Demihisar* – was at anchor at Nara Burnu in the Dardanelles, having returned from training exercises off the Lebanese coast. On 2 October the fleet sailed to Istanbul for repairs and then returned to Nara on 12 October; but it was kept there ostensibly to defend the Dardanelles against any Italian incursion.[34] But it was probably also sent there to keep the ships out of harm's way. This decision illustrates the futility of the Ottoman attempt to build up a 'big ship' battle fleet. Tucked away in the safety of the Dardanelles where they couldn't be attacked, the two Ottoman battleships were already more of a liability than an asset. All that remained of the Ottoman navy in the Mediterranean were the three old ironclads, *Muin-ı Zafer*, *Feth-ı Bülend* and *Avnillah*, used as stationary harbour defences at Izmir, Salonika and Beirut, and a handful of torpedo boats and destroyers.

In addition, a torpedo cruiser,* the *Peyk-ı Şevket*, was currently stationed in the Red Sea, and six seagoing gunboats were in the Arabian Gulf. The gunboats were immediately ordered to return to the Mediterranean via the Red Sea and the Suez Canal.

The following day an Italian squadron of seven warships including two battleships appeared off Tripoli, and emissaries were sent into the town under a white flag to demand its surrender. No satisfactory reply was received, and on the 3rd the bombardment of the town's four principal forts began. Although the Turkish gunners replied, their artillery had insufficient range to reach the Italian warships which stood off six miles from the coast, and one by one the forts were destroyed.

On 5 October, the armoured (heavy) cruiser *Giuseppe Garibaldi* entered Tripoli's harbour and a party of 1,600 sailors took possession of what remained of its defences. On 7 October Rear-Admiral Raffaele Borca Ricci d'Olmo disembarked and assumed the governorship of Tripoli. He was met by a reception party of local notables headed by Tripoli's mayor, Hasuna Paşa Karamanli, whose family had been dispossessed by the Turkish reoccupation of 1835 and who now pledged his loyalty to the Italians.[35] As for Tripoli's local Arab population, they appeared to give every indication that they would accept the occupation.

---

*　In spite of its designation as 'cruiser', the 'torpedo-cruiser' was simply a more heavily armed and faster version of the torpedo-boat, with torpedoes as its main armament. Some, like the Peyki-i Şevret, lacked any armour plating. They were a rather unsuccessful hybrid between destroyer and torpedo-boat, and by the early 1900s were generally being phased out by most European navies.

The first contingent of the army of occupation, commanded by the sixty-six-year-old General Carlo Caneva, finally arrived at Tripoli with 8,000 men on 10 October and began disembarking. Three days later, Caneva assumed the governorship of the town, replacing Admiral Borca Ricci. Meanwhile, on 4 October, the navy captured Tobruq on the coast of Cyrenaica, which it was believed would serve as an excellent naval base. Between the 16th and 20th of that month, Derna, al-Khums and Benghazi were also bombarded and captured, but not without some stiff resistance from their Turkish defenders.[36]

Meanwhile, with no hope of British support, on 4 October Grand Vezir Mehmed Said Paşa admitted to the German Ambassador at the Porte that 'the abandonment of Tripoli to Italian occupation and administration under the maintenance of the sultan's sovereignty is inevitable'.[37] But if that was all he feared, worse was to come. Nine days later, Antonio di San Giuliano, Italy's foreign minister, disclosed his government's real war aim: the outright annexation of Libya. For the Ottomans, full annexation was utterly demeaning and unacceptable. The Porte now decided to resist the invasion of Libya with all the resources it could muster.

CHAPTER 28

Unexpected Resistance:
The Arabs and Turks Fight Back

In early October 1911 the Ottoman cabinet and parliament had been uncertain how to react to the Italian declaration of war. Major Isma'il Enver (Enver Paşa) had travelled to Salonika where he addressed the Central Committee of the CUP. Until then, its young officers had generally let the elected parliament proceed in its own way. But now the CUP officers – the men who had actually brought about the Revolution of 1908 – decided to take matters into their own hands.

At a five-hour meeting Enver urged his comrades to fight the Italians with a guerrilla war in Libya.[1] At the same meeting, or shortly afterwards, they also agreed to establish the *Teşkilat-ı Mahsusa* (special organisation), whose original objective was to lead military operations in the *vilayet* of Cyrenaica (eastern Libya). The Italian navy commanded the sea and the British would not allow military supplies or personnel to pass through Egypt. Therefore the first of these officers – the Egyptian 'Aziz Bey al-Misri, Isma'il Enver Bey, his brother Nuri, Mustafa Kemal, and the Iraqis Nuri al-Sa'id and Ja'far al-'Askari* – were smuggled through Egypt to the border where they were able to cross into Libya in late October 1911. Enver, Mustafa Kemal and their comrades set up their camp on the Jebel Akhdar, the great calcareous mountain rising to a tableland which dominates northern Cyrenaica. They

---

* Enver would become Ottoman Minister of War in 1913 and in 1914 a member of the dictatorial triumvirate which declared war on the Allies. Mustafa Kemal would play a leading role in the defence of Gallipoli in 1915, and after the end of the war he became President of the first Turkish Republic. Al-Misri eventually deserted to the British during the First World War, and became commander of the Emir Faysal's small anti-Turkish Arab army. Nuri al-Sa'id and Ja'far al-'Askari also changed sides after being captured in 1916. After the war they became, respectively, prime minister and minister for war in the puppet 'Arab nationalist' government which the British set up in Iraq in 1920 (see Rutledge, 2014).

were followed by hundreds of enthusiastic, nationalist officers and civilians from all quarters of the Empire.

Initially these volunteers were unsure what reaction their plans would receive from the Arabs and Berbers, the vast majority of the Libyan population, many of them nomadic Bedouin. For their part, the Italian government thought that the Arabs would actually welcome the defeat of the Turkish regime which had dominated Libya since 1835, believing that they hated the Turks for their oppression. But in this, as in much else, the Italians were seriously mistaken. According to the US navy's Commodore William Beehler, 'Italian claims that the country was misgoverned and that untenable conditions existed, were not well founded.'[2] Already two local notables in the Ottoman parliament, Sulayman al-Baruni and Farhat Bey al-Zawi, were instrumental in organising the resistance. Both were strong supporters of the CUP, and they travelled throughout their districts calling for volunteers.[3]

While Enver and his comrades were establishing themselves in Cyrenaica, they received news from the *vilayet* of Tripoli (western Libya) that encouraged them to believe that the Arabs and Berbers would, indeed, fight the invasion. The first clear evidence of Arab-Turkish unity came shortly after the Italian capture of Tripoli. Brushing aside any potential resistance to the invasion, General Carlo Caneva deployed his troops no further than six kilometres from the coast and failed to reconnoitre further inland. Neither did he show much concern about the whereabouts of the Turkish regular troops which had withdrawn from Tripoli after the Italian bombardment. In fact the Turkish commander at Tripoli, Jamal Paşa, had set up his headquarters at 'Ain Zara, only fifteen kilometres southeast of the city, where his regular troops were being steadily reinforced by Arab tribesmen.

On 23 October Caneva got a rude awakening. Tripoli was notable for its large oasis which ran eastwards for a distance of about eighteen kilometres, extending inland towards the desert to a depth of around three kilometres. This oasis was dotted with small Arab houses and many gardens. Because there had been some occasional sniper firing west of the town, Caneva had positioned most of his troops on that side; he left the oasis only lightly defended by the 11th Bersaglieri Regiment.

At around 8 a.m. a force of Arabs and Turks mounted an attack on the western side of the Italian positions. This appears to have been a feint because, suddenly, a general uprising of Tripoli's Arab population began. At about the same time, the main force of Turkish and Arab troops attacked Caneva's left wing along the oasis, overrunning the Italian trenches. The 11th Bersaglieri battalion were attacked from both front and back, with Arabs firing on them from positions behind them in the oasis gardens. Although the Turko-Arab attack was eventually beaten off and the Arab uprising in the city crushed, the 11th Bersaglieri were almost completely wiped out, losing 343 of their original 400 strength, killed, wounded or missing.[4]

The fury of the Italian troops at what they believed to be Arab treachery is clearly expressed by Second-Lieutenant Messe in his diary for the day.

> This is terrible! ... How come the Arabs are in rebellion? So, they were lying when they made a display of being content with our occupation. They have forgotten that until yesterday our good soldiers had fed them. Cowards![5]

In response to the uprising, and the 'cowardly' revolt by the oasis Arabs, Caneva ordered what many journalists described as a 'massacre'. It was later claimed that as many as 4,000 men, women and children were slaughtered by the rampaging Italian troops. One of the units involved in the reprisal attack on the oasis was Messe's 3rd Battalion of the 84th. In his diary entry for 23 October he acknowledges that the fighting in the oasis was 'a vicious hunt without quarter'.[6] Six days later his unit was still 'searching' the oasis. While the figure of 4,000 men killed is probably an exaggeration, even a pro-Italian British writer (who was not actually in Tripoli at the time) would later state that 'It must be admitted that the *plan of reprisal* was severe.' [My emphasis.][7]

Two days later, another and more powerful Turko-Arab attack was made on the troops deployed around Tripoli. The fighting was fierce and this time Caneva was forced to withdraw his men from a number of outlying strongpoints. Although the attackers were again beaten off, this partial retreat and the drawing-in of the line of defence severely affected the morale of the Italian troops, most of whom were illiterate peasant conscripts. In his diary Lieutenant Messe acknowledges this setback but insists on following the 'official' line about the withdrawal, which he stresses was '*voluntarily* abandoned', underlining the word 'voluntarily'.[8] Caneva was now besieged in the town, with his men further afflicted by an outbreak of cholera which caused around 1,000 deaths.[9] The only other significant event during this first stage of the war was on 1 November when an Italian airman, flying a German-made Taube monoplane, dropped hand grenades on Turkish troops at 'Ain Zara and the Tagiura oasis – history's first instance of aerial bombardment.

From then on fighting on the Tripoli front followed very much the same pattern. The Italians would move out of their coastal enclave to attack Turko-Arab troop concentrations ('Ain Zara was attacked and captured on the 4 December). The superior weaponry of the Italians enabled them to inflict heavy casualties, mainly on the Arabs, and force them to retreat; but then General Caneva would order his forces to withdraw back to the safety of Tripoli.

Caneva's task was made all the more difficult by his having no maps. It was intended that this would be remedied by the use of photography from airships. However, it was not until mid-December that two zeppelin airships arrived; and not until 4 March 1912 that they were able to make their first flight, during which their crews dropped some small bombs on enemy positions, as well as taking photographs.[10]

The Italians now landed troops to the west of Tripoli, capturing the coastal town of Misurata on 15 June 1912. Even so, in May of that year, so perilous was the situation at Tripoli that Caneva ordered the building of a 12-foot-high wall along the trenches surrounding the town.[11] The military situation in the vilayet of Tripoli had now reached a stalemate.

In Cyrenaica the Turkish troops put up a fierce resistance at Benghazi after the first attack in mid-October 1911. They then withdrew with some of their artillery and established their headquarters at the town of Banina, twelve kilometres to the east. It was sometime later that they were contacted by the Ottoman officers who had arrived after their secret journey through Egypt. The Ottoman resistance in Cyrenaica then began to take a coordinated form. However, it had still received little support from the Arab population – though this was about to change.

For the Italians, their most serious disadvantage was their lack of any reliable knowledge about the Libyan interior. In particular they had only very vague knowledge of the Sanusiyya, the Sufi *tariqa* which, over the preceding fifty years, had come to dominate the vast tract of land south of the Libyan coast, stretching far into the Sahara and beyond.

Their founder was Sayyid Muhammad bin 'Ali bin Sanusi (1787–1859), born in the Ottoman regency of Algiers.[12] After embarking on a number of journeys to Fez, Cairo and the Arabian Hejaz to study from their holy men, Ibn Sanusi formed his own *tariqa*. He gathered around him a growing number of loyal adherents who became known as the Ikhwan (the brothers). The principal objective of the Sanusiyya was to conduct missionary work among the nomadic and semi-nomadic Bedouin, whose understanding of Islam and its principal tenets was very limited.

Unable to return to Algeria since its occupation by the French, Ibn Sanusi chose as his base the eastern region of Libya, Cyrenaica, known to the Arabs as Barqa.[13] It was in 1843, on the great plateau of Jebel Akhdar, that he established his first *zawiya* (centre of Islamic studies), Al-Bayda, which became the *tariqa*'s mother lodge.

Among Ibn Sanusi's students, one in particular would achieve a reputation as an Arab hero comparable to that of 'Abd al-Qadir. His name was 'Umar al-Mukhtar (c. 1862–1931), and he would later gain his greatest fame as leader of the Cyrenaica Arabs in their war of resistance against the Italian occupation.[14]

The Turks took a very pragmatic view of their relations with the Sanusiyya. All that concerned them was the collection of taxes and the maintenance of peace and communications. Both these objectives were acceptable to the Sanusiyya and, while the Bedouin were usually reluctant to pay Ottoman taxes, the revenue collection system was organised in collaboration with the Sanusiyya and appears to have been generally successful.

Under Ibn Sanusi's successor, his son Sayyid Muhammad al-Mahdi (1884–1902), the realm of the Sanusiyya expanded exponentially, not only throughout North Africa but into the southern Sahara and beyond into sub-Saharan Africa. But as the Sanusiyya extended its influence it came into conflict with the French, who were advancing east across the Sahara and imposing their control over the whole Central African region. By 1897 French forces were already attacking and destroying Sanusi *zawiya*s in southern Libya and northern Chad, and Sanusi troops were involved in constant fighting with them. 'Umar al-Mukhtar played an important role in this ultimately unsuccessful struggle against the French. The Sanusiyya had to move their headquarters back north to the isolated oasis of Kufra, 500 kilometres from the Mediterranean coast. Muhammad al-Mahdi is reputed to have said later of 'Umar al-Mukhtar, 'If only I had ten men like 'Umar, it would be sufficient'.[15]

By 1908, leadership of the Sanusiyya had fallen to Sayyid Ahmad al-Sharif, the son of al-Mahdi's brother who had predeceased him, with 'Umar al-Mukhtar appointed head of the *zawiya* of al-Qasr in Cyrenaica, on the plateau of Jebel Akhdar. When news of the CUP revolution and the events of April 1909 reached al-Sharif, his attitude was initially one of anxiety, if not hostility. The Sanusiyya was essentially a conservative Islamic institution and regarded Abdülhamid, both sultan and caliph, with deep reverence. This hostility increased as Ahmad al-Sharif learnt of the increasingly secular tendency of the CUP and the apparent threat to the rule of the Shari'a. However, when the Italians invaded Libya, in a repeat of the European occupations of Tunis and, Egypt, he felt compelled to support the Turkish authorities in Libya. As yet, however, he made no formal declaration of jihad against the invaders.

At the time of the invasion 'Umar al-Mukhtar was at the Jalu oasis, about 370 km south of al-Qasr, returning from a conference with Ahmad al-Sharif at Kufra.[16] When he heard of the Italian invasion and occupation of the coastal towns he hurried back to the al-Qasr *zawiya* and enlisted all the armed men of the neighbouring 'Abid tribe, more than a thousand in total.[17] Many more tribesmen poured into Banina, the Ottoman base, after the Sanusi representative in Benghazi and the head of its *zawiya*, Sheikh Ahmad al-'Isawi, wrote to all the sheikhs of the lodges in the neighbourhood asking them to send volunteers to fight the Italians. Moreover, once al-Mukhtar learned of the Turkish officers' presence on the Jebel Akhdar plateau, he and his men went to join them.[18]

Al-Mukhtar was no man of letters and never appears to have recorded his battlefield experiences; but we can get a brief glimpse of the kind of action in which he took part, and some idea of the reverence in which his men held him, in the following brief account of a battle at Salawi (near Benghazi) in late 1911. The words are attributable to one of al-Mukhtar's comrades, Sheikh Muhammad al-Akhdar al-'Issawi, who was himself present on this occasion:

> We fell upon the enemy's frontline with the mujahidin cavalry.
> But meanwhile they were hitting us with machine gun fire and

forced us to dismount in a low-lying position cultivated with barley. The ears of corn were flying all over the place under the hail of bullets, as if the enemy were reaping us with scythes. While we were like this suddenly we spotted a place lower down than the one we were in. We urged Sayyid 'Umar to shelter there because we feared for him, but he fiercely refused until one of his followers reached him and appealed to the Sayyid and was forced to compel him to move to the place where he could shelter.[19]

The principal target of the Turko-Arab forces in Cyrenaica was the town of Derna, occupied by around 15,000 Italian troops. The geographical position of Derna favoured the Muslims since it was overlooked by the Jebel Akhdar which, at this point, falls steeply to the sea. The only access to the plateau from the coast was the Wadi (valley of) Derna. The Arabs fiercely attacked an attempt by the Italians to advance up the left bank of the wadi to reconnoitre a route to the plateau, and their troops were saved from disaster only by the arrival of a battalion of elite Alpine troops.[20] Apart from a few further forays outside the town, from now on, as in Tripoli, the

'Umar al-Mukhtar (photographed at the time of his execution by the Italians in 1931)

Italians were forced to remain in Derna and fortify their position with a number of redoubts.

With the Italian army making little headway in Libya, the Italians were forced to widen the war, contrary to their previous declarations to the other European powers. They hoped to use their supremacy at sea to put pressure on the Porte to get an early peace, one which could be portrayed as some kind of victory to the Italian nationalists who had so fervently backed the war.

The Italian naval campaign which had begun in late September 1911 at the 'Battle of Preveza', continued in late December. The Italians reinforced their naval presence in the Red Sea by sending three cruisers and two destroyers through the Suez Canal. Shortly after their arrival, they attacked the Ottoman torpedo cruiser *Peyk-ı Şevket* which was damaged and fled into the British-occupied Arabian port of Hudayda, where it was interned.

By now the six seagoing Ottoman gunboats which had been ordered to return from the Arabian Gulf to the Mediterranean had reached the Red Sea. But on 7 and 8 January 1912, they were driven into the Arabian port of Kunfuda by the Italian cruiser *Piemonte* and two destroyers. The Italian cruiser, with an armament of six 6-inch guns, stood off the port and opened fire at a range of 4,500 yards. In the very one-sided 'Battle of Kunfuda Bay' it sank four of the gunboats and forced the other two to beach themselves.

Then, in a major expansion of hostilities, on 24 January 1912 the heavy cruisers *Giuseppe Garibaldi* and her sister ship *Francesco Ferruccio* bombarded the port of Beirut, killing over 140 civilians and driving thousands of citizens out of the town. At 11.00 hours the two cruisers stopped the bombardment and the *Giuseppe Garibaldi* entered the harbour and torpedoed the old ironclad guard-ship, *Avnillah*, killing forty-nine crew and two officers. The captain of the only other Ottoman ship in the harbour, the torpedo boat *Ankara*, decided that the powerful Italian cruiser could not be resisted and scuttled his ship.[21]

With little real progress still evident in Libya, the Italians finally decided to attack the Turkish mainland. On 18 April 1912 they sent the cruisers *Giuseppe Garibaldi* and the *Varese* into the Dardanelles where they shelled two of the main Turkish forts, causing considerable damage. After that they imposed a blockade on the Straits. In retaliation the Ottomans closed the Straits completely by laying mine barrages at Çanakkale, thus trapping 170 merchant ships of various nationalities in the Sea of Marmara.

The Ottoman's closing of the Straits inflicted heavy losses on Russian trade,[22] and, once again, raised the profile of the Straits in Russian strategic thinking. According to Prince Grigorii Trubetskoi, who headed the key Foreign Ministry department that ran Russian policy in the Balkans and the Ottoman Empire, 'The present situation in which Turkey can lock the door to the trade of our entire southern region cannot be seen as tolerable for a great power.'[23]

Meanwhile, the Italians continued their naval campaign in the Mediterranean. On 4 and 16 May they seized the predominantly Greek-occupied island of Rhodes and a further eleven of what were known as the Dodecanese Islands. But thereafter the war again settled into a stalemate

As the war dragged on, the CUP-backed government acted with increased ferocity against those who challenged its heavy-handed imposition of conscription and higher taxes, especially in its two most contentious regions – Macedonia and Albania. Inter-ethnic murders and atrocities raged in the former's three *vilayet*s, while in Albania demands for an independent state gathered force, encouraged by the government's centralising attempt to suppress the Albanian language. As a result, 'even being an Albanian, for some ardent CUP men, was enough to implicate someone in seditious behaviour'.[24] The CUP victory in the general elections of January 1912 was won only by outright violence and fraud.

Three days later, with Raymond Poincaré recently installed as French prime minister, there occurred a series of events which threatened to destroy the friendly relationship established between France and Italy in the agreements of 1900 and 1902. It had been this colonialist pact that had given the go-ahead for Italy's invasion of Libya.

As the Italian invasion, literally, ran into the sand, its navy had become convinced that French and other gun-runners were smuggling armaments from Europe by sea to Tunis, and from there across the border to the Libyan resistance. On 15 January 1912 the French mail ship *Carthage*, en route from Marseilles to Tunis, was intercepted by the Italian cruiser *Agordat* and conveyed to Sardinia on the suspicion that was carrying parts of an aircraft to be assembled by the Turks. On the 18th the *Agordat* seized another French vessel, the *Manouba*, because of suspicions it was carrying Turkish officers.[25] These actions caused violent recriminations in the French press, to which Poincaré added his own bellicose voice, since he had recently declared he would pursue a strong foreign policy and therefore felt obliged to take a nationalistic line on this issue..[26] Consequently, in late 1912, Italy reaffirmed its friendship with the other two members of the Triple Alliance, thus notably declaring its support for Austria.[27] It was a realignment lasting for only a few years, but it would have a profound effect on the growing international crisis threatening the outbreak of a European-wide war.

In July a group of Turkish officers belonging to the opposition Liberal Party staged a coup in the Macedonian *vilayet* of Monastir, spreading to the capital. On 21 July it forced the resignation and replacement of all the CUP-backed ministers. The war minister Mahmud Shevket Paşa was replaced by Nazim Paşa and the grand vezir Said Paşa was replaced by the elderly Crimean War hero Ahmed Mukhtar Paşa. Without any coordination or discussion with its officers fighting in Libya, the new government began peace negotiations with the Italians at Caux (Switzerland) and later at Ouchy. But the discussions got nowhere, largely because the Ottoman delegates made various demands – for example, that any action on the part of the delegates must be sanctioned by their respective parliaments – which the Italians viewed as playing for time. By early October 1912 there had still been no progress. So, 'finally, the Italians played the Balkan card'.[28]

CHAPTER 29

'Playing the Balkan Card':
From Imperialism to World War

'Playing the Balkan card' was the Italians' last chance to bring an end to what was proving to be an unexpectedly difficult war with poor results. The stubborn resistance of the Arabs and Turks had forced it to increase its army in Libya to around 100,000. In addition, so far, it had suffered over 4,000 casualties. It was also proving to be an unexpectedly costly war. By 1912 Italy's war costs had risen to 498 million lire, on top of an expanded military budget of 837 million, together amounting to 46.9 per cent of total state expenditure.[1]

The Italian Crown was related by marriage to King Nikola I of Montenegro. King Emmanuel III of Italy was married to one of Nikola's daughters, Elena. Nikola had already agreed with the Serbo-Bulgarian Balkan League that his tiny state would join any future attack on the Ottoman Empire. However, on 8 October 1912 the Italians encouraged their Montenegrin ally to declare war on the Ottomans independently.[2] In this way, the Italian invasion of Libya 'created the conditions for the outbreak of the Balkan Wars.'[3]

After Montenegro declared war, the bulk of its 55,000 army surged into the *vilayet* of Shkodër (Scutari) laying siege to the Albanian-inhabited city of the same name. Ten days after the Montenegrin attack, the Bulgarian, Serbian and Greek armies, with a total of 715,000 men, outnumbering the available Ottoman troops by more than two to one, poured across the Macedonian frontier. At the same time the Greek navy was preventing Ottoman troops from Anatolia sending reinforcements across the Aegean.

On the same day, at Ouchy in Switzerland, the Ottoman delegates, facing the catastrophe of a war against five enemies, were forced to sign a peace agreement with Italy. Under its terms the Italians received sovereignty over Libya with the sultan retaining only nominal religious authority as caliph of Islam.

Italy's imperialist war merged seamlessly into a much greater Balkan one, which, in turn, would become 'the first phase of the First World War':⁴ 'The catalyst for calamity'.⁵ In the words of the historian Dominic Lieven, 'Italy's war with the Ottomans played a big part in ratcheting up international tensions, undermining the status quo in the Balkans, and leading Europe to the outbreak of world war in 1914.'⁶ The biographer of 'Umar al-Mukhtar, 'Asam 'Abd al-Fatah, agrees: 'The Italy-Turkey War ... formed a first step towards the First World War.'⁷ In 1924 Miroslav Spalajkovic, the former political head of the Serbian Foreign Ministry, said of the Italian invasion of Libya that he believed 'all subsequent events [were] nothing more than the evolution of that first act of aggression'.⁸

Russia's foreign minister, Sergei Sazonov, was one of the principal architects of the Balkan League and a passionate believer in 'pan-Slavism'. However, Sazonov failed to grasp the extent to which the two aggressive little Slavic polities which he himself had reared would be willing to ignore the advice of their 'big brother' when it suited them. Serbia and Bulgaria knew all too well that an increasingly vocal Russian public opinion was now almost fanatically determined that Russia should support its 'Slav brothers'. Too late, Sazonov discovered his mistake.

Under the terms of the Treaty of Ouchy the Ottomans withdrew a large number of their troops from Tripoli. But it made little difference to the military situation in Cyrenaica, where a substantial number of Turkish military personnel, including Enver Paşa and Mustafa Kemal, remained to provide a disciplined core of support to the resistance movement of al-Mukhtar and his Arab tribesmen. However, when the severity of the threat to Istanbul from the Bulgarian army became clear, both Enver and Mustafa Kemal decided they must return to defend the homeland. Command of the resistance in Libya was handed over to 'Aziz Ali al-Misri.

Before he left, Enver made a remarkable journey in the Turks' only motor vehicle to distant Jaghbub, an oasis in the Libyan desert, where he held discussions with Ahmad al-Sharif. Although previously ambivalent in his response to the Italian invasion, by now the Grand Sanusi had let it be known that he could not agree to peace with the Italians. So when Enver asked him, in the name of Sultan Mehmed V, to carry on the struggle, he agreed, but under certain conditions. Henceforth, all official correspondence and documents from the headquarters of the movement would be stamped

Al Hukuma al-Sanusiyya (The Sanusiyya Government).[9] In short, this was no longer an Italo-Ottoman war but an Arab jihad for the liberation of Libya.

'Umar al-Mukhtar now became one of the two closest companions of Ahmad al-Sharif and commander of the guerrillas in the Jebel Akhdar.[10] And although the Italian forces were able to mount a number of major campaigns against the resistance in both Tripoli and Cyrenaica, by the beginning of the First World War their only securely held territory remained their few coastal enclaves.

As the first of the Balkan Wars began, the Bulgarian army made spectacular advances, crushing an Ottoman army at Kirk Kilisse in Thrace on 24 October and encircling the ancient Ottoman capital of Edirne the following day. By 3 November they had reached the Çatalaca line, only 40 kilometres from Istanbul and its last line of defence. Meanwhile the Serbs stormed through the predominantly Albanian *vilayet*s in the west, committing numerous atrocities, and reaching the Adriatic on 10 November. The previous day the Greeks had seized the great maritime city of Salonika, while the Greek navy was capturing all but one of the Ottomans' Aegean islands.

On 29 October 1912, the Grand Vezir, Kamil Paşa, who had always been pro-British, was brought back to office; and on 7 November, with the loss of Edirne looming, he appealed to Sir Edward Grey to intervene and stop the war.[11] His letter contained many emotional references to the historic links between the two countries, especially during the Crimean War, and he urged Britain to induce its de facto ally Russia to prevent the final disintegration of Ottoman Europe. But once again Grey refused to assist, and informed Kamil Paşa that it would be best to surrender Edirne.[12] Grey seemed oblivious to the danger of the Bulgarians seizing Istanbul, something even the Russians were alarmed about. Indeed, on 4 November the Russian government warned the Bulgarians against such a move. The idea of the Austro-Germanic self-styled 'Tsar' Ferdinand (known in diplomatic circles as 'Foxy Ferdinand') holding the Straits had little appeal to the Russians.

Then, in mid-November, Serbia's Prime Minister Nikola Pašić dropped a diplomatic bombshell. With Serbian forces overrunning large swathes of Albanian territory, in a letter to *The Times* he declared that Serbia must have a coastline of some fifty kilometres along the Adriatic. Since he knew that this was anathema to Austria-Hungary, this was a clear attempt to force Russia into supporting Serbia.[13]

Two questions must now receive further attention: why was the presence of a Russian-backed Serbian enclave on the Adriatic so appalling to the Austrians? And precisely why did this possibility ultimately lead to the Balkan Wars becoming the 'Prelude to the First World War'?[14]

By 1912, the Austro-Hungarian battle fleet included three modern semi-dreadnoughts, the Radetzky class, completed in 1910–11, with a main armament of four 12-inch guns, a secondary armament of eight 9.4-inch (four per broadside) and a top speed of 20 knots. In June 1911 and March 1912 the first two dreadnoughts were launched, the *Tegetthoff* and the *Viribus Unitis*. Protected by a belt of 11-inch thick Krupp steel, they carried a main armament of twelve 12-inch guns, and they too were capable of making 20 knots.[15] Built later than many of the earlier British and German dreadnoughts they were considerably ahead in design: for example they had Marconi wireless rooms and anti-aircraft guns. The Austro-Hungarian fleet was projected to have a tonnage of 129,711 by 1914, which would make it the second largest fleet in the Mediterranean after France.[16]

Historians of the First World War have placed sea-power rivalry towards the top of all the factors leading to the war's outbreak. But it has always been the rivalry between Britain and Germany that has been their focus. It is true that Germany desired to become a global trading power to accommodate the needs of its industrial base. Its construction of a High Seas Fleet to support and protect that global influence certainly meant that, once hostilities had started, joining sides with France and Russia was the only option for Britain.[17] But the remarkable growth of the Austro-Hungarian navy in the Mediterranean has been ignored. This development put the seal on the fatal rivalry between Austria and Russia. The existence of this large modern fleet presented a massive obstacle to Russia's plans to seize Istanbul and the Straits and break through into the Mediterranean with its less powerful Black Sea Fleet. At the same time, however, the Austro-Hungarian fleet was itself vulnerable.

This modern and powerful Austrian battle fleet was based mainly at Pula on the tip of the Istrian peninsula at the northern head of the Adriatic. But to support its massive naval build-up Austria-Hungary had also expanded its port facilities and naval construction yards at Trieste, Rijeka and Kotor, together with a number of smaller ports and naval fortifications along the Dalmatian coast.

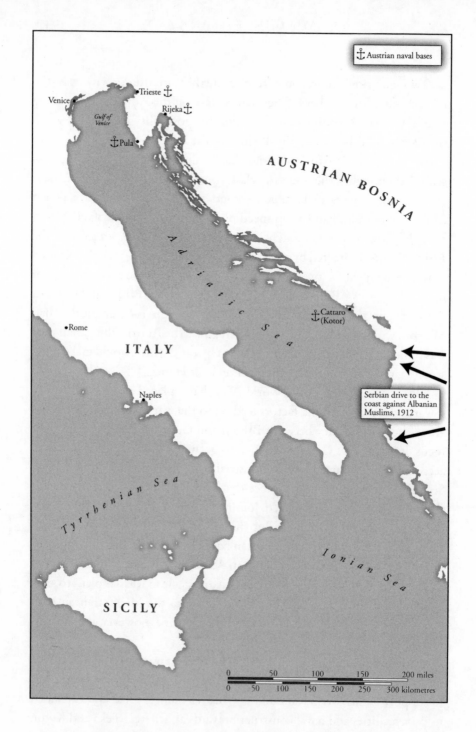

SERBIAN-OCCUPIED TERRITORY AND THE
THREAT TO AUSTRO-HUNGARIAN NAVAL BASES
IN THE MEDITERRANEAN, 1912

Consequently, the Austrians were determined that not under any circumstances should Serbia be permitted to push its frontiers to the Adriatic coast. As the Canadian historian Margaret MacMillan puts it, 'Its naval base at Pola which had already absorbed a good deal of Austria-Hungary's resources might well become useless and the very important port of Trieste, at the head of the Adriatic, could be strangled.'[18] Worse still, with several ports newly occupied, a new Russian naval base might now be established, with Belgrade's blessing.[19] At the same time both Austria-Hungary and Italy insisted that Albania must be founded as an independent state, 'since any port that Serbia acquired would of necessity lie in the midst of an Albanian-inhabited country'.[20]

However, Serbian forces surged on, occupying not only the whole of the *vilayet* of Kosovo but a swathe of territory in the north of the projected Albanian state, including the port city of Durazzo (Durrës) captured on 30 November. Meanwhile the Montenegrins were still laying siege to the city of Scutari and its 30,000 Albanian inhabitants. In the huge areas they had conquered, the Serbs and Montenegrins continued to commit atrocities. According to the Vienna correspondent of a Ukrainian newspaper, Leon Trotsky, Serbian troops and irregulars were 'engaged quite simply in the extermination of the Muslim population'.[21] Not only were civilians massacred but Turkish and Albanian prisoners of war were mutilated by having their noses and ears cut off, after which they were hidden from inspections by visiting Red Cross personnel.[22]

The issue of a Serbian enclave on the Adriatic now brought Austria-Hungary and Russia to the brink of war. The Austrians were particularly incensed that Adriatic ports had been captured by the Serbians, whom they saw as agents of Russia.[23] Indeed, the Tsar now stated that he was firmly in support of Serbia's Adriatic ambitions. Austria-Hungary was adamant that the Serbs should be blocked. Italy, angered at France's high-handed seizure of its shipping, came out in full support of its Triple Alliance partner, giving strength to Austria's stance.

At the end of September 1912, Russia carried out what it described as a 'trial' mobilisation of its Warsaw military district bordering both Austria-Hungary and Germany. With the Serbs now settling down for an occupation of a sizeable stretch of Adriatic coastline, Austria-Hungary responded by putting its troops in Bosnia and Dalmatia on a war footing and increasing its garrisons in Galicia, near the Russian border. The Tsar's top commanders were now arguing for a showdown with Austria-Hungary.[24] On 22 November the Tsar and his generals took the decision for another military district (Kiev) to be mobilised and another prepared for mobilisation. A general European war seemed imminent, and even though the correspondent of the *Daily Mirror* took a less pessimistic view, he could identify the likely cause. 'It would seem inconceivable that six great civilised nations should go to war because an infant state wants a port on the Adriatic Sea.'[25]

For nineteen months war was avoided. Vladimir Kokovtsov, Russia's minister of finance, argued that Russia was simply not ready for war, either militarily or financially.[26] Characteristically, the Tsar now changed his mind and stated that he didn't support Serbia's Adriatic ambitions after all. Nevertheless the warning bell had rung. It would be the fear of that infant state acquiring a port on the Adriatic Sea which would be the most important consideration in leading Austria-Hungary's leaders to decide to crush Serbia, even if it meant confronting Russia in a wider war.

Meanwhile, the Ottoman navy had proved unable to make any significant contribution to the war effort and once again underlined the mistake of trying to create a 'big ship' navy. During the Italian war its two former-German battleships *Barbaros Hayreddin* and *Torgud Reis* had been withdrawn to home waters to keep them out of harm's way. However, the intention had also been to prepare them for an anticipated Balkan war and continue training their crews; but from May 1912 onwards nothing was done to allow the necessary repairs to begin. Requests from the captains of the ships for material and engineers failed to elicit any response from the Ministry of Marine. The battleships were now suffering from corroded piping, the breakdown of their telephone systems and faulty watertight doors. Worse still both ships' rangefinders and ammunition hoists had been removed. In spite of this two further battleships, both dreadnoughts, had been ordered from the British.

The two Brandenburg-class battleships, which should have been able to wreak havoc on the small Greek navy, made only two sorties out of the Straits. On 16 December 1912 an operation was planned to attack the Greek-held island of Imbros just off the mouth of the Dardanelles. The two battleships were accompanied by the torpedo boat *Sivrihisar* and the two old central-battery ironclads *Mesudiye* and *Asar-I Teyfik*, supported by the cruiser *Mecidiye* and two destroyers. They soon encountered a Greek squadron consisting of the modern armoured cruiser *Giorgios Averoff* accompanied by two old Hydra-class ironclads. Although the Greek cruiser was more lightly armed than the Ottoman battleships it was much faster, its crew fully trained and its equipment in good condition. At 09.00 hours the Ottomans opened a sluggish fire at 9,000 metres without any hits, but a quarter of an hour later the *Giorgios* performed the Nelsonian manoeuvre 'crossing the T', firing simultaneously at both the Ottoman battleships. As the Ottoman commander broke off the action and headed back to the Dardanelles, *Barbaros Hayreddin* received a hit from the *Giorgios* on its afterdeck and shortly afterwards another which put the after turret out of action. Both *Torgud Reis* and *Mesudiye* also received hits from the *Giorgios*. The Ottoman squadron eventually reached safety with fifty-nine casualties, of which eighteen dead.[27]

A second attempt to attack a nearby Greek-held island on 18 January ended in a similar fashion with the *Giorgios* hitting the middle turret of the *Barbaros Hayreddin,* as well as the *Torgud Reis* and *Mesudiye.* All were badly damaged and there were 145 casualties including forty-one dead.[28] After this engagement both Ottoman battleships remained in port, more of a liability than an asset.

On 6 December 1912, with tens of thousands of Muslim refugees pouring into Istanbul and Anatolia, the Ottoman government was forced to agree an armistice with Serbia, Bulgaria and Montenegro.* Belatedly, Grey now appears to have become anxious about the way events were moving. On 16 December he brought together the ambassadors of the Great Powers and the Ottoman Empire in London, who began discussions on a solution to the Balkan crisis. But on 23 January 1913, fearing that the Ottoman negotiators were about to surrender Edirne, Enver and the other leaders of the CUP staged a coup d'état, killing Nazim Paşa, the defence minister, and replacing the grand vezir Kamil Paşa with their own man, Mahmud Shevket Paşa.

The conference reconvened in July 1913, but its only significant decision was to ratify the action of a small group of Albanian notables on 24 November 1912 to establish Albania as a sovereign state, a decision which

---

* Although Greece refused to join it. Hence the naval actions described above.

was accepted by the Ottoman government five days later. The creation of Albania was much favoured by Austria-Hungary, which envisaged the new state as an Austrian puppet and a defensive obstacle to Serbian ambitions on the Adriatic. Nevertheless, the conference decision on Albania's borders left between 30 and 49 per cent of the total Albanian population excluded and in the hands of Serbia and Greece, thereby sowing the seeds of further conflict and atrocities in years to come.

The London conference was the last gasp of the Concert of Europe. In the words of the American historian Richard Hall, 'By 1912 the Great Powers, who had maintained peace in the Balkan Peninsula since 1878 through the mechanism of the Berlin settlement, lacked the determination to enforce it when confronted by Balkan unity. Because of this failure they would find themselves at war within two years.'[29]

Hostilities now recommenced; but the renewal of war brought further losses to the Ottomans, including the surrender of Edirne to the Bulgarians on 26 March 1913. The first Balkan War ended with the signing of the Treaty of London on 30 May, leaving the Ottoman Empire in Europe with only a tiny remnant of territory in eastern Thrace to shield Istanbul. In the general atmosphere of fear, hatred and recrimination in the city, in June the CUP carried out a brutal purge of their political enemies, creating, in effect a CUP dictatorship in which Talat Paşa, Enver Paşa and Jamal Paşa emerged as the Empire's rulers.

The ability of Serbia and Greece to make substantial territorial gains during 1912 had been greatly facilitated by the Bulgarian army, which had borne the brunt of the heavy fighting against the Ottoman troops. Now Bulgaria felt cheated at the way the spoils of war had been shared out at the Treaty of London. On the night of 29–30 June 1913 the Bulgarian army launched a surprise attack on its rivals in the hope of gaining more territory. But this second Balkan War, started recklessly and foolishly by Bulgaria, not only gave Romania the chance to seize territory on the Black Sea coast from Bulgaria, but also gave the CUP leaders in beleaguered Istanbul the opportunity to counter-attack and recover the city of Edirne and part of Thrace. Enver Paşa, now minister of war, led the campaign and became a national hero.

Subsequently, at the Treaty of Bucharest, signed on 10 August 1913, Serbia and Greece increased their share of the Ottoman spoils at the expense of Bulgaria. Since the beginning of the first Balkan War, Serbia had doubled its territory and increased its population by a third. Bulgaria lost much of its gains in the first Balkan War but retained some of its acquisitions, including a corridor through Thrace to the Aegean. But for the Ottoman Muslims the consequence of the two Balkan Wars – or, more accurately, the invasion and occupation of the three Macedonian *vilayet*s of Kosovo, Monastir and Salonika – were catastrophic: 1,450,000 Muslim civilians were killed, and, in what was one of the most serious episodes of ethnic cleansing in modern times, 410,000 Muslim refugees were forced to flee to Istanbul and Anatolia.[30]

Russia was now alienated from Bulgaria as a result of the latter's opportunistic attack upon its allies in the second Balkan War. In Russian eyes, this showed that Bulgaria's devious and Germanic 'Tsar' Ferdinand was unwilling to accept Russian tutelage. Consequently, Russia's leaders were compelled to consider Bulgaria a potential enemy – all the more so since Bulgaria now had access to the northern Aegean and proximity to the Straits which had been blocked during the Balkan Wars. That event had demonstrated, yet again, just how important the Straits were as an outlet for Russia's exports.

For its part, Serbia recognised that it was Russia's only real ally in the southern Balkans, a sentiment reciprocated by the Russians who saw its 'little brother' as the only state it could now count upon to block any hostile Austrian move. In turn, this Serbian leverage with Russia gave Serbian extreme nationalists – who saw their next move as incorporating Bosnian Serbs into a greatly expanded 'pan-Slav' polity – the confidence to begin subversive activities in neighbouring Bosnia-Herzegovina.

During the Adriatic crisis Austria-Hungary and Russia had come close to war on a number of occasions, especially since around 100,000 Serbian troops remained on the territory of the newly independent Albania when the Balkan wars ended. Eventually, faced with an Austrian ultimatum to quit Albania, on 25 October 1913 the Serbian army units were forced to leave.[31] The following day the Kaiser paid a visit to Vienna and congratulated the Austrian foreign minister, Leopold von Berchtold, on Austria's firmness, promising that Germany was always ready to support its ally.[32]

If the second Balkan War raised Russian anxieties about the Straits, they were increased to almost panic levels by the surprise arrival of a forty-two-man German military mission in the Ottoman Empire in December

1913. The mission was headed by General Otto Liman von Sanders, an experienced Prussian cavalry officer. Both the Empire's CUP leaders and the Germans themselves argued that the mission's presence was simply to restore the capabilities of the Ottoman army which had so recently displayed its deficiencies. Liman von Sanders was given a five-year appointment and also a seat on the Ottoman war council, plus command of the Ottoman corps stationed in and around the capital.

According to Sazonov, the German mission and in particular the command appointment of Liman von Sanders was 'a mortal blow' to Russia's aspirations in the Black Sea and the Straits. With the German general given control of the Ottoman corps based at Istanbul, it appeared that the Germans had effectively taken control of the Ottoman capital, which Sazonov considered 'the nodal point ... at the junction of Europe and Asia' and 'the most important point on the Berlin to Baghdad railway'.[33]As a consequence German-Russian relations fell into an abyss. For the time being, however, neither side could contemplate war and, in the event, a face-saving device was produced: the Germans promoted Von Sanders to a higher rank, which made him ineligible to command the 'mere' army corps at Istanbul.

Nevertheless, the presence of the German military mission at Istanbul continued to exacerbate Russian anxieties about the Straits. When the Russian Council of Ministers met in February 1914 the Straits – and reclaiming 'Constantinople' for Orthodox Christianity – re-emerged as a key object of Russian foreign policy. Moreover, it was decided that the best opportunity to seize these objectives would arise in the context of a general European war. Tsar Nicholas II approved these recommendations in April and committed his government to create the necessary forces to occupy Istanbul and the Straits at the earliest such opportunity.[34]

For their part, the Austrians were utterly shocked by the doubling of Serbia's territory as a result of its conquest of most of western Macedonia, in spite of the fact that Serbia had now withdrawn from its enclave on the Adriatic. The possibility that Serbia and Russia might eventually cooperate to bring about Austria's maritime isolation was still a nightmare for Vienna.[35] What also shocked Austria-Hungary's leaders was the fact that none of the Great Powers, even Germany for a time, seemed to appreciate Austria's genuine anxiety over this issue. The Balkan Wars changed everything for

Austria-Hungary. More than anything, they revealed how isolated Vienna was and how little understanding there was in the foreign chancelleries for its fear about Balkan events.'[36]

Had the Concert of Europe still been functioning it is quite possible that Austria-Hungary's 'nightmare' could have been removed. After all, Austria did have genuine security concerns. Its fears for the safety of its large Adriatic naval bases and its fleet were not illusory. This matter could have been dealt with through negotiation and giving Austria certain security guarantees. But such an outcome was no longer possible. The Concert was now irredeemably split into the Anglo-Franco-Russian Triple Entente and the Italo-Austro-German Triple Alliance.

Consequently, the hugely enlarged Serbia remained, in Austrian eyes, an existential threat to its naval presence in the Adriatic and the Mediterranean. It was this consideration, as much as any subversion from gangs of Bosnian Serbs, that convinced them that Serbia had to be defeated in war. Once again, all that was required was a certain 'incident', in this case an 'accident waiting to happen'. And a handful of Bosnian Serb fanatics, probably supported by elements within the Serbian military secret service, were not long in providing it – the assassination of the Austrian Grand Duke Franz Ferdinand and his wife in Sarajevo on 28 June 1914.

Austria-Hungary promptly sent Serbia an ultimatum, and at least one of its terms was impossible for the Serbs to accept. The subsequent Austrian preparations for an attack on Serbia compelled the Tsar and his government – under extreme pressure from the great force of popular 'pan-Slav' sentiment – to defend Russia's remaining 'little brother' in the Balkans. In an age when honour, both national and individual, meant everything to Europe's aristocrats, the Tsar and his ministers were determined not to endure, for a second time, the 'shameful' diplomatic defeat by Austria-Hungary which they had experienced during the Bosnian crisis of 1908.

Consequently on 23 July Foreign Minister Sazonov proposed to the Russian Chief of Staff General Nikolai Yanushkevich a 'partial mobilisation' against Austria-Hungary (the nearest thing to a declaration of war). The following day the proposal was adopted 'in principle' by the Council of Ministers. On the 25th the Council authorised a batch of regulations known as 'Period Preparatory to War Measures'. These pre-mobilisation regulations were not confined to the regions bordering Austria-Hungary but applied across the whole of European Russia, including districts bordering Germany. Then, on 28 July, the Russian government decided to announce officially that it would conduct a 'partial mobilisation' against Austria-Hungary.[37]

The problem was that Russia had no existing plans for a 'partial mobilisation', in an age when mobilisation plans were rigid and mobilisation was all or nothing. Consequently, when the announcement was actually made on the 29th, news of this 'partial' Russian mobilisation, combined with numerous reports of troop movements, were interpreted by the other European states, including crucially Germany, as nothing less than 'mobilisation' *full stop*.[38] Especially since, the previous day, Austria-Hungary had declared war on Serbia.

Any such general mobilisation would therefore be aimed not only at Austria-Hungary but also against Germany. On the 31st, news arrived from the German Ambassador in Moscow that Russia had indeed ordered total mobilisation from midnight the previous night.[39] Germany therefore demanded an end to the Russian mobilisation. With no Russian response, on 1 August Germany declared war on Russia. With Germany and Russia now at war, and France pledged to support Russia, on 3 August Germany attacked France.

Britain had no treaty obligation to enter the war on France's side. As we have seen, the famous Entente Cordiale of 1904 was primarily about colonies. Moreover the majority of the Liberal Party government had strong pacifist inclinations. But since the beginning of the century Britain and Germany had been locked in a fierce economic rivalry and German industrial and mercantile competition had a significant influence upon the thinking of the country's leaders, including Grey himself.[40] If Germany defeated France and the whole of Europe fell under its political *and economic* sway, Britain would certainly have lost its imperial hegemony. And in the corridors of power some believed a war between the two countries was inevitable anyway, so why not fight Germany now, when Britain had two powerful allies? As yet there was little enthusiasm for war in the country: that would come. However, at 11 p.m. on 4 August, after Germany had invaded Belgium – infringing its neutrality and killing hundreds of civilians – Britain declared war on Germany.

Because its military preparations were still not complete, Austria-Hungary delayed its declaration of war on Russia until 6 August.

The question remains: does the only explanation for Russia's reckless 'partial' and 'pre-mobilisation' decisions – decisions almost guaranteed to spark a European war – lie in the Russian public's pressure to support their Serbian 'little brothers', and the reluctance of Russia's aristocratic leaders to lose face a second time in dealing with the Austrians? Was this done on Serbia's behalf only? According to the historian Christopher Clark:

> The robustness of the Russian response fully makes sense only if we read it against the background of the Russian leaderships' deepening anxiety about the future of the Turkish Straits ... Russian control of the Balkans would place St Petersburg in a far better position to prevent unwanted intrusions on the Bosphorus. Designs on the Straits were thus an important reinforcing factor in the decision to stand firm over the threat to Serbia.[41]

What is indisputable is that the acquisition of Istanbul and the Straits was one of Russia's explicit war aims, and one that would be agreed with Britain and France, as we shall see in the next chapter.

In early July 1914, as the chances of a European war were accelerating, the Ottoman government began desperately seeking a defensive alliance with one or other of the major European states. Its leaders, especially Enver Paşa and Jemal Paşa, believed that neutrality counted for nothing without such a pact. But with no hope of an alliance with Britain, and after attempts by Jemal Paşa to obtain one from France failed, Enver Paşa and the grand vezir, Said Halim Paşa, decided they must turn to Germany. By mid-July secret negotiations between Enver and the German government were underway, and on 24 July the Kaiser gave his blessing to an Ottoman-German defensive pact. Four days later there occurred the event which would provide Enver with the popular support for the agreement it required.

On 28 July the First Lord of the Admiralty, Winston Churchill, proposed to the cabinet the requisition of the two dreadnoughts, the *Reshadieh* and the *Sultan Osman*, which were being completed for the Porte on the Tyne. In fact, a Turkish crew had already arrived to man both vessels, which had cost the impoverished Ottoman Empire £7.5 million, mainly through public subscription. Three days later the British cabinet approved his proposal. With the Turkish people appalled at this act of betrayal, on 2 August Enver concluded the secret pact with Germany, having called for full mobilisation to begin the previous day; and on the 3rd the Turkish Straits were closed. In the words of the Turkish historian Feroz Ahmad, 'The German alliance was a gamble and the outcome of the war proved that [the Ottomans] had backed the wrong horse. But events had shown that they had no other horse to back.'[42]

The Great War was now raging across most of mainland Europe. Noting the stalemate on the Western Front, elements in the Ottoman government reckoned that neutrality was still an option. So, while mobilisation slowly continued, the Porte procrastinated in the final decision to go to war in alliance with Germany and Austria-Hungary. In response, the exasperated Germans, who had already sent £2 million worth of gold bullion to Istanbul to finance the Ottoman mobilisation, now promised a further £3 million.

On 3 August two German warships, the battleship *Goeben* and light cruiser *Breslau*, were sent into the Mediterranean to attack French transports carrying troops from North Africa. When the Royal Navy tried to hunt them down the two ships fled to the Turkish Straits where the Ottoman authorities allowed them to steam up to Istanbul. The Ottoman Empire was still a neutral state and according to international law should have either expelled or interned the two warships. Instead Jemal Paşa, minister of marine, announced the Empire had decided to 'buy' them and they were absorbed into the Ottoman navy.

Two months passed as the Ottoman mobilisation continued and uncertainty grew within and without the Ottoman government as to whether it should enter the war. Then, on 24 October, Jemal Paşa gave orders for the *Goeben* and *Breslau* to enter the Black Sea. Three days later the reflagged warships passed through the Bosphorus. On the 29th they sank two small Russian warships and bombarded Sevastopol. The 'Ottoman' navy had begun hostilities. All that remained was for the sultan to meet with twenty-nine religious scholars and prepare *fetvas* commanding jihad against Russia, Britain, France, Serbia and Montenegro. On 14 October the jihad was announced to the Turkish people and to all Muslims throughout the world,[43] and on 31 October the Ottomans declared war on Russia, Britain and France.

Around a third of the Ottoman Army consisted of regular Arab soldiers – mainly from Syria and Iraq – and to the very end of the war they generally fought with loyalty and courage.[44] The Shi'i Arabs of Iraq also rallied to the call of jihad and resisted the British invasion until conflict emerged with their Turkish overlords.[45] In Libya, Ahmad al-Sharif initially resisted the call to jihad against all the states the sultan had named. However, by way of encouragement, Sultan Mehmed V sent him a message in which he conferred upon him 'absolute military and civilian power in North Africa'.[46] Enver Paşa also sent two Arab officers, Nuri al-Sa'id and Ja'far al-'Askari, to provide military advice and training as in 1911; and after the British defeat at Gallipoli in November 1915, Ahmad al-Sharif ordered his forces to attack them across the Libyan-Egyptian border. For a time, they threatened the whole British presence in the northwest of the country, until they were defeated in March the following year. Meanwhile, 'Umar al-Mukhtar remained in Cyrenaica waging guerrilla war against the Italians who, by now, had abandoned the Triple Alliance and were allies of the British.[47]

But as far as the rest of the Islamic Mediterranean was concerned the Ottoman call to jihad had only meagre results. The call was barely heard in the lands of the Maghreb, now fully under French control, and especially in Morocco, in the grip of the collaborating Glaoua 'Lords of the Atlas'.

Nevertheless, the French remained worried about the Ottoman sultan-caliph's call to jihad. On 3 November 1914 they set up the Comité Interministériel des Affaires Musulmanes (CIAM), tasked with finding a counterweight to the sultan-caliph's message. The Comité recognised the threat it still posed in this deeply religious country and they decided that 'the problem had to be solved within the religious field and according to an Islamic rationale'.[48] Using the coercive power of their chief collaborators, Madani and Thami Glaoui and their tame Sufi leaders, the CIAM engineered a *majlis al-baladi* (national council) at Fez which declared that the Turks were not the true defenders of Islam because the Ottomans had usurped the Caliphate.[49] In this way the French were able to impose their own interpretation of 'holy war' upon their illiterate Moroccan subjects, one which legitimised the French recruiting agents who were now touring the colony.

By early August 1914 around 15,000 Moroccans had been recruited into *les batailions de chasseurs indigènes*, and were despatched to France to fight on the Western Front. They were used as 'shock troops', the most dangerous infantry role, and, of the initial 4,000 who arrived, between 17 August and 23 September, only one fifth survived.[50] In total, around 42,000 Moroccans were brought to France during the war, either as front-line troops or ancillary workers.[51]

The Ottomans won some significant victories over the Allies, notably at Gallipoli and at the siege of Kut in Iraq. In the end, however, they did not have the resources, either in men or materiel, to defeat the forces ranged against them. On 30 October 1918 an armistice was signed with Britain at Moudros on the Aegean island of Lemnos. The signatories were the Ottoman minister of marine, Rauf Bey, and Admiral Somerset Gough-Calthorpe representing the British Empire. Meanwhile, the CUP triumvirate, Enver, Talat and Jamal, had fled, fearing retribution for the death march of the Ottoman Armenian community which they had ordered in 1915.

On 13 November 1918, having recently cleared the minefields of the Dardanelles, an Allied fleet steamed into Istanbul's great harbour, led by the British dreadnought HMS *Agamemnon*. For the Ottomans, perhaps the most bitter irony was that this was a battleship of the power which had spent most of the past century protecting Istanbul and the Straits from the designs of its principal imperialist rival; and it would now head the convoy of Europeans coming to occupy their capital.

CHAPTER 30

From World War to Imperialism

In July 1920 Vladimir Lenin wrote an article with the title 'Imperialism and Capitalism' which was first published in the *Communist International*, No. 18, October 1921. It would later be published as the preface to the French and German edition of his book *Imperialism: The Highest Stage of Capitalism*. The article is significant in that, for the first time, it carries Lenin's explicit statement about the relationship between imperialism and the First World War.*

> The war of 1914–18 was imperialistic (that is, an annexationist, predatory, plunderous war) on the part of both sides; it was a war for the division of the world, for the partition of colonies, 'spheres of influence' of finance capital etc.[1]

However, Lenin fails to give any empirical evidence for this statement. The two examples he gives in his original *Imperialism* ('German appetite for Belgium, France's appetite for Lorraine') are not very convincing. As Lenin himself concedes, the German invasion of neutral Belgium was actually a military-strategic move to attempt the encirclement of the allied armies: 'Belgium is chiefly necessary to Germany as a base for operations against England.'[2] In the case of 'France's appetite for Lorraine' [i.e. Alsace-Lorraine] Lenin was on somewhat stronger ground. The recovery of Alsace-Lorraine was certainly a French war aim – but it was a recovery. This French region had originally been annexed by the German Empire in 1871.

Lenin's apparent lack of interest in the historical reality of his 'annexationist, predatory, plunderous war' is all the more strange, given that four years earlier, on 23 November 1917, the Bolsheviks had made

---

* In his *Imperialism* of 1917, Lenin refers to the First World War, but only obliquely, as part of a passage attacking Kautsky. (See pp. 113–14.)

public all the secret treaties between the imperialist powers carving up the colonial world; and they subsequently renounced all Russia's secret agreements.

In fact, the Allies' plans for an 'annexationist' and 'predatory' war had begun as early as 4 March 1915. The Tsar's government demanded from Britain that, after an Allied victory, it would gain possession of Istanbul, the Straits, territory on both the European and Asian sides of the Straits, and the Aegean islands of Imbros and Tenedos. In other words, the whole of the territory Russia had coveted since the eighteenth century and which, for most of that period, Britain had done its best to protect. Eight days later, Britain gave its full agreement.

This Anglo-Russian agreement was the subject of Sir Maurice de Bunsen's opening remarks on 30 June, when he chaired a committee consisting of all the heads of Britain's government departments to discuss the disposal of the Ottoman Empire's non-European possessions. Not a single voice was raised in opposition to the Anglo-Russian deal.[3] A policy which had been the bedrock of Britain's diplomatic and military strategy in the Mediterranean for nearly a century was quietly abandoned. Thereafter, between 1915 and 1917 a further series of secret treaties and agreements divided what remained of the Ottoman Empire into Russian, British, French and Italian colonies and zones of influence.

Among these was the infamous Sykes-Picot Agreement of May 1916 which, in effect, divided the Middle East between Britain and France. But it was also revealed that Britain had secretly promised the Sharif Husayn of Mecca and his sons a vast Islamic empire, carved out of Ottoman Syria and Iraq, in return for his rebellion against the Turks in the Hejaz. The whole question of the division of the spoils would therefore have to be revisited and untangled after the end of the war.

Part of the solution was found in the 'Mandate' system. It was first discussed at a meeting of the Allied Supreme Council on 30 January 1919.

The idea was that the former colonial and other dependencies of Germany, Austria-Hungary and the Ottoman Empire would be classified according to their ability to become fully independent 'civilised' nations. Some – for example the European elements of the Austro-Hungarian Empire, like the Czechs and Hungarians – qualified immediately for full statehood. At the other end of the spectrum of 'civilisation', Germany's

African colonies were deemed unfit for independence for the foreseeable future and were given to France and Britain as virtual colonies. In the middle were the Arab *vilayet*s of the Ottoman Empire's 'Asian' provinces. These were deemed to be, as yet, incapable of 'civilised' statehood, but should be placed in trust to 'mandatory powers' (i.e. Britain and France), whereby the policies carried out by each power aimed to bring the territory in question to a stage of 'fitness' for independence. The distribution of the mandates was finalised at the San Remo Conference on 24 April 1920. Britain was granted the mandates of Palestine and Iraq, and France the mandate of Syria (including Lebanon). In reality these turned out to be little different from simple colonies.

There remained the problem of Anatolia, the Turkish heartland of the Ottoman Empire. This was dealt with at the Treaty of Sèvres of 10 August 1920. Anatolia was to be divided up between France, Italy, Greece and a proposed state for the Armenians, leaving only a rump Turkish entity in the north of the region. For the time being Istanbul and the Turkish Straits would remain in the hands of Britain and France, who controlled a puppet sultan, Mehmed VI.

But in central Anatolia forces were gathering which would eventually recover much of the Turkish heartland. Resistance against the Allies had been growing for some time. At the armistice, General Kazim Karabekir had been in Azerbaijan. Returning to Istanbul, now ruled by a puppet government, he was offered the position of Head of the General Staff. However, on learning of the terms that were to be imposed on what remained of the Ottoman Empire, he rejected the offer. Instead, together with some loyal troops, he secretly crossed the Straits back into Anatolia where he took command of the 14th Army Corps, which had never surrendered.[4] On 15 May 1919 Sultan Mehmed VI sent Mustafa Kemal, the hero of Gallipoli, to eastern Anatolia to organise the demobilisation of the 14th Corps; but instead Kemal joined Kazim in what was the beginning of a Turkish nationalist rebellion against the sultan and the Allied forces of occupation. On 8 July the sultan dismissed Mustafa Kemal and declared him a traitor. On 23 July and 9 September 1919, nationalist congresses were held at Erzurum and Sivas respectively, where the delegates pledged to recover all the territory which had been in Ottoman hands at the time of the 1918 armistice, including Istanbul.

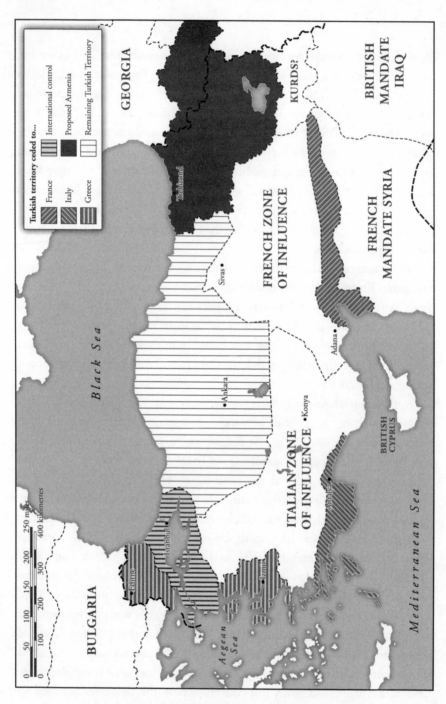

THE CARVE-UP OF THE OTTOMAN EMPIRE
AT THE TREATY OF SÈVRES, AUGUST 1920

When most representatives in the Ottoman parliament also adopted this objective, the Allies cracked down. Around 150 nationalists were arrested and on 16 March 1920 the puppet sultan dissolved the parliament. On 11 May, the Allies informed the Porte of the partition of Anatolia, and on 14 August Turkey's nominal rulers gave their reluctant acceptance.

However, in the aftermath of the Great War, the Allies lacked the military capacity to defeat the Turkish nationalists in Anatolia and enforce the partition. For example, Britain had already demobilised most of its conscript armies in France and its colonial forces were spread thinly throughout its empire. The French, whose troops in Anatolia had already been defeated by the Turkish nationalists, faced similar problems and calculated that at least twenty-seven divisions would be required to crush the rapidly growing forces under Mustafa Kemal. For its part, the Italian government was faced with revolutionary socialism in its major industrial zones, and the emergence of Mussolini's ultra-nationalist Fascist movement; so it was losing interest in asserting its claims in Anatolia.

As the British government found itself increasingly isolated, Prime Minister David Lloyd George, an extreme Turkophobe, saw a solution in using the Greek army as a proxy to reconquer Anatolia. Greece had been promised territorial gains in Anatolia after its entry into the war, and Greek forces had already established a significant foothold at Izmir and were advancing inland. As Greece's largely illiterate and ill-trained peasant conscripts marched on, they randomly killed Muslims, actions for which their co-religionists in Anatolia would later pay dearly.

Beginning in October 1920, the Greek army advanced deep into Anatolia and defeated the Turks in a number of battles until they reached the Sakarya River, forty-five kilometres from Ankara. Here the Turks fought a major defensive action between August and September 1921, stopping the Greek advance. Between 21 September and 22 August 1922 the Greek and Turkish forces were locked in stalemate, during which time the Turks received substantial armaments and gold from the infant Bolshevik government which had recently defeated an Allied military intervention in support of the counter-revolutionary Russian 'Whites'.

On 26 August the Turks mounted an overwhelmingly successful counter-offensive. As the Greeks retreated they conducted a 'scorched earth' policy and again committed numerous atrocities against Turkish villagers. By 8

September Turkish cavalry had reached the outskirts of Izmir, and entered the city the following day. Over the next few weeks thousands of Greeks and Armenians were killed by the city's Muslims, assisted by Turkish troops, and fire destroyed most of the Christian quarters. 'Smyrna', the centuries-old great cosmopolitan Ottoman trading city, had ceased to exist.[5]

Turkish forces now marched north and British troops were sent to Çanakkale to prevent them from entering the Straits zone. On 24 September 1922 Mustafa Kemal's men entered the zone. The British government was divided as to whether to engage in a new war against the Turks. In the event, the British commander General Charles Harington made his own decision and ordered his men not to open fire.

The Turkish nationalists had won. At the Treaty of Lausanne – signed on 24 July 1923 between the Ottoman Empire and all the states which had fought against it during the Great War – they obtained most of their objectives, including eastern Thrace and the city of Edirne, as well as Istanbul itself. But at the same time they renounced most of their former imperial territories in the Mediterranean and the Middle East – Syria, Palestine, Libya and Iraq – which remained in the hands of the surviving imperialists, Britain, France and Italy.

After over 150 years of intermittent struggle against the Christian European powers, the state which was the descendent of that great Ottoman Empire of the mid-eighteenth century – where our narrative began – remained, straddling its European and Asian shores.

But it was no longer Ottoman, nor was it Islamic. In 1924 the Caliphate was abolished and from then on, and especially after Mustafa Kemal's purges of 1926, the Turkish Republic became a radical secular state. Soon all the trappings of the old Islamic Ottoman Empire, including its Arabic-based alphabet and even that ubiquitous male headwear, the fez, were abolished. Until his death in 1938 Mustafa Kemal ruled as dictator, under his newly minted surname, Atatürk. His 'secular revolution' encouraged the growth of a new, Western-orientated middle class, but left behind, in the vast Anatolian countryside, a peasantry which still cherished the old ways and the old religion.

Appendix A

Large cities of the Mediterranean Region c. 1750–c. 1800
(Greater than or equal to 50,000 inhabitants). Various sources.

EUROPEAN/CHRISTIAN REGION

	City size (in 1,000s of inhabitants)	Approx. Date of count
Naples	350	1750
Rome	163	1790
Lyon	146	1790
Palermo	139	1715
Milan	135	1800
Venice	134	1802
Barcelona	115	1800
Marseille	110	1790
Valencia	100	1800
Barcelona	92	1799
Genoa	91	1799
Seville	81	1799
Granada	80	1800
Cadiz	71	1799
Bologna	71	1791
Toulouse	53	1790
Malaga	50	1800
No. of 'large' cities	**17**	
Total population	**1,981**	
Average inhabitants per city	**142**	
Median inhabitants per city	**100**	

There is virtually no difference between the two sub-regions in the number of 'large cities' nor their average or median size.

ISLAMIC REGION

	City size (in 1,000s of inhabitants)	Approx. Date of count
Old Istanbul	350	1800
Istanbul suburbs	250	1800
Cairo	250	1800
Izmir (Anatolia)	100	1800
Aleppo	100	1800
Edirne (Thrace)	100	1800
Tunis	100	1750
Bursa (Anatolia)	100	1800
Fez	88	1780
Salonika	70	1799
Damascus	65	1800
Scutari (Albania)	60	1793
Ankara	60	1800
Meknes (Morocco)	56	1780
Algiers	50	1788

No. of 'large' cities	15
Total population	1,799
Average inhabitants per city	138
Median inhabitants per city	100

Appendix B

Indicators of standard of living in the eighteenth-century Mediterranean region:
Southern Europe (the Christian Mediterranean) and the Ottoman Empire compared.

A. FOOD CONSUMPTION AND DIET

Diet (and therefore nutrition) is the most direct indicator of 'standard of living'. Without
adequate consumption of nutritious food, human beings are unable to work or to enjoy the
other common elements of the standard of living, such as possessions and culture.

While information on the food consumption of the elites in both societies is plentiful,
data for the 'ordinary people' – peasants, urban artisans, soldiers, etc. – is sparse. The
foregoing therefore comprises only some brief notes on the subject.

i) Meat consumption

In late eighteenth-century Europe, meat generally cost at least eleven times as much as grain
when taking calorific content into consideration. Consequently (except for England
and the Netherlands), in the 1770s 'Grain represented approximately half a man's daily
existence'.[1] In his classic account of social life in eighteenth-century France, the historian
Henri Sée comments that even for a self-employed artisan – a social stratum well above 'the
poor' – 'meat is too expensive'.[2] As for the French peasant, Sée states, 'Meat appeared on
the table but rarely' and 'in the poorest regions the peasants ate biscuits and porridge made
of buckwheat [a seed of the flowering rhubarb or sorrel plant], or even chestnuts or maize.'[3]

For France as a whole meat consumption averaged around 23.5 kilos per year.[4] For Rome
per-capita annual meat consumption fell from 38.3 to 21.5 kilos between the seventeenth
and eighteenth centuries.[5] Indeed, it seems that, except in England, meat consumption in
eighteenth-century Christian Europe was in general decline and this regression was more
pronounced in the Mediterranean region.[6]

In Istanbul the state ensured that the city was well supplied with meat (mainly mutton
and lamb). The average annual mutton consumption of an 'ordinary' inhabitant of Istanbul
(i.e. a non-*askeri*) was substantial, 50–58 kilos per person year,[7] although like all averages
this figure would have included consumption by many non-*askeri* wealthy individuals. The
food consumption of the poor was usually supplemented by public 'soup kitchens', where
not only soup but a second course, which usually included some meat, was included. A
similar pattern existed in the other major cities of the Empire, in keeping with the sultan's
duty of *hisba*.

Among the Ottoman peasantry, however, meat consumption would probably have been
as low as in the Christian Mediterranean, although there must have been great regional
variations (see below).

ii) Grains and vegetables

As noted above, in eighteenth-century Europe, the diet of the ordinary man was dominated by
bread made from a variety of different grains, some of very poor nutritional value. A peasant
with some land would have done better than a landless rural wage-labourer. In Andalusia,
where around 70 per cent of the rural population were landless labourers, their daily wage
of 3.35 *reales* in the 1780s barely sufficed to buy the 2.5 kilo of bread (at a daily cost of 1.3
reales per kilo) which a family would have required to live 'at the limit of subsistence'.[8]

According to the Comte de Volney, who travelled widely in Egypt and Syria between
1783 and 1785, the diet of the Egyptian fellah (peasant or rural wage labourer) was 'bread
[made from millet] ... eaten with water and raw onions, *their only food throughout the year*
[my emphasis]; and they esteem themselves lucky if they can sometimes procure a little
honey, cheese, sour milk and dates. Flesh, meat and animal fat which they love with passion
only appear at the great feast days.'[9]

However, in Volney's case we need to be on our guard against prejudice and exaggeration.
He is an example of the 'Enlightenment' writers who were eager to paint the condition of
the peoples of the Ottoman Empire in the darkest colours.

This certainly appears to be the case in his description of the fellah's diet. Only a few
decades after Volney's account (and we have no reason to believe the general condition of
the fellah would have changed), the British Arabist Edward William Lane recorded his
own account of a fellah's diet. While confirming that the bread they ate was often made
of millet, Lane adds the following items of which 'his food generally consists': 'milk, new
cheese, eggs, small salted fish, cucumbers and melons, gourds ... onions and leeks, beans,
chickpeas, lupins, the fruit of the black egg-plant [aubergines], lentils, etc. dates (both fresh
and dried) and pickles',[10] although he agrees with Volney that 'flesh-meat they very seldom
taste'.

This is a far cry from the meagre repast of millet-bread and onions described by Volney.
In particular, it should be noted that, while detailing a predominantly vegetarian diet,
Lane's list of foodstuffs contains both animal protein (small salt fish) and vegetable
protein (lentils).* Perhaps most important of all, Lane's description of the fellah's diet
concludes with his expressing surprise at 'how robust and healthy' is the Egyptian fellah,
in spite of a diet which he himself (no doubt a typical British heavy meat-eater) thought
'simple and poor'.

iii) Famine

Where adverse weather and poor harvests struck the peasantry in both Christian and Muslim
societies, mere poverty quickly slid into outright famine. In 1763–64 the countryside
around Naples suffered a disastrous famine with thousands of starving peasants flooding
into the city to die miserably in its back streets. Thousands also died of starvation in
Egypt in 1784 and Tunis in 1784–85. In France severe droughts in 1785 and 1786 brought
starvation in their wake.[11] The Mediterranean World of the eighteenth century did not
discriminate in its periodic failure to offer the poor the most basic necessities of life.

---

*   Perhaps today, we would consider it an example of the venerated 'Mediterranean diet'?

B. HUMAN STATURE

Many studies have shown that human stature is closely correlated with nutrition. Eighteenth-century military records include considerable information about the height of new recruits, who would have been drawn mainly from the peasantry. Soldiers in Northern European and American regiments had heights ranging from 1.65 metres to 1.72 metres.[12] However, in parts of the Christian Mediterranean the picture appears to have been different. A record of the heights of regimental recruits drawn from Liguria (southern Italy) over the years 1792–79 shows that 72 per cent were less than 1.5 metres (5 ft 2 in) tall.[13] By both modern and ancient standards this is remarkably small and suggests a generally poor diet.

Mouradgea d'Ohsson's extremely detailed description of the characteristics of Ottoman men and women written in 1784 omits any mention of their heights, which strongly suggests they were not different from those of Christian Europe with which he was familiar. Otherwise, the best we can do is for a somewhat later period – a cohort of adult males from central Anatolia born in the 1840s. The average height was 1.66 metres and above, the same as for northern European military personnel.[14]

C. LIFE EXPECTANCY

Average life expectancy is probably the best, overall, indicator of human welfare. It has been estimated that in Spain in 1797 it was twenty-seven years and in France, for males, it was twenty-seven-and-a-half years in the mid-1780s. Unfortunately, the best we can do for the Ottoman Empire is a figure of twenty-five years for early nineteenth-century Serbia; but Serbia was an overwhelmingly Christian province. Whether religion would have made any difference we really cannot say.

However, it is worth noting a revealing comment about life expectancy made by a Frenchman living in Istanbul in 1766. He observed that – were it not for the visitations of the plague – the life expectancy of a Turk was the same as that of one of his own countrymen.[15]

D. MATERIAL CULTURE (POSSESSIONS)

Europeans commented on the fact that Muslims were likely to own less furniture and other items of domestic utility and adornment than in the Christian West.[16] For example, in 1796 the American consul in Algiers, Joel Barlow, described the city's houses as having 'hardly any furniture'.[17] 'Neither Turks or Moors ever use chairs, their tables are six inches high and sometimes there is not one in the house. Their beds are straw mats or sometimes mattresses laid on the floor.' Similarly, Edward Lane described Egyptian houses, even those of the rich, as having in their public rooms little more than a cushioned mattress covered with printed calico, while the plastered walls might be decorated with 'crude paintings' of religious subjects or flowers. In the upstairs apartments – exclusively for the owner and his family – 'no chambers are furnished as bedrooms ... A mat, or carpet ... and a deewan [mattress] constitute the complete furniture of a room'.[18]

In contrast, in the expanding cities of France the later eighteenth century witnessed what one historian has described as a 'democratisation of luxury'. At least for the middle classes, domestic interiors were being transformed, with space more differentiated; wardrobes and cupboards were replacing the old linen chests; wallpaper, curtains, writing tables, coat stands, cups, china and mirrors were beginning to appear.[19]

However, in making such comparisons it should be noted that, in many Ottoman cities, houses were built of wood and were notoriously prone to fire damage which could obliterate any prized domestic adornments; so more portable forms of wealth were preferred. The comments of Consul Barlow on the lack of any display of fancy furnishings in Muslim houses is accompanied by the statement that 'a Turk living like this ... may be worth a hundred thousand *piastres* [and] his clothes are richly embroidered and his fingers stiff with precious rings'.[20] Differences of these kinds suggest that the average Ottoman householder wasn't necessarily poorer than his Christian European counterpart – only that his environment was different.

Appendix C

**Some data for the Ottoman Empire's trade balance with Western Europe
in the late eighteenth century (figures in *livres tournois*)**

	Date	Exports	Imports
Alexandria	1782	6,678,000	5,008,000
Salonika	1788	6,764,000	4,573,000
Smyrna	1788	32,402,000	20,938,000
Tripoli	1766	495,000	364,000
Istanbul	1785	3,300,000*	11,500,000
Totals	-	**49,639,000**	**42,383,000**

Source: Panzac (1992)

Rough estimate based in Panzac's text

*Note: Because the data for each port are for different years,
and data for some smaller ports are unavailable,
the totals can give us only a rough indication of the overall
trade balance during the second part of the eighteenth century.*

Appendix D

Calculating the amount actually received and the 'effective' interest rate of the first two Ottoman foreign loans.

OTTOMAN LOAN OF 1854

Amount of money required by the Porte (in Turkish pounds) = £3.3 million
Face value of bonds (total) = £3.3 million
Repayment date (n.a.)
Coupon (nominal interest rate) = 6 per cent (usually paid in quarterly instalments)
Interest payment therefore = £3.3 x 6/100 = £198,000 per annum

But because of the believed riskiness of the loan the total offer for the bonds fell short of the amount requested and the bonds were finally sold at 80 (i.e. 80 per cent of their face value), so the cash received by the Porte was only £3.3 x 80/100 = £2.64 million.

Banks' expenses reduced this to £2.515 million.

However, recall that the 6 per cent interest rate on the loan (the 'coupon') was based on the original face value of the bonds and remains at a total of £198,000 . Therefore the *effective* rate of interest to be paid on the loan is now (in millions):

£0.198/£2.5 x 100 = **7.9 per cent**

OTTOMAN LOAN OF 1855

Amount of money required by the Porte (in Turkish pounds) = £5.5 million
Face value of bonds (total) = £5.5 million
Repayment date (n.a.)
Coupon (nominal interest rate) = 4 per cent
Interest rate therefore = £5.5 x 4/100 = £220,000

But because repayment of the loan was guaranteed by the British government the demand for the bonds exceeded the original amount on offer and the bonds were finally sold at 102.6 (i.e. 2.6 per cent higher than their face value) so the cash received by the Porte was £5.5 x 102.6/100 = £5.64 million.

Banks' expenses reduced this to £5.58 million (still more than amount originally requested).

Since the coupon was equal to £220,000, the effective rate of interest to be paid on the loan was now (in millions):

£0.220/£5.58 x 100 = **3.94 per cent (almost the same as the original 4 per cent coupon)**

Examples based on Owen (2009) p. 104.
For Egyptian loans see Owen p. 127.

Glossary of Arabic and Ottoman Turkish Words

(See note on transliteration. Plurals are given only when they appear in text.)

Language identifying suffixes	Meaning
Turkish = (T), Arabic = (A), Persian = (P), European = (E).	

'abid (A)	(lit. 'slaves'), the black African slave-soldiers originally raised by Moroccan Sultan Isma'il
'alim (A), pl. 'ulama (A) ulema (T)	Muslim religious scholar or member of the judiciary
amir al-hajj (A)	Officer in charge of annual caravan carrying pilgrims to Mecca and Medina during the Hajj
ağa (T), agha (A)	Military officer; lord, master
agha al-arab (A)	Commander of auxiliary Arab cavalry (Algiers)
ashraf (A)	Nobles. Title attributed to those claiming lineal descent from the Prophet Muhammad through his grandson Hasan ibn 'Ali (Sunni usage)
akçe (T)	Turkish silver coin. Smallest denomination of Turkish currency. 120 akçes = 1 kuruş (piastre)
alay (T & A)	Regiment
amir al-hajj (A)	Commander of annual pilgrimage from Egypt to Mecca
askeri (T), 'askari (A)	(lit. 'soldier) Tax-exempt Ottoman class; Ottoman elite. From Arabic 'askari
avarid (T)	A tax levied by a sultan or other ruler which is not sanctified by religious law
ayan (T), a'yun (A)	Provincial notables, governors, often outside the askeri class
Bab-ı Ali (T)	The 'Sublime Porte' (lit. the High Door). The European name for the Ottoman government and residence of the grand vezir; after 1908, the Foreign Ministry

487

baraka (A)	(lit. 'blessing') Divine quality believed possessed by Sufi masters, 'saints' and/or sharifs (mainly in Morocco)
bedel-i askari (T)	Military exception tax introduced as part of the 1856 Tanzimat reforms. It replaced the old Islamic cizye
belediye (T)	Subdivision of sancak, township; subdivision of qada From Arabic baladiya
berat (T)	Certificate, licence
beşe (T)	Term for Janissary; honorific term for any Turkish military
bey (T)	Ruler of an autonomous Ottoman province, 'regency' (specifically, Tunis); ruler of a region of the Regency of Algiers.
beylerbeyi or bey (T)	Ruler of Ottoman province; abbreviation of sanjacbeyi (Egypt). See also emir
binbashi (T)	Colonel (in European-style Ottoman Army)
bled al-makhzan (A)	Moroccan term for territory under government control (bled = Moroccan corruption of balad, country)
bled al-siba (A)	Moroccan term for territory outside government control
bölük (T)	Janissary company
çiftlik (T)	Semi-private landed property or tax farm
cizje (T), jizye (A)	Poll tax paid by non-Muslims.
dar al-sultan (A)	Government-controlled territory (Algiers)
devşirme (T)	Levy of boys from Christian rural population for incorporation in the corps of Janissaries
dey (T)	Ruler of an autonomous Ottoman province, 'regency' (specifically, Algiers)
dhimmi (T & A)	Non-Muslim belonging to a millet, Christian or Jew
divan (P & T), diwan (A)	State council, advisory council
efendi (T)	Honorific name for member of religious or judicial establishment
elhac (T), hajji (A)	Title for one who has performed the Hajj pilgrimage
emir (T & A)	Commander, governor. See also sancakbey

esnaf (T)	'Guilds', organisations representing, and controlling, specific occupations
eyalet (T)	Province of Ottoman Empire
faranji (A)	(lit. 'French') Term used for all Europeans
fallahin (A)	Egyptian peasants
fetva (T), fatwa (A)	Legal opinion by authority in Islamic law
fiqh (A)	Islamic jurisprudence
firman (T)	Decree issued by sultan
grand vezir (T & E)	Chief minister in Ottoman government.
hadith (A)	Reputed saying of the Prophet Muhammad
harka (A)	Moroccan Arabic corruption of Arabic haraqa military campaign (to collect revenue)
Hatt-ı Şerif (of Gülhane) (T)	Imperial Edict of Gülhane 1839 (Sultan Abdülmecid's announcement of reforms. Beginning of Tanzimat period)
Hatt-ı Hümayun (T)	Imperial Edict of 1856 (announcement of Sultan's implementation of reforms; continuation of Tanzimat)
hisba (T & A)	Responsibility of sultan to conduct himself so as to 'command the right and forbid the wrong'
hiyal (A)	(lit. 'tricks') Device to avoid Qur'anic prohibition on lending at interest (riba)
'id al-fitr (A)	Muslim feast-day, ceremony of fast-breaking at end of Ramadan
ijtihad (A)	Exercise by a jurist of independent reasoning in situations where the Qur'an and hadiths did not give clear guidance
ikhwan (A)	(lit. 'Brothers') Name of the adherents of the Sanusi Sufi tariqa
iltizam (A) see also mukataa (T) and muqata'a (A)	Tax farm auctioned, usually on short-term lease; may apply to land, customs duties or any other taxable source
iqta' (A)	Semi-feudal system of landholding (Mount Lebanon)
Janissary (E). See also yeni çeri (T)	(lit. 'New Soldiers') Originally raised from a 'tithe' of young boys from the Balkans and Greece
jihad (A), cihad (T)	Holy war against Christian states

kada (T)	Jurisdiction of judge
kadı (T), qadi (A)	Muslim judge
kafes (T)	(lit. 'cage') Place of imprisonment for sultan's siblings
kahya (T?)	Title of the head of an esnaf (guild)
kaid (E)	European transliteration for Moroccan qaid (Arabic qa'id)
kapıkulu (T)	Janissary (lit. slave of the sultan's household). Sometimes also used to refer to the court and bureaucracy and, more generally, all those who received regular allocations of food and other stipends from the Palace.
kapudan paşa (T)	Turkish admiral, or commander of a corsair fleet
kashif (A)	A Mamluk governor of a province or city, rank below a bey
kaymakam (T), qa'imaqam (A)	Deputy governor of sancak or eyalet
kethüda (T & P), katkhuda (A)	Official acting as deputy; e.g. second in command of a military unit; title of the head of an esnaf (guild)
khalifa (A)	(lit. 'deputy') In this context, officer or official commanding a region
khaznaji (A)	Chief financial officer (Algiers)
khedive	Viceroy of Egypt
khoja (A)	(lit. 'teacher') Secretary or principal secretary (Algiers)
khoja al-khayl (A)	(lit. 'horse secretary') Collector of taxes (Algiers)
khushdash (T?) pl. khushdashiya	Comrade or bondsman (among junior Mamluks) belonging to a particular Mamluk household
kis (A)	Large denomination in Egyptian currency 1 kis = 25,000 paras
kul (T)	Lit. 'slave', but 'slaves of the sultan': the elite stratum of a sultan's servitors based in Istanbul
Kuloğlu (T)	Offspring of Turkish soldier and Arab woman. From kul (slave [of the sultan]) and oğlu (son)
kuruş (T)	Unit of Turkish currency; 1 kuruş = 120 akçes; see also piastre
levend (T & P)	Irregular Ottoman provincial militia

lisan al-faranji (A)	Lingua franca used especially in trade between European and Muslim merchants, especially in the Levant
ma'una (A)	Type of non-Qur'anic tax, e.g. 'Abd al-Qadir's war tax
madhhab (A)	School of Islamic jurisprudence
Maghreb (A)	(lit. 'sunset') Refers to North African states: Morocco, Algeria, Tunis and Libya
mahbub (A)	Gold coin, varying in value but generally worth between 2 kuruş 90 akces and 4 kuruş
mahmal (A)	Banner carried from Egypt or Damascus to Mecca during Haj
makhzan, makhzan al-kabir (A)	(lit. treasury, government) Refers to Arab tribes employed by state to assist in tax collection (Algiers)
malikane (T)	Life-time tax farm
Mamluk (A)	(lit. 'owned man', 'slave') Self-perpetuating class of military rulers of Egypt who drew their recruits mainly from enslaved Caucasian boys.
marabout (E), murabit (A)	Europeanisation of Arabic term (lit. N. African garrison soldier). Later used for itinerant Sufi holy man
millet (T)	Autonomous religious community recognised by the Ottoman state (mainly Jews and Orthodox Christians)
miri (land) (T & P)	State land, whose usufruct is taxable
miri (tax) (T)	Agricultural tithe (typically one-tenth of value of production but with wide regional variations). The principal Ottoman tax
molla (T & A)	Honorific name for member of Ottoman religious or judicial establishment
muderris (T)	Religious teacher or scholar. From Arabic mudarris
mufti (A)	One who is qualified to issue a judgement in Islamic law (fetva, fatwa)
muhtasib (T & A)	Official responsible for monitoring and regulating market prices
mujahidin (A)	General term for those fighting for a jihad

mukataa (T), muqata'a (A)	Tax farm, auctioned, usually on short-term lease; may apply to land, customs duties or any other taxable source
mulay (A) (alt., moulay)	Moroccan Arabic title of nobility, 'prince'
multezim (A)	Holder of a tax farm (iltizam)
muqata'aji (A)	Holder of a tax farm (muqata'a), especially used in Mount Lebanon
müstahfizan (T & A)	(lit. 'guardians') Janissary troops serving as city garrison troops; one of the 'seven regiments' of Cairo
mütesellim (T)	Tax collector, deputy of a multezim
mütasarrif (A)	Administrator of a region which came directly under the Porte (mutasarrifate) rather than a provincial vali
narh (T & P)	Ceiling price of a commodity, typically set in times of scarcity
Nizam-ı Cedid (T)	(lit. 'New Order') European-style regular army established by Sultan Selim III
nauba (A)	Turkish garrison (Algeria)
ocak (T)	Janissary corps or regiment
okka (T & A)	Measure of weight equal to 1.28 kg
orta (T)	Janissary regiment
'ushr (A)	Tithe on miri land. See also miri tax
Padishah (T & P)	Lord of lords (originally a Persian expression) attributable to Ottoman sultan.
para (A)	Unit of Ottoman currency: 40 paras = 1 kuruş (piastre), commonly used in Egypt
paşa (T)	Pasha; governor of Ottoman province (see also vali and beylerbey)
pataque (E)	French unit of currency used in the Mediterranean. 1 pataque = 90 paras= 3,600 kuruş
piastre (E)	European name for kuruş
(The) Porte (E)	(lit. 'the door'), usually written 'The Sublime Porte'. European name for residence of the grand vezir and the Ottoman government.

qantar (A)	Egyptian unit of weight = 45 kg
qa'id (A); see also kaid (A)	Leader, provincial ruler
reaya (T), ra'aya (A)	(lit. 'flock') Tax-paying Ottoman lower (non-askeri) class.
reis (T)	Captain of a North African corsair ship
reisülküttub (T)	Head of chancery and, later, Ottoman foreign minister
riba (A)	Usury, charging interest or 'excessive' interest, forbidden by Qur'an
sancak (T), sanjaq (A)	Subdivision of eyalet
sancakbey (T)	Governor of sancak, adressed as bey or emir
sayyid (A)	Claiming descent from the Prophet Muhammad and his family. More commonly used by Shi'is. See also sharif
serasker (T)	Commander-in-chief of reformed Ottoman army
şeyhülislam (T)	Most senior Ottoman cleric
Shari'a (A)	Sacred law of Islam
Shahada	The Muslim evocation, 'There is no god but Allah and Muhammad is the messenger of Allah'
sharif (A), pl. ashraf	Claiming descent from the Prophet Muhammad and his family; commonly used by Sunnis. See also sayyid
shashiya (A)	Conical men's headware produced mainly in Tunis; variants include the Turkish fez and tarbush
shaykh or sheikh (A & E)	Generic term for elder, leader; Sufi master of a zawiya
shaykh al-balad (A)	(lit. 'elder of the city') In different regions it had different meanings. In Mamluk Egypt it meant 'civil governor', but it could also simply mean 'village headman'. In Algiers it meant 'head of city administration'
Shi'i (A)	Member of minority sect in Islam
shura (A)	An advisory body
silihdar (T)	Sultan's sword-bearer
sipahi (P)	Turkish cavalryman

smala (A)	Name for 'Abd al-Qadir's mobile 'war city' (etymology unknown)
Sufism	The mystical and heterogeneous tendency in Sunni Islam (see also tariqa and Ikhwan)
Sunni (A)	Member of majority sect in Islam
ta'ifa (A)	Council of North African corsair captains
Tanzimat (T)	Period of Radical Ottoman reforms implemented over 1839–76
tariqa (A)	A Sufi brotherhood
tereke (T)	Inventory of a deceased person's bequeathed property deposited with the kadi
timar (T & P)	Semi-feudal system of landholding whereby the holder of the timar enjoys the taxes raised from his peasantry in return for military service in the imperial army when required
ulema (T), 'ulama (A), s. 'alim	Muslim clergy and judiciary
'ushr (A)	Tithe; tax on miri land
ustadh (A)	Head of a Mamluk military household
vakif (T), waqf (A)	Inalienable endowment of an asset whose usufruct is dedicated to charitable (or sometimes family) purposes
vali (T)	Governor of Ottoman province (see also beylerbey, bey, paşa)
vezir (T) wazir (A)	Minister, as in grand vezir
vilayet (T), wilaya (A)	Ottoman province replacing eyalet in nineteenth century
wakil al-kharj (A)	Senior official responsible for marine and foreign relations (Algiers)
wushah	(lit. 'sword-belt') Abbreviation of title of 'Abd al-Qadir's military instruction manual.
yeni çeri (T)	(lit. 'new army') Known in Europe as Janissaries
zawiya (A)	A college of Islamic learning; Sufi community of scholars and teachers

Acknowledgments

This book has been eight years in preparation. It would never have got off the ground without the favourable comments upon its first few chapters by Saqi's external consultant, Lawrence Joffe.

During that passage of time one person more than any other has been my right-hand woman: the publisher and owner of Saqi Books, Lynn Gaspard. Since Lynn accepted my current project without the customary intervention of an agent, she has in effect carried out what would otherwise have been the agent's function, continuously involved in the process of editing and commenting upon my various offerings. But much more than that, while keeping Saqi afloat during the prolonged pandemic, she has also kept me afloat during periods when I have experienced my own crises. I cannot even begin to thank her enough for her enduring kindness and moral support.

I must also extend my thanks to Lynn's excellent staff at Saqi who have supported me during these critical years.

There are two other individuals to whom I offer my heartfelt thanks: Charles Peyton who read the first full draft of the book and advised me on a crucial reorientation of the book's final chapters, and my copyeditor, Brian David. Brian's historical imagination and his meticulous professionalism have knocked the book into shape.

Finally, in the realm of personalities, I thank our cartographer, Martin Lubikowski of ML Design, who converted my sketch maps into real works of graphic art (as he did in my previous book for Saqi). Working on these with Martin was a real pleasure.

Over the eight years of the book's gestation, a significant change took place in the world of historical research. Whereas most of the research for my previous books and articles was conducted in libraries, there has since then been an explosive growth in the number of institutions that have made available online both primary source material and antiquarian books – works which it would have otherwise been almost impossible to access. In this respect, I must acknowledge the support and help of the following institutions: the Hathi Trust, Internet Archive, the Wellcome Trust, Gallica, and the Online Books Page of the University of Pennsylvania, as well as the National Archive in London. In addition, I must thank the University of Southampton's Hartley Library for providing me with photocopies of a selection of Palmerston's papers relating to the French invasion of Algiers, 1830.

A further web resource which is of particular utility to Arabists is the growing scope and efficiency of Arabic-language online booksellers, especially those based in Lebanon. Accessing this important source of literature would otherwise have been impossible.

It is customary to end the Acknowledgements section with a paean of praise for one's spouse or partner. But in this book (at the age of seventy-six, probably my last) and looking back over fifty-six years of marriage, there is little more I can add to the remark which concluded my previous one: 'But above all, I must thank my wife Diana ... for putting up with my dereliction of domestic duties, closeted in my office, in pursuit of an objective which I suspect she frequently doubted would ever come to fruition.'

Credits

1: John Young (1755–1825), *A Series of Portraits of the Emperors of Turkey*, William Bulmer & Co, London, 1815. Current locations: Metropolitan Museum of Art, New York.

2: Octavien d'Alvimart (1770–1854), *The Costume of Turkey*, Vol. VI of *Costumes of Various Nations*, William Miller, London, 1804. Current locations: Aikaterini Laskaridis Foundation, Athens.

3: Octavien d'Alvimart (1770–1854), *The Costume of Turkey*, Vol. VI of *Costumes of Various Nations*, William Miller, London, 1804. Current locations: Aikaterini Laskaridis Foundation, Athens.

4: Artist unknown. From Henry Maundrell, *A Journey from Aleppo to Jerusalem*, Oxford, 1703. Author's collection.

5: Octavien d'Alvimart (1770–1854) (5a and 5b); John Heaviside Clark (1770–1863) (c). From: William Miller (ed.), *The Military Costume of Turkey*, Vol. VII of *Costumes of the Various Nations*, William Miller, London, 1818. Current locations: Aikaterini Laskaridis Foundation, Athens, and Victoria and Albert Museum, London.

6: Artist: John Heaviside Clark (1770–1863). Publication: William Miller (ed.), *The Military Costume of Turkey*, Vol. VII of *Costumes of the Various Nations*, William Miller, London, 1818. Reproduced: Tamer el-Leithy (ed.) *Military Costume of the Ottoman Empire*, Zeitouna, Cairo, 2000. Current locations: Aikaterini Laskaridis Foundation, Athens; Victoria and Albert Museum, London.

7: Artist unknown (eighteenth century). Publication unknown. Current locations: Ministry of Culture. Museum of Sidi Muhammad Ben Abdellah, Essaouiria.

8: Artist unknown. Publication: *Encylopaedia Britannica*.

9: Artist: Cobija, 2014. Current locations: Mersin Naval Museum.

10: Artist: Duterte. From: *Description de l'Egypte* 1809. Current locations: Paris National Archives and National Museum.

11: Vivant Denon (Engraved by W. Cooper), Vivant Denon (Translated E. A. Kendal), *Travels in Upper and Lower Egypt*, Vol. 2, London 1802. Author's collection.

12: Vivant Denon (Engraved by W. Cooper), Vivant Denon (Translated E. A. Kendal), *Travels in Upper and Lower Egypt*, Vol. 1, London 1802. Author's collection.

13: Vivant Denon (Engraved by W. Cooper), Vivant Denon (Translated E. A. Kendal), *Travels in Upper and Lower Egypt*, Vol. 1, London 1802. Author's collection.

14: Octavien d'Alvimart (1770–1854), *The Costume of Turkey*, Vol. VI of *Costumes of Various Nations*, William Miller, London, 1804. Current locations: Aikaterini Laskaridis Foundation, Athens.

15: Artist: Sydney Hall (1788–1831). Publication: 1816. Current locations: Unknown.

16: John Young (1755–1825), *A Series of Portraits of the Emperors of Turkey*, William Bulmer & Co, London, 1815. Current locations: Metropolitan Museum of Art, New York.

17: Artist: Henri-Guillaume Schlesinger (1814–1893). Publication: 1839. Current locations: Topkapı Museum, Istanbul.

18: Artist: Charles Etienne Motte (1785–1836). Publication: Augustin Bernard, *L'Algérie*, 1929. Current locations: Musée de l'Armée, Paris.

19: Artist: Louis Dupré c. 1830. From: Frontispiece of Edouard-Pierre-Marie de Cadalvène and Jules-Xavier Saguez de Breuvery, *L'Égypte et la Nubie*, 1841. Current location: Collection of Actia Nicopolis Foundation, Preveza, Greece.

20: Artist: Emile Prisse d'Avennes (1807–1879). From *Oriental Album*, James Madden, London, 1848.

21: Artist unknown. From: Rev. Joseph Williams Blakesley, *Four Months in Algeria*, MacMillan & Co., Cambridge 1859. Author's Collection.

22: Photograph by Etienne Carajat (1828–1906). From: Mrs Richard Burton, *The Inner Life of Syria*, Henry King & Co., London, 1865.

23: Artist unknown (nineteenth century). Current locations: Pera Museum, Istanbul.

24: Artist: John Henry Rimbault (1820–1888). From: *Engineering*, 20 May 1870.

25: Unknown photographer (1883).

26: Artist: Eduardo Ximenes (1852–1932). From: *Le Monde Illustré*, 1882.

27. Unknown photographer.

28: Unknown photographer, Marina Militare.

29: Unknown photographer. From: *Cassier's Magazine* (New York) Vol. 25, 1903.

30: Unknown photographer, 1911.

31: Photograph believed to be by the Italian General Graziani, 1931.

Notes

A NOTE ON TERMINOLOGY

1. Braudel, Fernand, *The Mediterranean and the Mediterranean World in the Age of Philip II* (trans. Sian Reynolds), 2 vols, Fontana Press, William Collins & Son, London 1972–73.

2. Abulafia, David, *The Great Sea: A Human History of the Mediterranean*, Allen Lane, London 2012. 'This book is a history of the Mediterranean Sea, rather than a history of the lands around it' (p. xvii).

3. Norwich, John Julius, *The Middle Sea: A History of the Mediterranean*, Chatto & Windus, London, 2006.

INTRODUCTION

1. The same starting point, and for the same reason, was chosen by H.A.R. Gibb and H. Bowen, *Islamic Society and the West*, Vol. 1, Oxford University Press, London, 1950, p. 19.

2. See Hodgson, Marshall G. S., *The Venture of Islam*, Chicago University Press, Chicago, 1974, and McNeill, William H., 'The Age of the Gunpowder Empires, 1450–1800', in Michael Adas, *Islamic and European Expansion: The Forging of a Global Order*, Temple University Press, Philadelphia, 1993. The term 'gunpowder empires' reflects the fact that, although the empires in question arose in the later Middle Ages, they quickly adopted European gunpowder weaponry, including hand arms and artillery, which, for a time, put them on equal footing with their enemies.

3. Bayly, C. A., *Imperial Meridian: The British Empire and the World, 1780–1830*, Longman, Harlow Essex, 1989, p. 18.

4. Bayly, C. A., 'The First Age of Global Imperialism c. 1760–1830', *Journal of Imperial and Commonwealth History*, Vol. 26, No. 2, 1998. The difference between my own periodisation (1750–1815) and that of Bayly (1760–1830) is, I would argue, immaterial.

5. The term 'classical imperialism' is that of Winfried Baumgart, *Imperialism: The Idea and Reality of British and French Colonial Expansion 1880–1914*, Oxford University Press, Oxford 1982. An alternative used by many historians is 'late imperialism'. As to the dates, there are as many periodisations as there are historians.

6. Russo-Turkish wars occurred in 1768–74, 1787–92 and 1806–12. All three were Russian victories.

7. Laurens, Henry, 'Europe and the Muslim World in the Contemporary Period', in John Tolan, Gilles Veinstein and Henry Laurens, *Europe and the Islamic World: A History*, Princeton University Press, 2013, p. 279.

8. According to the terms of the so-called Treaty of Allahabad, 12 August 1765, the

Mughal Emperor Shah Alam was forced to hand over to the East India Company the Diwani (right to collect taxes) of his three richest provinces, Bengal, Bihar and Orissa. (See Dalrymple, William, *The Anarchy; The Relentless Rise of the East India Company*, Bloomsbury, London, 2019, pp. 207–09).

9.   Laurens 2013, p. 265.

10. Mouradgea d'Ohsson, Ignatius, *Tableau général de l'empire othoman*, Vol. 1, Imprémerie de Monsieur, Paris, 1788.

11. Bayly, C. A., *The Birth of the Modern World 1780–1914*, Blackwell Publishing, Maldan MA, 2004, p. 2

12. Gibb & Bowen 1950, Vol. 1, p. 199. Although this is unquestionably a great work of scholarship, the title 'Islamic Society and the West' is highly suggestive of their general approach and tone. For criticism of Gibb, see Said, Edward, *Orientalism: Western Conceptions of the Orient*, Routledge and Kegan Paul, London 1978.

13. Hanioğlu, M. Şükrü, *A Brief History of the Late Ottoman Empire*, Princeton University Press, Princeton, 2008, pp. 1–2.

14. Yapp, M. E., *The Making of the Modern Near East, 1792–1923*, Routledge, Abingdon, Oxford, 1987, p. 96.

15. Baumgart 1982, p. 8.

16. Well-known works on imperialism which are focused on Africa include Hobson, John A., *Imperialism: A Study*, James Nisbet & Co., London, 1902; Pakenham, Thomas, *The Scramble for Africa, 1876–1912*, Abacus, London, 2003 (reprint of 1991); Robinson, Ronald, and John Gallagher, *Africa and the Victorians: The Official Mind of Imperialism*, Macmillan and Company, London 1961; Baumgart 1982, p. 179. Baumgart describes the division of Africa as 'the most spectacular event in the general movement of expansion after 1880', but he too includes the southern shore of the Mediterranean in his 'African' category.

17. MacMillan. Margaret, *The War that Ended Peace: How Europe Abandoned Peace for the First World War*, Profile Books, London, 2014, p. xxii.

18. The first version of *Imperialism* was written in 1915–1916 and published in Russian in 1917. This was the original title. In the second (French and German) edition, published with a preface written in 1920, the adjective 'Latest' was changed to 'Final'.

19. Stokes, Eric, 'Late Nineteenth-Century Colonial Expansion and the Attack on the Theory of Economic Imperialism: A Case of Mistaken Identity?', *Historical Journal*, Vol. 12, No. 2, 1969, p. 291.

20. Lenin, *Imperialism*, p. 157

21. Ibid., p. 98.

22. Ibid., pp. 98, 101.

23. Langer, William, *The Diplomacy of Imperialism, 1890–1902*, 1st edition, Alfred A. Knopf, 1951.

24. Robert L. Tignor, introduction to Al-Jabarti, 'Abd al-Rahman, Napoleon' in *Egypt, Al-Jabarti's Chronicle of the French Occupation*, 1798, Markus Wiener Publishing, Princeton and New York, 1993, p. 5.

25. The one notable exception is Cain, P. J., and A. G. Hopkins, *British Imperialism*

1688 to 2015, Routledge, Abingdon, Oxon, 2016.

26. Judd, Denis, *Empire: The British Imperial Experience from 1765 to the Present*, Harper Collins, London, 1996.

27. Darwin, John, *Unfinished Empire: The Global Expansion of Britain*, Penguin, London, 2012.

28. Darwin, John, *The Empire Project: The Rise and Fall of the British World-System*, Cambridge University Press, Cambridge, 2009.

29. Hyam, Ronald, *Britain's Imperial Century 1815–1914: A Study of Empire and Expansion*, Palgrave Macmillan, Basingstoke, 2002, p. xi.

CHAPTER 1

1. Mouradgea d'Ohsson 1788, Vol. 1, pp. ii–iii.

2. Findley, Carter V., 'A Quixotic Author and His Great Taxonomy: Mouradgea d'Ohsson and his Tableau General de L'Empire Othoman', University of Oslo, 2000, p. 4; available at https://www.oslo2000.uio.no/program/papers/m1b-findley.pdf

3. See Laurens 2013 pp. 262–63; Said, Edward, *Orientalism: Western Conceptions of the Orient*, Routledge & Kegan Paul, London 1978, p. 81.

4. Findley, p. 43.

5. Quoted in Freely, John, *Inside the Seraglio: The Private Lives of the Sultans in Istanbul*, Viking, London 1999, p. 208.

6. Quataert, Donald, *The Ottoman Empire, 1700–1922* (2nd ed), Cambridge University Press, Cambridge, 2005, p. 91.

7. Palmer, Alan, *The Decline and Fall of the Ottoman Empire*, Faber & Faber, London 2011 (1992), p. 20.

8. Quataert 2005, p. 92.

9. Gibb, H. A. R., and H. Bowen, *Islamic Society and the West*, Oxford University Press, London, 1950 and 1951, Vol. 1, p. 339. The word Padishah (lord of lords) was of Persian origin. The word caliph was not used officially until much later.

10. Palmer 2011 (1992), p. 44.

11. Baron de Tott, François, *Memoires sur les Turcs et les Tartars*, Paris, 1785, Vol. 1, pp. 70–71.

12. Ibid., pp. 18–19.

13. Bayly 2004, p. 2.

14. Braudel, Fernand, *Civilization and Capitalism, 15th–18th Century, Vol. 3: The Perspective of the World* (trans. Sian Reynolds), William Collins & Son, London, 1984 p. 467.

15. Mouradgea d'Ohsson 1788, Vol. 1, Dedication.

16. The figure of 55,000 *kapikulus* is based on Tülay Artan's definition of what he refers to as the Ottoman 'elite', defined as those receiving regular (and large) supplies of food from the imperial kitchens. This total is made up of around 40,000 Janissariers and 15,000 'palace dependents' (Artan, Tülay, 'Aspects of the Ottoman Elites Food Consumption', in Donald Quataert (ed.) *Consumption Studies and*

the History of the Ottoman Empire 1550–1922, State University of New York Press, 2000, p. 136. In most of the relevant literature the precise relationship between the *kapikulus* and the wider body of *askeris* is unclear. For example, Suraiya Faroqui refers to the *kapikulus* rather confusingly as the 'military establishment' which 'formed part of the askeri'. Suraiya Faroqui in İnalcik, Halil and Donald Quataert (eds), *An Economic and Social History of the Ottoman Empire, 1300–1914*, Cambridge University Press, 1994, p. 435. Gibb and Bowen are also unclear as to whether the ulema were askeris, although like the askeri military they were tax-exempt.

17. Schinder, Joel, 'Career Line Formation in the Ottoman Bureaucracy, 1648–1750: A New Perspective', *Journal of the Economic and Social History of the Orient*, Vol. 16, No. 2/3, 1973, pp. 227, 236n.

18. Somel, Selcuk Aksin, *Historical Dictionary of the Ottoman Empire*, Scarecrow Press, Lanham Maryland, 2003, p. 165; and http://www.osmanli700.gen.tr/english/individuals/k16.html

19. Hanioğlu 2008, pp. 33–37. See also 'Ottoman Turkish Language', https://en.wikipedia.org/wiki/Ottoman_Turkish_language

20. Findley, p. 5.

21. Shaw, Stanford J., 'The Ottoman Census System and Population, 1831–1914', *International Journal of Middle East Studies*, Vol. 9, No. 3, 1978, p. 326.

22. Jones, Colin, *The Great Nation: France from Louis XV to Napoleon*, Penguin, London, 2003, p. 159.

23. Barton, Simon, *A History of Spain* (2nd ed.), Palgrave/Macmillan, Basingstoke, 2009, p. 166.

24. Black, Jeremy, *Eighteenth-Century Europe* (2nd ed.), Macmillan, Basingstoke, 1999, p. 4.

25. Both quotations from Morland, Paul, *The Human Tide: How Population Shaped the Modern World*, John Murray, London, 2019, p. 20.

26. Karaman, K. Kivanç, and Şevket Pamuk, 'Ottoman State Finances in European Perspective 1500–1914', *Journal of Economic History*, Vol. 70, No. 3, 2010, p. 612.

27. McGowan, Bruce, 'Population and Migration', in İnalcik and Quataert 1994, p. 646

28. Yapp 1987, pp. 14–15.

29. See, for example, Bayly 2004.

30. Van Zanden, Jan L.,'Wages and the Standard of Living in Europe, 1500–1800', *European Review of Economic History*, Vol. 2, 1999, p. 175.

31. Malanima, Paolo, 'The Long Decline in a Leading Economy: GDP in Central And Northern Italy 1300–1913', *European Review of Economic History*, Vol. 15, 2010, pp. 169–219.

32. Ibid., p. 189.

33. Pamuk, Şevket, 'Institutional Change and the Longevity of the Ottoman Empire, 1500–1800', *Journal of Interdisciplinary History*, Vol. 35, No. 2, 2004, p. 243.

34. Özmucur, Süleyman, and Şevket Pamuk, 'Real Wages and Standards of Living in the Ottoman Empire, 1489–1914', *Journal of Economic History*, Vol. 62, No. 2,

2002, 293–321.

35. Pamuk 2004, p. 244.

36. See the graphs on pp. 312–13 of Özmucur and Pamuk, 2002.

37. Ergene, Boğaç A. and Ali Berker, 'Wealth and Inequality in 18th-Century Kastamonu: Estimations for the Muslim Majority', *International Journal of Middle East Studies*, Vol. 40, Vol. 1, 2008, p. 28.

38. Ibid., p. 27.

39. Establet, Colette, Jean-Paul Pascual and André Raymond, 'La mesure de l'inégalité dans la societé Ottomane: Utilisation de l'indice de Gini pour le Caire et Damas vers 1700', *Journal of the Economic and Social History of the Orient*, Vol. 37, No. 2 1994, pp. 176, 180.

40. Alfani, Guido, and Sergio Sardone, *Long-Term Trends in Economic Inequality in Southern Italy*, Bocconi University, Milan, 2012, available at eh.net/eha/wp-content/uploads/2015/05/Alfani.pdf, p. 28.

41. Hanioğlu 2008, p. 30.

42. Baron de Tott, François, *Memoirs of Baron de Tott: Containing the State of the Turkish Empire and the Crimea During the Late War with Russia* (2nd edn) Vol. 1, Part 2, G. G. J. and J. Robinson, London, 1786, pp. 144–45.

43. For a study of the varieties of ayan, see Zens, Robert, 'Provincial Powers: The Rise of the Ottoman Local Notables (Ayan)', *History Studies*, Vol. 3, No. 3, 2011, pp. 433–47.

44. Yapp 1987, p. 21.

45. Gibb and Bowen 1950/51, Vol. 2, p. 142.

46. See, for example, Quataert 2005, p. 167.

47. Christian state literacy rates for 1750 taken from http://ourworldindata.org/data/education-knowledge/literacy

48. Hanna, Nelly, 'Literacy and the "Great Divide" in the Islamic World, 1300–1800', *Journal of Global History*, Vol. 2, 2007, pp. 176–78.

49. Ibid., p. 183.

50. Ibid., p. 187.

51. Lewis, Bernard, *The Arabs in History*, Oxford University Press, Oxford, 1993 (reprint of 1958), p. 189.

52. Rubin, Jared, *Rulers, Religion and Riches: Why the West Got Rich and the Middle East Did Not*, Cambridge University Press, New York, 2017, pp. 105, 110.

53. Schwartz, Kathryn A., 'Did Ottoman Sultans Ban Print?', *Book History*, Vol. 20, 2017, pp. 12–13.

54. Ibid., p. 7.

55. See Gencer, Yasemin, 'Ibrahim Müteferrika and the Age of the Printed Manuscript', in Christiane Gruber, *The Islamic Manuscript Tradition*, Indiana Press, Bloomington, 2010, p. 183.

56. Sabev, Orlin, 'Formation of Ottoman Print Culture (1726–1746): Some General Remarks',NewEuropeCollege,*RegionalProgram2003-04and2004-05*,p.306,availableat https://www.academia.edu/728136/Formation_of_Ottoman_Print_Culture_1726-1746_Some_General_Remarks

57. Hanioğlu 2008 pp. 38–41.
58. Lane, Edward, *An Account of the Manners and Customs of the Modern Egyptians* (3rd popular edition, three volumes in one), Charles Knight & Co., London, 1846, Vol. 2, p. 20.
59. Hanioğlu 2008, p. 38.
60. Anderson, M. S., *The Eastern Question 1774–1923*, Macmillan Press, London, 1966, p. xviii.
61. Flournoy, Francis, R., *British Policy towards Morocco in the Age of Palmerston* (1830–1865), P. S. King & Son, Westminster, 1935, p. 6. Flournoy is actually referring to the University of Fez the mid-nineteenth century.
62. Marino, John A., *Early Modern Italy*, Oxford University Press, 2002, pp. 221–22, 246.
63. Al-Jabarti, *'Abd al-Rahman, Napoleon' in Egypt, Al-Jabarti's Chronicle of the French Occupation, 1798* (trans. Shmuel Moreh), Markus Wiener Publishing, Princeton, 1975, 1978, 1993, p. 110.
64. See, for example, Nasr, Seyyed Hossein, *Islamic Science: An Illustrated Study*, World of Islam Festival Publishing Co. Ltd, 1976.
65. Rubin 2017.
66. See Ihasanoğlu, Ekmeleddin, *An Overview of Ottoman Scientific Activities: Foundation for Science, Technology and Civilisation*, Manchester, 2006, available at https://muslimheritage.com/uploads/An_Overview_of_Ottoman_Scientific_Activities1.pdf

CHAPTER 2

1. İnalcık, Halil, 'The Ottoman Economic Mind and Aspects of the Ottoman Economy', in M. A. Cook, *Studies in the Economic History of the Middle East*, Oxford University Press, 1970, p. 218.
2. Quoted in Shechter, Relli, 'Market Welfare in Early-Modern Ottoman Economy: A Historiographical Overview with Many Questions', *Journal of the Economic and Social History of the Orient*, Vol. 46, No. 2, 2005, p. 259.
3. Ibid., p. 253.
4. İnalcık, Halil, 'The Ottoman State: Economy and Society 1300–1600' in İnalcık and Quataert (eds), *An Economic and Social History of the Ottoman Empire, 1300–1914*, Cambridge University Press, 1994, p. 45.
5. Shechter 2005, p. 265.
6. See, for example, Rubin 2017, pp. 99–148.
7. Sabev, 2007, pp. 302–03.
8. Ibid., pp. 314–15.
9. Marsigli, Le Comte de, *L'etat militaire de l'empire ottoman: ses progrès et sa décadence*, Paris, 1732, Vol. 1, p. 40.
10. Braudel 1984, p. 616.
11. Schechter 2005, p. 262
12. Yapp 1987, p. 23.

13. Baer, Gabriel, 'The Administrative and Social Functions of Turkish Guilds', *International Journal of Middle East Studies*, Vol. 1, No. 1, 1970, p. 32.

14. İnalcık, 1970, pp. 216–17.

15. Baer, 1970, p. 34.

16. Ibid., p. 49. Although Baer acknowledges some exceptions from this pattern where the esnaf were more independent.

17. Olson, Robert W., 'The Esnaf and the Patrona Halil Rebellion of 1730: A Realignment in Ottoman Politics?', *Journal of the Economic and Social History of the Orient*, Vol. 17, No. 3, 1974, p. 329.

18. Schechter 2005, p. 269.

19. Valensi, Lucette, 'Islam et capitalisme: production et commerce des chéchias en Tunisie et en France aux XVIIIe et XIXe siècles', *Revue d'Histoire Moderne et Contemporaine*, Vol. 16, No. 3, 1969, p. 400. See also Largueche, Abdelhamid, Julia Clancy-Smith and Caroline Audet, 'The City and the Sea: Evolving Forms of Mediterranean Cosmopolitanism in Tunis 1700–1881', *Journal of North African Studies*, Vol. 6, No. 1, 2001, p. 122, whose authors describe the Tunisian shashiya industry as 'proto-capitalist'.

20. Valensi 1969, pp. 385, 387

21. Largueche et al., 2001, p. 122.

22. La Force, J. C., 'Royal Textile Factories in Spain, 1700–1800', *Journal of Economic History*, Vol. 24, No. 3, 1964, pp. 337–63.

23. Sée, Henri, *Economic and Social Conditions in France During the Eighteenth Century* (translated Edwin H. Zeydel), Batoche Books, Kitchener, 2004 (original 1927), pp. 86–94.

24. See Rodinson, Maxime, *Islam and Capitalism*, Allen Lane, London, 1974 (reprint of original French, 1966), p. 36.

25. Pamuk, Şevket, 'Prices in the Ottoman Empire, 1469–1914', *International Journal of Middle East Studies*, Vol. 36, 2004, p. 461.

26. İnalcık 1970, p. 212.

27. Mansel, Philip, *Levant: Splendour and Catastrophe in the Mediterranean*, John Murray, London 2010, p. 9.

28. Largueche et al 2001, pp. 120–23

29. Mansel 2010, p. 14.

30. Ibid., p. 13.

31. Lewis, Bernard, *Emergence of Modern Turkey*, Oxford University Press, London, 1961, p. 28.

32. Braudel 1984, Vol. 3, p. 468; Panzac, Daniel, 'International and Domestic Maritime Trade in the Ottoman Empire during the 18th Century', *International Journal of Middle East Studies*, Vol. 24, No. 2, 1992, pp. 191–92.

33. Davis, Ralph, 'English Imports from the Middle East. 1580–1780', in M. A. Cook (ed.) *Studies in the Economic History of the Middle East*, Oxford University Press, Oxford, 1970, p. 202.

34. Owen, Roger, *The Middle East in the World Economy 1800–1914* (2nd edition), I. B. Tauris, London, 2009 (reprint of 1981), pp. 6–7.

35. Ibid., p. 192.

36. See the table in Crecelius, Daniel, *The Roots of Modern Egypt: A Study of the Regimes of 'Ali Bey al-Kabir and Muhammad Bey Abu al-Dhahab, 1760–1775*, Biblioteca Islamica, Mineapolis, 1981, p. 13.

37. Braudel 1984, Vol. 3, p. 473.

38. Hansen, Thorkild, Arabia Felix: *The Danish Expedition of 1761–1767*, Collins, London, 1964, p. 103. On the importance of the Ottoman caravan trades, see also Braudel 1984, Vol. 3, pp. 475–76.

39. Braudel 1984, Vol. 3, pp. 473–74.

40. Ibid., p. 474

41. Owen 2009, p. 52.

42. Panzac 1992, p. 202.

43. Ibid., p. 193

44. Panzac, Daniel, *Barbary Corsairs: The End of a Legend 1800–1820*, Brill, Leiden, 2005, p. 11.

45. Ibid., pp. 53, 16.

46. Ibid., p. 53.

47. Ibid., p. 138.

48. Wright, John, *The Trans-Saharan Slave Trade*, Routledge, London, 2007, p. 59.

49. Hansen 1964, p. 104.

50. Wright 2007, p. 3.

51. Marx, Karl, Capital, Vol. III, Lawrence & Wishart, London, 1984, pp. 327–28.

52. Panzac 1992, p. 202.

53. Schechter 2005, p. 273.

54. Ibid., p. 272.

55. Küçükkalay, A. Mesud, and Numan Elibol, 'Ottoman Imports in the 18th Century: Smyrna (1771–72)', *Middle Eastern Studies*, Vol. 42, No. 5, 2006,, p. 724.

56. Owen 2009, p. 10; Braudel 1984, Vol. 3, p. 474.

CHAPTER 3

1. For example, Hobsbawm, Eric, *The Age of Revolution, 1789–1848*, Abacus, London, 2003 (reprint of 1962).

2. See Ralston, D. B., *Importing the European Army: The Introduction of European Military Techniques and Institutions into the Extra-European World 1600–1914*, Chicago University Press, 1990, 'Introduction'.

3. Parker, Geoffrey, *The Military Revolution: Military Innovation and the Rise of the West 1500–1800* (2nd edition), Cambridge University Press, 1996, p. 43.

4. Nicolle, David, *Armies of the Ottoman Empire, 1775–1820*, Osprey, Botley, Oxford, 1998, p. 11. The terminology differs in different sources: 'ocak' is sometimes translated as 'regiment'.

5. McGowan, Bruce, 1994, p. 704.

6. Panzac 2005, pp. 17, 20.

7. Crecelius 1981, p. 21, citing Leila 'Abd al-Latif Ahmad.

8. Raymond, André, 'Soldiers in Trade: The Case of Ottoman Cairo', *British Journal of Middle East Studies*, Vol. 18, No. 1, 1991, 1991.

9. Ibid., pp. 29–30, 32.

10. Wheatcroft, Andrew, *The Ottomans: Dissolving Images*, Penguin, London, 1993, pp. 89–100.

11. Quoted in Parker 1996, p. 128.

12. See Zorlu, Tuncay, *Innovation and Empire in Turkey: Sultan Selim III and the Modernisation of the Ottoman Navy*, Tauris Academic Studies, London, 2008.

13. Ibid., p. 64.

14. Ibid., pp. 12, 64, 119–20.

15. Bayly 2004, p. 92. Bayly mistakenly refers to 'Abraham' – not Ambrose – Crowley. Abraham was a poet.

16. Storrs, Christopher, 'The Savoyard Fiscal-Military State in the Long Eighteenth Century', in Christopher Storrs (ed.), *The Fiscal Military State in the 18th Century*, Ashgate Publishing, Farnham, 2009, pp. 206, 217.

17. O'Brien, Patrick, 'The Political Economy of British Taxation, 1660–1815', *Economic History Review*, Vol. XLI, No. 1, 1988, p. 2.

18. Erginbaş, Vefa, 'Enlightenment in the Ottoman Context: İbrahim Müteferrika and His Intellectual Landscape', in *Historical Aspects of Printing and Publishing in Languages of the Middle East* (ed. Geoffrey Roper), Brill, Leiden, 2014, p. 53.

19. Aksan, Virginia H., 'Ottoman Political Writing 1768–1808', *International Journal of Middle East Studies*, Vol. 25, No. 1, 1993, pp. 56, 188.

20. Zens 2011, pp. 433–35.

21. Hanioğlu 2008, p. 12.

22. Rood, Judith Mendelsohn, *The Sacred Law in the Holy City: The Khedival Challenge to the Ottomans as seen from Jerusalem, 1829–1841*, University of Chicago Press, 1993, p. 39.

23. Rood 1993, p. 51.

24. Aksan, Virginia H., 'Whatever Happened to the Janissaries', *War in History*, Vol. 5, No. 1, 1998, p. 26.

25. Quoted in Owen 2009, p. 19.

26. Cohen, Amnon, *Palestine in the 18th Century*, Magnes Press, Jerusalem, 1973, p. 15.

27. Ibid., p. 40.

28. Winter, Michael, *Egyptian Society under Ottoman Rule, 1517–1798*, Routledge, London, 1992, p. 19.

29. Winter, Michael, 'The Re-Emergence of the Mamluks Following the Ottoman Conquest', in Philipp and Haarmann (eds), *The Mamluks in Egyptian Politics and Society*, Cambridge University Press, 1998, p. 104.

30. Hathaway, Jane, '"Mamluk Households" and "Mamluk Factions" in Ottoman Egypt: A Reconsideration', in Philipp and Haarmann (eds) 1998, p. 107.

31. Crecelius, Daniel, 'The Mamluk Beylicate of Egypt...', in Philipp and Harmann (eds) 1998, p. 130.

32. Philipp, Thomas, 'Personal Loyalty and Political Power of the Mamluks in the Eighteenth Century',, in Philipp & Harmann (eds) 1998, p. 124.

33. Ayalon, David, 'Studies in al-Jabarti: Notes on the Transformation of Mamluk Society under the Ottomans', *Journal of the Economic and Social History of the Orient*, Vol. 3, No. 3 1960, pp. 304–05.
34. Ibid., p. 303
35. Ibid., p. 124; Crecelius, Daniel, and 'Abd al-Wahhab Bakr (trans.), *Al-Damurdashi's Chronicle of Egypt, 1688–1755*, E. J. Brill, Leiden, 1991, pp. 365–66.
36. Al-Sayyid-Marsot, Afaf Lutfi, *Women and Men in Late Eighteenth-Century Egypt*, University of Texas Press, Austin, 1995, p. 21, citing Shaw 1978, pp. 37, 80, 82.
37. Livingston, John W., 'The Rise of Shaykh al-Balad 'Ali Bey al-Kabir: A Study in the Accuracy of the Chronicle of al-Jabarti', *Bulletin of the School of Oriental and African Studies*, Vol. 33, No. 2, 1970, pp. 287–88.
38. Crecelius 1981, p. 29.
39. Karaman and Pamuk 2010, pp. 610–11, and database at http://www.ata.boun.edu.tr/faculty/Şevketpamuk/JEH2010articledatabase
40. Quoted in Ibid., p. 602.
41. Ibid., p. 597.
42. Ibid., p. 609.
43. Pamuk, Şevket, 'Prices in the Ottoman Empire, 1469–1914', *International Journal of Middle East Studies*, Vol. 36, 2004, p. 455.

CHAPTER 4

1. Blunt, Wilfrid, *Black Sunrise: The Life and Times of Mulai Ismail, Emperor of Morocco, 1646–1727*, Methuen & Co., London, 1951, pp. 258–65.
2. Ibid. p. 265.
3. Abun-Nasr, Jamil M., *A History of the Maghrib*, 2nd edn, Cambridge University Press, 1975, p. 230.
4. Flournoy 1935, pp. 8–9.
5. Abun-Nasr 1975, p. 231.
6. Maxwell, Gavin, *Lords of the Atlas: The Rise and Fall of the House of Glaoua, 1893–1956*, Longman, London, 1966, p. 33.
7. Rogers, P. G., *A History of Anglo-Moroccan Relations to 1900*, Foreign and Commonwealth Office, n.d., pp. 86–95
8. Ibid., p. 98
9. Brown, James A. O. C., *Anglo-Moroccan Relations in the Late 18th and Early 19th Centuries, with Particular Reference to the Role of Gibraltar*, PhD thesis, Faculty of Asian and Middle East Studies, University of Cambridge, 2009, p. 44.
10. Flournoy 1935, p. 35.
11. Brown J. 2009, p. 45.
12. Ibid., p. 65
13. Davis 1970, p. 202.

CHAPTER 5

1. On Sicard's corsairing, see Dearden, Seton, *A Nest of Corsairs: The Fighting Karamanlis of the Barbary Coast*, John Murray, London, 1976, pp. 75, 83.
2. Ibid., pp. 74–75.
3. Quoted in Panzac 2005, pp. 21–22.
4. Dearden 1976, pp. 21–22.
5. Ibid., p. 21; Barnby, H. G., *The Prisoners of Algiers: An Account of the Forgotten American-Algerian War, 1785–1797*, Oxford University Press, 1966, p. 24; Davis, Robert C., 'Counting European Slaves on the Barbary Coast', *Past and Present*, No. 172, 2001, p. 96.
6. Clissold, Stephen, *The Barbary Slaves*, Purnell Book Services, Abingdon, 1977, p. 34.
7. Barnby 1966, p. 252.
8. Venture de Paradis, Jean-Michel (ed. E. Fagnan), *Alger au XVIIIe Siècle*, Algiers, Typographie Adolphe Jourdan, 1898 (reprint of original), p. 7. Panzac 2005, p. 48, quoting a nineteenth-century source, gives a lower number of xebecs for the period 1785–87 but a larger number of smaller craft – six barques and three galliots.
9. Panzac 2005, p. 47.
10. Davis 1970, pp. 98–101.
11. Barnby 1966, p. 241.
12. Panzac 2005, pp. 68–69.
13. Ibid., p. 308n
14. There are some small differences in the names and precise number of members of this inner Turkish elite and I have tried to identify those most commonly mentioned in the literature.
15. Ruedy, John, *Modern Algeria: The Origins and Development of a Nation*, Indiana University Press, Bloomington, 1992, p. 36.
16. Boyer, Pierre, 'Introduction à une Histoire intérieure de la régence d'Alger', *Revue Historique*, 235/2, 1966, p. 313.
17. Emerit, Marcel, 'Les tribus privilégiées en Algérie dans la première moitié du XIXe siècle', *Annales: Histoire, Science Sociales*, 21e Année No. 1, 1966, pp. 46–47.
18. Boyer, 1966, p. 314.
19. Ruedy 1992, p. 35.
20. See Emerit 1966, pp. 49–58.
21. Ruedy 1992, pp. 35–36.
22. On the network of Jewish merchants and financiers throughout the Mediterranean, see Abulafia 2012, various entries.
23. Barnby 1966, p. 58.

CHAPTER 6

1. Aksan, Virginia H., *Ottoman Wars 1700–1870: An Empire Besieged*, Pearson Education, Harlow, 2007, p. 142.

2.   Charles-Roux, François, *Les origines de l'expedition d'Égypte*, Librairie Plon, Paris 1910, p. 39, 'C'est à la instigation de notre ambassadeur Vergennes que le Sultan avait declaré la guerre aux Russes.'

3.   Anderson, M. S. 1966, p. 2.

4.   Anderson, M. S., 'Great Britain and the Russo-Turkish War of 1768–74', *English Historical Review*, Vol. 69, No. 270, 1954, p. 42.

5.   Aksan 1998, p. 29.

6.   Ibid., pp. 25–29.

7.   Baron de Tott 1786, p. 159.

8.   Anderson, R. C. 1951, *Naval Wars in the Levant, 1559–1853*, Liverpool University Press, 1951, pp. 279–80.

9.   Anderson, M. S., 1954, pp. 44, 44n.

10. Anderson, M. S., 'Great Britain and the Russian Fleet, 1769–70', *Slavonic and East European Review*, Vol. 31, No. 76, 1952, pp. 149–50.

11. Ibid., p. 152.

12. Accounts of the size and composition of the Ottoman Fleet vary somewhat. The data I have used are based on R. C. Anderson (1951), pp. 286, 286n and 287.

13. Anderson, M. S., 1952, p. 287.

14. Ibid., pp. 290–91.

15. Anderson, M. S., 1952, p. 53.

16. Ibid., p. 163.

17. Cohen 1973, p. 20.

18. Mansel 2010, pp. 36–37

19. Quoted in Hanioğlu 2008, p. 6.

20. Anderson, M. S., 1966, p. xi.

21. The English Translation of the full text of the key articles of the Treaty is published in Anderson, M.S., *The Great Powers and the Near East 1774–1923* (Documents of Modern History), Edward Arnold, London, 1970, pp. 9–14.

22. Anderson, R. C., 1951, p. 304.

CHAPTER 7

1.   Crecelius, Daniel, 'Egypt in the Eighteenth Century', in M. W. Daly (ed.), *The Cambridge History of Egypt*, Vol. 2, Cambridge University Press, 1998, pp. 73–74.

2.   Ibid., p. 75.

3.   Quoted in ibid., p. 76.

4.   Livingston 1970, pp. 283–94.

5.   Winter 1992, p. 25.

6.   Ghali, Ibrahim Amin, *Ali Bey El-Kebir et les origines de la pénétration Russe en Egypte*, Publications d'Atelier d'Alexandrie, Alexandria 1979, pp. 13–14.

7.   Crecelius 1981, p. 56.

8.   Percy Kemp, 'An Eighteenth Century Turkish Intelligence Report', *International Journal of Middle East Studies*, Vol. 16, No. 4, 1984, pp, 499, 506n.

9.   See Crecelius, Daniel, 'A Late Eighteenth-Century Austrian Attempt to Develop

the Red Sea Trade Route', *Middle Eastern Studies*, Vol. 30, No. 2, 1994, pp. 262–80.

10. Ibid., pp. 262–63.
11. Ingram, Edward, 'From Trade to Empire in the Near East – 1: the End of the Spectre of the Overland Trade, 1775–1801', *Middle Eastern Studies* Vol. 14, No. 1, 1978, p. 5.
12. Ghali 1979, p. 26.
13. Ibid., p. 28.
14. Aksan 2007, p. 235.
15. Charles-Roux 1910, 148–51.

CHAPTER 8

1. Fernández Duro, Cesáreo, *Armada Española (desde la unión de los reinos de Castilla y Aragon)*, Madrid, 1903, Vol. 7 pp. 165–66.
2. Ibid., p.167.
3. Brown, James A. O. C, *Crossing the Strait: Morocco, Gibraltar and Great Britain in the 18th and 19th Centuries*, Brill NV, Leiden, 2012 p. 50.
4. Fernandez Duro 1903, p. 169.
5. See the brief report in *Gentleman's Magazine*, Vol. XLV, London, 1775, p. 205.
6. Herrera Hermillosa, Juan Carlos, 'La expedición contra Argel de 1775: una misión impossible de Carlos III', p. 2, available at http://anatomiadelahistoria.com/2011
7. M. B., 'General Count O'Reilly's Attack upon Algiers', *National Magazine*, Vol. 1 No. 3, 1830, p. 348.
8. Fernandez Duro 1903, pp. 170–71; Herrera Hermillosa, p. 2. There are some small discrepancies between the numbers recorded by these two sources.
9. Barnby 1966, p. 77.
10. Fernandez Duro 1903, p. 172.
11. Barnby 1966, p. 77.
12. Fernandez Duro 1903, p. 173.
13. Ibid. p. 174
14. Herrera Hermillosa, p. 4.
15. Barnby, *The Prisoners of Algiers*, p. 17n.
16. Quoted in Panzac 2005, pp. 283–84.

CHAPTER 9

1. Quoted in Mansel, Philip, *Constantinople: City of the World's Desire, 1453–1924*, John Murray, London, 1995, p. 205.
2. Charles-Roux 1910, p. 72.
3. Volney, C.-F., *Voyage en Syrie et en Égypte pendant les années 1783, 1784 et 1785* (4th edn), Paris, 1807, p. 144.
4. Said 1978 (Penguin reprint, 1995), p. 81.
5. See Irwin, Robert, *For Lust of Knowing: The Orientalists and their Enemies*, Allen Lane, 2006, p. 114.

6.   Charles-Roux 1910, p. 212.
7.   Volney, C.-F., *Considérations sur la guerre actuelle des Turcs*, London, 1788, pp. 125–28.
8.   Charles-Roux 1910, pp. 252, 252n.
9.   Ibid., p. 262.
10. Ibid., pp. 221–73.
11. Ibid., p. 273.
12. Ibid., pp. 274–75.
13. Quoted in Herold 2005, p. 14.
14. Charles-Roux 1910, pp. 323–26.
15. Herold 2005, p. 20.
16. Ibid., pp. 21–22; Dwyer, Philip, *Napoleon: The Path to Power 1769–1799*, Bloomsbury, London, 2007, p. 402n.
17. Quoted in Coller, Ian, 'Egypt in the French Revolution', in Suzanne Desan, Lynn Hunt and William Max Nelson (eds), *The French Revolution in Global Perspective*, Cornell University Press, 2013, p. 125.
18. Quoted in Charles-Roux 1910, p. 313.
19. Quoted in Coller 2013, p. 125.
20. On the ambiguous attitude of the Directory and of Bonaparte himself towards the 'home grown' Italian republican movements, see Dwyer 2007, pp. 277–82.

CHAPTER 10

1.   Other representations of the battle include the drawing by François-André Vincent (1746–1816) exhibited in 1800, and the much later painting by the Polish artist Wojciech Kossak (1857–1942).
2.   Martin, Pierre Dominique, *Histoire de l'éxpedition Française en Égypte*, Vol. 1, J. M Eberhart, College Royal de France, Paris, 1815, pp. 203–04.
3.   Cole, Juan, *Napoleon's Egypt: Invading the Middle East*, Palgrave Macmillan, New York, 2007, p. 8.
4.   Dwyer 2007, pp. 362–63.
5.   Quoted in Crowdy, Terry, *The French Soldier in Egypt 1798–1801*, Osprey Publishing, 2003, p. 16.
6.   Quoted in Herold 2005, p. 69.
7.   Ibid., p. 70.
8.   Quoted in Cole 2007, p. 63.
9.   Dwyer 2007, p. 371.
10. Martin 1815, Vol. 1, p. 204.
11. Crecelius 1981, p. 21.
12. Herold 2005, p. 98n.
13. Ibid., p. 100
14. Ibid., p. 122
15. Ayalon 1960, p. 218.
16. Ibid., p. 239

17. Al-Jabarti 1975, 1978, 1993, p. 22.
18. See, for example, Al-Azmeh, Aziz, 'Barbarians in Arab Eyes', *Past & Present*, No. 134, 1992, p. 7.
19. Al-Jabarti 1975, 1978, 1993, pp. 28–29.
20. Ibid., p. 50.
21. Bayly 2004, p. 97.
22. Aksan 1993, p. 57.
23. Shaw, Stanford J., 'The Origins of Ottoman Military Reform: The Nizam-i Cedid Army of Sultan Selim III', *Journal of Modern History*, Vol. 37, No. 3, 1965, pp. 298–99.
24. Aksan 2007, p. 230.
25. Al-Jabarti 1975, 1978, 1993, pp. 84–7.
26. Ibid., p. 95.
27. Cole 2007, p. 213.
28. Cohen 1973, p. 21.
29. On the weak state of the Palestinian Army in the eighteenth century, see Cohen, Amnon, 'The Army in Palestine in the Eighteenth Century – Sources of its Weakness and Strength', *Bulletin of the School of Oriental and African Studies*, Vol. 34, No. 1, 1971, pp. 36–55.
30. Quoted in Dwyer 2007, p. 410.
31. Al-Jabarti 1975, 1978, 1993, p. 82.
32. Herold 2005, p. 276.
33. Ibid., p. 367–68.
34. Ibid., p. 388.

CHAPTER 11

1. Beaty, Charles, *Ferdinand de Lesseps: A Biographical Study*, Eyre & Spottiswoode, London, 1956, p. 14.
2. Anderson, M. S. 1966, p. 34.
3. Fortescue, J. W., *A History of the British Army: Vol. VI 1807–1809*, Macmillan & Co., London, 1910, p. 9.
4. Ibid., p. 10.
5. This account of al-Alfi Bey's death is given by Driault, E., 'Les Anglais devant Constantinople et Alexandrie 1807', *Revue Historique*, Vol. 73, 1900, p. 55. Other sources simply refer to his sudden death.
6. Ibid., p. 28.
7. Mackesy, Piers, *The War in the Mediterranean 1803–1810*, Longmans Green & Co., London, 1957, p. 161.
8. Ibid., p. 167.
9. Duckworth to Collingwood, 6 March 1807, *The New Annual Register for the Year 1807*, p. 121.
10. Ibid.
11. Driault 1900, p.48. Fortescue (1910) gives lower total casualty figures – '160 killed

or wounded'.

12. Palmer 2011, p. 69.

13. Fortescue 1910, p. 12.

14. Ibid., p. 7.

15. Ibid.

16. Ibid., pp. 7–8.

17. General Mackenzie-Fraser to General Fox, 6 April 1807, *The New Annual Register for the Year 1807*, pp. 147–48.

18. Driault 1900, p. 57.

19. Ibid., p. 58.

20. Fortescue 1910, p. 18n.

21. Brigadier Stewart to General Mackenzie-Fraser, 25 April 1807, *The New Annual Register for the Year 1807*, p. 169.

22. Ibid., 18 April 1807, p. 168.

23. Ibid.

24. Ibid., p. 169.

25. Stewart's account of the disaster which befell his column has been supplemented by Fortescue (1910), pp. 20–23.

26. Fortescue 1910, pp. 23–24.

27. Ibid., p. 25.

28. Sim, Katherine, *Desert Traveller: The Life of Jean Louis Burckhardt*, Victor Gollancz, London, 1969, pp. 308, 417. For the histories of the many thousands of other 'white victims' of British imperialism, see Colley, Linda, *Captives: Britain, Empire and the World 1600–1850*, Pimlico, London, 2003 (2nd edn of Jonathan Cape, London, 2002).

29. Holland, Robert, *Blue-Water Empire: The British in the Mediterranean Since 1800*, Allen Lane, London, 2012, p. 30.

30. Panzac 2005, p. 262n.

31. Holland 2012, p. 15.

32. Owen 2009, pp. 84–87.

33. Ibid., p. 67.

CHAPTER 12

1. James, Lawrence, *The Rise and Fall of the British Empire*, Abacus, London, 2007 (reprint of 1994), p. 157.

2. On the concept of 'informal empire' see Gallagher, John, and Ronald Robinson, 'The Imperialism of Free Trade', *Economic History Review*, New Series, Vol. 6, No. 1, 1953.

3. Kissinger, Henry, *A World Restored: Metternich, Castlereagh and the Problems of Peace, 1812–1822*, Echo Points and Media, 2013 (original 1957).

4. Ibid., pp. 5–6.

5. Dearden 1976, p. 163; Anderson R. C. 1951, p. 413.

6. Dearden 1976, pp. 158–61; Anderson R. C. 1951, pp. 411, 413–14.

7. Barnby 1966, p. 151.
8. Panzac, Daniel, *Barbary Corsairs: The End of a Legend 1800–1820*, Brill, Leiden, 2005, p. 103.
9. Ibid., pp. 130–31.
10. Ibid., p. 171.
11. The words of the French consul-general in Algiers quoted in Ibid., p. 261.
12. Perkins, Roger, and K. J. Douglas-Morris, *Gunfire in Barbary*, Kenneth Mason, Homewell Havant, Hampshire, 1982, pp. 67–68.
13. Perkins and Douglas-Morris 1982, p. 130.
14. Shaler, William, *Sketches of Algiers, Political, Historical and Civil*, Cummings Hilliard & Co, Boston, 1826, p. 139. However, in his initial report to Washington Shaler estimated the Algerine losses at around 2,000. It can only be assumed that the 600 figure published in the main text of his 1826 book was based on a somewhat later investigation.
15. Perkins and Douglas-Morris 1982, p. 151.
16. Shaler 1826, p. 139.
17. Ibid., p. 44.
18. Panzac 2005, p. 289.
19. Ibid., p. 295.
20. Ibid., p. 310.
21. Shaler 1826, p. 79 (original data in Spanish dollars).
22. Barnby 1966, p. 244.
23. Ruedy 1992, p. 46.
24. Abun-Nasr 1975, p. 237.
25. Ruedy 1992, pp. 47–48.
26. Todd, David, 'A French Imperial Meridian, 1814–1870', *Past & Present*, No. 210, 2011, p. 170.
27. Ibid.
28. Earl of Aberdeen to Lord Stuart de Rothesy, 5 March 1830, *British & Foreign State Papers*, Vol. XIX, 1831–1832, Foreign Office London, 1834, p. 942.
29. Ibid., pp. 945–46.
30. Lord Stuart de Rothesey to the Earl of Aberdeen, 30 April 1830, ibid., p. 953.
31. Shaler 1826, p. 12.
32. Khodja, Hamdan, *Le Miroir: Aperçu historique et statistique sur la Regénce de Alger*, introduction by Abdelkader Djeghloul, Sindbad, Paris, 1985 (original, 1833), p. 45.
33. Ruedy 1992, p. 21.
34. Ibid., p. 25.
35. Shaler 1826, p. 47. Danziger, Raphael, *'Abd al-Qadir and the Algerians*, Holmes & Meier Publishers, New York and London, 1977, p. 4, states that the population of Algiers in 1830 was only 35,000, but this estimate appears to have been based on the city after thousands had fled the French occupation.
36. Ibid., p. 45.
37. Lord, Perceval Barton *Algiers, with Notices of the Neighbouring States of Barbary*, London, 1835, p. 86.

38. Ibid., p. 88
39. Ruedy 1992, p. 48.
40. Gallissot, René, 'Abd el-Kader et la nationalité algérienne. Interpretation de la chute de la Régence d'Alger et des premières résistances a la conquête française (1830–1839)', *Revue Historique*, Vol. 233, No. 2, 1965, p. 342.
41. 'Traité de Navigation et de Commerce entre La France et la Régence de Tunis, signé à Bardo, le 8 Août, 1830', and 'Traité de Navigation et de Commerce entre La France et la Régence de Tripoli, signé en rade de Tripoli, le 11 Août, 1820', published in *British & Foreign State Papers*, Vol. XIX, 1831–1832, Foreign Office London, 1834, pp. 1050–56.
42. Panzac 2005, p. 334.

CHAPTER 13

1. Troop numbers from Shaw 1965, p. 300.
2. *The Gentleman's Magazine and Historical Chronicle*, Vol. LXXVII, London, November 1807, p. 1069. The original report refers to the 'Byzantine' Empire.
3. Hanioğlu 2008, pp. 60–61.
4. Brewer, David, *The Greek War of Independence*, Overlook Duckworth, New York and London, 2001, p. 121. Note that Brewer is generally sympathetic to the Greek cause. On the Greek atrocities see also McCarthy, Justin, *Death and Exile: The Ethnic Cleansing of Ottoman Muslims, 1821–1922*, Darwin Press, New Jersey, 1995, pp. 10–13.
5. Mansel 2010, p. 58.
6. Fahmy, Khaled, *All the Pasha's Men: Mehmed Ali, His Army and the Making of Modern Egypt*, American University in Cairo Press, Cairo, 2003, pp. 92–93.
7. Ibid., p. 92.
8. Owen 2009, pp. 70–71.
9. Levy, Avigdor, 'The Officer Corps in Sultan Mahmud II's New Ottoman Army', *International Journal of Middle East Studies*, Vol. 2, No. 1, 1971, p. 21.
10. However Fahmy 2003, pp. 252–53, gives a different description of the two flags for which I have found no other evidence.
11. Ralston 1990, p. 55.
12. Palmer 2011, p. 93.
13. Levy 1971, pp. 21, 23.
14. Quoted in Mansel 2010, p. 107.
15. Quoted in Brewer 2001, p. 246.
16. Anderson, M. S., 1966, p. 65.
17. Ibid., p.67.
18. Palmer 2011, p. 98.
19. Anderson, M. S., 1966, p. 74. The protocol 'drew the frontiers of the new Greek state considerably south of the Arta-Vola line.'
20. Aksan 2007, p. 357.
21. Erdem, Y. Hakan, *Slavery in the Ottoman Empire and its Demise, 1800–1909*,

Macmillan, Houndsmills, Basingstoke, 1996, p. 59

22. Anderson, M. S., 1966, p. 79.
23. Webster, Charles, *The Foreign Policy of Palmerston, 1830–1841*, G. Bell & Sons, London, 1951, Vol. 1, p. 284.
24. Treaty of Unkiar-Skelessi (Hünkar İskelesi), 8 July 1833, Separate Article, in Anderson, M. S., *The Great Powers and the Near East 1774–1923* (Documents of Modern History), Edward Arnold, London, 1970, p. 43.
25. Hanioğlu 2008, p. 85.

CHAPTER 14

1. Abun-Nasr 1975, p. 238.
2. Webster 1951, Vol. 1, p. 261.
3. Ruedy 1992, pp. 51–52.
4. Gallissot 1965, pp. 343–44.
5. Brower, Benjamin Claude, *A Desert Named Peace: The Violence of France's Empire in the Algerine Sahara, 1844–1902*, Columbia University Press, New York, 2009, p. 16.
6. Temimi, Abdeljelil, *Le Beylik de Constantine et Hadj Ahmed Bey 1830–1837*, Publications d'Histoire Maghrébine, Vol. 1, Tunis, 1978, p. 86.
7. Ibid., p. 93.
8. Gallissot 1965, pp. 344–48.
9. Quoted in Ibid., p. 63.
10. Temimi 1978, pp. 56–59.
11. Ibid., pp. 57, 62.
12. Gallissot, René, 'Présentation', in Marcel Emerit, *L'Algérie à L'Epoque d'Abd el-Kader*, Editions Bouchene, Paris, 2002, p. 11.
13. Kiser, John W., *Commander of the Faithful: The Life and Times of Emir Abd el-Kader*, Monkfish Book Publishing Co., New York, 2008, p. 22.
14. Gallissot 1965, p. 351.
15. Churchill, Charles Henry, *The Life of Abdel Kader, Ex-Sultan of the Arabs of Algeria*, Chapman & Hall, London, 1867, p. 24.
16. Al-Sallabi, 'Ali Muhammad, *Al Amir 'Abd al-Qadir al-Jaza'iri, Qa'id Rabbani wa mujahid Islami* (The Amir 'Abd al-Qadir, Religious Leader and Islamic fighter), Dar Ibn Kathir, Beirut, 2015, pp. 116–17.
17. Kiser 2008, pp. 15, 57.
18. Danziger 1977, p. 75.
19. Churchill 1867, p. 31.
20. 'Abd el-Kader', *Gentlemen's Magazine*, Vol. 192–193, London, 1852, p. 575.
21. Churchill 1867, p. 37.
22. Bennison, Amira K., 'The "New Order" and Islamic Order: The Introduction of the Nizami Army in the Western Maghrib and Its Legitimation, 1830–73', *International Journal of Middle East Studies*, Vol. 36, 2004, p. 595.
23. Al-Hasani al-Jaza'iri, Al-Imara Badi'a, *Fikr al-Amir 'Abd al-Qadir, Haqa'iq wa*

Watha'iq (The Beliefs of the Amir 'Abd al-Qadir, facts and documents), Dar al-Fikr li al-Tiba'a wa al-tawzi' wa al-nashr, Damascus, 2000, p. 59. However, there are a number of sources stating that the *wushah* wasn't disseminated until around 1839: e.g. Danziger 1977 (p. 188), Al-Sallabi 2015, (p. 124).

24. Al-Hasani al-Jaza'iri 2000, p. 59.
25. Ibid., p. 61. According to Bennison, p. 97, this particular Sura was commonly used to legitimise the establishment of 'European' armies elsewhere, for example in Morocco.
26. Al-Sallabi 2015, p. 123.
27. Al-Hasani al-Jaza'iri 2000, pp. 61–62.
28. Al-Sallabi 2015, p. 125. Bennison states that the companies were divided into units of 33 men known as 'tents'.(p. 595).
29. Al-Hasani al-Jaza'iri 2000, p. 61.
30. Danziger 1977, p. 97.
31. Quoted in Kiser 2008, pp. 47-8
32. Ageron, Charles-Robert, *Modern Algeria: A History from 1830 to the Present*, Hurst & Co., London, 1991 (Paris 1961), p. 11.
33. Khodja 1985.
34. Ibid. pp. 37–38.
35. Ibid., p. 155.
36. Ibid., pp. 210–11.
37. Ibid., p. 45.
38. Quoted in Ruedy 1992, p. 50.
39. Ibid., p. 54.
40. Windrow, Martin, *Uniforms of the French Foreign Legion, 1831–1981*, Blandford Press, Poole, 1981, p. 10.
41. Ibid., pp. 10–11
42. Churchill 1867, p. 51.
43. Ibid., pp. 51-2.
44. Ibid., p. 53.
45. Quoted in Kiser 2008, p. 63.
46. Windrow 1981, p. 12.
47. Churchill, presumably informed by 'Abd al-Qadir himself, states that the French had 5,000 infantry (Churchill 1867, p. 75).
48. Churchill 1867, p. 76.
49. Ibid., p. 77.
50. Kiser 2008, p. 85.
51. Churchill 1867, pp. 77–78.
52. *The Annual Register for 1835*, Vol. 77, Chapter XV, London, 1836, p. 424.
53. Quoted in Kiser 2008, p. 95.
54. Churchill 1867, p. 123.
55. Temimi 1978, p. 132.
56. Quoted in Ibid., p. 145.
57. Dearden 1976, pp. 297–310,

58. Temimi 1978, p. 152.
59. Anon, 'L'oeuvre de l'arme du génie en Algérie', *Revue du Génie Militaire*, Vol. LXVIII, Jan. 1931, p. 93.
60. Ibid., p. 95.
61. Ibid., p. 96.
62. Kiser 2008, p. 96; Sessions, Jennifer E., *By Sword and Plow: France and the Conquest of Algeria*, Cornell University Press, 2011. A much lower figure for the losses (2000 men) is given by Pélissier 2001.
63. Brower 2009, p. 43.

CHAPTER 15

1. The standard work on the subject is Gallagher and Robinson 1953.
2. Mathias, Peter, *The First Industrial Nation: An Economic History of Britain 1700–1914* (2nd edn), Methuen, London, 1983, p. 454.
3. Ibid., p. 457.
4. Quoted in Brown 2002, p. 27.
5. See Gallagher and Robinson 1953, p. 13.
6. Webster 1951, Vol. 1, pp. 750–51.
7. Quoted in Ibid., p. 540.
8. Anderson, M. S., 1966, p. 88.
9. Karaman and Pamuk 2010, pp. 619, 621.
10. Ibid., p. 620.
11. Webster 1951, Vol. 2, p. 549.
12. Pamuk, Şevket, *The Ottoman Empire and European Capitalism, 1820–1913*, Cambridge University Press, 1987, p. 20.
13. Webster 1951, Vol. 2, p. 613.
14. Panza, Laura, and Jeffrey G. Williamson, 'Did Muhammad Ali Foster Industrialization in Early Nineteenth-Century Egypt?', *Economic History Review*, Vol. 68, No. 1, 2015, p. 82.
15. Frederick Engels, 'Persia–China'. *New York Daily Tribune*, 5 June 1857, reproduced in Shlomo Avineri, *Karl Marx on Colonialism and Modernization*, Anchor Books, New York, 1969, p. 186.
16. Quoted in Ibid., p. 273.
17. Levy 1971, pp. 26–31.
18. Ibid., p. 25
19. Fahmy 2003, p. 275.
20. Anderson, M. S., 1966, p. 96
21. Driault, Edouard, *La question d'Orient depuis ses origines jusqu' à la paix de Sèvres*, Librairie Félix Alcan, Paris, 1921, p. 147.
22. Hanioğlu 2008, pp. 72–73.
23. Palmer 2011, p. 107.
24. Quoted in Flournoy 1935, pp. 57–58.
25. Anderson, M. S., 1966, p. 99.

26. Ibid.
27. Webster 1951, Vol. 2, p. 623.
28. Ibid., p. 672
29. *Report of the Select Committee on Steam Communication with India*, House of Commons, Parliament, London, July 1837, pp. iii, 2–6.
30. Anderson, M. S., 1966, pp. 97, 97n.
31. Quoted in Waterfield, Gordon, *Sultans of Aden*, John Murray, London 1968, p. 131.
32. Ibid., p. 57.
33. Anderson, M. S., 1966, p. 101.
34. Webster 1951, p. 706.
35. Anderson, R. C., 1951, pp. 562–64.
36. Holland 2012, p .66.
37. Quoted in Fahmy 2003, p. 246.

CHAPTER 16

1. Kiser 2008, p. 107.
2. Quoted in Temimi 1978, p. 166.
3. Letter of Hajj Ahmad Bey to 'Ali Ben Aissa, July 1839, in Emerit 2002, p. 230.
4. Bugeaud's words as reported in the *Revue des Deux Mondes*, Quatrième Séries, Vol. XIV, Paris, 14 June 1838, p. 861.
5. *Revue des Deux Mondes*, 14 June 1838, p. 861.
6. Churchill 1867, p. 189.
7. Bugeaud's words as reported in the *Revue des Deux Mondes*, 14 June 1838, p. 860.
8. Al-Sallabi 2015, p. 124.
9. Scott, Colonel James, *A Journal of Residence in the Esmailla of Abd-el-Kader and of Travels in Morocco and Algiers*, Whittaker & Co., London, 1842, pp. 71, 100.
10. Kiser 2008, pp. 137–39.
11. Abun-Nasr 1975, p. 245.
12. Churchill 1867, p. 191.
13. Ibid., p. 80. In fact this quotation refers to an earlier fight between 'Abd al-Qadir's regular troops and those of the French; nevertheless it can be equally applied to the Battle of the Gorges of Mouzaïa.
14. Scott 1942, pp. x–xi.
15. Ibid., p. 137.
16. Ibid., pp. 131–32.
17. Ibid., pp. 170–71.
18. For a detailed analysis of the role of the razzia in the conquest of Algeria, see Gallois, William, *A History of Violence in the Early Algerian Colony*, Palgrave Macmillan UK, Basingstoke, Hants, 2013, especially pp. 100–121.
19. Quoted in Brower 2009, p. 143.
20. Ibid., p. 287.
21. See PP/MM/AL/1, *Notes by Lord Palmerston on Diplomatic Proceedings in 1830*

(1844), Hartley Library, University of Southampton.

22. Flournoy 1935, pp. 64–66, 91–93.
23. Ibid., p. 85.
24. Ibid., p. 93.
25. 'Abd al-Kader', *Gentleman's Magazine* 1852, p. 577.
26. Temimi 1978, p. 205.
27. Brower 2009, p. 48.
28. Danziger 1977, p. xi.
29. For the full account of the war in the Algerian Sahara, see Brower 2009.
30. Ibid., p. 43.

CHAPTER 17

1. Farah, Caesar E., *The Politics of Interventionism in Ottoman Lebanon, 1830–1861*, Centre for Lebanese Studies and I.B. Tauris, London, 2000, p. 703.
2. Ibid., p. 274.
3. Issawi, Charles, 'British Trade and the Rise of Beirut, 1830–1860', *International Journal of Middle East Studies*, Vol. 8, 1977, pp. 91–101, p. 92.
4. Calculated from Farah 2000, p. 748.
5. Harik, Iliya F., 'The Iqta' System in Lebanon: A Comparative Political View', *Middle East Journal*, Vol. 19, No. 4, 1965, pp. 405–21. In contrast Chevalier rejects the use of such terms as 'feudal' and 'fief'. See Chevalier, Dominique, 'Les cadres sociaux de l'économie agraire dans le Proche-Orient au debut du XIXe siècle: le cas du Mont Liban', in M. A. Cook, *Studies in the Economic History of the Middle East*, Oxford University Press, 1970, p. 344. My own view is that, in most (but no all) respects the comparison with feudalism is valid.
6. Porath, Yehoshua, 'The Peasant Revolt of 1858–61 in Kisrawan', *Asian and African Studies*, Vol. 2, 1966, pp. 79–80.
7. Porath 1966, p. 79.
8. Wagstaff, J. M., 'A Note on Nineteenth-Century Population Statistics for Lebanon', *Bulletin of the Society for Middle Eastern Studies*, Vol. 13, No. 1, 1986, pp. 27–28.
9. Akarli, Engin, *The Long Peace: Ottoman Lebanon, 1861–1920*, University of California Press, Berkeley, 1993, available at http://ark.cdlib.org/ark:/13030/ft6199p06t/, pp. 11, 15–16.
10. Karam, Rizk, 'The Shihab Emirship (1697–1841): Bashir II's Emirship (1789–1840', in *Politics, Religion and State Building (11th–16th/19th Centuries* (ed. Dominique Avon), Université du Maine, Le Mans, 2011, p. 3, available at http://hemed.univ-lemans.fr/cours2011/en/co/module_Eomed(2)_17.html
11. Ibid., p. 2.
12. Akarli 1993, pp. 23–24.
13. Kisirwani, Maroun, 'Foreign Interference and Religious Animosity in Lebanon', *Journal of Contemporary History*, Vol. 15, No. 4, 1980, p. 695.
14. Churchill, Charles Henry, *The Druzes and the Maronites under Turkish Rule,*

1840–1860, Bernard Quarich, London, 1862, p. 39.

15. The term 'proxy-war' is my own but this rather sweeping interpretation is backed up by all the major modern works on the subject, notably in Farah's great study, a work of scrupulous objectivity.

16. Farah, Caesar E., 'Protestantism and British Diplomacy in Syria', *International Journal of Middle East Studies*, Vol. 7, No. 3, 1976, p. 332.

17. Farah 2000, p. 76.

18. Quoted in Ibid.

19. Ibid., p. 329.

20. Ibid., p. 328.

21. Quoted in Ibid., p. 95.

22. Ibid., p. 96.

23. Ibid., p. 94.

24. Churchill 1862, p. 20.

25. Wagstaff 1986, p. 28.

26. Farah 2000, p. 748.

27. Ibid., p. 380.

28. Ibid., p. 393.

29. Ibid., p. 398.

30. Quoted in Ibid., p. 4.

31. Figes, Orlando, *Crimea: The Last Crusade*, Allen Lane, London, 2010, p. xxiii.

32. Cain, P. J., and A. G. Hopkins, 'Gentlemanly Capitalism and British Expansion Overseas: 1. The Old Colonial System, 1688–1850', *Economic History Review*, New Series, Vol. 39, No. 4, 1986, p. 371.

33. Figes 2010, p. 104.

34. Ibid., p. 108.

35. Ibid., pp. 108–09.

36. Quoted in Ibid., p. 158.

CHAPTER 18

1. Emerit, Marcel, 'La Crise syrienne et l'expansion économique française en 1860', *Revue Historique*, Vol. CCVII, 1952, p. 225.

2. Owen 2009, p. 155.

3. Churchill, Charles Henry, *Mount Lebanon: A Ten Years' Residence from 1842 to 1852 Describing the Manners, Customs and Religion of the Inhabitants*, Vol. 1, Saunders & Otley, London, 1853, pp. 98–99.

4. Porath 1966, p. 85.

5. Traboulsi, Fawwaz, *A History of Modern Lebanon*, Pluto Press, London, 2007, p. 30.

6. Farah 2000, p. 586.

7. Traboulsi 2007, p. 39; Farah 2000 gives 3,600 to 4,000 as the probable death toll.

8. Farah 2000, p. 592.

9. Ibid., p. 215.

10. Quoted in Abu Shukran, ʿUsama Kamil, *ʾAuda ila Asbab Ahdath al-Qarn al-Tasiʿ ʿashar fi Jabal Lubnan* (A Return to the Causes of the Events of the Nineteenth Century in Mount Lebanon), Dar Al-ʿArabiyya Al-ʿulum Nashirun, Beirut, 2017, p. 126.

11. Ibid.

12. Traboulsi 2007, p. 37.

13. Farah 2000, p. 613.

14. Ibid., p. 652.

15. Karabell, Zachary, *Parting the Desert: The Creation of the Suez Canal*, John Murray, London, 2003, p. 137.

16. Bell, K., 'British Policy Towards the Construction of the Suez Canal 1859–65', *Transactions of the Royal Historical Society*, Vol. 15, 1965, p. 128.

17. Wilson, Sir Arnold, *The Suez Canal: Its Past, Present and Future*, Oxford University Press, London, 1933, p. 20.

18. Karabell 2003, p. 142.

19. Ibid., p. 160.

20. Anderson, M. S., 1966, p. 156.

21. Farah 2000, p. 706.

22. Gates, Carolyn, *The Merchant Republic of Lebanon: Rise of an Open Economy*, Centre for Lebanese Studies and I.B. Tauris, London, 1998, p. 14.

23. Emerit 1952, pp. 224–25.

24. Farah 2000, p. 651.

25. Kiser 2008, p. 263.

26. Emerit 1952, p. 216.

27. Kiser 2008, pp. 286–87.

28. Ibid., p. 309

29. Quoted in Choueiri, Youssef M., 'Ottoman Reform and Lebanese Patriotism', in Nadim Shehadi and Dana Haffar Mills (eds), *Lebanon: A History of Conflict and Consensus*, Centre for Lebanese Studies and I.B. Tauris, London, 1989, p. 73.

30. Quoted in Emerit 1952, p. 215.

31. Ibid., p. 218.

32. Kiser 2008, p. 310.

33. Quoted in Emeri 1952, pp. 218–19.

34. Quoted in Farah 2000, p. 660.

35. Quoted in Emerit 1952, p. 221.

36. Ibid., pp. 218, 221.

37. Quoted in Emerit 1952, p. 216n.

38. Farah 2000, pp. 695–96.

39. Owen 2009 (1981), p. 156.

40. See Marx, Karl, *The Eighteenth Brumaire of Louis Bonaparte*, 1852, available at https://www.marxists.org/archive/marx/works/1852/18th-brumaire/ch01.htm

41. Farah 2000, p. 668.

42. Wilson 1933, p. 29.

43. Goudar, Ange, *Les intérêts de France mal entendus*, Vol. 1, Chez Jacques Coeur,

Amsterdam, 1756, p. 5.

44. Ruedy 1992, p. 68.

CHAPTER 19

1. See Loizos, Dimitris, 'Economic History Problems of 18th c. Ottoman Greece: The Case of Ambelakia in Thessaly' (preliminary report), p. 1, available at http://www.anistor.gr/english/enback/e011.htm

2. Felix Beaujour, *Tableau du Commerce de la Grece*, Paris 1800, quoted in Urquhart, David, *Turkey and Its Resources: Its Municipal Organization and Free Trade...*, Saunders & Otley, London, 1833, pp. 50–51.

3. Urquhart 1833, p. 47.

4. Ibid., p. 52.

5. Hobsbawm, Eric, *The Age of Capital, 1848–1875*, Abacus, London 2004 (reprint of 1975), p. 360.

6. Quataert, Donald, 'The Age of Reforms: Manufacturing', in Inalcik and Quataert, *An Economic and Social History of the Ottoman Empire*, Vol. 2, Cambridge University Press, Cambridge, 1994, p. 770.

7. Pamuk 1987, p. 32.

8. Owen 2009, p. 85.

9. Compare, for example, Issawi, Charles, 'Decline of Ottoman Industry in the 1840s', in Charles Issawi (ed.), *The Economic History of the Middle East 1800–1914*, University of Chicago Press, Chicago, 1966, pp. 41–45, with Quataert, Donald, *Ottoman Manufacturing in the Age of the Industrial Revolution*, Cambridge University Press, Cambridge, 1993. However, in a later paper Issawi somewhat modified his views about the extent of the destruction of handicraft industry. See: 'De-industrialisation and Re-industrialisation in the Middle East since 1800', *International Journal of Middle East Studies*, Vol. 12, No. 4, 1980, pp. 469–79.

10. Pamuk 1987, p. 123.

11. Quataert 1994, p. 906.

12. Pamuk 1987, p. 123.

13. See various passages in Quataert 1994, pp. 888–943; and Quataert 1993.

14. Hutton, Catherine, *The Tour of Africa*, Baldwin, Cradock & Joy, London, 1821, p. 461.

15. Brown, L. Carl, *The Tunisia of Ahmad Bey*, 1837–1855, Princeton University Press, Princeton NJ, 1974, p. 191.

16. Quataert 1993, p. 176.

17. Clark, Edward C., 'The Ottoman Industrial Revolution', *International Journal of Middle East Studies*, Vol. 5, No. 1, 1974, p. 66.

18. Ibid.

19. Ibid.

20. Owen 2009, p. 72.

21. Panza and Williamson 2015, p. 84.

22. St John, James Augustus, *Egypt and Mohammed Ali; Or, Travels in the Valley of the*

Nile (2 vols), Longman et al., London, 1834, Vol. 2, pp. 408–09.

23. Ibid., pp. 412–13.
24. Warburton, Eliot, *The Crescent and the Cross; or, Romance and Realities of Eastern Travel* (15th edn), Hurst & Blackett, London, 1859, p. 81.
25. Saleh, Mohamed, 'A Pre-Colonial Population Brought to Light: Digitization of the Nineteenth Century Egyptian Censuses', *Historical Methods: A Journal of Quantitative and Interdisciplinary History*, January 2013, Vol. 46 (1), pp. 5–18.
26. St John 1834, p. 425.
27. MacFarlane, Charles, *Turkey and Its Destiny: The Results of a Journey Made in 1847 and 1848 to Examine into the State of the Country*, Vol. 2, Lea and Blanchard, Philadelphia, 1850, p. 356
28. MacFarlane, Charles, *Turkey and Its Destiny: The Results of a Journey Made in 1847 and 1848 to Examine into the State of the Country*, Vol. 1, John Murray, London, 1850, p. 58.
29. MacFarlane 1850, Vol. 2, p. 356.
30. Clark 1974, p. 68.
31. Pamuk 1987, p. 21.
32. Owen 2009, p. 63.
33. And to a lesser extent Mount Lebanon. See Chapter 18.
34. Quataert 1993, p. 122.
35. Quoted in Tok, Alaaddin, *The Ottoman Mining Sector in the Age of Capitalism: An Analysis of State–Capital Relations 1850–1908*, PhD thesis, Atatürk Institute for Modern Turkish History, Boğaziçi University, 2010, p. 24.
36. Quataert 1993, p. 171.
37. Fahmy 2003, p. 50.
38. Urquhart 1833, p. 176n.
39. Quataert, Donald, *Miners and the State in the Ottoman Empire: The Zonguldak Coalfield, 1822–1920*, Berghahn Books, New York, 2006, p. 21.
40. Ibid., p. 28.
41. Ibid., p. 7.
42. Ibid.
43. Ibid, p. 28.
44. Ibid., p. 4.
45. See, for example, Notz, William, 'The World's Coal Situation during the War', *Journal of Poliitical Economy*, Vol. 6, No. 6, 1918, p. 568.
46. Panza, Laura, 'De-Industrialization and Re-Industrialization in the Middle East: Reflections on the Cotton Industry in Egypt and in the Izmir Region', *Economic History Review*, Vol. 67, No. 1, 2014, p. 159.
47. Ibid., p. 148.
48. Owen 2009, p. 114.
49. Ibid., p. 136.
50. Braudel 1984, Vol. 3, p. 484.

CHAPTER 20

1. Hobson 1902, p. 19.
2. Ibid., p. 23.
3. Lenin, V. I., *Imperialism: The Highest Stage of Capitalism*, Penguin, London 2010 (reprint of 3rd edn c. 1922), pp. 98–99.
4. Hobsbawm, Eric, *The Age of Empire, 1875–1914*, Abacus, London, 1996 (reprint of 1987), p. 59.
5. Ibid.
6. Ibid.
7. Pakenham 2003 (1991).
8. Baumgart 1982.
9. Cain and Hopkins 2016, p. 123.
10. Hobsbawm, Eric, *The Age of Capital, 1848–1875*, Abacus, London 2004 (reprint of 1975), pp. 252–53.
11. Percentage increases based on the price indices constructed by Pamuk 1987, Appendix A2.2.
12. Issawi, Charles (ed.), *The Economic History of the Middle East 1800–1914*, University of Chicago Press, Chicago, 1966, p. 448.
13. Cooke, W. S., *The Ottoman Empire and Its Tributary States*, B. R. Grüner, Amsterdam, 1968 (reprint of 1876), p. 60.
14. Vatikiotis, P. J., *The History of Egypt from Muhammad Ali to Mubarak* (3rd edn), Weidenfeld & Nicolson, London, 1985, p. 73.
15. Marlowe, John, *Spoiling the Egyptians*, Andre Deutsch, London, 1974, pp. 105–06.
16. Shaw, Stanford J., 'Ottoman Expenditures and Budgets in the Late Nineteenth and Early Twentieth Centuries, *International Journal of Middle East Studies*, Vol. 9, No. 3, 1978, p. 374.
17. Owen 2009, p. 104.
18. Shaw 1978, p. 374.
19. Marsden, Arthur, *British Diplomacy and Tunis, 1875–1902*, Scottish Academic Press, Edinburgh, 1971, p. 30.
20. Abun-Nasr 1975, p. 267.
21. Vatikiotis 1985, pp. 84–85.
22. Owen 2009, p. 127.
23. Hobsbawm 2004, p. 62.
24. Ibid.
25. Hobsbawm 1996, pp. 36–37.
26. Glenny, Misha, *The Balkans, 1804–2012*, Granta Publications, London, 2012 (reprint of 1999), p. 100.
27. Owen 2009, p. 104.
28. Wilson, Sir Arnold, *The Suez Canal: Its Past, Present and Future*, Oxford University Press, London, 1933, pp. 44–45.
29. Karabell, Zachary, *Parting the Desert: The Creation of the Suez Canal*, John Murray, London, 2003, p. 264.

30. *Manchester Guardian*, 27 November 1875, 'The Suez Canal and the Government', Guardian Archive, available at: https://www.theguardian.com/theguardian/2010/nov/29/archive-the-suez-canal-and-the-government-1875

31. Mowat, R. C., 'From Liberalism to Imperialism: The Case of Egypt 1875–1887', *Historical Journal*, Vol. 16, No. 1, 1973, p. 112.

32. Tunçer, Ali Coşkun, *Sovereign Debt and International Financial Control: The Middle East and the Balkans, 1870–1914*, Palgrave Macmillan, Basingstoke, 2015, p. 36.

33. Vatikiotis 1985, p. 129.

34. Ramm, Agatha, 'Great Britain and France in Egypt, 1876–1882', in P. Gifford and W. M. R. Lewis (eds), *France and Britain in Africa*, Yale University Press, New Haven, 1971, p. 100.

35. Tunçer 2015, p. 38.

36. Schölch, Alexander, 'The "Men on the Spot" and the English Occupation of Egypt in 1882', *Historical Journal*, Vol. 19, No. 3, 1976, p. 776.

37. Ibid., p. 776n.

38. Quoted in ibid. See also Chamberlain, M. E., 'The Alexandria Massacre of 11 June 1882 and the British Occupation of Egypt', *Middle Eastern Studies*, Vol. 13, No. 1, 1977: 'Taxation increased and the methods employed to secure the payment of taxes became more and more brutal', p. 16.

CHAPTER 21

1.Ković, Miloš, 'The Beginnings of the 1875 Serbian Uprising in Herzegovina: The British Perspective', *Balcanica* 41: 2010, p. 55.

2. Quoted in ibid., p. 59.

3. Ibid., p. 60.

4. Rogan, Eugene, *The Fall of the Ottomans: The Great War in the Middle East 1914–1920*, Allen Lane, London, 2015, p. 2.

5. McCarthy, Justin, *Death and Exile: The Ethnic Cleansing of Ottoman Muslims, 1821–1922*, Darwin Press, New Jersey, 1995, p. 339.

6. Rogan 2015, p. 3.

7. Anderson, M. S., 1996, pp. 198–210.

8. The words contained in an official despatch to London from the French foreign minister William Waddington (a Frenchman of English descent), recording the minister's recollection of Salisbury's own words. Quoted in Marsden 1971, p. 56.

9. Quoted in McClure, W. K., *Italy in North Africa: An Account of the Tripoli Enterprise*, Constable & Co., London, 1913, p. 8.

10. Owen 2009, p. 194.

11. Ibid., p. 193.

CHAPTER 22

1. Marsden 1971, p. 28.
2. Ibid.,p. 30.
3. Abun-Nasr 1975, p. 270.
4. Marsden 1971, p. 24.
5. Quoted in Ibid., p. 24.
6. Ibid., p. 32
7. Abun-Nasr 1975, p. 275.
8. Brunschwig, Henri, *French Colonialism, 1871–1914, Myths and Realities*, Pall Mall Press, London, 1966, pp. 55–57.
9. For a longer, and very entertaining account of the events preceding, during and after the French invasion of Tunisia, see Pakenham 2003, pp. 109–22.
10. There is much disagreement about the exact dates of the French military intervention and its arrival at Tunis. Abun-Nasr 1975, Pakenham 2003 and Ganiage, Jean, 'France, England and the Tunisian Affair', in P. Gifford and W. M. R. Louis (eds), *France and Britain in Africa*, Yale University Press, New Haven, 1971, all give different chronologies.
11. Quoted in Brunschwig 1966, p. 59.
12. Ibid.
13. McCarthy, Justin, 'Nineteenth-Century Egyptian Population', *Middle Eastern Studies*, Vol. 12, No. 3, 1976, p. 33.
14. Ibid., p. 29; Reimer, Michael J., 'Colonial Bridgehead: Social and Spatial Change in Alexandria, 1850–1882', *Middle East Studies*, Vol. 28, 1988, p. 534,
15. Ibid., p. 531.
16. Ibid., pp. 536–37.
17. Vatikiotis 1985, p. 127.
18. Beeri, Eliezer, 'Social Origin and Family Background of the Egyptian Army Officer Class', *Asian and African Studies*, Vol. 2, 1966, pp. 1–7.
19. Quoted in Keddie 1968, p. 62.
20. Vatikiotis 1985, p. 132.
21. Ibid., pp. 377–78.
22. Mowat 1973, p. 114.
23. Schölch 1978, p. 776.
24. Al-Najar, Husayn Fawzi, *Ahmad 'Arabi, Misr li al-Misriyyin* (Ahmad Arabi, Egypt for the Egyptians), Matabi'a al-Hai'a al-Misriyya al-'Ama li al-Kitabat, Cairo, 1992, p. 71.
25. Ibid., p. 73.
26. Ibid., p. 76.
27. Blunt, Wilfrid Scawen, *The Secret History of the English Occupation of Egypt*, History Press, Cheltenham UK, 2007, p. 157.
28. Ibid., p. 154.
29. Ibid., p. 68.
30. Galbraith, John S., and Afaf Lutfi Al-Sayyid-Marsot, 'The British Occupation of

Egypt: Another View', *International Journal of Middle East Studies*, Vol. 9 No. 4, 1978, p. 473.

31. Schölch 1978, p. 780n.
32. Galbraith and Al-Sayyid-Marsot 1978, p. 474.
33. Ibid.
34. Pakenham 2003, p. 115.
35. Quoted in Galbraith & Al-Sayyid-Marsot 1978, p. 476.
36. Quoted in Schölch 1978, p. 775.
37. Schölch 1978, p. 776.
38. Chamberlain 1977, pp. 14, 24.
39. Reimer 1988, p. 547.
40. Chamberlain 1977, p. 34.
41. Hopkins, A. G., 'The Victorians and Africa: A Reconsideration of the Occupation of Egypt, 1882', *Journal of African History*, Vol. 27, No. 2, 1986, pp. 363–91, p. 384.
42. Galbraith and Al-Sayyid-Marsot 1978, p. 485.
43. Quoted in ibid., p. 385.
44. Reproduced in Blunt 2007, pp. 348–54.
45. Schölch 1978, p. 780.
46. Ibid., p. 784.
47. Ibid., p. 773, 773n; see also Hopkins 1986, especially pp. 373–74.
48. Galbraith and Al-Sayyid-Marsot 1978, p. 472.
49. Ramm 1971, p. 110.
50. 'Supply forces in the Mediterranean', Parliamentary Debates (Hansard), House of Commons, 25 July 1882, col. 1778. Quoted in Wikipedia, available at https: en.wikipedia.org/wiki/Bombardment_of_Alexandria
51. Pakenham 2003, p. 134.
52. Ibid., pp. 138–39.
53. Quoted in Galbraith and Al-Sayyid-Marsot 1978, p. 478.
54. Jenkins, Roy, *Gladstone*, Macmillan, London, 1995, p. 507.
55. Jenkins presents some arguments in Gladstone's defence against the accusation of 'pecuniary interest'. See ibid., p. 508.
56. Hopkins 1986, p. 386.
57. Ramm 1971, pp. 114–17.

CHAPTER 23

1. Eric Hobsbawm 1996, pp. 61–62.
2. Quoted in Baumgart 1982, p. 42.
3. Ibid., pp. 36–37.
4. Langer, William, *The Diplomacy of Imperialism, 1890–1902*, 1st edn, Alfred A. Knopf, 1951, pp. 84–85.
5. Montbard, Georges, *Among the Moors: Sketches of Oriental Life*, Sampson Low, Marston & Company, London, 1894, p. vi.
6. Quoted in MacMillan 2014, p. 103.

7. Calderwood, Eric, 'The Beginning (or End) of Moroccan History: Historiography, Translation, and Modernity in Ahmad B. Khalid Al-Nasiri and Clemente Cerdeira', *Journal of Middle East Studies*, No. 44, 2012, p. 409.

8. Parsons, F. V., 'The "Morocco Question" in 1884: An Early Crisis', *English Historical Journal*, Vol. 77, No. 305, 1962, p. 661.

9. Ibid., p. 666.

10. Ibid. p. 667.

11. Parsons, F. V., 'The Proposed Madrid Conference on Morocco, 1887–88', *Historical Journal*, Vol. 8, No. 1, 1965, p. 74.

12. Ibid., pp. 79, 86.

13. Ibid., p. 92.

14. Cooke, James J., *New French Imperialism 1880–1910: The Third French Republic and Colonial Expansion*, David & Charles, Newton Abbot, 1973, p. 15.

15. Ibid., p. 37.

16. Ibid., p. 110.

17. Harris, Walter, *Morocco that Was*, Eland, London, 1983 (reprint of 1921).

18. James Chandler, Afterword to ibid., p. 335.

19. Maxwell 1966, p. 39.

20. Ibid., p. 50.

21. Harris 1983, p. 65.

22. Ibid., p. 80.

23. Ibid., p. 79.

24. Forrest, A. S. (illustrator), and S. L. Bensusan, *Morocco*, Adam Charles & Black, London, 1904, Chapter VIII.

25. Ibid., p. 141.

26. Harris 1983, p. 69.

27. Hart, D. M., 'The Saint and the Schoolmaster, or Jbala Warlord and Rifian Reformer Revisited: Conflicting Views of Islam in a Confrontation and Power Clash in Colonial Northern Morocco, 1924–24', *Journal of North African Studies*, Vol. 6, No. 2, pp. 29, 34.

28. Abun-Nasr 1975, p. 298.

CHAPTER 24

1. Langer 1951, p. 797.

2. Ibid., p. 3.

3. Ibid., pp. 19–20.

4. Ibid., pp. 47–48.

5. Ibid., p. 46.

6. Ibid., p. 49.

7. Ibid., p. 50.

8. Ibid., p. 342.

9. Grenville, J. A. S., 'Goluchowski, Salisbury, and the Mediterranean Agreements, 1895–1897', *Slavonic and East European Review*, Vol. 36, No. 87, 1958, p. 341.

10. See Langer 1960, especially pp. 157–58.

11. Ibid., pp. 205–06.

12. Grenville 1958, p. 366.

13. Ibid., p. 367.

14. Burnikel, Catherine T., *Camille Barrère and Franco-Italian Rapprochement 1898–1902*, Thesis, Loyola University, Chicago, 1972, available at https://ecommons.luc.edu/cgi/viewcontent.cgi?article=2166&context=luc_diss

15. Ibid., p. 82.

16. Quoted in ibid., p. 159.

17. Nogué, Joan, and José Luis Villanova (eds), *España en Marruecos (1912–1956): Discursos geográficos e intervención territorial*, Editorial Mileno, Lleida, 1999, p. 38.

18. Ibid., pp. 187–205.

19. Cooke, J. J., 1973, pp. 111–12.

20. Ibid., pp. 113–15.

21. Ibid., p. 116.

22. See Nogué and Villanova 1990, pp. 106n–107.

23. MacMillan 2014, p. 195.

24. Quoted in Cain & Hopkins 2016.

25. Clark, Martin, *Modern Italy, 1871 to the Present* (3rd edn), Routledge, Abingdon, Oxon, 2008 (original 1984), p. 144.

26. Ibid.

27. Mitchell, B. R., *European Historical Statistics, 1750–1970*, Macmillan, London 1978.

28. Mathias 1983, p. 279.

29. Gibbons, H. A., *The Reconstruction of Poland and the Near East*, New York, 1917, quoted in Earle, Edward M., *Turkey, the Great Powers and the Bagdad Railway: A Study in Imperialism*, Macmillan, London, 1923, p. 51.

30. Kinross, Lord, *The Ottoman Centuries: The Rise and Fall of the Turkish Empire*, Jonathan Cape, London, 1977, p. 565.

31. Baumgart 1982, p. 27.

32. Lenin 2010, p. 5.

33. Earle 1923, pp. 30–33.

34. Kinross 1977, p. 566.

35. Earle 1923, p. 77.

36. Ibid., p. 99.

37. Ibid., p. 227.

38. Ibid, p. 165.

39. Pamuk 1987, pp. 65–66.

40. Hendrickson, Jon K., *Crisis in the Mediterranean: Naval Competition and Great Power Politics, 1904–1914*, Navy Institute Press, Annapolis, 2014, p. 37.

41. Vego, Milan, *Austro-Hungarian Naval Policy 1904–14*, Routledge, London, 1966, p. 6.

42. Ibid., p. xvi.

43. Hendrickson 2014, p. 53.

44. Ibid.
45. Calculated from Hendrickson 2014, pp. 37, 61.
46. Ibid., p. 70.
47. MacMillan 2014, p. 381.

CHAPTER 25

1. Wank, Solomon, 'Aehrenthal and the Sanjak of Novibazar Railway Project: A Reappraisal', *Slavonic and East European Review*, Vol. 42, No. 99, 1964, p. 355.
2. Ibid., p. 368.
3. Lieven, Dominic, *Towards the Flame: Empire, War and the End of Tsarist Russia*, Allen Lane, London, 2015, p. 210.
4. Zürcher, Erik J., *The Young Turk Legacy and Nation Building*, I.B. Tauris, London, 2010, pp. 31, 34–35, 39–30.
5. Ibid., pp. 31–33.
6. Lieven 2015, p. 211.
7. Rogan 2015, pp. 7–8.
8. Zürcher 2010, pp. 76–82. It should be noted that Zürcher's interpretation of the counter-revolution departs from some of the traditional accounts.
9. Lieven 2015, p. 217.
10. Ibid., p. 218.
11. Ibid., p. 223.

CHAPTER 26

1. Cooke, W. S., 1968, p. 133.
2. Ibid., p. 132.
3. Ibid. p. 133.
4. Abun-Nasr 1975, p. 301.
5. Cooke, W. S., 1968, p. 134.
6. Katz, Jonathan, 'The 1907 Mauchamp Affair and the French Civilising Mission in Morocco', *Journal of North African Studies*, Vol. 6, No. 1, 2011, pp. 144, 147.
7. Maxwell 1966, p. 99.
8. Martin Corrales, Eloy, 'El protectorado español en Marruecos (1912–1956): Una perspectiva histórica', in Nogué and Villanova 1999, p. 145.
9. Ibid., p. 149.
10. See Venier, Pascal R., 'French Imperialism and Pre-Colonial Rebellions in Eastern Morocco, 1903–1910', *Journal of North African Studies*, Vol. 2, No. 2.
11. MacMillan 2014, p. 413.
12. Ibid., p. 414.
13. Quoted in Ibid., p. 420.
14. Maxwell 1966, p. 141.
15. Lieven 2015, pp. 238–39.

CHAPTER 27

1.   See Clark, Christopher, *The Sleepwalkers: How Europe Went to War in 1914*, Penguin Books, London, 2013, pp. 242–49. The only full-length post-war book on the war is Timothy W. Childs's *Italo-Turkish Diplomacy and the War over Libya 1911–12*, but this was published in 1990 and as the title indicates is largely a diplomatic history.

2.   Finkel, Caroline, *Osman's Dream: The Story of the Ottoman Empire 1300–1923*, John Murray, London 2005, p. 522.

3.   Howard, Douglas A., *A History of the Ottoman Empire*, Cambridge University Press, Cambridge 2017, p. 299.

4.   Hendrickson 2014, p. 37.

5.   Papastratigakis, Nicholas, 'British Naval Strategy: The Russian Black Sea Fleet and the Turkish Straits, 1890–1904', *International History Review*, Vol. 32, No. 4, 2010, p. 649.

6.   Hendrickson 2014, p. 1.

7.   Ibid., p. 61.

8.   Data on the Italian navy from Darr, Karl Wilhelm Augustus, *The Ottoman Navy 1900–1918: A Study of the Material, Personnel, and Professional Development of the Ottoman Navy from 1900 through the Italian, Balkan and First World Wars*, M.A. Thesis, University of Louisville, 1998, p. 3, available at https://ir.library.louisville.edu/cgi/viewcontent.cgi?article=4015&context=etd

9.   Darr 1998, p. 3.

10.   Calculations based on Shaw, 'Ottoman Expenditures and Budgets in the Late Nineteenth and Early Twentieth Centuries', pp. 374–76'

11.   Darr 1998, p. 4.

12.   Ibid., p. 23.

13.   Ibid., 42.

14.   Hendrickson 2014, p. 90.

15.   Ben-Ghiat, Ruth, and Mia Fuller (eds), *Italian Colonialism*, Palgrave Macmillan, New York, 2008, p. xvi.

16.   Clark, M., 2008, p. 185.

17.   Ahmad, Feroz, 'Great Britain's Relations with the Young Turks 1908–1914', *Middle Eastern Studies*, Vol. 2, No. 4, 1966, p. 302.

18.   FO 800/79, 11 August 1908, National Archive, London.

19.   The Ottoman reply is referred to in FO 371/1252, Grand Vizier to Tewfik Pasha [Ottoman Ambassador] Communicated to FO 30 September 1911, National Archive, London.

20.   Messe, Giovanni, *La guerra italo-turca 1911–1912: Diario* (ed. Nicola Labanca), Ugo Mursia Editore, Milan, 2016, p. 61. Messe's Diary was recently brought to light for the first time by his son, Giancranco Messe.

21.   Beehler, Commodore W. H., *The History of the Italian-Turkish War*, Advertiser-Republican, Annapolis MD, 1913, p. 5.

22.   Herrmann, David G., 'The Paralysis of Italian Strategy in the Italian-Turkish War,

SEA OF TROUBLES

1911–1912', *English Historical Review*, Vol. 104, No. 411, 1989, p. 351.

23. FO 371/1252, 30 September 1911, National Archive, London.
24. Ibid.
25. FO. 800/80, Grey to Said Paşa, 2 November 1911, National Archive, London.
26. Heller, Joseph, *British Policy towards the Ottoman Empire 1908–1914*, Frank Cass, Abingdon, 1983, pp. 45–46.
27. See Wrigley, W. David, 'Germany and the Turkish–Italian War, 1911–1912', *International Journal of Middle East Studies*, Vol. 11, No. 3, 1980.
28. Ibid., p. 320.
29. Quoted in MacMillan 2014, p. 435.
30. Ibid., p. 318.
31. Beehler 1913, p. 13.
32. Ibid., p. 15,
33. Langensiepen, Bernd, and Ahmet Güleryüz, *The Ottoman Steam Navy, 1828–1923*, Naval Institute, Annapolis, Maryland, 1995, p. 15.
34. Ibid.
35. McClure 1913, p. 50.
36. Ibid., pp. 47–58.
37. Quoted in Herrmann 1989, p. 338.

CHAPTER 28

1. Rogan 2015, pp. 15–16.
2. Beehler 1913, p. 7.
3. Anderson, Lisa, 'The Development of Nationalist Sentiment in Libya, 1908–1922', in Rashid Khalidi, Lisa Anderson, Muhammad Muslih and Reeva Simon (eds), *The Origins of Arab Nationalism*, Columbia University Press, New York, 1991, pp. 229–30.
4. McClure 1913, p. 65.
5. Messe 2016, p. 68.
6. Ibid.
7. McClure 1913, p. 76.
8. Messe 2016, p. 80.
9. McClure 1913, p. 96.
10. Ibid., pp. 113, 145.
11. Ibid., p. 156.
12. Al-Sallabi, 'Ali Muhammad, *Tarikh al-Haraka al-Sanusiyya* (The History of the Sanusi Movement), Dar al-Marefah, Beirut, 2011, p. 21.
13. Ibid., p. 49.
14. 'Abd al-Fatah, *'Asam, 'Umar al-Mukhtar: Hakathan Yakun al-Rijal* (Omar al-Mukhtar, Men Should Be Like This), Dar al-Kitab al-'Arabi, Beirut, 2008, pp. 25–26. Other sources give 1859 or 1860 for his birth.
15. Anon., *Al-Batal Libiyyi, al-shadid 'Umar al-Mukhtar; Nasha'athu wa Jihadhu* (al-juz' al-awal) (The Libyan Hero, the Martyr 'Umar al-Mukhtar; His Early Years

and Struggle [part one]), p. 2, available at http://libyanet.com/omar11.htm

16. 'Abd al-Fatah 2008, p. 33.
17. Al-Sallabi 2011, p. 429.
18. 'Abd al-Fatah 2008, p. 33.
19. Quoted in al-Sallabi 2011, p. 429.
20. McClure 1913, p. 192.
21. Langensiepen and Güleryüz 1995. Some very different dates are given by other sources for the attack on Beirut. Rogan 2015, p. 17, gives March 1912 while the entry in Wikipedia on the 'Italo-Turkish War' gives 24 February.
22. Lieven 2015, p. 244.
23. Quoted in Ibid., p. 247.
24. Gingeras, Ryan, *Fall of the Sultanate: The Great War and the End of the Ottoman Empire, 1908–1922*, Oxford University Press, Oxford, 2016, p. 67.
25. McClure 1913, pp. 315–16.
26. Ibid. p. 317.
27. Ibid., p. 319.
28. Rogan 2015, p. 17.

CHAPTER 29

1. Herrmann 1989, p. 349.
2. Rogan 2015, p. 17.
3. Herrmann 1989, p. 332.
4. Hall, Richard C., *The Balkan Wars 1912–1913: Prelude to the First World War*, Routledge, London, 2000, p. 132.
5. Hooton, E. R., *Prelude to the First World War: The Balkan Wars 1912–1913*, Fonthill Media Ltd, UK, 2014, p. 7.
6. Lieven 2015, p. 245.
7. 'Abd al-Fatah 2008, p. 18.
8. Quoted in Clark, C., 2013, p. 244.
9. Evans-Pritchard, E. E., *The Sanusi of Cyrenaica*, Clarendon Press, Oxford, 1954 (reprint of 1949), p. 116.
10. Al-Sallabi 2011, p. 429.
11. FO 800/80, 7 November 1912, National Archive, London.
12. Ahmad 1966, pp. 319–20.
13. MacMillan 2014, pp. 450–51.
14. The title/subtitle of of both Hall and Hooton's books on the wars.
15. Hendrickson 2014, p. 145.
16. Vego 1966; Hendrickson 2014, p. 116.
17. Cain and Hopkins 2016, p. 425.
18. MacMillan 2014, p. 454.
19. Hooton 2014, p. 102.
20. Clark, C., 2013, p. 282.
21. Quoted in Malcolm, Noel, *Kosovo: A Short History*, Macmillan, London, 1998,

p. 253.

22. Ibid.

23. Hooton 2014, p. 154.

24. MacMillan 2014, p. 455.

25. 'European War Cloud Lifting', *Daily Mirror*, 27 November 1912. Republished in Welch, Ian, *Great War: The Countdown to Global Conflict*, Haynes Publishing, Sparkford, 2014, p. 91.

26. MacMillan 2014, p. 456.

27. Hooton 2014, p. 145.

28. Ibid., p. 146.

29. Hall 2000, p. 21.

30. McCarthy 1995, p. 339.

31. MacMillan 2014, p. 465.

32. Ibid.

33. Ham, Paul, *1914: The Year the World Ended*, Doubleday, London and Australia, 1913, p. 242. In the original quotation from Sasonov by Ham, Sasonov refers to the 'Hamburg to Baghdad Railway'; I have changed the original to 'Berlin to Baghdad'. Ham doesn't offer any explanation as to why Sasonov might have so strangely misconceived the railway's starting point.

34. Rogan 2015, pp. 32–33.

35. Hall 2000, pp. 54–55.

36. Clark C. 2013, pp. 288–89.

37. Ibid., p. 478

38. Clark, C., 2013, pp. 477–79.

39. Ibid., p. 526

40. Cain and Hopkins 2016, p. 425.

41. Ibid., pp. 484, 486.

42. Ahmad 1966, p. 325.

43. Rogan 2015, p. 52.

44. See Rutledge, Ian, *Enemy on the Euphrates*, Saqi Books, London, 2014, pp. 57, 90–91, 396.

45. See Ibid., pp.41–48.

46. Al-Sallabi 2011, p. 284.

47. I have no direct evidence of this, but it should be noted that none of the two Arabic-language sources I have consulted nor two English-language ones make any mention of 'Umar al-Mukhtar fighting against the British at this time. Since we know that al-Mukhtar was certainly fighting the Italians in 1923, it seems most likely that he was in combat with them during 1915–17.

48. Maghraoui, Driss, 'The "Grande Guerre Sainte": Moroccan Colonial Troops and Workers in the First World War', *Journal of North African Studies*, Vol. 9, No. 1, 2004, p. 15.

49. Ibid.

50. Ibid.

51. Ibid., p. 3.

CHAPTER 30

1. Lenin, V. I., Preface to the second (French and German) edition of *Imperialism: The Highest Stage of Capitalism*, p. 4.
2. Ibid., p. 114.
3. Minutes, CAB/27/1, *British Desiderata in Turkey in Asia*, 30 June 1915, National Archive, London.
4. Zürcher 2010, pp. 19–20.
5. On the destruction of Izmir (Smyrna) see Milton, Giles, *Paradise Lost: Smyrna 1922 – The Destruction of Islam's City of Tolerance*, Sceptre, London, 2008.

APPENDIX B

1. Braudel 1984, p. 133.
2. Sée 2004, pp. 95–96.
3. Ibid., p. 27.
4. Braudel 1984, p. 196.
5. Artan, Tülay, 'Aspects of the Ottoman Elite's Food Consumption: Looking for "Staples", "Luxuries" and "Delicacies" in a Changing Century', in Donald Quataert (ed.) *Consumption Studies and the History of the Ottoman Empire 1550–1922*, State University of New York Press, 2000, p. 136.
6. Braudel 1984, pp. 190–91.
7. Artan 2000, p. 136.
8. Solana Ruiz, José Luis, 'Las clases sociales en Andalucía: un recorrido sociohistórico', *Gazeta de Antropología*, No. 16, articulo 08, 2000, pp. 1–2. See also Simon Barton 2009, p. 166.
9. Volney 1807, pp. 162–63.
10. Lane 1846, Vol. 1, p. 251.
11. Jones 2003, p. 361.
12. Stekel, Richard H., 'Stature and the Standard of Living', *Journal of Economic literature*, Vol. 33, No. 4, 1995, p. 1919.
13. See Hobsbawm 2003, p. 21.
14. Stegl, Mojgan, and Joerg Baten, 'Tall and Shrinking Muslims, Short and Growing Europeans: The Long-Run Welfare Development of the Middle East, 1840–1980', University of Tübingen, available at www.ehs.org.uk/dotAsset/05b192a5-d56a-4718-9669-739a616f5cb.pdf
15. Braudel 1984, Vol. 1, p. 91.
16. Hanioğlu 2008, pp. 27–33.
17. Quoted in Barnby 1966, p. 226.
18. Lane 1846, pp. 35, 41.
19. Jones 2005, p. 356.
20. Barnby 1966, p. 226.

Bibliography

PRIMARY SOURCES

British Cabinet and Foreign Office Papers
CAB/27/1, The National Archive, Kew, London
FO/371/1252, The National Archive, Kew, London
FO/800/79, The National Archive, Kew, London
FO/800/80, The National Archive, Kew, London

Published official documents
British & Foreign State Papers, Vol. XIX, 1831–1832, Foreign Office London, 1834
'Supply forces in the Mediterranean', Parliamentary Debates (Hansard), House of
    Commons, 25 July 1882, col. 1778, available at https://en.wikipedia.org/wiki/
    Bombardment_of_Alexandria
Report of the Select Committee on Steam Communication with India, House of
    Commons, Parliament, London, July 1837
US Department of State Bulletin, *Right of Protection in Morocco; extraterritorial
    jurisdiction in Morocco relinquished by the United States, October 6 1956*

Other Archival Sources
PP/MM/AL/1, *Notes by Lord Palmerston on Diplomatic Proceedings in 1830* (1844),
    Hartley Library, University of Southampton

Contemporary Press and Other Contemporary Reportage
The Gentleman's Magazine, Vol. XLV, London, 1775
The Gentleman's Magazine and Historical Chronicle, Vol. LXXVII, London,
    November 1807
The New Annual Register for the Year 1807, John Stockdale (Printer), London, 1808
The National Magazine, London, Vol. 1 No. 3, Dublin, 1830
The Annual Register for 1835, Vol. 77, Chapter XV, London, 1836
Revue des Deux Mondes, Quatrième Séries, Tome XIV, Paris, 14 June 1838
New York Daily Tribune, 5 June 1857, Frederick Engels, 'Persia-China'. Reproduced
    in Shlomo Avineri, *Karl Marx on Colonialism and Modernization*, Anchor Books,
    New York, 1969, pp. 184–90
The Manchester Guardian, 27 November 1875, 'The Suez Canal and the
    Government', The Guardian Archive, available at: https://www.theguardian.com/
    theguardian/2010/nov/29/archive-the-suez-canal-and-the-government-1875
The Daily Mirror, 'European War Cloud Lifting', 27 November 1912. Republished

in Ian Welch, *Great War: The countdown to Global Conflict*, Haynes Publishing,
Sparkford, 2014

SECONDARY SOURCES

Books and Articles in the Arabic Language
'Abd al-Fatah, 'Asam, *'Umar al-Mukhtar: Hakathan Yakun al-Rijal* (Omar
al-Mukhtar, Men Should Be Like This), Dar al-Kitab al-'Arabi, Beirut, 2008

Abu Shukran, 'Usama Kamil, *'Auda ila Asbab Ahdath al-Qarn al-Tasi' 'ashar fi Jabal
Lubnan* (A Return to the Causes of the Events of the Nineteenth Century in
Mount Lebanon), Dar Al-'Arabiyya Al-'ulum Nashirun, Beirut, 2017

Anon, *Al-Batal Libiyyi, al-shadid 'Umar al-Mukhtar; Nasha'athu wa Jihadhu (al-juz'
al-awal)* (The Libyan Hero, the Martyr 'Umar al-Mukhtar; His Early Years and
Struggle [part one]), p. 2, available at http://libyanet.com/omar11.htm

al-Hasani al-Jaza'iri, al-Imara Badi'a, *Fikr al-Amir 'Abd al-Qadir, Haqa'iq wa Watha'iq*
(The Beliefs of the Amir 'Abd al-Qadir, facts and documents), Dar al-Fikr li
al-Tiba'a wa al-tawzi' wa al-nashr, Damascus, 2000

al-Najar, Husayn Fawzi, *Ahmad 'Arabi, Misr li al-Misriyyin* (Ahmad Arabi, Egypt for
the Egyptians), Matabi'a al-Hai'a al-Misriyya al-'Ama li al-Kitabat, Cairo, 1992

al-Sallabi, 'Ali Muhammad, *Tarikh al-Haraka al-Sanusiyya* (The History of the Sanusi
Movement), Dar al-Marefah, Beirut, 2011

al-Sallabi, 'Ali Muhammad, *Al Amir 'Abd al-Qadir al-Jaza'iri, Qa'id Rabbani wa
mujahid Islami* (The Amir 'Abd al-Qadir, Religious Leader and Islamic fighter),
Dar Ibn Kathir, Beirut, 2015

Books in European Languages
Abulafia, David, *The Great Sea: A Human History of the Mediterranean*, Allen Lane,
London 2012

Abun-Nasr, Jamil M., *A History of the Maghrib*, 2nd edn, Cambridge University Press,
1975

Adas, Michael, *Islam and European Expansion: The Forging of a Global Order*, Temple
University Press, Philadelphia, 1993

Ageron, Charles-Robert, *Modern Algeria: A History from 1830 to the Present*, Hurst &
Co., London, 1991 (Paris 1961)

Akarli, Engin, *The Long Peace: Ottoman Lebanon, 1861–1920*, University of California
Press, Berkeley, 1993, available at http://ark.cdlib.org/ark:/13030/ft6199p06t/

Aksan, Virginia H., *Ottoman Wars 1700–1870: An Empire Besieged*, Pearson Education,
Harlow, 2007

Anderson, M. S., *The Eastern Question 1774–1923*, Macmillan Press, London, 1966

Anderson, M. S., *The Great Powers and the Near East 1774–1923 (Documents of
Modern History)*, Edward Arnold, London, 1970

Anderson, R. C., *Naval Wars in the Levant, 1559–1853*, Liverpool University Press, 1951

Avineri, Shlomo, *Karl Marx on Colonialism and Modernisation*, Anchor Books, New York, 1969

Barnby, H. G., *The Prisoners of Algiers: An Account of the Forgotten American-Algerian War, 1785–1797*, Oxford University Press, 1966

Baron de Tott, François, *Memoires sur les Turcs et les Tartars*, Tome 1, Paris, 1785

Baron de Tott, François, *Memoirs of Baron de Tott: Containing the State of the Turkish Empire and the Crimea During the Late War with Russia* (2nd edn) Vol. 1, Part 2, G. G. J. and J. Robinson, London, 1786

Barton, Simon, *A History of Spain* (2nd ed.), Palgrave/Macmillan, Basingstoke, 2009

Baumgart, Winfried, *Imperialism: The Idea and Reality of British and French Colonial Expansion 1880–1914*, Oxford University Press, Oxford 1982

Bayly, C. A., *Imperial Meridian: The British Empire and the World, 1780–1830*, Longman, Harlow Essex, 1989, p. 11

Bayly, C. A., *The Birth of the Modern World 1780–1914*, Blackwell Publishing, Maldan MA, 2004

Beaty, Charles, *Ferdinand de Lesseps: A Biographical Study*, Eyre and Spottiswoode, London, 1956

Beehler, Commodore W. H., *The History of the Italian-Turkish War*, The Advertiser-Republican, Annapolis MD, 1913

Ben-Ghiat, Ruth, and Mia Fuller (eds), *Italian Colonialism*, Palgrave Macmillan, New York, 2008

Black, Jeremy, *Eighteenth-Century Europe* (2nd ed.), Macmillan, Basingstoke, 1999

Blunt, Wilfrid Scawen, *Black Sunrise: The Life and Times of Mulai Ismail, Emperor of Morocco, 1646–1727*, Methuen & Co., London, 1951

Blunt, Wilfrid Scawen, *The Secret History of the English Occupation of Egypt*, The History Press, Cheltenham, 2007

Bovill, E. W., *The Golden Trade of the Moors* (2nd ed.), Oxford University Press, 1968

Bowen, H. V., *The Business of Empire: The East India Company and Imperial Britain 1756–1833*, Cambridge University Press, Cambridge, 2006

Braudel, Fernand, *The Mediterranean and the Mediterranean World in the Age of Philip II* (trans. Sian Reynolds), 2 vols, Fontana Press, William Collins & Son, London 1972–73

Braudel, Fernand, *Civilization and Capitalism, 15th–18th Century, Vol. 1: The Structures of Everyday Life* (trans. Sian Reynolds), Fontana Press, William Collins & Son, London, 1984

Braudel, Fernand, *Civilization and Capitalism, 15th–18th Century, Vol. 3: The Perspective of the World* (trans. Sian Reynolds), William Collins & Son, London, 1984

Brewer, David, *The Greek War of Independence*, Overlook Duckworth, New York and

London, 2001

Brower, Benjamin Claude, *A Desert Named Peace: The Violence of France's Empire in the Algerine Sahara, 1844–1902*, Columbia University Press, New York, 2009, p. 16

Brown, David, *Palmerston and the Politics of Foreign Policy 1846–55*, Manchester University Press, Manchester 2002

Brown, James A. O. C., *Anglo-Moroccan Relations in the Late 18th and Early 19th Centuries, with Particular Reference to the Role of Gibraltar*, PhD Thesis, Faculty of Asian and Middle East Studies, University of Cambridge, 2009

Brown, James A. O. C, *Crossing the Strait: Morocco, Gibraltar and Great Britain in the 18th and 19th Centuries*, Brill NV, Leiden, 2012

Brown, L. Carl, *The Tunisia of Ahmad Bey, 1837–1855*, Princeton University Press, Princeton NJ, 1974

Brunschwig, Henri, *French Colonialism, 1871–1914, Myths and Realities*, Pall Mall Press, London, 1966

Cain, P. J., and A. G. Hopkins, *British Imperialism 1688 to 2015*, Routledge, Abingdon, Oxon, 2016

Charles-Roux, François, *Les origines de l'expédition d'Égypte*, Librairie Plon, Paris 1910

Churchill, Charles Henry, *Mount Lebanon: A Ten Years' Residence from 1842 to 1852 Describing The Manners, Customs and Religion of the Inhabitants*, Vol. 1, Saunders & Otley, London, 1853

Churchill, Charles Henry, *The Druzes and the Maronites under Turkish Rule, 1840–1860*, Bernard Quarich, London, 1862

Churchill, Charles Henry, *The Life of Abdel Kader, Ex-Sultan of the Arabs of Algeria*, Chapman and Hall, London, 1867

Clark, Christopher, *The Sleepwalkers: How Europe went to War in 1914*, Penguin Books, London, 2013

Clark, Martin, *Modern Italy, 1871 to the Present* (3rd edition), Routledge, Abingdon, Oxon, 2008 (original 1984)

Clissold, Stephen, *The Barbary Slaves*, Purnell Book Services, Abingdon, 1977

Cohen, Amnon, *Palestine in the 18th Century*, Magnes Press, Jerusalem, 1973

Cole, Juan, *Napoleon's Egypt: Invading the Middle East*, Palgrave Macmillan, New York, 2007

Colley, Linda, *Captives: Britain, Empire and the World 1600–1850*, Pimlico, London, 2003 (2nd edition of Jonathan Cape, London, 2002)

Cook, M. A. (ed.), *Studies in the Economic History of the Middle East*, Oxford University Press, 1970

Cooke, W. S., *The Ottoman Empire and its Tributary States*, B. R. Grüner, Amsterdam, 1968 (reprint of 1876)

Cooke, James J., *New French Imperialism 1880–1910: The Third French Republic and Colonial Expansion*, David & Charles, Newton Abbot, 1973

Crecelius, Daniel, *The Roots of Modern Egypt: A Study of the Regimes of 'Ali Bey al-Kabir and Muhammad Bey Abu al-Dhahab, 1760–1775*, Biblioteca Islamica, Mineapolis, 1981

Crecelius, Daniel, and 'Abd al-Wahhab Bakr (trans.), *Al-Damurdashi's Chronicle of Egypt, 1688–1755*, E. J. Brill, Leiden, 1991

Crowdy, Terry, *The French Soldier in Egypt 1798–1801*, Osprey Publishing, 2003

Dalrymple, William, *The Anarchy; The Relentless Rise of the East India Company*, Bloomsbury, London, 2019

Daly, M. W. (ed.), *The Cambridge History of Egypt*, Vol. 2, Cambridge University Press, 1998

Danziger, Raphael, *'Abd al-Qadir and the Algerians*, Holmes & Meier Publishers, New York and London, 1977

Darwin, John, *Unfinished Empire: The Global Expansion of Britain*, Penguin, London, 2012

Darwin, John, *The Empire Project: The Rise and Fall of the British World-System*, Cambridge University Press, Cambridge, 2009

Dearden, Seton, *A Nest of Corsairs: The Fighting Karamanlis of the Barbary Coast*, John Murray, London, 1976

Denon, Vivant, *Travels in Upper and Lower Egypt During the Campaign of General Bonaparte*, Crosby and Co., London, 1802

Desan, Suzanne, Lynn Hunt and William Max Nelson (eds), *The French Revolution in Global Perspective*, Cornell University Press, 2013

Driault, Edouard, *La question d'Orient depuis ses origines jusqu' à la paix de Sèvres*, Librairie Félix Alcan, Paris, 1921

Duggan, Christopher, *A Concise History of Italy*, Cambridge University Press, Cambridge, 2005 (reprint of 1997)

Dwyer, Philip, *Napoleon: The Path to Power 1769–1799*, Bloomsbury, London, 2007

Earle, Edward M., *Turkey, the Great Powers and the Bagdad Railway: A Study in Imperialism*, Macmillan, London, 1923

Emerit, Marcel, *L'Algérie à l'époque d'Abd-el-Kader* (Presented by René Gallissot), Editions Bouchène, Paris, 2002 (1951)

Erdem, Y. Hakan, *Slavery in the Ottoman Empire and its Demise, 1800–1909*, Macmillan, Houndsmills, Basingstoke, 1996

Evans-Pritchard, E. E., *The Sanusi of Cyrenaica*, Clarendon Press, Oxford, 1954 (reprint of 1949)

Fahmy, Khaled, *All the Pasha's Men: Mehmed Ali, His Army and the Making of Modern Egypt*, American University in Cairo Press, Cairo, 2003

Farah, Caesar E., *The Politics of Interventionism in Ottoman Lebanon, 1830–1861*, Centre for Lebanese Studies and I. B. Tauris, London, 2000

Faroqhi, Suraiya, *A Cultural History of the Ottomans*, I.B. Tauris, London 2016

Ferguson, Niall, *Empire: How Britain Made the Modern World*, Penguin, London, 2003

Fernández Duro, Cesáreo, *Armada Española (desde la unión de los reinos de Castilla y Aragon)*, Madrid, 1903

Figes, Orlando, *Crimea: The Last Crusade*, Allen Lane, London, 2010

Finkel, Caroline, *Osman's Dream: The Story of the Ottoman Empire 1300–1923*, John Murray, London 2005

Flournoy, Francis, R., *British Policy towards Morocco in the Age of Palmerston (1830–1865)*, P. S. King & Son, Westminster, 1935

Forrest, A. S. (illustrator) and S. L. Bensusan, *Morocco*, Adam Charles and Black, London, 1904

Fortescue, J. W., *A History of the British Army: Vol. VI 1807–1809*, Macmillan & Co., London, 1910

Freely, John, *Inside the Seraglio: The Private Lives of the Sultans in Istanbul*, Viking, London 1999

Gallois, William, *A History of Violence in the Early Algerian Colony*, Palgrave Macmillan UK, Basingstoke, Hants, 2013

Gates, Carolyn, *The Merchant Republic of Lebanon: Rise of an Open Economy*, Centre for Lebanese Studies and I.B. Tauris, London, 1998

Ghali, Ibrahim Amin, *Ali Bey El-Kebir et les origines de la pénétration Russe en Egypte*, Publications d'Atelier d'Alexandrie, Alexandria, 1979

Gibb, H. A. R., and H. Bowen, *Islamic Society and the West*, 2 vols, Oxford University Press, London, 1950/1951

Gifford, P., and W. R. Lewis (eds), *France and Britain in Africa*, Yale University Press, New Haven, 1971

Gingeras, Ryan, *Fall of the Sultanate: The Great War and the End of the Ottoman Empire, 1908–1922*, Oxford University Press, Oxford, 2016

Glenny, Misha, *The Balkans, 1804–2012*, Granta Publications, London, 2012 (reprint of 1999)

Goudar, Ange, *Les intérêts de France mal entendus*, Vol. 1, Chez Jacques Coeur, Amsterdam, 1756

Gruber, Christiane (ed.), *The Islamic Manuscript Tradition*, Indiana Press, Bloomington, 2010

Hall, Richard C., *The Balkan Wars 1912–1913: Prelude to the First World War*, Routledge, London, 2000

Ham, Paul, *1914: The Year the World Ended*, Doubleday, London and Australia, 1913, p. 242

Hanioğlu, M. Şükrü, *A Brief History of the Late Ottoman Empire*, Princeton University Press, Princeton, 2008

Hansen, Thorkild, *Arabia Felix: The Danish Expedition of 1761–1767*, Collins, London, 1964

Harris, Lawrence, *With Mulai Hafid at Fez: Behind the Scenes in Morocco*, Smith Elder & Co., London, 1909

Harris, Walter, *Morocco that Was*, Eland, London, 1983 (reprint of 1921)

Hastings, Max, *Catastrophe: Europe Goes to War 1914*, William Collins, London, 2013

Heller, Joseph, *British Policy towards the Ottoman Empire 1908–1914*, Frank Cass, Abingdon, 1983

Hendrickson, Jon K., *Crisis in the Mediterranean: Naval Competition and Great Power Politics, 1904–1914*, Navy Institute Press, Annapolis, 2014

Herold, J. Christopher, *Bonaparte in Egypt*, Pen & Sword Military, Barnsley, 2005 (Reprint of 1962)

Hobsbawm, Eric, *The Age of Revolution, 1789–1848*, Abacus, London, 2003 (reprint of 1962)

Hobsbawm, Eric, *The Age of Capital, 1848–1875*, Abacus, London 2004 (reprint of 1975)

Hobsbawm, Eric, *The Age of Empire, 1875–1914*, Abacus, London, 1996 (reprint of 1987)

Hobson, John A., *Imperialism: A Study*, James Nisbet & Co., London, 1902

Hodgson, Marshall G. S., *The Venture of Islam*, Chicago University Press, Chicago, 1974

Holland, Robert, *Blue-Water Empire: The British in the Mediterranean Since 1800*, Allen Lane, London, 2012

Hooton, E. R., *Prelude to the First World War: The Balkan Wars 1912–1913*, Fonthill Media Ltd, UK, 2014

Howard, Douglas A., *A History of the Ottoman Empire*, Cambridge University Press, Cambridge 2017

Hyam, Ronald, *Britain's Imperial Century 1815–1914: A Study of Empire and Expansion*, Palgrave Macmillan, Basingstoke, 2002

İnalcik, Halil, and Donald Quataert (eds), *An Economic and Social History of the Ottoman Empire, 1300–1914*, Cambridge University Press, 1994

Irwin, Robert, *For Lust of Knowing: The Orientalists and Their Enemies*, Allen Lane, 2006

Issawi, Charles (ed.), *The Economic History of the Middle East 1800–1914*, University of Chicago Press, Chicago, 1966

Issawi, Charles, *An Economic History of the Middle East and North Africa*, Methuen & Co., London, 1982

al-Jabarti, 'Abd al-Rahman, *Napoleon' in Egypt, Al-Jabarti's Chronicle of the French Occupation, 1798* (trans. Shmuel Moreh), Markus Wiener Publishing, Princeton, 1975, 1978, 1993 (original c. 1798)

James, Lawrence, *The Rise and Fall of the British Empire*, Abacus, London, 2007, p. 157 (reprint of 1994)

Jenkins, Roy, *Gladstone*, Macmillan, London, 1995

Jones, Colin, *The Great Nation: France from Louis XV to Napoleon*, Penguin, London, 2003

Judd, Denis, *Empire: The British Imperial Experience from 1765 to the Present*, Harper Collins, London, 1996

Karabell, Zachary, *Parting the Desert: The Creation of the Suez Canal*, John Murray, London, 2003

Keddie, Nikki R., *An Islamic Response to Imperialism: The Political and Religious Writings of Sayyid Jamal ad-Din 'al-Afghani'*, University of California Press, Berkeley, 1968

Kelly, Walter Keating, *Syria and the Holy Land: Their Scenery and Their People*, Chapman and Hall, London, 1844

Kennedy, Paul, *The Rise and Fall of the Great Powers*, Vintage Books, New York, 1987

Khalidi, Rashid et al. (eds), *The Origins of Arab Nationalism*, Columbia University Press, New York, 1991

Khodja, Hamdan, *Le Miroir: Aperçu historique et statistique sur la Regénce de Alger*, introduction by Abdelkader Djeghloul, Sindbad, Paris, 1985 (original, 1833)

Kinross, Lord, *The Ottoman Centuries: The Rise and Fall of the Turkish Empire*, Jonathan Cape, London, 1977

Kiser, John W., *Commander of the Faithful: The Life and Times of Emir Abd el-Kader*, Monkfish Book Publishing Co., New York, 2008

Kissinger, Henry, *A World Restored: Metternich, Castlereagh and the Problems of Peace, 1812–1822*, Echo Points and Media, 2013 (original 1957)

Kuran, Timur, *The Long Divergence: How Islamic Law Held Back the Middle East*, Princeton University Press, Princeton NJ, 2010

Lane, Edward, *An Account of the Manners and Customs of the Modern Egyptians* (3rd popular edition, three volumes in one), Charles Knight & Co., London, 1846

Lane-Poole, Stanley, *The Story of Cairo*, J. M. Dent & Sons, London (reprint), 1924

Langensiepen, Bernd, and Ahmet Güleryüz, *The Ottoman Steam Navy, 1828–1923*, Naval Institute, Annapolis, Maryland, 1995

Langer, William, *The Diplomacy of Imperialism, 1890–1902*, 1st edition, Alfred A. Knopf, 1951

Langer, William, *The Diplomacy of Imperialism, 1890–1902*, 2nd edition, Alfred A. Knopf, 1960

Lenin, V. I., *Imperialism: The Highest Stage of Capitalism*, Penguin, London 2010 (reprint of 3rd edition c. 1922)

Lewis, Bernard, *The Arabs in History*, Oxford University Press, Oxford, 1993 (reprint of 1958), p. 189

Lewis, Bernard, *Emergence of Modern Turkey*, Oxford University Press, London, 1961

Lieven, Dominic, *Towards the Flame: Empire, War and the End of Tsarist Russia*, Allen Lane, London, 2015

Loizos, Dimitris, 'Economic History Problems of 18th c. Ottoman Greece: The Case of Ambelakia in Thessaly' (preliminary report), p. 1, available at http://www.anistor. gr/english/enback/e011.htm

Lord, Perceval Barton *Algiers, with Notices of the Neighbouring States of Barbary*, London, 1835

Mackesy, Piers, *The War in the Mediterranean 1803–1810*, Longmans Green and Co., London, 1957

MacFarlane, Charles, *Turkey and Its Destiny: The Results of a Journey Made in 1847 and 1848 to Examine into the State of the Country*: Vol. 1, John Murray, London, 1850; Vol. 2, Lea and Blanchard, Philadelphia, 1850

MacMillan, Margaret, *The War that Ended Peace: How Europe Abandoned Peace for the First World War*, Profile Books, London, 2014

Malcolm, Noel, *Kosovo: A Short History*, Macmillan, London, 1998

Mansel, Philip, *Constantinople: City of the World's Desire, 1453–1924*, John Murray, London, 1995

Mansel, Philip, *Levant: Splendour and Catastrophe in the Mediterranean*, John Murray, London 2010

Marlowe, John, *Spoiling the Egyptians*, Andre Deutsch, London, 1974

Marino, John, A., *Early Modern Italy*, Oxford University Press, 2002

Marsden, Arthur, *British Diplomacy and Tunis, 1875–1902*, Scottish Academic Press, Edinburgh, 1971

Marsigli, Le Comte de, *L'etat militaire de l'empire ottoman: ses progrès et sa décadence*, Paris, Vol. 1, 1732

Martin, Pierre, *Histoire de l'expedition Française en Égypte*, Vol. 1, J. M Eberhart, College Royal de France, Paris, 1815

Marx, Karl, *Capital: A Critique of Political Economy*, Vol. III, Lawrence and Wishart, London 1984

Marx, Karl, *The Eighteenth Brumaire of Louis Bonaparte*, 1852, available at https:// www.marxists.org/archive/marx/works/1852/18th-brumaire/ch01.htm

Mathias, Peter, *The First Industrial Nation: An Economic History of Britain 1700–1914* (2nd edn), Methuen, London, 1983

Maxwell, Gavin, *Lords of the Atlas: The Rise and Fall of the House of Glaoua, 1893–1956*, Longman, London, 1966

McCarthy, Justin, *Death and Exile: The Ethnic Cleansing of Ottoman Muslims, 1821–1922*, Darwin Press, New Jersey, 1995

McClure, W. K., *Italy in North Africa: An Account of the Tripoli Enterprise*, Constable & Co., London, 1913

Messe, Giovanni, *La guerra italo-turca 1911–1912: Diario* (ed. Nicola Labanca), Ugo Mursia Editore, Milan, 2016

Milton, Giles, *Paradise Lost: Smyrna 1922 – The Destruction of Islam's City of Tolerance*, Sceptre, London, 2008

Mitchell, B. R., *European Historical Statistics, 1750–1970*, Macmillan, London 1978

Montbard, Georges, *Among the Moors: Sketches of Oriental Life*, Sampson Low, Marston and Company, London, 1894

Morland, Paul, *The Human Tide: How Population Shaped the Modern World*, John Murray, London, 2019

Mouradgea d'Ohsson, Ignatius, *Tableau général de l'empire othoman*, Vol. 1, Imprémerie de Monsieur, Paris, 1788

Nasr, Seyyed Hossein, *Islamic Science: An Illustrated Study*, World of Islam Festival Publishing Co. Ltd, 1976

Nicolle, David, *Armies of the Ottoman Empire, 1775–1820*, Osprey, Botley, Oxford, 1998

Nicolle, David, *The Janissaries*, Osprey, London, 1995

Nogué, Joan, and José Luis Villanova (eds), *España en Marruecos (1912–1956): Discursos geográficos e intervención territorial*, Editorial Mileno, Lleida, 1999

Norwich, John Julius, *The Middle Sea: A History of the Mediterranean*, Chatto & Windus, London, 2006.

Owen, Roger, *The Middle East in the World Economy 1800–1914* (2nd edition), I.B. Tauris, London, 2009 (reprint of 1981)

Pakenham, Thomas, *The Scramble for Africa, 1876–1912*, Abacus, London, 2003 (reprint of 1991)

Palmer, Alan, *The Decline and Fall of the Ottoman Empire*, Faber & Faber, London, 2011 (reprint of 1992)

Panzac, Daniel, *Barbary Corsairs: The End of a Legend 1800–1820*, Brill, Leiden, 2005

Pamuk, Şevket, *The Ottoman Empire and European Capitalism, 1820–1913*, Cambridge University Press, 1987

Parker, Geoffrey, *The Military Revolution: Military Innovation and the Rise of the West 1500–1800* (2nd edition), Cambridge University Press, 1996

Perkins, Roger, and K. J. Douglas-Morris, *Gunfire in Barbary*, Kenneth Mason, Homewell Havant, Hampshire, 1982

Philipp, Thomas, and Ulrich Haarmann (eds), *The Mamluks in Egyptian Politics and Society*, Cambridge University Press, 1998

Quataert, Donald, *Ottoman Manufacturing in the Age of the Industrial Revolution*, Cambridge University Press, Cambridge, 1993

Quataert, Donald, *The Ottoman Empire, 1700–1922* (2nd edition), Cambridge University Press, Cambridge, 2005

Quataert, Donald, *Miners and the State in the Ottoman Empire: The Zonguldak Coalfield, 1822–1920*, Berghahn Books, New York, 2006

Ralston, D. B., *Importing the European Army: The Introduction of European Military Techniques and Institutions into the Extra-European World 1600–1914*, Chicago University Press, 1990

Riasanovsky, Nicholas V., and Mark D. Steinberg, *A History of Russia* (7th edition), Oxford University Press, New York and Oxford, 2005

Robinson, Ronald, and John Gallagher, *Africa and the Victorians: The Official Mind of Imperialism*, Macmillan and Company, London 1961

Rodenbeck, Max, *Cairo: The City Victorious*, American University in Cairo Press, 1998

Rodinson, Maxime, *Islam and Capitalism*, Allen Lane, London, 1974 (reprint of original French, 1966)

Rogan, Eugene, *The Fall of the Ottomans: The Great War in the Middle East 1914–1920*, Allen Lane, London, 2015

Rogers, P. G., *A History of Anglo-Moroccan Relations to 1900*, Foreign and Commonwealth Office, n.d.

Rood, Judith Mendelsohn, *The Sacred Law in the Holy City: The Khedival Challenge to the Ottomans as Seen from Jerusalem, 1829–1841*, University of Chicago Press, 1993

Rubin, Jared, *Rulers, Religion and Riches: Why the West Got Rich and the Middle East Did Not*, Cambridge University Press, New York, 2017

Ruedy, John, *Modern Algeria: The Origins and Development of a Nation*, Indiana University Press, Bloomington, 1992

Rutledge, Ian, *Enemy on the Euphrates*, Saqi Books, London, 2014

Said, Edward, *Orientalism: Western Conceptions of the Orient*, Routledge and Kegan Paul, London 1978

al-Sayyid-Marsot, Afaf Lutfi, *Women and Men in Late Eighteenth-Century Egypt*, University of Texas Press, Austin, 1995

Scott, Colonel James, *A Journal of Residence in the Esmailla of Abd-el-Kader and of Travels in Morocco and Algiers*, Whittaker & Co., London, 1842

Sée, Henri, *Economic and Social Conditions in France During the Eighteenth Century* (trans. Edwin H. Zeydel), Batoche Books, Kitchener, 2004 (original 1927)

Sessions, Jennifer E., *By Sword and Plow: France and the Conquest of Algeria*, Cornell University Press, 2011

Shaler, William, *Sketches of Algiers, Political, Historical and Civil*, Cummings Hilliard & Co, Boston, 1826

Shehadi, Nadim, and Dana Haffar Mills (eds), *Lebanon: A History of Conflict and Consensus*, Centre for Lebanese Studies and I. B. Tauris, London, 1989

Sim, Katherine, *Desert Traveller: The Life of Jean Louis Burckhardt*, Victor Gollancz, London, 1969

Somel, Selcuk Aksin, *Historical Dictionary of the Ottoman Empire*, Scarecrow Press, Lanham Maryland, 2003

St John, James Augustus, *Egypt and Mohammed Ali; Or, Travels in the Valley of the Nile*

(2 vols), Longman et al., London, 1834

Storrs, Christopher (ed.) *The Fiscal-Military State in Eighteenth-Century Europe*, Ashgate Publishing, Farnham, Surrey, 2009

Temimi, Abdeljelil, *Le Beylik de Constantine et Hadj Ahmed Bey 1830–1837*, Publications d'Histoire Maghrébine, Vol. 1, Tunis, 1978

Tolan, John, Gilles Veinstein, and Henry Laurens, *Europe and the Islamic World: A History*, Princeton University Press

Traboulsi, Fawwaz, *A History of Modern Lebanon*, Pluto Press, London, 2007

Tunçer, Ali Coşkun, *Sovereign Debt and International Financial Control: The Middle East and the Balkans, 1870–1914*, Palgrave Macmillan, Basingstoke, 2015

Urquhart, David, *Turkey and Its Resources: Its Municipal Organization and Free Trade*, Saunders & Otley, London, 1833

Vatikiotis, P. J., *The History of Egypt from Muhammad Ali to Mubarak* (3rd edition), Weidenfeld & Nicolson, London, 1985

Vego, Milan, *Austro-Hungarian Naval Policy 1904–14*, Routledge, London, 1966

Venture de Paradis, Jean-Michel (ed. E. Fagnan), *Alger au XVIIIe Siècle*, Algiers, Typographie Adolphe Jourdan, 1898 (Reprint of original)

Volney, C.-F., *Considérations sur la guerre actuelle des Turcs*, London, 1788

Volney, C.-F., *Voyage en Syrie et en Égypte pendant les années 1783, 1784 et 1785* (4th edition), Paris, 1807

Warburton, Eliot, *The Crescent and the Cross; or, Romance and Realities of Eastern Travel* (15th edition), Hurst & Blackett, London, 1859

Waterfield, Gordon, *Sultans of Aden*, John Murray, London 1968

Webster, Charles, *The Foreign Policy of Palmerston, 1830–1841*, Vol. 1, G. Bell & Sons, London, 1951

Welch, Ian, *Great War: The Countdown to Global Conflict*, Haynes Publishing, Sparkford, 2014

Wheatcroft, Andrew, *The Ottomans: Dissolving Images*, Penguin, London, 1993

Wilson, Sir Arnold, *The Suez Canal: Its Past, Present and Future*, Oxford University Press, London, 1933

Windrow, Martin, *Uniforms of the French Foreign Legion, 1831–1981*, Blandford Press, Poole, 1981, p. 10

Winter, Michael, *Egyptian Society under Ottoman Rule, 1517–1798*, Routledge, London, 1992

Wright, John, *The Trans-Saharan Slave Trade*, Routledge, London, 2007

Yapp, M. E., *The Making of the Modern Near East, 1792–1923*, Routledge, Abingdon, Oxford, 1987

Zorlu, Tuncay, *Innovation and Empire in Turkey: Sultan Selim III and the Modernisation of the Ottoman Navy*, Tauris Academic Studies, London, 2008

Zürcher, Erik J., *The Young Turk Legacy and Nation Building*, I.B. Tauris, London, 2010

Articles in Academic Journals, Chapters in Books and Articles/Theses on Internet Sites

Ahmad, Feroz, 'Great Britain's Relations with the Young Turks 1908–1914', *Middle Eastern Studies*, Vol. 2, No. 4, 1966, pp. 302–29

Ahmida, 'Ali 'Abdullatif, 'State and Class Formation and Collaboration in Colonial Libya', in Ruth Ben-Ghiat and Mia Fuller (eds), *Italian Colonialism*, pp. 59–73

Aksan, Virginia H.,'Ottoman Political Writing 1768–1808', *International Journal of Middle East Studies*, Vol. 25, No. 1, 1993, pp. 53–69

Aksan, Virginia H., 'Whatever Happened to the Janissaries', *War in History*, Vol. 5, No. 1, 1998, pp. 23–36

Alfani, Guido, and Sergio Sardone, *Long-Term Trends in Economic Inequality in Southern Italy*, Bocconi University, Milan, 2012, available at http://eh.net/eha/wp-content/uploads/2015/05/Alfani.pdf, pp. 1–29

Anderson, Lisa, 'The Development of Nationalist Sentiment in Libya, 1908–1922', in Rashid Khalidi, Lisa Anderson, Muhammad Muslih and Reeva Simon (eds), *The Origins of Arab Nationalism*, Columbia University Press, New York, 1991, pp. 225–42

Anderson, M. S., 'Great Britain and the Russian Fleet, 1769–70', *Slavonic and East European Review*, Vol. 31, No. 76, 1952, pp. 148–63

Anderson, M. S., 'Great Britain and the Russo-Turkish War of 1768–74', *English Historical Review*, Vol. 69, No. 270, 1954, pp. 39–58

Anon, 'L'oeuvre de l'arme du génie en Algérie', *Revue du Génie Militaire*, Vol. LXVIII, Jan. 1931, pp. 16–121

Artan, Tülay, 'Aspects of the Ottoman Elites Food Consumption: Looking for "Staples", "Luxuries" and "Delicacies" in a Changing Century', in Donald Quataert (ed.) *Consumption Studies and the History of the Ottoman Empire 1550–1922*, State University of New York Press, 2000

Atalay, Figen, 'The History of the Coal Mining Industry and Mining Accidents in the World and Turkey', *Turkish Thoracic Journal*, Vol. 16 (Suppl. 1), 2015

Ayalon, David, 'The Historian al-Jabarti and his Background', *Bulletin of the School of Oriental and African Studies*, Univ. of London, Vol. 23, No. 2, 1960, pp. 217–49

Ayalon, David, 'Studies in al-Jabarti: Notes on the Transformation of Mamluk Society under the Ottomans', *Journal of the Economic and Social History of the Orient*, Vol. 3, No. 3 1960, pp. 275–325

al-Azmeh, Aziz, 'Barbarians in Arab Eyes', *Past & Present*, No. 134, 1992, pp. 3–18

Baer, Gabriel, 'The Administrative and Social Functions of Turkish Guilds', *International Journal of Middle East Studies*, Vol. 1, No. 1, 1970, pp. 28–50

Bayly, C. A., 'The First Age of Global Imperialism c. 1760–1830', *Journal of Imperial and Commonwealth History*, Vol. 26, No. 2, 1998, pp. 28–47

Beeri, Eliezer, 'Social Origin and Family Background of the Egyptian Army Officer Class', *Asian and African Studies*, Vol. 2, 1966, pp. 1–40

Bell, K., 'British Policy Towards the Construction of the Suez Canal 1859–65', *Transactions of the Royal Historical Society*, Vol. 15, 1965, pp. 121–43

Bennison, Amira K., 'The "New Order" and Islamic Order: The Introduction of the *Nizami* Army in the Western Maghrib and its Legitimation, 1830–73', *International Journal of Middle East Studies*, Vol. 36, 2004, pp. 591–612

Boyer, Pierre, 'Introduction à une Histoire intérieure de la régence d'Alger', *Revue Historique*, 235/2, 1966, pp. 297–314

Burnikel, Catherine T., *Camille Barrère and Franco-Italian Rapprochement 1898–1902*, Thesis, Loyola University, Chicago, 1972, available at https://ecommons.luc.edu/cgi/viewcontent.cgi?referer=https://www.google.com/&httpsredir=1&article=2166&context=luc_diss

Cain, P. J., and A. G. Hopkins, 'Gentlemanly Capitalism and British Expansion Overseas: 1. The Old Colonial System, 1688–1850', *Economic History Review,* New Series, Vol. 39, No. 4, 1986, pp. 501–25

Calderwood, Eric, 'The Beginning (or End) of Moroccan History: Historiography, Translation, and Modernity in Ahmad B. Khalid al-Nasiri and Clemente Cerdeira', *Journal of Middle East Studies*, No. 44, 2012, pp. 399–420

Chamberlain, M. E., 'The Alexandria Massacre of 11 June 1882 and the British Occupation of Egypt', *Middle Eastern Studies*, Vol. 13, No. 1, 1977, pp. 13–49

Chevalier, Dominique, 'Aspects sociaux de la Question d'Orient: aux origines des troubles agraires Libanais en 1858', *Annales: Economies, Societés, Civilisation*, Year 14, No. 1, 1959, pp. 35–64

Chevalier, Dominique, 'Les cadres sociaux de l'économie agraire dans le Proche-Orient au debut du XIXe siècle: le cas du Mont Liban', in M. A. Cook, *Studies in the Economic History of the Middle East*, Oxford University Press, 1970, pp. 333–45

Choueiri, Youssef M. 'Ottoman Reform and Lebanese Patriotism', in Nadim Shehadi and Dana Haffar Mills (eds), *Lebanon: A History of Conflict and Consensus*, Centre for Lebanese Studies and I.B. Tauris, London, 1989, pp. 64–78

Clark, Edward C., 'The Ottoman Industrial Revolution', *International Journal of Middle East Studies*, Vol. 5, No. 1, 1974, pp. 65–76

Cohen, Amnon, 'The Army in Palestine in the Eighteenth Century – Sources of its Weakness and Strength', *Bulletin of the School of Oriental and African Studies*, Vol. 34, No. 1, 1971, pp. 36–55

Coller, Ian, 'Egypt in the French Revolution', in Suzanne Desan, Lynn Hunt and William Max Nelson (eds), *The French Revolution in Global Perspective*, Cornell University Press, 2013, pp. 115–31

Coşgel, Metin, and Boğaç A. Ergene, 'Intergenerational Wealth Accumulation and Dispersion in the Ottoman Empire: Observations from Eighteenth Century Kastamonu', *European Review of Economic History*, Vol. 15, 2011, pp. 255–76

Crecelius, Daniel, 'Egypt in the Eighteenth Century', in M. W. Daly (ed.), *The Cambridge History of Egypt*, Vol. 2, Cambridge University Press, 1998, pp. 59–86

Crecelius, Daniel, 'The Mamluk Beylicate of Egypt', in Philipp and Harmann (eds), *The Mamluks in Egyptian Politics and Society*, Cambridge University Press, 1998

Crecelius, Daniel, 'A Late Eighteenth-Century Austrian Attempt to Develop the Red Sea Trade Route', *Middle Eastern Studies*, Vol. 30, No. 2, 1994, pp. 262–80

Darr, Karl Wilhelm Augustus, *The Ottoman Navy 1900–1918: A Study of the Material, Personnel, and Professional Development of the Ottoman Navy from 1900 through the Italian, Balkan and First World Wars*, M.A. Thesis, University of Louisville, 1998, p. 3, available at https://ir.library.louisville.edu/cgi/viewcontent.cgi?article=4015&context=etd

Davis, Ralph, 'English Imports from the Middle East. 1580–1780', in M. A. Cook (ed.) *Studies in the Economic History of the Middle East*, Oxford University Press, Oxford, 1970, pp. 192–206

Davis, Robert C., 'Counting European Slaves on the Barbary Coast', *Past & Present*, No. 172, 2001, pp. 87–124

Driault, E., 'Les Anglais devant Constantinople et Alexandrie 1807', *Revue Historique*, Vol. 73, 1900, pp. 24–60

Emerit, Marcel, 'La Crise syrienne et l'expansion économique française en 1860, *Revue Historique*, Vol. CCVII, 1952, pp. 221–23

Emerit, Marcel, 'Les tribus privilégiées en Algérie dans la première moitié du XIXe siècle', *Annales: Histoire, Science Sociales*, 21e Année No. 1, 1966, pp. 44–58

Ergene, Boğaç A., and Ali Berker, 'Wealth and Inequality in 18th-Century Kastamonu: Estimations for the Muslim Majority', *International Journal of Middle East Studies*, Vol. 40, Vol. 1, 2008, pp. 23–46

Erginbaş, Vefa, 'Enlightenment in the Ottoman Context: İbrahim Müteferrika and His Intellectual Landscape', in *Historical Aspects of Printing and Publishing in Languages of the Middle East* (ed. Geoffrey Roper), Brill, Leiden, 2014, pp. 53–100

Establet, Colette, and Jean-Paul Pascual, 'Damascene Probate Inventories of the 17th and 18th Centuries: Some Preliminary Approaches and Results', *International Journal of Middle East Studies*, Vol. 24, No. 3, 1992, pp. 373–93

Establet, Colette, Jean-Paul Pascual and André Raymond, 'La mesure de l'inégalité dans la societé Ottomane: Utilisation de l'indice de Gini pour le Caire et Damas vers 1700', *Journal of the Economic and Social History of the Orient*, Vol. 37, No. 2 1994, pp. 171–82

Farah, Caesar E., 'Protestantism and British Diplomacy in Syria', *International Journal of Middle East Studies*, Vol. 7, No. 3, 1976, pp. 321–44

Faroqhi, Suraiya, 'Crisis and Change', in Halil İnalcık and Donald Quataert, *An Economic and Social History of the Ottoman Empire, Vol. Two 1600–1914*, Cambridge University Press, 1994, pp. 411–623

Findley, Carter V., 'A Quixotic Author and His Great Taxonomy: Mouradgea d'Ohsson and his Tableau General de L'Empire Othoman', University of Oslo, 2000, p. 4; available at https://www.oslo2000.uio.no/program/papers/m1b-findley.pdf

Galbraith, John S., and Afaf Lutfi al-Sayyid-Marsot, 'The British Occupation of Egypt: Another View', *International Journal of Middle East Studies*, Vol. 9 No. 4, 1978, pp. 471–88

Gallagher, John, and Ronald Robinson, 'The Imperialism of Free Trade', *Economic History Review*, New Series, Vol. 6, No. 1, 1953, pp.1–15

Gallissot, René, 'Abd el-Kader et la nationalité algérienne. Interpretation de la chute de la Régence d'Alger et des premières résistances a la conquête française (1830–1839)', *Revue Historique*, Vol. 233, No. 2, 1965, pp. 339–68

Gallissot, René, 'Présentation', in Marcel Emerit, *L'Algérie à L'Epoque d'Abd el-Kader*, Editions Bouchene, Paris, 2002, pp. 7–18

Ganiage, Jean, 'France, England and the Tunisian Affair', in P. Gifford and W. M. R. Louis (eds), *France and Britain in Africa*, Yale University Press, New Haven, 1971, pp. 35–72

Gencer, Yasemin, 'Ibrahim Müteferrika and the Age of the Printed Manuscript', in Christiane Gruber, *The Islamic Manuscript Tradition*, Indiana Press, Bloomington, 2010, pp. 154–93

Grenville, J. A. S., 'Goluchowski, Salisbury, and the Mediterranean Agreements, 1895–1897', *The Slavonic and East European Review*, Vol. 36, No. 87, 1958, pp. 340–69

Hanna, Nelly, 'Literacy and the "Great Divide" in the Islamic World, 1300–1800', *Journal of Global History*, Vol. 2, 2007, pp. 175–194

Harik, Iliya F., 'The Iqta' System in Lebanon: a Comparative Political View', *Middle East Journal*, Vol. 19, No. 4, 1965, pp. 405–21

Hart, D. M., 'The Saint and the schoolmaster, or Jbala Warlord and Rifian reformer revisited: conflicting views of Islam in a confrontation and power clash in Colonial Northern Morocco, 1924–24', *Journal of North African Studies*, Vol. 6, No. 2

Hathaway, Jane, '"Mamluk Households" and "Mamluk Factions" in Ottoman Egypt: A Reconsideration', in Thomas Philipp and Ulrich Haarmann (eds), *The Mamluks in Egyptian Politics and Society*

Herrera Hermillosa, Juan Carlos, 'La expedición contra Argel de 1775: una misión impossible de Carlos III', available at http://anatomiadelahistoria.com/2011

Herrmann, David G., 'The Paralysis of Italian Strategy in the Italian-Turkish War, 1911–1912', *English Historical Review*, Vol. 104, No. 411, 1989, pp. 332–356

Hoexter, Miriam, 'Waqf Studies in the Twentieth Century: The State of the Art', *Journal of Economic and Social History of the Orient*, Vol. 41, No. 4, 1998, pp. 474–95

Hopkins, A. G., 'The Victorians and Africa: A Reconsideration of the Occupation of Egypt, 1882', *Journal of African History*, Vol. 27, No. 2, 1986, pp. 363–91

Hutton, Catherine, *The Tour of Africa*, Baldwin, Cradock & Joy, London, 1821

Ihasanoğlu, Ekmeleddin, *An Overview of Ottoman Scientific Activities: Foundation for Science, Technology and Civilisation*, Manchester, 2006, available at https://muslimheritage.com/uploads/An_Overview_of_Ottoman_Scientific_Activities1.pdf

İnalcık, Halil, 'The Ottoman Economic Mind and Aspects of the Ottoman Economy', in M. A. Cook, *Studies in the Economic History of the Middle East*, Oxford University Press, 1970, pp. 207–18

İnalcık, Halil, 'The Ottoman State: Economy and Society 1300–1600' in Halil İnalcık and Donald Quataert (eds), *An Economic and Social History of the Ottoman Empire, 1300–1914*, Cambridge University Press, 1994, pp. 11–409

Ingram, Edward, 'From Trade to Empire in the Near East – 1: The End of the Spectre of the Overland Trade, 1775–1801', *Middle Eastern Studies* Vol. 14, No. 1, 1978, pp. 3–21

Issawi, Charles, 'Decline of Ottoman Industry in the 1840s', in Charles Issawi (ed.), *The Economic History of the Middle East 1800–1914*, University of Chicago Press, Chicago, 1966, pp. 41–45

Issawi, Charles, British Trade and the Rise of Beirut, 1830–1860, *International Journal of Middle East Studies,* Vol. 8, 1977, pp. 91–101

Issawi, Charles, 'De-industrialisation and Re-industrialisation in the Middle East since 1800', *International Journal of Middle East Studies*, Vol. 12, No. 4, 1980, pp. 469–79

Karam, Rizk, 'The Shihab Emirship (1697–1841): Bashir II's Emirship (1789–1840', in *Politics, Religion and State Building (11th–16th/19th Centuries* (ed. Dominique Avon), Université du Maine, Le Mans, 2011, p. 3, available at http://hemed.univ-lemans.fr/cours2011/en/co/module_Eomed(2)_17.html

Karaman, K. Kivanç, and Şevket Pamuk, 'Ottoman State Finances in European perspective 1500–1914', *Journal of Economic History*, Vol. 70, No. 3, 2010, pp. 593–629

Katz, Jonathan, 'The 1907 Mauchamp Affair and the French Civilising Mission in Morocco', *Journal of North African Studies*, Vol. 6, No. 1, 2011, pp. 143–66

Kemp, Percy, 'An Eighteenth-Century Turkish Intelligence Report', *International Journal of Middle East Studies,* Vol. 16, No. 4, 1984

Kisirwani, Maroun, 'Foreign Interference and Religious Animosity in Lebanon', *Journal of Contemporary History*, Vol. 15, No. 4, 1980, pp. 685–700

Ković, Miloš, The Beginnings of the 1875 Serbian Uprising in Herzegovina: The British Perspective', *Balcanica* 41: 2010, pp. 55–71

Küçükkalay, A. Mesud, and Numan Elibol, 'Ottoman Imports in the 18th Century: Smyrna (1771–72)', *Middle Eastern Studies*, Vol. 42, No. 5, 2006, pp. 723–40

La Force, J. C., 'Royal Textile Factories in Spain, 1700–1800', *Journal of Economic History*, Vol. 24, No. 3, 1964, pp. 337–363

Largueche, Abdelhamid, Julia Clancy-Smith and Caroline Audet, 'The City and the Sea: Evolving Forms of Mediterranean Cosmopolitanism in Tunis 1700–1881', *Journal of North African Studies*, Vol. 6, No. 1, 2001, pp. 117–28

Laurens, Henry, 'Europe and the Muslim World in the Contemporary Period', in John Tolan, Gilles Veinstein and Henry Laurens, *Europe and the Islamic World: A History*, Princeton University Press, 2013, pp. 257–387

Levy, Avigdor, 'The Officer Corps in Sultan Mahmud II's New Ottoman Army', *International Journal of Middle East Studies*, Vol. 2, No. 1, 1971, pp. 21, 23

Livingston, John W., 'The Rise of Shaykh al-Balad 'Ali Bey al-Kabir: A Study in the Accuracy of the Chronicle of al-Jabarti', *Bulletin of the School of Oriental and African Studies*, Vol. 33, No. 2, 1970, pp. 283–94

Loizos, Dimitris, 'Economic History Problems of 18th c. Ottoman Greece: The Case of Ambelakia in Thessaly (preliminary report)'. Available at http://www.anistor.gr/english/enback/e011.htm

M. B., 'General Count O'Reilly's Attack upon Algiers', *National Magazine*, Vol. 1 No. 3, 1830, p. 348

Maghraoui, Driss, 'The "Grande Guerre Sainte"; Moroccan Colonial Troops and Workers in the First World War', *Journal of North African Studies*, Vol. 9, No. 1, 2004, pp. 1–21

Malanima, Paolo, 'Urbanisation and the Italian Economy During the Last Millennium', *European Review of Economic History*, Vol. 9, No. 1, 2005, pp. 97–122

Malanima, Paolo, 'The Long Decline in a Leading Economy: GDP in Central And Northern Italy 1300–1913', *European Review of Economic History*, Vol. 15, 2010, pp. 169–219.

Mardin, Serif, 'Power, Civil Society and Culture in the Ottoman Empire', *Comparative Studies in Society and History*, Vol. 11 No. 3 , 1969, pp. 258–81

Martin Corrales, Eloy, 'El protectorado español en Marruecos (1912–1956): Una perspectiva histórica', in Joan Nogué and José Luis Villanova, *España en Marruecos (1912–1956): Discursos geográficos e intervención territorial*, Editorial Mileno, Lleida, 1999

McCarthy, Justin, 'Nineteenth-Century Egyptian Population', *Middle Eastern Studies*, Vol. 12, No. 3, 1976, pp. 1–39

McGowan, Bruce, 'The Age of the Ayans, 1699–1812', in İnalcık, Halil and Donald Quataert (eds), *An Economic and Social History of the Ottoman Empire*, Vol. 2, Cambridge University Press, 1994, pp. 639–758

McNeill, William H., 'The Age of the Gunpowder Empires, 1450–1800', in Michael Adas, *Islamic and European Expansion: The Forging of a Global Order*, Temple University Press, Philadelphia, 1993

Medlicott, W. N., 'The Mediterranean Agreements of 1887', *Slavonic Review*, Vol. 5, No. 13, 1926, pp. 66–88

Mowat, R. C., 'From Liberalism to Imperialism: The Case of Egypt 1875–1887', *Historical Journal*, Vol. 16, No. 1, 1973, pp. 109–24

Notz, William, 'The World's Coal Situation during the War', *Journal of Poliitical Economy*, Vol. 6, No. 6, 1918

O'Brien, Patrick. 'European Economic Development: The Contribution of the Periphery', *The Economic History Review*, Vol. 35, No. 1, 1982, pp. 1–18

O'Brien, Patrick, 'The Political Economy of British Taxation, 1660–1815', *Economic History Review*, Vol. XLI, No. 1, 1988, pp. 1–32

Olson, Robert W., 'The Esnaf and the Patrona Halil Rebellion of 1730: A Realignment in Ottoman Politics?', *Journal of the Economic and Social History of the Orient*, Vol. 17, No. 3, 1974, pp. 329–44

Özmucur, Süleyman, and Şevket Pamuk, 'Real Wages and Standards of Living in the Ottoman Empire, 1489–1914', *Journal of Economic History*, Vol. 62, No. 2, 2002, pp. 293–321

Pamuk, Şevket, 'The Ottoman Empire in the "Great Depression" of 1873–1896', *Journal of Economic History*, Vol. 44, No. 1, 1984, pp. 107–18

Pamuk, Şevket, 'Institutional Change and the Longevity of the Ottoman Empire, 1500–1800', *Journal of Interdisciplinary History*, Vol. 35, No. 2, 2004

Pamuk, Şevket, 'Prices in the Ottoman Empire, 1469–1914', *International Journal of Middle East Studies*, Vol. 36, 2004, pp. 451–68

Panza, Laura, 'De-Industrialization and Re-Industrialization in the Middle East: Reflections on the Cotton Industry in Egypt and in the Izmir Region', *Economic History Review*, Vol. 67, No. 1, 2014, pp. 146–69

Panza, Laura, and Jeffrey G. Williamson, 'Did Muhammad Ali Foster Industrialization in Early Nineteenth-Century Egypt?', *Economic History Review*, Vol. 68, No. 1, 2015, pp. 79–100

Panzac, Daniel, 'International and Domestic Maritime Trade in the Ottoman Empire During the 18th Century', *International Journal of Middle East Studies*, Vol. 24, No. 2, 1992, pp. 189–206

Papastratigakis, Nicholas, 'British Naval Strategy: The Russian Black Sea Fleet and the Turkish Straits, 1890–1904', *International History Review*, Vol. 32, No. 4, 2010, pp. 643–59

Parsons, F. V., 'The "Morocco Question" in 1884: An Early Crisis', *English Historical Journal*, Vol. 77, No. 305, 1962, pp. 659–83

Parsons, F. V., 'The Proposed Madrid Conference on Morocco, 1887–88', *Historical Journal*, Vol. 8, No. 1, 1965, pp. 72–94

Philipp, Thomas, 'Personal Loyalty and Political Power of the Mamluks in the Eighteenth Century', in Thomas Philipp and Ulrich Haarmann (eds), *The Mamluks in Egyptian Politics and Society*

Porath, Yehoshua, 'The Peasant Revolt of 1858–61 in Kisrawan', *Asian and African Studies*, Vol. 2, 1966, pp. 77–157

Quataert, Donald, 'The Age of Reforms: Manufacturing' in İnalcık and Quataert, *An Economic and Social History of the Ottoman Empire,* Vol. 2, Cambridge University Press, Cambridge, 1994, pp. 888–943

Ramm, Agatha, 'Great Britain and France in Egypt, 1876–1882', in P. Gifford and W. M. R. Lewis (eds), *France and Britain in Africa*, Yale University Press, New Haven, 1971

Raymond, André, 'Soldiers in Trade: The Case of Ottoman Cairo', *British Journal of*

Middle East Studies Vol. 18, No. 1, 1991, pp. 16–37

Reimer, Michael J., 'Colonial Bridgehead: Social and Spatial Change in Alexandria, 1850–1882', *Middle East Studies*, Vol. 28, 1988, pp. 531–53

Rizk, Karam, 'The Shihab Emirship (1697–1841)', in *Politics, Religion and State Building (11th– 16th/19th Centuries* (ed. Dominque Avon), Université du Maine, Le Mans, 2011, p. 3, available at http://hemed.univ-lemans.fr/cours2011/en/co/module_Eomed(2)_17.html

Sabev, Orlin, 'Formation of Ottoman Print Culture (1726–1746): Some General Remarks', New Europe College, *Regional Program 2003–04 and 2004–05*, p. 306, available at https://www.academia.edu/728136/Formation_of_Ottoman_Print_Culture_1726-1746_Some_General_Remarks

Saleh, Mohamed, 'A Pre-Colonial Population Brought to Light: Digitization of the Nineteenth Century Egyptian Censuses', *Historical Methods: A Journal of Quantitative and Interdisciplinary History*, January 2013, Vol. 46 (1), pp. 5–18.

Schinder, Joel, 'Career Line Formation in the Ottoman Bureaucracy, 1648–1750: A New Perspective', *Journal of the Economic and Social History of the Orient*, Vol. 16, No. 2/3, 1973, pp. 217–37

Schölch, Alexander, 'The "Men on the Spot" and the English Occupation of Egypt in 1882', *Historical Journal*, Vol. 19, No. 3, 1976, pp. 773–85

Schwartz, Kathryn A., 'Did Ottoman Sultans Ban Print?', *Book History*, Vol. 20, 2017, pp. 1–39

Shaw, Stanford J., 'The Origins of Ottoman Military Reform: The Nizam-ı Cedid Army of Sultan Selim III', *Journal of Modern History*, Vol. 37, No. 3, 1965, pp. 291–306

Shaw, Stanford J., 'The Nineteenth-Century Ottoman Tax Reforms and Revenue System', *International Journal of Middle East Studies*, Vol. 6, No. 4, 1975, pp. 421–59

Shaw, Stanford J., 'Ottoman Expenditures and Budgets in the Late Nineteenth and Early Twentieth Centuries, *International Journal of Middle East Studies*, Vol. 9, No. 3, 1978, pp. 373–78.

Shaw, Stanford J., 'The Ottoman Census System and Population, 1831–1914', *International Journal of Middle East Studies*, Vol. 9, No. 3, 1978, pp. 325–38

Shechter, Relli, 'Market Welfare in Early-Modern Ottoman Economy: A Historiographical Overview with Many Questions', *Journal of the Economic and Social History of the Orient*, Vol. 46, No. 2, 2005, pp. 253–76

Solana Ruiz, José Luis, 'Las clases sociales en Andalucía: un recorrido sociohistórico', *Gazeta de Antropología*, No. 16, articulo 08, 2000, pp. 1–17

Stanev, Kaloyan, Edward Josep Alvarez-Palau and Jordi Marti-Henneberg, 'Railway Development and the Economic and Political Integration of the Balkans c. 1850–2000', *Europe–Asia Studies* Vol. 69, No. 10, pp. 1601–25

Stegl, Mojgan, and Joerg Baten, 'Tall and Shrinking Muslims, Short and Growing Europeans: The Long-Run Welfare Development of the Middle East, 1840–1980',

University of Tübingen, available at www.ehs.org.uk/dotAsset/05b192a5-d56a-4718-9669-739a616f5cb.pdf

Stekel, Richard H., 'Stature and the Standard of Living', *Journal of Economic literature*, Vol. 33, No. 4, 1995, pp. 1903–1940

Stokes, Eric, 'Late Nineteenth-Century Colonial Expansion and the Attack on the Theory of Economic Imperialism: A Case of Mistaken Identity?', *Historical Journal*, Vol. 12, No. 2, 1969, pp. 285–301

Storrs, Christopher, 'The Savoyard Fiscal-Military State in the Long Eighteenth Century', in Christopher Storrs (ed.), *The Fiscal Military State in the 18th Century*, Ashgate Publishing, Farnham, 2009

Todd, David, 'A French Imperial Meridian, 1814–1870', *Past & Present*, No. 210, 2011, pp. 155–86

Tok, Alaaddin, *The Ottoman Mining Sector in the Age of Capitalism: An Analysis of State-Capital Relations 1850–1908*, PhD thesis, Atatürk Institute for Modern Turkish History, Boğaziçi University, 2010

Valensi, Lucette, 'Islam et capitalisme: production et commerce des chéchias en Tunisie et en France aux XVIIIe et XIXe siècles', *Revue d'Histoire Moderne et Contemporaine*, Vol. 16, No. 3, 1969, pp. 376–400

Van Zanden, Jan L., 'Wages and the Standard of Living in Europe, 1500–1800', *European Review of Economic History*, Vol. 2, 1999, pp. 175–97

Venier, Pascal R., 'French Imperialism and Pre-Colonial Rebellions in Eastern Morocco, 1903–1910', *Journal of North African Studies*, Vol. 2, No. 2, 1997, pp. 57–67

Wagstaff, J. M., 'A Note on Nineteenth-Century Population Statistics for Lebanon', *Bulletin of the Society for Middle Eastern Studies*, Vol. 13, No. 1, 1986, pp. 27–35

Wank, Solomon, 'Aehrenthal and the Sanjak of Novibazar Railway Project: A Reappraisal', *Slavonic and East European Review*, Vol. 42, No. 99, 1964, p. 355

Winter, Michael, 'The Re-Emergence of the Mamluks Following the Ottoman Conquest', in Philipp and Haarmann (eds), *The Mamluks in Egyptian Politics and Society*

Wrigley, W. David, 'Germany and the Turkish-Italian War, 1911–1912', *International Journal of Middle East Studies*, Vol. 11, No. 3, 1980, pp. 313–38

Zens, Robert, 'Provincial Powers: The Rise of the Ottoman Local Notables (Ayan)', *History Studies*, Vol. 3, No. 3, 2011, pp. 433–47

Websites

http://ourworldindata.org/data/education-knowledge/literacy/

http://www.osmanli700.gen.tr/english/individuals/k16.html

Sevket Pamuk, Coins and Currency of the Ottoman Empire, http://www.pierre-marteau.com/currency/coins/turk.html#intro

SOURCES OF QUOTATIONS HEADING EACH SECTION

Title
Henry Laurens, 'Europe and the Muslim World in the Contemporary Period', in Tolan, John, Gilles Veinstein and Henry Laurens, *Europe and the Islamic World: A History*, Princeton University Press, Princeton, and Oxford 2013, p. 257.

Part One
Mouradgea d'Ohsson, Ignatius, *Tableau général de l'empire othoman*, Paris, 1788, Vol. 4, Part 1, pp. 372–73.

Part Two
Lord Palmerston quoted in Brown, David, *Palmerston and the Politics of Foreign Policy 1846–55*, Manchester University Press, Manchester 2002, p. 162.

Part Three
Quoted in Keddie, Nikki R., *An Islamic Response to Imperialism: The Political and Religious Writings of Sayyid Jamal ad-Din 'al-Afghani'*, University of California Press, Berkeley, 1968, p. 72.

Part Four
Langer, William, *The Diplomacy of Imperialism, 1890–1902*, 2nd edition, Alfred A. Knopf, 1960, p. 96.

Index